Wissenschaftliche Monographien zum Alten und Neuen Testament

Begründet von
Günther Bornkamm und Gerhard von Rad

In Verbindung mit
Erich Gräßer und Hans-Jürgen Hermisson
herausgegeben von
Ferdinand Hahn und Odil Hannes Steck

Vol. 61
Helge S. Kvanvig
Roots of Apocalyptic

Neukirchener Verlag

Helge S. Kvanvig

Roots of Apocalyptic

The Mesopotamian Background
of the Enoch Figure and of the Son of Man

1988

Neukirchener Verlag

Financially supported by the Norwegian Research Council for Science an Humanities

Cover-Design: Kurt Wolff, Düsseldorf-Kaiserswerth
Manufactured: Breklumer Druckerei Manfred Siegel KG
Typeset on HP LaserJet with TMS Proportional 2 Font
Typesetting and paste up: Bodil Sunde, Oslo, Norway
Printed in Germany – ISBN 3-7887-1248-1

CIP-Kurztitelaufnahme der Deutschen Bibliothek

Kvanvig, Helge S.:
Roots of apocalyptic : the Mesopotamian background of the
Enoch figure and of the Son of Man / Helge S. Kvanvig. -
Neukirchen-Vluyn : Neukirchener Verl., 1988
  (Wissenschaftliche Monographien zum Alten und Neuen Testament ;
  Vol. 61)
  ISBN 3-7887-1248-1
NE: GT

To Anne-Grete

Preface

My studies in apocalyptic literature were initiated in 1972/73 when I was engaged as a research assistant at the "Arbeitsstelle zur Erforschung der profetischen und apokalyptischen Sprache und Literatur" in the Old Testament Department of the University of Hamburg. During the following years as Faculty lecturer at the Free Faculty of Theology in Oslo I continued the studies, although other duties occupied most of my time. The research project got a new impetus in 1979 when I was granted a three years scholarship by the Norwegian Research Council for Science and the Humanities, which also granted financial means for travelling abroad. The scholarship was extended by half a year by the Free Faculty of Theology. The first year of this period I stayed in Oxford studying at the Oriental Institute, University of Oxford. The next seven months I spent at the Hebrew University, Jerusalem. The rest of the period I stayed at the Free Faculty of Theology in Oslo, interrupted by a further period in Oxford in the spring of 1981.

The first part of this study was accepted for the doctor's degree in theology at the University in Oslo, September 1984.

I am most grateful to those scholars who have helped and encouraged me. In Oxford I worked with Professor James Barr and conferred frequently with him as the project developed. Dr. Stephany Dalley was my supervisor in Akkadian language and literature during both periods in Oxford. Without her help I would not have been able to enter into a detailed discussion of the Mesopotamian material. During my stay in Jerusalem I worked with Professor Jonas Greenfield who advised me in my study of the Aramaic Qumran fragments to the Books of Enoch. In Jerusalem I had also the pleasure of discussing my project in detail with Professor Menachem Haran and Professor Moshe Greenberg. At my own faculty I am greatly thankful to Professor Edvin Larsson whose constructive advice has been of great help in the final completion of the manuscript. Professor Ebbe Knudsen at the Semitic Institute, University of Oslo, has examined the linguistic aspects of the manuscript critically, and I also express my gratitude to him. Dr. Frederick Hale and Rev. David Foster MA have corrected my English with great diligence.

Fifteen years have gone by since I started my studies in apocalyptic. During all these years I have been encouraged and advised by Professor Klaus Koch, Hamburg University. He has read the drafts to my study, offering constructive criticism and suggested substantial improvements. He has kept me informed about new developments in the field of apocalyptic and he has invited me to the "Arbeitsgruppe Apokalyptic innerhalb der Wissenschaftlichen Gesellschaft für Theologie", which sessions have been of great importance for me. I am greatly indebted to him.

I also wish to express my gratitude to the Norwegian Research Council for granting financial means for the publication of this study, and to Professor Odil Hannes Steck for accepting my study for the series WMANT.

A preface must allow a personal remark at the end. The person who during these years has known my work in greatest detail as it developed is my wife Anne-Grete. She accompanied me to Hamburg, Oxford, Jerusalem, sharing with me the strange apocalyptic dream visions in discussions reaching into the late hours of night. Without her support the whole enterprise would have been a lonely affair.

Ammerud, 1986   Helge S. Kvanvig

Contents

Roots of Apocalyptic

To write a study about the "roots of apocalyptic" is at first sight to turn the apocalyptical universe upside down. Apocalyptic presents itself as literature not grown out of anything in this world, but given through heavenly revelations. No other Jewish or Christian sources from antiquity seem to contradict the modern rational approach to reality so sharply as the apocalyptical literature. This causes a great challenge for modern researchers. One has to cross the border to another world, the world of apocalyptical imagination.

Now, the question whether the apocalyptics in their visions and visionary journeys actually crossed the border to another reality shall not be our concern in this study. This is ultimately a question of theological hermeneutics and religious philosophy. But whatever experience lay behind the writing down of the revelations, they cannot be lifted out of human history. If one assumes underlying visionary experiences, these were nevertheless perceived through human eyes, understood by a human mind and communicated in a human world.

The roots of apocalyptic can be sought in different places. One can ask about the "roots" in the human mind, which demands a psychological analysis; or the "roots" can be sought in contemporary society, which demands a sociological analysis. But before these questions can be put, one needs an inquiry with a broader frame of reference than the individual and the contemporary society. Neither the individual, nor a society, nor groups within a society, create a *novum* without any connection to previous history. We need an inquiry into the history of tradition shaping the apocalyptical imagery.

This question is not new. It has accompanied apocalyptical research in its whole history. The fact that the apocalyptical literature seems to appear so suddenly in post-exilic Judaism and to distinguish itself so clearly from previous and contemporary traditions, has not reduced interest, but rather sharpened curiosity. The basic problems dealt with in research are on the one hand the connection between Old Testament traditions, i.e. prophecy and wisdom, and apocalypticism, and on the other hand the relationship between the apocalyptical imagery and contemporary non-Jewish religions. The opinion that the first Biblical apocalyptic, Daniel, belonged to the prophets has been traditional in the Church, and most scholars from the beginning of historical critical research have seen a close relationship between prophecy and apocalyptic. But the assumption that apocalyptic is simply to be regarded as a "child of prophecy" has, nevertheless, been challenged through new discoveries of both Jewish and non-Jewish religious texts. On the Jewish side these discoveries have gradually increased the knowledge of apocalyptic and related literature as a broad literary current in Judaism of peculiar speculative character which distinguished it from prophecy. On the non-Jewish side religious texts have been published with a content and an imagery resembling those of apocalyptic.

I do not find it necessary to start this study with a comprehensive review of the research history. The research history of apocalyptic in general from the beginning of scholarly research up to the publications of the Qumran manuscripts was written by J.M. Schmidt.[1] The latest decades are covered by K. Koch.[2] Further reports about the more recent developments were given by K. Koch, J. Barr, C. Rowland, K. Rudolph and P.D. Hanson.[3] In my study the first part is introduced by a review of the research history to the Enoch figure, and the second part is introduced by a discussion of the present state of research, since a full report of the research history to Daniel has already been written by K. Koch.[4]

Nevertheless, I think that the reader will find it helpful to have a

1   J.M. Schmidt, Die Jüdische Apokalyptik, Neukirchen-Vluyn 1969.
2   K. Koch, "Einleitung", Apokalyptik, K. Koch and J.M. Schmidt (eds.), WdF, Darmstadt 1982.
3   K. Koch, Ratlos vor der Apokalyptik, Gütersloh 1970; J. Barr, "Jewish Apocalyptic in Recent Scholarly Study", BJRL, 58, 1975; C. Rowland, The Open Heaven, London 1982, pp. 191-213; K. Rudolph, "Apokalyptik in der Diskussion", Apocalypticism in the Mediterranean World and the Near East, D. Hellholm (ed.), Tübingen 1983, pp. 771-89; P.D. Hanson, "Introduction", Visionaries and their Apocalypses, idem, Philadelphia-London 1983, pp. 4-15.
4   K. Koch et al., Das Buch Daniel, EdF, Darmstadt 1980.

broader framework for the discussions in both parts. Such a summary review could very well outline the main trends in the development of new methods applied to the material, and the theological context of the various methods. But in the field of apocalyptical studies — more than for instance in the study of the Old and New Testament — the discoveries of new sources have played a major role. The research history of apocalyptic is accordingly not the history about how new methods have been applied to the same texts, but the history of an ongoing expansion of relevant sources directly affecting the basis of research, not least in the question of the roots of apocalyptic.

On the Jewish side this concerns the source material from the time of the second temple and shortly afterwards.[5] The discoveries of new sources from this period enabled scholars to separate the apocalyptic writings as a special kind of literature over against other contemporary scriptures. Thus the basis for apocalyptical studies was laid by F. Lücke in 1832 and 1852, and further developed by A. Hilgenfeld in 1857 through the classification of writings resembling the Revelation of John as apocalyptical.[6] The most important sources used by Lücke and Hilgenfeld were 4 Ezra, which was known through the Vulgate; the Sibylline Oracles, which were known in Europe through its whole Christian history, but first properly edited in the first halt of the nineteenth century; and as the most important source concerning non-Biblical Jewish apocalyptic, the Book of Enoch, which was only known through Greek quotations before it was edited on the basis of Ethiopic manuscripts in 1821.[7]

The great interest in apocalyptical studies around the turn of the century was influenced both through new editions of the previous sources, and through new sources, among them the Book of Jubilees, which was first edited in 1850 from Ethiopic manuscripts, and the Syriac Baruch Apocalypse, which was edited in 1866. Through these sources the basis for apocalyptical studies in our century was laid.

---

5 Cf. for the following the review by Koch in "Einleitung", Apokalyptik, pp. 1-11.
6 F. Lücke, Versuch einer vollständigen Einleitung in die Offenbarung des Johannes, 1st ed. 1832, 2nd ed. Bonn 1852; A. Hilgenfeld, Die jüdische Apokalyptik in ihrer geschichtlichen Entwickelung, Jena 1857.
7 Cf. Lücke, op.cit., pp. 89-92.

A new impetus came in 1947 through the discovery and subsequent publishing of the Qumran scrolls.[8] Although the writings
composed by the Qumran community cannot be regarded as
apocalyptical,[9] they gave a new knowledge about Judaism in the
last centuries B.C. Of greater importance, however, was the
discovery of mainly Aramaic fragments not composed, but copied
by the Qumran community, which were either clearly related to
apocalyptic, or belonged to this genre.[10] Among these texts there
were fragments belonging to the Danielic traditions, for instance
the Prayer of Nabonidus, 4Q OrNab, closely related to Dan 4,[11]
and as the most important, fragments of the original Aramaic
version of the Books of Enoch.[12]

When Lücke and Hilgenfeld wrote the first comprehensive studies
of apocalyptic, the starting point was the canonical apocalyptical
books, the Revelation of John and the Book of Daniel. Accordingly the emphasis in the definition of apocalyptic was laid on
those features that dominated in these books, above all the historical and eschatological perspective that corresponded with the
central parts of the Old and New Testament. Until the publication
of the Qumran fragments to the Books of Enoch it was a presupposition among most scholars that the Book of Daniel was the first
apocalyptical book, and that the examination of the origin of
apocalyptic had to start there. This situation has changed radically.
The Qumran Enoch fragments demonstrate clearly that two
Enochic books were composed before the final edition of the Book
of Daniel. Accordingly the Enochic books and the broad current
of traditions in Judaism relating to these books have suddenly been

---

8   The Qumran writings proper are easily available in E. Lohse, Die Texte aus
Qumran, Darmstadt 1971.
9   Cf. H. Stegemann, "Die Bedeutung der Qumranfunde für die Erforschung
der Apokalyptik", Apocalypticism in the Mediterranean World and the Near
East, pp. 495-530.
10   The texts are edited with English translation by J.A. Fitzmyer and D.J.
Harrington, A Manual of Palestinian Aramaic Texts, BibOr 34, Rome 1978; and
recently with German translation by K. Beyer, Die aramäischen Texte vom
Toten Meer, Göttingen 1984. In this study we use the publication by Fitzmyer
and Harrington.
11   Published by J.T. Milik, " 'Prière de Nabonide' et autres écrits d'un cycle de
Daniel", RB 63, 1956, pp. 407-15. Cf. also the edition and the discussion of the
fragments in A. Mertens, Das Buch Daniel im Lichte der Texte vom Toten
Meer, SBM 12, Stuttgart 1971.
12   Published by J.T. Milik, The Books of Enoch. Aramaic Fragments of
Qumran Cave 4, Oxford 1976.

seen as the centre of gravity in the early apocalyptical traditions. This demands new inquiries and interpretations of the origin and nature of apocalyptic.

But not only the increasing knowledge of Jewish sources has affected the understanding of apocalyptical literature; just as important has been the new material from the surrounding non-Jewish religions.

Long before Lücke separated apocalyptic as a special genre, scholars had realised that several post-exilic writings were marked by traditions different from the pre-exilic Old Testament scriptures. This was particularly the case with angelology and demonology, and the emphasis on divination in the Book of Daniel and the known Greek quotations of the Book of Enoch. On the basis of a general impression of "Chaldean religion" from Greek sources, and since the Book of Daniel explicitly referred to "Chaldean" practice, these features were generally held to be of Mesopotamian origin. Thus J.S. Semler in his epilogue to an anonymous book about demonology noted that demonology was younger than the Hebrew scriptures and belonged to the Apocrypha, especially the Book of Enoch. He referred to the Chaldeans and the Assyrians for its origin.[13] J.G. Eichhorn in his introduction to the Old Testament referred to the Chaldeans for the origin of divination in the Book of Daniel.[14]

The first primary source which should play a decisive role in research was the Persian Zend-Avesta in the publication by Perron in 1774. When Biblical scholars became aware of this source, Persian religion gradually moved into focus concerning the origin of strange features in post-exilic writings. In H. Corrodi's book about the history of chiliasm from 1781 the Persians feature together with the Chaldeans as the source of Jewish demonology.[15] In his later book about the Bible canon he referred to the Persians for the origin of the angelology of the Book of Daniel.[16]

---

13 J.S. Semler (ed.), Versuch einer biblischen Demonologie. Mit einer Vorrede und einem Anhang von D.J.S. Semler, Halle 1776, pp. 320ff.
14 J.G. Eichhorn, Einleitung im Alten Testament III, Leipzig 1787, pp. 344f.
15 H. Corrodi, Kritische Geschichte des Chiliasmus I, Frankfurt-Leipzig 1781, pp. 31f.
16 H. Corrodi, Versuch einer Beleuchtung der Geschichte des Jüdischen und Christlichen Bibelkanons I, Halle 1792, pp. 80-95.

In the first half of the nineteenth century the Zend-Avesta was increasingly quoted as the most important source not only for angelology and demonology (thus Bauer 1802 and de Wette 1818),[17] but also for the resurrection of the dead, the judgment of the world, and the dualistic concept of reality (thus Vatke 1835).[18] The most extensive list of parallels was made by von Cölln in 1836.[19] Persian religion had influenced Judaism in the concept of God as a god of light, in demonology and angelology, in the concept of history divided into fixed periods ending with the Messianic kingdom and the judgment of the world, in the understanding of the divine word as a hypostasis, in the concept of a final individual judgment where the dead receive reward or punishment, and is sent to "Paradise" or "Hell", and in the resurrection of the body.

In view of this clear tendency it is interesting to notice Lücke's reservation in seeing too marked an influence from Persian or other religions. Indeed, he did not exclude Persian influence in for instance the division of history into periods and the transcendental concept of eschatology, but this influence concerned more the appearance than the content and dynamic of Jewish apocalyptic.[20] Lücke's position can be explained on the basis of his definition of apocalyptic which placed the Revelation of John in the centre. But it is also clear that there was a growing awareness among scholars about the methodological problems relating to the comparison of different religions.

This is illustrated through three quotations that should significantly demonstrate the different positions. For Corrodi "Es hat vielmehr das Ansehen, dass die eigentlich sogenannte Philosophie der Juden nicht anders, als eine Vermischung von allerhand Meinungen gewesen, welche sie von ihrer Nachbarn und andern Nationen, mit welchen sie von Zeit zu Zeit Verkehr gehabt, gehört, und die sie sodann ungeprüft adoptierten, obwohl sie nicht selten auf diese

---

17   G.L. Bauer, Hebräische Mythologie des alten und neuen Testaments, Leipzig 1802, pp. 151-9; W.M.L. de Wette, Biblische Dogmatik Alten und Neuen Testaments, Berlin 1818, pp. 146ff.
18   V. Vatke, Die Religion des Alten Testaments, Berlin 1835, pp. 542-51.
19   D.G.C. von Cölln, Biblische Theologie, D. Schulz (ed.), Leipzig 1836, pp. 346-52.
20   Lücke, op.cit., pp. 55-60.

Weise wichtige, und schätzbare Wahrheiten erlernt haben mögen".[21] Vatke (1835), who goes far in seeing a Persian influence on post-exilic Judaism, has nevertheless a more historical perspective of the "process of assimilation": "Alle diese Einflüsse, welche grösstenteils auf den Parsismus zurückgehen, vermittelten sich allmälig mit den älteren Jehovareligion, und das Zeitalter des Exils bietet nur erst die Keime dar von dem grossen Assimilationsprocesse, wodurch mit der Zeit die Hauptmomente persischer Religion und Weisheit in's Judenthum und durch dessen Vermittelung in Christenthum aufgenommen wurden".[22]

What is different in Lücke's hermeneutical considerations is the emphasis on the Jews not only as adopters, but also as transformers of the material: "So entstand besonders von diesem Punkte aus ein merkwürdiger Assimilationsprocess zwischen Jüdischen und Persischen Religionslehre, in welchem der lebendige Jüdische Monotheismus bei aller Aufnahme und Aneignung des Fremden das constitutive umbildende Element war".[23]

From these quotations it is clear that broader knowledge of the supposed relevant source material did not necessarily lead to greater general acceptance of influence, but rather sharpened the methodological considerations about the nature of interrelationship. The publications of the Akkadian cuneiform sources that started in the second half of the nineteenth century did not reduce the interest in the Persian traditions as the background for Jewish apocalyptic.[24] Influential scholars like W. Bousset, H. Gressmann and A.F. von Gall argued for a Persian background, especially because of the close resemblance in the eschatological teaching.[25] In recent scholarship the theory still has supporters.[26]

---

21 Corrodi, Chiliasmus, p. 27.
22 Vatke, op.cit., p. 551.
23 Lücke, op.cit., pp. 56f.
24 Cf. the review of the positions in the religio- and traditio-historical school in Schmidt, Die jüdische Apokalyptik, pp. 206ff.
25 Cf. W. Bousset and H. Gressmann, Die Religion des Judentums im Spät-hellenistischen Zeitalter, HNT 21, Tübingen 1926, pp. 500-20; A.F. von Gall, Basileia tou Theou, Heidelberg 1926, pp. 219-351.
26 For the recent discussions of the relevant Persian material, cf. J.J. Collins, "Persian Apocalypses", Semeia 14, 1979, pp. 207-17; G. Widengren, "Leitende Ideen und Quellen der iranischen Apokalyptik", Apocalypticism, D. Hellholm (ed), pp. 77-162; A. Hultgård, "Forms and Origins of Iranian Apocalypticism", idem, pp. 387-412. For a close examination of the parallels between Enochic and

As previously noted scholars assumed right from the beginning of
critical research, that many of the new features of post-exilic
Jewish religion had their background in "Chaldean" religion. But
the knowledge about this religion was scanty. This changed
radically through the excavations in Mesopotamia and the discovery of cuneiform tablets containing religious texts.
The first notable influence on the field of apocalyptic came
through F. Lenormant's presentation and discussion of Babylonian
magical and divinatory texts in 1887.[27] Lenormant himself used
the new material to criticise the dating of the whole Book of
Daniel at the time of the Maccabean revolt, that was commonly
accepted in contemporary critical research. At the least, the
legends in Dan 1-6 had their background in Babylonian mantic
practice.[28] The broader knowledge about Babylonian wisdom and
divination led many scholars to date the Aramaic part of the Book
of Daniel back in the Persian age either as a literary unit or at
least through a line of preceeding traditions, and in some cases to
hold the Babylonian diaspora as the place of origin.[29] For the
scholars who held to a long period of growth for the Book of
Daniel, this also influenced their understanding of apocalyptic.
The speculative interest in unfolding the future that characterized
mantic practice, marked the apocalyptical traditions from their
very beginning and through their history.[30]
Just as important as the knowledge about Babylonian divination
was the direct access to Babylonian mythological texts that

Persian literature, cf. G. Widengren, "Iran and Israel in Parthian Times with
Special Regard to the Ethiopic Book of Enoch", Religious Syncretism in Antiquity, B.A. Pearson (ed.), Missoula, Montana 1975, pp. 85-129.
27 F. Lenormant, Die Magie und Wahrsagekunst der Chaldäer, Jena 1879.
28 Lenormant, pp. 525ff.
29 Cf. the review in W. Baumgartner, "Ein Vierteljahrhundert Danielforschung", ThR NF 11, 1939, pp. 59-83, 125-44, 201-28, pp. 126-30. This theory was
substantiated through the literary criticism of G. Hölscher, "Die Entstehung des
Buches Daniel", ThStKr 92, 1919, pp. 113-38. It led to a more dynamic understanding of the growth of the Danielic traditions, cf. M. Noth, "Zur Komposition
des Buches Daniel", ThStKr 98/99, 1926, pp. 143-63; and recently O.H. Steck,
"Weltgeschehen und Gottesvolk im Buche Daniel", Kirche, Festschr. G. Bornkamm, Tübingen 1980, pp. 53-78, also in Wahrnehmungen Gottes im Alten
Testament, TB 70, München 1982, pp. 262-90.
30 Cf. G. Hölscher, Geschichte der israelitischen und jüdischen Religion,
Giessen 1922, pp. 187-93; and more recently H.-P. Müller, "Magisch-mantische
Weisheit und die Gestalt Daniels", UF 1, 1969, pp. 79-94; "Mantische Weisheit
und Apokalyptik", VT.S 22, 1972, pp. 268-93; and "Märchen, Legende und
Enderwartung", VT 26, 1976, pp. 338-50.

previously could only be traced very fragmentarily in Greek sources. Above all the Babylonian Epic of Creation, Enuma Elish, influenced the research into the Old Testament as well as in apocalyptical literature.[31] The first parts of the epic was published by G. Smith in 1876, and soon more extensive editions appeared in English and German translations.[32] Through this epic scholars got an immediate impression of the Babylonian mythological imagery for the first time. The first scholar to utilize the epic in the field of apocalyptic was H. Gunkel in 1895.[33] Gunkel's study was primarily an investigation of the background of Gen 1 and Rev 12, but he also paid special attention to Dan 7.[34] The underlying mythical theme in these texts, and many others included by Gunkel, was the fight against the chaos-monster, in Enuma Elish represented by the fight between Marduk and the sea-monster Tiamat. In Dan 7 the four monsters from the sea were derivations of this sea-monster, and Gunkel suggests that the Son of Man could be a derivation of the one who conquered this monster.

The knowledge about ancient near eastern mythology in our century through excavations of Egyptian, Hittite and Canaanite texts created a new basis for the understanding of Old Testament and Jewish religious texts. Of special importance in the field of apocalyptic were the excavations in Ras Shamra, ancient Ugarit, which started in 1929.[35] Through these excavations ancient Canaanite myths were discovered where the leading god of the pantheon, Baal, was defeating a sea-monster Lotan, obviously the same monster referred to in the Old Testament as Leviathan. Here the fight against the chaos-monster, known from Enuma Elish, re-occurred in environments much closer to Israel with protagonists known from the Old Testament. The first to revive Gunkel's theory about a chaos-myth behind Dan 7 and other apocalyptical texts, based, however, on the Ugaritic texts, was O. Eissfeldt in

---

31 Cf. H.-J. Kraus, Geschichte der historisch-kritischen Erforschung des Alten Testaments, 2nd ed., Neukirchen-Vluyn 1969, pp. 297f, 302-14.
32 Cf. A. Heidel, The Babylonian Genesis, 2nd ed., Chicago 1951, pp. 1ff.
33 H. Gunkel, Schöpfung und Chaos in Urzeit und Endzeit, 2nd ed., Göttingen 1921(1895).
34 Gunkel, pp. 323-35.
35 For the excavated tablets, cf. H.-J. Kraus, op.cit., pp. 436-8; and D. Kinet, Ugarit — Geschichte und Kultur einer Stadt in der Umwelt des Alten Testaments, SBS 104, Stuttgart 1981, pp. 10-6, 59-64.

1932.[36] But the theory became first really influential through the analysis by J.A. Emerton in 1958, and has still many supporters in recent scholarship.[37]

The access to the mythical universe of the Ancient Near East led inevitably to the question about common patterns in the ancient myths, and to analyse Old Testament and Jewish texts according to these patterns. In apocalyptical research especially two tendencies have been prevailing. The one is as previously noted to locate the basic pattern of apocalyptic in mainly eastern traditions through the juxtaposition of Babylonian, Persian and even Indian texts, often combined with Hellenistic syncretistic traditions.[38] This current of research has especially emphasized the dualistic concept of reality and the doctrine of salvation as the most characteristic features of apocalyptic. The other current is of more recent date and a consequence of the increasing knowledge about Babylonian, Canaanite and Hittite mythology. Here the essential mythical pattern in apocalyptic is either understood on the basis of the chaos-myth or of a "rebellion myth", two mythical themes that are interrelated.[39]

The latest publications of ancient near eastern texts have, however, again moved Babylonian traditions into focus. In 1964 A.K. Grayson and W.G. Lambert published a series of Akkadian prophecies, later supplemented by further prophetic texts.[40] These

36 O. Eissfeldt, Baal Zaphon, Zeus Kasios und der Durchzug der Israeliten durchs Meer, Halle 1932, pp. 23-30.

37 J.A. Emerton, "The Origin of the Son of Man Imagery", JThS 9, 1958, pp. 225-42.

38 For the location of the Enoch concept in mainly Babylonian traditions, cf. H.L. Jansen, Die Henochgestalt. Eine vergleichende religionsgeschichtliche Untersuchung, Oslo 1939. For tracing the concept of era of salvation and the Son of Man back to Persian and Indian traditions, cf. R. Otto, Reich Gottes und Menschensohn, München 1933. For the supposed Persian and Hellenistic concept of the Primeval Man as background for apocalyptical savior figures, cf. for instance. S. Mowinckel, Han som kommer, København 1951, pp. 273-84; English edition He that Cometh, Nashville-New York 1954, pp. 420-37.

39 Cf. P.D. Hanson, "Jewish Apocalyptic Against its Near Eastern Environment", RB 78, 1971, pp. 31-58; and "Rebellion in Heaven, Azazel, and Euhemeristic Heroes in 1 Enoch 6-11", JBL 96, 1977, pp. 195-233.

40 Cf. A.K. Grayson and W.G. Lambert, "Akkadian Prophecies", JCS 18, 1964, pp. 7-30; R.D. Biggs, "More Babylonian 'Prophecies' ", Iraq 29, 1967, pp. 117-32; and A.K. Grayson, Babylonian Historical Literary Texts, TSTS 3, Toronto 1975, pp. 13-37. For the evaluation of the material in relation to apocalyptic, cf. W.G. Lambert, The Background of Jewish Apocalyptic, London 1978. For a recent short presentation of the texts, cf. H. Ringren, "Akkadian Apocalypses", Apocalypticism, D. Hellholm (ed.), pp. 379-86.

prophecies showed close resemblance with the prophecies in the visions of the Hebrew part of the Book of Daniel both in style and content. As previously noted, scholars had often supposed a "Babylonian" background for the Aramaic part of the book, and claimed that the book had grown out of a continuous tradition. Now these observations seemed to get support from the new publications. Even the Hebrew part of the book, which is particularly linked to the Maccabean revolt, and certainly written in Palestine, seemed to be marked by a literary genre closely resembling Babylonian texts.

One can be in doubt whether one should call the research history of apocalyptic exciting or confusing. I think both characteristics fit the present state of research. The increasing source material combined with broader philological knowledge and refined methods have enabled scholars to penetrate more deeply into the apocalyptical imagery. There is also a wide-ranging consensus about how to delimit and describe apocalyptical literature. On the other hand the more complex questions about the origin, growth and nature of apocalyptic are still under intense discussion. Overlooking the research history it is evident that these questions are intimately connected with the question about the roots of apocalyptic, i.e. not only the question about when and why the apocalyptical literature was composed, but also about the origin of the apocalyptical concept of reality and imagery.

The problem of the roots of apocalyptic is as already noted connected with two observations that have been present in the whole history of research. On the one hand it is evident that apocalyptic is marked by what can be called a historical eschatological perspective of reality. This is a heritage from the Old Testament prophetic preaching, a fact which is pointed out in nearly every handbook written about apocalyptic. On the other hand, however, apocalyptic is marked by what can be called a mythical or symbolical universe. This universe with its special imagery seems to have closer resemblance with non-Israelite religions than with the Israelite religion known from the main body of the Old Testament. These two observations evoke a series of questions:

1. What kind of traditions, alien to the main body of Old Testament scriptures, were adopted in the apocalyptical literature?

2. Are the apocalyptical writings based on one or several distinct traditions, or are they an amalgam of disparate motifs which first find a unity in the apocalyptical perspective of reality?

3. How are the non-Israelite traditions to be related to the prophetic heritage? Are they a sort of outer decoration of the inherited historical eschatological perspective, or do they constitute the inner nerve? Is there a harmonious development from prophecy to apocalyptic, or is there a break?

4. Were the non-Israelite traditions alien to the people living in Israel in the Old Testament period, or did they exist as a sort of popular belief, that first "came to the surface" in the apocalyptical writings? If these traditions were new, why were they adopted at that special time?

5. Was there a development in the apocalyptical literature in one direction or another? Can we trace a development from more authentically prophetic traditions to a more speculative or mythical concept of reality, or does the development go in the other direction?

It is obvious that these questions can be approached in different ways. They could lead to a comprehensive study of apocalyptical literature as a whole, trying to separate, classify, date and trace the different traditions. My research has led me in another direction. The question about the roots of apocalyptic must first of all be answered on the basis of the earliest apocalyptical traditions, those traditions that launched the special apocalyptical imagery and concept of reality in Judaism. I have therefore concentrated on the early Enochic literature as the first occurrence of apocalyptic, and on Dan 7, which in the Book of Daniel is the first fully developed apocalyptical text. The Enochic traditions are of variegated character. What holds them together is the protagonist himself, who is regarded both as originator and hero. Dan 7 is transmitted as one composition, where history moves towards a final goal represented by the Son of Man. Thus both the Enochic apocalyptic and Dan 7 introduce individual figures (at least so portrayed within the apocalyptical imagery), that became central in apocalyptical theology and expectations. I shall concentrate on these two figures, instead of aspects of content of motifs, because the characteristics attributed to them form the focal point in the traditions.

The study is not aimed to give a comprehensive review of all traditions that might have influenced the Enochic and Danielic apocalyptic, but is based on what I will characterize as the main sources. The sources dealt with are mostly of Mesopotamian origin. Many of them are not at all considered in this context before, while others have to be examined anew in relation to the new source material.

The point of departure has not been a distinct theory about the origin and nature of apocalyptic, nor the wish to apply a new method to the apocalyptical literature. The various aspects of methodology shall be discussed in connection with the comparison of the sources. The study has grown out of years of searching, analyzing and classifying concrete sources. Slowly the sources began to form a historical pattern, and gradually this pattern gave rise to reflections on what factors shaped it, leading over to a theory about the basic historical dynamic underlying the growth of apocalyptic and the characteristics of this kind of literature. The study has to be read in the light of this developing awareness. The concrete work on the sources has not been carried out as an illustration of a general theory or methodology, but rather forms the basis of the study. The reflection and theorizing is the subsequent result of the concrete work. Of course, one could, after the study is finished, be tempted to write another book, paying more attention to apocalyptic literature as a whole. But I hope the reader will agree that the present documentation had to be written first.

Part 1
The Mesopotamian Background
of the Enoch Figure

חנוך נמצא תמים
והתהלך עם ייי ונלקח
אות דעת לדור ודור

"Enoch was found blameless,
and he walked with the Lord and was taken away,
a sign of knowledge for generations."
(Cairo Geniza Ms.B, Sirach 44, 16)

I
Introduction

a) Why Enoch?

The question introducing this chapter concerns a very simple observation arising from a comparison of Enoch's place in the Bible and later Jewish literature. In the Old Testament Enoch is dealt with twice, namely in Gen 4,17-18 and 5,18-24, two passages totalling a mere nine verses. When one turns to Jewish literature from the fourth or third to the first centuries B.C., however, one finds a totally different picture. Here Enoch becomes a person of utmost importance. Whole books are ascribes to him. Why did such an amount of literature deal with a person whose place in the Bible is so modest?

Of course a quantitative observation like this does not way a great deal. But it indicates a discrepancy between Biblical literature and the later Jewish traditions. What is recorded explicitly about Enoch in Gen 4 and 5 does not amount to much. Cain named a city after him (4,17). He lived for 365 years and walked with God, but then disappeared because God took him away (5,23-24). These two statements are significant enough. Both Enoch's relation to God and his fate are extraordinary and attract attention. Nevertheless, there seems to be quite a distance between the pious man who went to God and the revealer of the wisdom of God par excellence in the later Jewish traditions. Why did circles within the Jewish community choose Enoch as the ultimate revealer of wisdom when the Genesis stories about him do not explicitly mention revelation of wisdom at all?

The tradition of grouping literature around persons is well known from the Old Testament. The Law is ascribed to Moses, the Wisdom to Solomon, the Psalms to David, and the prophecies to the great prophets.[1] But these persons are all described as distinguished individuals in the Old Testament. According to the great compilations within the Old Testament formed either during the exile or shortly thereafter, such as the Deuteronomic work of history and the Pentateuch, they all belong to the classical period of Israel's history from the exodus to the exile. But why Enoch? He is not portrayed as one of the great personalities of the Old Testament, nor does he belong to the history of Israel. Rather, Enoch appears on the stage of primeval history. Strictly speaking, he is not even a Jew.

I am not, of course, the first to raise the question, which in fact is very old. Enoch enjoyed great popularity in Jewish circles up to the first century A.D. His popularity in the main body of the Christian Church continued until the third century A.D.[2] But the Books of Enoch (1 Enoch) did not become a part of either the Jewish or the Christian canon of the Old Testament. The Christians were here influenced by the Jews.[3] The reason why 1 Enoch did not acquire canonical status among the Jews is to be found in the doctrine of history which determined the discussion about the limits of the canon.

This doctrine was clearly formulated by the Jewish historian Josephus in 95 A.D.: ". . . we do not possess myriads of inconsistent books, conflicting with each other. Our books, those which are justly accredited, are but two and twenty, and contain the record of all time. Of these, five are the books of Moses, comprising the laws and the traditional history from the birth of man down to the

1 On anonymity and pseudepigraphy in Old Testament and Jewish tradition, cf. M. Smith, "Pseudepigraphy in the Israelite Literary Tradition", EnAnC 18, 1972, pp. 191-215.
2 The Book of Enoch, 1,9, is explicitly quoted in the New Testament, Jud 14-15. The book was also frequently quoted and referred to by the early Church fathers, cf. W. Adler, "Enoch in Early Christian Literature", P.J. Achtemeier (ed.), SBL 1978, Seminar Papers Vol. I, Missoula, Montana 1978, pp. 171-5. Enoch's position in rabbinic literature was quite different: "The Talmudic period is characterized by relatively little mention of Enoch. The Talmuds do not mention him at all, and only one reference is to be found in tannaitic literature. The comments of the late third and early fourth century rabbis in Genesis Rabbah suggest that Enoch had become an extremely controversial figure", M. Himmelfarb, "A Report on Enoch in Rabbinic Literature", Achtemeier (ed.), op.cit., pp. 259-69, p. 266.
3 For the exclusion of 1 Enoch from the sacred writings of the Church, cf. A.C. Sundberg, The Old Testament of the Early Church, HThS 20, Cambridge 1964, pp. 163-9.

death of the lawgiver. This period falls only a little short of three thousand years. From the death of Moses until Artaxerxes, who succeeded Xerxes as king of Persia, the prophets subsequent to Moses wrote the history of the events of their own times in thirteen books. The remaining four books contain hymns to God and precepts for the conduct of human life. From Artaxerxes to our own time the complete history has been written, but has not been deemed worthy of equal credit with earlier records, because of the failure of the exact succession of the prophets."[4] Basically the same doctrine of history, although expressed in another context, is classically formulated in the beginning of the rabbinical Aboth: "Moses received Torah from Sinai and delivered it to Joshua, and Joshua to the Elders, and the Elders to the Prophets, and the Prophets delivered it to the Men of the Great Synagoge. These said three things; Be deliberate in judging, and raise up many disciples, and make a hedge for the Torah."[5]

In both cases a period of history is singled out as normative. In Josephus this period is defined as the age of prophetic inspiration, while in Aboth it is the period of the transmission of the Law.[6] In both cases, however, the same period is meant — that extending from Moses to Ezra. This period was regarded as the history of revelation. Accordingly, only books believed to originate in this period acquired canonical status.[7] Why approve the claim of authority in the Enochic literature when Enoch did not belong to the period of revelation history?

---

4 Josephus, Against Apion, I,38-41. Text according to H.St.J. Thackeray, Josephus I, LCL, London-Cambridge, Mass., 1927-28 (1976), pp. 178f. The same position is reflected in a tannaitic saying quoted in Tossephta Sota XIII,2: Yoma 9b; Sota 48b; Sanhedrin 11a: "After the later prophets Haggai, Zechariah, and Malachi had died, the Holy Spirit departed from Israel." For discussion, cf. J. Maier and K. Schubert, Die Qumran-Essener, UTB 224, München 1982, pp. 19ff.
5 Aboth I, 1. Text according to R.T. Herford, Pirke Aboth. The Ethics of the Talmud: Sayings of the Fathers, New York 1945 (1962), p. 19.
6 For concepts of the normative period of history in the Jewish community, cf. J.C.H. Lebram, "Aspekte der alttestamentlichen Kanonbildung", VT 18, 1968, pp. 173-89.
7 There seems to be a univocal agreement in the research that this was the decisive criterion in the discussion about the limitations of the canon, cf. Sundberg, op.cit., pp. 12-28, and "The Bible Canon and the Christian Doctrine of Inspiration", Interpretation 29, 1975, pp. 352-71; H. von Campenhausen, Die Entstehung der Christlichen Bibel, BHTh 39, Tübingen 1968, pp. 6-10; O. Eissfeldt, Einleitung in das Alte Testament, 3rd rev. ed., Tübingen 1964, pp. 762-65; L. Rost, Einleitung in die alttestamentlichen Apokryphen und Pseudepigraphen, Heidelberg 1971, pp. 15-18.

The doctrine of the normative period seems not to have been formulated before the first century A.D., but it was not a totally new invention. Traces of it can be followed in previous centuries; both in a negative way, in the experience that there was no legitimate prophet in Israel after the Ezra period, and in a positive way, in the concentration on "the torah and the prophets" as sacred writings, i.e. the scriptures that formed the basis for the doctrine about the normative period.

Both features have roots in the Old Testament. In Lam 2,9 the poet laments the "the prophets have received no vision from Yahweh" after the destruction of the temple. And Ps 74,9 states that "there is no longer a prophet". The polemic against the prophets in Zech 13,2-6 also seems to presuppose that at least some circles did not approve of a true prophetic charisma in those days. Later in history the lack of prophets is referred to several times in 1 Macc,4,44-46; 9,27; 14,41.[8]

The process of canonization started in the pre-exilic period.[9] But Ezra's introduction of the Law in the post-exilic Jewish community had decisive importance (Neh 8) and was the basis for the canonization of the Pentateuch.[10] About 300 B.C. the prophetic writings were regarded as canonical at least in some circles within the Jewish community.[11]

The reading of the Torah and later also the prophets became a part of the synagogical liturgy.[12] In the prayers we find a concentration on the "salvation history" of the Old Testament.[13] Rabbinic Judaism, which later formed the doctrine of the normative period, had its roots in the Pharisaic groups close connected to the

8   Cf. R. Leivestad, "Das Dogma von der Prophetenlosen Zeit", NTS 19, 1973, pp. 288-99.
9   Cf. J.A. Sanders, Torah and Canon, Philadelphia 1975, pp. 31-53; B.S. Childs, Introduction to the Old Testament as Scripture, Philadelphia 1979, pp. 62-7.
10   Cf. W.S. McCullough, The History and Literature of the Palestinian Jews from Cyrus to Herod, Toronto 1975, pp. 45-8; G.F. Moore, Judaism I, Cambridge 1927 (1962), pp. 29-36.
11   Cf. Eissfeldt, op.cit., pp. 765-68.
12   Cf. P. Schäfer, "Der Synagogale Gottesdienst", J. Maier and J. Schreiner (eds.), Literatur und Religion des Frühjudentums, Würzburg 1973, pp. 391-413; S. Safrai, Das jüdische Volk im Zeitalter des Zweiten Tempels, Neukirchen-Vluyn 1978, pp. 51-3.
13   Cf. K. Müller, "Geschichte, Heilsgeschichte und Gesetz", Maier and Schreiner (eds.), op.cit., pp. 73-105, pp. 97-105.

synagogue.[14] It is therefore likely that the process of canonization developed within the synagogues, although we hardly can presuppose the same development in all of them.

The Enoch literature differs from this tradition in Judaism in two ways. First, it shows that there were groups in post-exilic Judaism which continued to produce revelation literature with a claim of divine authority. Secondly, this literature was not dated back in the classical history of Israel, but in primeval history.

The first feature the Enoch literature has in common with a broad current in post-exilic Judaism. In Qumran, for instance, where the Aramaic Enoch fragments were found, the community regarded itself as sharing in the revelation history. According to the Damascus Document the history of Israel demonstrates a basic pattern in the relationship between God and man: The multitude transgresses the Law, while only a remnant shares in the covenant and revelation. That was also the case in the time of the community. The multitude had left the covenant of god, "but for those who kept the commandments of God, for those who were left from them, God established his covenant for Israel for everlasting time, in order to reveal to them the hidden things in which whole Israel has erred."[15] But very often when new literature was written, it borrowed authority from the classical period of Israel's history, either as commentaries on or retellings of Old Testament books, anonymous prophecies ascribed to Old Testament prophets, or as pseudepigraphical literature written in the name of one of the great personalities of Israel's classical history.[16] To some extent this scribal activity only underscored the awareness in post-exilic Judaism of a special period of divine revelation dating back to the period before Ezra.

But Enoch does not belong to this special period, and that makes the Enoch literature different. Yet it is not without parallels. At least three other compilations from the fourth or third to the first

---

14 Cf. C. Thomas, "Der Phariseismus", Maier and Schreiner (eds.), op.cit., pp. 254-72.
15 Dam Doc III,12-14. Text in E. Lohse (ed.), Die Texte aus Qumran, Darmstadt 1971, p. 70. Cf. O. Betz, Offenbarung und Schriftforschung in der Qumransekte, WUNT 2, Tübingen 1960, pp. 8-15; E. Janssen, Das Gottesvolk und seine Geschichte, Neukirchen-Vluyn 1971, pp. 112-23.
16 Cf. J. Schreiner, Alttestamentlich-jüdische Apokalyptik, München 1969, pp. 74-9; D.S. Russel, The Method and Message of Jewish Apocalyptic, London 1964, pp. 127-39.

century B.C. concern primeval figures. "The Life of Adam and
Eve" is commonly dated in the first century B.C.[17] The book is
extant only in a latin translation, making the original content
difficult to determine. In form it is a haggadic work which records
incidents supplementary to the Biblical story. In an early Christian
list of apocryphical writings a "Book of Lamech" is included
together with among others a "Book of Adam" and the "Book of
Enoch".[18] There are no known manuscripts or fragments from this
Book of Lamech.

More interesting for our subject is the reference to a Book of
Noah in Jub 10,13 and 21,10. A reference to a Book of Noah is
also found in a Greek fragment to the Testament of Levi.[19]
Traditions from this book or closely related to it seem to have
been incorporated in the Books of Enoch.[20] In the last of the
"Noah-sections" in the Books of Enoch Noah's birth is told, En
106-107. The same story is told in the Genesis Apocryphon of
Qumran Cave 1.[21] Another text also relates the birth of Noah,
namely 4 Q Mess ar.[22] It tells about the birth of the Elect of God,
the revealer of the secrets of mankind. In these texts Noah is
portrayed in the same way as Enoch, i.e. as a revealer of the
wisdom of God belonging to primeval history.

According to J.T. Milik the original Aramaic Testament of Levi

---

17   Cf. Schreiner, op.cit., pp. 52-4; Russel, op.cit., pp. 59f; Rost, op.cit., pp.
114-6.
18   Cf. Russel, op.cit., pp. 66f. and p. 393. An Aramaic fragment from Qumran
cave 1 was published by D. Barthélemy and J.T. Milik as an apocalypse of
Lamech, cf. D. Barthélemy and J.T. Milik, DJD I, Oxford 1956, pp. 86f.; cf. also
J.T. Milik, Ten Years of Discovery in the Wilderness of Judea, SBT 26, London
1959, pp. 35f. When the whole scroll to which the text belonged was examined,
it was realized that the name was a mistake. The composition is now called the
Genesis Apocryphon, cf. J.A. Fitzmyer, The Genesis Apochryphon of Qumran
Cave 1, BibOr 18A, 2nd rev. ed., Rome 1971, pp. 4-6.
19   Cf. R.H. Charles, The Greek Versions of the Testament of the Twelve
Patriarchs, Oxford 1908 (repr. Darmstadt 1960), p. 252, verse 57. The groups of
Greek fragments agree word for word with Aramaic fragments where they co-
exist, Charles, p. liii.
20   Cf. below, pp. 87-90.
21   Column II-VII. For text and commentary, cf. Fitzmyer, op.cit., pp. 51-5
and 78-99.
22   Cf. P. Grelot, "Hénoch et ses écritures", RB 82, 1975, pp. 481-500. The text
is easy available in J.A. Fitzmyer and D.J. Harrington, A Manual of Palestinian
Aramaic Texts, BibOr 34, Rome 1978, pp. 97-101. A Hebrew version of a summary from the Book of Noah may be preserved on a fragment from Qumran
cave 1 (1Q 19), cf. Barthelemy and Milik, DJD I pp. 84-6; and J.T. Milik (ed),
The Books of Enoch. Aramaic Fragments of Qumran Cave 4, Oxford 1976, p. 55.

was composed in the course of the third, if not towards the end of the fourth century B.C.[23] The Book of Noah must then have been composed as early as the fourth century B.C., which also seems to be the date of the earliest Enoch texts. In any case, the reflections of the book in such a variety of second and first century B.C. writings seem at least to indicate a date at the end of the third or beginning of the second century B.C.

The groups behind the Enoch and Noah traditions operated with a view of revelation history different from the view that later was "canonized" in rabbinic Judaism. The new revelations were not ascribed anonymously or pseudepigraphically to the great revealers of Israel's history, but pseudepigraphically to sages of the primeval history. The question "Why Enoch?" is accordingly not only a question about the background and significance of this particular figure, but also a question about different concepts of history. In one the wisdom of God was linked to the Torah of Moses and interpreted by the prophets.[24] In the other the wisdom of God was already revealed to the sages of primeval history. While the first conception easily could base its understanding on the Old Testament "picture" of the great revealers of the will of God, the second has far less support in the Old Testament. Neither Enoch, Noah, nor any other figure of Old Testament primeval history is portrayed as a revealer in this sense. What is then the background of this concept of history?

b) Research History

A survey of the history of research on Enoch must be divided into two sections, one dealing with Enoch in the Genesis texts and the other with the later Jewish material. The research has developed along these two lines. This is partly dependent on a division of Old Testament and Jewish studies into two distinct fields and partly on a fairly late dating of the Jewish Enoch traditions in the second

23 Cf. J.T. Milik, The Books of Enoch, pp. 24 and 56.
24 For the identification of torah and wisdom in Judaism, cf. M. Hengel, Judentum und Hellenismus, WUNT 10, 2nd rev. ed., Tübingen 1973, pp. 275-318; E. Zenger, "Die Späte Weisheit und das Gesetz", Maier and Schreiner (eds.), op.cit., pp. 43-56.

and first centuries B.C. This had the consequence that the Jewish
Enoch traditions seemed to belong to a different setting than the
Enoch of the Genesis texts.

1.   Enoch in the Genesis Texts

The similarity between Mesopotamian material and the Biblical
primeval history was already seen by Eusebius in his work
Chronica. Here Eusebius quotes extracts from the work "Babyloniaca" written in Greek by the Babylonian priest Berossos.[25] But
prior to the rise of the historical-critical research it was always a
presupposition that the Babylonian work was dependent on the
Biblical stories and not the other way round.
Excavations of Mesopotamian cuneiform texts led to a new
understanding of the relation between Mesopotamian and Biblical
literature. It now became clear that the Primeval history of the
Bible was influenced by the Mesopotamian traditions.[26] This also
led to a reexamining of Berossos' work, which showed that to a
great extent he was reliable in his transmission of Mesopotamian
traditions.
H. Zimmern in his article of 1902, "Urkönige und Uroffenbarung", perceived three basic similarities between the ten antediluvian patriarchs in Gen 5 and the ten antediluvian kings recorded in
Berossos' work.[27] 1) A similarity in names: Since the names of the
kings were extant only in the Greek text of Berossos, Zimmern
presupposed that they reflected Akkadian words. He suggested the
following similarities between Berossos and Gen 5 (in the sequence
Greek-Akkadian-Hebrew): Amelon = amēlu = 'Enōš, "man";
Ammemon = ummânu = Qēnān, "craftsman"; Euedoranchos =
Enmeduranki = Ḥanōk, "high priest, dedicated"; Amempsinos =
amēl Sin = Mᵉtū Šälaḥ, "man + name of god". 2) The similarity
between Enmeduranki and Enoch: Enmeduranki is the seventh
king in Berossos' list as Enoch is the seventh in Gen 5. The king

---

25   The work of Berossos is commented on below, p. 162f.
26   Cf. H.J. Kraus, Geschichte der historisch-kritischen Erforschung des Alten
Testaments, 2nd ed., Neukirchen-Vluyn 1969, pp. 302-9.
27   H. Zimmern, "Urkönige und Uroffenbarung", E. Schrader (ed.), Die Keilschriften und das Alte Testament III, Giessen 1902, pp. 530-43.

Enmeduranki is also described in a cuneiform text from the library of Ashurbanipal.[28] This text describes how Enmeduranki is taken to the gods, among them the sun god Šamaš, and taught divination and astrology. Enmeduranki is also located to Sippar, the city of the sun god. This corresponds to the notice that Enoch lived 365 years and was taken to heaven. The number 365 indicates a connection between Enoch and solar cult. It also corresponds to later Jewish traditions where Enoch is portrayed as the founder of astrology, astronomy and the art of writing. 3) The remarkable longevity: In both Berossos' list and in Gen 5 the figures are said to have lived for an enormous number of years.

H. Gunkel agreed with Zimmern's analysis and underscored some of his arguments.[29] Gunkel recorded the following correspondences: 1) Both lists describe a period between creation and deluge. 2) Both lists contain ten names. 3) In both lists a very high number of years is added to the names. He also called attention to outstanding details, such as the names (cf. Zimmern above) and that in both cases the tenth was the name of the hero of the flood, i.e. the Babylonian Ziusudra and the Biblical Noah.

But later discoveries of Mesopotamian material showed that Zimmern, Gunkel and others worked on partly false presuppositions. In 1923 two cuneiform lists of antediluvian kings were published.[30] This was the Mesopotamian tradition behind Berossos. The language of the cuneiform lists was Sumerian and not Akkadian. Zimmern's approach presupposing an Akkadian background of the Greek words was accordingly mistaken. Considering that the original language was Sumerian, he admits that his conclusions were wrong: "Es fallen also damit all die Schönen Kombinationen, die sich bisher an Gleichsetzungen wie Alaparos (Adaparos), Adapa und gar Adam; Amelon, amēlu und 'Enōš; Ammenon, ummānu und Qain — Qēnan; Amempsinos, Amēl-Sin und Metū Šelah usw. angeschlossen hatten, erbarmungslos dahin."[31]

---

28 The new edition of the text will be discussed below, pp. 184-9.
29 H. Gunkel, Genesis, HK 1/1, 3rd ed., Göttingen 1910, pp. 131f.
30 The antediluvian king lists will be discussed below, pp. 160ff.
31 H. Zimmern, "Die altbabylonischen vor- (und nach-) sintflutlichen Könige nach neuen Quellen", ZDMG NF 3, 78, 1924, pp. 19-35. Cf. also A. Deimel, "Die babylonische und biblische Überlieferung bezüglich der vorsintflutlichen Urväter", Orientalia 17, 1925, pp. 33-47. On the background of the publication

The discovery of the Sumerian originals of the list of antediluvian
kings caused a change in the research. But *von Rad*, for instance,
still saw a relationship between the Mesopotamian lists and Gen 5;
"There are also connections between this list and one with ten
Babylonian primeval kings, who are said to have ruled until the
Flood ... The relationship, however, is not so close as one hereto-
fore thought ... Nevertheless, the Babylonian tradition relates that
the seventh king was actually carried off to the gods and shared in
their secrets (like Enoch); and in that list the tenth king is also the
hero of the flood."[32]

But in the recent commentary on Genesis written by *C. Westermann* in 1971 the evaluation is quite different.[33] Summarizing
previous research, Westermann states three facts about the
Mesopotamian king list: 1) The Primeval king list is an independent entity, originally not connected to a postdiluvian list. 2) The
original number of kings is eight or seven, not ten. 3) The names
of the kings are Sumerian and not Akkadian. He refutes the
correspondences between the Mesopotamian list and Gen 5 put
forward by Gunkel: 1) Although it is correct to consider both lists
as primeval, it is not correct to consider the Sumerian lists as
antediluvian. The dating "before the flood" is not original in the
lists. 2) The number ten is given only in one Sumerian list.
Accordingly it is impossible to compare each name in the two lists.
3) The high number of years is not original either in the Sumerian
lists, nor in Gen 5. It is likely that P (the author of Gen 5) did
know the high number of years in the Sumerian lists, but it is not
necessary to suppose a dependence. 4) There are no correspondences in the names. Westermann concludes: "Es kann jetzt als sicher
gelten, dass P in der Reihe der Namen nicht von einer altbabylon-
isher Liste der Urkönige abhängig ist."[34]

Concerning the figure of Enoch Westermann states: 1) That he

of the cuneiform tablets in 1923 it is rather remarkable that the Genesis commentary of the ICC, 2nd ed., Edinburgh 1930, by J. Skinner hoped that a cuneiform original may be discovered. That this hope is still expressed in the latest
impression of 1969, p. 137, fortysix years after the publication of the two first
lists, and when in all five lists had been published, is astonishing.

32   G. von Rad, Das erste Buch Mose. Genesis, ATD 2/4, Göttingen 1949.
Quoted from the English translation, Genesis. A Commentary, OTL, 2nd rev.
ed., London 1963, p. 69.

33   C. Westermann, Genesis, BK I, Neukirchen-Vluyn 1971, pp. 473-77.

34   Westermann, op.cit., pp. 484-6.

lived for 365 years is not to be regarded as a reference to a solar deity; it is only a round number. 2) There is no relationship between Enoch and Enmeduranki, the seventh king of Berossos' list, since there is no relationship between the Mesopotamian lists and Gen 5. As a parallel, the Mesopotamian figure Adapa comes closer. He was the first of the seven primeval sages and was taken away to the gods and bestowed with wisdom.[35] 3) The taking away of Enoch is expressed in two different elements of tradition. The first is the disappearance of a person, "he was no more"; the second is the rationalizing, mythological explanation, "because God took him away" (Gen 5,24). Westermann finds the same elements in the Mesopotamian traditions about the taking away of the hero of the flood, Ziusudra. But he does not seem to suppose a relationship between this Mesopotamian material and Gen 5.

All the beautiful correspondences between the Mesopotamian primeval king lists and Gen 5 put forward at the beginning of our century ended in a total denial of any connection. But we must ask: Are there sound reasons for this, or is it rather to be explained as a reaction to the mistake in earlier research of seeing a direct relationship in the names?

2. Enoch in Jewish Literature

Interest in Mesopotamian literature as the background for the figure of Enoch resulting from the discovery of the cuneiform tablets also influenced the research in Jewish literature.[36] The context of Enoch in this literature, however, is partly different from the Genesis texts. In the Jewish material Enoch is primarily portrayed as a primeval sage, the ultimate revealer of divine secrets. This led research to focus more on the figure of Enoch

---

35 Westermann sees in general a correspondence between the Cainite genealogy, Gen 4,17-26, and Mesopotamian lists about the seven sages, op.cit., pp. 463f. For these lists, cf. below, pp. 191ff.
36 R. Otto, Reich Gottes und Menschensohn, München 1933, pp. 132ff, is here an exception. Otto does not even discuss the Mesopotamian material, but finds the roots of the figure of Enoch in Persian and Indian traditions. For the influence of the Mesopotamian sources on the research of apocalyptic in general, cf. J.M. Schmidt, Die jüdische Apokalyptik. Die Geschichte ihrer Erforschung von den Anfängen bis zum den Textfunden von Qumran, Neukirchen-Vluyn 1969, pp. 204-214.

himself and less on the genealogical framework. Consequently the negative effect of the mistake in the identification of names has been less influential.

In their study of 1926, *Die Religion des Judentums, Bousset* and *Gressmann* regarded the figure of Enoch as rooted partly in Mesopotamian and partly in Persian traditions.[37] In the Mesopotamian material they found three parallel figures: 1) The seventh antediluvian king Enmeduranki, who, like Enoch, according to a cuneiform text, knew the secrets of heaven and earth. 2) The Babylonian hero of the flood, who, like Enoch, according to the Babylonian flood story, was taken away to Paradise at the end of the earth. 3) The Babylonian god Nabu who resembles Enoch as the scribe of God. In the Persian material Bousset and Gressmann found parallels in the journeys of Zoroaster to receive divine revelations, and, concerning Noah, not Enoch, the legends about Zoroaster's birth.

The first larger analysis of the figure of Enoch was *H.L. Jansen*'s work of 1939, *Die Henochgestalt*.[38] He included the Mesopotamian material already considered but also to a large extent added new material.

According to Jansen Enoch is in 1 Enoch portrayed both as a prophet and a sage. As a prophet he is a terrestrial figure, as a sage a transcendent figure. The terrestrial Enoch is a prophet and wise man who embodies features both from the activity of a native prophet and from a Chaldean wise man and apocalyptic. The transcendent Enoch is a Jewish reception of the Babylonian-Chaldean conception of Ea-Oannes (pp. 5-13).
The transcendent Enoch is primarily connected to the flood story (pp. 22-52). Here Enoch is portrayed in two ways. In the first role he acts as the wise saviour situated in heaven. In the second role he is the wise hero of the flood situated in Paradise. The Babylonian background of the first conception is the role of Ea-Oannes. The god of wisdom Ea is according to the Babylonian flood stories the one who instructs the hero to build a boat and escape the deluge. On the other side Ea under the name of Oannes is the god who brings all wisdom according to Berossos (p. 30). The Babylonian background of the second conception is primeval sages as Gilgamesh, Utnapištim and Adapa. These are however to be regarded as variations of one motif, the primeval sage (p. 33). In the Babylonian flood stories this primeval sage is taken away to the gods. This primeval figure, however, was no ordinary human being. In the Epic of Gilgamesh the hero is described as 2/3 god and 1/3 man. In the myth of Adapa the hero is called "son of Ea". The primeval sage is accordingly the terrestrial antitype of the god Ea (p. 37). He is the representation of the god on earth (p. 38).

37 W. Bousset and H. Gressmann, Die Religion des Judentums im Späthellenistischen Zeitalter, HNT 21, Tübingen 1926, pp. 490f.
38 H.L. Jansen, Die Henochgestalt. Eine vergleichende religionsgeschichtliche Untersuchung, Oslo 1939.

The same two basic motifs are thus according to Jansen extant in both the Babylonian and the Enoch myths of the flood: The god or divine figure who brought heavenly wisdom, and the hero who was saved through this wisdom (p. 50).

The terrestrial Enoch appears as a prophet of judgment and salvation, both features rooted in native Jewish traditions. But he also appears as a Chaldean wise man, a teacher of astronomy and cosmology. This feature has its background in the Babylonian traditions about the primeval sages as Oannes and Adapa. Besides that Enoch also appears as a apocalyptic teacher with a message rooted in Babylonian and Persian wisdom. This terrestrial Enoch is a historical person, a Jewish prophet and wise man who in his teaching includes both the native prophetic traditions and the Chaldean wisdom (p. 66-85).

Enoch is also entitled "the Son of Man". Accordingly this appellation is interesting for a correct understanding of Enoch (pp. 86-110). The description of the Son of Man by the throne of God is on the one side rooted in Old Testament traditions about an eschatological saviour. On the other side this figure has its background in the Babylonian conception of the god-man Ea (p. 105). According to Babylonian sources Ea lives in the water, and according to Berossos he ascended from the sea under the name of Oannes and lived on earth as a human being. This explains the strange features connected to the Son of Man: His wisdom, his preexistence, his ascension from the sea (cf. 4 Ezra 13), and the designation "man". The Book of Enoch describes accordingly three figures: The transcendent Enoch and the Son of Man, both influenced by the Ea-Oannes figure, and the terrestrial Enoch who is a historical person and who acted as a prophet and Chaldean wise man (pp. 111-3). How are these features related?

The question is how the historical person Enoch could regard himself as a representation of the primeval transcendent Enoch (pp. 114-32). Again Jansen finds the key in the Babylonian material. On the one hand the primeval sages as Adapa and Oannes were regarded as an incarnation of the god Ea. On the other side the Mesopotamian kings were regarded as manifestations of their gods. Some of the kings could also regard themselves as incarnations of primeval sages. Sennacherib regarded himself as an incarnation of Adapa, Ashurbanipal as an incarnation of Gilgamesh (pp. 120-1). The kings were accordingly the incarnation of the primeval man. This explains both how the historical Enoch could regard himself as a representation of the primeval Enoch and how he could identify himself with the Son of Man. In the same way as the Mesopotamian kings regarded themselves as an incarnation of the god-man Ea-Oannes, the historical Enoch regarded himself as an incarnation of the primeval sage, the Son of Man.

There is no need to go into any detailed criticism of Jansen's work. Our presentation and discussion of the Mesopotamian material later will clearly illustrate the different position of the recent cuneiform research. But some remarks have to be made. Jansen reflects the position of research of his own time, both methodologically and in the concrete knowledge of the sources. Methodologically this approach can hardly be called history of religion because it works basically synchronically and not diachronically with the sources. It lacks any real attempt to understand the sources according to their genre and intention and against the background of their different historical setting. Only then would it be possible to postulate one historical person behind the different books of Enoch and to construct a Mesopotamian conception of the god-man Ea-Oannes incarnated in historical persons. To state the point clearly, there has never existed a Mesopotamian conception like this. It is nothing but a pure construction based on a misinterpretation of the sources. If we keep this in mind, the basic idea behind Jansen's work falls into pieces, even though some of his observations still have value.

A large step forward in the analysis of the background of Enoch was made by *P. Grelot* in his article of 1958, "La légende d'Hénoch dans les Apocryphes et dans la Bible".[39] Grelot's article is characterized both by a broad presentation of the Biblical and Jewish material analysed according to the different setting of the texts and through a treatment of the Mesopotamian sources without premature syntheses. Much of the material he refers to both in Mesopotamian and Jewish literature will be presented and discussed later. Therefore we will here give only an outline of this important article.

The basic thesis put forward by Grelot is not new. Behind the figure of Enoch as he is presented in the three most important sources — Genesis, the Books of Enoch and the Book of Jubilees — Grelot finds two Mesopotamian figures: Enmeduranki, the seventh antediluvian king; and Ziusudra, the Mesopotamian hero of the flood.

Enmeduranki forms the background when Enoch is portrayed as the heavenly scribe who invented the art of writing, read the heavenly tablets, composed books about astronomy and the future of mankind, and gave these books to later generations.

Ziusudra (and his Akkadian counterpart Utnapištim and Greek counterpart Xisouthros in Berossos) forms the background for the removal of Enoch and his settling down either in Heaven or in Paradise.

Of special importance is Xisouthros' role in the account of Berossos. Here Xisouthros is commanded by the gods to hide the antediluvian books in Sippar, so that they can be transmitted to future generations after the flood. The same idea of transmission

---

39 P. Grelot, "La légende d'Hénoch dans les Apocryphes et dans la Bible: Origine et signification", RSR 46, 1958, pp. 5-26 and pp. 181-210.

of antediluvian wisdom also occurs in the Enoch traditions. In this way Enmeduranki forms the background of Enoch as the initiator of civilization and Xisouthros (Ziusudra) as the transmitter of the antediluvian wisdom.

We will later indicate agreement with many of Grelot's arguments, although we will define the role of Enmeduranki and Ziusudra somewhat differently with regard to both the Mesopotamian material and the influence on the Enoch figure.

The latest great achievement in research on Enoch is the publication of the Aramaic fragments of 1 Enoch from Qumran cave 4 by *J.T. Milik* in 1976.[40] Since this is a text edition, it does not primarily concern our subject. Nevertheless, Milik suggests a Babylonian background for much of the material, such as the background for Enoch as a sage in Mesopotamian traditions about the antediluvian sages (p. 13); the background of the Enochic picture of the world in a Babylonian map (pp. 15-18); the background of the "fall of angels" in the Babylonian model of antediluvian kings and sages (pp. 29-30). But the main importance of this publication is that it gives a new perspective on the unfolding of the Enoch traditions and literature.

The Qumran Enochic corpus was composed essentially of five Aramaic literary works: The Astronomical Book (Ethiopic Enoch ch. 72-82), the Book of Watchers (Eth En 1-36), the Book of Giants (not extant in Eth En), the Book of Dreams (Eth En 83-90) and the Epistle of Enoch (Eth En 91-107). The Similitudes of Enoch (Eth En 37-71) did not belong to this Enochic corpus, nor are any references to the book found in sources before Christ.[41]

The fragments belong to eleven scrolls stemming from different times. On the basis of paleography and orthography they are dated as follows: Enastr[a]: End of the third or beginning of the second century B.C.; En[b]: Middle of the second century B.C.; En[f]:

---

40 J.T. Milik, The Books of Enoch. Cf. also the review by J.A. Fitzmyer, "Implications of the New Enoch Literature from Qumran", TS 38, 1977, pp. 332-45.

41 Milik, op.cit., pp. 89-100, regards the book as a Christian composition and dates it about 270 A.D. This theory is questionable. J.C. Greenfield and M.E. Stone argue for a Jewish origin and date the book before the destruction of the second temple; cf. J.C. Greenfield and M.E. Stone, "The Enochic Pentateuch and the Date of the Similitudes", HThR 70, 1977, pp. 51-65.

Third quarter of the second century B.C. The rest of the fragments belong to the first centuries B.C. and A.D.

The fragments Enastr[a] show that astronomical writings attributed to Enoch with certainty existed in the third century. The fragments En[a] correspond only to the Book of Watchers. They show that this book existed in the first half of the second century. Since the book is a compilation of different parts, the oldest of these (ch. 1-19) must also have existed at the end of the third century. This is the terminus ante quem for both books. The actual date of origin must be earlier. Also the fragments En[b] only correspond to the Book of Watchers. The Book of Dreams and the Epistle of Enoch are only extant on the later fragments.

The early date of two books attributed to Enoch sheds new light on the Enochic traditions. They are no longer to be regarded as a result of the "apocalyptic wave" which arose in the Maccabean age in the middle of the second century B.C.[42] They are also earlier than the final redaction of the Book of Daniel which often has been regarded as the earliest apocalyptic work.[43] There is also not a large time span between the end redaction of the Pentateuch and the Jewish Enoch traditions. Accordingly, a common background for the Enoch of the P source of the Pentateuch and the Enoch of the Jewish literature cannot be excluded.

The present position on the Enoch figure is confusing.[44] In his analysis of Enoch in Genesis, Westermann states that there is no direct relationship between this figure and any Mesopotamian one. Grelot, including the Jewish material, points out a clear relationship with Mesopotamian figures, and Milik supports him. Westermann analyses Gen 5 isolated from the Jewish material. This approach presupposes that the traditions in Gen 5 and the Jewish

---

42   Thus for instance, M. Hengel, Judentum und Hellenismus, pp. 319-30; and D.S. Russel, The Method and Message of Jewish Apocalyptic, pp. 15-20.

43   Thus for instance, P. Volz, Die Eschatologie der jüdischen Gemeinde, Tübingen 1934 (repr. Hildesheim 1966), pp. 11, 16; and H.H. Rowley, The Relevance of Apocalyptic, 3rd rev. ed., London 1963, pp. 93-9.

44   J.C. VanderKam's study, Enoch and the Growth of an Apocalyptic Tradition, CBQ.MS 16, Washington DC 1984, was published about a year after I had handed in my thesis to be defended for the doctor's degree. This study is accordingly not included in the research history and the concrete analysis of the sources. In my concluding chapter to Enoch I give a brief comparative outline of VanderKam's study and mine, cf. note 331, p. 319f.

traditions had different origins and settings. But the early date of the Aramaic Enoch fragments does not point in that direction. The research thus ends with an open question which demands an answer.

c) A New Basis for the Study of Enoch

The discovery of the Enochic fragments in Qumran calls for a new emphasis on the historical growth of the Enochic traditions and literature. It is no longer possible to presuppose that there existed only one concept of the Enoch figure in Jewish literature. A glance at the variegated material to Enoch from the fourth to the first centuries B.C. makes this presupposition very unlikely. Enoch is portrayed in different sorts of literature arising from different historical settings. This demands an analysis first of each part individually and, as the next step, an analysis of the relationships between the various Enoch portraits.

Emphasis on the historical perspective also concerns the relationship between the Genesis sources and the Jewish material. One has the impression that the Enoch of the Priestly source (Gen 5) has been separated from the Jewish Enoch because the former belongs to the canon. The canonical Enoch is the basis and the Jewish Enoch only an elaboration. But in a historical perspective this is a false presupposition. The time span between the earliest Jewish Enochic sources and the Priestly source is not so large as to rule out a common background. To what extent the Jewish material is dependent on Gen 5,18-24 must be investigated, for a general dependence cannot be presupposed. When a dependence is confirmed, we must ask what new elements the Jewish material add.

The historical perspective also concerns our treatment of the Mesopotamian material. Instead of pointing out sporadic similarities or dissimilarities between the Old Testament/Jewish and Mesopotamian material, we need a proper survey of the Mesopotamian material itself on its own premises. And instead of pointing out correspondences in general ideas, we need a detailed textual approach. Individual texts must be analysed and compared before more general conclusions concerning concepts or ideas can be drawn.

It is not correct, however, to claim that C. Westermann, for instance, does not record the Mesopotamian material properly. But as our analysis will reveal, he seems to suffer from a false impression of the importance of the original shape of the Sumero-Babylonian traditions. This, of course, is of great importance if one wants to analyse these traditions in isolation, but it is not the crucial question if one wants to compare this material with the Priestly source of Genesis. The idea of an original shape in this case confuses historical reality. What is crucial for understanding the Priestly source and, consequently, the Jewish material is not what the Sumerian traditions looked like at the end of the third millennium, but rather the content of the available Sumerian and Babylonian texts and traditions more than 1500 years later, about 500-400 B.C., when the Priestly source was composed.

Our theory is accordingly that the portrayals of Enoch are dependent upon fixed Mesopotamian traditions which during a certain period were adopted by Jewish scribes. We shall also deal with cultural and religious concepts in a broader scale when they shed light on the Enochic traditions. But this is not the primary issue. The primary issue is to demonstrate historical dependence between traditions which, although they share some common features with conventional patterns in ancient near eastern and Greek literature, nevertheless have distinguishing characteristics of their own.

Accordingly we have not developed a methodology for comparing religious or mythical patterns. There are mythical elements both in the Mesopotamian literature we shall deal with and in the Enochic traditions, in the sense that they recount events dealing with origins in primordial time in which gods or semi-gods are protagonists. But neither the Mesopotamian compositions nor the Enochic traditions can be classified as genuin myths. The mythical elements are woven together with legendary elements dealing with humans as protagonists and placed in some sort of historical framework. The affinity to myths varies. In the cases where the affinity is closest we shall adopt broad designations as for instance "mythical narrative", which simply means a narrative based on mythical elements, or "mythical etiology", which classifies a composition as a story about origin based on mythical elements. But the relationship between such compositions and myth shall not be made a subject of its own. Our aim is not to give a structural analysis of mythical patterns and elements, but to uncover historical relationship and dependence between fixed traditions.

In our introductory chapter we pointed out that the choice of Enoch as the ultimate revealer of the wisdom of God had theological consequences. That the revealer appeared in primeval time and not in the "canonical" period of Israel's history demonstrated a theological position different from the main current of Old Testament and Jewish traditions. This observation has significance because it indicates a relationship between the figure of Enoch itself and the structure of thought appearing in the sources dealing with him. This means that we cannot draw a sharp line between the portraits of Enoch on the one hand and the literary framework in which he appears on the other. Rather, the enigmatic characteristics of the figure shed light on the enigmatic literature dealing with him. And the other way round, the kind of literature in which he appears contributes to an understanding of the nature of the figure.

This concerns the subjects dealt with in the Enochic traditions, such as astronomy, cosmology, mythical geography, divination. These are subjects which in a Jewish setting appear for the first time in the Enochic sources, at least in a so extensive form. There seems to be an intimate relationship between the figure itself and the kind of skills in which he was trained.

This also concerns the genre of the literature attributed to Enoch, commonly designated as "apocalyptic". To examine the origin and growth of the Enochic traditions is not the same as examining the origin and growth of apocalyptic. This is demonstrated by the simple fact that these traditions are also reflected in non-apocalyptic literature. Nevertheless, it is quite clear that the origin and growth of the Enoch traditions have something to do with the question of the origin and growth of apocalyptic. Whatever scholars think about apocalyptic, they agree that the Enoch literature belongs to this genre. And even more than that: Since the discovery of the Aramaic Enoch fragments and the redating of the Astronomical Book and the Book of Watchers it has become clear that the Enoch literature is a cornerstone in the earliest apocalyptic.

There is in recent research no consensus on the question of precisely how to define the nature of apocalyptic, but there seems to be some sort of consensus in a more broad description of apocalyptic literature. This description is primarily based on the collections of apocalypses found in the Books of Enoch, the Book

of Daniel, 4 Ezra, the Book of Revelation and 2 Baruch. The description is
synchronic, i.e. it does not concern the origin of the literature, but only the
characteristics as they appear in the extant books. Both in the descriptions by K.
Koch[45] and the more detailed classification by J. Collins[46] the form and content
are considered. As constitutive for the literary Gattung "apocalypse" Koch
recorded the kind of revelation as a vision, a didactic discourse between
heavenly and terrestrial representatives, or as a journey to heaven (or hell); the
characterization of the revealed matters as a mystery; and in most of the cases
the pseudonymity of the compositions. As the most important subjects dealt with
Koch listed the present time as the ultimate time; resurrection, universal judgment and a new aion; the imminent end of this era and individual ethics; the
succession of the empires; a division of history into periods; and the impact of
evil.[47]
The list presented by Collins is more detailed. He places the formal characteristics under the rubric "manner of revelation" and classifies the content according
to a temporal and spatial axis.[48] On the basis of this classification he also gives a
definition of the genre apocalypse: "'Apocalypse' is a genre of revelatory
literature with narrative framework in which a revelation in mediated by an
otherworldly being to a human recipient, disclosing a transcendent reality which
is both temporal, insofar as it envisages eschatological salvation, and spatial
insofar as it involves another, supernatural world."[49]
We find Collins' definition appropriate for the fully developed apocalypse. We
also think he has demonstrated the validity of the definition in his description of
the various kinds of apocalypses and their elements.[50] But the problem of the
nature of apocalyptic is not solved by this definition and classification. Collins
examines the finished building, but he admits that he does not examine the building activity and the bricks. The question how and why this building came into
being must be answered before we can say anything definite about its nature.

The debate in earlier research has to a large extent dealt with the
question of whether apocalyptic was a further development of the
Old Testament prophecy[51] or of Old Testament sapiential tradi-

45   Cf. K. Koch, Ratlos vor der Apokalyptik, Gütersloh 1970, pp. 19-31; and:
"Einleitung", K. Koch and J.M. Schmidt (eds.), Apokalyptik, WdF 365, Darmstadt 1982, pp. 1-29.
46   J. Collins, "Introduction: Towards the Morphology of a Genre", Semeia 14,
1979, pp. 1-20.
47   Koch, "Einleitung", pp. 12-8.
48   Collins, op.cit., pp. 6f.
49   Collins, op.cit., p. 9.
50   J. Collins, "The Jewish Apocalypses", Semeia 14, pp. 21-59.
51   The opinion that apocalyptic to a large extent had its roots in Old Testament
prophecy has gained far-reaching support among the researchers. The connecting
link between prophecy and apocalyptic is held to be the concern about history
and eschatology, and the belief in divine inspiration as the source of the revelations, cf. in general, J.M. Schmidt, Die jüdische Apokalyptik, pp. 212ff. and
265-77; K. Koch, Ratlos vor der Apokalyptik, pp. 37-51. The opinion has been
advanced most strongly in Anglo-American research, cf. R.H. Charles, Religious
Development between the Old and the New Testaments, London 1914, pp. 12-
26; H.H. Rowley, The Relevance of Apocalyptic, pp. 13-53, p. 15; D.S. Russel,
The Method and Message of Jewish Apocalyptic, pp. 88-100. But the opinion has
also gained support in German research, cf. above all O. Plöger, Theokratie und
Eschatologie, WMANT 2, Neukirchen-Vluyn 1968, pp. 129-42, and below, pp.
155f.

tions.[52] Recently the former point of view has been argued strongly by P.D. Hanson.[53] Hanson uses "apocalyptic" as a broad designation covering three phenomena: "apocalypse" as a literary genre, "apocalyptic eschatology" as a particular religious perspective and structure of thought, and "apocalypticism" as a religious movement expressing itself in a sociological ideology. He sees the growth of apocalyptic as an interplay of these three levels — the literary genre, the dominant theme, and the socio-religious conditions. Nevertheless, the generating process seems to go in one direction.

The starting point is the socio-religious milieu. "Apocalypticism" is based on the experience of alienation, either by one group over against its own nation or by a broader segment of a nation reacting against a foreign power. This experience of alienation led to "apocalyptic eschatology". This exchatology is partly the heritage of earlier prophetic eschatology, but unlike the prophets the apocalyptics did not expect a change within history. Theirs was outside history in a transcendent realm.

---

52 This more controversial opinion was advanced by G. Hölscher in 1922. Hölscher emphasized the speculative aspects of the apocalyptic literature, such as astronomy, cosmology, botany and medicine, magic and demonology, besides the historical and eschatological concerns, cf. G. Hölscher, Geschichte der israelitischen und jüdischen Religion, Giessen 1922, pp. 187-93. In more recent research the same opinion has been argued by G. von Rad. Theologie des Alten Testaments II, 5th ed., München 1968, pp. 316-31; and Weisheit in Israel, Neukirchen-Vluyn 1970, pp. 347-63. Like Hölscher von Rad emphasized the speculative character of apocalyptic. In dealing with history the apocalyptics distinguished themselves from the prophets in the belief that the periods of history were determined by God. The topics of the apocalyptic literature, such as astronomy, cosmology and interpretations of dreams, were not limited to apocalyptic. These topics were a part of the sapiential traditions. According to von Rad the same was the case with the belief in a determination of history. The problem is, however, the lack of literature from the fourth and the third centuries B.C., which could shed light on the development preceding the known apocalypses. Von Rad wrote this before the publication of the Aramaic Enoch fragments. The redating of the earliest Enochic books caused by this publication has to some extent contributed to solve the problem pointed out by von Rad. It is now possible with a greater degree of certainty to separate the Enochic books from each other and date them in a chronological order, which enables us to trace some of the main lines in the development of Enochic apocalyptic.
53 Cf. P.D. Hanson, "Appendix: An Overview of Early Jewish and Christian Apocalypticism", The Dawn of Apocalyptic, rev. ed., Philadelphia 1979, pp. 427-44; and "Old Testament Apocalyptic Reexamined", Interpretation 25, 1971, pp. 454-79.

H. Stegemann has chosen another approach.[54] He describes apocalyptic as an exclusive literary phenomenon, understood as the composing of revelatory literature whose intention it is to reveal subjects which could not be experienced through perception of the given reality, but had to be unveiled through a heavenly revelation. In a more precise characterization he operates with three designations: "Apocalypses" are literary compositions which in content have the character of a revelation of heavenly subjects, and in which the whole composition, including the literary framework, is composed with the intention of giving a heavenly revelation. "Apocalyptic" is the composing of "apocalypses" and also the apocalypses themselves as a phenomenon in the history of literature, including the immediate impact of these compositions on later history. "Apocalyptical" (used as an adjective) are subjects, imaginations, genres, notions and images, presupposed that they occur in apocalypses and are limited to this field and the immediate derivations from it.

The difference between Hanson and Stegemann is that the former sees the generating process starting in socio-religious conditions, while the latter regards apocalyptic as an exclusively literary phenomenon. The most challenging aspect of Stegemann's definition is that it implies a clear distinction between "apocalyptic" and "eschatology", two designations that often have been confused. "Eschatology" is a theme, while "apocalyptic" is a literary way of expression. "Eschatology" is something one writes about, "apocalyptic" is the way one writes. Eschatology is not the only theme of apocalyptic. Apocalyptic writers also handled such topics as astronomy, cosmology, and geography as well.

But this strictly literary approach, which we think has done away with many misunderstandings, cannot be completely isolated from thematic considerations and analyses of socio-religious conditions. It has to be explained why this kind of literature appeared in exactly this period, how its characteristic style came into being and why the apocalyptic writers of the Enochic tradition and predilection for special themes.

---

54   H. Stegemann, "Die Bedeutung der Qumranfunde für die Erforschung der Apokalyptik", D. Hellholm (ed.), Apocalypticism in the Mediterranean World and the Near East. Proceedings of the International Colloquium on Apocalypticism, Uppsala 1979, Tübingen 1983, pp. 495-530.

Our study does not aim at giving solutions to all these problems. Nevertheless, we think it shall contribute to a solution. By following fixed traditions from a non-apocalyptic setting into their apocalyptic dress in the Enoch literature, it shall demonstrate how literature became apocalyptic, and thus shed new light on the origin of the phenomenon.

Since we are interested primarily in the background of the Enoch figure and the traditions in which he appears, the emphasis will be on the earliest Enoch traditions. In concrete terms that means we shall analyse the two Genesis sequences Gen 4,17-18 and 5,18-24; the oldest Enochic writings — the Astronomical Book, the Book of Watchers and the Book of Dreams; and the earliest Jewish and Samarian sources dealing with Enoch — Pseudo-Eupolemus, Ben Sira and the Book of Jubilees. Naturally we shall add information from other sources when necessary.

II
The Enoch Figure in the Old Testament and in Jewish/Samaritan Literature

a) The Genesis Sequences

1. Enoch According to the Jahwistic Source

In the Jahwistic source which commonly is dated to the first half of the tenth century, Enoch is dealt with in Gen 4,17-18. The context is the Cainite genealogy, 4,1-2.17-24. In this genealogy J records the names of the primeval patriarchs and the inventions connected to them. The genealogy therefore tells about the origin of civilization: agriculture, nomadic and urban life, music and metalworking.[1] The genealogy falls into two parts: vv. 1-2.17-18 record the names of the first seven patriarchs according to the direct line Adam—Cain: Adam - Cain - Enoch - Irad - Mehujael - Lamech, and vv. 19-24 record the descendants of Lamech.

The short notice about Enoch in v. 17 runs as follows:

וידע קין את אשתו ותהר ותלד את חנוך ויהי
בנה עיר ויקרא שם העיר כשם בנו חנוך

"Cain knew his wife and she conceived and bore Enoch. And it happened that he built a city and he gave name to the city according to the name of his son, Enoch."

The syntax is not without difficulties. There are three possibilities: 1) The subject of the second clause is Cain. The problem is, however, that *wayhī* in the beginning of the second clause most naturally takes up again the last figure mentioned before as the subject, which is Enoch. 2) If Enoch is the subject of the second clause, the city is named *kešem benō* "according to the name of his son", who is Irad. This however, contradicts the text as it reads where the name of the son is Enoch. Furthermore, the birth of Irad is first recorded in the next verse. 3) If Enoch is the subject of the second clause and also the name of the city, we have to

---

1 Cf. C. Westermann, Genesis, pp. 438-42.

emend the text. Westermann, following Budde, suggests *kišmō*, "according to his name", instead of *kešem benō*, "according to the name of his son".[2] The problem is that there is weak basis for this emendation in the ancient text witnesses.

The question is whether it is possible to solve the problem on the basis of textual criticism. As the text now reads the first solution is most likely, despite the strange syntax.

But syntactical problems very often reveal a complex history of tradition before the present wording of a text. The tension in the text is in fact between *wayhī*, "and it happened", at the beginning of the clause which most naturally implies Enoch as subject, and Enoch at the end of the line. The beginning of the clause cannot be emended without changing its whole structure, but Enoch at the end can very easily be elided. If we read the text this way, a tradition before the present text could have had Enoch as the first founder of a city. If so, the name of the city would be Irad according to the name of his son (solution 2).

The second great question is connected to the name Enoch, in Hebrew *ḥanōk*. Besides Gen 4 and 5 the name occurs in Gen 25,4; 46,9; Ex 6,14; Num 26,5; and 1 Chr 1,3.33; 5,3. The genealogy in 1 Chr 1,3 is dependent on Gen 5. In Gen 25,4 and 1 Chr 1,33 Enoch is the name of Midian's third son. In Gen 46,9; Ex 6,14; Num 26,5 Enoch is one of Reuben's sons. According to Num 26,5 he is the ancestor of the family of Enoch.

These occurrences show that besides the occurrences in the primeval context, Enoch occurs as ancestor of tribes. It is tempting to regard Enoch in Gen 4 as a parallel to Cain. As Cain is portrayed as the primeval ancestor of the Cainite tribe, Enoch could be the primeval ancestor of the Enochic tribe.[3]

The stem ḤNK occurs in two derivations in Hebrew. The one derivation is *ḥek* (from *ḥink*) which means "palate, gums, mouth". The other is *ḥānak* which means "train, dedicate". It is not clear whether the two derivations were related semantically in Hebrew. An abstract meaning of *ḥek* besides the concrete "organ

2 Westermann, op.cit., pp. 443f.
3 Ch. K. Koch, "Die Hebräer vom Auszug aus Ägypten bis zum Grossreich Davids", VT 19, 1969, pp. 37-81, pp. 57f., note 4.

of taste and sound" is not known.[4] In Arabic *ḥanaka* means "understand" and *ḥunk* means "wisdom, prudence". In Ethiopic *ḥanaka* means "perceive, understand". These more psychologically-centered values may correspond to the concrete Hebrew *ḥek*.[5]

On the basis of the Arabic and Ethiopic meaning of the stem P. Grelot argues that at least the Priestly source has interpreted *ḥᵃnōk* as "the sage".[6] This may be the meaning in the Priestly source, but for the Jahwistic source a derivation from the common verb *ḥanak* seems more likely. The verb is used in the sense of "train youth" (Prov 22,6), "dedicate" as at the formal opening of a new house (Deut 20,5), and "consecrate" the temple (1 Kings 8,63). The meaning of the name *ḥᵃnōk* in Gen 4,17-18 can be explained in analogy to other names in the genealogy. Most likely the names of the sons of Lamech "Jabal, Jubal, Tubal" are understood as derivations from the root YBL.[7] In Hebrew the hiph'il form of the verb means "conduct, bear along".[8] In Aramaic the pe'al and haph'el forms can have the meaning "bring".[9] In Hebrew the noun *yᵉbūl* means "produce".[10] The three sons are thus understood as "producers", i.e. inventors of different sorts of occupations and skills (4,20-22). A relationship between name and occupation also occurs in the second name of Lamech's third son, *tūbal-qaīn*. The root QYN occurs in several Semitic languages in the sense of "metal worker, smith".[11] Tubal-cain made tools of bronze and iron, 4,22.

Also in the name *ḥᵃnōk* there is a relationship between name and activity. This is the case regardless of whether the city was named after Enoch, which seems to be the meaning of the present text, or Enoch was the founder of the city, as the original wording may

---

4 Cf. W. Gesenius and F. Brown (ed.), A Hebrew and English Lexicon of the Old Testament, Oxford 1907 (1966), sub ḥek and ḥānak, p. 335; L. Koehler and W. Baumbartner (eds.), Lexicon in Veteris Testamenti Libros, Leiden 1953, sub ḥek, p. 296, sub ḥānak, p. 315.
5 Cf. P. Grelot, "La légende d'Hénoch dans les Apocryphes et dans la Bible", RSR 46, 1958, p. 186.
6 Cf. Grelot, op.cit.
7 Thus Westermann, op.cit., p. 449.
8 Cf. Gesenius and Brown, op.cit., sub yābal, pp. 384f.
9 Cf. E. Vogt, Lexicon Linguae Aramaicae Veteris Testamenti, Roma 1971, sub yᵉbal, pp. 69f.
10 Cf. Gesenius and Brown, op.cit., sub yᵉbūl, p. 385.
11 Cf. Gesenius and Brown, op.cit., sub qaīn, pp. 883f.

have been. In both cases $ḥ^anōk$, "dedicated", fits very well the founding of a city.

2. Enoch According to the Priestly Source

The Priestly source or sequences of the Primeval history were written down during the exilic period in Babylonia before Ezra introduced "the torah of Moses" in the postexilic Jewish community in the beginning of the fourth century.[12] The context of the Enoch sequence, Gen 5,21-24, is the genealogy of the antediluvian patriarchs from Adam to Noah (Gen 5). This genealogy is partly parallel to the two genealogies recorded in the Jahwistic source: the Cainite genealogy in 4,1-2.17-18 and the Sethite genealogy in 4,25-26.

---

12 The dating of the Priestly source depends on the whole question of the origin of the Pentateuch/Hexateuch. Attempts also have been made in recent research to date the final redaction of the Priestly source before the exile. So for instance A. Hurvitz, "The Evidence of Language in Dating the Priestly Code", RB 81, 1974, pp. 24-56, who argues on linguistic reasons. But the massive arguments based on tradition and literary criticism still point toward an exilic age, cf. on the earlier research, O. Eissfeldt, Einleitung in das Alte Testament, 3rd rev. ed., Tübingen 1964, pp. 208-26, 271-6; cf. on more recent research, B.S. Childs, Introduction to the Old Testament as Scripture, Philadelphia 1979, pp. 122-4; for arguments based on content, cf. R. Kilian, "Die Priesterschrift. Hoffnung auf Heimkehr", J. Schreiner (ed.), Wort und Botschaft des Alten Testaments, Wartsburg 1967, pp. 226-43. It also seems clear that the Priestly source was a part of the "scroll of the law of Moses" (Neh 8,1) introduced by Ezra in the Jewish community about 398 B.C., cf. McCullough, The History and Literature of the Palestinian Jews from Cyrus to Herod, Toronto 1975, pp. 45-8. Whether the scroll contained the whole Pentateuch, as Eissfeldt argues, pp. 755-6, or a shorter form is debated. This problem implies the whole discussion about the character of the Pentateuch/Hexateuch sources. In recent research R. Rendtroff, in his analysis of the Patriarchal history, has argued that the Priestly source did not exist as an independent unit which later was joined to the earlier material of the Pentateuch; cf. R. Rendtroff, Das überlieferungsgeschichtliche Problem des Pentateuch, BZAW 147, Berlin-New York 1977, pp. 112-42. B.S. Childs has argued the same concerning the Primeval history, op.cit., p. 147. I basically agree with this analysis. In the Primeval history there have been independent traditions used by the exilic author, the clearest example being Gen 1,1-2,4a, but there did not exist an independent Priestly account of the Primeval history which was composed without knowledge of the Jahwistic source. It is possible that the Priestly sequences of the Primeval history contain elements from different authors, but the basic features of the sequences must have been created by one author, cf. above all the basic structure: Creation — ten generations — flood — ten generations.

Gen 4

Cainite genealogy	Sethite genealogy	Antediluvian genealogy
1. Adam	1. Adam	1. Adam
2. Cain	2. Seth	2. Seth
3. Enoch	3. Enosh	3. Enosh
4. Irad		4. Kenan
5. Mehujael		5. Mahalalel
6. Methushael		6. Jared
7. Lamech		7. Enoch
		8. Methuselah
		9. Lamech
		10. Noah

Comparison of the genealogies:

The names: Five names are identical: Adam, Seth, Enosh, Enoch, and Lamech. The fourth name in Gen 5 קֵינָן, *qēnān,* looks very much like קַיִן, *qaīn,* in Gen 4. The fifth name in Gen 5 מהללאל, *mahªlal'el,* looks very much like, מחויאל *mᵉḥuyā'el,* in Gen 4. The meaning of Mehujael in Gen 4 is unknown, but Mahalalel in Gen 5 is known as a proper name (Neh 11,4), meaning "praise God!" or "praising God". The sixth name in Gen 5 ירד, *yārād* or *yäräd,* resembles, עירד *'irad,* in Gen 4. The meaning of Irad in Gen 4 is unknown, but Jared in Gen 5 is known as a proper name (1 Chr 4,18) and is most likely to be derived from the stem YRD, "descend". The eighth name in Gen 5 מתושלח, *mᵉtušalāḥ* or *mᵉtušälaḥ,* looks like מתושאל, *mᵉtušā'el,* in Gen 4. The last name is most likely composed of mut(u), "man" + *šᵉ'ōl,* "underworld". The name in Gen 5 seems to have a similar content; mut(u) + *šalaḥ* — "a god of the underworld".[13] The tenth name in Gen 5 is the hero of the flood, Noah, in the Jahwistic source.

This comparison of names should clearly demonstrate that Gen 5 was not composed without an awareness of the names in Gen 4. One must of course consider the possibility that the priestly author knew a list similar to that of Gen 4 and closer to Gen 5, but I cannot see that such an assumption is necessary. The similarity between the names is close enough to assume that the priestly author knew the Jahwistic genealogies in one form or another.

The order: The priestly author of Gen 5 added the two genealogies of Gen 4 to get nine names before adding Noah, the hero of the

13   Cf. Westermann, op.cit., p. 446.

flood, to make ten. This is in accordance with his postdiluvian list which also has ten generations from Shem to Abraham (Gen 11,10-26). The basic structure of the priestly account of the Primeval history is accordingly: Creation (Gen 1,1-2,4a) — ten antediluvian generations from Adam to Noah (Gen 5) — the flood (Gen 6-8) — ten postdiluvian generations from Shem to Abraham (Gen 11,10-26).

What is rather confusing is that the priestly author changes the order of the names in his list in Gen 5. If we add the Cainite genealogy to the Sethite in Gen 4 and compare this with Gen 5, the order is the same ut to the fourth name in Gen 5, Cain — Kenan. The order is also the same in the last three names. What has happened is that when the author of Gen 5 came to the name Enoch in Gen 4, he moved this name from the fifth place, where it should have been, to the seventh. He also changed the order of Mahalalel (Mehujael) and Jared (Irad) so that Jared (Irad) became Enoch's father. There may be an explanation for this last change. In Jewish sources the name Jared clearly is interpreted as "descend", and the "fall of angels", recorded in Gen 6,1-4, is placed in his time as something that happened in the generation before Enoch.[14] The priestly author may have known similar traditions. But there is no explanation for the first change, other than that it must have been important for the priestly author to have Enoch at the seventh place of the list. We know that the number seven was a highly significant number for P through his account of creation, Gen 1,1-2,4a.

But why did P choose Enoch from the Jahwistic genealogies as the seventh extraordinary patriarch? There seems to be no relationship between what is told in Gen 4,17-18 and P's account in 5,18-24. The only direct link between the texts seems to be the name $h^an\bar{o}k$ itself. We have earlier argued that this name in the Jahwistic source was derived from the verb $h\bar{a}nak$ with the two meanings "dedicate" and "train".[15] P could have interpreted these values as a description of the person himself. If so, Enoch was perceived as a "dedicated and trained man". For the latter meaning one can compare Gen 14,14 where the $h^an\bar{\imath}k\bar{\imath}m$ are the trained men of

---

14 Cf. below, pp. 91f.
15 Cf. above, p. 41.

Abraham. The former would mean that Enoch was a man dedicated to God. The second value "trained" comes close to Grelot's suggestion that P interpreted $ḥ^anōk$ as "the sage".[16] In the context of P the two values describe a man dedicated to and trained by God, corresponding to the passage "Enoch walked with God", 5,22.24.

The account of Enoch is incorporated into the framework of the genealogy. The pattern of the genealogy is interrupted twice: in v. 22 with the passage "Enoch walked with God", and in v. 24: "Enoch walked with God, then he was no more, because God took him away." Besides these alterations the Enoch sequence is like the other genealogical sequences of Gen. 5.[17] Accordingly P had three statements about the seventh patriarch that made him special when compared to the others.

In Hebrew:

ויתהלך חנוך את האלהים	And Enoch walked with god,
ואיננו	then he was no more,
כי לקח אתו אלהים	because God took him away.

Besides these, the 365 years for the life of Enoch attract attention. His span of life was less than half that ascribed to the other figures of the genealogy.

1) *Enoch walked with God*. This passage can be interpreted in different ways. It can have a concrete meaning, i.e. Enoch lived in a kind of physical closeness to God. It can also have a metaphoric meaning, i.e. Enoch lived a life dedicated to God. A. Schmitt gives a list of the occurrences of $hālak$, "walk", in the Old Testament followed by different prepositions including *'ät*, "with". The list shows that both meanings are possible.[18]

The same result can be drawn from Jewish literature dealing with the passage. The Septuagint quite clearly understands the passage

---

16   Cf. above, p. 42.
17   I see no necessary reason to split up the text according to different sources on basis of literary criticism. The interruptions in the genealogical pattern are the work of P; cf. the discussion in A. Schmitt, Entrückung — Aufnahme — Himmelfahrt. Untersuchungen zu einem Vorstellungsbereich im Alten Testament, FoBib 10, Stuttgart 1973, pp. 153-8.
18   Cf. Schmitt, op.cit., pp. 158-160.

metaphorically: καὶ εὐηρέστησεν Ἐνωχ τῷ θεῷ, "And Enoch was pleasing to God." The Book of Jubilees, however, interprets the passage literally, understanding *'älohīm* as the angels.[19] The interpretation in Jubilees is influenced by other Jewish literature telling about Enoch's stay with the angels, which may reflect the traditions behind the priestly account of Genesis. We shall return to this problem in the analysis of the Jewish material.

The context of the phrase in Gen 5 clearly shows that a concrete meaning there is hardly likely. In v. 22 the passage is woven into the genealogy. In the three hundred years Enoch walked with God he begot sons and daughters. This means that he lived a normal life on earth and not in heaven or any other transcendent realm. That God in one form or another should be physically present on earth is an impossible assumption, given P's theology.

But also the metaphoric interpretation, which emphasizes the close spiritual relationship between Enoch and God, can have different connotations. The Septuagint quite clearly understands the passage in a moral sense.[20] But this is not the only possibility. The closest parallel to this passage in the Old Testament is the description of Noah in Gen 6,9: נח איש צדיק תמים היה בדרתיו את האלהים התהלך נח "Noah was a righteous man, he was blameless among his contemporaries. Noah walked with God." A. Schmitt regards the first clause as an explication of the second.[21] But this is not certain. The first clause describes Noah in relation to his contemporaries, while the second describes him in relation to God. The clause does not explicitly say that Noah was righteous because he walked with God or that he walked with God because he was righteous. The clauses say *first* that Noah was a righteous man and, *second*, that he walked with God. Accordingly Noah's walking with God may signify more than his righteousness in a moral sense. This is exemplified in the subsequent narrative in which God reveals his plans about the flood to Noah. We shall see that this interpretation corresponds very well with the Jewish Noah traditions.[22]

If this is a correct interpretation concerning Noah, the passage can

---

19 Cf. below, pp. 130f.
20 Cf. our discussion to the Book of Ben Sira, p. 125.
21 Cf. Schmitt, op.cit., p. 160.
22 Cf. below, p. 93.

have the same meaning with regard to Enoch. The seventh patriarch also had an extraordinarily intimate relationship with God implying that he had access to his plans. This also corresponds very well with the meaning of Enoch's name ad "dedicated, trained".

2) *And he was no more.* The simple nominal clause ואיננו, *'enännū* used in this context can have two meanings. It can signify death as in Job 7,21; and Ps 39,14; 103,16. It can also signify the sudden disappearance of a person. The mysterious character of the disappearance is often emphasized, as in the story of Joseph, Gen 37,29.30; 42,13.32.36, and in 1 Kings 20,40; as is the traceless disappearance, as in Ps 37,36; Jer 50,20; and Ezek 26,21.[23]
The possibility that "he was no more" should indicate the death of Enoch is unlikely. The notice of death belongs to the general pattern of the genealogy in Gen 5 and is always expressed through מות, *mūt*, "die", cf. vv. 5.8.11.14.17.20.27.31 *'enännū* is an alteration of this phrase, occurring at the same place as *mūt* in the other genealogical sequences. The alteration of phraseology must also mean an alteration of content. The phrase emphasizes the sudden, mysterious and traceless disappearance of Enoch.

3) *Because God took him away.* The verb לקח, *lāqah*, "take", used with God or a divine power as subject and a person as object, occurs in several contexts in the Old Testament.[24] We must limit our investigation to the occurrences which are closest to Gen 5,24.

i. The taking away of a dead person as an act of liberation from the power of the underworld, sheol. This is the meaning in Ps 49,16 and 73,24.[25]

ii. The taking away of a living person as an act of final removal from the earth. This is the case in the story about the ascension of Elijah, 2 Kings 2,1-18, cf. vv. 3.5.9.10.[26]

23 Cf. the discussion in Schmitt, op.cit., pp. 163-5.
24 For a survey of the occurrences, cf. Schmitt, op.cit., pp. 85-91; and H.H. Schmid, "Iqh nehmen", THAT I, München 1971, cols. 875-9.
25 Cf. Schmitt, op.cit., pp. 242ff and 300ff.
26 Schmitt, op.cit., pp. 110, 114 claims that the ascension of Elijah is a description of his death. His reason is the lamentation over Elijah in 2 Kings 2,12 which occurs in the same wording upon the death of Elisha in 2 Kings 13,14. There is of course a possibility that the text is based on a tradition about the death of Elijah, but as the text now reads Elijah is very much alive when the

iii. The taking away of a living person as an act of temporal transference. This is the case in the visionary experiences of Ezekiel, Ezek 3,12.14; 8,3: 11,24; 37,1; 40,2. The verb lāqaḥ is used in 3,14 and 8,3.

Comment on point i: In Ps 49,16 lāqaḥ stands alone. Parallel is pādā, "liberate". In Ps 73,24 lāqaḥ stands alone. There are no parallel verbs with the same connotations. The subject in both cases is Yahweh. There is no destination linked to lāqaḥ.

Comment on point ii: In 2 Kings 2,3.5.9.10 lāqaḥ stands alone. The same incident is described in v. 1 and v. 11. with the verb 'ālā, in v. 1 in hiph'il, "lift up", in v. 11 in qal, "ascend". In a suggestion about what may have happened to Elijah, his disciples use the verb nāsā', "lift up", v. 16. Subject to lāqaḥ is Yahweh. The destination for the ascension is "heaven", vv. 1.11.

Comment on point iii: In Ez 3,14 lāqaḥ stands together with three other verbs describing a course of event: "And the spirit (or "the wind") lifted me up and took me away and I went . . ." Here the verb nāsā', "lift up", is used together with lāqaḥ. In Es 8,3 lāqaḥ also stands together with other verbs: "He stretched out what seemed a hand and took me by the forelock of my head, and the spirit (or "the wind") lifted me up between earth and heaven and brought me to Jerusalem in visions from God." Here lāqaḥ is used together with nāsā' and bū' in hiph'il, "bring". But lāqaḥ has here not the meaning "take away", but the meaning "seize", i.e. "the seized me by the forelock".

The verb lāqaḥ used with God as subject and a person as object occurs one other time in the Primeval history besides Gen 5,24, namely in the Jahwistic "Paradise story" in Gen 2,15. ויקח יהוה אלהים את האדם וינחהו בגן עדן "And Yahweh God took the man (Adam) away and placed him in the garden Eden", cf. also 2,8. The verb lāqaḥ is here combined with nūaḥ in hiph'il, "place". A. Schmitt lists this occurrence under the rubric "removal as a temporal accident" together with the occurrences in the Book of Ezekiel.[27] I doubt that this classification is correct. The intention in Gen 2,8.15 is not to tell about a trip to Paradise in the same way as Ezekiel made a trip to Tel Aviv and Jerusalem. The result of the events in Gen 2-3 was that Adam's stay in Paradise became temporal, but the intention of the removal was that the garden of Eden should be Adam's permanent residence. Gen 2,15 accordingly forms a fourth possibility: The taking away of a person to Paradise.

Syntactically, the use of lāqaḥ in Gen 5,24 comes closest to our points i and ii, since lāqaḥ in these cases is used in an absolute

---

incident happens: "They went on, talking as they went, and behold!, chariots of fire and horses of fire, which separated them one from the other, and Elijah ascended in the storm to heaven," 2 Kings 2,11.
27   Cf. Schmitt, op.cit., pp. 310-4.

sense, not connected to other verbs. In the two psalms and in the story about Elijah there is also no destination linked directly to *lāqaḥ*, although the destination "heaven" occurs in 2 Kings 2,1.11. In content the removal of Elijah comes closest because he is taken away alive. This is also the case with Adam in Gen 2,15, but here the verb *lāqaḥ* is used together with another verb. The similarities, especially to the story of the ascension of Elijah, however, are not of that kind there is any reason to suppose a relationship between this story and Gen 5,24. The motif is the same, and the verb *lāqaḥ* is used in the same way, but there are no indications in the text that the fate of Elijah should have inspired the author of P in his account of the fate of Enoch. Such an assumption would demand some sort of signal in the sequence Gen 5,21-24 or its context that Enoch was patterned on Elijah. This is not the case. The similarities show that the basic motif of "removal" expressed through the verb *lāqaḥ* was known in Old Testament context and available to the author of P when he was to describe the fate of the seventh patriarch.

A. Schmitt emphasizes the difference between Gen 2,15 and 5,24 for two reasons. First, the removal in 2,15 is supposedly temporal (which is not the case); secondly, *lāqaḥ* in 2,15 is used together with another verb.[28] I am not convinced about the validity of the second argument either.

As will be demonstrated later under the treatment of the Book of Jubilees, the Enoch sequence there is structured according to Gen 5,21-24.[29] The sentence "... and he was no more, because God took him away," has the following corresponding clause in Jub 4,23: "And he was carried away from amongst the children of men and we conducted him into the garden of Eden in majesty and honour." The Ethiopic verbs used are *naś'a* in Ili (causative) and *wasada*. The first verb is the same as Hebrew *nāśā'* and has the same values: "lift up, carry, take away". The second verb has no similar root in Hebrew with the same meaning. In Ethiopic it means "conduct". The two verbs quite clearly describe the same sort of event as in Gen 2,15. There the verbs *lāqaḥ*, "take away" and *nûaḥ* in hip'il, "place", were used. The destination is also the

---

28 Cf. Schmitt, op.cit., pp. 311f.
29 Cf. below, pp. 127ff.

same: the garden of Eden. But Jub 4,23 is not a commentary on Gen 2,15, but on Gen 5,24! We do not know exactly which Hebrew verbs the original author of the Book of Jubilees used, but we know that he had no difficulty in applying verbs closely related to Gen 2,15 to the Enoch incident in Gen 5,24.

This should indicate that arguments based on syntactical observations, in this instance *lāqaḥ* used isolated, should not be stressed too heavily. The author of the Book of Jubilees could in a commentary on Gen 5,24 express the incident in words closely related to Gen 2,15. Of course, this does not automatically lead to the conclusion that the author of P was inspired by the incident described in Gen 2,15, or some similar traditions, but we cannot on the basis of syntax exclude the possibility. We shall return to the problem later in our analysis of the background of the P account in Mesopotamian material.

4)   *The 365 years*. Enoch is said to have lived 365 years, less than half as long as the other figures in Gen 5. C. Westermann sees a connection between this number and the number of days in a solar year. The question is then why this specific number was chosen. Westermann does not regard it as more than a round number which signified that Enoch lived a complete time on earth: "Dieser Entrückung zu Gott entspricht es, dass die Lebenzeit des Henochs eine volle, runde, ganzheitliche Zeit war. Diese runde Zahl konnte eine kurze sein, weil sie ja nicht mit dem Tod endete."[30] But he does not ask why precisely the "number of the sun" was chosen as the round number. This is a significant question since this number is not common in the Old Testament, nor is the solar year commonly used as an indicator of time.

This last observation led A. Schmitt to deny that the number 365 was meant to have any connection with the sun.[31] He suggests the possibility that it was meant only as a relatively short number signifying that Enoch was removed to God before the deluge. But this does not fit the context, as Schmitt admits. If so, the other patriarchs as Jared, Methuselah and Lamech should have died in

30   Westermann, op.cit., p. 485.
31   Cf. Schmitt, op.cit., pp. 171-3.

the flood. But this is certainly not the meaning of the short "then he died" at the end of each genealogical sequence.

Furthermore, it is very unlikely that the number 365, which is the number of the solar year, should have been chosen by accident. Although it is correct that the solar year not commonly is used as an indicator of time in the Old Testament — where the calendar is primarily a lunar one — it occurs in the Old Testament in a context closely connected to Gen 5.

According to Gen 7,11 the flood started on the seventeenth day of the second month. According to Gen 8,14 it ended on the twenty-seventh day of the second month of the next year. Hence, the flood lasted twelve months and eleven days. The lunar year encompasses 354 days. Adding eleven days we get 365 days, exactly on solar year.[32]

It is highly unlikely that the same author in one sequence should use the number 365 arbitrarily without any connection to the sun or a solar year, but in the next sequence calculate the duration of the flood at exactly 365 days, i.e. a solar year.

It is also rather remarkable that Schmitt argues on the basis that the solar year plays no important role in the Old Testament but does not mention Jewish literature, in which Enoch is made the advocate of a solar year.[33] The authors of this literature certainly saw a connection between Enoch and the number of the sun.

Both Westermann and Schmitt deny the possibility that the number 365 signifies a connection between Enoch and solar cult.[34] We shall discuss that later. But I cannot find any sound reasons to deny that P chose the number 365 to signify a connection between Enoch and some kind of speculation about the sun or the solar year.

We have reached the following conclusions about Gen 5,21–24 and the context in Gen 5:

* The names of the ten patriarchs in Gen 5 are derived from Gen 4 by adding the two genealogies given there.

---

32 Cf. R. de Vaux, Ancient Israel. Its Life and Institutions, London 1961 (Paperback ed. 1973), pp. 188f.
33 Cf. below regarding the Astronomical Book, pp. 69ff.
34 For this opinion, cf. our research history, p. 25.

* The names of the lists in Gen 4 are rearranged in Gen 5 so that Enoch comes at the seventh place.
* P seems to have interpreted the meaning of *ḥᵃnōk*, "dedicated, trained", to describe Enoch as a dedicated and trained man corresponding to the passage that "Enoch walked with God".
* P breaks the pattern of genealogy in the Enoch sequence. This indicates that P had available traditions about the seventh patriarch that he wanted to incorporate in the genealogy.
* "Enoch walked with God" means in P that he lived in an intimate spiritual relationship with God. As in Noah's case, this can mean that he had access to God's plans corresponding to his name as "dedicated, trained".
* "Enoch was no more" signifies his sudden, mysterious disappearance.
* "God took Enoch away" has its closest parallel in the Old Testament in the story about the ascension of Elijah, although other parallels, such as Adam's removal to Paradise, cannot be excluded.
* "Enoch lived 365 years" indicates a connection between Enoch and some sort of speculation about the sun or the solar year.

b) Jewish Enochic Writtings

1. The Astronomical Book

1.1 The Versions

The Astronomical Book covers ch. 72-82 of the Ethiopic Book of Enoch (Eth En).[35] There has been a Greek translation, but it is no

---

35 We use the following Ethiopic text editions to the Books of Enoch: R.H. Charles, The Ethiopic Version of the Book of Enoch ... together with the fragmentary Greek and Latin Versions, Oxford 1906; M.A. Knibb, The Ethiopic Book of Enoch. A new edition in the light of the Aramaic Dead Sea Fragments. Vol I. Text and Apparatus, Oxford 1978. For the Ethiopic text we use the translation of M.A. Knibb, The Ethiopic Book of Enoch. Vol II. Introduction, Translation and Commentary, when not otherwise stated.

longer extant.[36] Fragments of an Aramaic astronomical book were found at Qumran. J.T. Milik has published fragments belonging to three scrolls and given a description of a fourth (Enastr[a]). He dates the scrolls as follows: Enastr[a]: end of the third or beginning of the second century B.C.; Enastr[c]: middle of the first century B.C.; Enastr[d]: second half of the first century B.C.; Enastr[b]: early years A.D.[37] The discovered scrolls contain only material of astronomical and cosmological character. Judging from the fragments, the Aramaic Astronomical Book at Qumran was copied as a separate scroll not including other Enochic writings.

The fragments belonging to the oldest scroll (Enastr[a]) contain only calculations which synchronize the movements of the sun and moon. As a whole these calculations are not extant in Eth En, but Milik suggests that a résumé may be found in Eth En 73,1-74,9 or only in 74,3-9.[38] Enastr[b] and Enastr[c] contain passages which correspond to various paragraphs of Eth En. Enastr[b] has also fragments from the synchronistic calculations of Enastr[a]. Enastr[d] provides remains of the final part of the Aramaic book, which is lost in Eth En. Comparing the fragments, Milik states that the oldest scroll must have contained both the synchronistic calculations, sequences corresponding to Eth En, and a final part lost in Eth En.[39]

The discrepancy between the Ethiopic shorter version and the longer Aramaic original Milik ascribes to the creators of the Greek version: "It can be seen clearly that the Egyptian Jews responsible for the translation from Aramaic were at pains to shorten the voluminous, prolix and terribly monotonous original."[40]

The dating of the oldest scroll to the end of the third or the beginning of the second century gives the terminus ante quem for the origin of the Jewish astronomical Enochic traditions. The terminus ab quo will be discussed later.

36   J.T. Milik, The Books of Enoch, pp. 19f claims to have identified small parts of the book in Greek fragments.
37   Milik, op.cit., pp. 273f.
38   Milik, op.cit., p. 275.
39   Milik, op.cit., p. 8.
40   Milik, op.cit., p. 19.

1.2   The Content of the Ethiopic Astronomical Book[41]

The book begins with the headline "The book of the revolutions of the lights of heaven" (72,1), which signifies its astronomical content. The first section is introduced through the headline "And this is the first law of the lights. The light the sun . . ." (72,2). This section contains a calculation of the movements of the sun during one year. The system is based on a division of the eastern and the western horizon into twelve gates, six in the east and six in the west. The first pair of gates forms the most southern point of the sun's journey and the sixth pair of gates the most northern. The sun advances from the southern first gates to the northern sixth gates during the first six months. In this period the days grow longer. The next six months the sun returns to the first gates, and the days become shorter.[42] The calculation is based on a system of one year consisting of twelve months. The whole year is estimated at 364 days (72,32). The months are estimated at 30 days adding one month of 31 days after each third month. The days and nights are divided in 18 parts. The shortest day is estimated as 6/18, the longest as 12/18, which gives a ratio 2:1 for the extremal daylight.[43]

The next section is introduced by the headline "And after this I saw another law for the smaller light, named the moon" (73,1). This section deals with the lunar light in relation to the sun. Both this section and the following about the moon are incomplete; only parts of the course of the moon are described.[44] The light of the full moon is estimated at 1/7 of that of the sun (73,3). This estimation is then coordinated with the course of the moon during one month of alternatively 29 and 30 days, giving a lunar year of 354 days.

The lunar month is divided into two parts: During the first part the moon waxes from new moon to full moon in 14 days when the month is 29 days, or in 15 when the month is 30 days, and conversely wanes during the second part. The system did not work without adjustments, but applied to a month of 29 days we have the following calculation: the new moon has 1/14 parts of the lunar light, while the full moon has 14/14 parts. The system is based on the number 7. The moon increases from 1/2 (1/14) to 7 (14/14), estimated on the basis that the lunar light is 1/7 parts of the solar light.[45]

The next section is introduced by the headline "And another journey and (another) law I saw for it" (74,1). Also this section deals with the courses of the moon and the sun. The basic idea is the same as in the section above, but the purpose is now to synchronize the lunar with the solar year. This is first done by introducing the gates of the horizon known from the first section in order to

---

41   Our aim is not to give an analysis of the system of computation behind the astronomical calculations, but to give an outline of the structure and content of the Astronomical Book as a composition. For a recent analysis of the system underlying the astronomical calculations, cf. O. Neugebauer, The 'Astronomical' Chapters of the Ethiopic Book of Enoch (72 to 82), KDVSMfM 40:10, København 1981.

42   Cf. the description of the system in R.H. Charles, The Book of Enoch, Oxford 1912, pp. 153f; and Neugebauer, op.cit., pp. 6-13.

43   Cf. the table in O. Neugebauer, "Notes on Ethiopic Astronomy", Orientalia NS 33, 1964, pp. 49-71, p. 49. Cf. also Neugebauer above, note 41.

44   Cf. E. Rau, Kosmologie, Eschatologie und die Lehrautorität Henochs. Traditions- und formgeschichtliche Untersuchungen zum äth. Henochbuch und zu verwandten Schriften, unpubl. diss. Hamburg 1974, p. 202.

45   Cf. for further description, Charles, op.cit., p. 157; and Milik, op.cit., p. 283.

coordinate the courses of the sun and moon in one year (74,3-9).[46] The author
continues in his attempt to reconcile the lunar and solar years, estimated over
longer intervals of time, 3, 5 and 8 years (74,10-17).[47] There follows a sequence
about the four intercalary days, one day added to each third month of a year.
Most likely the section ends in 75,3, which sums up the previous calculations and
states that they were revealed by the angel Uriel.

The next part of the book has no clear headlines. It starts with a reference to the
angel Uriel and is thus linked to the end of the previous section: "Likewise Uriel
showed me twelve gate openings" (75,4). The section is a compilation of
variegated material. The first subsection seems to end in 75,9. It contains a
further elaboration of the twelve gates of the sun and moon known from the
previous sections.[48]
Most likely the next subsection starts in 76,1: "At the end of the world I saw
twelve gates open to all the winds." This section is cosmological rather than
astronomical.[49] It applies the system of the twelve gates of the horizon to twelve
gates of the winds. These gates are located according to the four quarters of
heaven, three in each quarter. This subsection seems to end in 76,14 with the
remark that Enoch showed all this to his son, Methuselah.
What seems to be a new subsection is linked to the previous one without any
headline or introduction (77,1). It deals with the four quarters of heaven from
the previous section.
This subsection is linked directly to a new one comprising cosmic geography,
77,4-8. Here each sequence is introduced by the phrase "I saw", 77,4.5.8.
In 78,1 begins a new astronomical section introduced "The names of the sun
(are) as follows . . ." This section contains names of the sun and moon and leads
to a new calculation of the relationship between the sun and moon with the same
content as 73,1ff and 74,1ff.

A clearly marked new section follows in 78,10 and is introduced by the title
"And Uriel showed me another law, (namely) when light is transferred to the
moon." The content of this section is the same as the previous synchronistic
calculations of the sun and moon. The section seems to come to an end with a
concluding remark in 79,1-2. But then a new calculation is added, 79,3-5, with a
new concluding remark in 79,6.

Three speeches follow. In two of them Uriel is addressing Enoch, and in the
third Enoch is addressing his son, Methuselah. The first speech, 80,1-7, refers
back to the astronomical material already presented, but also includes the law of
the stars which comes after the three speeches. The content of the speech is the
disorder in nature which will appear when the celestial bodies go astray. The
second speech, 81,1-10, has no reference to astronomical material but contains
moral teaching. The third speech, 82,1-8, refers to the astronomical material.
Here Enoch admonishes Methuselah to hand the correct astronomical calculations
over to future generations.

The book continues with a section introduced "This is the law of the stars," 82,9.
This section ends abruptly in 82,20, the end of the whole book.

46   For a detailed discussion we refer to Neugebauer, op.cit., pp. 51-8.
47   For a detailed discussion, cf. Charles, op.cit., pp. 160f; Rau, op.cit., pp. 210-23.
48   Rau's suggestion that En 75,4 does not mean twelve gates in the disc of the
sun, but twelve gates in the circle of the chariot of the sun in heaven, i.e. in the
horizon, seems plausible; Rau, op.cit., pp. 186f.
49   We use the word "cosmological" when the subject concerns natural phenomena, although it is clear that no sharp distinction was made in ancient astronomical, astrological and cosmological systems.

This short description of the content of the Ethiopic Astronomical Book demonstrates clearly that it cannot be regarded as a straightforward manuscript written by one author. The complicated arrangements of sections and the variegated material signify a complicated history of transmission. To analyze this history is difficult both because the translators of the book into Greek (or Ethiopic) have changed the structure of the Aramaic original, and because the Aramaic original itself is a compilation.

72,1: The Book of the Revolutions of the Lights of Heaven

72,2-37: The first law of the lights, The light the sun
73,1-8: I saw another law, for the smaller light named the moon
74,1-75,3: Another journey and another law I saw for it

75,4-9: Likewise Uriel showed me twelve gate-openings
76,1-14: At the end of the world I saw twelve gates open to all the winds
77,1-3: They call the first quarter eastern
77,4: I saw seven high mountains
77,5-7: I saw seven rivers
77,8: I saw seven large island
78,1-9: The names of the sun (are) as follows

78,10-79,6: And Uriel showed me another law, (namely) when light is transferred to the moon
80,1-8: In those days Uriel answered me and said to me
81,1-10: He said to me
82,1-8: And now my son Methuselah, all these things I recount to you and will write down for you
82,9-20: This is the law of the stars

1.3   The Ethiopic Text and the Aramaic Fragments

The Aramaic fragments can be arranged in three groups: 1) Those dealing with the synchronistic calculations with no directly corresponding texts in Eth En. 2) Those dealing with passages contained in Eth En. 3) A fragment which is to be placed after the end of Eth En (Enastr^d).[50] The fragments demonstrate that the Ethiopic Astronomical Book is an abridged version of the Aramaic original. The fragments which clearly correspond to Eth En contain the following passages, according to Milik: 76,3-10; 76,13-77,4; 78,6-8; 78,9-12; 79,3-5 + 78,17-79,2; 82,9-13.[51]

---

50 Cf. Milik, op.cit., p. 274.
51 Milik, op.cit., pp. 284-96.

The Aramaic fragments indicate that strange features in the
Ethiopic text in some cases have their origin in the translators'
rearrangement of the material. In the previous chapter we noticed
that the section beginning in 78,10 had a strange end. The section
seems to end with the concluding remark in 79,1-2, but then a
new astronomical sequence comes in 79,3-5 with a new concluding
remark in 79,6. The Aramaic fragments show that 79,3-5 is to be
placed before 78,17-79,2, which gives a clear structure.[52]

Another strange feature is that Eth En 79,1 refers to the calculation of the stars. So does 80,7. In Eth En 79,5 we have a similar
sort of reference, but the wording of the Aramaic original may be
different, cf. 4Q Enastr[b] 26, lines 3-4 (Milik, p. 294). The problem is that no calculation of stars is given before Eth En 82,9ff.
This may also indicate a rearrangement of the sections by the
translators. The Aramaic wording to Eth En 79,1-2, which according to the Aramaic fragments comes after 79,3-5, may differ from
the Ethiopic text. Eth En 79,1-2 refers back to the previous section, but the Aramaic text of 4Q Enastr[b] 26, lines 6-7 (Milik, p.
294), may introduce a new. First line reads: וכען מחוא אנה לך אנה
(ברי). "And now I demonstrate for you, my son ..." In the next
line חשבון, "calculation" is clearly visible. Milik also claims to see
traces of אחרן, reading "another calculation". If this is a correct
reading, the original wording in 79,1-2 cannot have introduced the
following text, ch. 80, because this is a speech. The only calculation left after 79,1-2 is that of the stars in Eth En 82,9ff. The
original Aramaic text may have had this calculation after 79,1-2
and the speeches from ch. 80ff at the end of the book. This would
explain why 80,7 refers to the law of the stars. The fragment 4Q
Enastr[b] 28 (Milik, p. 295), which corresponds to Eth En 82,9-13,
belongs to a different leaf than 4Q Enastr[b] 26 and cannot shed
light on the problem.

But although the structure of the original Aramaic scroll seems to
have been clearer than the present Ethiopic translation, the
Aramaic fragments show that also the Aramaic scroll contained
variegated material. Several passages from Eth En ch. 76-79 are
extant in Aramaic and indicate that the Aramaic original by and
large had the same composite character.

52   Milik, op.cit., pp. 294f.

1.4 The Original Aramaic Astronomical Book

The next question concerns the original shape of the Aramaic Astronomical Book and is one of literary criticism. The question about the underlying traditions will be discussed in the next chapter.

Charles thinks that both Eth En 80,2-8 and 81,1-10 are additions to the original book.[53] He characterizes 80,2-8 as "ethical and nothing else". This is contrary to the rest of the book which is a "scientific treatise". I cannot see that this characterization of the speech in 80,2-8 is correct. On the contrary, the speech of Uriel is not ethical in the sense of moral behaviour, but contains a prediction about a future disorder in the celestial and natural laws based on the previous descriptions of these laws. Nothing in its content indicates that this speech is not an original part of the Aramaic Astronomical Book.

Ch. 81 is different, however. Its content is ethical, and there are no links to the astronomical or cosmological teaching in the rest of the book. Milik demonstrates a close relationship between this text and the Book of Dreams. I agree with Charles and Milik that this section is to be regarded as an addition.[54]

It may seem hazardous to suggest an outline of the original Aramaic version, but, as we have seen, the Aramaic fragments considered in relation to the Ethiopic version give some indications. The book may have started with a solar calculation as in Eth En 72, followed by the synchronistic calculation of the sun and moon preserved on Enastr[a] and Enastr[b] of which there are different résumés in Eth En 73-75. Eth En 76-79 seems broadly to render the Aramaic text. Most likely "the law of the stars" in 82,9ff followed after ch. 79. If so, the book ended with two speeches, i.e. 80,1-8: Uriel addressing Enoch, and 82,1-8: Enoch addressing Methuselah.

---

53 Charles, op.cit., pp. 147f.
54 Milik, op.cit., p. 14. Cf. also our discussion below, pp. 76ff.

1.5   The Aramaic Book as a Compilation

1.5.1   The Astronomical Calculations

We have already noted that the main structure of the book is formed by titles containing the word "law" in the Ethiopic version, cf. 72,2; 73,1; 74,1; 78,10; 82,9. Two Ethiopic words are used in this connection. The one is *tě'zāz*, "law, precept", cf. 72,2.35; 73,1; 74,1; 76,14; the other is *šěr'at*, "arrangement, instruction precept", cf. 78,10; 79,1.2.5; 80,7; 82,9. There is no need to suppose that the Aramaic original had two different words here because the context in which the two Ethiopic words occur is exactly the same and the meanings of the words are very close. The change in wording occurs in the middle of the Astronomical Book and may go back to different translators.

The Greek word behind *tě'zāz* and *šěr'at* is most likely τάξις. In Eth En 2,1 the two Ethiopic roots are used together: "How each rises and sets in order" — *šěru'*; "they do not transgress their law" — *tě'zāz*. The last word is rendered τάξις, "correct order", in the Greek translation. The first corresponds to the participle τεταγμένος (from the same Greek root as τάξις), "appointed".[55]

Traces of the Aramaic text are visible in the last sentence, 4Q En^a lii, line 1 (Milik, p. 145, and Plate II, line 1). Milik restores: ולא מעב(רין) בסרכן M.A. Knibb claims to see less than Milik (and so do I):רכו ( ) מ ולא[56] Considering the Greek and Ethiopic text the reconstructionלא מעבריו, "not transgressing", seems likely. Both Milik and Knibb assume the following word to be סרכו, an assimilated form of סרכהוו. The word סרך, *säräk*, does not occur in Biblical, Palestinian or Targumic Aramaic in the sense of "rule, law" but is attested in Qumran Hebrew. It occurs in the title of the Rule of the Community, 1QS I, line 1: ספר סרך היחד, "The book of the rule of the community".[57] In an astronomical context it also occurs in 4Q 186,2, col. I, line 1.[58]

säräk comes in meaning close to the word hōq, which is common in the Old Testament as a designation fo both the order of the community and the order of

55   For the Greek text edition, cf. note 129, p. 85.
56   M.A. Knibb, The Ethiopic Book of Enoch II, p. 61.
57   Text in E. Lohse (ed), Die Texte aus Qumran, Darmstadt 1971, p. 4. Cf. the text critical note.
58   Text in J.M. Allegro, DJD V. Qumran Cave 4, Oxford 1968, p. 91.

nature.[59] In the meaning "law of nature" the word is used in the Qumran "Book of Hymns", IQH I, line 10: "and the mighty winds according to their laws".[60] The word ḥōq occurs in rabbinic Aramaic with the same meaning as in Hebrew.[61] In Nabatean Aramaic the verb ḥqq occurs in the sense of "determine".[62]

The observations above could indicate that the most likely words behind Ethiopic tĕ'zāz/šĕr'at in the Astronomical Book were Greek τάξις and Aramaic säräk or ḥōq. This is the presupposition behind E. Rau's analysis of the material.[63] The laws in the Astronomical Book would accordingly be laws as a part of cosmos, governing the nature and celestial bodies.

As we shall see, the Astronomical Book presupposes such laws, but this is not the meaning of the original Aramaic word behind Ethiopic tĕ'zāz and šĕr'at. The original Aramaic word is preserved in two places, 4Q Enastrᵇ 25, line 3 (Milik, p. 293, and 4Q Enastrᵇ 26, line 7 (Milik, p. 294). This word is חשבון, ḥāšbōn.

The verb with the same root is the common Hebrew and Aramaic חשב, ḥāšeb/ḥāšab, meaning "think, estimate, calculate, count". ḥāšbōn means "plan, estimation, calculation, number".[64] ḥāšbōn in the Astronomical Book is accordingly the thinking, counting, estimation of celestial phenomena; in short, ḥāšbōn is an astronomical calculation.

The occurrences of the word underscore this. In nearly all cases the Ethiopic tĕ'zāz or šĕr'at are used they are related to astronomical phenomena, either to the sun, the moon or the stars. There is one significant exception. In 76,14 the Ethiopic text reads: "And all their laws, and all their punishments, and all their benefits I have shown to you, my son Methuselah." The laws here do not refer to astronomical phenomena, but to the twelve gates of the

---

59 Cf. G. Liedke, "ḥqq einritzen, festsetzen", THAT I, cols 626-33.
60 Text in E. Lohse (ed.), op.cit., p. 112.
61 Cf. M. Jastrow, Dictionary of Talmud Babli, Yerushalami, Midrashic Literature and Targumim I, New York 1950, sub ḥōq, p. 438.
62 Cf. the Hever Nabatean contract, pap 5/6 Hev A nab, recto, frg. 1, line 10. Text in J.A. Fitzmyer and D.J. Harrington, A Manual of Palestinian Aramaic Texts, p. 164.
63 E. Rau, op.cit., pp. 158ff.
64 For the occurrences in the Hebrew Old Testament, cf. W. Schottroff, "ḥšb denken", THAT I, cols 641-46. For the occurrences in Biblical and Palestinian Aramaic, cf. for instance: 4Q Mess ar, col 1, lines 9.10 (Fitzmyer and Harrington, pp. 98f); ḥāšbōn, "plan"; Gen ap (proper), col 2, line 1 (Fitzmyer and Harrington, pp. 104f); hᵃšab, "think"; Dan 4,32: hᵃšab, "count"; 4Q Enᶜ lxiii, line 24 (Milik, p. 203): ḥāšbōn, "number".

winds. The wording is indeed strange. Fortunately a part of the Aramaic text is preserved and can be reconstructed as follows: ‏ושלמו (תרי עשר תרעי ארבע רוחי) שמיא שלמהון ופרשהון אח(זית‎ ‏לך ברי מתושלח‎ "And the twelve gates of the four quarters of heaven are complete. Their completeness and their separation I have shown to you, my son Methuselah", Enastr[b] 23, line 2 (Milik, p. 289).[65] The Aramaic text does not use a word for "law" or "calculation" here. This indicates that the Ethiopic translators understood the laws as "laws of nature". The Greek text may have used τάξις, "correct order" and caused the difference from the aramaic original.

The word "calculation" occurs either in the titles or in the conclusions of each section; in the titles: 72,2; 73,1; 74,1; 78,10; 79,1-2[66]; 82,9; in the conclusions; 72,35; 80,7. Accordingly the word functions as a classification of this special kind of astronomical literature. We thus come to the result that the main body of the Astronomical Book is composed of tables containing calculations of the sun, moon and the stars. These astronomical tables form the basis and, as we shall demonstrate, the oldest part of the book.

The framework of the book is that the knowledge is shown to Enoch by the angel Uriel (72,1; 74,2; 75,3.4; 78,10; 79,2.6; 80,1). Subsequently Enoch showed it to his son Methuselah (76,14; 79,1; 82,1). How is this framework related to the astronomical calculations?

The angel Uriel is describes in the following way:

* Uriel, Aramaic, 'ōri'el, means "light of God".
* This meaning is especially referred to in the description of his function. He is the leader of the lights of heaven (72,1; 74,2).
* Whenever Uriel's function is described, it is always in connection with celestial phenomena. He is placed in charge of the lights of heaven that they might rule the face of heaven (75,3). He has power over the orbits of the celestial phenomena (82,8). Since there is a close connection between the celestial and natural orders (80,2-6), Uriel is placed in charge of the cosmic order.
* Uriel is the revealer of astronomical science (72,1.2; 75,3.4; 78,10; 79,2.6; 80,1; 82,7). He is not connected to the cosmical and geographical material.

---

65   For the reconstruction "the four quarters of heaven", cf. the same fragment, line 4: "And the great quarter, the west quarter". Literally the word behind "quarter" rūah, should be translated "wind". The "four rūhē of heaven" do also occur in Dan 7,2 and there rūah means "wind".
66   Cf. the Aramaic text above, p. 58.

There should be no doubt that Uriel is most intimately connected to the astronomical material of the book.

Methuselah plays a more modes role. He is described twice in relation to the astronomical material (79,1; 82,1-2), and once in relation to the teaching about the winds (76,14). His connection to both kinds of material could indicate that he was not originally part of the framework of the astronomical tables. But other conclusions are also possible. The passage about Methuselah in 76,14 functions poorly in the context. This can mean that the passage about Methuselah was added in order to make him receiver of the cosmical teaching as well. The speech in 82,1-8 shows that Methuselah was connected primarily to astronomical teaching. But the fact remains that Methuselah is mentioned only once in connection with the astronomical tables themselves (79,1). Considering the observations together, it seems that he at an early point was connected to the astronomical material in the line of transmission Uriel — Enoch — Methuselah, but he is less intimately connected to the material than is Uriel.

There remains the question how Enoch is related to the material. His name is mentioned only in Uriel's speech (80,1). He is presupposed three times as the father of Methuselah (76,14; 79,1; 82,1). The whole book is autobiographical, and there is no doubt that in the framework of the whole Astronomical book "I" is meant to be Enoch. Whether this was the case already in the composition of each individual calculation is impossible to determine.

Considering the three figures together, it is quite clear that Uriel is the figure of the book most intimately connected to the astronomical calculations. The book also presents itself as the revelations of Uriel (72,2).

The next question is how the transmission of the astronomical knowledge is to be understood. In three places traces of the Aramaic text dealing with the issue are preserved: En 76,14: Enoch — Methuselah; 78,10; Uriel — Enoch; 79,1: Enoch — Methuselah. In all places the Ethiopic translation has a II i form (causative) of

the verb "to see", *'ar'aya*, "to show". The Aramaic fragments have
the following wording: שלמהון ופרשהון אח(זית לך ברי מתושלח
Enastr[b] 23, line 2 (Milik, p. 289), "Their completeness and their
explanation I have s[hown to you, my son Methuselah.".
Enastr[b] 25, line 3 (Milik, p. 293): (ואחויני אוריאל ח)שבון אחרן
אחזית לה

Milik translates: "And Urî'el demonstrated to me a further calculation, by
having shown it unto me that . . ." The translation is not without problems. If we
reconstruct as Milik, the syntax is complicated. Nothing indicates a second
subordinate clause. The form of the verb is also not clear. If Milik is right in his
reconstruction of the first example above, the form there must be aph'el, "I have
shown". This can hardly be the case in the present example. The Ethiopic text
would then be completely wrong because it reads *'ar'ayani*, "he showed me". If
we shall keep the meaning of the Ethiopic text, we must understand the form as
oph'al (causative passive), "I was shown". We also have this form in the same
context in 4Q En[c] lxii, line 27 (Milik, p. 201) = En 31,2; and 4Q En[e] lxxvii,
line 1 (Milik, p. 234) = En 32,3.

We leave out Milik's reconstruction at the beginning of the passage
and translate: ". . . another calculation I was shown it".[67] וכען
מחוא אנה לך ברי, Enastr[b] 26, line 6 (Milik, p. 294). "And now I
demonstrate to you my son."
The fragments show that both the causative form (aph'el, oph'al)
אחזית, "show", and the pa'el form מחוא, "demonstrate", are used
about transmission. Rau has pointed out that the verb "show"
corresponds to the phrase "I saw" which is used several times in
the Astronomical Book (72,3; 73,1; 74,1.9; 75,6.8; 76,1; 77,4.5.8).
He also called attention to the occurrence of the phrases in the
Gattung "vision".[68] Not often, but sometimes the two phrases are
used in the same context.[69] In the visions of Amos we find the
hiph'il (causative) form הראני, "he showed me" in 7,1.4.7; 8,1,
while we find the qal form ראיתי, "I saw", in 9,1. But it is not
certain that the visions in ch. 7-8 and ch. 9 belong together. Quite
certain is the use of both forms in the visions of Zechariah, where
we find the qal forms ארא / ראיתי, "I saw", in 1,8; 2,1.5; 5,9; 6,1;
and the hiph'il form יראני, "he showed me", in 2,3; 3,1.
In the Books of Enoch we have the combination in the vision in

---

67   M. Black doubts that Milik's identification of the fragment as corresponding
to En 78,10 is correct. Cf. M. Black, "Additional Notes to the Aramaic
Fragments", in Neugebauer, The 'Astronomical' Chapters, p. 38.
68   Cf. Rau, op.cit., p. 172.
69   Cf. the synopsis of vision formulas in the Old Testament, in S. Reimers,
Formgeschichte der prophetischen Visionsberichte, unpubl. diss. Hamburg 1976,
pp. 56ff.

ch. 13-14. In 14,8 the Greek text, Gr^{Pan}, reads: καὶ εμοὶ ἐφ' ὁράσει οὕτως ἐδἐιχϑη.[70] "And to me in a vision it was shown thus." The passive Greek verb demands here either an original Aramaic (h)itpa'el form אתחזית[71] or an oph'al form אחזית. Within the same vision Gr^{Pan} reads to En 14,14-15: ἐϑεώρουν ἐν τῇ ὁράσει μου καὶ ιδού. "I saw in my vision, and behold!" This clearly demands the Aramaic reconstruction: חזית בחזיתי וארו, cf. the Aramaic text to En 13,8, 4Q En^c lvi, line 5 (Milik, p. 193): ויחזית חזיון דרגוז"I saw a vision of wrath."

The combination of the phrases "I was shown" and "I saw" in the Astronomical Book could accordingly indicate that the reception of knowledge is thought of as a visionary experience. There is evidence, however, that points in another direction. First a more general observation: With few exceptions (to which we shall return in the next chapter) the Astronomical Book lacks the other characteristics of the genre vision. Then a semantic observation: As far as we can judge from the Ethiopic translation, we have the same kind of transmission repeated twice: Uriel — Enoch and Enoch — Methuselah. In the traces of the Aramaica fragments the verb חוא, ḥawwī, "demonstrate", is used together with אחזא, 'āḥᵃzī, "show". This tends to emphasize 'āḥᵃzī as a part of a teaching situation, not necessarily implying a visionary experience. If the transmission is imagined as like in both cases, it seems strange to think that Methuselah had a visionary experience of Enoch, his father, at least when it is nowhere stated that Enoch should be a transcendent figure.

The material demands a cautious conclusion: The phraseology of transmission functions within two semantic patterns where the one does not necessarily exclude the other. The one pattern is a phraseology corresponding to a visionary experience; the other is the phraseology of a teaching situation. It is quite possible that this double correspondence is caused by the object concerned. The object which is shown/demonstrated is the hidden laws of the universe. The "showing/demonstration" is accordingly a revelation of and instruction in the divine secrets.

---

70 For the Greek text edition, cf. note 129, p. 85.
71 For the passive meaning of reflexive forms, cf. S. Segert, Altaramäische Grammatik, Leipzig 1975, 6.6.7.6.4., p. 396.

1.5.2 The Cosmological Material

The sections in 75,4-77,8 are of a different character from the rest of the Astronomical Book. These sections are not introduced as calculations, but by a simple "I saw", 75,6.8; 76,1; 77,4.5.8. The same phrase also occurs in the astronomical material, but there it is related to the astronomical calculations, 72,2-3; 73,1; 74,1.9. In the cosmological part we get the impression that Enoch is on a journey "to the end of the earth", 75,6; 76,1.

Narratives of "the journeys of Enoch" occur in the Book of Watchers, Eth En 17-19;20-36. The composition 20-36 begins with a list of seven angels who accompany Enoch.

At the head of this list we find Uriel. In the Greek translation he is describes as follows: "Uriel, one of the holy angels, who is over the world and Tartarus." That Uriel in charge of the cosmos corresponds to his position in the Astronomical Book. In this text he is also in charge of Tartarus, which is the Greek name for the lowest part of the underworld. According to Hesiod's Theogony, 732-819, this gloomy place was inhabited by the Titans and the monster Typhoeus. The Titans were imprisoned there after the revolt of the younger gods under the leadership of Zeus.[72] Josephus knew the designation Tartarus as well as the myth about the imprisonment of the Titans, Con. Ap. II,240. The designation is also known in the New Testament, 2 Pet 2,4, in a passage which refers to the "fall of the angels" in Enoch.

It is hardly likely that the Aramaic text used the Greek world Tartarus here. One possible explanation is that the Aramaic text had the common Old Testament word for the underworld, šeʾōl.[73] But the word is not common in Aramaic and is generally translated "hades" in Greek.[74]

In the Aramaic original of En 22,4, 4Q En^e lxxii, line 1 (Milik, p. 229), the chambers of the underworld are called "pits for their house of ʾaganōn".[75] The verb ʾagan, "imprison", occurs in the Book of Giants, 4Q En Giants^a 7i, line 7 (Milik, p. 313). The concept here, the underworld as prison, is the same as the Greek concept of Tartarus. In the Book of Watchers the underworld is also the prison for rebelling divine figures, cf. ch. 19 and 21. The Aramaic text may have had an expression like bēt ʾagan, "house of incarceration", which led the Greek translator to use the term Tartarus.

The description of Enoch's journeys in En 20-36 follows a clear pattern which with only slight variations occurs in each section: Movement: "And I went (from there)"; Vision: "And I saw / And

---

72 Cf. M.L. West, Hesiod. Theogony. Edited with Prolegomena and Commentary, Oxford 1966, pp. 336-8, 356-9. Text: pp. 138-42. The Greek text and translation also in H.G. Evelyn-White, Hesiod. The Homeric Hymns and Homerica, LCL, London-Cambridge (Mass.), 1914 (1977), pp. 132-38.
73 šeʾōl occurs also in Aramaic, cf. the Targum of Job, 11 QtgJob, col I, line 2 (Fitzmyer and Harrington, p. 10).
74 Cf. G. Gerleman, "šeʾōl Totenreich", THAT II, cols. 837-41.
75 The verb ʾagan or ʾagan means "to tie, to imprison". As a noun the word occurs in the meaning "prison", cf. Jastrow, Dictionary, Vol. II, sub ʿGN, p. 1042.

he showed me"; Remark/Question: "Then I said"; Answer: "Then X, one of the holy angels who was with me, answered me (and said)":

Grelot and, subsequently, Milik have called attention to the similarity between the mythical geography presented in the Book of Watchers and the Astronomical Book and the mythical geography of Greek and especially Mesopotamian sources.[76] Both Greek and Mesopotamian sources tell about mythical journeys like that of Enoch. Grelot finds many close parallels especially between the journeys of Enoch and the journeys of Gilgamesh. But here is one main difference: Into the genre "mythical journey" the author of Enoch has incorporated another Gattung.

This becomes clear when one compares the journeys of Enoch with the visions of Zechariah, 1,8-17; 2,1-2; 2,3-4; 4,1-14; 5,1-4; 5,5-11; 6,1-8. In four of these visions we find the same main structure as in the Enoch sequences, 1,8-17; 2,1-2; 2,3-4; 6,1-8: Vision; Question of the visionary; Answer by the *angelus interpres*. The difference is that the passage about movement is lacking in Zechariah. The *angelus interpres* of the Zechariah visions is described as המלאך הדבר בי, "the angel who talked to me" (1,9; 2,2; 4,4; 5,5; 6,4). The corresponding passage in Enoch reads: "One of the holy angels who was with me". As already noted, the visionary experience in Zechariah can either be expressed in qal, "I saw", or in hip'il, "he showed me", which is also the case in Enoch. Accordingly, there should be no doubt that the journeys of Enoch are formulated as visionary experiences with a structure similar to that of Zechariah. We also find this Gattung "visionary journey" in Ezekiel, ch. 8-11.[77]

Traces of the Gattung "visionary journey" also occur in the Astronomical Book, especially in the cosmological and geographical part. This concerns both the phrase "I saw" and the description of location (75,6; 76,1). It also concerns a sequence of the title of the book where Uriel is introduced as "the holy angel who was with me", 72,1.

---

[76] P. Grelot, "La géographie mythic d'Hénoch et ses sources orientales", RB 65, 1958, pp. 33-69; Milik, op.cit., pp. 15-8, 29-30, 35-41. Cf. also below, pp. 246-54.

[77] Cf. above, p. 49.

There are also other indications of mutual contact between the visionary journeys in En 20-36 and the Astronomical Book. En 33,2-4 quite clearly breaks the main structure of the journey sequences. A comparison of this astronomical sequence and the Astronomical Book shows that En 33,2-4 was written under the influence of this book (En 33,2-4 compared to 76,1; 75,6; 82,1.9-10; 72,1; 80,1; 79,1; 76,14). The only difference is that Enoch according to 33,4 receives the calculation of the stars as a written document. In the Astronomical Book it is Enoch who writes down the calculations and hands them over to Methuselah together with oral instruction (82,1-2; 79,1; 76,14).

Accordingly there seem to be good reasons to suppose a mutual contact between the author(s) of the journeys of Enoch and the composers of the Aramaic Astronomical Book. Not only is the structure of the journey sequences also found in the Astronomical Book, especially in its cosmological and geographical part, but a sequence based on information given in the Astronomical Book is found in the journeys of Enoch, as well.

This analysis suggests that the astronomical calculations are the oldest part of the book. They are intimately connected to the angel Uriel. Later the book was enlarged by adding the cosmological and the geographical material, and the two speeches: Uriel — Enoch, Enoch — Methuselah. At the latest stage En 81 was added.

1.6   The Character of the Astronomical Calculations

There are no parallels to the astronomical calculations in the Old Testament or earlier Jewish literature. This makes the analysis of the material extremely difficult. That concerns both the character, the background and the purpose. Moreover, there is no consensus in the research about these problems. A thorough analysis of these problems would demand a separate study comparing the system argued in the Astronomical Book with Old Testament calendars as well as Babylonian, Egyptian and Greek astronomy.[78] We shall refer briefly to some of the problems involved but concentrate on some basic features of the system that we find significant for an understanding of the Enoch figure.

In his analysis of the basic system behind the astronomical calculations O. Neugebauer states: "Thus we are dealing with an extremely primitive level of astronomy which shows no relation to the sophisticated Babylonian astronomy of the Seleucid period nor to its hellenistic Greek sequel." And concerning the calculation of the length of daylight: "The strict linearity of the variation of the length of daylight — in obvious contradiction to the most elementary "observation" of the factual change — is a striking example of the primitivity of the methods at the disposal of this level.[79] As we have already noticed the calculations operate with a ratio of 2:1 for the extremal daylight. This ratio is also attested to in Babylonian calculations.[80] But Neugebauer sees no sufficient basis for the assumption of mutual contacts: "Very primitive methods offer very little freedom of choice. Operating with the simplest integer difference, 1, determines all remaining numbers for a given ratio of the extrema or a given mean value."[81]

R.H. Charles argues that there is a clear correspondence between the twelve gates in the horizon and the twelve signs of the zodiac.[82] Neugebauer denies also this: "One of the reasons for my interest in the Ethiopic material was the fact that the customary interpretation of the "gates" of heaven as zodiacal signs is obviously untenable since, e.g. the moon can never remain 7 or 8 days in the same sign as would be required by our text if the "gates" were identical with the signs of the zodiac."[83]

What Neugebauer denies is that the twelve gates of the sun depend on the twelve signs of the zodiac, not that the zodiac was unknown to the author of the astronomical calculations. The author also writes about the twelve gates of the stars, 75,6. Milik claims to find an explicit reference to the zodiac in the Aramaic text to Eth En 82,9, which introduces the calculation of the stars, 4Q Enastr[b] 28, line 1 (Milik, p. 295). It is also quite clear that the zodiac was known to the Qumran community and used in horoscopes.[84]

If Milik is correct, knowledge of the zodiac most likely was transmitted from a Babylonian environment. Judging from the sources, there was no widespread use of the zodiac in the Greek or Egyptian world as early as the fourth or third century B.C. The Babylonians seem to have invented the system in the fifth century.[85]

There is no doubt that the Astronomical Book argues a solar year of 364 days, 72,32; 82,6. As far as we know there are no parallels to this in the astronomical systems of the Babylonians, Egyptians or Greeks. The Babylonian calendars were

---

78 A discussion of the material is recently carried out by R.T. Beckwith, "The Earliest Enoch Literature and its Calendar", RevQ 10, 1981, pp. 365-403, pp. 373-87.
79 O. Neugebauer, "Notes on Ethiopic Astronomy", pp. 58.60.
80 Cf. O. Neugebauer, "The History of Ancient Astronomy: Problems and Methods", JNES 4, 1945, pp. 2-38, p. 13.
81 Neugebauer, "Notes", p. 60.
82 Charles, op.cit., p. 153.
83 Neugebauer, "Notes", p. 50.
84 Cf. 4Q 186. Text in J.M. Allegro, DJD V, pp. 88-91.
85 Cf. A. Sachs, "Babylonian Horoscopes", JCS 6, 1952, pp. 49-75; and J. Oates, Babylon, London 1979, p. 190.

based on a lunar year.[86] But the Babylonians also used for predictions a schematic year of 360 days, divided into 12 · 30 days.[87] The Egyptians developed a calendar based on a solar year consisting of 12 · 30 days. At the end of each year they added five days. This calendar was used by the hellenistic astronomers.[88] Another unsolved question is the relationship between the 364 days of the Astronomical Book and Old Testament and Jewish calendars. The Old Testament calendar is based on a lunar year.[89] But as we have shown, the solar year of 365 days was known to the priestly author of the Pentateuch.[90] A. Jaubert has argued that a calendar year corresponding to 364 days was used by the latest redactors of the Pentateuch, by Ezekiel and by the Chronicler.[91] But this is denied by R. de Vaux: "The recent attempts to connect this with an ancient priestly calendar, whose influence may be found in the redaction of the Pentateuch, is still no more than a hypothesis."[92] There is no doubt, however, that a calendar based on the same calculations as in the Astronomical Book later was put into practice in Qumran[93] and also formed the basis for the calendarian and historiographical speculations in the Book of Jubilees.[94] But as far as the Astronomical Book is concerned we do not know whether it was written in defence of an already existing cultic calendar or formed the basis for later cultical calendarian speculations.

The problems connected to the character of the astronomical calculations, however, must not overshadow the fact that the system is basically very simple and determined by two factors. The first is that the year is determined by the course of the sun, the second is that the universe is governed by a "law of seven".

The calculation of the course of the sun starts the Astronomical Book. And this section concludes: "And the year amounts to

---

86   Cf. O. Neugebauer, The Exact sciences in Antiquity, Copenhagen-Princeton-London 1951, p. 101. For a survey of late Babylonian astronomy, cf. G. Sarton, "Chaldean Astronomy in the Last Three Centuries B.C.", JAOS 75, 1955, pp. 166-73.

87   Cf. O. Neugebauer, "The History of Ancient Astronomy", p. 13.

88   Cf. O. Neugebauer, The Exact Sciences, pp. 80ff. For Egyptian astronomy, cf. the account by Herodot, Book II,4: "The Egyptians, they said, were the first men who reckoned by years and made the year to consist of twelve divisions of the seasons. They discovered this from the stars (so they said). And their reckoning is, to my mind, a juster one than that of the Greeks; for the Greeks add an intercalary month every other year, so that the seasons may agree; but the Egyptians, reckoning thirty days to each of the twelve months, add five days in every year over and above the number, and so the completed circle of seasons is made to agree with the calendar." Cf. A.D. Godley, Herodotus, LCL, London-Cambridge (Mass.) 1926 (1975), p. 279.

89   Cf. R. de Vaux, Ancient Israel. Its Life and Institutions, pp. 183-6, 188-90.

90   Cf. above, p. 52.

91   A. Jaubert, "Le Calendrier des Jubilés et de la secte de Qumrân. Ses origines bibliques", VT 3, 1953, pp. 250-64.

92   R. de Vaux, op.cit., p. 188. Critical of Jaubert is also E. Kutsch, "Der Kalender des Jubiläenbuches und das Alte und das Neue Testament", VT 11, 1961, pp. 39-47. For a thorough discussion of Jaubert's theory and a rejection of it, cf. also Beckwith, "The earliest Enoch Literature", pp. 386f.

93   Cf. J.T. Milik, Ten Years of Discovery in the Wilderness of Judea, pp. 107-13. Cf. also 4Q AstrCrypt, described by Milik in The Books of Enoch, pp. 68f.

94   Cf. J. van Goudoever, Biblical Calendars, 2nd rev. ed., Leiden 1961, pp. 62-70.

exactly three hundred and sixty four days. And the length of the day and night, and the shortness of the day and night — they are different because the journey of that sun" (72,32b-33). The year is divided into twelve months which gives 360 days, but four intercalary days are added, one each third month (75,1-2; 82,4-6). The light of the sun determines the light of the moon (73,3). The sun is the "great eternal light" (72,35), the moon is the "smaller light" (73,1).

The reason why the solar year is estimated at 364 and not 365 days as in the Priestly source of Genesis (and which is approximately the correct number) lies in the second factor. The number 364 is divisible by the number 7, which gives exactly 52 weeks of seven days. The number 7 also determines the numbers given in the estimation of the lunar light. The starting point there is that the moon has 1/7 parts of the light of the sun. The "law of seven" also occurs in the cosmic geography. There are "seven high mountains" (77,4), "seven rivers" (77,5), "seven large islands" (77,8).

We know that fixed numbers corresponding to calendarian units played an important role in Essene historiography as well as in other Jewish writings, such as the Book of Jubilees. The chief number was 7.[95] K. Koch has demonstrated that historiographical speculations based on fixed numbers started much earlier than the third or second century.[96]

The redactors of the Deuteronomistic work of history calculated 480 years from the exodus from Egypt to the first temple, and another 480 years from the first temple to the end of Babylonian exile, based on $40 \cdot 12$ as basic numbers. In the last period the years from the first temple to the beginning of the exile are counted as 430. The exile is accordingly predicted to last 50 years, i.e. the period of one jubilee, or $7 \cdot 7$ years, with the fiftieth year as the year of liberation. The calculation corresponds to Jer 34,17, understanding d^erōr as liberation, cf. Lev 25,10. In 2 Kings 25,27ff king Jehojachin is pardoned by the Babylonian king 37 years after he was captured, i.e. 25 years after the destruction of the temple, which is half of the period of 50 years.

The Chronicler calculated the period of exile at 70 years according to Jeremiah's prophecy in Jer 25,11f, cf. 2 Chr 36,21. If we add the 430 years from the first temple to the beginning of the exile, also presupposed by the Chronicler, we get a total sum of 500 years. If we add to this number the 480 years from the exodus to the first temple, Israel's total history from the exodus to the end of exile lasted 980 years. This number equals $2 \cdot 490$, which again equals $2 \cdot 49^{10}$. 49 is the

95 Cf. R.T. Beckwith, "The Significance of the Calendar for Interpreting Essene Chronology and Eschatology", RevQ 10, 1980, pp. 167-202.
96 K. Koch, "Die Mysteriösen Zahlen der judäischen Könige und die apokalyptischen Jahrwochen", VT 28, 1978, pp. 433-41.

basic number corresponding to one jubilee, 7 · 7 years, cf. Lev 25,8-17. 490 years is a basic unit for calculation of time both in Dan 9,24 — 70 year weeks = 70 · 7 = 490,[97] and in the Apocalypse of Weeks, Eth En 93,1-10; 91,11-17, where one week equals 490 years, at least in most of the cases.[98]

The use of 7 as a fixed number to interpret the meaning of history corresponds to the importance of the number in the cultic life of exilic and postexilic Judaism. This importance is clearly connected to the sabbatical institution which moved to the centre of Israel's faith in the exile and during the century afterwards.[99] But the number is also connected to other aspects of the cultic life, especially in the regulations in the Priestly source of the Pentateuch.

G. Robinson gives the following survey of the importance of the number 7 in the Priestly source:[100]

* Seven days is the period of ordination of priests and consecration of altars, Ex 29,35-37.
* Seven is often the number of sacrificial victims, Num 23,1-2.29; 28,11.
* Seven is the number of altars, Num 23,1-2.4.14.29.
* Seven times must the anointing oil and the sacrificial blood be sprinkled, Lev 4,6.17; 14,16; 16,14; Num 19,4.
* Seven days are the period when certain ritual defilements last; at the end of seven days one becomes clean, Lev 15,19.28; Num 19,11.14.16.
* The seventh day is the sabbath, Ex 20,8-11; 31,15-17; 35,2-3.
* The seventh year i the sabbatical year, Lev 25,1-7.

But according to the Priestly source "seven" was not only a law of the cultic life, but also a basic law of the cosmos. In the account of creation, Gen 1,1-2,4a, the priestly author used earlier traditions. Scholars do not agree whether these had a more formal influence on the account in the principle of listing natural phenomena,[101] or P took over an already fixed tradition.[102] But it is certain that the use of the seven-day week as the pattern of creation is the work of P.[103]

---

97   Cf. O. Plöger, "Siebzig Jahre", Aus der Spätzeit des Alten Testaments, Göttingen 1971, pp. 67-73.
98   Cf. K. Koch, "Sabbatstruktur der Geschichte", ZAW 95, 1983, pp. 403-30, pp. 413-20.
99   Cf. H.-J. Kraus, Gottesdienst in Israel. Grundriss einer alttestamentlichen Kultgeschichte, 2nd rev. ed., München 1962, pp. 107-8; R. de Vaux, op.cit., pp. 480-3.
100   G. Robinson, The Origin and Development of the Old Testament Sabbath, unpubl. diss. Hamburg 1975, p. 353.
101   So O.H. Steck, Der Schöpfungsbericht der Priesterschrift, FRLANT 115, Göttingen 1975, pp. 199-223.
102   So W.H. Schmidt, Die Schöpfungsgeschichte der Priesterschrift, WMANT 17, 3rd ed., Neukirchen-Vluyn 1973, pp. 160-3.
103   Cf. Steck, our note 101; Schmidt, op.cit., pp. 67-73.

We have now seen that the number seven was known as a key number in the first postexilic period (Persian age). This concerns the interpretation of history (Chronicler), the regulation of the cult (Priestly source), and the understanding of cosmos (Priestly source). The transference of this number to the course of the celestial bodies corresponds to all three aspects. The course of the celestial bodies determines time and consequently history. It also determines the time of festivals and is a part of the cosmic order.

The same role is ascribed to the celestial bodies in the priestly account of creation, Gen 1,14-18. The celestial bodies are a part of the cosmic order. They are placed at the vault as signs for festivals, days and years (v. 14). The great light, the sun, is given power to govern the day, and the small light, the moon, power to govern the night. The role of the celestial bodies in this account is generally seen in relation to a Near Eastern and especially a Babylonian background. On the one hand the author "demythologizes" the Babylonian reverence for the divine character of the celestial bodies by making them part of the created universe and nothing more. On the other hand there remains a reminiscence of the mythological background in that the lights are described as "rulers".[104]

Especially with regard to the stars the author of the Astronomical Book is closer to the mythological background. In a hierarchic system each star is placed under the rule of an angelic leader who governs the movements of the stars, which in turn govern the seasons of the year (En 82,9ff). This of course differs from mythological thinking according to which the celestial bodies themselves are regarded as divine, but the difference is not great.

Thus the stars in the Astronomical Book are both part of the cosmic order and governed by heavenly beings. Their twofold character underlies the prediction contained in the speech of Uriel, 80,2-8.

The speech is a combination of "prophetic prediction" and "astronomical observation" which is new to the Old Testament and the Jewish context. The speech concerns "the days of the sinners" (80,2) when nature will become disorderly and the moon and sun

---

104   Cf. C. Westermann, Genesis, pp. 175-86; Schmidt, op.cit., pp. 117-20.

will change their customary practice (80,2-5).[105] So far the text
corresponds to prophecies in the Old Testament about disorder in
nature and celestial phenomena, cf. Hos 4,1-3; Am 8,9; Joel 2,10;
Jer 4,23-26; and especially Jer 5,22-25. The difference comes in
the next sequence: "And many heads of the stars in command will
go astray, and these will change their courses and their activities,
and will not appear at the times which have been prescribed for
them", 80,6. In the Old Testament prophetic tradition disorder in
nature was caused by the sin of the people and God's judgment of
them. This is only partly the case in the speech of Uriel. The time
of confusion happens "in the days of the sinners" according to the
Old Testament tradition, but it is not said that it is caused by the
sinners or by the judgment of God. The time of confusion is
caused by the stars which govern the seasons but go astray.

The prophecy is based on a concrete experience.[106] A year of 364
days is 1 1/4 days too short compared to a real solar year. A year
that is 1 1/4 days too short will develop a one-month discrepancy
in 24 years and a two-month discrepancy in 48 years. After such
a period the calendar and the seasonal crops corresponding to the
appearance of the celestial bodies will be in total disharmony. The
transmitters of the calendar then had two possibilities: They could
try to develop a system adjusted to reality, or they could produce
an explanation for why reality did not follow the calendar. In
short, they could change the map, or they could try to change the
terrain. The transmitters were so convinced of the correctness of
their system that they chose the second alternative.

Accordingly the calendar remained the fixed point of reality, the
standard of what should be the normal behaviour of the celestial
bodies. It then appeared that the celestial bodies governing the
seasons had "gone astray". As seen above, Old Testament prophecies offered the necessary framework for such an assumption
by foretelling a period of disorder in the sky in the days of the
sinners.

What in fact had its background in a miscalculation of the length
of the year developed into a prediction. Once in primeval time

---

105   Verse 80,5 is corrupt in the Ethiopic text. I assume with Charles, op.cit.,
pp. 171f that the text deals with the sun; cf. also Knibb, The Ethiopic Book of
Enoch II, pp. 185f.
106   Cf. Beckwith, "The Earliest Enoch Literature", pp. 386f.

Uriel had told Enoch what would happen, and Enoch had predicted the future disorder in the sky and in nature. He had also given his successors the means by which they could determine when this period of disorder would occur, namely the correct astronomical calendar.

The prediction is accordingly a confusion of prophecy and astrology. The astrological system is, however, of a special kind. The author of the Astronomical book did not believe that the constellations directly communicated the future will of gods, as was the case in Mesopotamian judicial astrology.[107] This was excluded because the author's monotheistic faith and his setting in Old Testament traditions where the celestial bodies were a part of the order of the created universe. Nevertheless, he did share the two basic presuppositions which underlie astrology, namely that earthly happenings depend on the celestial bodies and that a properly trained person could predict the future by interpreting celestial constellations.[108] When the stars "went astray", when they did not "appear at the times which were prescribed for them", the author knew that the period of confusion had come.

As already stated, there are no parallels to this combination of prophecy and astrology in the Old Testament or, as far as I know, in other Jewish literature. Nor can a direct parallel be expected outside the Jewish tradition since En 80 also involves a mode of thinking which is unique to the Old Testament and Judaism. Nevertheless, the technique of combining prophecy and astrology is known from two Babylonian texts. Copies from the first were found in Ashurbanipal's library in Nineveh, while the second, very fragmentary, tablet is from the Seleucid period, probably from Babylon.[109] The texts resemble the Babylonian written prophecy: predictions concerning a longer interval of time composed as vaticinia ex eventu (predictions after the event). These predictions are linked to observations of specific constellations.

107 Cf. H.W.F. Saggs, The Greatness that was Babylon, London 1962, pp. 454-6; Sachs, "Babylonian Horoscopes", pp. 49-53; A.L. Oppenheim, Ancient Mesopotamia. Portrait of a Dead Civilization, rev.ed., Chicago 1977, pp. 224f.
108 Cf. for this understanding of astrology, N.G.L. Hammond and H.H. Scullard (eds.), The Oxford Classical Dictionary, 2nd ed., Oxford 1970, "Astrology", pp. 133f.
109 There is some uncertainty how to classify the compositions. The first one was published by Grayson and Lambert as a prophecy text. Cf. A.K. Grayson and W.G. Lambert, "Akkadian Prophecies", JCS 18, 1964, pp. 7-30. Text B, pp. 16-9. A new sequence was added by Biggs who also published the second composition, LBAT 1543. Biggs classified both texts as "prophecies". Cf. R.D. Biggs, "More Babylonian 'Prophecies'", Iraq 29, 1967, pp. 117-32. In a more recent discussion of Akkadian prophecies Grayson doubts that this classification was correct. The texts demonstrate close affinity to astrological literature. Cf. A.K. Grayson, Babylonian Historical-Literary Texts, TSTS 3, Toronto 1975, p. 15.

In both speeches the author argues his astronomical system over against a group called "the sinners" (80,7; 82,4). This group is characterized in two ways: Their astronomical knowledge is faulty (80,7; 82,4f), and they think the stars to be gods (80,7). Who are these "sinners"? Are they people who calculate the year as 354 days according to the course of the moon? This is the case in the Book of Jubilees which has the same calendar as the Astronomical Book, cf. Jub 6,28-38. The Astronomical Book would then argue for a solar calendar of 364 days over against the official Jewish calendar based on a luni-solar year. But this is nowhere stated in the Astronomical Book. According to 82,5-6 the "sinners" do not estimate a year based on a lunar calendar, but they err in the counting of the four additional days. That means that the "sinners" share the basic calculation $12 \cdot 30 = 360$, but not the intercalary days. As we have seen, the calculation $12 \cdot 30 = 360$ was known both in Egypt and Babylonia, but the four intercalary days were unique to the Astronomical Book. The accusation that the "sinners" worship the stars also points toward groups heavily influenced by gentile astrology. If we take into account that the author himself reveals clearly non-Jewish mythological features in his system, the discussion in the book indicates disagreement between groups which in this respect remain at the border of the main current in Judaism. On the other hand, the book also has features which clearly correspond to Old Testament and Jewish tradition, such as the use of "seven" as a key number and the understanding of the celestial bodies as part of the order of the universe.

1.7   En 81 and the Tablets of Heaven

We have already argued that En 81 was not part of the original Astronomical Book. There are several similarities with the Book of Dreams (Eth En 83-90). In the Apocalypse of Animals which constitutes the main body of this book, three holy ones appear, 87,2-4; 90,31, as in En 81,5. In this apocalypse Enoch is lifted up to the heavenly temple, 87,3-4, which also seems to be his location in En 81, cf. v. 5. And as in this apocalypse, Enoch recounts the heavenly revelation to his son Methuselah, comp. 83,1-2; 85,1-2 and 81,5.

En 81,1-2 tells that Enoch is invited to look at the book of the tablets of heaven and read their contents. The tablets contained the whole world history. Afterwards Enoch is sent back to the earth in order to instruct Methuselah and his other children and write down the contents of the heavenly tablets for them, 81,5-6.

The concept of the heavenly tablets is also found in the Epistle of Enoch (Eth En 91-107), a composition commonly dated at the end of the second century B.C. or the beginning of the first, cf. 93,1-3; 103,2; 106,19-107,1.[110]

The oldest occurrence of the tablets seems to be in the Apocalypse of Weeks which often is dated at the first half of the second century (Eth En 93,1-10; 91,11-17).[111] The Aramaic text to Eth En 93,1-3 is fragmentary. Milik restores and reconstructs as follows:

אנה הוא חנוך אחזי(ת אנה כלא בחזית שמין ומן) ממר
עירין וקדשין אנה כלא ידעת (ובלוחת שמיא אנה כל)א
קר(ית ואתבוננ)ת

Eth En 93,2b = 4Q En⁵ liii, lines 20-22 (Milik, p. 264). "I am Enoch. [I] was show[n everything in a heavenly vision and from] the word of the Watchers and the Holy Ones I have known everything [and on the tablets of heaven I] have read everything and understood."

There is no Aramaic text of Eth En 103,2, but the Greek text reads: ἐπισταμαι τὸ μυστήριον τοῦτο· ἀνέγνων γὰρ τας πλάκας του οὐρανοῦ καὶ εἶδον τὴν γραφὴν αναγκαίαν "I understand this mystery, because I have r[ead] the tablets of heaven and know the necessary book."[112]

---

110 Cf. Charles, op.cit., pp. 221; Milik, op.cit., pp. 48-9. G.W.E. Nickelsburg, Jewish Literature between the Bible and the Mishnah, Philadelphia 1981, pp. 149f, dates it at the beginning of the second century.

111 So Hengel, Judentum und Hellenismus, p. 345; Schreiner, Alttestament-liche-jüdische Apokalyptik, p. 29; Russel, The Method and Message of Jewish Apocalyptic, p. 53. Milik,op.cit., pp. 255f, thinks, however, that the author of the apocalypse is the same as the author of the whole epistle.
The Aramaic fragments now prove what has been claimed in the main translations of the Ethiopic text, that Eth En 93,1-10 and 91,11-17 belong together in one apocalypse, cf. Charles, op.cit., pp. 228ff; G. Beer, "Das Buch Henoch", E. Kautzsch (ed.), Die Apokryphen und Pseudepigraphen des Alten Testaments II, Tübingen 1900, pp. 299ff; E. Hammershaimb, "Første Enoksbog", De Gammeltestamentlige Pseudepigrafer 2, København 1956, pp. 155ff. The proof is given in 4Q En⁵liv (Milik, pp. 265ff), which combines the two texts.

112 Greek text in M. Black (ed.), Apocalypsis Henochi Graece, Fragmenta Pseudepigraphorum quae supersunt Graeca, Leiden 1970, p. 42. The text belongs to the Chester Beatty Papyri, cf. Milik, op.cit., pp. 75f.

The best preserved Aramaic text is of En 106,19-107,1, 4Q En^c 5ii, lines 26-28 (Milik, pp. 209f). The text as in Milik:

בד)י ידע אנה ברזי (מריא די) קדישין אחויוני (ודי
בלוחת) שמיא קרית וחזית כתיב בהון די (ד)ר מן דר
יבאש בכדן ובאש להוא (עד די יקומון) דרי קושטא

"For I know the mysteries of [the Lord which] the Holy Ones demonstrated for me and showed me and which I read [on the tablets] of heaven. And I saw written on them that [generation] after generation would continue to do evil in this way and that evil would persist [until there arose] generations of righteousness."[113]

If one compares the words used about transmission of knowledge here with the words used in the Astronomical Book, the correspondence becomes clear. In both places the verb חזה, *ḥazā*, is used in pe'al and aph'el (causative), "to see", "to show". And both places this verb is combined with a form of חוה, in pa'el, *hawwī*, or aph'el, *'aḥawī*, "to demonstrate". There is also a correspondence in what is seen, shown, demonstrated. In the Astronomical Book it is the *ḥäšbōnīn*, the astronomical calculations. In Eth En 81 and The Epistle of Enoch it is the לוחת שמיא, *luḥāt šᵉmayyā*, "the tablets of heaven". These tablets contain רזי מריא, *razē māryā*, "the mysteries of the Lord".

In all four cases in which the tablets of heaven are mentioned (81,1-2; 93,2; 103,2; 106,19-107,1) their content is predictions. Specifically, they refer to the Apocalypse of Weeks and the Apocalypse of Animals. The mystery of the tablets is the future of mankind. The correspondence in wording between the transmission of the astronomical calculations and the contents of the heavenly tablets indicates a relationship. The authors of the apocalypses of Enoch have related his ability as soothsayer to his instruction by the heavenly beings in the same way as the author of the astronomical calculations related Enoch's ability as astronomer and astrologer to the instruction by Uriel. It seems that the distance between Enoch the astronomer and Enoch the soothsayer is not so

---

113 For the reconstruction, lūaḥ, "tablet", cf. 2Q En Giants (2Q26), lines 1-3 (Fitzmyer and Harrington, p. 72), — for a possible literary context of the fragment, cf. Milik, op.cit., pp. 333ff; 4Q Giants^a, frg. 2, line 3 (Fitzmyer and Harrington, p. 72); 4Q Testuz ar, lines 3.5 (Fitzmyer and Harrington, p. 126). In a Hebrew commentary on a "Book of Periods", the periods of history are engraved on the tablets of heaven, cf. 4Q 180, I, line 3 (Milik, p. 249).

great. As we already have seen, Enoch's training in astronomy
enabled him to predict the future. This also answers the question
why En 81 is inserted in the Astronomical Book. It serves as an
extension of Uriel's speech in which the calculations are related to
predictions. En 81 links to the predictions in En 80 in order to
underscore the fact that Uriel also instructed Enoch in the secrets
of the future.

1.8 The Relationship between the Astronomical Book and Gen 5,21-24

The only direct conformity between the Astronomical Book and
Gen 5,21-24 is that Enoch is the father of Methuselah in both.
Since the arrangement of the names in Gen 5 most likely is the
work of P, we can assume that the author of the Astronomical
Book knew Gen 5.

The question is then whether the figure of Enoch in the Astronomical Book is patterned on Gen 5,21-24. If this was the case we
can expect, *first*, that the basic motifs in Gen 5 are referred in the
Astronomical Book, and *secondly*, that the basic motifs in the
Astronomical Book also are present in Gen 5.

This is not the case. There is no explicit reference in the Astronomical Book to Enoch walking with God. That Enoch was taken
away, which is the most significant motif in Gen 5, is not mentioned at all. And in the opposite order: The basic motif in the
Astronomical Book is that Uriel taught Enoch astronomy. Neither
Uriel nor astronomy is mentioned in Gen 5. The conclusion must
be that although the author of the Astronomical Book most likely
knew Gen 5, his composition did not depend on it.

There are several contacts between the two sources, however,
similar motifs that are used in different ways:

*   In both sources Enoch has an intimate relationship with a divine being,
    either God or Uriel.
*   In both sources Enoch is portrayed as an educated man; he is "trained" and
    an astronomer.
*   In both sources Enoch is connected to the number "seven"; he is the seventh
    patriarch, and seven is a basic number in astronomy and cosmology.
*   In both sources Enoch is connected to the sun — his life span of 365 years
    corresponding to the number of the sun and a solar calendar of 364 days.

These observations point clearly in one direction: The figure of
Enoch in the Astronomical Book is not patterned on the figure of
Enoch in Gen 5, but there are so many mutual contacts that both
sources must have been influenced at least partly by the same
traditions.

The portrait of Enoch in En 81 has clear connections to the
Astronomical Book, but there are also differences. It is not said in
the Astronomical Book that Enoch stayed in heaven as presupposed in En 81,1-4. Nor are the "tablets of heaven" mentioned in
the Astronomical Book. According to En 81,5ff Enoch returned to
the earth for one year to teach Methuselah and his other children.
That Enoch instructed Methuselah we find in the Astronomical
Book, but not that it happened in a one-year leave from heaven.

The idea that Enoch visited heaven corresponds to other aspects of
the Enoch tradition. In the Apocalypse of Animals Enoch ascends
to heaven. Even closer comes the Book of Watchers where Enoch
stays in heaven and is sent back to the earth again. He thereafter
returns to heaven in a vision (En 12-15).

Between En 81 and Gen 5 there are no direct parallels except that
Methuselah is the son of Enoch in both. But there are contacts in
motifs. Enoch's stay in heaven and communication with a divine
being correspond both to "Enoch walked with God" and "Enoch
was taken away" in Gen 5.

1.9   The Date and Setting of the Astronomical Book

The oldest Qumran manuscript where astronomical speculations are
attributed to Enoch can be dated at the end of the third or the
beginning of the second century. As already noted, this scroll most
likely contained the whole Astronomical Book. That means that the
oldest part of the book, the calculations, must have an earlier date.
There is also no reason to suppose that the Qumran manuscript was
the original scroll. Milik thinks that the astronomical calculations
are older than the P source of the Pentateuch. He believes that the
number 365 connected to Enoch in Gen 5,23 is a reference to these
calculations. Originally the Biblical text had the number 364 as the

Astronomical Book, but this was later corrected to 365.[114]
The oldest reference to the Astronomical Book in non-Biblical
sources Milik finds in the work of the so-called Pseudo-Eupolemus.[115] This work has a clearly Samaritan origin. Milik thinks it
was written by a Samaritan priest, and he dates it fairly far back
in the third century. On the basis of these observations he draws
the following conclusion: "The invention of the calendar of 364
days, its application to Biblical chronology, and the composition of
the astronomical work attributed to Enoch could have been
affected just as easily by the Samaritan priests of Sichem as by the
Judean priests of Jerusalem."[116]
It is not clear in Milik's argumentation how he relates the two
observations to each other. If Gen 5,23 reflects at least parts of the
Astronomical Book, it must consequently reflect a book written by
Samaritan priests. When is then the final redaction of the Pentateuch to be dated?
Milik's theory has been criticized by J.C. Greenfield and M.E.
Stone.[117] About Milik's first opinion they write: "Nothing in Gen
5,23 implies, alludes or suggests that its author knew astronomical
works circulating under the name of Enoch. The number 365
might imply an astronomical connection or astronomical traditions,
but not any astronomical writings. No evidence at all indicates the
correction of a putative original 364 year life-span to 365
years."[118]
We deviate from this criticism at only one point. If the number
365 implies an astronomical connection or traditions, it cannot be
excluded that the traditions were in written form. What can be
excluded is that the number 365 refers to those calculations which
we find in the Astronomical Book.
Greenfield and Stone doubt the early date of Pseudo-Eupolemus
in Milik's Samaritan theory. They also doubt that the reference to
Enoch as astrologer in his work implies an awareness of the
Astronomical Book. We shall later align ourself those scholars who
argue for a possible date of Pseudo-Eupolemus near the end of the

114   Milik, op.cit., pp. 8ff.
115   To Pseudo-Eupolemus, cf. below, pp. 111-18.
116   Milik, op.cit., pp. 9f.
117   J.C. Greenfield and M.E. Stone, "The Books of Enoch and the Traditions
of Enoch", Numen 26, 1979, pp. 89-103.
118   Greenfield and Stone, op.cit., p. 93.

third century. We shall also argue that it is quite likely that
Pseudo-Eupolemus knew at least Enoch's association with the
astronomical calculations of the book.[119]

But this does not mean that the astronomical calculations are of
Samaritan origin. Enoch is connected to astronomy/astrology in all
the early sources, such as the P source of Genesis and the Book of
Watchers, and in one text tradition to Hebrew Ben Sira.[120] What
Pseudo-Eupolemus and the other sources show are the spread of
the traditions about Enoch as astronomer/astrologer as early as the
beginning of the second century. Besides, it is highly unlikely that
a Samaritan calendar was adopted by the orthodox Qumram
community.

We have the following limits for the association of Enoch to the
astronomical calculations: The terminus ab quo is the Priestly
source of the Pentateuch, composed about 500 or 400 in Babylonia
and brought to Jerusalem by Ezra in 398.[121] The terminus ante
quem is about 200, the date of the earliest manuscript.

R.T. Beckwith has in his most recent study of the early Enoch
literature argued for 251 B.C. as the date of the Astronomical Book
in its original shape.[122] He bases this exact date on the following
observations:

1. The Astronomical Book was later copied by members of the Qumran
   community. In calendarian and other religious matters there are so many
   similarities between the Astronomical Book and the Essenes of Qumran that
   the Astronomical Book must have been composed in a group which stood in
   historical continuity with the Essenes. Beckwith calls this group "the pre-
   Essenes".
2. The Apocalypse of Animals in the Book of Dreams dates the rise of the
   Essenes to the same time as the rise of Judas Maccabeus. Then "the eyes of
   the sheep were opened" (En 90,9-10).[123] At the beginning of the same
   period the apocalypse records that the lambs "began to open their eyes" (En
   90,6). According to the Apocalypse this period lasted 84 years. Also including
   observations made in the Damascus Document and the Testament of Levi,
   Beckwith estimated the beginning of this period at about 251 B.C.

Beckwith's computation presupposes that the numerical calculations
in the Apocalypse of Animals and similar literature are to be
treated as fairly exact and correct historical information. Taking

119 Cf. below, pp. 115ff.
120 For Ben Sira, cf. below, pp. 123f.
121 Cf. above, note 12, p. 43; and below, note 183, p. 103.
122 Cf. Beckwith, "The Earliest Enoch Literature", pp. 365-77.
123 Cf. Beckwith, "The Significance of the Calendar", p. 180f; and below, pp.
107f.

into consideration that the system in the Apocalypse of Animals is based on 12 and 7 as fixed numbers, we think it wise to be a little more cautious. Nevertheless, Beckwith is probably right that the Essenes had some knowledge of a movement dating back in the third century that had some spiritual affinity with them. We also find it plausible to relate this movement to the earliest Enochic books, the Astronomical Book and the Book of Watchers. Beckwith ascribes the composing of the astronomical calculations to this group at the fixed date 251 and dates En 80 about fifty years later. We doubt that we can determine the date so precisely, and we have arrived at partly different conclusions concerning the development of the book.

We have argued above that the oldest stratum of the book consisted of astronomical calculations. The present Aramaic Astronomical book was composed at the next stage, containing the astronomical calculations, the cosmological material, and the two speeches, En 80 and 82. Later En 81 was added.[124] Since the cosmological material shows a close affinity with the Book of Watchers in its present shape, it seems likely that the Aramaic Astronomical Book and the Book of Watchers were composed at approximately the same time. Both can probably be ascribed to the group Beckwith calls "the pre-Essenes".

If so, the origin of the astronomical calculations must be earlier. If we use Beckwith's argument that En 80,2-8 presupposes a rather long period before the transmitters realised the discrepancy between the calendar and the seasons,[125] the origin of the calendar must be dated no later than the beginning of the third century.[126]

There are also other indications in the Astronomical Book and in Jewish sources that point toward an earlier date than the earliest

---

124   Cf. above, p. 59.

125   Cf. Beckwith, "The Earliest Enoch Literature", pp. 386ff; and above, pp. 74f.

126   The astronomical calculations may at the earliest stage have circulated as isolated compositions without any connection to the Enochic traditions. "What we have is not the work of one author (or "redactor") but a conglomerate of closely related versions made by generations of scribes who assembled, to the best of their knowledge, the teaching current in their community about the structure and the laws of the cosmos." So Neugebauer, The 'Astronomical' Chapters, p. 3. There seems to be reasons to suggest, however, that the calculations were associated with Uriel, and possibly with Enoch and Methuselah, at a stage prior to the composing of the Aramaic Astronomical Book, cf. above, pp. 62f.

manuscript about 200. On the one hand Enoch is well known as an astronomer/astrologer in sources from this period. The spread of these traditions both geographically (Samaria/Judea) and in different milieus (the Book of Watchers, Pseudo-Eupolemus, Ben Sira) indicates a much earlier date for the origin of the traditions. The Astronomical Book does also not explicitly refer to Gen 5 or other Biblical texts as is the case in the two other early Enochic books, the Book of Watchers an the Book of Dreams. This argument is of course not decisive for an early date for the traditions, but it could indicate a time when new literature could be produced also implying Biblical persons but without the need to borrow authority from the Biblical text. That would mean a time not too long after the introduction of the Torah in the beginning of the fourth century. A dating of the astronomical calculations to the Persian age (fourth century) can therefore not be excluded.

Concerning the setting of the calculations we are not better off, for also here the material is scanty. More generally, it can be argued that the speculative interest of this kind of literature points towards a learned scribal milieu.[127] Furthermore, the correspondence between astronomy and calendarian interests could point toward a priestly milieu. More special observations seem to support this. The number "seven", although it gained a general importance in post-exilic Judaism, is especially emphasized in the Priestly source. The author of this source extends the number from cultic life to the cosmos, Gen 1. The closest parallel to the description of the heavenly bodies is also in this source, Gen 1,14-18. Taken together, the indications we have, though they are not many, point toward an origin of the traditions in what we can describe broadly as priestly circles. We have previously argued that the book was influenced by a non-Jewish astrological thinking and that it polemicizes against groups influenced by foreign astral cults. This could indicate that the astronomical calculations had their origin in a group that struggles to reconcile the older Jewish traditions and the impact of astronomy and astrology from other cultures.

---

127 For the speculative interest in the early Enochic sources, cf. M.E. Stone, Scriptures, Sects and Visions. A Profile of Judaism from Ezra to the Jewish Revolts, Philadelphia 1980, pp. 37-47. For the scribal activity in this period, cf. below, p. 101.

2. The Book of Watchers

2.1 The Versions

The Book of Watchers covers ch. 1-36 in Eth En.[128] Most of the book is extant in two Greek translations: Eth En 1-32 is covered in GrPan, with a duplicate version of ch. 19,1-21,9. Extracts from the book are found in quotations by Syncellus, GrSyn.[129]

Five Aramaic Qumran scrolls contain fragments of the book: 4Q Ena dates from the first half of the second century B.C.; 4Q Enb from the middle of the second century; 4Q Enc, End, Ene, date from the first century.[130] The two first copies were brought to Qumran from elsewhere. Both probably contained only the Book of Watchers, while the three others, copied in Qumran, formed a part of the Enochic corpus.

The Aramaic fragments show that the original Aramaic version had the same length and content as the Greek and Ethiopic translations.

2.2 The Book of Watchers as a Compilation

The Book of Watchers is composed of different parts. General agreement in the research how to delimit these parts has not been changed after the discovery of the Aramaic fragments: Ch. 1-5: Introduction; 6-11: The Watcher Story; 12-16: The Dream vision of Enoch; 17-19: Enoch's first journey, 20-36: Enoch's second journey.[131]

The Aramaic fragments show that the Book of Watchers existed as a unit at beginning of the second century. This means that En 1-5

---

128   For the Ethiopic text editions, cf. note 35, p. 53. In quotations we use the critical edition by R.H. Charles, The book of Enoch, when not otherwise stated.

129   Cf. M. Black, Apocalypsis Henochi Graece, Leiden 1970, pp. 7-9; M.A. Knibb, The Ethiopic Book of Enoch II, pp. 15-7. For the Greek text I use the edition by Black.

130   Cf. Milik, The Books of Enoch, pp. 5 and 22.

131   Cf. G. Beer, "Das Buch Henoch", E. Kautzch (ed.), Die Apokryphen und Pseudepigraphen des Alten Testaments II, pp. 220-2; Charles, The Book of Enoch, pp. xlvii-xlviii; O. Eissfeldt, Einleitung in das Alte Testament, p. 837; L. Rost, Einleitung in die alttestamentlichen Apokryphen und Pseudepigraphen, p. 102; G.W.E. Nickelsburg, Jewischen Literature between the Bible and the Mishnah, pp. 48-55.

not was written as an introduction to the whole Enochic corpus as
previously often claimed,[132] but only to the Book of Watchers. As
far as we can see it does not, however, mean that "all the labor-
ious 'vivisection' of our document made by 'many hands' (Charles,
p. 1) accomplished during the last century and a half is shown to
be useless and mistaken . . .," as Milik claims.[133] The finds of the
Aramaic fragments do not give a final answer about the growth of
the book but rather new perspectives for the analysis of this
growth.

Within the Book of Watchers En 19,3 clearly ends a section. Gr[Pan]
reads: κἀγὼ ῾Ενὼχ ἴδον τὰ θεωρήματα μόνος, τα πέρατα
πάντων, καὶ οὐ μὴ ἴδη οὐδὲ εἷς ἀνθρώπων ὡς ἐγὼ ἴδον.
"And I Enoch saw the visions alone, the ends of everything, and
no man shall see what I have seen."[134] Most likely this concluding
remark refers to the composition En 6-19. In En 20 begins a new
composition with the list of the seven angels, telling about Enoch's
journeys, which ends in En 36. We therefore agree with Milik's
literary criticism regarding En 6-19 as a unit which was subsequently incorporated into a larger work with the inclusion of En
20-36 and 1-5.[135]
In En 19,3 the material in En 6-19 is characterized as "visions". In
Enoch's introductory speech to the Book of Watchers the whole
book is characterized in the same way: "The vision of the Holy
one and of heaven was shown to me, and from the words of the
watchers and the holy ones I heard it all," En 1,2.[136] Strictly
speaking only En 14-16 is a vision. En 17-19; 20-36 must be
characterized as visionary journeys. The other material consists of
either speeches or epic stories. The composers of En 6-19 and 1-
36 obviously emphasized the visionary features of the material.

---

132   Cf. Beer, op.cit., pp. 220ff; Charles, op.cit., pp. 2f.
133   Milik, op.cit., p. 25.
134   I am not quite convinced about Milik's reconstruction of an original
Aramaic wording "end of everything" = "end of the book", Milik, op.cit., p. 35.
135   Milik, op.cit., p. 25.
136   Translation based on Milik's reconstruction of the traces in 4Q En[a] li, lines
2-3 (Milik, p. 142), which seems more reliable for the original Aramaic wording
than the Greek translation.

But also within the composition En 6-19 it is possible to separate subsections. In the Watcher story, ch. 6-11, Enoch is not mentioned at all. This composition can be read independently of all the other parts of the book but is clearly presupposed in the other parts. In 12,1 Enoch is introduced. This section ends in 16,4. The section 12-16 is again presupposed in En 17-19. In 18,13-19,2 we have a combination of the "stars which went astray" from the Astronomical Book (ch. 80) and the "fallen angels" from En 6-11; 12-16. I therefore agree with Nickelsburg in regarding En 6-11 as the oldest part, then adding 12-16, and finally 17-19.[137]

2.3 The Noahitic Traditions

As already noted, Enoch is not mentioned in the oldest part of the Book of Watchers, ch. 6-11. This section, the Watcher story, draws on Gen 6,1-4, the story about the "fall of the angels". The Watcher story and Gen 6,1-4 have the leading motif in common: sexual relations between heavenly beings and human women causing the birth of giants. But in the Genesis text this is not directly connected to Noah and the deluge, which is the case in En 6-11, cf. En 10,2-3.22.[138]

In the Book of Watchers Gen 6,1-4 is combined not only with Noah and the flood, for in 12,1-3 the sequence is also connected to Enoch. He was taken away to heaven during the watcher incident, and in En 12 he is commissioned to go and reprove the watchers. This combination of Gen 6,1-4, Noah traditions and Enoch traditions occurs not only in En 6-16, but also in sections which Charles classified as fragments of a "Book of Noah". According to Charles, the following sections of the Books of Enoch and the Book of Jubilees should originate from this book; from the Books of Enoch: 6-11; 39,1.2a; 54,7-55,2; 60; 65,1-69,25; 106-107;[139] from the Book of Jubilees: 7,20-39; 10,1-15.[140]

---

137 Nickelsburg, op.cit., pp. 48-55; cf. also C.A. Newsom, "The Development of 1 Enoch 6-19: Cosmology and Judgment", CBQ 42, 1980, pp. 310-29.
138 For the connection Noah and the flood, cf. J.P. Lewis, A Study of the Interpretation of Noah and the Flood in Jewish and Christian Literature, Leiden 1968, pp. 10-41.
139 Charles, op.cit., xlvi f and pp. 106f.
140 R.H. Charles, The Book of Jubilees, London 1902, pp. lxxi f.

The Book of Noah is referred to twice in the Book of Jubilees, namely in 10,13 and 21,10. It is also clear that both the Books of Enoch and the Book of Jubilees contain traditions which have Noah in the central role. This is explicitly stated in En 60,8 and 65,1ff. En 60 also shows clearly how the interpolator of the Noah sequence into the Enoch corpus tried to adapt the material. The vision in En 60 is in v. 1 dated at the five hundredth year of Enoch's life. As we know, Enoch lived only 365 years according to Gen 5,23. 500 is however a number given about Noah before the flood in Gen 5,32. In En 60,8 the visionary calls Enoch his great-grandfather. Hence, the visionary can not be Enoch and must be Noah.[141]

But the fact that there existed a Book of Noah and the observation that several texts are centered around Noah do not automatically lead to the assumption that these texts are actually fragments of it. We rather prefer to use the designation "Noahitic traditions" which may in different ways reflect this book.

Among the texts which contain Noahitic traditions, we shall concentrate on two groups. The one describes Noah in relation to the coming judgment and the other his birth.

I. In En 60 vv. 1-10 and 24c-25 belong together.[142] The text can be divided into two sequences: vv. 1-6 contain a throne vision leading to a pronouncement of judgment; vv. 7-10.24c-25 tell about the destruction of two monsters. Noah is the visionary of the text. Enoch plays no active role, but he is referred to in the sequence about the monsters. He is called "the seventh from Adam" and is situated west of an immense desert "in the garden where the chosen and righteous dwell" (60,8).

In En 65 Noah realises that the destruction of the earth is near, and he seeks Enoch to ask the reason. Enoch is situated at "the ends of the earth" (65,2). He appears to Noah in what resembles a theophany (65,4-5) and tells him that the destruction will come because the earth is corrupted by the teaching of the angels and satans, but Noah will be saved (65,6-12).

---

141 Cf. J.C. VanderKam, "The Righteousness of Noah", J.C. Collins and G.W.E. Nickelsburg (eds.), Ideal Figures in Ancient Judaism, Chico 1980, pp. 13-32, esp. pp. 18ff.
142 Cf. Knibb, op.cit., pp. 142f, notes to 60,1.6.

II. There are three texts which recount the birth of Noah. En 106-107 is formed as a story told by Enoch. Lamech's wife gives birth to Noah who appears to have extraordinary features:

τέκνον ἐγεννήθη μου ἀλλοῖον, οὐχ ὅμοιον τοῖς ἀνθρώποις ἀλλὰ τοις τέκνοις τῶν ἀγγέλλων τοῦ οὐρανοῦ, καὶ ὁ τύπος ἀλλοιότερος, οὐχ ὅμοιος ἡμῖν τα ὄμματά ἐστιν ὡς ἀκτῖνες τοῦ ἡλίου, καὶ ἔνδοξον το πρόσωπον καὶ ὑπολαμβάνω ὅτι οὐκ ἔστιν ἐξ ἐμοῦ ἀλλὰ ἐξ ἀγγέλου ...

(En 106,5-6a).[143] "I have begotten a strange son, not like men, but like the sons of the angels of heaven, and of a different type, not like us. The eyes are like the rays of the sun, and the face glorious. And it seems to me that he is not from me, but from an angel..." Thus the complaint of Lamech.

Methuselah, Lamech's father, seeks Enoch to ask whether Noah is the son of Lamech or not. Enoch has his dwelling "with the angels", "at the end of the earth" (106,7-8). He recounts for Methuselah the Watcher story and predicts the coming destruction. He assures him that Noah is indeed the child of Lamech and that Noah will be saved.

The Genesis Apocryphon, 1Q apGen (proper), cols. 2-5, has a story which by and large is the same as En 106-107.[144] But this time the story is told by Lamech. To reach Enoch, Methuselah this time travels to Parwaim (col II, line 23). The land is mentioned in 2 Chr 3,6 as the place from where the gold for the temple came. Most likely it is used in Gen Ap as a designation for an exotic, far-off country, parallel to the distant area in which the Garden of the Righteous is situated, cf. En 60,23.[145]

The third text, 4Q Mess ar, is of a different kind.[146] It has the form of a prediction; more specifically it resembles the Gattung

---

143 Text from the Chester Beatty Papyri according to M. Black, cf. note 112, p. 77 above.
144 Text in J.A. Fitzmyer and D.J. Harrington, A Manual of Palestinian Aramaic Texts, pp. 104-7.
145 Cf. P. Grelot, "Parwaïm des Chroniques à l'Apocryphe de la Genèse", VT 11, 1961, pp. 30-8; J.A. Fitzmyer, The Genesis Apocryphon of Qumran Cave 1, pp. 94 f; Milik, op.cit., p. 41, note 1.
146 For text, cf. Fitzmyer and Harrington, op.cit., pp. 96-101.

"message of child birth" which occurs several times in the Old as well as the New Testament (Gen 16,11-12; Judg 13,3-5; Is 7,10-17; Luk 1,11-15.28-38).[147] The identity of the child is not revealed in the preserved text, but Grelot has argued convincingly that the child must be Noah.[148] In col I, lines 4-5 it is said that the child in his youth will become skilled in three books. This corresponds to the three books of Enoch in Jub 4,17-26 that Enoch was to hand over to his descendants. In the following lines the child is predicted to be wise and know the secrets of mankind. Noah is described in the same way in the so-called Noahitic fragments in the Book of Jubilees (7,20-39; 10,1-15). According to our text Noah will also become visionary, which corresponds to the Noahitic traditions in 1. Enoch. In the very fragmentary text of col II there is clearly a description of the deluge and the watcher incident, which also indicates that Noah is the person involved.

Unfortunately there remain only traces of the description of Noah's actual birth: שבונוהי בדי בחיר אלהא הוא מלדה ורוח(ח נשמוהי col I, line 10. ". . . his plans, because he is the Elect of God. The birth and the spirit of his breath." Most likely the line is to be understood in the light of the other birth texts that at his birth Noah appeared to have extraordinary features.

Our observations can be summarized thus:

* In the texts containing Noahitic traditions Noah is described as a visionary and a sage. He is the Elect of God, the one who was saved through the destruction.
* Noah's birth is extraordinary. As a newborn child he reveals divine features, although his divine origin is denied.
* Enoch's role in these traditions is modest. He is situated in Paradise (the Garden of the Righteous) at the ends of the earth where his descendants can seek him to get advice.

2.4 The Relationship between the Noahitic and the Enochic Traditions

In the Genesis narrative we find three events which are not explicitly related: 1) Enoch who walked with God and was taken away, Gen 5,21-24; 2) The sons of God who had intercourse with

147 For this Gattung, cf. H. Gese, "Natus ex virgine", Probleme biblischer Theologie, Festschr. G. von Rad, München 1971, pp. 73-89, esp. pp. 74-7.
148 P. Grelot, "Hénoch et ses écritures", RB 82, 1975, pp. 481-500.

human women and begat giants, Gen 6,1-4; and 3) Noah who was saved through the flood, Gen 6,5-9,17. The special character of several Jewish Enochic and Noahitic texts is caused by a combination of these three themes.

The combination "fallen angels"/watchers and the Flood story:

* In the Genesis narrative it is possible to read the "angel incident" as one of the reasons for the corruption of mankind. But the flood affects only mankind and not the "sons of God" or the giants, who are not mentioned in the Flood story. In both En 6-11 and the Noahitic traditions the flood motif is altered to become a destruction which primarily affects the sons of God/watchers and the giants. Mankind plays a marginal role. It follows that En 6-11 and the Noahitic traditions are based on an interpretation of the flood as a catastrophe affecting divine beings.
* Noah is involved in the Watcher story because of the above-mentioned combination. His modest role in En 6-11 shows that he hardly can be regarded as the fixed point in the combination. He is moved into the Watcher story because of an interpretation of the flood which involved Gen 6,1-4.
* As a part of the Watcher story Noah is portrayed differently from Noah in the Genesis account. In Genesis it is said that he was righteous and that he walked with God (Gen 6,9). Most likely this implies that he had an intimate relationship with God which gave him access to God's plans (Gen 6,13ff).[149] But Noah is not portrayed as a visionary and sage in Genesis. This is a new feature in the Noahitic traditions.
* Noah's divine appearance at his birth corresponds to the Watcher story. He resembles the divine beings that were destroyed in the catastrophe. It also underscores his special gift as a visionary and a sage.

These observations show that Noah in the Noahitic traditions and En 6-11 belongs to a different understanding of the Flood story than the one found in Genesis, one where the actors were divine or semi-divine figures and where the hero was understood as a visionary and a sage. One has the impression that the description of Noah's birth tries to maintain two seemingly contradictory elements. First, the description of Noah's appearance elevates him above ordinary human beings; secondly, his human descent is underscored. It is possible that the tradition is polemic, that the story is composed to refute what it denies, namely that Noah was divine.

The combination fallen angels/watchers and Enoch:

I. In Genesis there is no connection between Enoch and the account of the flood. There is a possibility, however, that already P dated the incident of Gen 6,1-4 back into the time of Enoch's

149   Cf. above, p. 47.

father and the early years of Enoch's life. As previously noted, P changed the name Irad to Jared (descent) and made Jared Enoch's father, Gen 5,15-20.[150] The author of the Book of Jubilees quite clearly saw a connection between the name Jared and the watcher incident: "... he called his name Jared; for in his days the angels of the Lord descended on earth," Jub 4,15. In the Ethiopic translation we have a pun involving the name $y\bar{a}r\bar{e}d$, "descent", and the verb $waradu$ (3 p. plur.), "descend". The original Hebrew version must have had a pun involving the name ירד, $y\bar{a}r\bar{a}d$, and the verb ירדו, $y\bar{a}r\bar{a}du$ (3 p. plur.). Such a pun is also presupposed in En 6,6 where Gr^{Syn} reads: οἱ καταβάντες εν ταῖς ἡμέραις Ἰάρεδ, "who descended in the days of Jared". Parts of the passage are also preserved in Aramaic, 4Q En^a liii, lines 3-4 (Milik, p. 150). Using the Greek text, the whole sentence can be reconstructed as: די נחתו) ביומי ירד. Since there is no word play between Hebrew ירד, $y\bar{a}r\bar{a}d$, and Aramaic נחת, n^ehat, "descend", the author must either have read the connection from the Genesis text or known another Hebrew tradition where this connection occurs. As already noted, the possibility that already P knew such a tradition cannot be excluded.

II. If already P dated the fall of the angels at the time of Enoch, En 6-11 is not the oldest source where this connection occurs. Also in the Noahitic traditions Enoch is the one who know and tells about the watcher incident. One could of course consider the possibility that the authors of En 6-16 were the first to combine Enoch and the watcher incident and that the Noahitic traditions simply depended on En 6-16. But besides the indication already considered that P knew the connection, there is an obstacle to this model. In En 12,1-3 Enoch is situated in the heavenly temple, while in the Noahitic texts he is situated in Paradise, at the end of the earth. There is also no explicit support for this placement of Enoch in Gen 5,24. Most likely both the authors of En 6-16 and of the Noahitic texts were aware of a tradition where the primary antediluvian sage was connected to a catastrophe affecting divine and semi-divine beings, and was removed to heaven or to Paradise. This connection may be alluded to already in P.

---

150   Cf. above, p. 45.

Enoch and Noah: We have already noted that the interpolator of the Noahitic traditions in En 60 confuses Enoch and Noah. Already P saw a similarity between the two figures; they were the only ones among the antediluvian patriarchs who had an intimate relationship with God (Gen 5,22.24; 6,9). Also in the Book of Watchers there is a similarity between the two figures: Both were removed during the catastrophe that struck the earth at the time of the watchers (En 10,2-3; 12,1-2). In the Noahitic traditions Noah is portrayed as a sage and a visionary, a feature commonly attributed to Enoch. The two figures are certainly treated as separate, but they appear in the same roles. There must have been traditions which caused this connection.

2.5   Enoch in En 12-16 and Gen 5,21-24

Enoch is introduced in the Book of Watchers according to Gr[Pan]:

Πρὸ τούτων τῶν λόγων ελήμφθη ʾΕνώχ, καὶ οὐδεὶς τῶν ἀνθρώπων ἔγνω ποῦ ελήμφθη καὶ ποῦ ἐστιν καὶ τί ἐγένετο αὐτῷ.

"Before these events Enoch was taken away, and nobody among men knew where he was taken away and where he was and what had happened to him", En 12,1. The text clearly draws on Gen 5,24, the passive verb ελήμφθη, "taken away", reflecting the Hebrew לקח, lāqah, "take away", through an Aramaic link. The passage elaborates the question which arises out of Gen 5,24: When Enoch was no more, when he was taken away, what had become of him? The author of En 12-16 knew the answer: He was taken away to the heavenly temple, to the assembly of the Lord, 12,2, cf. 9,1; 14,23.

An ascension to heaven is also told in En 14. The Gattung of this text is "night vision", and it is clearly inspired by Ezekiel's throne vision in Ezek 1-3.[151] The difference is that Ezekiel only looks into the throne room of God, while Enoch is lifted into it. Gr[Pan] reads to the passage where Enoch is lifted ut to heaven, En 14,8b-9a: καὶ ἄνεμοι ἐν τῇ ὁράσει μου εξέπετάσαν με καὶ ἐπῆράν με ἄνω καὶ εἰσήνεγκάν με εἰς τὸν οὐρανόν,

---

151   Cf. C. Rowland, "The Visions of God in Apocalyptic Literature", JSJ 10, 1979, pp. 137-54, pp. 140ff.

"... and winds in my vision made me fly and lifted me upwards and brought me into heaven." A part of the passage is visible in Aramaic: לעלא ואובלוני ואע(לו)ני ב(שמיא), En^c lvi, line 21, (Milik, p. 194). "... upwards and brought me and made me e[enter] into [heaven". The verb יבל, *y^{e}bal*, in aph'el, "to carry away", "bring", corresponds in meaning to לקח, *lāqaḥ*, in Gen 5,24. The destination "heaven" corresponds to Enoch's location in En 12,1-3. Enoch is in his nightly vision brought back to the heavenly assembly.

The whole section En 12-16 has the following structure: Enoch has been taken away to heaven and is situated among the angels, 12,1-3; he is commissioned to go to the fallen watchers as a messenger, 12,4-6; he (descends and) goes to the watchers (on earth), 13,1-6; on their behalf he goes to the waters of Dan and reads a record of their petition (for God or the angels) and falls asleep, 13,7; he receives a vision, 13,8; and brings its contents back to the watchers, 13,9; in the vision he ascends to heaven and is brought before the throne of God, ch. 14; he is commissioned to go and reprove the watchers, ch. 15-16.

There are two cornerstones in the narrative: Enoch is taken to heaven twice. The link between the cornerstones is the role of Enoch as a messenger and an intercessor. The reports about Enoch's ascensions clearly draw on Gen 5,24. But the second ascension is clearly coloured by the throne vision of Ezekiel. This corresponds to Enoch's role as a messenger, which can be described as a prophetic mission. In addition to this mission Enoch also acts as an intercessor on behalf of the watchers. This feature cannot be derived directly from the vision of Ezekiel and needs further investigation, to which we shall return later.

It seems clear that the portrait of Enoch in Gen 5,24 inspired the author of En 12-16. But he added new information. He knew where Enoch was taken away, namely to the heavenly assembly. He also placed the ascension of Enoch into a new framework, the watcher incident, apparently corresponding to the Noahitic traditions where this connection also occurs. He also gave Enoch the new roles of a prophet and an intercessor.

2.6   The Date and Setting of the Book

The oldest manuscript, 4Q En[a], dates from the first half of the second century B.C., and this is the terminus ante quem for the composing of the whole book. Since there is no reason to assume that this manuscript was the original, paleographical and linguistic arguments point toward a pre-Maccabean date of the book. This confirms the analysis by Charles,[152] and more recently Rost[153] but utterly disproves the late date given by Rowley and many other scholars who have regarded the Maccabean age as the terminus ab quo.[154]

A pre-Maccabean age is supported by attestation of the book. Thus the Apocalypse of Animals (En 85-90) in the Book of Dreams clearly presupposes the Book of Watchers. This apocalypse can be dated to about 164 B.C.[155] Milik has found a reference to En 6-19 in an Aramaic fragment of the Testament of Levi, 4Q Test Levi[a] 8iii, lines 6-7.[156] He claims that the Aramaic Testament of Levi was written in the course of the third century, if not toward the end of the fourth. But this early date is doubted by R.T. Beckwith, who argues for a date in the second century.[157]

On basis of the geographical and historical information which can be derived from Enoch's journeys in En 26-32, Milik dates the whole book to the middle of the third century.[158] But he dates the unit, ch 6-19, in an original shape much earlier. By comparing the Watcher story in Enoch with Gen 6,1-4 he claims that Gen 6,1-4 relies on Enoch and not the other way round. The Watcher story in Enoch he dates in the fifth century: "If my hypothesis is correct, the work incorporated in En 6-19 is earlier than the definite version of th first chapters of Genesis."[159] What Milik exactly means with "the work incorporated in En 6-19" is not stated. It may be something like En 6-11. We doubt this early dating for two reasons. First, Gen 6,1-4 is not only the work of P,

---

152   Charles, op.cit., pp. lii f.
153   Rost, Einleitung, pp. 103f.
154   H. Rowley, The Relevance of Apocalyptic, pp. 93-9, cf. the list of suggested datings pp. 94f.
155   Cf. below, pp. 110f.
156   Milik, op.cit., pp. 23f. Cf. also p. 141 below.
157   R.T. Beckwith, "The Significance of the Calendar", pp. 173f.
158   Milik, op.cit., pp. 25-8.
159   Milik, op.cit., p. 31.

for vv. 2 and 4 belong to the Jahwistic source.[160] Secondly, En 6-11 reflects later historical circumstances, as will be demonstrated below.

What we can conclude is that there are good reasons to assume that the Book of Watchers existed as a whole at least by the end of the third century. The composition, En 6-19, must be earlier, and the Watcher story, En 6-11, which is incorporated in this composition, must have a still earlier date.

What is the date, then, of En 6-11? The question applies to the present composition and not the underlying traditions, which will be dealt with later. Before answering it, I have to mention briefly two observations which also will be discussed in more detail later.

The first relates to the character of En 6-11, which is that of a mythical narrative. Accordingly the text cannot be interpreted as though it were a simple allegory or parable which retells events in symbolic language. The basic elements of the text are formed in earlier myths and reproduced by the author of En 6-11. The mythical material is used as a framework for his interpretation of reality, reflecting the events of his time in a correct perspective. But the reproduction of the mythical material is not mechanical. The author has formed the narrative through selection, emphasizing and elaborating some elements but neglecting others.

The second observation concerns its relationship to Gen 6,1-4. I agree with R. Bartelmus that Gen 6,1-4, which is used in En 6-11, must be characterized as a mythical etiology whose intention is to explain the origin of giants on earth.[161] I disagree with his opinion that the giants in 6,1-2.4 (v. 3 is held to be an addition) are regarded positively as heroes whose task is to fight the monsters (nefilim). I rather think that the giants both in Gen 6,1-4 and En 6-11 are understood as mighty warriors whose power surpasses human bounds also in a negative way. This negative aspect is elaborated in En 6-11, but is present both places.

This is not the whole of the mythical narrative in En 6-11, but it is one of the basic structures. And we think it is the structure which most clearly reflects the author's historical setting. This

160   For the origin of Gen 6,1-4, cf. below, pp. 280-83.
161   R. Bartelmus, Heroentum in Israel und seiner Umwelt, AthANT, 65, Zürich 1979, pp. 22ff.

"structure of power" tells that among other things the narrative reflects the acts of mighty warriors on earth.

These mighty warriors are said to be of divine origin, as they are the product of the sexual relations between the watchers and human women, 7,2. They devour the toil of men, 7,3. When men cannot sustain them any more, they devour the men, 7,4. In the end they devour the flesh of one another, 7,5. Thus, the power of the mighty warriors is totally destructive.

The last feature is repeated once more in En 10,9, where it is closer to historical reality. The mighty warriors will be sent into a "war of destruction", cf. 4Q En^b liv, line 6 (Milik, p. 175). En 6-11 accordingly describes a period of wars which are characterized as wars of greed in which the warriors oppress the people economically and physically. At the same time the warriors fight each other.

Both Rowley and Bartelmus think that the description reflects the oppression under Antiochus IV.[162] That is very unlikely for two reasons. First, the decade 170-160 B.C. is too late with regard of all the other evidence for the date of the narrative. Secondly, the description above hardly suits the circumstances under Antiochus IV. There are many warriors fighting each other, and their oppression is economical and physical rather than religious.

The description suits very well, however, another historical period, namely the Diadochan wars, as also Nickelsburg has argued.[163] In these wars, dating from 323 to 302, the successors of Alexander the Great fought for supremacy over Palestine. The people there felt the burden of a long period of oppression and violence.[164] During this period Palestine changed hands seven times. The political government was in chaos as each ruler sought to gain so much income as possible during his brief reign.

In a more general way the motif of the divine origin of the giants seems to have been used to reflect the claim of divinity put forward by the hellenistic rulers. This deification, rooted in Greek religion, started already with Alexander the Great when he was

---

162 Rowley, op.cit., p. 97; Bartelmus, op.cit., pp. 180-3.
163 G.W.E. Nickelsburg, "Apocalyptic and Myth in 1 Enoch 6-11", JBL 96, 1977, pp. 383-405, p. 391; Jewish Literature, p. 52.
164 Cf. A. Schlatter, Geschichte Israels von Alexander dem Grossen bis Hadrian, 3rd rev. ed., Stuttgart 1925, pp. 9-23; W.S. McCullough, The History and Literature of the Palestinian Jews, pp. 83-8; Nickelsburg, op.cit., pp. 43-5.

celebrated in Egypt as the successor of Pharaoh and acclaimed son
of the god Ammon. The ideology was taken over by his successors.[165]

Besides the "structure of power" in En 6-11 there is a "structure
of knowledge". The watchers reveal divine secrets which lead the
people astray from the true knowledge, cf. En 8,1; 9,6-7; 10,7-8.
Also this feature seems to have been used as a reaction against the
new hellenistic wisdom and way of life which rapidly influenced
groups within the Jewish community, not least the aristocracy and
the influential families around the priesthood in Jerusalem.[166]

There is no indication in En 6-11 that the wars have come to an
end. Indeed, En 10,9 points in the direction that they were still
being fought, for divine judgment is that the giants shall destroy
each other completely in a battle. This could indicate that En 6-11
was written before Ptolemy gained control over Palestine after the
battle at Ipsus in 301. If so, En 6-11 can be dated at the end of
the fourth century.

En 12-16 was written after En 6-11, but exactly how much later is
impossible to say. En 6-11 functions as a mythical narrative where
past and present are woven together. En 12-16 is more complex in
this regard. On the one hand, the incidents described are treated as
past events. This can be seen in En 15,8-12 where the spirits of
the giants were set loose in the world as evil spirits when they
died. Here the giants are an ancient race. The misery and sin on
earth in the time of the author are caused by their spirits. On the
other hand, there are indications that the story about the fall of
the watchers reflects actual circumstances in the author's own
days. We shall return to this issue below.

The authors of the different parts of the Book of Watchers
nowhere reveal their identity directly. The only way to trace it is
by analyzing the kind of language they used and how they applied
the mythical material. We find here several interesting details.

165 Cf. P. Wendland, Die hellenistisch-römische Kultur in ihren Beziehungen
zum Judentum und Christentum, HNT 2, Tübingen 1912 (4th ed. 1972), pp. 123-
7; R. Bartelmus, op.cit., pp. 176ff.
166 Cf. M. Hengel, Judentum und Hellenismus, pp. 486-503.

I. D. Dimant has shown that there is a striking similarity between the crimes of the watchers and giants, and the prohibitions of the Noahitic commandments as they appear in the Old Testament and later Jewish sources.[167] In Gen 9,1-7 there are two prohibitions: Eating of blood, 9,4; murder, 9,5b-6. Other prohibitions were added in later post-exilic and rabbinic sources. Dimant makes the following list of prohibitions compared to the crimes: Watchers: fornication — lusting after women, being defiled, begetting bastards; blasphemy — taking oaths; sorcery — teaching sorcery. Giants: robbery — devouring men's possessions; murder — devouring men and one another; eating a limb from a living animal — sinning against animals; blood drawn from a living animal — drinking blood. Asael: murder — making arms; idolatry — working gold and silver; fornication — cosmetics, dying cloths, working precious stones (ornamentation).[168]
This observation is confirmed by the Book of Jubilees. In Jub 7,20-25, which is a part of the Book of Noah according to the author of Jubilees, the connection between the fall of the watchers and the Noahitic commandments is made explicit. The flood had to come because the watchers and the giants had broken fundamental primeval laws. They had committed fornication and iniquities and been unclean, 7,21. Fornication and uncleanliness are exemplified by the sexual relations between the watchers and the women, 7,21, and iniquity by the cruelty of the giants, 7,22-24. These crimes are seen retrospectively in the light of the Noahitic commandments.

II. There are indications that this halakhic perspective is also extant elsewhere. In En 10,9 the offspring of the watchers are called, Greek mazerus, Ethiopic manziran. Both words render Aramaic mamzerīn, the Ethiopic word most clearly. In Old Testament Hewbrew a mamzer designates a child from a mixed marriage. Deut 23,2 reads: "a mamzer shall not come to the assembly of Yahweh." A child from the union between an Israelite and a gentile is not allowed to be a member of the congregation. D. Suter has argued that a sociological code of matrimony lies behind the wording in En 6-16[169]: "It would appear that a sociological code — the halakhic marriage rules — is being used to express the chaos that results when the cosmic order is violated by the marriages of the angels with women."[170] Suter claims that En 6-16 in the present form reflects the marriage rules of the priests; they are not allowed to marry women outside certain Jewish families which can with certainty be regarded as racially pure. As far as I can see En 10,9 is the only example from the section En 6-11 which may reflect such a matrimonial code. The word mamzer can have been used here to designate an illegitimate child without any implication of the whole code of matrimony as framework for the meaning.
En 12-16, however, gives more indications. Here it seems clear that the angels are portrayed as priests. The watchers should have stayed in heaven, "the holy eternal place", 12,4. Before the fall they must have been situated in the heavenly temple as the other holy ones, 14,22-23. Their task was to intercede for men, 15,2. But they who were holy and spiritual defiled themselves with women, 15,3.
I am not sure that this is the case in En 6-11 — at least it was not emphasized there — but the author of En 12-16 seems to have interpreted the Watcher story in the light of the priestly matrimonial rules. This also explains why the sexual motif is emphasized more in En 12-16 than in En 6-11. The sexual crime is the only one mentioned in the accusations in 12,4-6 and 15,2-7, while both the sexual crime, revelation of secrets and violence are mentioned in the accusation

---

167   D. Dimant, "1 Enoch 6-11: A Methodological Perspective", P.J. Achtemeier (ed.), SBL 1978, Seminar Papers, vol. I, Missoula, Montana, pp. 323-39.
168   Cf. Dimant, op.cit., p. 328.
169   D. Suter, "Fallen Angel, Fallen Priest: The Problem of Family Purity in 1 Enoch 6-16", HUCA 50, 1979, pp. 115-35.
170   Suter, op.cit., p. 119.

in En 9,6-9. This observation has also support from other Jewish interpretations of the Watcher story, in the Greek Testament of Levi, 14,1-16,5, and in the Aramaic Testament of Levi, 4Q Test Levi[a] 8iii, lines 6-7.[171]
The background of the matrimonial code of priestly purity is to be found in two places. Lev 21 gives rules for priestly purity also concerning marriage, cf. Lev 21,13-15. Neh 13,23-29 and Ezra 9-10 deal with the problem of mixed marriages concerning the whole Jewish community. There seems to have been a development in the two concerns: "While the law prohibiting marriage with inhabitants of the land is of primary importance in the fifth century, by the third century as T. Levi 9,10 . . . indicates, it has become a facet of the more stringent priestly marriage laws and the associated problems of priestly purity."[172]

III. P.D. Hanson and D. Dimant have called attention to similarities in the description of 'a_s̄ā'el in En 10,4-8 and the enigmatic figure 'a_zā'zel in the ritual of Yom Kippur in Lev 16,8-10.[173] In En 10,4 the angel Raphael is commissioned to bind Asael and throw him into the darkness in the desert. This could be a reminiscence of the ritual dispatching the scapegoat to Azazel as it was practiced in the time of the Second Temple. According to rabbinic sources the scapegoat was pushed down from a rock in the desert. The commissioning of Raphael to ascribe Asael all sins, En 10,8, could be an allusion to Lev 16,22.
A Hebrew fragment from Qumran supports an identification of the originally separate figures. The fragment belongs to a "pesher", a commentary on the Watcher story. Here the name of the chief angel is written 'a_zāz'el, which may be a confusion of 'a_s̄ā'el in Enoch and 'a_zā'zel in Lev 16, cf. 4Q 180 I, lines 7-8.[174]

IV. The same Hebrew fragment begins with a "pesher", a commentary, on the periods of history: "Pesher to the periods created by God," line 1. A commentary like this presupposes a book to be commented. Milik thins that the commentary was written on a lost "Book of Periods".[175] If we combine 4Q 180 I and 4Q 181 2, which seem to be two copies of the same text, it appears that the commentary presupposes a composition in which history is divided into ten periods and the ten units are combined in a larger period of seventy weeks, cf. 4Q 180 I, line 5 and 181 2, line 5 (Milik, p. 249). Milik thinks that the same composition is referred to in En 10,12 cf. 4Q En[b] liv, line 10 (Milik, p. 175), where it is said that Shemihazah and his companions shall be bound for seventy generations until the day of judgment. That may be so. What is clear is that the Watcher story, both in the pesharim from Qumran and in En 6-11, is placed into a chronological scheme based on the number 7, the same basic number that we found in the Astronomical Book.
The author of En 6-11 has also used a scheme of ten. Two of the fallen watchers are describes as leaders. The one is Shemihazah, who is designated as leader and king of the others: ". . . and Shemihazah, to whom you have given authority to rule they who were together with him, "cf. 4Q En[a] liv, line 21 = En 9,7 (Milik, p. 158) and Gr[Pan]. The other figure is Asael, who is associated with the revelation of divine secrets, En 9,6; 10,8. In the Aramaic version of the list of the twenty angels the king Shemihazah appears at the top of the list, and the sage Asael is number ten. His placement on exactly this number is hardly accidental.

---

171   Milik, op.cit., pp. 23f. Cf. below, p. 140.
172   Suter, op.cit., p. 122.
173   P.D. Hanson, "Rebellion in Heaven, Azazel, and Euphemeristic Heroes in 1 Enoch 6-11", JBL 96, 1977, pp. 195-233, esp. pp. 220-6; Dimant, op.cit., pp. 326f.
174   Cf. Milik, op.cit., p. 249.
175   Milik, op.cit., pp. 251ff.

Ten is the basic unit in the calculation. In all there are 20 angels who are the leaders of 200 others (En 6,6), each presiding over 10. The author has made the following computation: $10 + 10 = 20; 20 \cdot 10 = 200$.[176]

V. In En 12-16 Enoch is called scribe of righteousness, 12,4; 15,1; Aramaic safar qušta. In pre-exilic Israel the title sofer was used for officials at the royal court. The scribe was the king's private secretary and the secretary of state.[177] In post-exilic Israel Ezra is designated as a scribe. This may indicate that he had some sort of official status at the royal court in Persian Susa before he left for Jerusalem.[178] What is quite clear, however, is that the title corresponds to his knowledge in the divine law: Ezra 7,6: "and he was a skilled scribe in the Law of Moses"; Ezra 7,11: ". . . to Ezra, the priest and scribe, a scribe of the matters concerning the commandments of Yahweh and his statues for Israel"; Ezra 7,12: ". . . to Ezra, the priest, scribe of the Law of the God of Heaven."

The description of Ezra seems to reflect circumstances in the fourth century. The scribal activity was connected to or carried out in close relation to the priestly office (cf. also 2 Chr 34,13; Neh 13,13). If we compare this with the description of the scribe in Ben Sira, there has clearly been a change during the third century. Ben Sira presupposes scribal activity independent of the priestly office and cult, cf. the Wisdom of Ben Sira 38,24-39,11.[179]

There are some similar features in the descriptions of Ezra and Enoch. Ezra is entitled safar data, "scribe of the Law", and Enoch safar qušta, "scribe of Righteousness". There are also indications that Enoch, like Ezra, is portrayed as a priest. His visit to the heavenly temple is inspired by the vision of the priest and prophet Ezekiel (Ez 1-3).[180]

But more interesting is Enoch's role in relation to the watchers in En 12-16 compared to Ezra's role in relation to the inhabitants of Jerusalem in Ezra 9-10. Ezra is informed that the inhabitants of Jerusalem have married gentile wives, Ezra 9,1-2; Enoch is commissioned to go to the watchers who have married human women, En 12,1-6. Ezra intercedes in prayer on behalf of the inhabitants, Ezra 9,5-15; Enoch intercedes on behalf of the watchers, En 13,3-7. Ezra spends the night fasting, Ezra 10,6; Enoch has a dream during the night, En 13,8. Ezra settles the problem in a court decision the following day, Ezra 10,7-14; Enoch pronounces judgment on the watchers the following day, En 13,10-16,4.

The structure is so close as to suggest not only that the two figures are cast in the same roles, but also that En 12-16 is based on a Ezra-Enoch typology. This typology would also explain the complicated structure of En 12-16: Why did Enoch not pronounce judgment on the watchers at once? Why did he first descend to the earth, then ascend (in a vision) to God and thereafter go to the watchers? The answer seems to be that the author of En 12-16 wanted to portray Enoch in the role of intercessor, similar to that of Ezra, in a case that had some of the same implications, forbidden marriage.

176 Milik, op.cit., p. 29.
177 Cf. the list of the Davidic senior officials in 2 Sam 8,16-18; 20,23-26, and the Solomonic list in 1 Kings 4,1-6. R. de Vaux, Ancient Israel. Its Life and Institutions, pp. 131f.
178 Cf. P.A. Ackroyd, Israel under Babylon and Persia, Oxford 1970, pp. 266ff.
179 Cf. for the scribe in ben Sira, D.J. Harrington, "The Wisdom of the Scribe according to Ben Sira", J.J. Collins and J.W.E. Nickelsburg (eds.), Ideal Figures in Ancient Judaism, pp. 181-8. For the development, cf. Hengel, Judentum und Hellenismus, pp. 143-52.
180 A clear distinction between the priestly and prophetic "office" was not made in the fourth and third century, cf. O. Plöger, "Priester und Prophet", Aus der Spätzeit des Alten Testaments, pp. 8-42, esp. pp. 38-42.

VI. The first part of the Book of Watchers, En 1-5, shows a close relationship with the most important cultic celebrations of post-exilic Judaism and is strongly influenced by cultic language. L. Hartmann has demonstrated that the basic referential background is the covenant between God and his people.[181] He denies the possibility that only the background is cultic, while the language of En 1-5 has become "eschatologized": "I am afraid, however, that such an objection rides counter to facts, for it is precisely those texts which show the greatest similarities to En 1-5 in terms of terminology and motifs, viz the Jub and Qumran examples, that are also the ones which represent people for whom the covenant celebration has demonstratively played a decisive role."[182]

To summarize the observations:

* The description of the crimes of the watchers and giants in En 6-16 is formed in accordance to halakhic rules derived from the Noahitic commandments found in the Priestly source of Genesis and later elaborated in Jewish literature, especially in the rabbinic tradition.

* The description of sexual relations between the watchers and the women is at least in En 12-16 influenced by a matrimonial code of priestly purity. This code is based on Lev 21 (Priestly source) and the tradition of legislation derived from the circumstances under Nehemiah and Ezra.

* The description of Asael seem to be influenced by the ritual of Yom Kippur, described in Lev 16 (Priestly source).

* The Watcher story, En 6-11, is placed in a chronological scheme based on the number 7. This is the basic number in the Priestly source and the Astronomical Book.

* Enoch is called "scribe" and portrayed as a prophet and priest. The structure of En 12-16 resembles the structure of Ezra 9-10. The portrait of Enoch seems to be based on Ezra-Enoch typology.

* The part En 1-5 is strongly influenced by cultic language and rooted in a cultic conception.

I think that these observations are sufficient to claim that the growth of the Book of Watchers has taken place in scribal circles closely related to the priestly office. Of special interest is the section 12-16 which introduces Enoch in the Watcher story. Both the use of "mixed marriage" as a basic motif and the typology

---

181 L. Hartmann, Asking for a Meaning. A Study of Enoch 1-5, CB.NT 12, Uppsala 1979. Cf. the conclusion on pp. 123f.
182 Hartmann, op.cit., p. 124.

Ezra-Enoch indicate a link between priestly circles around Ezra in the first half of the fourth century[183] and the author of En 12-16 possibly less than a century later.

G.W.E. Nickelsburg has made interesting observations concerning the location of at least the oldest parts of the Book of Watchers.[184] In En 13,7 it is said that Enoch went and sat by the waters of Dan in the land of Dan, which is southwest of Mount Hermon. In En 13,9 the watchers are "sitting and weeping at Abel Maīn, which is between Lebanon and Senir" (Hermon). The descent of the watchers takes place at the top of Mount Hermon, En 6,6. The location of Enoch's vision is clearly the immediate environment of the ancient sanctuary of the Danite tribe (Tel Dan). Abel Maīn is to be located some kilometers northwest of this ancient sanctuary. It is interesting that Levi's vision in the Aramaic Testament of Levi also is located to Abel Maīn. This vision is both in style and content closely related to Enoch's vision in En 14.[185]

The sanctuary at Dan had a long history. Judg 17-18 indicate Israelite cultic activity as early as the premonarchial period. Jeroboam I chose the site for the location of the northernmost of his two shrines (1 Kings 12,26-31). Archaeological evidences have demonstrated that the shrine in the Hellenistic and Roman period still had religious significance.[186]

The authors of the Book of Watchers have not only directly located the most important incidents to this area, their stories do also reflect this area in a more indirect way. The mythical

---

183 There is considerable disagreement in the research about the historical circumstances in which Ezra was involved and the literary sources dealing with the issue. For a survey of the recent positions, cf. R.W. Klein, "Ezra and Nehemiah in Recent Studies", Magnalia Dei. The Mighty Acts of God, in memory of G.E. Wright, New York 1976, pp. 361-76. For a review of the research history, cf. H.H. Rowley, "The Chronological Order of Ezra and Nehemiah", The Servant of the Lord and other Essays on the Old Testament, 2nd rev. ed., Oxford 1965, pp. 137-68. In my study I work with two presuppositions: 1) That Ezra was the one who introduced the P source in the post-exilic Jewish community, cf. our note 12, p. 43; 2) That Ezra came to Jerusalem in the first years of the fourth century, cf. the discussion in Ackroyd, op.cit., pp. 191-96; and in K. Galling, "Bagoas und Ezra", Studien zur Geschichte Israels im persischen Zeitalter, Tübingen 1964, pp. 149-84, esp. pp. 158-61.
184 G.W.E. Nickelsburg, "Enoch, Levi, and Peter: Recipients of Revelation in Upper Galilee", JBL 100, 1981, pp. 575-600, pp. 582-7.
185 Cf. Nickelsburg, op.cit., pp. 588f; cf. also below, p. 142.
186 Cf. Nickelsburg, op.cit., p. 583.

geography connected to the location of Paradise reflects the mountaneous area of Lebanon/Syria.[187] Some of the mythical traditions adopted into the Watcher story seem also to have the same area as background.[188]

When both direct location and indirect reflection point toward the same area, they must have some sort of significance. The most likely solution is that at least some of the Enochic traditions had their setting in upper Galilee. Nor can it be excluded that parts of the Book of Watchers were composed there. Yet there is no other reason to ascribe the stories to this area. Neither Enoch nor Levi has any connection with this area in the Old Testament.

3. The Book of Dreams

3.1 The Versions

The Book of Dreams covers ch. 83-90 in Eth En. Some brief extracts of the book exist in Greek.[189] Four Aramaic Qumran scrolls contain fragments of the book: 4Q En^c, En^d, En^e, En^f. The last scroll is the oldest and dates from the third quarter of the second century B.C. The three others date from the first century B.C. Milik estimates that a quarter of the original text can be recovered from the fragments with their Aramaic context restored.[190]

The first dream, En 83-84, has no direct equivalence in the Aramaic fragments, but the fragments classified as 4Q En Giants^a, 9 and 10, have a text similar to En 84,2-6.[191] The second dream, En 85-90, is well represented in the Aramaic fragments. A comparison with the Ethiopic text shows that the Ethiopic version is longer. Milik thinks that this may be the result of the paraphrastic work of the Ethiopic translators, since the Greek extracts are fairly close to the Aramaic text.[192]

---

187   Cf. below, pp. 246-53.
188   Cf. below, pp. 300-4.
189   Cf. Milik, The Books of Enoch, pp. 42, 45-7.
190   Milik, op.cit., p. 41.
191   Cf. Milik, op.cit., pp. 316f.
192   Milik, op.cit., pp. 41f.

3.2   The Contents

The first dream vision, En 83-84, contains an introduction (83,1-2), a vision (83,3-4), an interpretation (83,6-9), and ends with a blessing and a prayer (83,10-84,6). The contents of the vision are the cosmic catastrophe which will come upon the earth. Enoch is here placed into the same position as Noah in the Noahitic texts, as he also foresaw the coming catastrophe, cf. En 60 and 65.[193]

The second dream vision, En 85-90, is commonly called "the Apocalypse of Animals" because the actors in this tableau of world history are symbolized as various kinds of animals. The tableau starts with Adam and ends with the new world in the eschatological era. The style is *vaticinia ex eventu* formed in the Gattung "vision". We give below a survey of the structure of content, the symbolism and the numerical calculations.

The Apocalypse of Animals

85: History before the fall of angels	white bulls
86-88: The fall of angels	stars, animals, seven white men
89,1-9: The flood	white bull
89,10-11: Origin of nations	wild animals and birds
89,12-58: History of Israel	white sheep, wild animals
89,59-90,19: Reign of the empires	shepherds

Reign of the seventy shepherds				
	1:	Babylonian dominion; 89,65-72: $12 \cdot 7$	=	84 years
	2:	Persian dominion; 89,73-77: $23 \cdot 7$	=	161 years
	3:	Greek dominion; 90,1-5: $23 \cdot 7$	=	161 years
	4:	From resistance to judgment; 9,6-19: $12 \cdot 7$	=	84 years
		Total 70 yearweeks	=	490 years

90,20-27: The final judgment	stars, shepherds, blind sheep, seven white men
90,28-38: The new world	wild animals, white sheep, white bulls, white men.

---

193   Cf. above, p. 88.

I. The Symbolism: The first human beings before the fall of the angels are symbolized as bulls or heifers/cows. The angels i the Watcher story are symbolized as stars. We have here the same combination of the stars which went astray from the Astronomical Book, cf. 80,6, and the fallen angels from En 6-11, as in En 18,12-19,1. The two motifs were originally separate.[194] The fallen angels are contrasted with seven white men who are the angels known from En 20. The offspring of the copulation between the angels and the women, the giants, are described as camels, elephants and asses. Noah is again described as a bull. The nations which arose after the flood are described as various species of wild animals and birds, all of them unclean by Jewish standard. Shem, Abraham, and Isaac are again described as bulls. With Joseph comes a change in history. From now on the people of God are symbolized as sheep. During the whole history of Israel these sheep have to fight with the wild animals. The image of Israel as sheep is a common metaphor in the Old Testament.[195] A new change comes with the Assyrian conquest of Samaria (cf. below). From now on the sheep are placed under seventy shepherds.[196] The seventy shepherds correspond to the table of nations in Gen 10.

There are three symbols which quite clearly are used in a positive way. 1) The Jews are during their history from the sons of Jacob to the eschatological era symbolized as sheep. 2) Adam and his descendants in the direct line up to Jacob are symbolized as white bulls (85,3-10; 89,1.9-12). This symbolism is taken up again in the description of the eschatological era. In the "new world" a white bull will be born, clearly as an antitype to the first bull, Adam (90,37). After that event all animals will be transformed into white bulls (90,38). The history has achieved its goal.[197] 3) The seven archangels are described as "white men" (87,2; 90,21). In the sequence of the fall of the angels these heavenly white men are clearly contrasted with the fallen stars. One terrestrial figure is

---

194 Cf. above, pp. 73f. and below, pp. 296-300.
195 Cf. Nickelsburg, Jewish Literature, p. 92.
196 For this concept, cf. Nickelsburg, op.cit., p. 92; Hengel, Judentum und Hellenismus, pp. 342f.
197 A close parallel to this view of the world history is found in Rom 5,12-21.

described in the same way and that is Moses.[198] The Aramaic text can be restored as follows: וחזית בחלמא דן עד א(מר)א(א) דן אתהפך והוא אנוש, 4Q En^c 4, line 10 (Milik, p. 205) = Eth En 89,36a. "[And I looked in that dream until] that [s]heep was changed and became a man." Moses is there changed into the image of the divine beings in order to emphasize his importance.

II. The numbers: There are 70 shepherds signifying 70 yearweeks which gives a total amount of $70 \cdot 7 = 490$ years. These years are divided into four periods described in 89,65-72a; 89,72b-77; 90,1-5; 90,6-17. The duration of a period is partly designated by hours (89,72) and partly by the numbers of shepherds (90,1; 90,5; 90,17), both units signifying yearweeks. The first period is calculated as 12 hours (89,72). The first and second periods together are calculated as 37 shepherds (90,1). The third period is calculated as 23 shepherds (90,5). The first, second and third periods together are calculated as 58 shepherds (90,5). The fourth period is calculated as 12 shepherds (90,17).

At one point the computation must be wrong: If we add 23 to the 37 of the first and second periods, we get 60 and not 58 in 90,5. The number 58 must be correct, however, to reach 70 by adding 12, cf. 90,17. Accordingly, either the number 37 in 90,1 or 23 in 90,5 must be wrong. If the number 37 is correct, the second period must be $37 - 12 = 25$. The third period must be corrected to 21 in 90,5 to get 58 as a total sum for the three periods. If so, we have the numbers $12 + 25 + 12 = 70$. If we subtract 2 from 37, however, and not from 23, the first period will be $35 - 12 = 23$. The result is a symmetrical computation: $12 + 23 + 23 + 12 = 70$. I think this is the best solution.

For the division of periods R.T. Beckwith uses incidents from Israel's national history.[199] He starts with Manasseh in the time of the monarchy. To reach the return from the exile which ends the first period he has to correct the first number. He corrects 12 in 89,72 to 12 + 12 by supposing a mistranslation. The first period will then be $24 \cdot 7 = 168$ years from Manasseh to the return from the exile. The second period is $35 - 24 = 11$ to the high priest

198   In the Ethiopic translation Noah is also described in this way, Eth En 89,1. The Aramaic text has another wording, cf. 4Q En^e 4 i, lines 13ff (Milik, p. 238).
199   R.T. Beckwith, "The Significance of the Calendar", pp. 182-4.

Joiakim. The third period is 23 to the raise of the pre-Essene movement, and the last period is 12 to Judas Maccabeus.

There are two obstacles to this computation. The first is that it is based on a correction of the number in 89,72 for which there is no textual support. The second obstacle is that the author of the apocalypse for this period of history emphasized the reigns of gentile nations (89,59-64). The description of the oppression and violence under the shepherds signifies primarily the acts of the gentile rulers and not relations within the Jewish community. Accordingly, it is more natural to seek the historical basis for the four periods in the change of gentile empires, as also Milik does.[200]

The first period consists of 12 yearweeks, $12 \cdot 7 = 84$ years. At the beginning of this period 89,66a refers to the Assyrian conquest of Samaria, but relates directly to the destruction of the temple in Jerusalem by the Babylonians, En 89,66b. The following verses describe the deportation to Babylonia. The 12 yearweeks in 89,72 refer back to the incidents described in 89,65-69. In these verses the destruction of the temple and the acts of the Babylonians play the leading role. Although the description starts with the Assyrians as a prelude, the computation seems to begin with the Babylonians, cf. the wording in 89,72: "after this (the deportation by the Babylonians) the shepherds pastured for twelve hours." The next period of reign is the Persian empire, computated as $23 \cdot 7 = 161$ years, leading over to the Greek empire. The last period is the time of resistance against the gentile rulers. Since the author worked with fixed numbers the relation to the historical reality could not be exact, but it is not totally wrong.

A four scheme is also used in Dan 2 and 7 to signify the periods of gentile rule. There the scheme is applied to Babylonia, Medea, Persia and Greece.[201]

The Watcher story is incorporated in the vision, but it plays a modest role. The incident is regarded as a past event and recorded at its "proper place" in the history before the flood. The theme is taken up again at the end of history in the description of the final judgement. This is different in En 6-11 where the story reflects actual events and where the giants symbolize hostile military powers. The role as the enemies of the Jews is in our text taken over by the wild animals and the seventy shepherds symbolizing gentile power.

---

200   Milik, op.cit., p. 254.
201   Cf. H.S. Kvanvig, "Struktur und Geschichte in Dan 7", StTh 32, 1978, pp. 95-117, esp. pp. 99ff.

The use of animal symbolism resembles Dan 7 and 8, although there are no direct parallels in the details. The concept of angels presiding over nations resembles Dan 10,19-11,1. The depiction of heavenly beings as men resembles Dan 8,15.16; 10,5.18; 12,6. The basic chronological scheme is the same as in Dan 9,24-27; 70 yearweeks = 70 · 7 = 490 years; and the four scheme applied to gentile nations is used in Dan 2 and 7.

In the Apocalypse of Animals the symbols are used as allegories without interpretation. Each feature of the symbols is constructed according to the reality it signifies. We have no parallel to this in Dan. In Dan 7 there is a discrepancy between the images of the vision and the interpretation, which gives them an independent meaning. In Dan 8 the correspondence between the images and the history is closer,, but they nevertheless need interpretation. In Dan 10-12 we have the same kind of retelling of history in the style of <u>vaticinia ex eventu</u> as in our text, but there without symbols. We can conclude that the Apocalypse of Animals has several features in common with the visions of the Book of Daniel, but there is no indication of literary dependence. The similarities rather point toward an origin in the same milieu, at least with regard to the final redaction of the Book of Daniel.

3.3   The Description of Enoch

Both visions of Enoch are dated at the time before he married, the first before he learnt the art of writing (83,2), the second before he married Edna, Aramaic עדנא, meaning "Paradise" (85,3). In the first case Enoch reports the vision to his grandfather Malalel who interprets it (83,6ff). The information is here taken from Gen 5,15 and 21: Methuselah was born when Enoch was 65 years old (5,21); Mahalalel was Enoch's grandfather (5,15). The Genesis account, however, says nothing about Enoch's wife.

In the second vision Enoch is lifted up and placed in a high tower above the earth (87,3-4). The incident takes place just before the watcher incident. The high tower occurs again in 89,50.56.66.73. There it clearly means the temple. The high tower above the earth must accordingly be the heavenly counterpart to the temple. En 87,3-4 thus draws on En 12,1-3, where Enoch is said to have stayed in heaven during the watcher incident. Both texts correspond to the most likely location in Gen 5,24, although the text itself is not alluded to in En 87,3-4.

Enoch recounts both visions for his son Methuselah (83,1-2; 85,1-2). Here the framework is the same as in the Astronomical Book and En 81. In these texts Enoch instructs Methuselah about the astronomical calculations and the heavenly tablets containing an account of the world history.

The Book of Dreams thus draws on already existing Old Testament and Jewish sources in the portrait of Enoch. The only new information is the name of his wife, "Paradise". This may have connection to the Noahitic traditions in which Enoch is located to Paradise after his life on earth.[202]

3.4   The Date and Setting of the Book

There seems to be no doubt about an approximate date of the Apocalypse of Animals. The sheep with the big horn in the last period of history is Judas Maccabeus, cf. En 90.9.[203] Both Milik and Nickelsburg think that En 90,13-15 describes the battle of Bethsur in 164 B.C.,[204] cf. 2 Macc 11,6-12. Milik thinks that the book was composed just afterwards, while Nickelsburg has a more approximate date, 164-160 B.C.

The author belonged to the Jews who resisted the hellenization of Jewish society and religion. There are two indications in the text that reveal more about his standpoint in the Jewish revolt. One is his critical attitude toward the cult of the temple. In En 89,73 it is said that the bread on the altar was unclean. This can only be interpreted that the author did not recognize the cult of the second temple. This must be the reason why he does not tell about the profanation of the temple by Antiochus IV in 164 B.C. The second indication is his positive attitude toward the military resistance under Judas Maccabeus. The final act of this eschatological war is initiated when God gives the resistance troops a big sword (En 90,19.34).

These two standpoints are the opposite of the standpoint of the final redactor of the Book of Daniel, although both authors belonged to the antihellenistic movement. To the final redactor of the Book of Daniel, the defilement of the temple is the crucial point in the crimes of Antiochus IV, cf. Dan 8,11ff; 11,31. The military resistance is, however, characterized as "little help", cf. 11,34.[205]

---

202   Cf. above, pp. 88f.
203   Cf. Nickelsburg, op.cit., p. 93; Hengel, op.cit., p. 343.
204   Cf. Milik, op.cit., p. 44; Nickelsburg, op.cit., p. 93.
205   Cf. O. Plöger, Theokratie und Eschatologie, p. 27.

This indicates that the two authors belonged to two different groups within the antihellenistic movement. The author of the Book of Dreams could hardly have supported any of the competing candidated for the office of high priest.[206] His positive attitude toward Judas Maccabeus and his companions makes it likely that he belonged to this group.

c) The Description of Enoch in Samaritan and Jewish Sources

1. Pseudo-Eupolemus

The designation Pseudo-Eupolemus is given to two Greek extracts found in Eusebius' *Praeperatio Evangelica*, Praep. Ev. 9.17 and 18.2.[207] Eusebius quoted from Alexander Polyhistor, who ascribed one of the fragments to the Judean author Eupolemus and quoted the other as anonymous. It was J. Freudental who first demonstrated that the two fragments belonged to an unknown Samaritan author and that Polyhistor's information was wrong.[208] Most scholars in recent research date this source at the end of the third century and locate it in Samaria.[209]

The basic subject of the two fragments is the life of Abraham, who is portrayed as the father of civilization. On the command of God he left Babylonia and introduced the Chaldean sciences into Phoenicia and Egypt. This seems to have been a Jewish-Samaritan answer to the opinion found among Greek writers that civilized

---

206 Cf. Hengel, op.cit., pp. 503-15.

207 For the Greek text, cf. K. Mras, Eusebius Werke. Achter Band. Die Praeperatio Evangelica. Erster Teil, GCS, Berlin 1954, pp. 502-5; F. Jacoby, FGH III, C, Zweiter Band, Leiden 1958, pp. 678f; M. Black, Apocalypsis Henochi Graece . . ., una cum historicum et auctorum judaeorum hellenistrarum fragmentis, collegit et ordinavit A.-M. Denis, Leiden 1970, pp. 197f. English translation in B.Z. Wacholder, Eupolemus. A Study of Judaeo-Greek Literature, New York-Jerusalem 1974, pp. 313f. German translation in N. Walter, Fragmente jüdisch-hellenistische Historiker, JSHZ 1, Gütersloh 1976, pp. 137-43.

208 J. Freudenthal, Hellenistische Studien, Heft 1, Jahresbericht des jüdisch-theologischen Seminars, Breslau 1874, pp. 82-103.

209 The basic arguments are given in B.Z. Wacholder; "Pseudo-Eupolemus' Two Greek Fragments on the Life of Abraham", HUCA 34, 1963, pp. 83-113, esp. p. 84-7; cf. also his Eupolemus, pp. 287-93; cf. further N. Walter, "Zu Pseudo-Eupolemus", Klio 43-45, 1965, pp. 282-90, esp. pp. 283f; M. Hengel, Judentum und Hellenismus, pp. 162-9.

culture originated in Egypt.[210] It corresponds, however, to the picture of the Jews as a people of philosophers also found among Greek writers especially from Hekataios from Abdera at the end of the fourth century B.C. and later.[211] The anonymous Samaritan author is the first known writer in the Jewish-Samaritan milieu to deal with this issue, one which cropped up frequently in later Jewish historiography.[212]

Of special interest is Eupolemus, who lived in Judea and whose work "On the Kings of Judea" can be dated at 158/57 B.C.[213] One extract from this work reads as follows: "Eupolemus says that Moses was the first wise man; and he handed over the letters to the Jews first, the Phoenicians received them from the Jews, the Greeks from the Phoenicians. Moses was also the first who wrote laws for the Jews."[214]

Both fragments ascribed to Pseudo-Eupolemus start by telling about the flood and the tower of Babel. Fragment one starts as follows: ". . . the city Babylon was first founded by those who were saved through the flood. They were the giants who built the tower recorded in history. But when this fell down by the act of God, the giants dispersed over the whole earth." Fragment two deals with the same story in a somewhat different way: ". . . these (the giants), living in Babylonia, were destroyed by the gods because of their impiety, as one of them, Belus, escaping death, settled in Babylonia, and built a tower to dwell in it, which was called Belus after its builder, Belus." The differences between the two fragments are that in the first the one God is acting, in the second "the gods", and, secondly, that the act of God or the gods are related to different events — in fragment one the destruction of the tower, in fragment two the flood.

---

210   Cf. Wacholder, Eupolemus, pp. 79ff.
211   Cf. Hengel, op.cit., pp. 464-73.
212   Cf. M. Küchler, Frühjüdische Weisheitstraditionen, OrbBOr 26, Göttingen 1979, pp. 120-5; L.H. Feldman, "Abraham the Greek Philosopher in Josephus", TPAPA 99, 1968, pp. 143-56.
213   Cf. Wacholder, op.cit., pp. 5ff.
214   The extract is from Eusebius Praep Ev as quoted here. A somewhat different recension of the same text is found in Clement Alexandrinus, Stromata, I, 153, 4; cf. Wacholder, op.cit., pp. 307f whose translation we quote; for discussion, cf. Wacholder, pp. 71-96.

Both fragments reflect some reliance on the Genesis narratives in which the flood and the tower are recorded as two events following each other. But Genesis does not tell that the tower of Babel was built by those who escaped the flood. Neither are the giants involved in the Flood story. But there is a possibility of connecting the Genesis sequence about the origin of the giants, Gen 6,1-4, to the sequence about the tower, Gen 11,1-9. In Gen 10,10 Nimrod is made the ruler of Babel. In the Hebrew Bible he is described as follows: וכוש ילד את נמרד הוא החל להיות גבר בארץ, "And Cush begat Nimrod. He began to ge a mighty hero on the earth," Gen 10,8. The LXX version reads as follows: Χους δὲ ἐγέννησεν τὸν Νεβρωδ. οὗτος ἤρξατο εἶναι γίγας ἐπὶ τῆς γῆς. "Chus begat Nimrod. He began to be a giant on the earth." The Hebrew גבר, *gibbor*, "mighty hero", and the Greek, γίγας, "giant", can be read in the light of Gen 6,4 where the offspring of the fallen angels are described in the following way: הגברים אשר מעולם אנשי השם,"The mighty heroes from distant times, the men with a (famous) name". The LXX version reads γίγαντες, "giants", for Hebrew גברים, *gibborim*, "mighty heroes". The similarity in wording can lead to the interpretation that the giants of Gen 6,4 were those who built the tower in Gen 11,1-9. Whether this was intended in the Genesis narratives we shall leave unanswered for the present.

Fragment one continues:

δεκάτη δὲ γενεᾷ, φεσίν, ἐν πόλει της Βαβυλονίας Καμαρίνη, ἥν τινας λέγειν πόλιν Οὐρίεν (ειναι δὲ μεθερμηνευομένην Χαλδαιων πόλιν), <ἥ> ἐν τρισκαι-δεκάτη γενέσθαι ᾿Αβραὰμ γενεᾷ, ευγενεία καὶ σοφία πάντας ὑπερβεβηκότα, ὄν δὴ καὶ τὴν ἀστρολογίαν καὶ Χαλδαïκὴν εὑρεῖν ἐπί τε τὴν εὐσέβειαν ὁρμήσαντα εὐαρεστῆσαι τῷ θεῷ.[215] "In the tenth generation, he says, in a Babylonian city of Camarina, which some call the city of Urie (which is to be translated "the city of the Chaldeans"), in the thirteenth generation, Abraham was born, who surpassed everybody in nobility and wisdom, who also discovered astrology and Chaldean (science), and who on account of his piety was well-pleasing to God."

---

215 The Greek texts are quoted according to Denis, op.cit.

The text is not fully consistent. There is a contradiction between "in the tenth generation" in the beginning of the passage and "in the thirteenth generation" further down. The first computation is in accordance with Gen 11,10-26 where the priestly author counts ten generations from Shem (Noah's son) to Abraham. Wacholder suggests that Pseudo-Eupolemus could have added a different system of computation, beginning with the generation after Enoch.[216] The computation "ten generations" means ten generations from Noah and the flood. If the text is to be understood in the way that Pseudo-Eupolemus also counts from Enoch, he could have known traditions in which also Enoch was involved in the Flood story. We have previously shown that such traditions existed.[217]

Fragment two has a somewhat surprising statement about the origin of Abraham: ... ᾿Αβραὰμ ἀναφέροντα εἰς τοὺς γίγαντας, "Abraham traced his ancestry to the giants". The giants meant here are those who were destroyed in the flood, and from whom only one, Belus, escaped and built the tower of Babel. This statement about Abraham is based on Pseudo-Eupolemus' identification of Belus. Belus equated on the one hand Noah as the hero of the flood, on the other hand the giant (LXX) Nimrod as the builder of the tower of Babel.[218] When Noah is equated with one of the giants, Abraham, the descendant of Noah, can trace his ancestry to the giants. But this interpretation removes us far from the Genesis narratives.

According to both fragments Abraham left Babylonia and taught first the Phoenicians and then the Egyptians "the changes of the sun and moon and all other things" (fragm. I) and "astrology" (fragm. II). The Biblical material behind this portrait of Abraham is of course extremely scanty. Abraham is a nomad in the Genesis narratives, not a sage and astrologer. But if one wanted to prove that civilization originated among the ancestors of Israel, the life of Abraham provided a possible link. He emigrated from Babylonia, which had a reputation as an ancient civilization, to two

---

216 Wacholder, "Pseudo-Eupolemus' Two Greek Fragments", p. 100.
217 Cf. above, p. 92.
218 Cf. Wacholder, op.cit., pp. 89f; and B. Wacholder, "Biblical Chronology in the Hellenistic World Chronicles", HthR 66, 1968, now in Essays on Jewish Chronology and Chronography, New York 1976, pp. 106-36, pp. 113f.

other ancient seats of civilization according to the Greek mind, Phoenicia and Egypt. But it is an open question whether this outer framework of the life of Abraham was a good enough reason to choose him as a primary sage.

About Abraham's stay in Egypt fragment one records: "Abraham lived with the Egyptian priests in Heliopolis teaching them many things. And he introduced astrology and other things, saying that the Babylonians and himself discovered these things, but he traced the discovery back to Enoch, and he was the first to discover astrology, not the Egyptians." The introduction of Enoch here is surprising. Both in this and in the passage above it is stated that Abraham discovered astrology. This is the whole point in Pseudo-Eupolemus' argumentation: Abraham, the ancestor of Israel, discovered the sciences and brought them to other civilizations. It seems as if Pseudo-Eupolemus struggles to reconcile two traditions. In the first Abraham is the primary sage, a tradition which suits Pseudo-Eupolemus' own argumentation well. In the other Enoch is the primary sage. This tradition must have been so strong that it could not be ignored.

At the end of the fragment one Pseudo-Eupolemus writes:

Ἕλληνας δὲ λέγειν τὸν Ἄτλαντα εὑρηκέναι ἀστρο - λογίαν, εἶναι δὲ τὸν Ἄτλαντα τὸν αὐτὸν καὶ Ἐνώχ· τοῦ δὲ Ἐνὼχ γενέσθαι υἱὸν Μαθουσάλαν, ὃν πάντα δι᾽ ἀγγέλων θεοῦ γνῶναι καὶ ἡμᾶς οὗτος ἐπιγνῶναι.

"The Greeks say that Atlas discovered astrology, but Atlas is the same as Enoch. And Enoch had a son Mathusala, who learned everything through the angels of God and thus we learned to know."

In this passage Enoch is equated with Atlas, an ambiguous figure in Greek mythology. In sources from 400 B.C. and onwards he is described as the discoverer of astrology.[219] But in many texts he is also described with a cosmic function.

M.L. West distinguished four different versions of Atlas' cosmic function:[220] 1) He stands at the world's end and supports the sky on his head and hands. 2) He stands under the earth and supports both earth and sky. 3) He lives in the sea and supports the columns which hold the sky up from the earth. 4) "Atlas" is the North African mountain range and so he is himself the column that supports the sky.

---

219 Cf. Wacholder, "Pseudo-Eupolemus' Two Greek Fragments", p. 96 for references.
220 M.L. West, Hesiod, Theogony, Oxford 1966, p. 311.

This double function of Atlas as astrologer and cosmic guardian
has a parallel in the Enochic writings. In the Astronomical Book
Uriel is described in the same way. He is both the specialist in
astronomy and the cosmic guardian.[221] As one of the Titans Atlas
is in Hesiod's Theogony placed in Tartarus, the underworld.[222] In
the Book of Watchers, En 20,1, Uriel is according to the Greek
text described as the angel in charge of cosmos and Tartarus.[223]
There are also other contacts between this passage in Pseudo-
Eupolemus and the Astronomical Book. In both Enoch is connected with astronomy/astrology. In both Methuselah is described as
a link in the chain of transmission of astronomical knowledge. In
both the angels — in the Astronomical Book only one, Uriel — are
described as teachers of astronomy.[224]
But there is one striking difference. In the Astronomical Book the
angel Uriel is the first link who instructs Enoch as the second.
Enoch subsequently instructs Methuselah. In Pseudo-Eupolemus
Enoch is the first link, the discoverer of astrology. The angels do
not instruct Enoch, but Methuselah. One could of course consider
that the text is out of order, that the subordinate clause "who
learned everything through the angels of God" originally referred
to Enoch and not to Methuselah. But here is nothing in the passage
that indicated a change of syntax. We are then left with the
possibility that is was Pseudo-Eupolemus who changed the well-
established tradition that the knowledge of astrology was transmitted from the angel(s) to Enoch and then to Methuselah. The
reason for this change must be the identification of Enoch as the
Greek Atlas. As we have seen the divine figure Atlas had many
features in common with Uriel in the Astronomical Book. The
identification of Enoch and Atlas demands that Enoch take Uriel's
place in the chain of transmission. Like Atlas Enoch is the first
knower of astrology. The instruction of the angel(s) is then moved
to the second link in the chain of transmission, Methuselah. The
identification of Enoch as the same figure as Greek Atlas and
consequently in the same position as Uriel corresponds to Pseudo-
Eupolemus' treatment of other Biblical patriarch. As we already

---

221 Cf. above, p. 62.
222 Cf. Hesiod. Theogony, 746. Text in H.G. Evelyn White, Hesiod, pp. 132f.
223 Cf. above, p. 62.
224 Cf. above, pp. 62f.

have noted, Noah is equated with the semidivine Belus, and Abraham traced his ancestry back to the semi-divine giants.

There should be no doubt that Pseudo-Eupolemus knew one of the main currents of traditions connected with Enoch in Judaism, namely Enoch as astronomer. This is the case whether he is directly dependent on the astronomical material of the Astronomical Book, which we regard as probable, or he draws on the same traditions as the Astronomical Book. But Pseudo-Eupolemus seems also familiar with traditions closely related to the other main current of Enochic traditions, the Watcher story. Nothing indicates, however, that Pseudo-Eupolemus has read the book of Watchers or that he knew any of the Noahitic texts as we know them. But he seems to have known the same version of the Flood story which underlies the Book of Watchers and the Noahitic traditions.[225]
We find three points of contact: 1) Both places the flood or the primeval catastrophe affects giants and not the human race as in the Genesis story. 2) Both places the hero of the flood surpasses ordinary human conditions. This is explicitly the case in Pseudo-Eupolemus where Noah is equated with the divine or semi-divine Belus. And I think that we here have found the core of the Noahitic birth stories. The stories, first carefully telling all the good reasons for believing that Noah was divine and then refuting this possibility, seem to have been composed against a background where the hero of the flood was regarded as divine.[226] Pseudo-Eupolemus proves that such a tradition was known in Palestine in the third century B.C. 3) In the Noahitic traditions Noah and Enoch appear in the same roles. Such a confusion of the two figures also seems presupposed in the double computation by Pseudo-Eupolemus, first from Noah and the flood — ten generations, then from Enoch and the flood — thirteen generations.
We think that in this respect Pseudo-Eupolemus is of great

---

225 Cf. above, p. 91.
226 Wacholder, op.cit., pp. 89ff, claims that Pseudo-Eupolemus was the first who contaminated the Genesis account about the tower of Babel and the rebellion of the Titans in Hesiod's Theogony. We cannot see that this is a necessary conclusion. If Pseudo-Eupolemus knew a flood story about rebelling giants, it could be quite natural to transfer this motif to Gen 11 on the basis of Gen, 6,1-4 and 10,8.10. Hengel, op.cit., pp. 163f, shares Wacholder's opinion, while Walter, op.cit., p. 289 is critical. A contamination of Hesiod's Theogony and the "tower of Babel" is, however, quite clear in Or Sib III, 97-158.

importance for understanding the background of En 6-16 and the Noahitic traditions. He gives a version of the Flood story sharing many of the same motifs, but independent, it seems, of Enochic writings and traditions, one stemming from another milieu than the scribes of the Enochic writings.

2. The Wisdom of Jesus Ben Sirach

2.1 Date and Versions

In the case of the Wisdom of Ben Sira (Hebrew form of the name) we are in the fortunate position of knowing both the original Hebrew author and the translator of the book into Greek. In the prologue of the book and in the epilogue following the main part (Sir 50,27-29) the translator explains how it was composed by his grandfather and later brought to Egypt by himself. The author was Ben Sira, who lived in Jerusalem (Sir 50,27). According to the prologue the grandson went to Egypt in the 38th year of Ptolemäus Physeon VII. Euergetes II., or 132 B.C. The time of his grandfather must be about sixty years earlier, in the first quarter of the second century. The date is generally set at about 190 B.C.[227] Ben Sira was a scribe whose profession included the study of "the law of the Most High ... the wisdom of all the ancients ... and prophecies" (39,1).

The whole book is extant in Greek. The Hebrew version was known in Europe up to the Middle Ages, when it was lost. In 1896 fragments from five manuscripts were found in a synagogue in Cairo (Cairo Geniza).[228] They date from the eleventh or twelfth century A.D. Fragments of the Hebrew text were also found at Qumran and Masada.[229] The Masada scroll was written in the first third of the first century B.C.

---

227 For the introductory questions, cf. O. Eissfeldt, Einleitung in das Alte Testament, pp. 807ff; L. Rost, Einleitung in die alttestamentlichen Apokryphen und Pseudepigraphen, pp. 47ff; G.W.E. Nickelsburg, Jewish Literature between the Bible and the Mishnah, pp. 55f.

228 For the authenticity of the Cairo Geniza manuscripts, cf. H.P. Rüger, Text und Textform im hebräischen Sirach, BZAW 112, Tübingen 1970, pp. 112-5.

229 Y. Yadin, Masada. Herod's Fortress and the Zealots last Stand, London 1966, Abacus ed. 1978, pp. 175ff.

The references to Enoch are found in the last section of the book, ch. 44-50. This section lists famous men from Israel's past. According to the Greek text the list begins with Enoch (44,16) and records the great heroes in succeeding order up to Nehemia (49,13). It then turns to the patriarchal and primeval period again and records Enoch (49,14), Joseph, Shem, Seth, Adam (49,14-16). The first part of this section where the first Enoch sequence occurs is in Hebrew covered both by a Cairo Geniza manuscript, Ms. B, and by the Masada scroll. The second Enoch sequence is only covered by the Cairo Geniza manuscript.

The understanding of the Enoch figure in Ben Sira is linked up with textual problems. A correct interpretation is possible only through an evaluation of the versions and the history of the text.

2.2 Versions and History of the Text[230]

Below we give a synopsis of the text versions of the figures of Enoch and Noah in Genesis and Ben Sira:

Genesis

T.M. 5,24 Enoch:

ויתהלך חנוך את האלהים ואיננו כי לקח אתו אלהים

6,9 Noah:

נח איש צדיק תמים היה בדרתיו את האלהים התהלך נח

LXX 5,24 Enoch:

καὶ εὐηρέστησεν Ἐνὼχ τῷ θεῷ καὶ οὐχ ηὑρίσκετο, ὅτι μετέθηκεν αὐτὸν ὁ θεός.

6,9 Noah:

Νῶε ἄνθρωπος δίκαιος, τέλειος ὢν ἐν τῇ γενεᾷ αὐτοῦ τῷ θεῷ εὐηρέστησεν Νῶε.

230 Text editions. Greek: H.B. Swete (ed.), The Old Testament in Greek according to the Septuagint, 3rd ed., Cambridge 1905; A. Rahlfs, Septuaginta, 9th ed., Stuttgart 1935; J.W. Wevers (ed.), Genesis, SeptVTG I, Göttingen 1974; J. Ziegler (ed.), Sapientia Jesu Filii Sirach, SeptVTG XII/2, Göttingen 1965. Hebrew to ben Sira: R. Smend (ed.), Die Weisheit des Jesu Sirach. Hebräisch und Deutsch, Berlin 1906; M.S. Segal, Säfär ben Sira haššalem, Jerusalem 1959; Y. Yadin, The Ben Sira Scroll from Masada, Jerusalem 1965.

Ben Sira

Masada scroll
44,16 Enoch:
44,17 Noah (VII,24):

נוח צדיק נמצא תמים   ב)

Cairo Geniza, Ms. B.
44.16 Enoch:

חנוך (נמצ)א תמים   והתהלך עם ייי ונלקח
אות דעת לדור ודור

44.17 Noah:

(נ)ח צדיק נמצא תמים   לעת כלה היה תחליף

49.14 Enoch:

מעט נוצר על הארץ כחנוך   וגם הוא נלקח פנים

LXX

44,16 Enoch:

Ενωχ εὐηρέστησεν κυρίῳ καὶ μετεέθη, ὑπόδειγμα
μετανοίας ταῖς γενεαῖς.

44,17 Noah:

Νωε εὑρέθη τέλειος δίκαιος, ἐν καιρῷ ὀργῆς ἐγένετο
ἀντάλλαγμα.

49,14 Enoch:

Οὐδεὶς ἐκτίσθη ἐπί τῆς γῆς τοιοῦτος οἷος Ενωχ καὶ
γάρ αὐτὸς ἀνελήμφθη ἀπὸ τῆς γῆς.

Comparison of the Enoch passages:

Sir 44,16-17:   After v. 15 in the Greek text only the words נמצא
תמים ב,"was found blameless in . . .", are preserved on the Masada
scroll. They are written on the top of the large fragment. Yadin
joined a small fragment with the words נוח צדיק, "Noah the
righteous", at this place.[231] If this placement is correct, the
passage about Enoch in V. 16 was missing in the Masada scroll.
This passage is also missing in the Syriac translation,[232] which
reflects a Hebrew original.[233]

231   Yadin, The Ben Sira Scroll, p. 38.
232   Cf. F.V. Reiterer, "Urtext" und Übersetzungen. Sprachstudie über Sir
44,16-45,26 als Beitrag zur Siraforschung, MU, München 1980, p. 83.
233   Cf. Reiterer, op.cit., p. 238f.

In Cairo Geniza the passage contains three lines: "Enoch was found blameless, and he walked with the Lord and was taken away, a sign of knowledge for generation and generation.". The first line is missing in the Greek translation which reads: "Enoch was pleasing to God and was translated, an example of repentance to the generations." There are two differences between these versions. 1) In the first line Cairo Geniza follows TM to Gen 5,24, "walked with God", the Greek translation follows LXX to Gen 5,24, "was pleasing to God". 2) Cairo Geniza reads in the last line "a sign of knowledge", while the Greek translation has "an example of repentance". This last line has no support in the Genesis text.

Sir 49,14: The Masada scroll of this section is not preserved. Cairo Geniza and the Greek translation have broadly the same text: "Few (or nobody) like Enoch have been created on earth. He was also taken up from the earth." The last line causes some difficulties. Cairo Geniza reads פנים, *panīm*. We emend as G.H. Box/W.O.E.Oesterly מעל פניה, "from the face thereof", which corresponds to the Greek translation.[234]

History of the text:
We shall concentrate on Sir 44,16, which contains explicit information about Enoch which goes beyond Gen 5,24. Here we find also the most striking differences between the versions. As far as I can see there are five possible explanations for these differences.
1. The Masada scroll of this sequence is too fragmentary to be reliable. The original Hebrew version contained the passage in Sir 44,16.[235]
2. The words נוח צדיק from the small fragment which Yadin joined to the large are misplaced. They belong to a separate line.

---

234 G.H. Box and W.O.E. Oesterly, "Sirach", Apocrypha und Pseudepigrapha of the Old Testament, Vol I, Apocrypha, ed. R.H. Charles, Oxford 1913, p. 506. Another possibility is to take panīm as a reference to God: Enoch was taken away to the "divine presence".
235 So for instance A. Schmitt, Entrückung - Aufnahme - Himmelfahrt, p. 178; J. Marböck, "Henoch - Adam - der Thronwagen. Zu frühjüdischen pseudepigraphischen Traditionen bei ben Sira", BZ 25, 1981, pp. 103-11, pp. 103f

The two words on the large fragment נמצא תמים can introduce
44,16 and not 44,17, cf. Cairo Geniza.[236]

3. Some parts of 44,16 were placed in the Enoch sequence in ch.
49 in the original Hebrew version.[237]

4. The copyist of the Masada scroll and the translator of the
Syriac version have omitted 44,16 for theological reasons.[238]

5. There have been two Hebrew versions of the text. The elder of
them did not contain the sequence in 44,16. It was added in a later
Hebrew manuscript which formed the background of the Greek
translation, but not of the Syriac.

Evaluation of these explanations:

No. 1: It is correct that the Masada scroll is fragmentary at this
point, but the fact remains that words of the sequence are
preserved on two fragments which have to be placed in accordance
with the other textual witnesses.

No. 2: There is a possibility that נמצא תמים belonged to 44,16, but
it requires a rather complicated explanation. The basis for this
assumption is that these words are written in Cairo Geniza for
44,16. The problem is that the words are generally regarded as
dittography in Cairo Geniza, because LXX presupposes a text
starting with the second line in 44,16. Lührman (note 236) suggests
that the dittography was already present in the Masada scroll and
that LXX presupposes the original Hebrew version. Yet two
problems remain. The one is that the large fragment has a ב
introducing a new word after נמצא תמים. The word can very well
have been בעת, corresponding to Cairo Geniza 44,17 לעת, cf. also
the Greek ἐν καιρῷ, and the Syriac בדמנא, "in the time".[239] The
Enoch passage in 44,16 gives according to Cairo Geniza no
possibility of a ב introducing a second line. The other problem is
that this solution fails to explain why 44,16 is missing in the Syriac
version.

No. 3: Yadin's reconstruction (note 237) of an original wording of
the Enoch sequence in ch. 49 is interesting. The problem is that

236   So for instance D. Lührmann, "Henoch und die Metanoia", ZNW 66, 1975,
pp. 103-16, pp. 107ff.
237   So Yadin, op.cit., p. 38, who restores the Enoch sequence in ch. 49 as
49,14a-44,16b-44, 16a-49,14b.
238   Suggested by Milik, The Books of Enoch, p. 10f.
239   Yadin, op.cit.

there is no textual evidence for the attempt. Until this is found it can never be more than a suggestion.

No. 4: That both the copyist of the Masada scroll and the translator of the Syriac version should find 44,16 theologically problematic seems unlikely. As far as the copyist of the Masada scroll is concerned there is no evidence from the first century B.C. that Enoch was a controversial figure.

No. 5: As far as I can see this is the most likely solution. To judge from the Masada fragments this scroll did not contain Sir 44,16. The same version of the text must be reflected in the Syriac translation. LXX presupposes a Hebrew text similar to that of Cairo Geniza. There is no plausible reason why Enoch should have been omitted in the one Hebrew version, but that 44,16 should have been added can be explained. Someone wanted to include the Enoch figure known from the Enochic writings in the original list of Biblical heroes. If this is the case, the inclusion of 44,16 cannot have happened long after the composing of the original manuscript, since the passage existed in the Hebrew version known by Ben Sira's grandson.

2.3 The Portrayals of Enoch in the Hebrew and the Greek Text Versions

The only passage about Enoch which explicitly goes beyond Gen 5,24 is the third line in Cairo Geniza to Sir 44,16 אות דעת לדור ודור with the Greek translation ὑπόδειγμα μετανοίας ταῖς γενεαῖς. The Hebrew and the Greek passages differ considerably in meaning.

In the Hebrew version Enoch is called 'ōt da'at, "a sign of knowledge" for all generations. The closest parallel to this phrase is to be found in Jub 4,24b: "For there (in the Garden of Eden) he was given as a sign and that he should testify against all the children of men, that he should recount all the deeds of the generations until the day of condemnation." Here the Ethiopic tĕ'mĕrt, "sign", must go back to an original Hebrew אות, 'ōt. Sir 44,16 and Jub 4,24b correspond in three ways: 1) In both Enoch is called a "sign". 2) In Sir Enoch is called a sign after his translation, cf. נלקח, nilqāḥ, "taken away", at the end of the second line. The

same is the case in Jubilees. Enoch becomes a sign after his
removal to Paradise, cf. Jub 4,23. 3) In both the figure of Enoch
has significance for future generations.

The author of Jubilees does not say, however, what the sign refers
to. The copula between this clause and the following indicates that
the following two clauses hardly can be interpreted as an explication of the first.[240] The two following lines refer to an Enochic
writing of historiographical character, as does Jub 4,19.[241] There
is a possibility that the first line refers to astronomical writings, as
do Jub 4,17-18. If so, the order would be the same in Jub 4,17-19
and in 4,24b: Astronomical-historiographical. There could also be
a correspondence between the use of words: "he wrote down the
signs of heaven", 4,17; "he was given as a sign", 4,24b.

Be that as it may, the *da'at,* "knowledge" in Sir 44,16 hardly
refers to historiographical traditions. The closest parallel in the
Enochic writings seems to be in the Astronomical Book, in Enoch's
concluding speech to Methuselah: "I have given wisdom to you
and your children, and to those who will be your children, that
they may give their children for all generations for ever — this
wisdom (which is) beyond their thoughts", En 82,2. The passage
concerns "wisdom", Ehtiopic *ṭĕbab,* Aramaic חכמה, *ḥåkmā,* and
not *"knowledge",* Aramaic מנדע, *manda',* or מדע, *madda',* but
"wisdom" and "knowledge" were closely related in this kind of
literature.[242] The knowledge referred to in Sir 44,16 is accordingly the astronomy of the Astronomical Book. There are no
similar passages in the Book of Watchers, which certainly antedates
this Hebrew version of Ben Sira, or in the Book of Dreams and the
Apocalypse of Weeks which may antedate it.[243] This understanding also corresponds very well to the description of Enoch in
Pseudo-Eupolemus as a primeval sage and the discoverer of
astrology.[244]

---

240 The copula is, however, omitted in one of the Ethiopic manuscripts,
designated "A" by Charles. Cf. the Ethiopic text edition, R.H. Charles, The
Ethiopic Version of the Hebrew Book of Jubilees, Oxford 1895, text and
apparatus, p. 17, introduction, pp. xii–xiii.
241 Cf. below to the Book of Jubilees, p. 129.
242 Cf. 4Q En[g] liv, line 13 = En 93,10 (Milik, p. 265); and 4Q TLev ar[a], col 1,
line 14 (Fitzmyer and Harrington, p. 88), where the words are used as parallels.
243 For the dating, cf. above, pp. 110f.
244 Cf. above, pp. 115ff.

Thus, this version of Ben Sira combines the two earliest features associated with Enoch: The removal, known primarily from Gen 5,24 but also attested to in the Noahitic traditions and En 12-16; and Enoch as astronomer, known primarily from the Astronomical Book but also attested to in Pseudo-Eupolemus.

It is difficult to determine whether the grandson of Ben Sira knew the early Enochic traditions. His translation "example of repentance" shows clearly that he did not have the astronomical traditions in mind. He may have been inspired by Enoch's reproval of the watchers in En 12-16 or Enoch's speech of penitence in En 1-5. But his translation can also have been based on more general considerations.

In the line before the grandson follows the LXX version of Gen 5,24 that he knew, according to his own information in the prologue. This is not surprising, since the Septuagint originated in Egypt where the grandson lived when he translated the work.[245] The Septuagint reads "Enoch was pleasing to God" instead of TM "Enoch walked with God", clearly emphasizing the moral aspect: Enoch was a pious man. This interpretation of the Hebrew text may have caused the next line in the grandson's version of Sir 44,16: "Enoch was an example of repentance." As a pious man Enoch, like Noah, cf. the Greek versions of Gen 6,9 and Sir 44,17, distinguished himself from his contemporaries. Unlike the other people in the antediluvian generations he had repented for his sins. This interpretation is also attested to in later exegesis in the Jewish Alexandrian milieu in Egypt. In the Wisdom of Solomon Enoch's repentance is the main issue, cf. 4,10-15.[246] The same is the case in Philo from Alexandria's allegorical exegesis of Genesis: "The second place after hope is given to repentance for sins and to improvement, and, therefore, Moses mentions next in order him who changed from the worse life to the better, called by the Hebrews Enoch ... We are told of him that he proved "to be pleasing to God and was not found because God transferred him",

245 For the origin of the Septuagint, cf. E. Würtwein, Der Text des Alten Testaments, 3rd rev. ed. Stuttgart 1966, pp. 50-77.
246 For the date and setting of the Wisdom of Solomon, cf. Rost, op.cit., p. 43; Nickelsburg, op.cit., p. 184f. For the treatment of Enoch, cf. Lührmann, op.cit., pp. 110f; Schmitt, op.cit., pp. 181-92.

for transference implies turning and changing, and the change is to the better because it is brought about by the forethought of God" (On Abraham, 17-18).[247] The description of Enoch in the Letter to Hebrews 11,5-6 must be understood in the same line of influence from the Septuagint version of Gen 5,24, although the Christian writer here emphasized faith as the essential part of Enoch's piety.

3.   The Book of Jubilees

3.1   Date and Versions

The Book of Jubilees has usually been dated at the end of the second century.[248] More recently, however, earlier dates, just before the Maccabean revolt, or about 144-140 B.C., have been argued.[249] The Book is an elaboration of the text in Gen 1 to Ex 12, presented as a revelation to Moses on Mount Sinai. The specific feature of the exposition of the Genesis and Exodus texts is that the history of Israel is arranged according to a calendar based on a solar year of 364 days. The same calendar was argued in the Astronomical Book and Qumran writings.[250] The years are arranged in jubilees, and the history from creation to the entry of the Israelites into the promised land is placed in a framework of 50 jubilees, cf. Jub 50,4.[251] The same sort of chronographical speculations based on a jubilee are found in Old Testament historiographical literature and apocalyptic writings.[252]

---

247   Text in: F.H. Colson, Philo, Vol VI, LCL, London-Cambridge, Mass. 1935, p. 13. Philo deals with Enoch in the same way several places, cf. especially: "On Rewards and Punishments", 15-17; text in: F.H. Colson, Philo, Vol VIII, 1939, pp. 322f; and "Questions and Answers on Genesis I", 82-6; text in: R. Marcus, Philo, Supplement I, 1953, pp. 50-5. Cf. also als a whole the presentation of the material by R.A. Kraft, "Philo (Josephus, Sirach and Wisdom of Solomon) on Enoch", P.J. Achtemeyer (ed.), SBL 1978 Seminar Papers Vol I, pp. 253-7.
248   Cf. R.H. Charles, The Book of Jubilees, London 1902, pp. lviii-lxvi; L. Rost, Einleitung, p. 100.
249   Cf. G.W.E. Nickelsburg, Jewish Literature, pp. 78f; and K. Berger, Das Buch Der Jubiläen, JSHRZ II/3, Gütersloh 1981, pp. 298ff.
250   Cf. above, pp. 69f and 76.
251   Cf. R.T. Beckwith, "The Significance of the Calendar", p. 185.
252   Cf. above, pp. 71f and pp. 107f.

The book was written in Hebrew, but the Hebrew version is lost. The whole book is extant only in an Ethiopic translation of a lost Greek version. Parts of the book are also extant in Latin. During the excavations at Qumran fragments of the book in Hebrew were discovered.[253] The text of the Hebrew fragments is close to the Latin and Ethiopic versions.[254] Unfortunately, the Hebrew original of the Enoch sequence in Jub 4 was not among the preserved fragments.[255]

There is a close relationship between the Book of Jubilees and Qumran Essene literature, in calendarian and historiographical speculations as well as in religious attitudes. Several scholars therefore believe the author belonged to the Qumran community or at least was under its influence.[256] Others argue for a Pharisaic origin of the book.[257] If it is to be dated as early as the first half of the second century, the author most likely belonged to the pre-Essene movement.[258]

3.2   The Structure of the Enoch Sequence

Enoch is first referred to in Jub 4,9 in connection with Gen 4,17. The author obviously did not have any specific interest in this text. He only retells that Cain built a city and named it after Enoch. This is significantly different, though, when the author comes to the text of Gen 5,21-24 which he elaborates in Jub 4,17-26. The structure of this Enoch sequence in Jubilees is caused by the structure of the Genesis, as shown below.

---

253   Cf. the list of fragments in Berger, op.cit., p. 286.
254   Cf. J.T. Milik, Ten Years of Discovery in the Wilderness of Judea, p. 32.
255   The fragment 4Q 227, published by Milik, The Books of Enoch, p. 12, has a closely related text. For the Ethiopic version we use the edition by R.H. Charles, The Ethiopic Version of the Hebrew Book of Jubilees, Oxford 1895. In quotations we use, Charles, The Book of Jubilees, unless otherwise stated.
256   So Rost, op.cit., p. 100; Eissfeldt, Einleitung in das Alte Testament, p. 823.
257   So Charles, op.cit., p. lxxiii; W.S. McCullough, The History and Literature of the Palestinian Jews, p. 190.
258   So Nickelsburg, op.cit. Cf. also above, pp. 82f.

Gen 5,21-24   Jub 4,17-26

vv. 17-19:
And he was the first among men that are born on
earth who learnt writing and knowledge and wisdom
and who wrote down the signs of heaven according
to the order of their months in a book, that men
might know the seasons of the years according to
their separate months. And he was the first to write
a testimony, and he testified to the sons of men
among the generations on earth, and recounted the
week[259] of the jubilees, and made known to them
the days of the years, and set in order the months
and recounted the Sabbaths of the years as we made
(them) known to him. And what was and what will
be he saw in a vision of his sleep, as it will happen
to the children of men throughout their generations
until the day of judgment; he saw and understood
everything and wrote his testimony, and placed the
testimony on earth for all the children of men and
for their generations.

v. 20:

And it happened when   An in the twelfth jubilee, in the seventh week
Enoch was 65 years, he   thereof, he took to himself a wife, and her name
begat Methuselah.   was Ednî, the daughter of Dânêl, the daughter of
                         his father's brother, and in the sixth year in this
                         week she bore him a son and he called his name
                         Methuselah.

v. 21:

Enoch walked with God   And he was moreover[260] with the angels of God
for three hundred years these six jubilees of years, and they showed him
after he had begotten   everything which is on earth and in the heavens, the
Methuselah, and he begat rule of the sun and he wrote down everything. And
sons and daughters. All he testified to the watchers, who had sinned with
the days of Enoch were   the daughters of men; for these had begun to unite
365 years.   themselves, so as to be defiled, with the daughters
                         of men, and Enoch testified against them all.

vv. 23-26:

Enoch walked with God   And he was taken from amongst the children of
and he was no more,   men, and we conducted him into the Garden of
because God took him   Eden in majesty and honour, and behold there he
away.   writes down the condemnation and judgment of the
                         world, and all the wickedness of men. And on

---

259   Milik, The Books of Enoch, p. 61, has noted correctly that Charles translates plural "weeks" here, while he in his Ethiopic text edition prefers the
singular form of the word. Most of the Ethiopic manuscripts have the singular
subā'ēhomu, while the manuscripts C and D have the plural subā'ēyātihomu.
260   The Ethiopic conjunction 'ēnka, translated by Charles as "moreover",
introduces a statement whose content follows immediately after the foregoing, cf.
A. Dillmann, Grammatik der äthiopischen Sprache, Leipzig 1899 (repr. Graz
1959), § 169,2, p. 366. This observation is significant because v. 21 introduces a
new sequence of Enoch's life, not a continuation of a foregoing one.

account of it (God) brought[261] the waters of the
flood upon all the land of Eden; for there he was set
as a sign and that he should testify against all the
children of men, that he should recount all the
deeds of the generations until the day of condemnation. And there he burnt the incense of the sanctuary, (even) sweet spices, acceptable before the
Lord of the Mount. For the Lord has four places on
the earth, the Garden of Eden, and the Mount of
the east, and the mountain on which thou art this
day, Mount Sinai, and Mount Zion (which) will be
sanctified in the new creation for a sanctification of
the earth; through it will the earth be sanctified
from all (its) guilt and its uncleanness throughout
the generations of the world.

One question which arises out of the synopsis is to what extent the
Enoch sequence in Jubilees is meant as a biographical description.
This concerns above all the passages in vv. 17-19 which also can
be interpreted as a summary of Enoch's whole activity. A closer
examination, however, shows that this is not the case. In v. 19 the
author refers to Enoch's visionary ability, clearly drawing on the
Book of Dreams. According to this book Enoch had his two visions
before he married his wife Edna (En 83,2; 85,3).[262] Exactly the
same is told in Jubilees, where in v. 19 Enoch has his vision and in
v. 20 marries Edna and begets Methuselah. When the description of
Enoch in v. 19 is meant biographically, there is no need to doubt
that this also is the case in vv. 17-18. Hence, we can regard the
Enoch sequence in Jubilees as a short biography structured
according to Gen 5,21-24 and incorporating Jewish Enoch traditions.

261   J.C. VanderKam, "Enoch Traditions in Jubilees and other Second-century
Sources", P.J. Achtemeier (ed.), SBL 1978 Seminar Papers, Vol I, pp. 229-51, p.
236, suggests another interpretation of the passage. He thinks that Ethiopic
'amsë'a, "he brought" is a corrupt reading for 'imas'a, "did not come". The
meaning of the passage would then be that the waters of the flood did not come
over the Land of Eden. VanderKam claims to have support for this emendation
in the oldest extant manuscript of Jubilees, EMML 3. Unfortunately, he does not
give the text of this manuscript. The variant reading is not listed by Charles in
his apparatus. The reason why VanderKam prefers this reading is that if the
flood came over the Land of Eden, Enoch would have drowned. But this is not
the case. According to v. 23 Enoch is situated: wĕsta ganata 'edom, "in the
Garden of Eden", while the flood in v. 24 came over: kᵘĕllu mĕdra 'edom, "all
the Land of Eden". The Garden of Eden is obviously thought as the one place
left when the flood struck "all the Land of Eden". A similar distinction between
the Garden of Eden and the Land of Eden is made in Jub 8,18-21.
262   Cf. above, p. 109.

According to this biography, Enoch started his career as a sage and
was taught writing, knowledge and wisdom. He wrote an astronomical work, v. 17. He also taught men the correct cultic calendar, v. 18. Thus Enoch is portrayed as the primary human sage, the
one who brought the human race the basic cultural Benefits.

The next stage in Enoch's life is his activity as a visionary. The
whole history from primeval time to the day of judgment was
revealed to him. This vision he wrote down for future generations,
v. 19.

Neither of these features is explicitly extant in Gen 5,21-24. The
author of Jubilees accordingly places them in the first 65 years of
Enoch's life that are not commented on in the Genesis account.

The parallels between Genesis and Jubilees begin with the birth of
Methuselah, Jub, v. 20. After this event Genesis tells that Enoch
walked with God for three hundred years and begot sons and
daughters. The latter statement is neglected in Jubilees, but the
former is taken literally. Genesis tells that Enoch walked with the
'älohīm. Jubilees clearly interprets 'älohīm as divine beings, angels.
Enoch was with the angels for six jubilees of years. One jubilee is
here taken as 50 years, 50 · 6 = 300. The angels taught Enoch
cosmic geography, and he wrote a book about it, v. 21. During
these years comes also the fall of the angels, and Enoch testifies
against them, v. 22.

The Genesis account ends the report of Enoch by telling about his
removal from earth. The corresponding sequence in Jubilees also
starts by telling about Enoch's removal, v. 23. But while Genesis
says nothing about Enoch's destination, Jubilees states that Enoch
was conducted into the Garden of Eden. A similar combination of
verbs occurs in Gen 2,15, where Adam is "taken away" and
"placed" into the Garden of Eden.[263] Enoch's removal to Paradise
is linked up with a flood that was brought upon "the Land of
Eden", v. 24. In Eden Enoch wrote a new book about "the
condemnation and the judgment of the world", v. 23, and he
brought God a sacrifice on a holy mountain, vv. 25-26.

There are two significant features in Jubilees' elaboration. The one
is that "walked with the 'älohīm" in Gen 5,22.24 is taken literally
as "was with the angels". The other is that Enoch's removal is

263   Cf. above, pp. 49ff.

linked up with his stay in Paradise and a version of the Flood story. In both places Jubilees corresponds to Jewish Enoch traditions.

3.3 The Background of the Enoch Sequence in Enochic Writings and Traditions

v. 17a: There is no direct parallel to this clause in Enochic writings or traditions, but the elements are known. In the Book of Dreams, En 83,2, Enoch says that he had the first vision by the time he learnt the art of writing. In one of the Hebrew versions of Sir 44,16 Enoch is called "a sign of knowledge", and in the Astronomical Book, En 82,2, Enoch instructs Methuselah in his "wisdom".[264] But it is not explicitly said that Enoch was "the first". This feature corresponds, however, to Pseudo-Eupolemus, who wrote that Enoch was the first to discover astrology. Most likely Pseudo-Eupolemus and the author of Jubilees relied on the same kind of tradition which made Enoch the first sage.[265]

v. 17b: This passage quite clearly refers to the Astronomical Book, En 72-82.

v. 18a: It is not clear to what the two first passages refer. Milik found the Astronomical Book also intended here, especially the speeches in En 80-82.[266] J.C. VanderKam regarded the passages as a reference to the Epistle of Enoch, more specifically to the introduction to the Apocalypse of Weeks, En 93,1-2, cf. 4Q En^g liii, lines 18-22 (Milik, pp. 263f),[267] but we cannot see any specific similarities. Both v. 17 and v. 18b quite clearly refer to astronomical and calendarian documents, and it is not likely that v. 18a should break the pattern.

v. 18b: In none of the Enochic books is Enoch connected to a week of jubilees. Milik, however, has called attention to calendarian fragments from Qumran containing a cycle of seven jubilees.[268]

v. 19: Primarily this is a reference to the Apocalypse of Animals in the Book of Dreams, En 85-90. VanderKam saw again a reference to the Epistle of Enoch, especially the Apocalypse of Weeks, En 93,1-10; 91,11-17.[269] But the character of the vision as a "vision of his sleep" seems clearly to refer to En 85,3. The author of Jubilees, however, combines the Apocalypse of Animals and En 81, cf. v. 19b and En 81,2.6, a combination which is correct with regard to the content of En 81.[270]

v. 20: The name of Enoch's wife, Edni, also occurs in the Book of Dreams, En 85,3, although there in another spelling. The name of her father, Danel, does not occur in any known Enochic documents.

264 Cf. above, pp. 124f.
265 For Pseudo-Eupolemus, cf. pp. 116f.
266 Milik, op.cit., p. 11.
267 VanderKam, op.cit., p. 234.
268 4Q 260B. Cf. Milik, op.cit., pp. 61-8.
269 VanderKam, op.cit.
270 Cf. above, pp. 78f.

vv. 21-22: Enoch's stay with the angels quite clearly refers to the cosmological part of the Book of Watchers, En 17-19; 20-36. That he testified to the watchers refers to the central Enoch section of the same book, En 12-16. This part of Enoch's activity is also dealt with in a Hebrew fragment from Qumran, 4Q 227.[271]

vv. 23-26: This section has caused confusion in the research. Grelot thinks that v. 23 draws on the cosmological part of the Book of Watchers, in which Enoch twice visits Paradise, En 32,3-6, cf. 24,3-25,7.[272] But this is wrong. Enoch's journeys are referred to in v. 21, and they took place during his 300 years. V. 23 refers to another event. VanderKam correctly sees a connection with En 106-107 and the Genesis Apocryphon where Enoch is located in Paradise, but he has difficulties in placing the sequence within the Enoch traditions.[273] Most of the problems are solved, however, when one sees that v. 23 is a parallel to Gen 5,24. Vv. 23-24 presuppose a version of Enoch's removal similar to the Noahitic traditions and parallel to En 6-16.[274] In the Noahitic traditions the hero of the flood was portrayed as a sage and visionary who escaped the flood and was situated in Paradise. In the role of this hero could partly Noah and partly Enoch appear.

In v. 23 it is said that in Paradise Enoch wrote down "the condemnation and judgment of the world, and all the wickedness of the children of men". If we compare this with the Book of Watchers I think that also this writing of Enoch can be identified. En 6-11 recounts a version of the Flood story mixed up with the fall of the angels from Gen 6,1-4. According to En 12,1-3 Enoch was removed to heaven before the catastrophe happened. His location "in heaven" is here parallel to "Paradise" in the Noahitic traditions. In En 12-16 the acts of Enoch are directed toward the watchers with the Watcher story, En 6-11, as background. En 1-5 can easily be read in the same way as En 12-16, that Enoch here talks on the background of the catastrophe described in En 6-11. The difference between the two sections is that En 12-16 has the crimes of the watchers as the primary subject, which Jubilees dealt with in v. 22. En 1-5 has the crimes of men as its subject. When we read En 1-5 in this way, the speech in En 1-5 comes after Enoch's removal from earth, just as Enoch's activity in En 12-16. Jubilees has understood Enoch's removal as a translation to Paradise. Accordingly, En 1-5 must also be placed in this context. Regarding the content, Enoch's speech of penitence in En 1-5 suits the description in v. 23.

The author of Jubilees certainly knew the three oldest Enochic books: The Astronomical Book, the Book of Watchers and the Book of Dreams. The Astronomical Book and the Book of Dreams he treats as unities. The Book of Watchers he splits up according to the different kind of material it contains. The author also made use of other Enochic calendarian speculations known to us from fragments from Qumran. Finally, he used traditions similar to the Noahitic traditions in which the hero of the flood is described as a visionary and sage and removed to Paradise.

---

271   Cf. above, note 255.
272   Cf. P. Grelot, "Hénoch et ses écritures", p. 486.
273   VanderKam, op.cit., p. 236.
274   Cf. above, pp. 92f.

3.4   The Interpretation of the Enochic Writings and Traditions in Jubilees

I.   When one knows the sources behind the Enoch sequence, one becomes aware of the accuracy in the treatment of the material. The Astronomical Book is connected with the description of Enoch as a primeval sage. In these passages there is nothing which indicates a visionary experience. Enoch was taught writing, knowledge and wisdom and on the background of this instruction he wrote the Astronomical Book. v. 17. This corresponds to our own observation in the analysis of the astronomical material, where we saw that the phraseology of transmission primarily presupposed a teaching situation not necessarily implying a visionary experience.[275] The phraseology of vision in the Astronomical Books was connected primarily with the cosmological material corresponding to the cosmological section in the Book of Watchers.[276]

The next Enochic book dealt with, the Book of Dreams, is classified as a dream vision, v. 19. This corresponds to the Gattung of the book. The content is correctly described as historiographical.[277]

The Book of Watchers is dealt with in three parts corresponding to the trifold nature of the material. The cosmological material is treated as a unity, v. 21. This insight was revealed to Enoch when he stayed with the angels. Enoch's activity in the watcher incident, En 12-16, is described as a second unity, closely connected with the cosmological section, v. 22. As a third unity, separated from the two first, Enoch's speech of penitence, En 1-5, is described. This speech is connected with Enoch's stay in Paradise, due to the author's interpretation of En 6-16.

Thus the genres of the material can be characterized in the following way, corresponding to our own analysis:

Astronomical material — instruction
Cosmological material — visionary journey
Historiographical material — visions

In addition comes Enoch's speech of penitence and his testimony against the watchers.

---

275   Cf. above, pp. 63ff.
276   Cf. above, pp. 66ff.
277   Cf. above, p. 105.

II.   We have already noticed that the sequence 4,23-26 shows clear contact with Noahitic traditions. Some of the basic observations made in this material should be repeated. In the Genesis narratives three incidents are reported: The removal of Enoch; the fall of the angels; Noah and the flood. In the Noahitic traditions and in En 6-16 these three themes are combined in an often confusing way. The result of the combination is that the flood affects the fallen angels/watchers and that Enoch becomes involved in the Watcher story.[278] In Jubilees these three themes are separated again: The removal of Enoch, 4,23-26; the Watcher story, 5,1-12; Noah and the flood, 5.19-6,10. But each theme is marked by the transformation it underwent in Jewish literature. Thus the variations of the one catastrophe from Genesis in Jewish literature are split into three primeval catastrophes in Jubilees:

1) The flood which came over the Land of Eden
2) The condemnation of the watchers and giants
3) The flood which came over the whole earth

Consequently it becomes clear that Jub 4,23-26 is one variant of the primeval catastrophe reported in Genesis and the Jewish material. Similar to Genesis is above all that the catastrophe struck men and not divine and semi-divine beings. Similar to the Jewish material are Enoch's role as the protagonist and his removal to Paradise. This variant in Jubilees has three basic elements:

1) The flood strikes the Land of Eden.   This is a geographical limitation compared to the Noah flood story in which the flood strikes the whole earth, Jub 5,20. The Land of Eden is a part of Shem's lot in Jub 8,12-21. It is not easy to locate because of the author's confusing ideas about geography.[279] It seems to be located somewhere east of Palestine since Shem's lot included the areas between Lebanon and the Red Sea in the west to India in the east, Jub 8,21. The mountain where Enoch sacrificed is also called "the Mountain of the East" (cf. below).

---

278   Cf. above, pp. 90-3.
279   Cf. the discussion in Charles, op.cit., pp. 69-74.

2) The hero is removed to the Garden of Eden. The Garden of Eden is located close to the Land of Eden, Jub 8,16, and is regarded as one of the holy places of the earth, Jub 4,26; 8,19.

3) The hero sacrifices on a mountain. The mountain is not identical to the Garden of Eden. In Jub 8,19 three holy places are mentioned: Sinai, Zion, the Garden of Eden. Jub 4,26 adds a fourth: "the Mountain of the East". This must be the mountain meant in v. 25. The motif is similar to the Noah flood story in Jub 6,1-3: The hero sacrifices on a mountain after the flood.

The analysis sheds light on the complicated material concerning the primeval catastrophe. The Jewish-Samaritan authors must have known another version of the Flood story besides the Genesis version. This version must have contained elements that could cause confusion with the story of the fall of the angels and the Enochic traditions. It has been treated in different ways in En 6-16; the Noahitic traditions; Pseudo-Eupolemus;[280] and Jubilees.

3.5   The Antediluvian Traditions

3.5.1   The Enochic Antediluvian Traditions

In the book of Jubilees we find a description of how the Enochic writings and instructions were transmitted through history until they reached the group responsible for the Enochic traditions in the author's own time. The chain starts in the Enoch sequence, Jub 4,17-26, where we have seen that Enoch is described as the composer of the Astronomical Book, the Book of Dreams, the Book of Watchers and other writings containing calendarian calculations.

The next link of the chain is in Jub 7,38-39 where the Noahitic commandments are described. Noah insists that these go back to Enoch, designated as the seventh in his generation, through oral instruction: Enoch — Methuselah — Lamech — Noah. The background of this concept of transmission can be found in En 81,

---

280   Cf. above, pp. 117f.

where it is described how Enoch visits heaven and reads the heavenly tablets, 81,1. The tablets contain predictions, 81,2, but they are also connected to teaching about human conduct, 81,7-9. Enoch is commanded to leave heaven and go back to the earth to instruct Methuselah and all his other children, 81,5-6.10. In the final edition of the Astronomical Book En 81 was inserted before En 82 so that En 82 was to be read in the light of En 81.[281] En 82 tells that the wisdom Enoch has revealed to Methuselah is to be transmitted to future generations, 82,1-2.

Noah not only transmits the Enochic traditions but also forms new ones. In Jub 10,13-14 it is told that Noah wrote a book containing instructions about medicine and handed it over to Shem.

In Jub 12,25-27 it is told how Abraham through divine instruction is taught Hebrew, the language of creation. This language had disappeared from the earth after the confusion of tongues in the tower of Babel incident. Abraham then translates the books of his fathers, written in Hebrew, into his own language and studies them.[282] Although it is not said, Abraham's language must have been thought to be Chaldean (Aramaic) since Abraham grew up in Ur in Chaldea. Through this sequence the author of Jubilees gives an explanation of what must have been seen as a problem concerning the Enochic writings: If these books were written by Enoch, why did they exist in Aramaic and not in the ancient sacred language Hebrew? The author answers by means of a model of the history of language. The primeval language was Hebrew, but after the confusion of tongues it was no longer spoken. Abraham then translated the books into Aramaic.

At several points concerning the period of the patriarchs the books and traditions from Enoch and Noah are mentioned. In Jub 21,10 Abraham instructs Isaac about sacrifices and refers to the books of Enoch and Noah. In Jub 25,7 Jacob refers to the instruction by Abraham. In Jub 39,6-7 Joseph remembers the words that his father Jacob read from the words of Abraham.

The chain of transmission ends in Jub 45,16, where the passage reads: "And he (Jacob) gave all his books and the books of his fathers to Levi his son that he might preserve them and renew

281 Cf. above, p. 59.
282 In the Genesis Apocryphon, 1QapGen, col 19, line 25 (Fitzmyer and Harrington, pp. 112f), Abraham is also connected with the Enochic books.

them for his children until this day." There should be no doubt that the author of Jubilees claims that the descendants of Levi were responsible for the Enochic traditions from the time of their ancestor Levi up to the author's own time.

The chain of transmission established in Jubilees must be regarded as an etiology of the sacred knowledge of the descendants of Levi. This sacred knowledge is based on two kinds of transmission: 1) Oral instruction. This instruction concerns cultic and moral teaching. Although Enoch is depicted as a "priest" in Jub 4,25, it is not said there that he taught this kind of knowledge. But Noah refers to Enoch as the authority in Jub 7,38-39. 2) The primeval Books of Enoch. These are the main concern in Jub 4,17-26. Originally they were composed in the primeval language, Hebrew, but later Abraham translated them into Aramaic.

The problem is to define what is the meaning of "the children of Levi". Already at the end of the exile the leading Zadokite priests, who served as altar priests in Jerusalem both in the pre-exilic and post-exilic periods, started to trace their ancestry back to Levi (Ezek 40,46; 43,19; 44,15).[283] The Qumran community that copied the Enoch as well as the Levi literature had Zadokite priests as the leading element.[284] Accordingly "the children of Levi" do not necessarily mean "from the tribe of Levi" or "from the group of temple functionaries explicitly called Levites in post-exilic Judaism".

A. Hultgård dates the emergence of the concept of Levi as ideal priest to pre-Essene Zadokite circles at the beginning of the second century.[285] This is hardly correct. The idealization of Levi and the Levitical priesthood is already reflected in Malachi from the beginning of the fifth century, cf. Mal 2,4-9; 3,3-4. The concept of Levitical priesthood presupposed in Malachi again corresponds to the Deuteronomistic Law, Deut 18,1-8. Here "Levitical priests" clearly means "priests from the tribe of Levi". The code reflects

283   Cf. A. Cody, The History of Old Testament Priesthood, AnBib 35, Rome 1969, pp. 166ff.
284   Cf. A. Hultgård, "The Ideal 'Levite', the Davidic Messiah and the Savior Priest in the Testaments of the Twelve Patriarchs", Ideal Figures in Ancient Judaism, pp. 93-110, pp. 93f. Cf. also below, note 288, p. 138.
285   Hultgård, op.cit., p. 93.

the claim put forward by the members of the Levitical tribe that
they were the only ones who had the right to the priestly
office.[286]
The concept of Levi as the ideal priest accordingly has a long
history, and through this history it has been used polemically
against other claimants to the priestly office. In pre-exilic times it
was used by the Levitical tribe against the Zadokite priesthood in
Jerusalem. The same concept was taken over and further developed in the second century by a group that also used it polemically against the Jerusalemite priesthood. Since the Levi literature
enjoyed popularity in the Qumran community, it can probably be
assumed that this group was the one which developed into the
Essene movement.

The crucial question for our subject is why this group identified
itself so strongly with the Levitical lineage. It could of course only
be a reaction to the common post-exilic tradition that all true
priests were the "sons of Levi". But there are obstacles to this
theory. Although the official Zadokite priesthood bowed to the
Deuteronomistic claim that only Levites could be priests, their
Levitical ancestry was never emphasized. Aaron was introduced as
their most important ancestor and was regarded as a descendant of
Levi and the brother of Moses.[287] Later, at the beginning of the
second century, Ben Sira also makes Aaron the ancestor of the
priesthood, clearly reflecting the official Jerusalemite view at this
time, cf. ch. 45. The priests are "the sons of Aaron" (Ben Sira
50,13.16). In the Zadokite-influenced Qumran community the
expected priestly leader was called "the anointed of Aaron", cf.
the Rule of Community, 1QS ix, 11.[288]

The Levi traditions, however, concentrate exclusively on Levi as
ancestor. And as we have noticed, these traditions did not originate
late in the post-exilic period but can be traced back to the
beginning of this period. Here the idealization of Levi, presupposed in Malachi, corresponded to Levi's prominent place in the
Deuteronomistic law.

---

286 Cf. Cody, op.cit., pp. 129-34.
287 Cf. Cody, op.cit., pp. 170-4; A.H.J. Gunneweg, Leviten und Priester,
FRLANT 89, Göttingen 1965, pp. 206f.
288 Text in E. Lohse, Die Texte aus Qumran, p. 32. For further references, cf.
J. Maier and K. Schubert, Die Qumran-Essener, UTB 244, München 1982, pp. 30f.

I think these observations point in the direction of some sort of continuity between the Levi traditions of the pre-exilic and exilic time, when they functioned as a polemical defence of the Levitical priesthood, and the later post-exilic Levi traditions. If so, it is reasonable to assume that this continuity consisted of a group regarding itself as descendants of Levi over against the Zadokite priestly lineage.

One more observation supports these considerations. We have previously seen that both Enoch traditions in the Book of Watchers and Levi traditions are located to the vicinity of the ancient sanctuary at Dan in Upper Galilee.[289] The sanctuary at Dan was the ancient sanctuary of the Levites (Judg 17-18). In 1 Kings 12,26-31 it is told how Jeroboam I erected new sanctuaries, Bethel and Dan, after the division of the monarchy. Besides this he also built shrines on the hills and appointed non-Levitical priests to serve there. The last statement presupposes that the priesthood in Bethel and Dan was Levitical. If not, the author of the Book of Kings would have said so. When post-exilic Enoch traditions and Levi traditions are located at Dan, they are located to the ancient sanctuary of the Levites. I think this further supports the theory that the group that elaborated the Levi traditions in the post-exilic period stood in some sort of continuity with the earlier claim that only members of the Levitical tribe were the true priests of Israel.

Why did the author of Jubilees connect the Enoch traditions with the descendants of Levi?
I. It could be that he only wanted to emphasize the importance of a certain group identified as the Levitical priesthood, that he supported their claim as the true priests of Israel over against the established priesthood in Jerusalem. That the author of Jubilees strongly favoured a priesthood based on Levitical descendance is clear from Jub 30,18 and 32,1. Such a claim is also well attested to in both the Aramaic and the Greek Testament of Levi, cf. TLevi ar, Bod, col a, 6; Camb, col c, 67;[290] 1Q TLevi ar, frg 1,

---

289 cf. above, pp. 103f; and below, p. 142.
290 The Aramaic texts of the Cambridge University and Bodleian Library Geniza fragments are published in R.H. Charles, The Greek Versions of the Testaments of the Twelve Patriarchs, pp. 245-56. The fragments are analysed and commented anew by J.C. Greenfield and M.E. Stone, "Remarks on the Aramaic

line 2;[291] Greek Testament 5,2; 8,1-10; 9,3.[292] But although Enoch enjoyed considerable popularity in some circles during the second century, the etiology in Jubilees would hardly impress the priestly aristocracy in Jerusalem. At this time the torah and the prophets were well established as normative writings, and Enoch plays a modest role in them.[293] The priestly aristocracy traced its ancestry back to Aaron, the brother of Moses, a major figure in the normative writings.[294] The priority of the normative writings belonging to a normative period of history is in fact recognized by the author of Jubilees himself by making the Book of Jubilees a revelation given to Moses.

II.   Could it be that the group which identified itself as "Levitical" put forward such a claim, that they preserved the ancient antediluvian knowledge, and that this claim had its origin not in the second century, but in an earlier period?

We have previously noted that the two earliest Enochic books, the Astronomical Book and the Book of Watchers show marks of priestly influence.[295] But the marks were not specific enough to determine the identity of the group. Could it have been the group that also developed the Levi traditions?

There are in fact contacts between the Aramaic and Greek Testament of Levi and Enochic literature. In the Greek Testament of Levi 10,5; 14,1; 16,1 references are given to the Book of Enoch. In 14,1 and 16,1 this reference is missing in the A-group of manuscripts, but it is extant in the more valuable B-text.[296] Such references, however, are given not only in the Testament of Levi,

---

Testament of Levi from the Geniza", RB 86, 1979, pp. 214-230. For my references, cf. Greenfield and Stone, pp. 218,224.

291   The fragment was first published by Milik in D. Barthélemy and J.T. Milik, DJD I, pp. 87-91. The text is readily accessible in Fitzmyer and Harrington, pp. 80f.

292   Greek text in R.H. Charles, op.cit.; and M. de Jonge, Testamenta XII Patriarcharum, PsVTGr 1, Leiden 1964, (manuscript b).

293   Cf. above, pp. 17ff.

294   Cf. R. de Vaux, Ancient Israel. Its Life and Institutions, pp. 294-7; J. Maier, "Tempel und Tempelkult", J. Maier and J. Schreiner (eds.), Literatur und Religion des Frühjudentums, pp. 371-90, pp. 374ff; K. Koch, "Priestertum II. In Israel", RGG³, col. 577.

295   Cf. above, p. 84 and pp. 102f.

296   Charles, op.cit., pp. xix-xxiii, distinguished correctly between two groups of manuscripts, designated A and B. He preferred A to B. This is disproved in later research. The A-group is no more than a late and free recension of the B-text, cf. M. de Jonge, op.cit., p. xiii.

but occur several places in other Greek Testaments: TestSim 5,4; TestJud 18,1; TestDan 5,6; TestNaft 4,1; TestBenj 9,1. In all cases the references concern predictions made by Enoch. Three of the occurrences are in a context which deals with the Levitical priesthood, TestSim 5,4-6,1; TestDan 5,4-10; TestNaft 4,1-5,5. In all three cases the theme is the apostasy of the people and Levi is introduces as the true priest of the Lord. In TestDan and TestNaft the Levitical priesthood is persecuted by the apostates. In TestLevi 14,3-8 and 16,1-5 we hear more about this group of sinners who are contrasted with the Levites; the apostates are priests who have defiled the priesthood and the cult.

References to Enoch occur not only in the Greek Testament of Levi; most likely such a reference is also to be found in a fragment of the Aramaic Testament, 4Q Test Levi[a] 8iii, lines 6-7. I think Milik is correct in seeing Greek TestLevi 14,3-4 as a corresponding text. According to Milik the very fragmentary text reads (without all the reconstructions suggested by Milik):[297]

(שמשא וש)הרא וכוכביא
)   (מן
)   וכ(שהרא
(   )   הן אנ(תן תחשכון
(   )   א(הלא קבל חנוך
)   נא(ועל מן תהוא חובתא
(הן)   הלא עלי ועליכן בני

"[the sun and] the [m]oon and the stars. [   ] from [   ] the moon. If you are obscured [   ]. Did not Enoch accuse [   ]. And with whom will the blame lie, [if] not with me and with you, my sons?"

If TestLevi 14,3-4 is the correct context here (and I think it is), the fallen priests are likened to the heavenly bodies that shine on the vault, but can obscure their light. This accusation is similar to Enoch's accusation against the watchers portrayed as priests in En 12-16,[298] especially if we take into account that the watchers in En 18,13-19,1 are equated with the stars that went astray.

297   Milik, The Books of Enoch, pp. 23f.
298   Cf. above, pp. 99f.

This is not the only example of contact between the Enochic and the Levitical literature. A significant parallel to Enoch's visionary ascension to heaven in En 14 is to be found both in the Greek and the Aramaic Testament of Levi: Greek TestLevi 2,5-8; Aramaic 4Q TLevi ar[a], col 2, lines 11-18.[299] Both Enoch's visionary ascension and Levi's are located to the same place, Abel-Maīn or "the waters of Dan", close to Mount Hermon.[300]

Closely related to the Testament of Levi are the visions ascribed to his grandson Amran, 4Q Amram [abcde],[301] cf. 4Q Amram[c], frg 1, line 1 (Fitzmyer and Harrington, pp. 94f). These visions show that circles that regarded themselves as the true Levitical priesthood produced the same kind of revelatory visionary literature as found in the Books of Enoch.

Crucial in this respect, however, are the few lines preserved from the Testament of Qahat, Levi's son, 4Q TQahat, frg 1, lines 9-12 (Fitzmyer and Harrington, p. 96)

וכען לכה עמרם ברי מפק(ד אנה
ו(בנ)יכה ורבניהון אנה מפקד)
ויהבו ללוי אבי ולוי אבי לי (יהב
כול כתבי בשהדו די תזדהרון בהון)

"Now you, 'Amram, my son, [I] am comman[ding   ] and your sons and their sons I am commanding [   ] and they gave to Levi, my father, and Levi my father gave to me [   ] all my books in testimony, so that you might be forwarned by them [   ]." The books given to Levi here, that he subsequently handed over to Qahat and Qahat to Amram, can only be the books referred to in Jub 45,16, i.e. the books of the primeval patriarchs handed down through generations. When this is the case, the author of Jubilees has not constructed the concept of the Levites as the holders of the primeval books out of his own mind. The concept was present in circles producing Levitical literature.

---

299 Published by J.T. Milik, "Le Testament de Lévi en araméen: Fragment de la grotte 4 de Qumrân", RB 62, 1955, pp. 398-406. The text is readily accessible in Fitzmyer and Harrington, op.cit., pp. 88-91f.
300 Cf. 4Q TLevi ar[a], col 2, line 13; En 13,9; and Milik, op.cit., p. 404.
301 Published by J.T. Milik, "4Q Visions de Amram et une citation d'Origène", RB 79, 1972, pp. 77-97. The texts are readily accessible in Fitzmyer and Harrington, op.cit., pp. 90-7.

We summarize our observations:

1) The two earliest Enochic books, the Astronomical Book and the Book of Watchers, have features pointing toward a priestly origin.
2) The author of the Book of Jubilees claims that the "Levites" are the actual holders of the Enochic writings and traditions.
3) This claim has support in Levitical literature.
4) In Levitical literature and traditions Enoch is regarded as a great authority predicting the legitimacy of the Levitical priesthood.
5) The Levitical literature has several features in common with the Enochic, both in Gattung and content.

I think these observations are solid enough to claim that there must have been a connection between "Levites" and the Enochic literature, at least in the period when the Astronomical Book and the Book of Watchers were composed. And there seems to be good reason for supposing that these early Enochic writings actually were composed within these circles. But one problem remains: Why did this group trace its ancestry and authority back to Enoch? We shall return to that problem later.

3.5.2   The Tradition from the Watchers

In the description of the fall of the angels, the Book of Jubilees draws on En 6-16 and Gen 6,1-4. In Jub 4,22 Enoch testifies to the watchers as in En 12-16. In Jub 5,1-12 the Watcher story is told in close relationship to Gen 6,1-4 and En 6-11.

Yet there is an important difference. In the Book of Watchers the descent of the watchers is regarded as a conscious rebellion, cf. En 6,2-5. In Jubilees the descent is regarded positively: ". . . for in his days the angels of the Lord descended on the earth, those who are named the watchers, that they should instruct the children of men, and that they should do judgment and uprightness on the earth," Jub 4,15b. The clause describes the task of the watchers in two ways. On the one hand they should instruct men, which must be understood as bringing the human race divine wisdom; on the other hand they should advise men in moral and legal matters. In other words, the watchers are regarded as primeval divine sages coming from God to live on the earth.

The change in the position of the watchers came, according to Jubilees, when the watchers mixed sexually with the human race. This was a violation of the cosmic law and caused great evil on the earth, Jub 5,2-3. Although it is not explicitly said in Jubilees, we must assume that the perversion of the watchers' conduct caused a perversion of their teaching as well.

The theme is taken up again in Jub 8,2-3 related to Kainam, the son of Arpachshad. The sequence reads: "And the son grew, and his father taught him writing, and he went to seek for himself a place where he might seize for himself a city. And he found a writing which former (generations) had carved on the rock, and he read what was thereon, and he transcribed it and sinned owing to it; for it contained the teaching of the watchers in accordance with which they used to observe the omens of the sun and moon and stars in all the signs of heaven."

Josephus included a similar story but it related to the descendants of Seth: ". . . they also discovered the sciences of the heavenly bodies in their orderly array. Moreover, to prevent their discoveries from being lost to mankind and perishing before they were known — Adam having predicted a destruction of the universe, at one time by a violent fire and at another by a mighty deluge of water — they erected two pillars, one of brick and the other of stone, and inscribed these discoveries on both; so that, if the pillar of brick disappeared in the deluge, that of stone would remain to teach men what was graven thereon and to inform them that they had also erected one of brick" (Antiquities I, 69-71).[302] Josephus then continues to tell how the descendants of Seth were corrupted by the fallen angels.

Kainam, the discoverer of the inscription, is regarded in Jubilees as the son of Arpachshad (Jub 8,1). The Hebrew text of Genesis does not mention Kainam but goes directly from Arpachshad to Sjelah (Gen 10,24; 11,12). The Septuagint, however, lists Kainam as the son of Arpachshad (LXX 10,24; 11,12).

Arpachshad belongs to the Semitic genealogy in the Genesis table of nations (Gen 10). As sons of Shem are listed: Elam (the Elamites), Assur (the Assyrians), Arpachshad, Lud (the Lydians?), Aram (the Arameans), Gen 10,22.[303] The name Arpachshad is not attested to in any ancient sources. The name is written ארפכשד, 'arpakšad, in Hebrew. The last three letters KŠD are the same as the Hebrew word for the Babylonians, only that šin is used instead of sin, כשדים, kasdīm. It would also have been surprising

---

if the Babylonians were not mentioned among the Semitic nations.[304] Josephus quite clearly identifies Arpachshad as the ancestor of the Babylonians, cf. Antiquities I, 144.

In Jubilees Arpachshad begot two sons, Kainam and Kesed, Jub 8,6. Kesed begot Ur, who built the city of Ur, Jub 11,3. Ur named the city after himself and his father Kesed. This is obviously an explanation of the name of the city according to Gen 11,28, אור כשׂדים, 'ur kasdīm, "Ur of the Chaldeans". There is accordingly a clear connection between the descendants of Arpachshad and Babylonia in Jubilees. This is also clear from Jub 9,4, where Arpachshad is given the region of the Chaldeans as his portion.

The city of Ur is regarded in Jubilees as the seat of Chaldean science. In Jub 11,8 the following is told about Nahor's education: "And she bore him Nahor, in the first year of this week, and he grew and dwelt in Ur of the Chaldeans, and his father taught him the researches of the Chaldeans to divine and augur, according to the signs of heaven."

The place where Kainam found the inscription is not named. It is only told that he went out to seize for himself a city. Most likely the inscription that had survived from the flood was found in this city. The inscription was carved on a rock. The Ethiopic $k^uak^u\check{e}h$, "rock", has its equivalent in Hebrew צור, ṣur, which can be a part of a mountain or a large stone block cut free from the mountain.[305]

Thus Jubilees deals with a tradition about the origin of Babylonian science. This science was revealed to men in primordial time. The revelators were angels who descended from heaven and acted as sages among men. They transgressed the divine laws and were condemned to the underworld. Their teaching was carved on rock or a stone block and thereby survived the flood. It was redis- covered after the flood by the ancestors of the Babylonians and was taught in Ur of the Chaldeans as Chaldean science.

---

304 Cf. C. Westermann, Genesis, p. 684.
305 Cf. W. Gesenius and F. Brown (eds.), A Hebrew and English Lexicon of the Old Testament, sub ṣur, (V), p. 849.

3.5.3   The Origin of Wisdom in Traditions Related to Enoch

In the Palestinian sources we have found four models of the origin
of wisdom:

1) Enoch is the first sage. He was one of the antediluvian Babylonian giants.
2) Wisdom stems from the watchers, who led men astray with their teaching.
3) Wisdom stems from Enoch, who was instructed by an angel or angels.
4) Wisdom stems originally from the watchers but was divided into true and
false wisdom. True wisdom was transmitted through Enoch, false wisdom
through the rebellious watchers.

The first model is the one found in Pseudo-Eupolemus,[306] the
second in the Watcher story, En 6-11,[307] the third in the Astronomical Book,[308] and the fourth in the Book of Jubilees.
There is one basic difference. In Pseudo-Eupolemus, the Astronomical Book and Jubilees the origin of wisdom is regarded
positively, but in the Watcher story it is regarded negatively.
Within the first group there are also differences. Pseudo-Eupolemus treats Enoch as the first semi-divine sage. In the Astronomical Book Enoch is instructed by the angel Uriel. It is likely
that we have a similar idea in Jubilees, that the angels who
descended and lived on earth, Jub 4,15, were those who instructed
Enoch, Jub 4,17.
Three of the models contain a report about a rebellion among the
primordial divine or semi-divine figures. In Pseudo-Eupolemus
this does not affect his theory of the origin of wisdom. In Jubilees
this rebellion causes a division into two kinds of wisdom: true wisdom in the line from Enoch to Levi; false wisdom in the line from
the rebellious watchers to the Babylonians. In the Watcher story,
En 6-11, the rebellion takes place already in heaven and accordingly affects the teaching of the watchers from the beginning.
We do not think it is correct to ask what source contains the oldest
tradition, because we do not think there is one single Palestinian
tradition behind the sources. Rather, we think that they have
adopted material containing two basic elements which are interpreted in different ways. These two elements are not difficult to
isolate:

306   Cf. above, pp. 115ff.
307   Cf. above, p. 98.
308   Cf. above, pp. 63ff, and 76ff.

1) Wisdom had its origin among divine or semi-divine sages living
on earth in the antediluvian period.
2) These divine figures rebelled against the divine laws and
consequently were struck by a catastrophe.

d) Enoch as Sage, Visionary and Apocalyptic

I.   One of the most significant observations arising from the comparison of the Jewish material and the Genesis texts is the consis-
tent lack of interest by the Jewish authors in the Enoch figure in
Gen 4,17-18. This is clearly illustrated in the Book of Jubilees.
The Enoch figure in Gen 4,17-18 is only mentioned, while that in
Gen 5,21-24 is one of the leading figures of the book. When one
considers the variety of motifs corresponding to Gen 5,21-24 in
Jewish literature, it is surprising to find that not one corresponds
to the foundation of a city. There can only be one reason for this:
The Jewish authors clearly associated a large scale of motifs
reading Gen 5, while Gen 4 was rather indifferent to them.

The comparison of Gen 5,21-24 and the Jewish-Samaritan material
has shown different kinds of connections. The Astronomical Book
has only the name of Methuselah as Enoch's son directly in common with the Genesis account. Besides this there are similarities in
motifs, but they do not indicate that the Astronomical Book was
patterned on Genesis. The author of En 12-16 seems to have been
inspired by the Genesis account in his report of Enoch's ascension.
But he adds new motifs and places Enoch into a context totally
different from that of Genesis. In the Noahitic traditions Enoch is
removed to Paradise, something which cannot be derived from the
Genesis text. The author of the Book of Dreams seems to be the
one who collected most details from the Genesis text, but his portrayal of Enoch as a visionary is far removed from Genesis. One
Hebrew version of Ben Sira presents an elaboration of the Genesis
text but describes Enoch as "a sign of knowledge", an appellation
which has no explicit background there. Pseudo-Eupolemus also
seems to have known the Genesis text but presents Enoch in a different mythological setting. The author of Jubilees also offers an
elaboration of the Genesis text but includes a series of new motifs.

The relationship with Genesis varies in the sources, but none of
them seems totally determined by the content of Gen 5,21-24.
They all present a different Enoch from that of Genesis. However,
this Jewish-Samaritan Enoch corresponds in many features to the
Enoch of Gen 5, so the two Enoch figures must have some sort of
common basis. What seems quite clear is that the Jewish-Samaritan
Enoch cannot have been the result of only an elaboration of
Gen 5. Nor have the Enoch portraits in Jewish-Samaritan literature
grown out of one common source. There are too many differing
motifs to suppose that. The most obvious conclusion is that both
the priestly author of the Genesis account and the Jewish-Samaritan writers had available several traditions about antediluvian
time that in one way or another corresponded to each other and
that they utilized features of these traditions.

II.   The variety in the Enoch sources becomes clear when one
recognizes the distinguished characteristics connected with Enoch.
They can be summarized under five rubrics:
1) Enoch as a primeval sage, specialist in astronomy/astrology —
Genesis (to some extent), the Astronomical Book, Pseudo-Eupolemus, Ben Sira, Jubilees.
2) Enoch as a hero in a primeval catastrophe — The Book of
Watchers, the Noahitic traditions, the Book of Dreams, Jubilees.
3) Enoch as the discoverer of cosmic geography — The Astronomical Book, the Book of Watchers, Jubilees.
4) Enoch as a visionary apocalyptic — The Book of Dreams,
Jubilees.
5) Enoch as an example of piety — LXX and Alexandrian
exegesis.

Even a cautious dating and placing of the sources show that some
of the portraits are distinctly older than others. It is quite clear,
for instance, that Enoch became an example of piety from the
second century and onwards in the Alexandrian exegesis. Likewise,
it is clear that Enoch "became" a visionary apocalyptic occupied
with history and eschatology in the disturbances at the time of the
Maccabean revolt. In this context we use the word "apocalyptic"
in the most usual sense as a predictor of the future history of
mankind.

If we start at the other end, it seems clear that the oldest feature connected to Enoch is that of the primeval sage. Old is also the connection between Enoch and a primeval catastrophe. Enoch as the discoverer of cosmic geography seems, according to the date of the sources, to place himself between the sage and the hero on the one hand and the apocalyptic on the other. Of course one can object that this analysis only takes the age of the sources into account and that the age of the underlying traditions not depends on the age of the literary sources. But also a cautious evaluation of the Enochic traditions, seen in the light of their Gattungen, support the observation.

III.   I give below a survey of the Gattungen represented in the Enochic material. I can begin neither a detailed discussion of what constitutes a Gattung nor one of the character of each Gattung at this point. Nevertheless, I think that the survey and the discussion will be sufficient for our aims.

1) Primeval list, genealogy. Gen 4; Gen 5.
2) Astronomical tables in the form of instruction. The Astronomical Book.
3) Mythical narrative, the Watcher story, En 6-11, adding En 12-16.
4) Dream vision. En 13-16; En 83-84; cf. En 60 and 65.
5) Visionary journey. En 17-19; 20-36.
6) Historical apocalypse in the form of a vision. The Apocalypse of Animals, the Apocalypse of Weeks.

This survey demonstrates that the Gattung vision does not occur in the earliest sources. In the two oldest sources from the tenth and the sixth or fifth century Enoch occurs in primeval lists formed as genealogies. The first Enochic work, possibly from the beginning of the third century, is made up of astronomical tables placed into a framework of instruction of one figure by another. The Watcher story, stemming from the end of the fourth century and incorporated into the Enochic traditions, has the form of a mythical narrative.

The first vision associated with Enoch is the throne vision in En 13-16. It might be from the first half of the third century. The framework of the vision is the Watcher story telling of a primeval catastrophe. The Noahitic texts in 1 Enoch deal with the same theme. These texts also incorporate visions. The first vision in the Book of Dreams, En 83-84, also concerns the primeval catastrophe. In our analysis of the Noahitic traditions and En 6-16 we have found that a basic motif here is that the hero in the primeval catastrophe is portrayed as a visionary.[309] Regarding the occurrences of Gattungen, I think we can conclude that that of vision was introduced into the Enochic material in the description of Enoch as a hero in a primeval catastrophe, the role that Enoch shared with Noah.

The next occurrence of the Gattung vision is in Enoch's visionary journeys. These correspond to the earlier Enochic material in two ways. First, Enoch travels to see the final fate of the watchers. In this perspective the visionary journeys are an extension of the dream vision in En 13-16. Secondly, traces of the form visionary journey also occur in the cosmological parts of the Astronomical Book. Here Enoch is portrayed as the discoverer of cosmic geography, a feature also present in the journeys in En 17-19; 20-36. The visionary form here corresponds to the instruction of Enoch in the astronomical mysteries. The fields of astronomy and cosmology were closely related in the minds of ancient people. We have already observed that the instruction formulas in the astronomical part of the Astronomical Book tended toward the Gattung vision.[310] They were apparently interpreted in that way by the composers of the cosmological material.

Once he was established in the tradition as a visionary, it is not surprising that the antihellenistic groups in the first half of the second century chose Enoch as the visionary authority in their apocalypses. We shall later discuss in more detail how they related them to the earlier Enochic material.

This analysis is supported by the treatment of Enoch in the Jewish-Samaritan material. Neither Pseudo-Eupolemus nor the Ben Sira tradition which treats Enoch as a sage describes him as a visionary. In the Book of Jubilees Enoch is first introduced as a primeval sage in connection with the Astronomical Book and other calendarian speculations, then introduced as a visionary in connection with the Book of Dreams.[311]

IV.   The survey above demonstrated a growing tendency to use the Gattung vision in connection with the Enochic material. The

---

309   Cf. above, p. 88 and 93.
310   Cf. above, p. 65.
311   Cf. above, p. 133.

same tendency can also be demonstrated by examining the visions themselves.

We start with the observations drawn from the analysis above. At the very beginning of the Enochic traditions in Judaism, as far as we can judge from the dates of the sources and the use of Gattungen, Enoch is portrayed in two ways, as a primeval sage and as a hero in a primeval catastrophe. The use of the Gattung vision occurs first in the second context, while the phraseology in the first tends toward that of vision.

Observing that the Gattung vision was initially connected with the texts about the primeval catastrophe, we can examine how this Gattung expanded in the course of the tradition. The dream vision in En 13-16 is introduced as a "vision of wrath" affecting the watchers, En, 13,8 = 4Q En^c lvi, line 5 (Milik, p. 193).[312] Enoch is here placed into the same position as in En 83-84 and Noah in En 60 and 65 in that he foresees the coming primeval catastrophe. But instead of going into details about this catastrophe, which was not necessary because it was already recounted in En 6-11, the author of En 13-16 introduces other Enochic material. The vision in En 14 draws on the motif of Enoch's ascension in Gen 5,24.[313] The motif is clothed in the language of vision taken from Ezek 1-3.

Also the journeys of Enoch in En 17-19; 20-36 have as a starting point that Enoch is a visionary, drawing on En 13-16, but extend the Gattung vision to the area of cosmic geography. Mythical journeys including cosmic geography similar to that of Enoch are known from Mesopotamian sources.[314] What happens in the Enochic literature is that the mythical journeys are described in a language of vision similar to that of the visions of Zechariah.[315]

At the end the language of vision is extended to encompass the composition of the Book of Watchers. In En 19,3, the concluding line of En 6-19, the material is characterized as visions. In En 1,2, the introduction to the whole Book of Watchers, the visionary features are also emphasized.

The Book of Dreams contains two visions. The first contains a pre-

---

312 Cf. above. p. 65.
313 Cf. above, p. 93.
314 Cf. above, pp. 67f, and below, pp. 246ff.
315 Cf. above, p. 67.

diction of the coming catastrophe corresponding to the tradition of
the primeval visionary in the flood/watcher incident. In the second
vision, En 85-90, the perspective is extended. The primeval visionary sees not only the immediate approaching catastrophe, which
in the Enochic traditions is treated as a typos for the eschaton (cf.
below), he sees the whole history from the beginning to the end.
The same extension of the Gattung vision can be recognized in the
first context, Enoch as a primeval sage. In the Astronomical Book
Enoch is instructed in the content of the astronomical tables by the
angel Uriel. That Enoch communicated with one or several
transcendent figures is a well-established fact in the early Enochic
sources and is already extant in Gen 5,22.24.[316] In the speech of
Uriel, En 80, Enoch's knowledge of astronomy is related to
predictions.[317] In En 81 we have a new interpretation of Enoch's
position in En 80. Enoch is situated in heaven, i.e. the ascension
motif is incorporated, and the tablets of heaven are introduced as
a parallel to the astronomical tables. Now Enoch reads the future
of mankind directly from the document shown to him by Uriel.
We have previously noticed that the description of the heavenly
tablets resembles that of the astronomical tables.[318] In the
introduction to the Apocalypse of Weeks the heavenly tablets are
adopted into the Gattung vision. As in En 81 Enoch reads the
future of mankind out of the heavenly tablets, but the context is
a visionary experience.[319]

I think that the surveys above are sufficient to demonstrate two
facts:
1) There have been visionary elements connected with the Jewish
Enochic traditions from the beginning: On the one hand is the hero
in the Watcher/Flood story portrayed as a visionary; on the other
hand the motif "Enoch communicated with a divine being",
related to Enoch as a sage, tends toward the language of vision.
2) These visionary features are greatly expanded in the growth of
the traditions in Judaism to the extent that the visionary capacity
became the primary character of Enoch.

316   Cf. above, pp. 46ff.
317   Cf. above, pp. 74ff.
318   Cf. above, pp. 78f.
319   Cf. the text on p. 77.

V. The words "vision", "apocalyptic" and "eschatology" are very often used together.[320] It remains to see to what extent the early Enochic traditions can be characterized as eschatological.

In the earliest accounts of Enoch, Gen 4, Gen 5, Pseudo-Eupolemus, and Ben Sira, there are no indications of any eschatological implications. But both in Pseudo-Eupolemus and Ben Sira the teaching of Enoch is regarded as relevant to future generations. This is also the case in the Astronomical Book, which seems to have formed the background for the two sources. The teaching of Enoch should be transmitted to future generations (En 82). Enoch was also enabled to make predictions about the "days of the sinners" related to the astronomical calculations (En 80). But these predictions are not eschatological in the sense that history moves towards a final crisis or change.

Eschatology enters into the Enochic traditions in the Book of Watchers, but in a an ambiguous way.[321] The difficulty concerns especially the Watcher story which forms the basis of the book. To what extent is this story to be read as a report of primeval events which have influence the later history, and to what extent is it to be read as a description of events in the author's own days? We argued earlier that the story must be characterized as a mythical narrative which retells a primordial incident in the way that it reflects actual circumstances.[322] That means that the condemnation of the fallen watchers and the giants (En 9,1-10,16) and the healing of the earth (En 10,17-11,2) fit primarily the primordial context, but because the author used features in the material to reflect his own time they also become signs of what will happen in the author's future. In this respect the crisis and renewal have eschatological significance, even though the primary concern of the story is primeval events. The same observation can be made of the Noahitic traditions, En 60 and 65, and in En 83-84. The visions there concern primarily the primeval catastrophe, but this is regarded as a typos of the eschatological crisis.

I think that on the basis of these observations we can trace the

---

320 On eschatology in the Book of Watchers, cf. also below, pp. 317f.
321 Cf. the discussion in J.J. Collins, "Methodological Issues in the Study of Enoch: Reflections on the Articles of P.D. Hanson and G.W. Nickelsburg", P.J. Achtemeier (ed.), SBL 1978 Seminar Papers. Vol I, pp. 315-322, pp. 317ff.
322 Cf. above, pp. 96ff.

main line of development concerning Enoch and eschatology. 1) In the earliest Enochic writing Enoch as a sage is able to make predictions. 2) In the Watcher story a primeval crisis is used as a mirror for actual historical circumstances. 3) Since the historical circumstances are experienced in an eschatological perspective, the transference of the primordial story to a historical setting also gave the primordial story eschatological significance. 4) The heroes in the primeval catastrophe, Noah and Enoch, were able to predict it. 5) Since the primeval catastrophe was given eschatological significance, the predictions also became eschatological. 6) These basic features are then utilized in the later historical apocalypses in which Enoch is able to predict all of history from the primordial time to the eschaton.

This shows that the development of eschatology in the Enochic traditions has followed the same pattern as the development of the visionary forms. There are two cornerstones in the traditions. The one is the primeval sage bestowed with the capacity to predict. The other is the primeval catastrophe transferred to an actual historical setting and interpreted in an eschatological perspective. In this context the primeval hero appears and is able to predict this catastrophe.

VI. We know the approximate date of the earliest source of that Enoch figure which formed the basis for the Enochic traditions. The Priestly source was composed during the sixth and fifth century in Babylonia.[323] We also know approximately when the Enochic traditions appeared in Palestine. This must have happened in the course of the fourth century.

We also know the basic features which characterize the earliest Enochic traditions. They elaborate such mythological material as astrological mythology, mythological material concerning a primeval catastrophe, and mythical geography. The treatment of the material shows distinctively speculative interests. We find different kinds of estimations, computations, numerical symbolism, and astronomical and geographical teaching. But the treatment of

---

323 It seems quite clear that in the legal material P included pre-exilic sources, cf. M. Haran, "Behind the Scenes of History: Determining the Date of the Priestly Source", JBL 100, 1981, pp. 321-33. But the final composition of the work took place in the exile, cf. our note 12, p. 43.

the material also reveals priestly influence, as in calendarian speculations, the use of seven as the sacred number, priestly purity rules, interpretations based on halakcic rules, and cultic concerns. There is a growing tendency to clothe the traditions in a visionary language, a tendency parallel to that of interpreting the material in an eschatological perspective. This tendency is reflected in the portraits of Enoch. In the earliest sources he is depicted as a sage and hero, in the later ones as a visionary apocalyptic.

The problem is how to place this kind of literature in post-exilic Judaism. As far as the historical apocalypses are concerned their setting seem to be in the growing antihellenistic movement in the first half of the second century. But what is the setting of the earliest Enochic traditions?

In a well-known work about post-exilic Judaism, O. Plöger distinguished between a theocratical and an eschatological Israel.[324] The theocratical Israel had its basis in the Law and the Temple, while the eschatological Israel interpreted reality in the light of the coming acts of God, i.e. in an eschatological perspective. The theocratical ideal was expressed in the Priestly source and by the Chronicler, while the eschatological hope was expressed in such late prophetic scriptures as Joel, Trito-Zechariah and the Isaiah-apocalypse (Is 24-27).

Plöger's analysis is by and large confirmed and deepened by P.D. Hanson in his study of the origins of apocalyptic eschatology.[325] Starting with Trito-Isaiah, Hanson demonstrated a growing conflict in post-exilic Jewish society with "visionaries" on the one side and the established Zadokite priesthood on the other. The basic issue was the legitimacy of the cult. The "visionaries", who included lay disciples of Deutero-Isaiah and Levites, longed for a renewed Zion and expressed their hope in eschatological oracles, while the Zadokites established their power in a reformation of the cult based largely on the program in Ezek 40-48. Losing more and more of their influence in their concrete historical circumstances, the "visionaries" developed a more transcendent eschatology which became the typical mark of apocalyptic.

The problem is that the early Enochic traditions do not fit this

---

324   O. Plöger, Theokratie und Eschatologie, pp. 129-42.
325   P.D. Hanson, The Dawn of Apocalyptic. Cf. above, pp. 36ff.

pattern. Although they share motifs with the Priestly source and
the Chronicler, the basic interests are so different that an origin
among the groups behind these scriptures can be excluded. For
instance, the primeval and patriarchal age is only a prelude to
Moses and the Law in the Priestly source, while the whole
emphasis is laid on Enoch and primeval wisdom in the Enochic
traditions. But neither can the early Enochic writings be a
subsequently developed form of post-exilic prophecy. What are
the similarities between the Astronomical Book and the Book of
Watchers on the one hand and Trito-Isaiah on the other, except for
some features due to a common Jewish heritage? Nor is it possible
to regard the speculative character of the Enochic writings as a
framework and place the eschatological perspective in the centre.
On the contrary, the speculative character is the basis, while the
eschatological perspective was adopted and emphasized more and
more in the course of the traditions.

What happened during the fourth century which gave rise to this
new kind of literature? Two related events greatly overshadowed
the rest: Ezra's return from exile and the restoration of Jewish
society according to the laws of the Priestly code. Are there any
indications in the Enochic material which point toward these
events? In fact there are. In our analysis of En 12-16 we found
that this section was based on an Ezra-Enoch typology. The scribe
Enoch was portrayed in the role of an intercessor similar to the
scribe Ezra in a case that had the same implications, namely
forbidden marriage.[326] Ezra brought with him the Priestly source,
either as a part of the whole Pentateuch or as a separate scroll. In
this source the Enoch figure who corresponds to the Enochic
traditions is mentioned for the first time. This could point toward
an origin of the traditions in the Babylonian or Persian diaspora.

In the treatment of the visionary forms of the early Enochic
writings we have previously referred to Ezekiel and Zechariah.
These two prophets have several features in common: 1) They are
both priests, Ezek 1,3; Zech 1,1 compared to Ezra 5,1; 6,14; Neh
12,16.[327] 2) Their message included to a large extent visionary

---

326 Cf. above, p. 101.
327 Cf. W. Zimmerli, Ezechiel, BK XIII, Neukirchen-Vluyn 1969, p. 24; and
O. Eissfeldt, Einleitung, pp. 579f.

narratives, in Zechariah almost exclusively so.[328] 3) Their visions
make considerable use of mythical elements.[329] 4) They both had
connection to the exilic community. Ezekiel lived and preached in
Babylonia. Zechariah returned from the exile as a member of the
Zadokite Iddo family (Neh 13,4.16) and preached in Jerusalem.

To some extent Ezekiel and Zechariah share certain features with
the early Enochic writings: 1) The Enochic writings show priestly
influence. 2) The Enochic writings use a phraseology of vision
closely related to Ezekiel and Zechariah.[330] 3) The Enochic visions
deal with mythological themes.[331] I do not wish to exaggerate the
similarities, but they indicate that there existed learned milieus
among the Jews in Babylonia where priestly interests, knowledge
in mythic lore and a predilection for the visionary form were
combined.

We have argued that Levites were the bearers of the early Enochic
traditions.[332] That could not be the Levites involved in the
"visionary group" which, according to Hanson, stood behind the
oracles in Trito-Isaiah (cf. above note 325). According to the date
and the character of the Enochic traditions it must have been a
new group entering Jewish society some time during the fourth
century, most likely from the diaspora. Do we have any reports
about Levites coming from the diaspora in this period? In fact, we
have.

In the account of Ezra's return from the exile in the Book of Ezra
a sequence deals with Levites (Ezra 8,15-20).[333] After Ezra had
gathered the Zadokite priests and the heads of the families in
Babylonia, he realised that the Levites were missing. Apparently
they had no interest in joining Ezra and returning to Zadokite-

---

328 For a survey, cf. S. Reimers, Formgeschichte der prophetischen Visionsberichte, pp. 30ff.
329 Cf. O. Keel, Jahve — Visionen und Siegelkunst. Eine neue Deutung der
Majestätsschilderungen in Jes 6, Ez 1 und 10 und Sach 4, SBS 84/85, Stuttgart
1977, pp. 125-320; and K. Seybold, Bilder zum Tempelbau. Die Visionen des
Propheten Sacharja, SBS 70, Stuttgart 1974, pp. 65-75.
330 Cf. above, pp. 93 and 67.
331 A relation between the visions of Zechariah and apocalyptic is argued by
R. North, "Prophecy to Apocalyptic via Zechariah", VT.S 22, 1972, pp. 47-71,
and by H. Gese, "Anfang und Ende der Apokalyptik, dargestellt am Sacharjabuch", ZThK 70, 1973, pp. 20-49.
332 Cf. above, pp. 135-43.
333 For an analysis of the sequence, cf. H. Schneider, Die Bücher Ezra und
Nehemia, HSAT IV/2, Bonn 1959, pp. 140f; and L.H. Brockington, Ezra,
Nehemiah and Esther, CeB, London 1969, pp. 99-102.

dominated Jerusalem. Ezra then sends a deputation in order to persuade them. The deputation was sent: על אדו הראש בכספיא המקום, "to Iddo, the head at Casiphya, the place", Ezra 8,17a. It is not clear what המקום, *hammaqōm*, "the place", means here. It is repeated after Casiphya also in the next line so it obviously belongs together with Casiphya as a designation of the place. *hammaqōm* can mean "the area" or "the district" (Ex 3,8; 23,20). This would mean that the author wanted to distinguish the district Casiphya from, for instance, a city or a village with the same name. Unfortunately the location of Casiphya is uncertain, so we do not know whether such a distinction was necessary. Another question is whether it is likely that the author would have felt it necessary to make such a distinction and inform his Jewish readers about the exact geography of the place. *hammaqōm* can also mean a holy place, a sanctuary (cf. for instance Deut 12,5; Jer 7,3.6.7). I think this meaning suits the context better. Iddo is the head at Casiphya, the sanctuary, where it is a community of Levites and temple servants (8,18-20). The result of the mission to Casiphya was that 38 Levites joined Ezra in his return to Jerusalem.

It is quite clear that this argumentation is based on deduction from a series of observations and that there is nothing in the account in Ezra 8,15-20 which explicitly indicates a link between this specific group of Levites joining Ezra and the Enochic traditions. Nevertheless, the account in Ezra demonstrates that there existed a community of Levites in Babylonia and that a group of them came to Jerusalem at the beginning of the fourth century B.C. The account accordingly establishes a bridge between two basic observations: First, that the Enochic traditions appear in Palestine in the course of the fourth and third centuries in connection with Levites; secondly, that they seem to have their origin in the diaspora. I now turn to this second observation: Are there any indications that the Enochic traditions had their roots on Babylonian soil?

III
Mesopotamian Antediluvian Traditions

In analyzing the Mesopotamian material we shall confine ourself to two main currents of traditions: those about the antediluvian kings and those about the primeval sages. Although these traditions originated separately, they were later brought together in what can be regarded as a comprehensive view of the primeval antediluvian period. It is possible that the traditions originally had nothing to do with the primeval flood that according to Mesopotamian sources swept over the Mesopotamian area. But soon this catastrophe became a primary historical demarcation dividing the early history in two periods, the antediluvian and the postdiluvian. And in this way it appears in our sources, separating antediluvian kings and sages from postdiluvian kings and sages or scholars.

Our aim is to give a presentation of this material, which we think is of relevance to the Enochic traditions. Consequently, we shall not emphasize the earliest stage of the Mesopotamian traditions or present an analysis of their origin and original setting. Rather, the presentation is a survey of major trends in the development of the traditions as they are represented in cuneiform and Greek sources dating from different periods.

a) The Antediluvian King List

1.   The Texts

1.1   Publications

WB 62

The first edition of a tablet containing a list of antediluvian kings was by S. Langdon in 1923 (WB 62). The tablet belonged to the Weld-Blundell Collection given to the Ashmolean Museum at Oxford.[1] The same year Langdon also published the Weld-Blundell prism, containing both the antediluvian and

WB 444

postdiluvian kings of Sumer (WB 444).[2] A new edition of these texts was published by T. Jacobsen in 1939.[3]
New tablets to the antediluvian King List have been discovered since Jacobsen's critical edition of the Sumerian King List. In 1952 F.R. Kraus published a fragmentary tablet from the

Ni 3195

Istanbul Museum (Ni 3195).[4] In 1962 van Dijk published a tablet found during the excavations in Uruk-Warka containing

WB 20 030,7

both the names of ancient Sumerian kings and sages (W 20 030,7).[5] Another tablet, containing the antediluvian King List,

UCBC 9 1819

was published by J.J. Finkelstein in 1964.[6] The tablet belongs to the University of California in Berkeley (UCBC 9 1819).
The most recent publication was by W.G. Lambert in 1973.[7] Lambert had earlier joined an already published piece, K.

Ct 46,5 +
K. 12054

11624,[8] to the fragment K. 11261 (= CT 46,5). Now he joined ano her piece, K. 12054. The tablets are in the British Museum.

1   S. Langdon, "The Chaldean Kings before the Flood", JRAS 42, 1923, pp. 251-9.
2   S. Langdon, Oxford Editions of Cuneiform Texts II, Oxford 1923.
3   T. Jacobsen, The Sumerian King List, AS 11, Chicago 1939.
4   F.R. Kraus, "Zur Liste der älteren Könige von Babylonien", ZA NF 16 (50), 1952, pp. 29-60.
5   H.J. Lenzen, XVIII. vorlaufiger Bericht über die von dem Deutschen Archäologischen Institut und der Deutschen Orient-Gesellschaft aus Mitteln der Deutschen Forschungsgemeinschaft untergenommenen Ausgrabungen in Uruk-Warka, Berlin 1962, pp. 43-52.
6   J.J. Finkelstein, "The Antediluvian Kings: A University of California Tablet", JCS 17, 1963, pp. 39-51.
7   W.G. Lambert, "A New Fragment from a List of Antediluvian Kings and Marduk's Chariot", Symbolae Biblicae et Mesopotamicae, Francisco Mario Theodoro de Liagre Böhl dedicatae, Leiden 1973, pp. 271-5.
8   Cf. Jacobsen, op.cit., p. 60.

1.2   A Short Description of Versions

WB 62   The tablet was written in Larsa[9] and has been dated at the end of the third millenium.[10] Accordingly, it is the oldest known written source about the antediluvian king tradition. The text is fairly well preserved, but of the third and fourth names there are only traces. The tablets ends by summing up: "ten kings before the flood", line 18.

WB 444   The tablets were written in Larsa[11] and contain both the antediluvian King List and the postdiluvian King List. The latter ends with the reign of Sîn-magir (1827-1817 B.C.) in the dynasty of Isin. His reign is reported to be eleven years. If the list is up to date, it is written in 1817 B.C.[12] The text of the antediluvian section is nearly complete. Between the antediluvian and postdiluvian sections there is a notice about the flood. The antediluvian list contains eight kings.

Ni 3195   The tablet was found in Nippur and was written in the middle of the Old Babylonian period (about 1800 B.C.).[13] It was perhaps a student exercise.[14] The tablet is very damaged, and only some of the names from the central part are visible. It seems to have been an independent entity.[15]

W 20 030,7   The tablet was found in Uruk. The scribe has dated it to year 147 in the reign of Antiochus, cf. line 24. According to our chronology that is 165/4 B.C. under Antiochus IV.[16] The left part of the tablet is destroyed, but all the names of the kings are preserved. The text lists seven antediluvian kings parallel to seven apkallu's (sages). Then comes most likely the flood.[17] After the flood the text continues to list nine postdiluvian kings parallel to one apkallu and nine ummânu's (scholars). Since no cities ares mentioned in the list, the text cannot be regarded as belonging to the antediluvian King List proper. But since both the names of the kings are by and large the same as in the King Lists and the first sequence ends with the flood, it seems quite clearly to have been patterned on the King List. Here Berossos (cf. below) forms a connecting link. His list contains the names of the kings, the cities and the sages.

UCBC 9 1819   The tablet was found in ancient Tutub. It can be dated roughly in the time span between Sinmuballit̲ and Samsuiluna in the First Dynasty of Babylon (1812-1712 B.C.).[18] The tablet may have been a student exercise.[19] The central part of it is fairly well preserved. The first line is fragmentary and the end damaged. The text lists seven or eight kings. It is an independent entity.

---

9   Cf. Langdon, op.cit., p. 1.
10   Cf. H. Zimmern, "Die altbabylonischen vor-(und nach-)sintflutlichen Könige nach neuen Quellen", ZDMG NF3 (78), 1924, pp. 17-35, p. 20.
11   Cf. Langdon, op.cit., p. 1. For dating we use generally the chronology by J.A. Brinkman in L.O. Oppenheim, Ancient Mesopotamia, rev.ed. Chicago 1977, pp. 335-46.
12   Cf. Jacobsen, op.cit., p. 5
13   Cf. Finkelstein, op.cit., pp. 39f.
14   Cf. Kraus, op.cit., p. 31.
15   Cf. Kraus, op.cit., p. 31.
16   Cf. the list of dates in W.R. Mayer, Texte aus dem Reš-Heiligtum in Uruk-Warka, BaghM, Beiheft 2, Berlin 1980, p. 23.
17   Van Dijk's restoration here is likely, because Euechsios, i.e. Enmerkar is mentioned as the first king after the reference to the flood in Berossos. For the close connection between W 20 030,7 and Berossos, cf. pp. 195ff below.
18   Cf. Finkelstein, op.cit., pp. 39f.
19   Cf. Finkelstein, op.cit., p. 41.

Ct 46,5 + K. 12054 The pieces come from the library of Ashurbanipal in
Niniveh and can be dated to about 650 B.C.[20] Lambert considers the possibility
that the texts belonged to the same composition as a dynastic list and contained
Babylonian kings down to the first millennium.[21] What seems quite clear is that
the list has not been an independent entity but has continued with the Flood
story. In the fragmentary end of the text traces of the introduction to the Flood
story occur: "Enlil . . . the noise".[22] Cf. Atra-Ḫasis (Lambert/Millard, our note
21), Tabl. I, col v rev., lines 356-8: ["Enlil heard] their noise. [And addressed]
the great gods: 'The noise of mankind [has become too intense for me].'" The
text lists nine antediluvian kings.

1.3   The Antediluvian King List in Berossos' Babyloniaca

Already in the edition of the first tablets of the King List
Langdon[23] realised that this was the cuneiform version of the
antediluvian King List found in the Babylonian priest Berossos'
Babyloniaca.[24] The Babyloniaca of Berossos, written in Greek, is
to be dated 281 B.C. in Babylon.[25] Berossos gives a list of ten
antediluvian kings and seven beasts (sages) if we include Oannes as
the first beast in the beginning.[26] A connection between the

20 Cf. Lambert, op.cit., p. 273.
21 Cf. Lambert, op.cit., pp. 271f; and W.G. Lambert and A.R. Millard, Atra-
Ḫasis. The Babylonian Story of the Flood, Oxford 1969, pp. 17f.
22 T. Jacobsen restores more of the text, thus making the reference to the
flood even clearer: "Enlil took a dislike to mankind, the clamor of their shouting
. . . kept him sleepless". T. Jacobsen, "The Eridu Genesis", JBL 100, 1981, pp.
513-29, p. 520.
23 Langdon, op.cit., pp. 1f.
24 Cf. for Berossos: Text: P. Schnabel, Berossos und die Babylonisch-
Hellenistische Literatur, Berlin 1923, pp. 261-4; F. Jacoby, FGH III, C, Erster
Band, Leiden 1958, pp. 374-7. Translation: S.M. Burstein, The Babyloniaca of
Berossos, SANE 1/5, Malibu, California 1978. We use this translation when not
otherwise stated. The main source for Berossos' Babyloniaca is Eusebius'
Chronica which directly and through other sources in its excerpts from Berossos
is based on Alexander Polyhistor's epitome of Babyloniaca. The main sources to
Eusebius' Chronica are the Armenian translation and excerpts preserved in the
ninth century A.D. Byzantine Chronicle of George Syncellus. Cf. the table in
Schnabel, op.cit., p. 168; Burstein, op.cit., pp. 10f and C.F. Lehmann-Haupt,
"Berossos", RLA II, E. Ebeling and B. Meissner (eds.), Berlin-Leipzig 1938, pp.
1-17.
25 Cf. Schnabel, op.cit., pp. 3-15; Burstein, op.cit., pp. 5f.
26 The references to Berossos are based on F. Jacoby, FGH III, C, Erster Band,
where the Armenian translation of Eusebius' Chronica and the excerpts
preserved in the Chronicle of Syncellus are given in parallel columns. For the
translation we refer to the sequence number and page number in Burstein's
edition. The King List: Text: Euseb. (Arm.) Chron. p. 4,8-6,8; (9,2ff.) and
Syncellus p. 71,3. FGH III, C. 1. B, sequences 10-13, pp. 374-77. Translation:
Burstein, Book II, 1,1-11, pp. 18f. Oannes: Text: Euseb. (Arm.) Chron. p. 6, 8-9,
2 and Syncellus p. 49, 19. FGH III, C. 1. B, sequences 4-5, pp. 369f. Translation:
Burstein, Book I, 1,5, pp. 13f.

Greek names in Berossos and the Sumerian names of the cuneiform tablets can be established in nine of the cases.[27] The list of
Berossos links directly to his own account of the flood.

1.4 Chronological Order

We have accordingly seven versions of an antediluvian list of kings
dating from about 2000 to 165 B.C. We give the texts in chronological order:

WB 62: About 2000.
WB 444: 1817.
Ni 3195: About 1800.
UCBC 9 1819: About 1700.
CT 46,5 + K. 12054: About 650.
Berossos: 281.
W 20 030,7: 165/4.

2. The Origin of the List

It is quite clear that the antediluvian and postdiluvian King Lists
have different origins. This was already stated by T. Jacobsen[28]
and has been confirmed by the finds of new versions. WB 444 is
the only version of the King List proper which directly links the
antediluvian list to the postdiluvian. This must be regarded as a
secondary connection established by the author of this text.
The antediluvian list was accordingly an independent entity. There
are good reasons, however, to think that the tradition of the kings
was connected early to the tradition of the flood.[29] All the compositions where we have the final part preserved end by either
referring to the flood or connect directly to the flood story.

27 Cf. already Langdon, op.cit., p. 3; Zimmern, op.cit., pp. 22-7; Jacobsen,
op.cit., pp. 69-77. The name which causes trouble is the third name in Berossos'
list, "Ammenon". Jacobsen, op.cit., p. 73, note 18, thinks that this name only is
a doublet of Amelon, Berossos' second king. Finkelstein, op.cit., p. 47, thinks it
reflects the Sumerian name Enmenunna, a name identical with that of a ruler of
the first postdiluvian dynasty of Kish. Zimmern, op.cit., p. 23, note 4, argued
the same as Finkelstein and called attention to the fact that also Dumuzi occurred
both as an antediluvian and postdiluvian king.
28 Jacobsen, op.cit., pp. 55-68.
29 Cf. Jacobsen, op.cit., pp. 58ff; and W.W. Hallo, "Antediluvian Cities", JCS
23, 1970-71, pp. 57-67, esp. pp. 61-6.

There are also other indications. WB 444 introduces the King List in the following way:

> When the kingship was lowered from heaven
> the kingship was in Eridu.
>
> (lines 1-2)

The text continues to describe how the kingship was carried to four other cities: Badtibira, Larak, Sippar and Šuruppak. In the introduction to the Sumerian flood story we read:

> After the lofty crown and the throne of kingship
> had come down from heaven
> . . .
> Founded [   ] cities in [   ],
> Gave them their names, apportioned their capitals;
> The first of these cities, Eridu
> he gave to the leader Nudimud,
> The second, Badtibira
> he gave to the "nugig",
> The third, Larak
> he gave to Pubilsag,
> The fourth, Sippar
> he gave to the hero Utu,
> The fifth, Šuruppak
> he gave to Sud.
>
> (col ii, lines 89,91-97)[30]

The text describes how the first antediluvian cities were founded and each given to a chief god: Eridu to Nudimud (Enki); Badtibira to Inanna ("nugig" = "virgin", title of Inanna); Larak to Pubilsag; Sippar to Utu (the sun god); Šuruppak to Sud.[31]
Both in the King List of WB 444 and in the Sumerian flood story we find accordingly a clause about the origin of kingship followed by the same list of antediluvian cities. This city list occurs in all versions except W 20 030,7 which, however, differs much in style from the others, The order of the first and the last cities is usually the same, but the order of the three in the middle can vary. The reason may be that they existed contemporarily rather than successively.[32]

30 Text according to M. Civil, "The Sumerican Flood Story", W.G. Lambert and A.R. Millard, The Babylonian Story of the Flood, pp. 138-45, p. 141.
31 Cf. for the names of the gods, Langdon, "The Chaldean Kings before the Flood", p. 252; and Civil in Lambert and Millard, op.cit., p. 170, note 95.
32 Cf. Hallo, op.cit., p. 63. There are some differences in the recording of the two first cities. As the first city WB 62 has Ku'ara. — Hallo reads the signs HA.A.KI as Šu'ara, op.cit., p. 63. We follow the reading in D.O. Edzard, G. Farber and E. Sollberger, Repertoire géographique des textes cunéiformes I,

In both the Flood story and the antediluvian King List Eridu is regarded as the most ancient city. In a poetic text from Lagaš, according to Hallo one of the oldest known pieces of Sumerian mythology, there is a sequence about the creation of the world. In it Eridu is regarded as the first city.[33] This emphasis on Eridu as the first city of mankind in different text types may reflect Eridu as the venue of these compositions.[34] The antediluvian King List may therefore have been a part of the lore of Eridu in the second half of the third millenium. Whether there is any historical value in the information of the King List is difficult to determine. This also depends on how one regards the actual historical realities behind the Flood story. But if M.E.L. Mallowan is correct in dating the flood behind the Flood story to about 2900 B.C., the time span between this event and the first written sources is not overwhelming.[35]

3.   The Versions of the Antediluvian List: Cities and Kings

3.1   A Survey

The lists contain three basic elements: Recording of the cities, the kings, and the number of years the kings ruled. We give the opening sequence of the list in WB 444 as an example:

(In) Eridu Alulim (became) king
and reigned for 28,800 years;
Alalgar reigned 36,000 years.
2 kings
reigned its 64,800 years.

                                        (col i, lines 3-7)

Wiesbaden 1977, pp. 95f. — Both Jacobsen, op.cit., p. 70, note 5, and Finkelstein, op.cit., p. 46, note 22, think that Ku'ara in some way must represent Eridu. WB 62 continues with Larsa, a city not mentioned in the other versions. Both Jacobsen, pp. 71f, note 18, and Finkelstein, p. 46, agree in regarding this as a sort of local patriotism. In Berossos the first city is not Eridu, but Babylon. Hallo, p. 63, thinks that in the same way as Ku'ara was simply a subdivision of Eridu, it was later a subdivision of Babylon. Burstein, op.cit., p. 18, note 29, thinks that Berossos simply followed Enuma Elish, as he did in his record of the creation, in making Babylon the first city created after Marduk's victory over Tiamat, cf. Enuma Elish, Tabl. VI, lines 55-58, ANET[3], p. 68.

33 Cf. Hallo, op.cit., pp. 65f. The text is published by J. van Dijk, "Le motif cosmique dans la pensée Sumerienne", AcOr 28 1964, pp. 39-44.

34 Cf. Jacobsen, op.cit., pp. 59f.

35 M.E.L. Mallowan, "Noah's Flood Rediscovered", Iraq 26, 1964, pp. 62-82; cf. also Hallo, op.cit., pp. 61ff.

A CBS 10673	B WB 444	C WB 62	D Ni 3195
ERIDU	ERIDU 1. Alulim 2. Alalgar	KU'ARA (Eridu) 1. Alim 2. Alalgar	ERIDU
		LARSA 3. . . . 4. . . .	
BADTIBIRA	BADTIBIRA 3. Enmenluanna 4. Enmengalanna 5. Dumuzi	BADTIBIRA 5. Dumuzi 6. Enmeluanna	LARAK Enmegalanna Ensipazianna
LARAK	LARAK 6. Ensipazianna	LARAK 7. Ensipazianna	BADTIBIRA Dumuzi
SIPPAR	SIPPAR 7. Enmeduranna	SIPPAR 8. Enmeduranna	
ŠURUPPAK	ŠURUPPAK 10. Ubartutu	ŠURUPPAK 9. Šuruppak (son of Ubartutu) 10. Ziusudda (son of Šuruppak)	
Cities: 5	Cities: 5 Kings: 8	Cities: 6 Kings: 10	
Connects with the flood story	Reference to the flood Connects with king list after the flood	Reference to the flood Independent entity	Independent entity

E UCBC 9	F CT 46,5 + 12054	G Berossos	H W 20 030,7

ERIDU
1. . . .
 	
2. Alalgar
		BABYLON
		1. Aloros
		  (Alulim)
		2. Alaparos
		  (Alalgar)
		  (son of
		  Aloros)
			1. Ayalu
			  (Alulim)
			2. Alalgar

BADTIBIRA
 	
3. Ammeluanna
 	
4. Ensipasianna
5. Dumuzi
	BADTIBIRA
	
	4. Enmegalanna
	
	5. Dumuzi
		PAUTIBIBLON
		(Badtibira)
		3. Amelon
		  (Ammeluanna)
		4. Ammenon
		5. Amegalaros
		  (Ammegalanna)
		6. Daonos
		  (Dumuzi)
			3. Ammeluanna
			
			4. Ammegalanna
			5. Enmešugalanna
			
			6. Dumuzi

	SIPPAR 6. Enmeduranki	7. Euedorachos (Enmeduranki)	7. Enmeduranki
SIPPAR 6. Enmeduranki	**LARAK** 7. Ensipazianna	**LARAGCHOS** 8. Amempsinos (Enzipazianna)	
ŠURUPPAK 7. Ubartutu	**ŠURUPPAK** 8. Ubartutu	9. Otiartes (Ubartutu)	

8. (?) . . .	9. Ziusudra
	  (son of
	  Ubartutu)
		10. Xisouthros
		  (Ziusudra)
		  (son of
		  Otiartes)	

Cities: 4 Kings: 7 or 8	Cities: 5 Kings: 9	Cities: 3 Kings: 10	Kings: 7
	Connects with the flood story	Connects with the flood story	Reference to the flood Connects with king list after the flood
Independent entity			

Since we are primarily interested in the kings and cities, we need
not recount the number of years in the survey. In this connection
it is enough to emphasize that all the kings are supposed to have
reigned for enormous spans of time.

In the survey we include the list of antediluvian cities from the
Sumerican flood story, CBS 10673, referred above. We also include
W 20 030,7, although this text does not belong to the antediluvian
King List proper, but is a variation of it.

3.2   The Order of Cities and Kings

The number of cities differs:

(A), B, F: five cities
       C: six cities
       E: four cities
       G: three cities
       H: does not list cities

The number "six" in C comes from the inclusion of Larsa, which
may have reflected a sort of local patriotism (cf. note 32). The
number "four" in E may be a scribal error.[36] It seems then most
likely that the basic pattern at least up to Neo-Assyrian time was
five cities. The order of cities is according to (A), B, C, D(?), E:
Eridu, Badtibira, Larak, Sippar, Šuruppak.

The number of kings differs also:

B: eight kings
C: ten kings
E: seven or eight kings
F: nine kings
G: ten kings
H: seven kings

The number "ten" in C comes from the inclusion of Larsa with
two kings. If we exclude Larsa this tablet also has eight. Eight is
also a possible number for E. It seems likely, then, that a basic
pattern in the Old Babylonian period was eight kings. The
variation both in the numbers of cities and kings shows, however,
that the numbers by no means were regarded as absolute.

---

36 So Finkelstein, op.cit., p. 46.

The order of kings:

1. Alulim in all texts
2. Alalgar in all texts
3. Enmeluanna in B, E, G, H, F (most likely).
   C: name fragmentary, but not Enmeluanna
   D: seems to have Enmeluanna
4. Enmegalanna in B, F, H.
   C: name fragmentary
   D: seems to have Enmegalanna
   E: has Ensipazianna
5. Dumuzi in B, C, D (most likely).
   G: has Enmegalanna
   H: has Enmešugalanna
6. Ensipazianna in B.
   C: has Enmeluanna
   E, F: has Enmeduranki
   G, H: has Dumuzi
7. Enmeduranki in B, G, H.
   C, F: has Ensipazianna
   E: has Ubartutu
8. Ubartutu in B, F.
   C: has Enmeduranki
   G: has Ensipazianna
9. Šuruppak in C.
   G: has Ubartutu
   F: has Ziusudra
10. Ziusudra in C, G.

The lists show conformity only in regard of the first two kings. The reason for this is not difficult to find. The city Eridu (represented by Ku'ara in C, Babylon in G — cf. note 32) occurs first in all texts. A list showing the relations between cities and kings gives the following evidence:

ERIDU: Alulim — All
BADTIBIRA: Enmeluanna — All
Enmegalanna — B, F, G.
   D: listed under Larak
   C, E: not listed
   Dumuzi — All
LARAK: Ensipazianna — B, C, D, F, G.
   E: listed under Badtibira
SIPPAR: Enmeduranki — B, C, D, E, F.
   G: does not list Sippar
ŠURUPPAK: Ubartutu — B, E, F.
   C: Šuruppak, son of Ubartutu
   G: does not list Šuruppak
   Ziusudra — C, F.
   B: not listed
   G: does not list Šuruppak

This survey shows quite another degree of conformity. There is accordingly clear evidence to conclude that the stable factor in the list was neither the order of cities nor the order of kings, but rather the connection between cities and kings. This should indicate that the list was regarded basically as a list of city dynasties.

4.   Berossos and the Cuneiform Sources

4.1   Correspondence in the Names

Since our project is primarily an inquiry into the background of fairly late Old Testament and Jewish texts, the list of Berossos has special interest. As already stated, a cuneiform background can be found for all the names except the fourth, Ammenon (cf. note 27). If we exclude this name, a comparison of Berossos and the cuneiform texts is as follows:

Berossos	Cuneiform sources
Alulim	B, C, E, H, (most likely F)
Alalgar	B, C, E, H, (most likely F)
Enmeluanna	B, E, H, (most likely F)
(Ammenon)	
Enmegalanna	B, F, H
Dumuzi	B, C, D (probably), E, F
Enmeduranki	E, F
Ensipazianna	C, F
Ubartutu	B, F
Ziusudra	F

Since the names of the three first kings, not preserved in F, in all texts concerning the two first and generally concerning the third are "Alulim, Alalgar, Enmeluanna", it seems reasonable to restore these names in F, as well. If this is the case, it is highly significant that Berossos and F (The Neo-Assyrian text) show conformity in all the names. F is the only text which shows this conformity.

We can also mention other significant similarities:

1. F changes the order of Larak and Sippar, as the only cuneiform text represented. A similar change is presupposed in Berossos when Larak is placed before Ensipazianna and not before Enmeduranki.
2. F is the only cuneiform text represented which related directly to the flood story. The same connection also occurs in Berossos.

We can therefore conclude that Berossos presupposes a pattern similar to that represented by the Neo-Assyrian text from the library in Niniveh.

4.2 Stylistic Features

The cuneiform tablets do not have the same style.[37] Two of the texts, WB 444 and CT 46,5 + 12054, have stylistic similarities in that to some extent they use the same phraseology for changes of dynasty as the Sumerian king list. WB 62, on the other hand, omits this phraseology altogether and mentions the names of the cities only in connection with the summary number of kings representing the dynasty of each city. UCBC 9 and very likely Ni 3195, although having adopted the antediluvian tradition to the Sumerian king list format in terms of the change of dynasty formulas, omit introductory, summary, or concluding statements.

Below we give an extract from the same sequence in three of the cuneiform texts: WB 444; WB 62; CT 46,5 + 12054. We also include an extract from Berossos. A comparison between the style of the Greek text of Berossos which we only have through abridgements of Polyhistor-Eusebius,[38] and the cuneiform texts might seem hazardous. But the account of Berossos shows such accuracy in its rendering of the names that it is not likely that the style should have changed totally through the history of the text.

It is quite clear that among the cuneiform texts WB 444 and CT 46,5 + 12054 form one group over against WB 62. The basic idea expressed explicitly in the first two texts is the change of kingship from one city to another. This is lacking in WB 62 which only lists the kings and cities. The same is the case in Berossos. If we take into consideration that both UCBC 9 and Ni 3195 contain the phraseology for change of kingship, WB 62 and Berossos form a separate group. It is possible that this emphasis on the kings in Berossos and not on a successive city dynastic line caused the omission of two of the cities.[39] The late text W 20 030,7 shows that a king list could be used without mentioning the cities at all.

37 Cf. for the following, Finkelstein, op.cit., pp. 44f.
38 Cf. note 24 above. For the text, cf. note 26 above.
39 That they were omitted by the transmitter of Berossos' text, as Finkelstein supposes, seems less likely, op.cit., p. 46.

WB 444	WB 62	CT 46,5 + 12054	Berossos
In Larak Ensipazianna reigned its 28,800 years. One king reigned its 28,800 years.	Ensipazianna (ruled) 36,000 years. One king at Larak	In Sippar Enmeduranki, the king, [reigned] 50,400 + [ ] years. [One king,] the dynasty of Sippar reigned 54,600 + [ ] years.	Then Euedorachos from Pautibiblon became king and reigned for eighteen saroi.
I drop (the topic) Larak; its kingship to Sippar was carried.		[The dynasty] of Sippar changed: its kingship passed [to] Larak.	
In Sippar Enmeduranna became king and reigned 28,000 years. One king reigned its 28,000 years.	Emmeduranna (ruled) 72,000 years. One king at Sippar.	In Larak Ensipazianna, the king, reigned 37,200 + [ ] years. One king, the dynasty of Larak reigned 37,200 + [ ] years.	Then Amempsinos, a Chaldean from Laragchos, became king and reigned for ten saroi.

The basic features of Berossos' list occur accordingly also in the cuneiform texts. Berossos has the order of names and the connection with the Flood story in common with the Neo-Assyrian tablet CT 46,5 + 12054; he has the number of kings and the style in common with the oldest discovered text, WB 62.

b) Antediluvian Kings

Two of the kings from the antediluvian King List play an important role in other Mesopotamian traditions. They are the hero of the flood, Ziusudra, and the ancestor of the diviners, Enmeduranki.

1. Ziusudra and the Flood Story

1.1 Ziusudra in the King List

Ziusudra is mentioned as the last king in the oldest known text, WB 62; the Neo-Assyrian text, CT 46,5 + 12054; and in Berossos. In the two Old Babylonian texts, Ni 3195 and UCBC 9, the end is damaged, but Finkelstein considers the restoration of Ziusudra as the last king in UCBC 9 as likely.[40] Before the edition of CT 46,5 + 12054, WB 62 and Berossos were the only texts that mentioned Ziusudra. Since WB 62 showed some peculiarities, one could think that Ziusudra did not belong to the main tradition of antediluvian kings. Now it appears that WB 444 is the only text belonging to the King List proper which definitely does not mention Ziusudra.[41]

1.2 The Flood Story

Three cuneiform versions of the Flood story are known from Mesopotamia. In addition comes Berossos' version in Babyloniaca. Since our primary concern here is not the Flood story itself, we shall give only a brief outline of the versions.

I. The Sumerian Flood Story. The tablet can be dated about 1600, but the actual story is earlier: "The theme of the flood which wiped out all but a handful of the human race became popular during the Isin dynasty" (2000-1800).[42]
The sequence where Ziusudra is introduced is badly preserved. Quite clearly he is called a king, col iii, line 145; col v, line 209.

---

40 Finkelstein, "The Antediluvian Kings", p. 43.
41 Finkelstein argues that this has its reason in uncertainty about Ziusudra's royal status, op.cit., pp. 47f. Lambert argues that the Old Babylonian version of the flood story as it is known in the composition Atra-Ḫasis seems to have had a version of the antediluvian history different from that of the King Lists. The hero of the flood and the antediluvian King List may have belonged originally to different traditions that were not combined in WB 444, Lambert, Atra-Ḫasis, pp. 20f.
42 M. Civil, "The Sumerian Flood Story", in Lambert and Millard, op.cit., p. 139. For the dating, cf. Lambert and Millard, p. 4, and Civil, pp. 138f. The references below follow the edition by Civil, op.cit., pp. 138-45.

T. Jacobsen restores the sequence in col iii, lines 145-50 in the following way:

> At that time Ziusudra was king
> and lustration priest.
> He fashioned, being a seer, (a statue of)
> the god of giddiness (inducing ecstacy)
> and stood in awe beside it, wording (his
> wishes) humbly.
>
> As he stood there regularly day after day he heard
> something that was not a dream appearing: conversation
> a swearing (of) oaths by heaven and earth . . .[43]

The somewhat strange passage that Ziusudra did not have a dream, which seems to contradict both Atra-Ḥasis and Berossos (cf. below), must be understood as a scoring of the direct manner of revelation. The sequence is followed by Enki's warning about the deluge. Ziusudra's role is described as follows by Jacobsen: "The description of how Enki's warning came to his ward is interesting. It is intimately connected with the king's role as diviner, seer and prophet. This side of kingship was very important in older times; the king was, as priest-king, mediator between the people and the gods, and by discovering the gods' will and obeying it he ensured peace and prosperity."[44]

II. Atra-Ḥasis.   Most of the known tablets date from the reign of Ammiṣaduqa (1646-1626) in the Old Babylonian period.[45] These tablets, however, are only copies, and the text may have been composed a century or two earlier.[46]
Atra-Ḥasis is a fairly long composition of which the actual flood story is only a part, through an important enough one. The epic starts by telling how the weaker Igigu-gods had to do hard labour for the more powerful Anunnaku-gods (Tab I, col i). After a long period the Igigu-gods rebelled and surrounded the palace of the supreme god Enlil (Tabl I, col ii). In the assembly of the gods Enki proposed to create man so that man could suffer the toil of the gods (G rescension, col ii + Tabl I, col iv). The primeval man

---

43   T. Jacobsen, "The Eridu Genesis", p. 522.
44   Jacobsen, op.cit., p. 523.
45   Cf. Lambert and Millard, op.cit., pp. 5f., whose edition we use.
46   Cf. Lambert and Millard, op.cit., pp. 23f.

was made out of clay mixed from the flesh and blood of the leading rebel god and given his personality (Tabl I, cols iv-v).[47] This concept of creation is combined with the concept of creation by birth. The goddess Mami in the presence of Enki/Ea gives birth to man after nine months (Tabl I, col vi). According to the Assyrian recension seven pairs, male and female, were born (S recension, Obv. iii).

After a long period a new rebellion occurs. The noisy activity of the human race, which had multiplied enormously, deprived the gods of their rest (Tabl II, col i). The gods reacted against the tumult among men by sending three crises preceding the deluge as the final reaction. Each time the human race is saved by the intercession of Enki (Tabl II). In these crises Astra-hasis, "the most wise", is introduced. He is the favorite of Enki and is instructed how to escape the crises. Atra-hasis is described as the one among the human race who directly communicated with the god (Tabl I, lines 364-69). Besides this he is a visionary, "giving attention do drams" (Tabl II, col iii, lines 8.10). The introduction to the deluge seems to presuppose that he was warned through a dream (Tabl III, col i, lines 13-14).

Atra-hasis built a boat for his family and all kinds of animals and was thus saved from the flood. After it he brought a sacrifice to the gods (Tabl III, col v, lines 30-35). The epic ends by telling about the regulations that the gods imposed on human society after the flood.

III. The Flood Story in the Epic Gilgamesh.   We find the flood story on the eleventh tablet. The version was found in Ashurbanipal's library in Niniveh. The story is told by the hero himself, Utnapishtim. The composition is very similar to the flood story in Atra-Hasis. A new motif is that Utnapishtim sent out several birds to see whether the earth was dry (lines 145-154). Lambert states that there are no known copies earlier than about 750 to this sequence, but the text may well have been put in shape between 1200 and 1000.[48]

---

47   For a more detailed discussion of the sequence, cf. below pp. 291ff.
48   Cf. W.G. Lambert, "A New Look at the Babylonian Background of 'Genesis'", JThS 16, 1965, pp. 287-300, pp. 291f.

IV. The Flood Story in Berossos' Babyloniaca.[49] Berossos' account has similarities with all three cuneiform versions.[50] The name of the hero, Xisouthros, reflects the Sumerican name Ziusudra. Similar to Atra-Ḥasis is that the hero is warned through a dream. Similar to the Gilgamesh epic is the episode of the birds. What is new is that Xisouthros is located to Sippar. The Gilgamesh version states explicitly Šuruppak (line 11) which is in accordance with the tradition in the antediluvian King List. Lambert suggests that Berossos used a Sipparian version of the flood.[51] But the new location can also depend on other factors (cf. below pp. 178ff.).

1.3   The Fate of the Flood Hero

In both the Sumerian flood story, the Gilgamesh version and Berossos the further fate of the flood hero is described. This part is lost in Atra-Ḥasis.

I. In the Sumerian flood story the sequence reads as follows:

> The king Ziusudra prostrated himself before An (and) Enlil
> (Who) gave him life, like a god,
> Elevated him to eternal life, like a god.
> At that time, the king Ziusudra
> Who protected the seed of mankind at the time of destruction
> They settled him in an overseas country,
> in the orient, in Dilmun.
>
> (col vi, lines 254-60)[52]

Two things are stated about Ziusudra: He is given eternal life like the gods, and he is settled in a distant country with the name Dilmun. This country is especially known from the Sumerian poem *Enki and Ninhursag*.[53] The location of Dilmun is thought to be either on the eastern shores of the Persian Gulf or on an island in

---

49   Text: Euseb. (Arm.) Chron. 10,17-12,16 and Syncellus p. 53,19. FGH III, C, 1.B, sequences 14-17, pp. 378-81. Translation: Burstein, Book II, 2, 1-4, pp. 20f.
50   For the relationship between Berossos and the cuneiform sources, cf. Burstein, op.cit., notes to the translation. For a more detailed comparison of the versions, cf. A. Heidel, The Gilgamesh Epic and Old Testament Parallels, Chicago 1946, pp. 224-269; cf. also K. Komoróczy, "Berosos and the Mesopotamian Literature", AAH 21, 1973, pp. 125-52, pp. 133-39.
51   Lambert and Millard, Atra-Ḥasis, p. 137.
52   Translation according to Civil in Lambert and Millard, p. 145.
53   Translation in ANET[3], pp. 37-41. For a commentary cf. also S.N. Kramer, Sumerian Mythology, rev.ed., Philadelphia 1969 (paperb. ed. 1972), pp. 54-9.

it.[54] In Enki and Ninhursag the country is described in the following way:

> The land Dilmun is pure, the land Dilmun is clean;
> The land Dilmun is clean, the land Dilmun is most bright.
>
> . . .
>
> The ittidu-bird[55] utters not the cry of the ittidu-bird
> the lions kill not,
> the wolf snatches not the lamb.
> Unknown is the kid-devouring wild dog.
>
> . . .
>
> The dove droops not the head.
> The sick-eyed says not "I am sick-eyed".
> The sick-headed (says) not "I am sick-headed".
> Its old woman (says) not "I am an old woman".
> Its old man (says) not "I am an old man".
>
> (lines 5-6, 14-17, 21-25)[56]

Dilmun seems to be a land without death, violence and illness. The similarity to the concept of "Paradise" or "Utopia" in other cultures is striking. This was to be the new dwelling for Ziusudra.

II. In the Epic of Gilgamesh, Tabl XI, the sequence reads as follows:

> "Hitherto Utnapishtim has been but to human,
> Henceforth Utnapishtim and his wife shall be
> like unto us gods.
> Utnapishtim shall reside far away, at the mouth
> of the rivers!"
> Thus they took me and made me reside far away,
> at the mouth of the rivers.
>
> (Tabl XI, lines 193-96)[57]

"The mouth of the rivers" is the general area where the Tigris and the Euphrates flowed into the Persian Gulf through separate mouths. But this is scarcely the meaning here if we read the story in the light of the whole epic. When Gilgamesh is travelling to meet Utnapishtim he is clearly thought to travel through a mountainous area to the end of the world.

---

54 For discussion cf. references in D.O. Edzard and G. Farber, Répertoire géographique des textes cunéiformes 2, Wiesbaden 1974, pp. 192f.
55 Probably a bird whose cry is a mark of death and desolation, ANET[3], p. 38, note 17.
56 Translation according to ANET[3], p. 38.
57 Translation according to ANET[3], p. 95. The transliteration of the last line, 196, is as follows: ilqûnnima ina rûgi ina pî nârâti uštešibūnni. Cf. R.C. Thompson, The Epic of Gilgamish, Oxford 1930, p. 64.

The beginning of the story has perhaps another version of
Utnapishtim's dwelling place. Here Gilgamesh asks: "How did you
join the Assembly of the gods, in your quest for life?" (line 7).
But the sentence can also be meant to express the more general
idea that Utnapishtim has become like the gods. Berossos, however,
seems to have taken this tradition more literally.

III. The sequence in Berossos reads as follows:

After performing obeisance to the earth
and setting up an altar and sacrificing to the gods,
he and those who had disembarked with him disappeared.
When Xisouthros and the others did not come back in,
those remaining in the boat disembarked
and searched for him calling out his name.
Xisouthros was no longer visible to them,
but a voice from the sky ordered them to be reverent.
Because of his piety, he had gone to live with the gods;
and his wife and the pilot were to share the same honour.[58]

That Xisouthros "had gone to live with the gods" may imply that
he was taken up to heaven. There is accordingly a conformity
between the versions of the translation of the flood hero, expressed through the verb "reside", but possibly a slight difference
in the location of the hero's dwelling place.

1.4   The Antediluvian Books in Sippar

In the introduction to the flood story in Berossos' Babyloniaca
Xisouthros is ordered to bury "the beginnings and middles and
ends of all writings in Sippar the city of the sun", Greek:
κελεῦσαι οὖν <διὰ> γραμμάτων πάντων ἀρχὰς καὶ μέσα
καὶ τελευτὰς ὀρύξαντα θεῖναι ἐν πόλει Ἡλίου
Ζισπάροις.[59] After the flood the surviving men were ordered to
go to Sippar and dig up the writings and distribute them to
mankind.

---

58   Text according to Syncellus p. 53,19. FGH III, C. 1.B, sequence 15, p. 380.
Translation: Burstein, Book II, 2,2, p. 20.
59   Text according to Syncellus p. 53,19. FGH III, C, 1.B, sequence 14, pp.
378f. Translation: Burstein, Book II, 2,1, p. 20.

It is quite clear what books Berossos refers to. In the first section of Babyloniaca he recounts how the first sage Oannes taught mankind all the basic cultural benefits. Oannes also wrote books: τὸν δὲ 'Ωαννην περὶ γενεᾶς καὶ πολιτείας γράψαι, καὶ παραδοῦναί τόνδε τὸν λόγον τοῖς ανϑρώποις, "Oannes wrote about birth and government and gave the following account to men."[60] "The following account" clearly refers to Berossos' recension of Enuma Elish which follows in the context. The teaching of Oannes was later "explained in detail" by other antediluvian sages.[61] The antediluvian books accordingly contained primarily the teaching of the primary sage Oannes, but possibly also additions from later sages.

We have no cuneiform version of the whole tradition recorded by Berossos, but the elements put together in his account are known.[62] Already the Greek phraseology reveals Akkadian influence. A close parallel to the first quotation above is to be found in two prayers to Marduk and Nabu from the first millennium: "The beginning of the inscription and the end of the inscription shall be recited twice."[63] "The beginning and end of the inscription" mean "the whole inscription", just as "the beginnings and middles and ends of all writings" mean "the writings in their entirety" in Berossos.

Three elements of Berossos' account are known from cuneiform sources: 1) the conception of antediluvian writings; 2) the prominent place of Sippar, the city of the sun-god; 3) the digging up of ancient writings.

1) We shall later return to this issue in detail.[64] Here it is sufficient to emphasize that there existed a tradition in the Babylonian scribal milieu where literary compositions were dated back to the antediluvian sages, above all to the primary sage U-An or Adapa, the cuneiform equivalent to Oannes.

---

60   Text according to Syncellus p. 49,19. FGH III, C, 1.B, sequence 5, p. 370. Translation: Burstein, Book I, 1,5, p. 14.
61   Text: Syncellus p. 71,3. FGH III, C, 1.B, sequence 12, p. 376. Translation: Burstein, Book II, 1,8, p. 19.
62   The issue is discussed in G. Komoróczy, "Berosos and the Mesopotamian Literature", pp. 137ff.
63   Khorsabad 1932, 26. Obv. lines 12-13; Rev. lines 11-12. Cf. W.G. Lambert, "Literary Style in First Millennium Mesopotamia", JAOS 88, 1968, pp. 123-32, pp. 130ff.
64   Cf. below, pp. 209-13.

2)   The prominent place of Sippar is clearly reflected in the Poem
of Erra, Tabl IV, line 50 (to the poem cf. below). Here and in
other sources the city is called *al ṣâti*, "eternal" or "primeval
city".[65] The city was also related to the king Enmeduranki in the
antediluvian King List who was famous for his insight in divine
wisdom.[66] In the Poem of Erra (reference above) Sippar is said to
be the only city not destroyed in the flood. Both these features,
Sippar as the seat of antediluvian wisdom and as the city that
survived the flood, must be part of the background of Berossos'
account.

3)   The interest in monuments of the past increased toward the
end of the Neo-Assyrian period and in the time of the Neo-
Babylonian empire.[67] The rediscovery of ancient monuments was
often related to foundation of new temples. When digging up the
ground of old temples, ancient foundation deposits were found.
The deposits were of different kind, but often inscribed tablets of
clay, stone or metal had been placed in the foundation or lower
parts of the temple — below the floor level.[68] The most massive
deposits discovered in modern excavations are two stone blocks
from Tukilti Ninurta I's twin shrines of Ištar Aššurītu and of
Dinītu in Assur. They measure 2.68 · 1.25 · 0.40 m and
1.70 · 1.40 · 0.30 m.[69]

Most of the reports about rediscoveries of deposits from ancient
times we have from the Neo-Babylonian king Nabonidus.[70] A
series of these are connnected with Sippar, where Nabonidus
discovered the ancient foundation of Naram Sin when he rebuilt
the temple of Ebabbara. The deposit contained an ancient inscription from the former builder together with a statue of Naram Sin's
father, Sargon.[71]

---

65   Cf. Hallo, "Antediluvian Cities", p. 65.
66   Cf. below, p. 190.
67   For a survey, cf. G. Gossens, "Les recherches historiques à l'époque néo-
babylonienne", RA 42, 1948, pp. 149-59.
68   Cf. R.S. Ellis, Foundation Deposits in Ancient Mesopotamia, New Haven-
London 1968, pp. 94-107.
69   Cf. Ellis, op.cit., pp. 98f.; and W. Andrae, Das wiederstandene Assur,
Leipzig 1938 (repr. München 1977), pp. 160f.
70   The reports are collected in Ellis, op.cit., pp. 181-4.
71   Cf. W.G. Lambert, "A New Source for the Reign of Nabonidus", AfO 22,
1968-69, pp. 1-8. Obv. III, lines 21-36, pp. 5,7.

We do not know whether Berossos was the first to bring these elements together into a story about the antediluvian books which were hidden before the flood, dug up again and thus known in his own time. We do know that the elements are attested to in cuneiform literature. Since Berossos' aim was to reproduce Mesopotamian traditions for Greek readers, it is most likely that he used an already existing tradition.

1.5   The Poem of Erra

The Flood story has a curious echo in the Poem of Erra.[72] The literary genre of this composition is not easy to decide. The editor of the poem, L. Cagni, discussed the problem in relation to two genres: "epic" and "myth". Among other aspects the most characteristic feature of the epic genre is the indispensable element of a human or, in some cases, a semi-divine hero. Among other aspects the most characteristic feature of myth is that it deals with gods as protagonists of events of origin.[73] As an example for the first genre one can mention the Epic of Gilgamesh, as an example for the second Enuma Elish.

The Poem of Erra does not fit these characteristics. Its protagonists are gods and not humans, and it does not deal with events of origin. L. Cagni characterizes the poem in the following way: It "can only be a literary, and still more, a religious way of interpreting history." It is "to be located, consequently, in the current of religious didactic and sapiential poetry."[74] Further: "I would hold that one might hazard presenting the Poem of Erra as a sort of vast allegory not much different from what is read at least in the first part of the Biblical book of Job."[75]

The poem cannot be an allegory in the way that it only retells real events in symbolical language. The generating process has been much more complex. The main theme of the poem is the catastrophe that comes over Babylon when Marduk leaves his royal

---

72   Text edition: L. Cagni, L'epopea di Erra, SS 34, Roma 1969. Translation and commentary: L. Cagni, The Poem of Erra, SANE 1/3, Malibu, California 1974. We use this translation when not otherwise stated.
73   Cagni, The Poem of Erra, pp. 6-13.
74   Cagni, op.cit., p. 13.
75   Cagni, op.cit., p. 14.

seat and power is transferred to the god Erra. This is seen as a
repetition of what happened in primeval time when Marduk
resigned from power and let the flood strike mankind. There are
accordingly two poles in the narrative. One is the primeval
catastrophe which once came upon mankind. The other is the
actual historical circumstances which underlie the composing of
the poem. The narrative mediates between these two poles in the
way that the actual historical circumstances are interpreted in the
light of the ancient mythical story of the primeval catastrophe.

That historical circumstances are reflected in stories about the gods
is not extraordinary in Akkadian narratives. A characteristic of
Akkadian myths is that they reflect history in the meaning of
socio-political development and foundation of institutions, while
Sumerican myths were more concerned with the tension between
nature and culture.[76] What distinguishes the Poem of Erra from
other Akkadian mythical compositions is that the mythical material
is consciously linked to specific historical circumstances and that
the composition is consciously formed to reflect these circumstances. Although the nature of these historical circumstances is
obscure, the poem clearly reflects a severe political and military
crisis that struck Babylonia in the first half of the first millennium
B.C.[77]

What happened in primeval time was that Marduk left his royal
power and caused the deluge, here understood as a broader cosmic
catastrophe.

> "I got angry long ago: I rose from my seat
> and contrived the deluge.
> I rose from my seat, and the government
> of heaven and earth dissolved.
> And the sky, lo! it shook:
> the stations of the stars in the sky were altered,
> and I did not bring (them) back to their (former) positions,
> The lower world, lo! it quaked:
> the yield of the furrow became scanty:
> Forever difficult to levy taxes (on it)!
> Lo! the government of heaven and earth dissolved:
> springs became few, the overflow receded."
>
>   (Tabl I, lines 132-36)

---

76 Cf. G.S. Kirk, Myth. Its Meaning and Functions in Ancient and other Cultures, Cambridge 1970 (paperb. ed. 1973), pp. 118-31. A good illustration is
given by J. Jacobsen in his interpretation of Enuma Elish, cf. T. Jacobsen, The
Treasures of Darkness. A History of Mesopotamian Religion, New Haven-
London 1976, pp. 167-91.
77 For a discussion of the date, cf. Cagni, op.cit., pp. 20f.

In this catastrophe Marduk dispatched the primeval sages down to
the Apsu (the fresh water)(Tabl I, line 146), which meant that
there was nobody to take care of his royal insignia, and which
again made it impossible to establish the correct cosmic order.[78]
If Marduk again leaves his royal seat, the same catastrophe will
strike the people of Babylonia:

> "I shall rise [from] my seat and the government
> [of heaven and earth] will be dissolved.
> [The waters] will swell and [devasta]te the country.
> The shining [day will turn] into deep darkness.
> [the st]orm will rise and [blot out?] the stars in the sk[y]
> The malign [wind] will blow and [obscure?]
> the eyesight of men, the offspring of the living.
> The gallû-(demons) will come up and . . . will grasp
> The bare-lioned man who confronts them . . .
> The Anunnaki will come up and strike
> down the offspring of the living.
>
> (Tabl I, lines 170-78)

As seen also in the previous quotation, the catastrophe is understood not only as a deluge, but as a larger cosmic catastrophe. This
catastrophe implies that the celestial and natural laws will come
out of order and the demonic powers will attack men. When Erra
reveals his plans for the new regime we see that also the social and
human laws will turn into chaos:

> "I shall cut off [the life] of
> the righteous man who acts as intercessor.
> The evil man, who cuts throats,
> him I shall put in the highest(?) places(?).
> I shall change men's hearts
> that father will not listen to son
> And daughters will talk to mother with hatred.
> I shall cause them to speak ill
> and they will forget their god
> (And) speak gross blasphemy to their goddess."
>
> (Tabl III, fragm. A, lines 9-13)

Erra's rule thus led to the destruction of Babylon and other of the
great cities of Babylonia. But Ishum, Erra's counsellor, intervenes
and changes Erra's mind. (The role as saviour is to some extent
similar to the role of Enki/Ea in the flood story.) The cosmic and
socio-political order is reestablished:

---

78   Cf. for a further discussion of this issue, below, pp. 199f.

"May the governors of all the cities
draw their massive tribute into Šuanna.
May the ruined temples raise their heads
as (high as) the flaming sun.
May the Tigris and Euphrates
carry the waters of abundance.
As to the provisioner of the Esagila and of Babylon,
may the governors of all the cities effect
(all due) delivering to him."

(Table V, lines 35-38)

The poem ends with an epilogue by the author in which he reveals
his name and the circumstances under which the poem came into
being. The story was revealed to the scribe during the night in a
vision (to some extent a parallel to the flood hero in Atra-Ḫasis
and Berossos who also foresaw the catastrophe in a dream), and in
the morning when he recited it he did not skip a single line, nor a
single line of his own did he add to it (Tabl V, lines 42-44).[79]

2.   Enmeduranki and the Origin of Divination

2.1   Enmeduranki in the King List

Enmeduranki is mentioned in all the antediluvian King Lists,
except the fragmentary Ni 3195. His placement in the list varies:
WB 62: No. 8; UCBC 9 and CT 46,5 + 12054: No. 6; WB 444,
Berossos and W 20 030,7: No. 7. The placement depends on the
order of the cities. In all the antediluvian King Lists proper
Enmeduranki is associated with Sippar (except Berossos who does
not list this city). Like numerous other cuneiform texts, the
introduction of the Sumerian flood story makes Sippar the city of
the sun-god Utu.

---

79   For a further discussion of this sequence, cf. below, pp. 211f.

2.2   The Ancestor of the Diviners

2.2.1   The Text

The traditions about Enmeduranki are known especially from a tablet found in Nineveh. Our translation of and comments of the text are based on W.G. Lambert's edition from 1967.[80] The text combines elements of three categories: legend, ritual, and explanation of ritual.

The translation below is taken from Lambert but formed according to the structure of the text:

	A		B
1	Šamaš in Ebabbara [appointed] Enmeduranki		
2	king of Sippar, the beloved		
3	of Anu, Enlil [and Ea]		
		10	Then he, in accordance with their word(?)
4	Šamaš and Adad (brought him] into their assembly.	11	brought 11 men of Nippur, Sippar and Babylon into his presence
5	Šamaš and Adad [honoured him].	12	and he honoured them. He set them on thrones before [him].
6	Šamaš and Adad [set him] on a large throne of gold.		
7	They showed him how to observe oil on water, a mystery of Anu, [Enlil and Ea].	13	He showed them how to observe oil on water, a mystery of Anu, Enlil and Ea.
8	They gave him the tablet of the gods, the liver, a secret of heaven and [underworld].	14	He gave them the tablet of the gods, the liver, a secret of heaven and underworld.
9	They put in his hand the cedar (-rod), beloved of the great gods.	15	He put in their hand the cedar (-rod), beloved of the great gods.

C

16 The tablet of the gods, the liver,
      a mystery of heaven and underworld;
17 how to observe oil on water,
      a secret of Anu, Enlil and Ea;
18 "that with commentary", When Anu, Enlil;
      and how to make mathematical calculations.

80   W.G. Lambert, "Enmeduranki and Related Matters", JCS 21, 1967, pp. 126-38.

D

19 The learned savant, who guards the secrets
     of the great gods,
20 will bind his son whom he loves with an oath
21 before Šamaš and Adad by tablet and stylus
22 and will instruct him.
23 When a diviner, an expert in oil,
     of abiding descent, offspring of Enmeduranki,
     king of Sippar,
24 who set up the pure bowl and
     held the cedar(-rod),
25 a benediction priest of the king,
     a long-haired priest of Šamaš
26 as fashioned by Ninhursagga,
27 begotten by a <u>nišakku</u>-priest of pure descent:
28 if he is without blemish in body and limbs
29 he may approach the presence of Šamaš and Adad
     where liver inspection and oracle (take place).

2.2.2   The Structure

Sections A and B are deliberately parallel, as shown above. The structure underlines the scope of the sections: In the same way as the gods instructed Enmeduranki in the heavenly assembly, Enmeduranki instructed the men from the three cities Nippur, Sippar and Babylon. The intention is accordingly to emphasize: 1) the authority of the knowledge, which goes back to the time before the flood when Enmeduranki received it from the gods in the heavenly assembly, and 2) the importance of Nippur, Sippar and Babylon, the first seats of the divine secrets.

Section C deviates from the style of the previous text. It is a commentary and seems to have been inserted later in the text. To the two techniques of divination "observing oil on water" (lecona- mocy) and "observing liver" (hepatoscopy) is added a third, astrology (cf. below).

Section D introduces yet another element. In section A and B the scope was the authority of the divination traditions of three an- cient cities. In section D the scope is the transmission of the tra- ditions through physical descendants. In lines 19-22 Enmeduranki instructs his son in the divine secrets. In lines 23-29 the line is drawn up to the priesthood in the time of the author. The priests are physical descendants of the primeval king Enmeduranki.

As a whole the tablet can be characterized as an etiological myth about the origin of divination. Sections A and B constitute a unity where divination is linked to three ancient cities. Section C is a commentary on this unity. In section D the priesthood traces its ancestry and the legitimacy of their traditions back to Enmeduranki.

2.2.3 Commentary

The text emphasized Sippar in two ways. First Enmeduranki is the king of Sippar. Secondly, he is appointed by Šamaš (the sungod), who is affiliated with the temple Ebabbara in Sippar.[81]

Enmeduranki was brought to the assembly of the gods. The verb, pret. of the causative Š-stem of *erēbu, šurubu,* is a certain restoration here, since the verb is used in this form in the parallel B section. The gods were located in different places in Mesopotamian mythology, but the general idea seems to be that the assembly of the gods took place in heaven.[82]

Enmeduranki is seated on a golden throne among the gods,[83] which must mean that he was included in their assembly. There he was instructed in the two techniques of divination: observing oil on water and observation of liver.[84]

In the text the phrase "the tablet of the gods, the liver" is not quite clear. The Akkadian word *tuppi* is most likely singular, but a plural *tuppī* is also possible.[85] As a plural "tablets of the gods" it can refer to tablets of liver omens. As a singular it must refer to an inscribed liver model.[86]

---

81 For the temple, cf. E. Ebeling, "Ebabbara", E. Ebeling and B. Meissner (eds.), RLA II, Berlin-Leipzig 1938, p. 263.

82 For puhru, "assembly of the gods", cf. Gilg., Tabl XI, line 119; Atra-Ḫasis, Tabl I, lines 122.218.224; Tabl II, col vi, lines 16.18; Tabl III, col iii, line 36.

83 Cf. Descent of Ishtar, Rev., line 33, ANET[3], p. 108, where the Anunnaki-gods are seated on golden thrones.

84 Cf. for these techniques, A.L. Oppenheim, Ancient Mesopotamia, pp. 206-27. Oppenheim describes two types of divination techniques, i.e. techniques of predicting the future. In the first, operational divination, the diviner offers the deity the opportunity of directly affecting an object activated by the diviner. Pouring oil on water belongs to this type. In the second, magical divination, the deity produces changes in natural phenomena. Observation of liver belongs to this type (p. 208). The diviner addresses the oracle gods Šamaš and Adad, requesting them to write their message upon the entrails of the sacrificial animal (p. 212).

85 Cf. Lambert, op.cit., p. 133.

86 Numerous such models are found, cf. Oppenheim, op.cit., p. 213. An example is pictured in H.W.S. Saggs, The Greatness that was Babylon, London 1962, plate 27[B].

Lambert translates *šamê^e u erṣetim*tim as "heaven and underworld". We prefer "heaven and earth" as CAD records the phrase
(cf. the reference to CAD in notes 88 and 94). Used in this context
the phrase has the cosmological meaning of "the whole world".[87]
The tablet emphasizes the esoteric character of the divine wisdom
revealed to Enmeduranki. To the phrase "how to observe oil on
water" is added: *niṣirti* ^{d}*anim* ^{d}*enlil u* ^{d}*ea*, "a mystery of Anu,
Enlil and Ea", line 7 (repeated in line 13). To "the tablet(s) of the
gods" is added: *pirišti šamê^e u erṣetim*tim, "a secret of heaven
and earth", line 8 (repeated in line 14). Both clauses are repeated
in the lines 16-17, but there *niṣirtu* and *pirištu* have changed
places. *niṣirtu* means literally "that which is protected"; *pirištu*
"that which is separated". Used together the words can best be
translated as "mystery" and "secret".[88]
The divinatory technique was shown, *ušabrû*, "they showed" (line
7), to Enmeduranki. The *tuppi ilāni*meš, "tablet(s) of the gods",
were transmitted, *iddinū*, "they gave" (line 8). The same process is
repeated when Enmeduranki returns to Sippar from heaven. He
"shows" the men of Nippur, Sippar and Babylon the divinatory
technique, and he "transmits" the tablet(s) (lines 13-14). The same
process is also repeated down through history. Enmeduranki,
described as *ummânu mūdû*, "learned scholar" and *nāṣir pirišti
ilāni*meš *rabûti*meš, "the guardian of the secrets of the great
gods", will instruct this son in the divine secrets. The process of
transmission will continue in the line of priestly descendants from
Enmeduranki until the priesthood at the time of the author
(section D, lines 19-29).

The classification of parts of the cuneiform literature as a secret confined to
dedicated scholars and priests, is not unique to our tablet. R. Borger has collected
tablets containing secret knowledge and given a survey of their contents.[89]
Secret knowledge included, in other texts, the lists of names of the gods, the lists
of statues of the gods and liturgical requisites, the ritual books, omen-collections,
incantation. Among the astronomical texts from the Seleucid period published by
O. Neugebauer, some are classified as secret revelations of the Gods.[90]
The classification as secret occurs in the colophons of the texts. They can be
classified as ikkibu "tabu" of the great gods, or as niṣirtu and pirištu, "mystery"
and "secret" of "heaven and earth" or of "the great gods" as in our text. The

87   For other examples, cf. CAD, sub erṣetu, p. 309.
88   Cf. CAD, sub niṣirtu, i.e. 2', p. 277.
89   R. Borger, "Geheimwissen", E. Weidner and W. von Soden (eds.), RLA III,
Berlin 1964, pp. 188-91.
90   No. 135 (U) and No. 180 (S) according to O. Neugebauer, Astronomical
Cuneiform Texts I, London 1955, p. 12.

secret knowledge is ascribed to apkallu's, "experts", and to different kinds of divinatory priests, also as in our text.[91] In colophons from the library in Nineveh, the Neo-Assyrian king Ashurbanipal boasts of knowing the "nisirti of the wise apkallu's". In an inscription he says that he has learnt "the art of the wise Adapa, the hidden nisirtu, the art of writing tablets",[92] (for Adapa as the primary antediluvian sage, cf. below).

There has been a growing tendency to use colophons demanding secrecy. In the second millennium such colophons occur sporadically. In the first millennium the tendency developed into what can be called a concept of "secret science", especially in the second half of this period, from Neo-Babylonian times onwards.[93] But it is difficult to find a clear pattern why some texts were classified as secrets whose public character had not been limited earlier. There was apparently a growing awareness among the priests and scribes about the esoteric character of their knowledge.

In section C a further type of divination is added. The first line is difficult to interpret,[94] but the series *Enuma (when) Anu, Enlil* is well known. The three words are the first words in the "canonical" series of astrological omen texts, excavated mainly in Nineveh. The series consisted of at least 70 tablets. The moon is dealt with in twentythree tablets, then the sun, meteorological phenomena, the planets and the fixed stars.[95] The astrology is closely related to the mathematics mentioned at the end of the line. The Akkadian word *arû* is a mathematical table containing computations often connected to astronomical calculations.[96]

2.3   The Ancestor of Nebuchadnezzar I

In 1967 Lambert gave a new edition of a historiographic text.[97] It was composed in poetic phraseology and written as an adoration of Marduk, who saved his people from their enemies. Unfortunately the text had lacunas in crucial places. The names of two kings, for instance, where the first claimed that he was descendant of the

---

91   Cf. Borger, op.cit., p. 189.
92   The first example is from the colophon classified by Streck as O, line 13; the second is from the inscription classified by Streck as L⁴, col i, line 13. Cf. M. Streck, Assurbanipal II, Leipzig 1916, pp. 367 and 255.
93   Cf. G. Komoróczy, "Berosos and the Mesopotamian Literature", pp. 128f.
94   "That with commentary" refers possibly to a commentary to the series Enuma Anu Enlil, cf. Lambert, op.cit., p. 133. CAD sub abālu, 10, p. 27 and sub sâtu, 2, p. 119, offers other possible readings.
95   Cf. Oppenheim, op.cit., p. 225.
96   Cf. CAD, sub arû, A 2, p. 312.
97   W.G. Lambert, op.cit., pp. 126-31.

other, were lacking (lines 7-10). On the basis of a historical analysis of the text, Lambert suggested that the first king was Nebuchadnezzar I and the second Enmeduranki.

This assumption was confirmed in 1971 when R. Borger together with Lambert identified a new piece of the text.[98] A New edition was published by Lambert in 1974.[99]

The sequence which involves Enmeduranki reads as follows:

> Nebuchadnezzar, king of Babylon who supervises
> all the cult-centres and confirms the regular
> offerings, I am.
> Distant scion of kingship, seed
> preserved from before the flood.
> Offspring of Enmeduranki, king of Sippar,
> who set up the pure bowl and held the cedar-wood(rod),
> Who sat in the presence of Šamaš and Adad,
> the divine adjudicators.[100]

The text is important for the antediluvian traditions in several ways. First, the text can be dated to the reign of Nebuchadnezzar I (1125-1104). This means that the previous text "Enmeduranki and the diviners", or at least traditions similar to the basic parts of this text, can be dated earlier than 1100.

Secondly, these traditions must have been well-known and accepted. If not, there would have been no reason for Nebuchadnezzar to derive his authority from them.

Through this text Enmeduranki becomes not only the ancestor of the diviners, but also of one of the most important Babylonian kings, Nebuchadnezzar I. And Sippar, the city of the sun-god, receives quite a significant place in Mesopotamian traditions, which corresponds very well to the other traditions we have examined about Sippar as the seat of antediluvian wisdom.

---

98   Cf. R. Borger, "Die Beschwörungsserie Bīt Mēseri und die Himmelfahrt Henochs", JNES 33, 1974, pp. 183-96, pp. 184f. The new piece has the number K.6088.
99   W.G. Lambert, "The Seed of Kingship", XIXᵉ Recontre Assyriologique International, Paris 1974, pp. 427-40.
100   According to Lambert, op.cit., notes 74 and 76.

c) Primeval Sages

Research about the primeval sages yielded less results than about the antediluvian kings. Apart from the material in Berossos, only scattered references to the sages were found in the cuneiform sources. But this has changed in the last twenty years owing to the discovery of cuneiform texts containing lists of sages similar to the material in Berossos.

1. The Lists of Primeval Sages

1.1 The Cuneiform Texts

The full knowledge of such a list in cuneiform literature came in 1961 when E. Reiner published a text that she called "the Etiological Myth of the 'Seven Sages'".[101] The text was edited on the basis of tablets found in Assur and Nineveh. Reiner suggested that the text was a part of the incantation series *Bīt Mëseri*.[102] It contained four names of primeval apkallu's, "sages, experts". These four sages, however, seemed to be related to a larger group of seven, whose names were not preserved in the fragmentary text. A year later van Dijk published W 20 030,7, which contained a parallel list of sages and kings.[103] Seven sages were listed before the flood. Then follows a list of one postdiluvian apkallu and nine ummânu's, "scholars".

In 1974 R. Borger published a new translation of the fragmentary Apkallu List edited by Reiner.[104] Borger included numerous new pieces and came to the conclusion that the etiological myth was in fact a part of the series Bīt Mëseri, as Reiner had suggested. The text belongs to the third tablet of this series. It contains three incantations, each of which includes a list of apkallu's. Only the first list, however, is preserved; the two others are fragmentary.

---

101 E. Reiner, "The Etiological Myth of the 'Seven Sages'", Orientalia NS 30, 1961, pp. 1-11.
102 Cf. for this series, G. Maier, "Die zweite Tafel der Serie bīt mëseri", AfO 13, 1939-41, pp. 139-52.
103 Published in H.J. Lenzen, XVIII vorlaufiger Bericht . . . Uruk-Warka, pp. 43-52.
104 R. Borger, "Bīt Mëseri und die Himmelfahrt Henochs", pp. 183-96.

The translation by Borger gives quite a new understanding of the text. The list contains two groups of apkallu's: first a list of seven apkallu's born in the sea, then a list of four apkallu's of human descent.[105]

1.2   Berossos

Berossos tells about sages twice. He starts his *Babyloniaca* with the story about Oannes who ascended from the sea to teach men all wisdom.[106] He takes up the theme again in the antediluvian King List where he in the same manner as W 20 030,7 gives parallel lists of kings and apkallu's.

There are some difficulties involved in the text history of Berossos' Apkallu List. Eusebius, who is our source for Berossos here, quotes two sources, one directly from Polyhistor and the other from Abydenos, who again depends on Polyhistor.[107] When Eusebius quotes Polyhistor directly he gives a list of seven sages where three are named and four unnamed. When Eusebius quotes Abydenos, he gives also the names of the four apkallu's.[108] We follow below the list according to Polyhistor — Eusebius, and include the names from Polyhistor — Abydenos — Eusebius.

---

105   W.G. Lambert wrote with reference to this text: "An exorcistic text offers a quite different group of seven sages. Only four of these are named, but not one of them occur in the other lists," Atra-Ḥasis, p. 19. As we now know, the four sages in the list edited by Reiner are not a part of the list of seven sages, but belong to a separate group.

106   Text: Euseb. (Arm.) Chron. p. 6, 8-9, 2 and Syncellus p. 49, 19. FGH III, C, 1.B, sequences 4-5, pp. 369f. Translation: Burstein, Book I, 1,5, pp. 13f.

107   Cf. for the text history, Schnabel, Berossos, pp. 134-68. About Abydenos, pp. 164ff. Cf. also note 24 above, p. 162.

108   Text for Polyhistor — Eusebius: Euseb. (Arm.) Chron. p. 4, 8-6, 8; (9,2ff) and Syncellus p. 71,3. FGH III, C, 1.B, sequence 11, p. 376. Text for Polyhistor — Abydenos — Eusebius: Euseb. (Arm.) Chron. p. 15, 24-16, 8 and Syncellus p. 68, 21-70. FGH III, C, 1.B, sequence 2, p. 400. Translation: Burstein, Book II, 1, 6, p. 19.

1.3   The Antediluvian Sages

Bīt Mēseri	W 20 030,7	Berossos
1. U-Anna	U-An	Oannes
2. U-Anne-dugga	U-An-dugga	Annedotos
3. Enmedugga	Enmedugga	Euedokos
4. Enmegalamma	Enmebulugga	Eneuboulos
5. Enmebulugga	Enmebulugga	Eneuboulos
6. An-Enlilda	An-Enlilda	Anementos
7. Utuabzu	Utuabzu	Odakon

Taking into consideration the change of the names from Sumerian into Greek, we must conclude that the lists conform both in names and in the order of the names.[109]

1.4   The Postdiluvian Sages and Scholars

According to Josephus, Jewish Antiquities I, 158 (also quoted by Eusebius, Praep Ev 9.16.2,[110] Berossos tells about one great wise man after the flood: μετὰ τὸν κατακλυσμὸν δεκάτηι γενεᾶι παρα Χαλδαίοις τις ἦν δικαιος ἀνὴρ καὶ μέγας καὶ τὰ οὐράνια ἔμπειρος. "In the tenth generation after the flood

---

109 Tentatively we give a paraphrastic translation of the Sumerian values of the names: U-An — "light of the god heaven"; U-An-dugga — "light of the god heaven, the good one"; En-me-dugga — "lord of the good me" (for me, cf. p. 201); En-me-galamma — "lord of the me of the land"; En-me-bùlug-gá causes problems. The ending bulùg-gá is not clear. Van Dijk, in Lenzen, op.cit. p. 48, refers šurbûtu as an Akkadian equivalence, which means "enormous greatness" (cf. also AHW, sub šurbûtu, p. 1283). H. Limet, L'anthroponymie sumérienne, Paris 1968, p. 222, lists tarbû as the Akkadian equivalence to bulùg, which means "descendant" (cf. also AHW sub tarbû p. 1328). In the first case En-me-bulùg-gá is to be translated "lord of the me of enormous greatness". In the second case it is to be translated "lord of the me, the descendant". An-Enlilda is a combination of two divine names: An (heaven) and Enlil. Utu-abzu — "born in the Apsû (the fresh water)".
The names of the following four apkallu's in Bīt Mēseri: Nun-gal-pirig-gal-dim — "great prince, great lion"; Pirig-gal-nun-gal (a pun of the first name?) — "great lion, great prince"; Pirig-gal-abzu — "great lion of the Apsû"; Lu-Nanna — "man of the moon(god)".
In the names of the kings in W 20 030,7 I have not seen any attempts to explain Alalgar. The other names can tentatively be given the following paraphrastic translation according to the original forms of the names: Alulim — "deer"; En-me-lu-an-na — "lord of the me, man of heaven"; En-me-gal-an-na — "lord of the great me, of heaven"; En-me-ušumgal-an-na — "lord of the me, the dragon of heaven"; Dumuzi sipa — "Dumuzi (a god), the shepherd"; En-me-dur-an-na — "lord of the me, band of heaven" — Cf. the list given in D.O. Edzard, "Enmebaragesi von Kiš", ZA NF 19 (53), 1959, pp. 9-26, p. 18.
110   Cf. FGH III, C, 1.B, p. 385.

among the Chaldeans there was a man who was just, great and
knowledgeable about heavenly phenomena." Josephus equals this
man with the Biblical Abraham. The question is whether there is
any support for the passage in cuneiform literature. If this is the
case, it would prove both that Josephus quoted Berossos correctly
and that Berossos also here transmits traditions and not invents
stories.

Both Bīt Mēseri and W 20 030,7 recount sages after the first group
of seven. Bīt Mēseri gives a list of four: Nungalpiriggaldim,
Piriggalnungal, Piriggalabzu, and Lu–Nanna. W 20 030,7 makes the
flood the limit for the first seven apkallu's and recounts one
apkallu after the flood, whose name is the same as the first in the
group of four recounted in Bīt Mēseri. The similarity to Jose-
phus/Berossos is both that the flood is the limit and that one wise
man is recounted after the flood. The wise man in Josephus/-
Berossos could accordingly be Nungalpiriggaldim.

But there are arguments that contradict this identification.
Josephus/Berossos tells that the great wise man appeared in the
tenth generation after the flood, an assertion which has no support
in the cuneiform Apkallu Lists. There is, however, the possibility
that this information comes from Josephus himself in order to
make the identification with Abraham more exact. But this is not
the only obstacle. If Berossos had one apkallu after the flood, why
is he not recorded as a part of his Apkallu List as in the cuneiform
sources? The great wise man in Josephus/Berossos is also described
differently from the apkallu's. Both in Bīt Mēseri and in Berossos
the apkallu's are placed into a mythological framework. There are
no mythological allusions in Berossos' description of the great wise
man. These observations point in the direction that if Berossos had
a great wise man in the tenth generation after the flood, he cannot
have used the Apkallu Lists as sources, nor can he have meant that
the great wise man belonged to the primeval group of apkallu's.

As already noted, W 20 030,7 not only contains a list of apkallu's,
but also adds a list of ummânu's. In the last sequence of this list,
at the tenth place after the flood the ummânu Aba'enlidari is
recorded with the explanation: *[ša* ᴸᵘ*]aḫ-la-MI-mu-ū i-qab-bu-ú
ˡa-ḫu-'u-qa-a-ri, (Rev. line 20), "whom the Arameans call
Aḫuqar". The author is obviously aware that Aḫiqar, one of
Sennacherib's counsellors, had an international reputation. A novel

about this counsellor, written in Aramaic, together with a series of proverbs, was found in Elephantine in Upper Egypt. Prior to this discovery post-Christian recensions of the Book of Aḥiqar were known. Aḥiqar is also referred to in the Jewish Book of Tobit (Tobit 1,22; 14,10).[111] Van Dijk considers the possibility that both the Apkallu List and the Ummânu List were meant as selective genealogies.[112] The colophon seems to indicate this, at least in the case of the Ummânu List. The first ummânu is Sînleqeunnīnī. In the colophon the editor regards himself as mār sînleqeunnīnī, "descendant of Sînleqeunnīnī".

It is quite clear that Berossos has not read the present tablet from Uruk, which can be dated 165/4 B.C.,[113] since he wrote his work more than hundred years before. But Sînliqunnnīnī is known as scribal ancestor in Urukean texts dating from the Late Assyrian period and onwards.[114] The editor of our genealogy may very well have used an older model. Besides this, W 20 030,7 is the only cuneiform source which contains a parallel list of kings and sages. Here Berossos must have utilized a tradition similar to W 20 030,7.

The Ummânu List shows that here existed in cuneiform literature a list of great postdiluvian scholars, most likely in the form of a selective genealogy. The information about the great wise man ten generations after the flood in Josephus/Berossos is in good accordance with such a list. Furthermore, at the tenth place after the flood appears Aḥiqar, who had an international reputation for his wisdom. In the Elephantine Aḥiqar story he is described in the following way: אנת הו) ספרא חכימא ובעל עטתא טבתא זי גבר(צדיק: כלא אתור הות מלוהי עטתא ל(וע הוה. "[Are you] the wise scribe and a man of good counsel, who [was a righteous] man [and b]y whose counsel and words all of Assyria was guided" (col iii, lines 42-43).[115] He is also described as אחי) קר רב, "Aḥiqar, the

---

111 Cf. J.C. Greenfield, "Aḥiqar in the Book of Tobit", De la Torah au Messie, Mélanges Henri Cazelles, Paris 1981, pp. 329-36.
112 Cf. van Dijk in Lenzen, op.cit., p. 52.
113 Cf. above, p. 161.
114 Cf. W.G. Lambert, "Ancestors, Authors and Canonicity", JCS 11, 1957, pp. 1-14, p. 4; and W.G. Lambert, "A Catalogue of Texts and Authors", JCS 16, 1962, pp. 59-77, p. 76.
115 Text in A. Cowley, Aramaic Papyri of the Fifth Century B.C., Oxford 1923, pp. 204ff., 213f; and F. Rosenthal, An Aramaic Handbook I/1, PLO, Wiesbaden 1967, pp. 15f.

great man" (col iii, line 60). The correspondence with the great and knowledgeable man in Josephus/Berossos is clear. Both the wise man in Josephus/Berossos and Aḥiqar are described in a language conventional in description of great sages of the past.

We can conclude that there is support for the passage in Josephus/Berossos in what must have been the scribal milieu of Berossos, and that nothing contradicts the supposition that Berossos really had an information about a great and knowledgeable man in the tenth position in a selective genealogy of great scholars after the flood. This information can easily have been transformed to "in the tenth generation" by Josephus or other Jewish scribes in order to reconcile Mesopotamian and Jewish traditions.

1.5   Kings and Sages in W 20 030,7 and Berossos

Both Berossos and W 20 030,7 list kings and sages together. We give below the names from the antediluvian section.

As the table below shows, only two pairs conform: Alulim/U-An and Enmeduranki/Utuabzu. The most striking difference is that W 20 030,7 lists kings and sages as pairs, while Berossos places a group of four under Dumuzi.

According to our observations in the antediluvian section so far we can conclude:

—There must have existed a stable tradition at least from the Neo-Assyrian period and onwards listing seven antediluvian sages with the same names in the same order. [116]

—W 20 030,7 and Berossos seem to show that the connection king/sage in the pairs Alulim/U-An and Enmeduranki/Utuabzu was an established tradition. Besides this, the two texts show that there must have existed a tradition in which the King List and the Apkallu List were related prior to Berossos.

---

[116] The existence of different lists seems clear from the traces of the second Apkallu List in Bīt Mēseri, Borger, op.cit., p. 193.

BEROSSOS		W 20 030,7	
Kings	Sages	Kings	Sages
1. Aloros (Alulim)	Oannes (U-An)	1. Alulim	U-An
2. Alaparos (Alalgar)		2. Alalgar	U-An-dugga
3. Amelon (Ammeluanna)		3. Ammeluanna	Enmedugga
4. Ammenon	Annedotos (U-An-dugga)	4. Ammegalanna	Enmegalamma
5. Amegalaros (Enmegalanna)		5. Enmešugalanna	Enmebulugga
6. Daonos (Dumuzi)	Euedokos (Enmedugga) Eneugamos (Enmegalamma) Eneuboulos (Enmebulugga) Anementos (An-Enlilda)	6. Dumuzi	An-Enlilda
7. Euedorachos (Enmeduranki)	Odakon (Utuabzu)	7. Enmeduranki	Utuabzu
8. Amempsinos (Ensipazianna)			
9. Otiartes (Ubartutu)			
10. Xisouthros (Ziusudra)			

2. Characteristics of the sages in Bīt Mēseri

2.1 General Characteristics of the Seven Sages

The first part of the text contains an incantation to a group of seven apkallu's. All seven are characterized in the following way:

> They are the seven shining apkallu's,
> purādu-fish from the sea,
> seven apkallu's "grown" in the river,
> who insure the correct functioning
> of the plans of heaven and earth.
>
> (lines 5-9)[117]

---

117 Cf. for text and translation, Reiner, op.cit., pp. 2-5. We translate Akkadian namrutu as "shining".

We analyze three aspects of this information: 1) the origin of the
apkallu's; 2) the shape; 3) the function.

2.1.1   The Origin

The apkallu's are called "*purādu*-fish of the sea *(apsû)*", and they
are "grown in the river". A clear reference to the same we find in
the Poem of Erra where Marduk asks:

> Where are the seven [ap]kallu's of the Apsû,
> pure purādu-(fishes) who, like Ea, their lord,
> distinguish themselves by their sapiential skill?
>
> (Tabl I, line 163)[118]

The apkallu's are located to the Apsu, because they are created by
Ea who has his abode in the Apsu.[119] Since Ea is the god of
wisdom, this is also the reason for their divine wisdom. This origin
of the apkallu's is also clearly attested to by Berossos, both in his
initial story about Oannes and in his parallel list of kings and
apkallu's.[120]

2.1.2   The Shape

The origin in the sea is also the reason why the apkallu's were
imagined as fishes (*purādu*-fish seems to indicate a large carp).[121]
The most detailed description we find in Berossos:

> In the first year a beast named Oannes
> appeared from the Erythrean Sea
> in a place adjacent to Babylonia.
> Its entire body was that of a fish,
> but a human head had grown beneath the head of the fish
> and human feet had grown from the fish's tail.
> It also had a human voice.
> A picture of it is still preserved today.[122]

---

118   Cf. L. Cagni, The Poem of Erra, p. 34.
119   Cf. for the same in the Myth of Adapa, A, lines 6-7, ANET[3]. p. 101.
120   For Oannes: Text: Euseb. (Arm.) Chron. p. 6, 8-9, 2 and Syncellus p. 49,
19. FGH III, C, 1.B, sequences 4-5, pp. 369f. Translation: Burstein, Book I, 1, 5,
pp. 13f. For the list of kings and sages: Text: Euseb. (Arm.) Chron. p. 4, 8-6, 8;
(9, 2ff) and Syncellus p. 71, 3. FGH III, C, 1.B, sequences 10-13, pp. 374-77.
Translation: Burstein, Book II, 1, 1-11, pp. 18f.
121   Cf. Cagni, op.cit., p. 35, note 51.
122   Text according to Syncellus, p. 49, 19. FGH III, C, 1.B, sequence 4, p. 369.
Translation from Burstein, Book I, 1, 5, p. 13.

A relief from Nimrud, dated to the reign of Ashurnaṣirpal II (883-859) fits Berossos' description exactly.[123] It shows a figure wearing a fish-coat. The head of the fish covers half of the head of the figure. The mouth of the fish points upwards. Beneath it a man's face is visible, and beneath the coat we see clearly a man's feet.

2.1.3 The Function

The apkallu's "insured the correct functioning of the plans of heaven and earth". In Akkadian: *mušteširū uṣurāt AN-e ù KI-tim*.[124] Since the text in Bīt Mēseri is bilingual we shall also consider the Sumerican text: GIŠ.ḪUR AN.KI.A SI.SÁ.NE. The combination of the noun GIŠ.ḪUR (=Akk *uṣurtu*) and the verb SI.SÁ (= Akk *šutēšuru*) occurs several times in Sumerian.[125] The Sumerian GIŠ.ḪUR and Akkadian *uṣurtu* mean concretely "drawing", for example drawings of the plans of a house. Abstractly, they mean "plan, prefigurement" (German: "Planung, Vorzeichnung").[126] The verb, Sumerian SI.SÁ and Akkadian *šutēšuru*, means "to carry out according to regulations" (German: "massgerecht ausführen").[127] The closest parallel to our sentence seems to be in a hymn to the god Nusku: GIŠ.ḪUR.AN.KI.A SI.SA.SÁ.E.[128] The sentence reads in context (according to van Dijk's German translation):

---

123   Cf. T.A. Madloom, The Chronology of Neo-Assyrian Art, London 1970, Plate 67,4. Both the description in Berossos and the relief in Nimrud are similar to descriptions of the sea-monster kulullu, cf. CAD sub kulullu, p. 526. As a part of an apotropaic ritual published by Gurney we also find a description of the seven sages, O.R. Gurney, "Babylonian Prophylactic Figures and their Rituals", AAA 22, 1935, pp. 31-96. In the ritual we find descriptions how to make statues of the apkallu's, resembling bird and fish-features (cf. esp. pp. 52f). Figures like those described in the ritual were excavated in Nimrud, some of them depicting birds with four wings, others wearing fish-hoods. Cf. M.E.L. Mallowan, "The excavations at Nimrud", Iraq 16, 1954, pp. 85-92.
124   Transliteration according to Reiner, op.cit., p. 2, line 9. CAD sub ešēru, 12f, p. 363, translates: ". . . who correctly administers the regulations of heaven and earth".
125   Cf. G. Farber-Flügge, Der Mythos "Inanna und Enki" unter besonderer Berücksichtung der Liste der me, StP 10, Rome 1973, pp. 181-91.
126   Cf. AHW sub uṣurtu, p. 1440.
127   Cf. Farber-Flügge, op.cit., p. 188.
128   Cf. J. van Dijk, Sumerische Götterlieder, AHAW.PH,Abh.1, Heidelberg 1960. I, 14. Transliteration, p. 108; translation, p. 111.

Die Urformen von Himmel und Erde
in rechter Ordnung zu halten,
in die Weite von Himmel und Erde
den grossen Entscheidigungen den Weg zu bahnen,
die Kultordnungen vollkommen zu machen.

Nusku is here described as the god who is put in charge of the cosmic order. And this must also be the case when the sentence is used about the apkallu's: "To insure the correct functioning of the plans of heaven and earth" means accordingly to have responsibility for the cosmic order as it was prefigured by the gods when they created the world.

In the hymn quoted above, responsibility for the cosmic order is closely related to the cultic order. This responsibility we also find in the texts about the apkallu's. In the Poem of Erra Marduk tells how he removed both the persons and the materials which were necessary for the correct care of his divine statue.[129] Those given responsibility for his statue were the apkallu's:

I dispatched those (renowned) ummânu(-sages)
down into the Apsû:
I did not ordain their coming up again.

(Tabl I, line 147)

This act was related to the breakdown of the cosmic order, which meant that the powers of chaos and death broke into the world.[130]

In Berossos' account of the sages, they are said to have brought the human race all cultural benefits. Berossos wrote about Oannes:

It gave to men the knowledge of letters
and sciences and crafts of all types.
It also taught them how to found cities,
establish temples, introduce laws and measure land.
It also revealed them seeds and the gathering of fruits,
and in general it gave men everything
which is connected with the civilized life.[131]

The background of Berossos here is the Sumerian concept of the me.[132] The best illustration of this concept we find in the myth

---

129   Cf. the Poem of Erra, Tabl I, lines 124-141; Cagni, op.cit., p. 32.
130   Cf. above, pp. 182ff.
131   Text according to Syncellus p. 49, 19. FGH III, C, 1.B, sequence 4, pp. 369f. Translation from Burstein, Book I, 1, 5, pp. 13f.
132   The names of several of the apkallu's are also composed with me, cf. note 109 above.

Inanna and Enki.[133] In it are listed phenomena regarded as *me*. The list contain in fact an encyclopedic view of all the phenomena characteristic for human life: Human relations, social relations, political relations, occupations, sciences, crafts, arts, deeds, etc. According to Farber-Flügge these phenomena are manifestations of *me:* "Die göttliche Kraft *me* ist ein pluralistischer Begriff, der sich aus sämtlichen 'abstrakten' Begriffen zusammensetzt, die das Leben und die Kultur ausmachen."[134]

Accordingly, there is a close relationship between the Sumerian GIŠ.ḪUR (= Akkadian *uṣurtu*) and *me:* "*me* als die allem zu Grunde liegenden (göttliche) Kraft und giš.ḫur also die zu Grunde liegenden (göttliche) Konzeption überschneiden sich in ihrer Bedeutung oft stark und stehen daher in den Belegen oft in identischem Kontext."[135]

The apkallus's were accordingly both in charge of the cosmic order, related to their cultic responsibility and they brought mankind the divine power of wisdom which was regarded as fundamental to civilized life.

2.2   Individual Characteristics

2.2.1   Systematizing of Apkallu's and Ummanû's

There is a clear distinction between the group of seven and the group of four apkallu's in Bīt Mēseri. A similar distinction in the history of great wise men we find in W 20 030,7 which lists seven sages before the flood and one after it, and continues to list nine ummânu's. Berossos records seven sages before the flood and one ummânu in the tenth generation after it, presupposing a list similar to W 20 030,7.[136]

The distinction between the group of seven sages and the group of four in Bīt Mēseri, and between apkallu's and ummânu's in W 20 030,7, demonstrates a special way of interpreting history: the primeval history is "the history of revelation", and the history which follows is the time when this revelation is transmitted and unfolded.

---

133   For text and analysis, cf. Farber-Flügge, op.cit.
134   Cf. Farber-Flügge, op.cit., p. 197.
135   Cf. Farber-Flügge, op.cit., p. 198.
136   Cf. above, pp. 193ff.

The list in Bīt Mēseri seems in fact to have a three stage model. The first seven sages have their origin in the sea, the abode of Ea. They are accordingly semi-divine beings sent to mankind to reveal the wisdom of the gods. The next stage is the group of four, who are characterized as "four apkallu's of human descent whom the lord Ea endowed with broad understanding". The fourth sage seems to be in a stage of transition between the period of the apkallu's and the period afterwards: He is only "two third apkallu".

The way history is divided into periods can vary — Berossos, for instance, concentrates almost exclusively on the basic revelation of Oannes (cf. below). But the different models all seem to express the same basic idea: The history of human civilization starts with a "history of revelation" followed by a "history of transmission".

2.2.2   The Seven Sages and Adapa

The information given about each of the apkallu's differs.[137] There seems, however, to be a sort of order in the information. The three first are distinguished by extraordinary wisdom, while the three next are described according to their origin and setting.

The first apkallu, U-Anna, "completed the plans of heaven and earth". This resembles what is said about all the apkallu's[138] and underscores the special importance of the figure. What the word "complete" (German "vollendet") here exactly means is difficult to determine. But there can be a similarity to Berossos' account about Oannes who gave men all wisdom: "From that time on has nothing further been discovered."[139] The role of the following apkallu's is according to Berossos: ". . . these figures all together explained in detail the things that had been spoken summarily by Oannes.".[140]

---

137 Since the only source for the first six apkallu's is Borger's translation of the text, it is difficult to go into the text in detail.
138 Cf. above, pp. 199f.
139 Text according to Syncellus p. 49, 19. FGH III, C, 1.B, sequence 4, p. 370. Translation from Burstein, Book I, 1, 5, p. 14.
140 Text according to Syncellus p. 71, 3. FGH III, C, 1.B, sequence 12, p. 376. Translation from Burstein, Book II, 1, 8, p.29.

The second apkallu is given "a broad understanding". The third is given "a good fate".

The next three are described differently. The fourth is "born in a house"; the fifth "grew up on a field" (German "Weidegrund"). The sixth is the diviner from the city Eridu. These bits of information do not harmonize with the statement applied to all the apkallu's: they are fishes from the Apsu which have their origin in a river. There seems to be an attempt to bring together two different traditions, one mythical and one legendary. In the mythical tradition the apkallu's were semi-divine composite beings from the Apsu. In the legendary tradition they were great men of antiquity connected to important cities (cf. below).

The seventh apkallu, Utuabzu, had a special fate: "Utuabzu who ascended to heaven". The same line is repeated in the fragmentary second Apkallu List of Bīt Mēseri. The third list has a variation: "Utuaabba who descended from heaven". The name Utuabzu in the two first lists means "born in the Apsu" (fresh water). The name Utuaabba i the third list means "born in the salt water". Both the placement in the list and the similarity in name indicate that the third list contains a variation of the theme of the two first.

In a vocabulary list the Sumerian ù.tu.a.ab.ba is given the Akkadian equivalent *a-da-pu*.[141] The question is whether there is any connection between Utuabzu/Utuaabba and the well-known Adapa from the myth.[142]

Like the seventh sage in the Apkallu List Adapa is called apkallu: *ina u₄-me-šu-ma ina ša-na-a-ti ši-na-a-ti ap-kal-lu [mār] Eridu ᵈÉ-a ki-ma rid-di ina a-me-lu-ti ib-ni-šu*.[143] "To that time, in those years, Ea created the apkallu, the son of Eridu as a model for mankind."

141   Cf. W.G. Lambert, "Three Literary Prayers of the Babylonians", AfO 19, 1959-60, pp. 47-66. Cf. also CAD sub adapu, p. 102.
142   For the Myth of Adapa, cf. translation in ANET[3], pp. 101ff.
143   Myth of Adapa, Recension A, line 5, ANET[3], p. 101. Cf. for this transliteration and the transliteration below, B. Kienast, "Überlegungen zum 'Fluch' des Adapa", Festschrift Labor Matouš, Budapest 1978, pp. 181-200.

Like the seventh sage in the Apkallu List Adapa ascended to heaven:

Myth of Adapa: *a-da-pa . . . [ù šá] a-na šamê^e i-lu-u.*
Bīt Mēseri: *u.tu.ab.zu šá ana šamê^e i-lu-u.*[144]

The equivalence of u.tu.a.ab.a and *adapu*, the designation "apkallu", and the similar fate point clearly in the direction that Utuabzu/Utuaabba in Bīt Mēseri is the same as Adapa of the myth.

But the name Adapa relates not only to the seventh apkallu. There is also a clear correspondence to the first. In a catalogue of texts and authors this sage is called *u$_4$-an-na-da-pà*.[145] According to G. Komoróczy (cf. note above), the full name Uanadapa has two short forms: U-An and Adapa. The full name has the meaning "light shining in the sky (or with the god An)", which corresponds very well to the characteristics of the apkallu's as "shining" in Bīt Mēseri.[146] The one short form of the name, U-An, which occurs as the first name of the Apkallu Lists in Bīt Mēseri and W 20 030,7, written u$_4$-^{d}an in W 20 030,7,[147] has the meaning "light of the god heaven (or An)".

Adapa is accordingly a short form of the name of the first primary sage with the full name Uanadapa. U-An is another short form of the name. This figure equals Oannes in Berossos' account. But, as we have seen, Utuabzu/Utuaabba/Adapa also occurs at the seventh place in the list of Bīt Mēseri. The seventh figure of the Apkallu List is in W 20 030,7 and Berossos parallel to the seventh king Enmeduranki. As we have seen, Enmeduranki also went to heaven and distinguished himself with divine wisdom. The similarities between Adapa and Enmeduranki may have caused the appearance of Adapa at the seventh place in the list of Bīt Mēseri.

---

144 Myth of Adapa, Recension D, lines 12-14, ANET^3, pp. 102f. Transliteration according to Reiner, op.cit., lines 3-4. Utuabzu restored according to Borger, op.cit.
145 Cf. W.G. Lambert, "A Catalogue of Texts and Authors", I, 6 p. 65. For further references, cf. Komoróczy, "Berosos and the Mesopotamian Literature", p. 144.
146 Cf. above, note 117.
147 Cf. Plate 27, line 1 in Lenzen, op.cit.

2.2.3   The Four Sages

The first apkallu of this group is said to have lived during the time of king Enmerkar. This is in accordance with W 20 030,7, which associated the same apkallu with Enmerkar as the only one after the flood. In Berossos the first king after the flood is Euechsios who most likely reflects Sumerian Enmerkar.[148] The second apkallu is born in Kish which in the Sumerian King list in WB 444 is listed as the first postdiluvian dynasty.[149] The third apkallu is located to the city Adab. With the fourth apkallu we have reached a period within our knowledge of history. He is associated with the king Shulgi who ruled in the third dynasty of Ur (2094-2047).

What makes these apkallu's special are the acts that they performed. The first of them "brought down Ištar from heaven into Eanna", her temple.[150] The same line occurs also in W 20 030,7. The second apkallu "angered Adad in the heaven so that he let no rain and (hence) no vegetation be in the country for three years." The third apkallu placed his seal on one of Ea's holy animals and thus angered Ea in the Apsu.[151] The fourth apkallu "drove the *uššumgallu*-dragon from Eninkarnunna, the temple of Ištar of Šulgi".

---

148   Cf. Cf. W.W. Hallo, "Beginning and End of the Sumerian King List in the Nippur Recension", JCS 17, 1963, pp. 52-7, p. 52.

149   Cf. Jacobsen, Sumerian King List, p. 77.

150   For the four apkallu's, cf. Reiner's edition, lines 10-27. Concerning the first one I prefer the translation by Reiner and Borger, who have the apkallu as the subject of the sentence. Van Dijk, in Lenzen, op.cit., p. 49 and note 120, has Ishtar as the subject and translates: "Nungalpiriggal Apkallu, den Ištar vom Himmel ins E-anna hinabstiegen liess". According to this translation it is the apkallu and not the goddess who descends from heaven. Van Dijk gives the following explanation: "Grammatikalisch wäre es das Beste (the translation by Reiner), da in allen folgenden Sätzen der Apkallu im Nachsatz Subjekt ist. Aus dem Fehlen der Agentivpastposition -e hinter ᵈinanna möchte ich diese Übersetzung nicht für zwingend halten. Die Schlüsse aus der Religionsgeschichte sind aber hier wichtig, und es ist in der Theologie der Sumerer so abwegig, dass ein Mensch eine Göttin vom Himmel hinabsteigen lassen könnte, dass ich vorlaufig meine Übersetzung bevorzuge." We agree with van Dijk that an incident in which a man brings a goddess down from heaven is highly extraordinary in Sumerian religion, but the question is whether this is not the point in the text. It would not be less extraordinary, however, if a god brought down a man from heaven, and this does not seem to be the point according to the context.

151   The clause is extremely difficult to interpret also because the crucial words exist only in Borger's German translation: ". . . der sein Siegel an? einem Ziegenfisch aufhängte und dadurch den Gott Enki/Ea im Süsswassermeer erzürnte, so dass ein Walker ihn mit seinem eigenen Siegel erschlug.".

The background of these extraordinary incidents is not easy to trace. I shall start with the second one, where the logic is clear. The second apkallu angered the god of rain and thunder, Adad, so there was drought in the country for three years. This incident is similar to what is told about Adapa in the myth. There Adapa broke the wing of the south wind, the wind that brings rain, with the result that a drought came over the country.[152] B. Kienast has analyzed the Myth of Adapa in two publications.[153] He has argued that the Myth of Adapa is not a myth about rebellion, but an etiological one about the origin of a certain kind of wisdom: "Die Adapa Erzählung ist also eine aitiologische Sage, die eine religiös-ethisch bestimmte Weisheit des Helden aus einer reinen Herzens begangenen schweren Verfehlung und deren Folgen deuten möchte."[154] Since our topic is not the Myth of Adapa we cannot enter into a detailed discussion of it here. Kienast may be correct in his interpretation of the myth, but we do not think he is correct when he continues: "Es ist — wohl aus überlieferungs-geschichtlichen Gründen nur zufällig — die einzige uns erhaltene Geschichte dieser Art. Doch hat E. Reiner einen interessanten Text vorgelegt, demzufolge auch über andere Weise vergleichbare Erzählungen im Umlauf waren. In jenem Katalog wird immer nur von dem Vergehen der Weisen gesprochen, aber wir dürfen für jede einzelne Geschichte postulieren: Nicht eine bewusste 'Revolte' gegen die Götter, sondern ungewollter Frevel und spätere Reue bilden den Gegenstand dieser Legenden — wie auch bei der 'Mythe vom weisem Adapa'."

The first reason why we disagree is methodological. We doubt that there is enough evidence to use the Myth of Adapa as the key for the interpretation of the acts of the four apkallu's. The texts share the motif "an apkallu causes drought". But this is only one motif among many others in the Myth of Adapa. The other reason is that we are not sure that such a complicated "psychology" can be presupposed in the mythical background of the short references in Bīt Mēseri.

---

152 Cf. ANET³, B, lines 1-9, p. 101. For this interpretation, cf. B. Kienast, "Die Weisheit des Adapa von Eridu", Symbolae Biblicae et Mesopotamicae, Leiden 1973, pp. 234-9, pp. 235f.
153 Cf. notes 143 and 152 above.
154 Kienast, "Die Weisheit des Adapa", pp. 238f.

If the Myth of Adapa has any connection with the list in Bīt Mēseri, we would rather assume that its composer used stories about extraordinary incidents associated with the apkallu's and out of these composed the myth with its special scope. As we have seen, the "ascension motif" also occurs in Bīt Mēseri. This should point toward an understanding of the Myth of Adapa as a compilation of different motifs, among them the motifs "an apkallu caused drought" and "an apkallu went to heaven".

We do not know exactly what is meant in the three other cases in Bīt Mēseri. That the first apkallu brought down Ishtar from heaven is certainly an extraordinary event. Since the other events clearly describe acts of offence, it is natural also to interpret this one in the same way. The last two incidents seem to have been crimes against cultic objects belonging to the deities.

How it the list as a whole to be interpreted? As far as we can see, only two facts can form the basis of our understanding. One is the extraordinary character of the incidents. The acts of the apkallu's seem to reveal a power that transgresses that of ordinary man. The other fact is that it is clearly stated twice that the apkallu's *angered* the gods. Their extraordinary acts were regarded as a provocation. We do not think that the enigmatic notices allow an analysis of the underlying "psychology". If we seek parallels one could be the heroic tales about Gilgamesh, who in his power and quest for fame also provoked the gods. Another parallel from primeval time is the description of the human race before the flood. Created out of divine substance and given the personality of the leading rebel god, the human race rebelled against the gods, causing severe crises with the flood as the final result.[155]

3.   The Elements of the Apkallu Tradition

Reading the Myth of Adapa, no one would think that Adapa was a fish. When he goes out on the sea, it is to catch fish, not to meet his colleagues. On the other hand it is said that Adapa was created by Ea, who lived in the sea. And the apkallu's in Bīt Mēseri are both created in the sea and called fishes. Further we have seen

---

155   Cf. above, pp. 174f.

that *adapu* is listed as an Akkadian equivalent of Sumerian
u.tu.a.ab.ba, which means "born in the salt water".

We have already met the problem in Bīt Mēseri. The apkallu's are
fishes from the sea, but among them Enmegalamma was born in a
house and Enmebulugga grew up on a field. There are contra-
dictions in the texts. Berossos attempts to explain the contra-
dictions in the following way: "... this beast (Oannes) spent the
days with men but ate no food ... But when the sun set this beast
Oannes plunged back into the sea and spent the nights in the deep,
for it was amphibious. Later other beasts also appeared."[156]

We have already suggested that the apkallu tradition was based on
two elements: a mythical tradition and a legendary tradition. We
start with the latter.

According to Bīt Mēseri three of the apkallu's are connected to
cities. An-Enlilda was an exorcist in Eridu. Piriggalnungal was
born in Kish and Piriggalabzu in Adab. In a Neo-Assyrian
colophon quoted by Lambert the apkallu's seem to have been
connected to a number of cities: Sippar, Nippur, Babylon, Larsa,
Ur, Uruk, and Eridu.[157] The list given by Berossos at least
indirectly associated the apkallu's with cities: the first to Babylon,
the next six to Badtibira. In a colophon (referred to below, p. 210)
Lu-Nanna is called the apkallu of Ur.

There are clear indications that we have here a legendary culture
hero tradition about great inventors and wise men of the ancient
past. We find a similar tradition in the Jewish tradition in the
oldest source to Genesis, Gen 4 (J). From the Phoenician area Philo
of Byblos records traditions about ancestral figures credited with
discoveries and inventions.[158]

Both in Berossos and W 20 030,7 the apkallu's are listed together
with kings. Since the lists vary, we can at present not assume a
stable tradition, except in the pairs Alulim/U-an; Enmeduranki/-
Utuabzu which occur in both. But this does not mean that the
pairing of kings and apkallu's is a "new" invention. On a tablet
found in Sultantepe the first line of an apocryphal letter is

156 Text according to Syncellus p. 49, 19. FGH III, C, 1.B, sequence 4, p. 370.
Translation from Burstein, Book I, 1, 5, p. 14.
157 The Naẓimaruttaš colophon, KAR. 177. Cf. W.G. Lambert, "Ancestors",
pp. 8f.; cf. also W.W. Hallo, "Antediluvian Cities", p. 65, note 103.
158 Cf. below, pp. 215-22.

preserved: *a-na* ᵐ*a-lu-lu qí-bi-ma um-ma* ¹*a-da-pa ap-kal-um-ma,* "To Alulu speak, thus says Adapa, the apkallu".¹⁵⁹

A legendary tradition about great wise men of the past seems accordingly to be one element of the apkallu tradition. In this legendary tradition the apkallu's were associated with various cities and city kings.

The other element of the apkallu tradition is mythological. An ancient Sumerian temple hymn tells about "the seven wise ones" connected to Eridu.¹⁶⁰ The Poem of Erra also tells about the seven sages of the Apsu.¹⁶¹ This tradition clearly points toward Eridu as the place of origin. Eridu was the city of Enki/Ea and the apkallu's are closely related to this god. In ancient times Eridu was also situated close to the marsh land and sea which explains its connection with the water.¹⁶²

Although the legendary and mythical background form a unit in the texts, the two sides could be emphasized differently. There seem to have been two basic settings of the tradition. The one is reflected in Bīt Mēseri and other incantation and exorcistic rituals. Here the apkallu's are invoked together with other prophylactic semi-divine figures.¹⁶³ The emphasis is clearly on the mythological aspects. The apkallu's ascend from the Apsu and so do other semi-divine beings of benevolent or malevolent character.

The other setting is reflected in W 20 030,7 and Berossos. Here the apkallu's are a part of a learned scribal tradition. They are great men of antiquity, sent by the gods to reveal to mankind the basic cultural achievements.

4. Apkallu's and Authorship

The overwhelming majority of Babylonian texts circulated anonymously, but the Babylonian scholars made attempts to determine the authorship of many compositions. The most well

159 STT 176.14, LA. Text in W.G. Lambert, Atra-Ḥasis, p. 27.
160 Cf. A. Sjöberg and E. Bergmann, The Collection of the Sumerian Temple Hymns, New York 1969, No 10, line 139, p. 25.
161 Poem of Erra, Tabl I, lines 147.162; Cagni, op.cit., p. 33, note 40, and p. 34.
162 For Eridu and Ea/Enki, cf. the myth Enki and Eridu, S.N. Kramer, Sumerian Mythology, pp. 62f.
163 Cf. note 123 above.

known example is a catalogue of texts and authors published by
Lambert,[164] who dates it in the first quarter of the first millennium. In this catalogue the authors whose names are preserved fall
into four classes: gods, legendary and other humans of great
antiquity, men without indications of family origin, and men
described as "sons" of ancestral figures.

The general tendency in this and other attempts to determine the
authorship is described by W.W. Hallo as follows: "the Babylonians
regarded not anonymity (as was once thought) but antiquity of
authorship as a measure of authority. They therefore were not
above attributing texts and versions of obviously late date to
impossibly early authors or, conversely, associating a patently late
author with the time of an early king."[165]

Both in the catalogue and elsewhere apkallu's are listed as authors.
Lu-Nanna, the last sage in Bīt Mēseri, is regarded as the author of
the Etana myth (the Catalogue VI, 11). He is also regarded as the
author of a medical text, the colophon reads: "... a secret of Lu-
Nanna, sage of Ur.".[166] Enmedugga, the third sage in all three
Apkallu Lists, is listed as the author of several compositions in the
catalogue (IV, 11). In a colophon to a medical text it is stated:
"... according to the old sages from before the flood."[167]
Antediluvian knowledge was highly prized among the Babylonians
and Assyrians. Ashurbanipal states: "I understand the script of
stone inscriptions from before the flood, which are difficult,
obscure and confused."[168]

The sage that in the most cases is regarded as author of texts is U-
An Adapa. His name occurs twice in the catalogue. The first time
he is mentioned directly after Ea (I, 1-6), the second in connection
with compositions from before the flood (VI, 15-16). Also outside
the catalogue U-An Adapa is regarded as an author. In the so-
called *Verse Account of Nabonidus* Nabonidus is said to have
boasted of a wisdom greater than an astronomical series composed

---

164   Cf. note 114 above.
165   W.W. Hallo, "On the Antiquity of Sumerian Literature", JAOS 83, 1963,
pp. 167-76, p. 175.
166   The text to which the colophon belongs has the number K.8080, cf.
Lambert, "Ancestors", p. 7.
167   The text to which the colophon belongs has the number K.4023, cf.
Lambert, op.cit., p. 8.
168   VAB VII 256 18, cf. Lambert, "Catalogue", p. 72.

by Adapa.[169] This astronomical series is also listed in the catalogue (cf. below). As late as in Seleucid Uruk a tablet is found
with the remark: "... which Adapa wrote".[170] When Berossos
makes Oannes the author of Enuma Elish, he is in principle in
good accordance with a broad cuneiform tradition.

The reason for this pseudepigraphy is clearly the Babylonian
concept about the origin of Wisdom. As we stated earlier, the
primeval time and especially the period before the flood was "the
history of revelation" in Babylonian theology. In this period the
basis for all later knowledge was laid. Writings originating in this
period would accordingly have a special authority.

It is difficult to know how the Babylonians imagined the divine
authorship of some compositions, as for instance Ea's, in the
catalogue. But in two places we seem to get information about how
texts came into being through divine inspiration. The first example
concerns the authorship of the Poem of Erra. Here the catalogue
first quotes the first line of the poem and then continues: "[This is
what] was revealed to [Kabti-ilāni-Marduk, son of Dabībī], and
which he spoke" (III,1-2). The restoration of the text above is
according to Lambert who convincingly argues that this line is
quoted from the end of the Poem of Erra itself, which reads:

> ka-ṣir kam-me-šu ᵐkab-ti-ilāniᵐᵉˢ-ᵈmar-
>   duk mār da-bi-i-bi
> ina šat mu-ši ú-sab-ri-šu-ma k-i šá ina
>   mu-na-at-ti id-bu-bu
> a-a-am-ma ul iḫ-ṭi e-du šu-mu ul ú-
>   rad-di ina muḫ-ḫi
>
> "Kabti-ilani-Marduk, son of Dabibi, was
>   the compiler of its tablets.
> It was revealed to him in the night, and
>   when he spoke it in the morning
> He did not leave out a single line,
>   nor did he add one to it.
>   (Tabl V, lines 42-44)[171]

---

169 Cf. ANET³, p. 314, col v.
170 The remark occurs in a colophon to a ritual tablet, published by R.C.
Thompson, cf. Lambert, "Catalogue", p. 74; and van Dijk in Lenzen, op.cit., p. 48.
171 Text according to Lambert, op.cit., p. 70.

The second example also involves a restoration. Also here I think that Lambert argues convincingly when he restores the first reference to Adapa in the catalogue (I, 5-7) in accordance with the reference to the author of the Poem of Erra above:[172]

[an-nu-tum ša] ^{1}ūma-an-na a-da-p[à]
[ú-šab-ri-šu-m]a id-bu-bu

"[These are what was revealed to]
U-An-Adapa and which he spoke"[173]

The Šin stem of barû, "to see", šubrû, is well attested to in the meaning "reveal in a vision".[174] In the Poem of Erra this must certainly be the meaning considering the context: ina šāt mūši ušabrīšu, "it was revealed to him in the night". If the restorations above are correct, I think this must also be the meaning in the catalogue. This shows that scribal activity and visionary ability were not regarded as opponents.

If so, Adapa, like Atra-Ḥasis, was regarded as a visionary. Besides the similarities with the epilogue of the Poem of Erra, which form the basis for the restoration, there are also other indications. The preserved verb idbubu, "spoke", in the quotation above (Catalogue I, 7) seems clearly to indicate that Adapa was the second link in the chain of transmission. This is certainly the case in the other place Adapa is mentioned in the catalogue (VI, 15-16), where he is a composer of writings ša lām abūbu, "from before the flood". The next line reveals the circumstances of this composing: [a-da-] pà ina pi-i-šu iš-tu-ru, "[Ada]pa wrote at his dictation".
In the first Adapa sequence, he is regarded as the composer of the astronomical work The Lunar Crescent of Anu and Enlil, I, even I, am Enlil. Lambert restores part of this title from the Verse Account of Nabonidus.[175] In the Verse Account, Nabodinus' boasting of supreme wisdom is the context for the reference to this astronomical work:

172   Lambert, op.cit., p. 73.
173   In this translation we have to presuppose a god as subject for the verb, cf. the translation in Cagni, op.cit., Tabl V, line 43, p. 60.
174   Cf. CAD sub barû, A.5b, p. 118.
175   Cf. Lambert, op.cit., p. 70.

(It was) he (who) stood up in the assembly
to praise hi[mself]
(Saying): "I am wise, I know, I have seen
(what is) hi[dden].
(Even) if I do not know how to write (with a stylus),
yet I have seen se[cret things].
The god Ilte'ri has made me see a vision,
he has [shown to me] everything.
[I am] aw[are] of a wisdom which
greatly surpasses (even that of)
(The series) U_4.sar. ^{d}A.num. ^{d}En.líl.lá
which Adapa has composed.

(col v)[176]

In this sequence Nabonidus is said to have compared himself to
Adapa explicitly in astronomical knowledge. A closer examination
shows that also the other abilities mentioned in the sequence
belong to the conventional description of an apkallu: The apkallu's
distinguished themselves with supreme wisdom, Adapa was
regarded as the inventor of the art of writing, a "hidden mystery",
and the writings of the apkallu's could be regarded as a secret.[177]
When the framework here is the abilities of the apkallu's and
especially Adapa in wisdom, the art of writing, insight into
mysteries and astrological/astronomical knowledge, I think that
also the remaining one must belong to the characteristics of Adapa:
visionary ability. This is even more conclusive when we take into
consideration that Nabonidus is said to have referred to exactly
that composition where the traces of signs in the catalogue seemed
to indicate a visionary experience.

---

176   Translation according to ANET[3] , p. 314; cf. also B. Landsberger and Th.
Bauer, "Zu neuveröffentlichten Geschichtsquellen der Zeit von Asarhaddon bis
Nabonid", ZA NF 3 (37), 1927, pp. 61-98, p. 92.
177   Cf. above, pp. 200f, 189, 210.

IV
The Influence of the Mesopotamian Traditions on the Enochic Sources

Both in the Mesopotamian traditions we have analyzed and in the Enochic traditions two basic themes occur in different variants: the origin of wisdom in primeval time and the primeval catastrophe which once struck the earth. In the following comparison we shall concentrate on these two themes. We shall deal first with the background of the Enoch portraits and the origin of wisdom. Then we shall analyze the background of the concepts of the primeval catastrophe as they appear in the Old Testament and Jewish literature.

a) The Background of the Enoch Portraits and of the Primeval Wisdom

1. The Background of the Enoch Sequence of the Jahwistic Source

This is not the place for a detailed discussion of the background of the Jahwistic source as a whole in its accounts of primeval history. But we find it necessary to point out that at least two places there are distinguishing marks of Mesopotamian influence. One place is the Flood story, Gen 6-8*. There are so many corresponding details between this story in Genesis and the Mesopotamian versions that the assumption of an influence from the Mesopotamian side seems inevitable.[1] The other is in the story of the

---

[1] Cf. the comparison in A. Parrot, The Flood and Noah's Ark, SBAr1, London 1955, pp. 15-67 and W.G. Lambert, "A New Look at the Babylonian Background of Genesis", pp. 291f; W.M. Clark, "The Flood and the Structure of the Pre-patriarchal History", ZAW 83, 1971, pp. 184-211, pp. 184-88. For a survey of the Mesopotamian versions, cf. above, pp. 173-8.

Tower of Babel. Here the Jahwist seems to have brought together two different Mesopotamian traditions. The one is centered around the enormous ziqqurat Etemenanki in Babylon.[2] The other has the confusion of the tongues as its main issue, a story which also is recounted on a Sumerian tablet dating from the end of the third millennium.[3]

The similarities in these two stories show certainly that there must have been some sort of contact between the Israelite scribes of the tenth-century Solomonic area and the Mesopotamian milieu. But the Mesopotamian impact was not of the kind that influenced the structure of the Jahwistic primeval account. The similarities concern two Mesopotamian traditions which, as far as I can see, were not brought together in Mesopotamian literature.

Much closer in structure comes the antediluvian section in Philo of Byblos' *Phoenician History*. The work as a whole is lost, but extracts are known from Eusebius' Praeperatio Evangelica, Praep. Ev. 1.10.[4] Philo of Byblos, a Phoenician, lived in the second part of the first century and the first part of the second A.D. His "history" was written in Greek. He claimed to have based his book on sources from a certain Sanchuniathon, or in Semitic *Sakkunnaton*, "Sakkun (a god) has given", who should have lived about a thousand years earlier. In some ways Philo is a counterpart of Berossos, for both wanted to translate their native heritage into Greek. But there are differences. Berossos was a priest in Babylon. He had excellent access to the cuneiform libraries. His information can also be evaluated in detail in comparison with the cuneiform material. With Philo the situation is different. We do not know whether his Sanchuniathon source is fiction or reality. There has also been considerable disagreement among researchers as to what extent he records Phoenician or Semitic heritage, or only presents

---

2 Cf. W. von Soden, "Etemenanki vor Asarhaddon nach der Erzählung vom Turmbau zu Babel und dem Erra-Mythos", UF 3, 1971, pp. 253-63.
3 Cf. S.N. Kramer, "The 'Babel of Tongues': A Sumerian Version", JAOS 88, 1968, pp. 108-11.
4 Text: K. Mras, Eusebius Werke. Achter Band, Die Praeperatio Evangelica, GCS, Berlin 1953, pp. 43-54; F. Jacoby, FGH III, C, Zweiter Band, pp. 803-17. The Greek text and the translation are readily accessible in H.W. Attridge and R.A. Oden, Jr., Philo of Byblos, The Phoenician History, CBQ.MS 9, Washington D.C. 1981.

a compilation of hellenistic synchretistic material. After the discovery of new sources of the culture and religion of ancient Phoenicia and Syria there has been a clear tendency to regard the Phoenician History as a source of pre-hellenistic traditions, as well. The work must, however, be analyzed and evaluated critically. As a whole it reflects the process of assimilation between Palestinian/Phoenician and Greek traditions which was going on in the last centuries B.C.[5]

The part which is relevant to our subject is the one dealing with the origin of culture and civilization, the so called "technogony", Praep. Ev. 1.10. 6-14.[6] It is the part of the Phoenician History which most clearly reflects the ancient Semitic heritage.[7] An excellent monograph on this part was written by J. Ebach.[8] Concerning the age of the material he stated: "Obwohl Philo selbst im 1. und 2. Jh. n. Chr. schreibt, ... ergab die Untersuchung, dass das Material, das Philos Werk zugrundeliegt, im wesentlichen erheblich älter ist als Philos Niederschrift und in seinem Kern dem ersten Viertel des 1. Jt. angehören dürfte. Ein grosser Teil des verarbeiteten Überlieferungen reicht noch erheblich weiter zurück, wie der Vergleich insbesondere mit altägyptischen und ugaritischen Zeugnissen zeigt."[9] With this dating of the material underlying the technogony we are back in the period in which the Jahwistic source was composed.

I give below the text of the antediluvian section, inclusive the flood, structured according to the generations.[10]

5　Cf. J. Barr, Philo of Byblos and his "Phoenician History", reprinted from BJRL 57, No 1, Manchester 1974; M.L. West, Hesiod. Theogony, pp. 24-31; S.E. Loewenstam, "Philo of Byblos", Comparative Studies in Biblical and Ancient Oriental Literatures, Neukirchen-Vluyn 1980, pp. 390-404; H. Gese, "Die Religionen Altsyriens", Die Religionen Altsyriens, Altarabiens und der Mandäer, RM 10,2, Stuttgart 1970, pp. 30-34.
6　Text: FGH III, C, 2.B, pp. 807f; text and translation: Attridge and Oden, pp. 41-7.
7　Cf. J. Barr: "With the technogony we are on different ground. Neither the literary form nor the content particularly suggests Greek influence, apart from particular details which may have been introduced at a late date," op.cit., p. 50.
8　J. Ebach, Weltenstehung und Kulturentwicklung bei Philo von Byblos, BWANT 6, Stuttgart 1979.
9　Ebach, op.cit., p. 409.
10　Translation according to Attridge and Oden, op.cit., p. 40-3.

The History of Culture (Praep. Ev. 1.10.6-10)

1. Generation
The Origin of Nourishment

Then he says that from the wind Colphia
and his wife Baau (this means night)
were born Aeon and Protogonos, mortal
men, so called. Aeon discovered the
nourishment from the trees.

2. Generation

The Origin of the Cult	The Origin of Fire
Their offspring were called Genos and Genea, and they settled in Phoenicia. When droughts occurred, they raised their hands to heaven toward the sun. "For", he says, "they considered him, the lord of heaven, to be the only god and called him Beelsamen, which is "Lord of Heaven" in Phoenician, Zeus in Greek".	From the generation of[11] Aeon and Protogonos there were born mortal children, whose names are Light, Fire and Flame. He says, "These discovered fire by rubbing sticks of wood together, and they taught its usefulness."

3. Generation
The Origin of Power — the Giants

They begot sons greater in size
and stature, whose names were
given to the mountains over which
they ruled. Thus from them derive
the names of Mt. Cassios, the
Lebanon, the Anti-Lebanon and
Mt. Brathy.

4. Generation
The Generation before the Catastrophe

"From these", he says, "were born
Samemroumos, who is also called Hyposouranios
<and Ousos>."[12] He says, "They took their

---

11   Attridge and Oden translate: ". . . from Genos, son of Aeon and Protogonos
. . .". A similar translation has W.P. Roland, A Commentary to Philos Byblius'
"Phoenician History", unpubl. diss. University of Southern California 1968, p.
88. We prefer the translation by Ebach: ". . . from the generation of . . .", cf.
Ebach, op.cit., p. 428, and note 8, p. 117.
12   Roland, op.cit., p. 89, reads the first name as "Memroumos". He translates
the whole clause: "To these, he says, were born Memroumos and Hypsouranios".
The name "Samemroumos" occurs in Codex Parisiensis 451. It reflects Semitic
šmm rmm, "high heaven", which also is the meaning of "Hypsouranios" in
Greek. Accordingly, Samemroumos and Hypsouranios must be the same person

names from their mothers, since women
at that time mated indiscriminately
with whomever they chanced to meet."
Then he says that Hypsouranios settled
Tyre and that he invented huts made of
reeds, rushes, and papyrus. He quarreled
with his brother, Ousoos, who first
discovered how to gather a covering for
the body from the hides of animals which
he captured.

The Catastrophe

Once, when there were fierce rainstorms
and gales, the trees in Tyre rubbed
against one another and started a fire, and
it burned down their woodland. Ousoos took
part of a tree, cut off the branches and,
for the first time ever, dared to travel
on the sea. He dedicated two steles for
Fire and Wind. He worshipped them and
poured out to them libations of blood from
the animals which he had hunted. He says
that when these men died, those who
survived them dedicated staves to them.
They worshipped the steles and conducted
annual festivals for them.

The structure of the Jahwistic account of the antediluvian period:

The Jahwistic account of the antediluvian period is structured
basically according to a genealogical pattern which is extended by
narratives. We shall concentrate on the genealogical pattern:

1. First generation, Gen 2, 4b-3, 24,
   Adam and Eve: The origin of nourishment.
2. Second generation: Two families:
   The family of Cain, Gen 4,1-24: The origin of civilization.
   The family of Seth, Gen 4,25-26: The origin of cult.
3. The generation of the giants, Gen 6,1-4[*13]: The origin of power.
4. The antediluvian generation, Gen 6,5-8.
5. The Flood story, Gen 7-8[*].

called by both his Semitic and Greek names. We therefore translate "also called
'Hypsouranios'", as Ebach, pp. 428f. Like Ebach we also include Ousoos, since
the next clause presupposes a plural in the preceding.

13   I regard Gen 6,1-4, at least in the oldest literary form, as belonging to the
Jahwistic source, cf. below, pp. 280-3.

The similarity in structure between Philo and the Jahwistic source:

The accounts start with a pair of humans described as fruit growers. From these comes a second generation divided into two families. The one family is associated with the origin of cult, the other with the origin of civilization ("technical inventions"). Further, both in the Jahwistic source and in Philo the family associated with cult is isolated in the genealogical succession. The genealogy continues both places the line from the families of inventions.

In both places the sequence about the origin of cult is based on an anachronism. In Philo Ba'al Shamem, the supreme god of the Phoenicians, is born later in the genealogy of gods.[14] According to Israelite traditions Yahweh was intimately connected to Sinai and the religion of Moses.[15] Both places the sequence has the same intention of emphasizing the supremacy of the national god of the author by transposing his cult to primeval time.

In both places the origin of power is associated with a generation of giants.[16] The period before the flood is described in both as a time of moral laxity. The founding of a city in the antediluvian period is also recounted in both.

Similarity in types of names:

Among the names recounted in the Jahwistic source can be distinguished two main groups. One group contains names which classify a figure as primeval ancestor or archetype of the human race: אדם, 'adām, "man"; hawwā, חוה, "life" (Gen 3,20);[17] אנוש, 'ănōš, "man" (Gen 4,26).[18] The other contains names structured according to inventions or origins of benefits of civilization: hănōk, חנוך, "dedication" (of a city)(Gen 4,17); יבל, yabāl (Gen 4,20);

---

14 Cf. Ebach, op.cit., p. 351.
15 Cf. L. Perlitt, "Sinai und Horeb", Beiträge zur Alttestamentlichen Theologie, Festschrift für Walther Zimmerli, Göttingen 1977, pp. 302-22.
16 I regard this as the core of the Jahwistic account in Gen 6,1-4, cf. below, pp. 283ff.
17 Cf. the discussion in A. Kapelrud, "hawwāh", ThWAT II, Stuttgart 1977, cols. 794-8. The woman is called hawwā, "life", because she is the mother of future generations, cf. Gen 4,1.
18 'ănōš implies even stronger than 'adām a collective idea; cf. C. Westermann, "'ādām, Mensch", THAT I, cols. 42-57, cols. 43f. For the names below, cf. above, pp. 41f.

יוּבָל, *yūbāl* (Gen 4,21); תּוּבַל, *tūbal*, "producers" (Gen 4,22); קַיִן, *qaīn*, "smith" (Gen 4,22).

Among the names recorded in Philo we can make a similar distinction. As primeval ancestors or archetypes are recounted αἰών, which can mean "life, lifetime, generation" or, with more emphasis on the temporal aspect, "a long space of time";[19] πρωτογόνος, "first born, first crated";[20] γένος, "offspring, race, generation";[21] γενεά, "race, family, generation"[22] (or simply a female form of the preceding word). The three last words are derived from the same Greek root and belong to the same semantic field. As inventors are mentioned φῶς, "light"; πῦρ, "fire"; φλόξ, "flame". It is also possible that Ousoos, who invented the log-canoe, at one stage in the history of tradition was connected to Semitic *'ṣ*, Hebrew עץ, *'eṣ*, "wood".[23]

The names Protogonos, Genos, Gena all correspond to the Greek word for "generation" and classify the figures as ancestors in the context of a genealogy. The Hebrew equivalent in ordinary genealogies would be אב, *'āb*, "father".[24] But within genealogies which trace the ancestry back to the first primeval ancestor, the Old Testament does not use *'āb*, but אדם, *'ādām*, "man", cf. Gen 5,1.3; 1 Chr 1,1. Thus, although the Greek words in Philo are not direct translations of Semitic words similar to the Hebrew *'ādām*, the Greek words in Philo function semantically in the same way.

The name of the other primeval ancestor in Philo, Aeon, can be interpreted in different ways. If the emphasis in the name lies on the temporal aspect, Greek αἰών would equal Hebrew עולם, *'ōlām*, "remote or everlasting time",[25] a correspondence well known and commented on in the exegesis of the Old and New Testament and Jewish literature.[26] But αἰών can also mean "life,

---

19   Cf. H.G. Liddell and R. Scott, A Greek-English Lexicon, new rev.ed. by H.S. Jones, Oxford 1970, sub aiōn, p. 45.
20   Cf. Liddell and Scott, sub protogonos, p. 1545.
21   Cf. Liddell and Scott, sub genos, p. 344.
22   Cf. Liddell and Scott, sub genea, p. 342.
23   Cf. Ebach, op.cit., pp. 169f.
24   Cf. E. Jenni, "'āb Vater", THAT I, cols. 1-17, cols. 3-5.
25   Cf. E. Jenni, "'ōlām, Ewigkeit", THAT II, cols. 228-43.
26   Cf. in general the discussion in O. Cullmann, Christ and Time, rev.ed., London 1962, pp. 45-9; G. Delling, Zeit und Endzeit, BSt 58, Neukirchen-Vluyn 1970, pp. 24, 53; J. Barr, Biblical Words for Time, SBT, First Series 33, 2nd

generation". In this sense the word is semantically not far removed from the designation of the primeval mother as ḥawwā, "life", in Genesis. The primeval mother is designated "life" because she is the origin of the future generations of mankind (cf. above note 17).

With the comparison above we do not claim that Philo used a source with the same Semitic words as Genesis. There is no basis for such an assumption because we do not know the character of Philo's source or to what extent his record is a translation or, more probably, a paraphrastic elaboration. What we have tried to show is that whatever the Semitic source might have looked like, Philo uses Greek words which semantically function in a way similar to Biblical ones.

There is one more significant parallel. The group of words which classify figures as ancestors or archetypes of mankind occurs in the first generation in the Genesis account (Adam, Eve) and in the family associated with the origin of cult in the second (Enosh). The names classifying figures as inventors occur in the family associated with the origin of civilization in the second generation (Enoch, Yabal, Yubal, Tubal-Cain). This is exactly the same in Philo: Aeon and Protogonos in the first generation; Genos and Genea in the second generation and associated with the origin of cult; Phos, Pyr, Phlox, and possibly Ousoos in the family connected to the origin of civilization.

We think the observations above point in the direction that the similarity between Philo and the Jahwistic source can be regarded not only as a general correspondence in motifs conventionally used in the description of the primeval period. The similarities are more specific than that. On the other hand, it is not our intention to construct a theory about literary dependence one way or the other.

rev.ed., Edinburgh 1969, pp. 50-109, 122-28; W. Harnisch, Verhängnis und Verheissung der Geschichte, FRLANT 97, Göttingen 1969, pp. 90-106.
Ebach, op.cit., p. 114, identifies Aion with Ulomos in the cosmogony of Machos (cf. text in Ebach, pp. 431f). The name Ulomos seems to reflect Semitic ʿlm, Hebrew ʿōlām. The background of Aion should accordingly be this Semitic word. The problem is, however, that Ulomos occurs at quite another place and is described quite differently in Machos' cosmogony. The identification is therefore questionable.

Besides the obvious problems involved in such a theory arising
from our ignorance of Philo's source, nothing in his Greek record
indicates a direct relationship. Our point is simply that there are so
many similarities that Philo and the Jahwist must have used similar
traditions, or, as it seems, a similar block of traditions. With regard
to what can be said about the age and geographical location of the
material used in Philo this is not an impossible assumption.

We now turn to the Mesopotamian material. Finkelstein and after
him Hallo have suggested that the genealogies in Gen 4 and 5 are
parallels to the two kinds of lists in the Mesopotamian tradition,
the antediluvian Apkallu List and the antediluvian King List.[27]
There is a correspondence in number between the seven generations in the genealogical line Adam - Cain - Lamech, Gen 4,1.17-
18 and the seven apkallu's as well as between the ten generations
in Gen 5 and the ten kings in WB 62 and Berossos. Berossos also
records the two lists together. But this argument rides counter to a
basic observation in the Old Testament field: There are about five
hundred years between the composing of Gen 4 and Gen 5. This
means that the argument is relevant only to the youngest Priestly
source and the understanding of Gen 4 in it, not for the original
background of Gen 4.

There remains, however, the question whether the seven generations in Gen 4 in isolation could have been composed under the
influence of the Apkallu List. Westermann sees a correspondence
in the juxtaposition of names and inventions. He also calls
attention to the fact that the apkallu Nungalpiriggal in W 20 030,7
is described as the inventor of the lyre, which has a parallel in
Gen 4,21.[28] But there are obstacles to a theory of dependence.
There are no correspondences between names and inventions in the
Apkallu Lists. Furthermore, the achievements in Gen 4 are with
one exception, the founding of a city, not linked to the seven
generations from Adam to Lamech, but to the children of Lamech
(4, 19-20). If the Jahwist structured his account according to the
seven apkallu's, why did he place most of the inventions in the
generation afterwards?

27 Finkelstein, "Antediluvian Kings", p. 60, note 41; Hallo, "Antediluvian
Cities", pp. 63f.
28 C. Westermann, Genesis, pp. 441 and 463f.

There are, however, parallels to Gen 4,17-18 in Mesopotamian literature. As observed previously, both the antediluvian King List and the introduction to the Sumerian flood story recounts the founding of cities.[29] An account about the *building* of a city and the *dedication* of the overlordship of a city in primeval time (cf. the words in 4,17, "build", *ḥᵃnōk*, "dedicated") is found in a genealogy of gods in the form of a succession myth:

> [Third]ly, they built the city of Dunnu, the twin towers.
> Ḥain dedicated the overlordship in the city
> of Dunnu to himself.
>
> (BM 74329 Obv., lines 6-7)[30]

That a ruler of a city can have the same name as the city itself is found in the antediluvian King List WB 62 where Shuruppak, the ninth king, is the ruler of Shuruppak.[31]

Hallo makes a most intriguing suggestion concerning the name of the city in Gen 4,17. We have previously discussed the strange syntax of this clause and considered the possibility that the Jahwist could have adopted a tradition in which Enoch was the founder of the city. Accordingly the name of the city would be according to the name of Enoch's son, Irad.[32] Hallo calls attention to the similarity between Irad and Eridu.[33] Although this is not conclusive since it implies an emendation of the Biblical text, it is tempting to see a correspondence between the first city in Mesopotamian and Biblical literature.

To summarize our observations, the basic structure of the antediluvian account in the Jahwistic source is very similar to the antediluvian section of the technogony in Philo of Byblos' Phoenician History. The similarities are of such a kind as to point toward some sort of common background, probably a common block of traditions. In relation to the Mesopotamian material there are certainly contacts between the Jahwistic source and Mesopotamian traditions in the stories of the flood and the tower of Babel. In the antediluvian section there is a general correspondence

---

29 Cf. above, pp. 165ff.
30 Cf. W.G. Lambert and P. Walcot, "A New Babylonian Theogony and Hesiod", Kadmos 4, 1965, pp. 64-72.
31 Cf. the table on pp. 166f.
32 Cf. above, p. 41.
33 Hallo, op.cit., p. 64.

in that great inventions of civilatory benefits are placed in this
period and associated with culture heroes appearing in lists. There
is a more specific correspondence in the invention of the lyre and
in the founding of cities. But these similarities do not mean that
the Jahwist used a fixed Mesopotamian tradition like the Apkallu
List. It may indicate that the Jahwist selected different elements
with which he had become acquainted in Mesopotamian primeval
traditions without necessarily knowing that they were Mesopotamian, although this assumption depends on how strongly one
wants to emphasize the similarities pointed out above.

2.   The Background of the Enoch Sequence of the Priestly Source

2.1   An Examination of Westermann's Position

I shall begin by examining Westermann's arguments in which he
denies that P used a Mesopotamian antediluvian model for his list
of ten antediluvian generations and for Enoch in the seventh
generation.[34]
Westermann states three facts about the antediluvian King List:

1. It is an independent entity not originally connected to a postdiluvian list.
2. The original number is eight or seven, not ten.
3. The names of the kings are Sumerian, not Akkadian.

Commentary: The third point is certainly correct. The first is
correct as far as the postdiluvian Sumerian King List is concerned.
WB 444 is the only list which definitely connects the antediluvian
list to the Sumerian King List.[35] This observation is important
enough in the Mesopotamian field, but it does not touch the
relationship between P and the Mesopotamian material since, as far
as I know, nobody has claimed a correspondence between P's
postdiluvian ten generations and the list of Sumerian kings. Point 2
involves several elements. *First,* what does "the original number"
mean? Does it refer to a number existing in an oral tradition in
the third millennium, or does it signify the number in the oldest

34   Cf. Westermann, Genesis, pp. 474-7, 484ff; cf. also above, pp. 26f.
35   Cf. above, p. 163.

written sources? When Westermann considered the possibility that the list originally had only seven kings, it is Ziusudra, the last king and the hero of the flood, he would exclude. Whether Ziusudra was a part of the list at some stage prior to the oldest written sources, if such a stage existed, we do not know. What we do know is that Ziusudra is the last king in the oldest written source, WB 62, and in CT 46,5 + 12054 and Berossos. Consequently he is missing only in WB 444 among the lists with the final part preserved. The only list which with certainty has seven kings is W 20 030,7, but there the number is clearly constructed according to the number of sages. What can be said in this respect is that eight seems to have been a basic pattern in the Old Babylonian period.[36] *Secondly,* why should we ask about the original number? P wrote his work about 500-400 B.C., and I think we can be sure that he had no interest in what the lists looked like about 1500 years earlier.

In his direct refutation of Mesopotamian influence Westermann states four points:

1. The Mesopotamian lists can not be regarded as antediluvian because they originally had no connection to the flood.
2. The number "ten" is given in only one Sumerian list. Since the other lists contain eight (or seven) names, a comparison of the names is impossible.
3. The high number of years shows a general correspondence, but is not specific enough to demonstrate a dependence.
4. There is no correspondence in the names.

Commentary: If we use the written sources as a basis (and we have nothing else), Westermann's first point is wrong. All the lists in which the final part is preserved either refer to the flood or connect to the Flood story: WB 62; WB 444; WB 20 030,7 refer to the flood; CT 46,5 + 12054 and Berossos connect to the Flood story.[37]

The second point contains a correct observation, for only one cuneiform list has ten names. Since Westermann published his commentary, CT 46,5 + 12054 has been edited and contains nine names. The question, however, is how strongly we should emphasize an argument like this. If it is correct that a basic pattern in

36   Cf. above, p. 168.
37   Cf. the table above, pp. 166f.

the Old Babylonian period was eight, to what extent does this concern P? Should we not rather ask what sorts of lists could have been available for P in the middle of the first millennium B.C.? The two lists which are closest to P in time are the Neo-Assyrian text CT 46,5 + 12054 (about 650) and Berossos (281). The first contains nine names, the second ten. In our analysis of the style we have seen that Berossos is closest to CT 46,5 + 12054 in the order of names and cities, as well as in relating to the Flood story. He is closest, however, to WB 62 in the number of names and in style.[38] These lists also have a genealogical pattern connected to the last dynasty. The youngest list, W 20 030,7, only gives seven names. Concerning the number of names this demonstrates two things. First, none of the lists from the first millennium follows the pattern "eight". Accordingly, we cannot presuppose this as a pattern in the first millennium. Secondly, Berossos seems to have known the ancient list WB 62, or at least a list similar to it, giving ten names. We see no reason why P should not have known the same kind of list.

I agree with Westermann's third point. The high number of years alone is not specific enough to demonstrate a relationship. In point four we agree with Westermann as far as the names of the antediluvian kings are concerned.

Concerning the figure of Enoch Westermann states:

1. The 365 years is only a round number.
2. There is no relationship between Enoch and Enmeduranki, since the lists in which they occur are not related. As a parallel the figure Adapa comes closer.
3. There is a similarity in phraseology between the disappearance of Xisouthros in Berossos and the removal of Enoch. But Westermann does not seem to see a relationship.

Commentary: To begin with the second point, its validity depends on the validity of points 1 and 2 in the immediately preceding section. In the first, Westermann's argument is wrong, and I have questioned this reasoning in the second. Enmeduranki occurs in the seventh position, as does Enoch, in WB 444 and in the two youngest lists, Berossos and W 20 030,7. There is a firm tradition, recorded in two Akkadian texts, that he was carried

---

38   Cf. above, pp. 170-2.

away to heaven, as was Enoch. Furthermore, Enoch does not appear in the seventh position in P's list by accident. P rearranged the list from Gen 4 in order to give Enoch this number.[39] I do not think it is correct to regard Enmeduranki and Adapa as alternatives here. In Bīt Mēseri the seventh sage, Utuabzu, is described as Adapa. Also this seventh sage ascends to heaven. Utuabzu and Enmeduranki are listed as pairs in Berossos and W 20 030,7. The ascension motif is in the antediluvian tradition connected to Enmeduranki and Adapa, who normally appears as the first sage. Most likely the juxtaposition of Utuabzu and Enmeduranki has caused the transference of the motif to the seventh sage instead of the first.[40] In any case, Enmeduranki and Utuabzu/-Adapa were related in Mesopotamian literature, both in placement in the lists and in fate. Accordingly there was a broad tradition in Babylonian scribal milieu that the figure associated with the number seven went to heaven and received insight into divine wisdom. Semantically there is also a correspondence between P's interpretation of Enoch's name as "dedicated, trained",[41] and the Akkadian designation *apkallu* which means "sage, expert".

I now turn to point 1. Westermann sees nothing specific in the number 365. I disagree. I have previously demonstrated that P used the number 365 as the specific number of the solar year.[42] The next question is inevitably why P associated this number with Enoch. In the cuneiform sources Enmeduranki is associated with Sippar. That Sippar had the sun-god Utu as its chief god is attested to in numerous cuneiform sources. In Berossos the city is simply called "the city of the sun".[43] Besides this Sippar was known as a seat for antediluvian wisdom and the city not destroyed in the flood.[44] In P the connection between Enoch and the number 365 involves three components: the sun, astronomical and calendarian speculations, and the seventh figure. In Mesopotamian literature we have the following components:

39 Cf. above, pp. 44f.
40 Cf. above, p. 204.
41 Cf. above, pp. 45f.
42 Cf. above, p. 52.
43 Cf. above, p. 178.
44 Cf. above, pp. 179f.

1. Sippar, the city of the sun, was according to the text <u>Enmeduranki and the Diviners</u> the first place where the well-known Babylonian astrological series <u>Enuma Anu Enlil</u> was taught.[45]
2. This astrological series was taught by Enmeduranki, the seventh antediluvian king.
3. The parallel figure to Enmeduranki, the seventh sage in Bīt Mēseri, had the full name Uanadapa, which means "light shining in the sky", or "with the god An".[46] The name indicates a correspondence with astronomical speculations. Although it is not stated in cuneiform literature, "the light shining with the god in the sky" could easily be related to the sun.
4. Adapa, the primary sage, was regarded as the composer of an astronomical work.[47] According to Berossos all the antediluvian books were hidden in Sippar during the flood.[48]

I think these four points demonstrate that the three elements in P also were related in Mesopotamian literature, although P combines them differently.

I now turn to Westermann's third point. There is a similarity in the way the disappearance is described in Berossos and in P. There is also a correspondence between the Epic of Gilgamesh, Tabl. XI, line 196, and Gen 5,24. The same verb, Hebrew *lāqaḥ*, Akkadian *leqû*, "take", is used in both places.[49] But I do not think that the fate of the Mesopotamian flood hero inspired P in the passage about the removal in Gen 5,24. The parallel to the Mesopotamian flood hero is Noah on the tenth place in P's list. There is, however, the possibility that once P had taken over the ascension motif from the seventh figure in the Mesopotamian lists, he used a wording corresponding to the wording about the flood hero. As we have noted previously, there are similarities in the description of the two figures in P.[50]

My evaluation of the material has led to conclusions which differ from Westermann's. This is because of two factors. First, I have included two texts not published when Westermann wrote his commentary, the more complete text to Bīt Mēseri by Borger[51]

---

45   Cf. above, p. 189.
46   Cf. above, p. 204.
47   Cf. above, pp. 210ff.
48   Cf. above, pp. 178f.
49   Cf. also P. Grelot, "La légende d'Hénoch", p. 190. For the Akkadian text cf. our note 57, p. 177.
50   Cf. above, pp. 47f.
51   Cf. above, pp. 191f. Already Borger pointed out the similarity between Bīt Mēseri and the ascension motif in Gen 5,24. Cf. Borger, "Bīt Mēseri und die Himmelfahrt Henochs", pp. 185f.

and CT 46,5 + 12054.[52] Secondly, I think the difference is demonstrated clearly by the following statement in Westermann's commentary: "Die angenommenen Übereinstimmungen treffen zum grössten Teil nicht zu. Soweit Entsprechungen bleiben, wie die hohen Zahlen, die Zehnzahl, der letzte name in der Liste, sind sie traditionsgeschichtlich aus späten Stadien zu erklären und schliessen es aus, die alt-babylonische Königsliste in ihrer ursprünglichen Gestalt als Vorlage von Gen 5 anzusehen."[53] What amazes me in this statement is the complete lack of historical perspective. Why should we demand that P depended on "the Old Babylonian King List in its original shape"? Why should we reconstruct what an original King List might have looked like perhaps more than 1500 years earlier than P and claim that either P should correspond to this list, or there is no correspondence at all? And when there is correspondence with the existing (not original?) lists and especially with those closest in time to P, this should be of no importance, because the corresponding elements are only secondary? It is hard to understand the logic. The reason why Westermann chose this approach can perhaps be found in a passage further down: "Es kann jetzt als sicher gelten, dass P in der Reihe der Namen nicht von einer der altbabylonischen Liste der Urkönige abhängig ist."[54] If the problem is the correspondence in the names, that was suggested earlier in the research,[55] the time scale must be different, because the names are already recorded in the Jahwistic genealogy about five hundred years earlier than P. There is no correspondence, as Zimmern made totally clear about 45 years before Westermann's commentary.[56] But it seems that this problem determined Westermann's approach.

I shall now reexamine the material. The question is not, as should now be clear, whether P derived his names from the antediluvian lists, but whether P in his rearrangement of the names from the genealogies in Gen 4 used Mesopotamian antediluvian lists as models.

---

52 Cf. above, p. 162.
53 Westermann, op.cit., p. 476.
54 Westermann, op.cit., p. 477.
55 Cf. above, pp. 24ff.
56 Cf. above, p. 25.

2.2   A New Examination of the Correspondence

2.2.1   The Enoch Sequence

In the Enoch sequence, Gen 5,21-24, we find the following correspondence between P and Mesopotamian primeval traditions:

I. "Walked with God (the *'älohīm*)".   In P this phrase is meant to describe an "intimate relationship with God".[57] The same clause is used about Noah, where the intimate relationship also seems to imply "a direct communication". In the Book of Jubilees the passage is taken literally as "travelled with the angels", drawing on the cosmological parts of the Astronomical Book and especially the Book of Watchers.[58] All these three aspects are contained in the text *Enmeduranki and the Diviners*.[59]

1. Enmeduranki is <u>naram</u> <u>danim</u> <u>denlíl ùdea</u>, "the beloved of Anu, Enlil and Ea".
2. Enmeduranki communicated with the gods in the heavenly assembly.
3. Enmeduranki travelled with the gods Šamaš and Adad to heaven.

The Aspect of communication is parallel to Noah. In Mesopotamian literature Enmeduranki and Ziusudra are parallels in this respect. Ziusudra is portrayed as the one who communicated directly with his god.[60]

II. "And all the days of Enoch were 365 years." We have discussed the background of this passage.[61] Three elements are combined. 365 is definitely the number of the solar year. This involves both the sun and astronomical-calendarian speculations. These two elements are then linked to the seventh sage as the third element. We find the following elements in the Mesopotamian antediluvian traditions corresponding to P:

1. Enmeduranki, the seventh king in WB 444, Berossos and W 20 030,7, is located to Sippar, the city of the sun.
2. Sippar was the first place where the best known Babylonian astrological series was taught.
3. This series was taught by Enmeduranki, the seventh king.

---

57   Cf. above, p. 48.
58   Cf. above, p. 130 and pp. 66ff.
59   Cf. for text, pp. 185f.
60   Cf. above, p. 174.
61   Cf. above, pp. 226f.

4. The seventh sage, parallel to Enmeduranki, has a name implying astronomical connections: "The light shining with the god heaven". The name can easily be connected to the sun.
5. This sage is regarded as the composer of an astronomical work.
6. According to Berossos all the writings of this sage were hidden in Sippar, the city of the sun.

III. "And he was no more because God took him away."   We find the following Mesopotamian elements corresponding to P:

1. Enmeduranki, the seventh king in WB 62, Berossos and W 20 030,7, was brought to heaven.
2. Adapa/Utuabzu, the seventh sage in Bīt Mēseri, and parallel to Enmeduranki in Berossos and W 20 030,7, also ascended to heaven.
3. The name of Enoch most likely has the meaning "dedicated, trained", in P. Adapa is apkallu, meaning "sage, expert".

Also here there are similarities to the hero of the flood in Mesopotamian sources. The disappearance is emphasized in Berossos' version of the flood story. The same verb is used about the removal of the hero in the Epic of Gilgamesh, Tab. XI, line 196, and Gen 5,24.

2.2.2   The Context

The similarities between P's list and the Mesopotamian antediluvian traditions can be summarized in eight points:

1. P has a list of ten names in an antediluvian context. WB 62 and Berossos have a version of the antediluvian King List containing ten names.
2. The list in P is a genealogy. The King List is at least in the Old Babylonian period understood as a list of urban dynasties.[62] Later the cities may have lost some of their importance in the lists. Berossos has only three cities, W 20 030,7 omits the cities.[63] There are traces of a genealogical pattern in the last dynasty Shuruppak in WB 62; CT 46,5 + 12054, and Berossos. The same is true also of Berossos' account of the first dynasty of Babylon.[64] It is possible that the Apkallu List in W 20 030,7 was meant as a genealogy. At least this is very likely concerning the succeeding Ummânu List.[65]
3. Both in P and in the King Lists the figures are said to have lived an enormous number of years, although there is no correspondence in the numbers.
4. The list in P is affiliated with the Flood story. All the Mesopotamian lists in which the final part is preserved refer to the flood at the end. The King List which are closest to P in time, CT 46,5 + 12054 and Berossos, continue with the Flood story.

62   Cf. above, pp. 169f.
63   Cf. above, pp. 171f.
64   Cf. the table above, pp. 166f.
65   Cf. above, p. 195.

5. The Flood story recorded in J/P depends on a Mesopotamian model.
6. The last figure in P's list, Noah, is the hero in the Flood story. The last
    figure in WB 62, CT 46,5 + 12054 and Berossos, Ziusudra, is the hero in the
    Mesopotamian Flood story. In WB 62 and Berossos he appears in the tenth
    position, just like the hero in P.
7. The seven figure in P, Enoch, was taken to heaven, as was the seventh figure
    in WB 444, Berossos and W 20 030,7, Enmeduranki. His counterpart in the
    seventh position in the Apkallu Lists, Utuabzu/Adapa, also went to heaven
    according to Bīt Mēseri.
8. Only two kings in the Mesopotamian King Lists have special traditions linked
    to their fate: Enmeduranki and Ziusudra. Among the antediluvian patriarchs
    in Gen 5 only two are connected to special events according to P, that is
    Enoch and Noah.

These are the similarities between P and the Mesopotamian
material as it appears in cuneiform literature and in Berossos.
There are more similarities which especially concern the relation
between P and Berossos, and to a certain extent also the latest
cuneiform source W 20 030,7.

We have previously seen that Berossos followed a cuneiform
tradition in connecting the King List and the Flood story. According to Josephus, Berossos recorded a great wise man in the tenth
generation after the flood. We have previously analyzed this
passage in Berossos and found that the background lay in a
tradition similar to that recorded in W 20 030,7.[66] A comparison
of the structure in this source and Berossos yields the following:

W 20 030,7	Berossos
Seven kings and seven apkallu's	ten kings and seven apkallu's
flood	flood
one apkallu	
Genealogy of ummânu's	
Aḥiqar, the famous scholar at the tenth	A great wise man in the tenth genera-
place after the flood	tion

The fact that W 20 030,7 is the only known cuneiform source in
which kings and apkallu's are listed as pairs, indicates strongly that
Berossos followed a tradition similar to it. If this holds true for his
account about the great wise man, we have the following structure
presupposed in Berossos and compared to P:

66   Cf. above, pp. 194ff.

Priestly source	Berossos
ten patriarchs	ten kings and seven apkallu's
Flood story	Flood story
ten patriarchs	(10 wise men)
Abraham in the tenth position	a great scholar in the tenth position

As we previously have noted, Finkelstein and Hallo called attention to the possibility that the genealogies in Gen 4 and 5 together could form a parallel to the Mesopotamian juxtaposition of kings and apkallu's. Gen 4 counts seven generations from Adam to Lamech; Gen 5 counts ten generations from Adam to Noah. The numbers seven and ten would be the same as in Berossos. The Mesopotamian tradition could have been interpreted in that way by P, understanding the genealogy in J as a parallel to the Apkallu List.

Berossos not only brings together the two blocks of Mesopotamian primeval traditions, the King List and the Flood story (which is in accordance with the cuneiform sources), but also adds a third block in front of the two others, an account of creation taken from Enuma Elish. In the cuneiform literature Enuma Elish is an independent entity associated with neither the List of Kings nor the Flood story. Nevertheless, I think it is possible to trace how Berossos connected this account of creation to the King List and what sort of tradition he may have followed when he did it.
According to Polyhistor, Berossos ended his account of the flood with the notice that the surviving men went to Babylon and founded the city anew.[67] That must mean that it existed before the flood. This is in fact the case in Berossos, where Babylon appears as the first city in the King List. According to Abydenos, Berossos recounted the founding of Babylon already in his account of creation: "They say that everything originally was water and was called *Thalassa*. Bel restrained it, assigned a place to each thing, and he surrounded Babylon with a wall."[68] It is not difficult to trace Enuma Elish as the underlying source.[69] Bel's restraining of the water is a clear reflection of Marduk's victory of

---

67 Text: Euseb. (Arm.) Chron. p. 10,17-12,16 and Syncellus p. 53,19. FGH III, C, 1.B, sequence 17, pp. 318f. Translation: Burstein, Book II, 2,4, p. 21.
68 Text: Praep. Ev. 9.41.5. FGH III, C, 1.B, p. 399. Translation: Burstein, Book I, 5, p. 17.
69 Cf. Schnabel, Berossos und die Babylonisch-Hellenistische Literatur, pp. 41f.

Tiamat. Enuma Elish also tells how Marduk founded Babylon after this victory, Tabl V, lines 119-131.[70] Accordingly Berossos gave the following information about Babylon: The city was founded as a part of creation, it was the first city in the King List, and it was refounded after the deluge.

Thus Babylon is the connecting link between creation and the King List. Berossos regarded the founding of Babylon as the final goal in Enuma Elish, and through its founding he connected the account of creation to the cities in the King List. This connection does not appear in Enuma Elish. But does it occur elsewhere?

In his recension of Enuma Elish Berossos concentrates on three themes: creation of heaven and earth, creation of the human race, and the foundation of Babylon.[71] These three themes are then combined with the King List and the Flood story. We have previously called attention to the similarities between the King List and the list of antediluvian cities in the introduction to the Sumerian Flood story.[72] But the Sumerian Flood story does not begin with the founding of cities. As far as we can judge from the fragmentary beginning, the composition recounts two stages before the flood. The first starts with the creation of the human race (col i, lines 47-48), while the second contains the founding of the cities (col ii, lines 89-98).[73] This means that already the Sumerian Flood story combined the three blocks that form the basic parts of Berossos' primeval account: Creation — list of cities — Flood story. We shall not argue that Berossos actually utilized the Sumerian Flood story as source in his primeval account. This would demand a more thorough exploration. Our point in this respect is that the connection of the theme of creation to other blocks of Mesopotamian primeval traditions was not a new invention by Berossos. Enuma Elish combines creation and the founding of Babylon, while the Sumerian Flood story combines creation to the founding of cities and flood.

---

70   Cf. ANET[3], p. 502.
71   Text: Euseb. (Arm.) Chron. p. 6,8-9,2 and Syncellus p. 49,19. FGH III, C, 1.B, sequences 6-7, pp. 370ff. Translation: Burstein, Book I, 2,1-3, pp. 14f. For Babylon, cf. note 68 above.
72   Cf. above, pp. 163ff.
73   Cf. Civil in Lambert and Millard, Atra-Ḥasis, p. 141. T. Jacobsen concludes in the same way after having examined the sources relating to the composition. The story contains three parts: creation, earliest cities and the flood. Cf. T. Jacobsen, "The Eridu Genesis", pp. 514, 526-7.

What we have observed in our analysis of the Mesopotamian material is that the primeval traditions did not exist as isolated entities but were combined in different ways through the history of transmission: primeval kings and cities to the Flood story, creation of the human race to foundation of antediluvian cities and the Flood story, antediluvian kings to antediluvian sages, antediluvian sages to postdiluvian ummânu's, and the creation of the world and the human race to the founding of the first city. What happens in Berossos is that he records one kind of combination. He was not the first to combine the traditions. We think that the observations above give good reason for maintaining that Berossos cannot be regarded as a creative author, but as a transmitter of the primeval traditions as they were known in his own scribal milieu in Babylon.

If we can assume that Berossos did not invent his comprehensive view of primeval history, but that it originated in learned activity in his own scribal milieu, this has great significance for the comparison of P and the Mesopotamian material. According to our analysis above, the extracts from Berossos' Babyloniaca seem to presuppose the following basic structure of primeval history, here compared to P:

Berossos	Priestly source
creation	creation
ten antediluvian kings and seven apkallu's	ten antediluvian patriarchs
Flood story	Flood story
(ten postdiluvian wise men)	ten postdiluvian patriarchs
a great scholar in the tenth position	Abraham in the tenth generation

The similarities between P and the Mesopotamian material cannot be regarded as depending only on a conventional description of primeval time, appearing independently in different cultures. There are so many corresponding features, both in the details and the structure, that the only possible conclusion is that P used a Mesopotamian model.[74]

---

74 T. Jacobsen came to the same conclusion by comparing the Sumerian Flood story (by him called "the Eridu Genesis"), the Neo-Assyrian tablet (CT 46,5 + 12054) and the Priestly source. Cf. Jacobsen, op.cit., pp. 527-29.

With regard to Gen 5 we can conclude that P rearranged the list in Gen 4 in order to make an antediluvian list of ten figures similar to a Mesopotamian counterpart. He placed Noah as the last figure of the list parallel to Ziusudra, and he placed Enoch, "the dedicated, trained one" (as he interpreted the name) in the seventh position of the list parallel to the wise king Enmeduranki and the sage Utuabzu/Adapa. It must have made quite an impression on P that such extraordinary figures were to be found in the seventh position in the Mesopotamian lists, connected to the sacred number which had such great importance in P's own theology.

I think we also know the reason why P rearranged the genealogies from Gen 4. It was dependent upon the principle of recognition. P recognized the Jahwistic Flood story in the Mesopotamian Flood story on the one hand, and he recognized the Jahwistic genealogy of a family of inventors in Mesopotamian antediluvian lists on the other. Through this rearrangement he updated his native primeval traditions so that they corresponded to the general structure of the Mesopotamian traditions, but he did so without giving away his own religion.

3. The Origin of Astronomy/Astrology in the Astronomical Book and in Mesopotamian Antediluvian Traditions

In our analysis of the Astronomical Book we found that the oldest part consisted of astronomical tables.[75] The origin was ascribed to the time of Uriel, Enoch and Methuselah. We have already noted that also Mesopotamian scribes dated astrological works back to primeval time. The best known astrological series *Enuma Anu Enlil* was said to have been revealed to Enmeduranki in the heavenly assembly and taught by him in the antediluvian city Sippar. In addition, mathematical tables which served as basis for the astronomical calculations were revealed to Enmeduranki.[76]

In our analysis of the Astronomical Book we also observed that the figure most intimately associated with the astronomical calculations was neither Enoch nor Methuselah, but Uriel. The whole book is

75   Cf. above, pp. 60ff.
76   Cf. above, p. 189.

presented as an instruction given by this figure,[77] who is described as an angel. In seeking a counterpart to Uriel in Mesopotamian traditions, we therefore have to look for an equivalent semi-divine figure. The choice is not difficult. In the highest position among the Mesopotamian antediluvian figures stands the semi-divine Uanadapa.

In the *Myth of Adapa* Adapa is called "the son of Ea" and is "created by Ea".[78] The full name Uanadapa can be paraphrased as light shining together with the sky; the short name U-An "light of the god heaven (sky)".[79] The connection with "light" is also clear in Bīt Mēseri where U-An together with the other apkallu's, is described as "shining".[80] According to Bīt Mēseri the apkallu's should "insure the correct functioning of the plans of heaven and earth"; the same is also said explicitly about U-An. In our analysis of the clause we found that the apkallu's were appointed as guardians over the cosmic order as it was prefigured by the gods when they created the world.[81] The apkallu's were also closely associated with Apsu, originally the fresh water but later hardly distinguished from the underworld where other monstrous creatures lived, as in the Poem of Erra.[82] To the primary sage Adapa were attributed literary compositions, among them an astronomical work.[83]

After this repetition of the fundamental features associated with Uanadapa we can make the following list of parallels with Uriel:[84]

Uriel	Uanadapa
The name Uriel means "light of God".	The short form of the name, U-An, means "light of the god heaven".
Uriel is the leader of the lights of heaven.	Uanadapa can be paraphrased as "light that shines in the sky". Elsewhere he is characterized as "shining".
Uriel is in charge of the cosmic order.	Uanadapa is in charge of the cosmic order.

77 Cf. above, p. 63.
78 Cf. Recension A, line 6; Recension B, line 11. ANET³, p. 101.
79 Cf. above, p. 204.
80 Cf. above, p. 197.
81 Cf. above, pp. 199f.
82 Cf. Cagni, The Poem of Erra, notes 15, 55, 58. Cf. also our note 123, p. 199.
83 Cf. above, pp. 210ff.
84 On Uriel, cf. above, pp. 62, 66.

Uriel is in charge of the underworld, the dwelling place of divine beings.	Uanadapa has his dwelling in the Apsû, the dwelling place of divine beings.
Uriel is the teacher of an astronomical work.	Uanadapa is the composer of an astronomical work.

Some of these features may be of the kind that can appear independently. For instance in Greek mythology Atlas is described as both the cosmic guardian and the inventor of astronomy and placed in the underworld. This similarity between Atlas and Uriel may already have been noticed by Pseudo-Eupolemus.[85] But there is nothing in the name of Atlas which connects him to the lights of heaven. What points strongly in favour of a relationship between Uriel and Uanadapa is that we here both have similar functions and almost identical names.

According to En 33,4 Uriel not only instructed Enoch in the astronomical calculations but also wrote them down for him.[86] This is different in the Astronomical Book, in which Uriel "shows" and "demonstrates" the calculations, but Enoch is regarded as the actual composer of the book.[87] The Astronomical Book presupposes the following transmission of the material: Uriel shows and demonstrates the astronomical calculations for Enoch. Enoch writes them down in books (En 82,1) before instructing Methuselah and handing the books over to him to be passed on to future generations. The books are characterized as wisdom which is beyond human thoughts (En 82,2).

As the primeval composer of astronomical books Enoch is parallel to Uanadapa. The kind of transmission presupposed in the Astronomical Book also resembles what is said about Uanadapa as composer. Uanadapa also received his astrological knowledge from a divine being who dictated it to him.[88] This astrological work is also characterized as supreme wisdom.[89] According to Berossos, the books of Oannes (U-An) were preserved through the flood and distributed to mankind.[90]

---

85   Cf. above, p. 116.
86   Cf. above, p. 68.
87   Cf. above, pp. 63ff.
88   Cf. above, pp. 212f.
89   Cf. the quotation from the Verse Account of Nabonidus, p. 213.
90   Cf. above, pp. 178f.

Both the author of one of the Hebrew text versions of Ben Sira and Pseudo-Eupolemus interpreted the Astronomical Book, or at least traditions similar to those recorded in the book, in a way that made Enoch the primary sage and the discoverer of astronomy/astrology. In Pseudo-Eupolemus we noticed that Enoch was placed into the same position as Uriel in the Astronomical Book.[91] When Enoch in Ben Sira is called a "sign", a word commonly used about celestial bodies, this may indicate that Enoch is placed into some relationship with the phenomena of the sky, as Uriel was in the Astronomical Book.[92]

If these observations are correct, Uanadapa forms the background for both Uriel and Enoch in the Astronomical Book. That also Enoch was patterned on Uanadapa would correspond to the Priestly source of Genesis, where we claimed that both Enmeduranki and Adapa formed the background for the seventh figure who was taken to heaven. With regard to the Mesopotamian traditions about the antediluvian sages this splitting up of the Uanadapa traditions into two figures is not an impossible assumption. As we have noted, the apkallu traditions contained both legendary and mythical features.[93] According to the legendary features the apkallu's are described as great wise men from the ancient past corresponding to Enoch in the main current of the Enochic traditions. According to the mythological features the apkallu's were semi-divine beings coming from the realm of the god Ea, which would correspond to an angelic figure like Uriel.

4. The Tablets of Heaven in Enochic and Mesopotamian Traditions

In our analysis of the Astronomical Book we found that En 81 was an addition to the original composition.[94] The location of Enoch is different from that of the Astronomical Book. Nothing in the Astronomical Book indicates that Enoch should have been taken to

---

91 Cf. above, pp. 116f.
92 Cf. above, pp. 123f.
93 Cf. above, pp. 207ff.
94 Cf. above, p. 59.

heaven, while En 81 clearly presupposes that Enoch is situated in the heavenly assembly, similar to his position in En 12 and 14.[95] In the Astronomical Book astronomical calculations were revealed to Enoch, while in En 81 he reads "the tablets of heaven". The different origins of the two compositions do not mean, however, that they have nothing in common. When En 81 was inserted into the Astronomical Book, the redactor clearly saw the astronomical calculations and the tablets of heaven as parallels. The connecting link is Uriel's speech in En 80 where Enoch on basis of Uriel's instruction is enabled to predict.[96] The tablets of heaven thus correspond to the astronomical calculations on the one hand and on the other to predictions (in the style of vaticinia ex eventu) of the future of mankind, as becomes clear also in the other references to the tablets in the Epistle of Enoch (cf. note above).

In research on Enoch scholars have often claimed that the heavenly tablets were patterned after the tablet(s) of the gods in the Akkadian text Enmeduranki and the Diviners.[97] In the table below I list the similarities as they appear in En 81 and in the other references to the tablets in the Epistle of Enoch compared to the text about Enmeduranki.[98]

ENOCH	ENMEDURANKI
Location	
heavenly assembly	heavenly assembly
Designation of the tablets	
lūhāt š^emayyā, "tablets of heaven"	tuppi ilāni, "tablet(s) of the gods"
Characteristics of the tablets	
rāzē maryā, "mysteries of the Lord"	niṣirti anim enlil u ea, "a mystery of Anu, Enlil and Ea" pirišti šamê u erṣetim, "a secret of heaven and earth" pirišti ilāni rabûti, "the secrets of the great gods"

---

95 Cf. above, p. 80.
96 Cf. above, pp. 78f.
97 Cf. for instance Bousset / Gressmann and Grelot in our survey of the history of the research above, p. 28.
98 The textual basis for the comparison is to be found above on pp. 76ff (Enoch) and pp. 185ff (Enmeduranki).

Instruction

qaddišīn 'aḫᵃwōnī wᵉaḫᵃzōnī
  the holy ones demonstrated for
  me and showed me"

ušabrušu, "they showed him"
iddinušu,
  "they gave him (the tablets)

Content of instruction

astronomy/predictions

divination/astrology

Transmission

tell everything to your son,
  Methuselah
show all your children

he showed them (the men from the
  cities)

instruct your children
write down for them
testify for all your children

he gave them the tablets of the gods
he will instruct him (his son)

Commentary: When one compares the lists one must be aware that the texts stem from two totally different cultures. Consequently basic features will differ considerably. For instance, a Jewish author obviously could not write about the "the assembly of the gods", "tablets of the gods", or "secret of the gods". There were also no traditions in Judaism in divinatory techniques like the Mesopotamian, or of astrology. The heavenly assembly will accordingly in Judaism be the "assembly of the Lord and his angels". The tablets of the gods will be the "the tablets of the Lord" or the "tablets of heaven" since "heaven" often is used as a transcription for the divinity. The mysteries of the gods will be the "mysteries of the Lord". Divination, i.e. unfolding of the future, will be based on the Jewish experience that this is communicated directly from God, especially through a visionary experience.

With this in mind I find the parallels between the texts striking. They concern not only general ideas but also similar words used in the same way, such as "tablets, heaven, mystery, show, instruct". The basic pattern of the texts is also the same: A primeval hero is taken to the heavenly assembly and taught how to unfold the mystery of the future. He returns to the earth and instructs his son in his knowledge.

There are two main differences. One seems to be dependent on the different cultural and religious setting. In the Akkadian text Enmeduranki brings the tablet(s) of the gods back to the earth. I think it would be extremely difficult for a Jew to accept this. The variant in the Enochic text is that Enoch wrote down the content of the heavenly tablets when he returned to the earth. The other difference is that Enmeduranki instructs the men from the important ancient seats of wisdom. This feature is neglected in the Enochic text, which only recounts that the divine wisdom is passed on to the next generation, a feature which is in full accordance with the Akkadian text. But I do not think that these differences contradict the fact that the portrait of Enoch here is dependent on Enmeduranki.

5.   The Primeval Hero in the Noahitic Traditions and En 6-16

5.1   Noah and Enoch in the Noahitic Traditions

5.1.1   The Characteristics of Noah

In our discussion of the Noahitic traditions we concentrated on two groups of texts. One dealt with Noah before the flood, while the other had his birth as its main issue.[99] In En 60,1-10.24c-25 Noah is described as a visionary (as in 4Q Mess ar, cf. note 100 below), and in a vision he is warned about the coming catastrophe. This description of the flood hero as a visionary has its parallel in both Atra-Ḥasis and Berossos' version of the Flood story where the flood hero is warned in a dream.[100]

The birth texts emphasize Noah's extraordinary features as a newborn child. He looks like one of the giants, although his divine origin is strongly denied. No similar stories exist among the Mesopotamian antediluvian texts. As compositions the birth stories depend on the same combination of the fall of the angels and the Flood story that appear in En 6-11. The background of this amalgam will be analyzed later.

---

99   Cf. above, pp. 88ff.
100   Cf. above, pp. 175f. Cf. also 4Q Mess ar, pp. 89f above.

We have suggested, however, that the birth stories were composed to refute what they deny, namely that Noah was divine.[101] That this kind of opinion existed on Palestinian ground is attested through Pseudo-Eupolemus who equated Noah and Belus.[102] This motif has a parallel in the Mesopotamian texts. Both the Sumerian Flood story and the Gilgamesh version state that the flood hero had become like the gods.[103]

5.1.2 The Characteristics of Enoch

In the Noahitic texts Enoch is situated "in the Garden of the Righteous", in Paradise. This location of Enoch occurs only in texts which relate to the Noahitic traditions. Neither Uanadapa nor Enmeduranki was taken away to Paradise. In the Mesopotamian material this motif is reserved exclusively for the flood hero.[104]

In the Noahitic traditions humans can seek Enoch in Paradise to get advice. This motif does not occur in the Mesopotamian versions of the Flood story. It is, however, one of the leading themes in the Epic of Gilgamesh which has adopted the Flood story. Here Gilgamesh travels to meet Utnapishtim to ask how to get eternal life.

5.1.3 The Confusion of Enoch and Noah

In our analysis of the Noahitic traditions and En 6-16 we found that Enoch and Noah appeared in the same roles as visionaries and heroes in the primeval catastrophe.[105] I think that on basis of the Mesopotamian traditions we can trace the background of this confusion. (In the following table the traditional features attributed to Enoch in Jewish literature are placed in brackets.)

101   Cf. above, p. 91.
102   Cf. above, p. 114.
103   Cf. above, pp. 176f.
104   Cf. above, pp. 176ff.
105   Cf. above, p. 93.

Mesopotamian	Genesis		Noahitic traditions	
Ziusudra	Noah	Enoch	Noah	Enoch
intimate relationship with God[106]	intimate relationship with God	intimate relationship with God	intimate relationship with God	[intimate relationship with God]
visionary			visionary	[visionary]
saved through the flood	saved through the flood		saved through the flood	
translated to Paradise				translated to Paradise
Uanadapa				
sage		(sage)	sage	[sage]
visionary				[visionary]
taken to heaven		removed from the earth		[taken to heaven]

Commentary: In the Mesopotamian material Ziusudra and Uana-dapa had two basic features in common: They were both vision-aries,[107] and both were removed from the earth. The Genesis account, however, keeps the basic features separate. Noah is the one who, like Ziusudra was saved through the flood, while Enoch was removed from the earth like Uanadapa. P, however, sees a similarity between the figures in their close relationship with God. P does not record one of the most distinguishing features in the fate of Ziusudra, namely his translation to Paradise. Neither did the Jahwistic source record this feature in the account of the flood. It connects this motif to Adam (Gen 2,15). As we have seen, it is possible that P included it in the removal of Enoch, but it was not the primary background.[108] Nor does P explicitly portray Noah and Enoch as sages and visionaries, although he alludes to Enoch's connection to astronomy.

The composers of the Noahitic texts used not only Genesis but also Mesopotamian traditions as sources. In accordance with these

---

106   Cf. above, p. 175.
107   Cf. above, pp. 175f, and pp. 211ff.
108   Cf. above, p. 231.

traditions they portrayed Noah as a visionary, a feature not found
in Genesis. And in more general accordance with the Mesopotamian apkallu traditions they portrayed Noah as a sage, a feature
also missing in Genesis. They were faithful, however, to the
Genesis account in one respect: They did not recount the translation of the flood hero to Paradise. Instead they connected this
motif to Enoch in the way that his removal in Gen 5,24 was
interpreted as a translation to Paradise. This caused a change in the
"translation to Paradise" motif. In the Mesopotamian versions of
the Flood story the hero is translated after the deluge, but in the
Jewish traditions he is translated before.

We have accordingly come to the conclusion that the distinguishing
features of the Noahitic traditions depend on a special combination
of two sources: 1) the Genesis account which relies on Mesopotamian traditions about Uanadapa and Ziusudra; 2) a direct use of
Mesopotamian primeval traditions in which those centered around
Ziusudra played the dominant role in the formation of the
material.

5.2   The Background of Enoch in En 6-16

What combines En 6-11 and the Noahitic traditions is that in both
Enoch is associated with the primeval catastrophe. This makes it
likely to assume that also Enoch in En 6-16 has adopted features
from Ziusudra. In fact the description of Enoch's disappearance in
En 12,1 resembles what is recounted about Ziusudra, as Milik has
pointed out.[109] But the description can also be regarded as an
elaboration of "he was no more" in Gen 5,24, and the similarity to
the tradition recorded in Berossos may be accidental.

In our analysis of En 12-16 we have pointed out that both the
reference to Enoch's removal in 12,1 and his visionary ascension in
En 14 seem to depend on Gen 5,24. What distinguished the two
accounts is among other things that En 12 and 14 clearly state the
direction: Enoch was taken away to the heavenly assembly. This
motif is connected to all three leading figures in Mesopotamian
primeval traditions: Enmeduranki, Adapa and Ziusudra. In the

109   Cf. Milik, The Books of Enoch, p. 33. Cf. also above, pp. 93 and 178.

Myth of Adapa[110] and *Enmeduranki and the Diviners*[111] the heavenly assembly is described, but none of the descriptions is similar to En 14. The similarity is only in the motif.

We do not think that the motif "entry of a primeval hero into the heavenly assembly" is adopted from the Myth of Adapa. As far as we can see none of the Enochic texts seem to have been influenced by this myth as a composition. Enmeduranki comes closer since on the one hand he seems to be one of the sources behind Gen 5,24 which influenced En 12 and 14, and on the other hand he seems to be the main source behind En 81 which related to En 12 and 14. There are also similarities in the way the removal is expressed. Enmeduranki: "Šamaš and Adad brought him, *ušeribūsu*, into their assembly." Enoch: "winds ... brought me, *'ōbᵉlūnī*, and made me enter into heaven".[112]

In the Gilgamesh version of the Flood story Ziusudra is said to have joined the assembly of the gods.[113] Taking into consideration that the emphasis on the disappearance in En 12,1 also occurs in the description of Ziusudra, we are inclined to think that Enoch in En 6-16 has adopted features both from Ziusudra and Enmeduranki. This would be a parallel to the Noahitic traditions which are closely related to En 6-16, where the heroes also had features adopted from two Mesopotamian figures, Ziusudra and Uanadapa.

5.3 The Location of Paradise

The "garden where the chosen and the righteous dwell" is in En 60,8 located to the west of an immense desert in Ethiopic named Dendayn. The same desert must be meant in En 10,4 as the place where Asael is thrown into the nether world. Gr^Pan reads here: τὴν ἔρημον τὴ οὖσαν εν τῷ Δαδουήλ, "the desert which is in Dadouel".

In both cases Dendayn or Dadouel is connected to a desert. The same desert must be meant in En 77,3, where it occurs together with Paradise in the third section of the earth. The Aramaic text reads: למדבריו ולש(ב)ע ל(פרד)ס קושטא, 4 Q Enastr^b 23, line 9

---

110 Cf. Myth of Adapa, B. ANET³, pp. 101f.
111 Cf. above, pp. 185f.
112 Cf. above, pp. 187, 93f.
113 Cf. above, p. 178.

(Milik, p. 289), "for the deserts and the S[ev]en and the Pa[radi]se of Righteousness". In the book of Giants, 4Q EnGiants[b], col iii, line 5 (Fitzmyer and Harrington, p. 76), one has to pass over: שהוין מדברא רבא, "the wasteland, the great desert", to reach Enoch.

According to these texts Paradise is situated west of an immense desert which either is named or lies in the area of Dendayn or Dadouel.

Milik has argued convincingly that the Aramaic word behind Dendayn and Dadouel is דד, *dad*, "breast".[114] The Ethiopic translation of the word seems to presuppose the Aramaic form דדין, understood as dual *dedayīn*, "twin breasts". The Greek form seems to presuppose an Aramaic דדו אל, *dadū'el*, which can be read as a dual construct form with the meaning "the twin breasts of the god (El).[115] Milik has further argued (cf. note above) that this name is an Aramaic equivalent of the mountain named Mašu in the Epic of Gilgamesh, Tabl IX, col ii, lines 1-5. The name means "twins" in Akkadian.[116] The mountain is described as a mountain "whose peaks reach to the vault of heaven and whose breasts reach to the nether world below", lines 4-5.

Gilgamesh comes to this mountain on his journey in search of Utnapishtim, the hero of the flood. The question is whether there is any possibility of locating the area. According to Tabl IX, col v, lines 38-39, Gilgamesh travels towards the north of central Mesopotamia. According to Tabl IX, col iv, line 45, he travels "along the road of the sun". The clause is ambiguous. Does it mean the course of the sun from east to west in the day, or in the opposite direction in the night, as it was imagined in Mesopotamian mythology? That Gilgamesh travels through the mountain in darkness, may indicate the night.[117]

---

114 Cf. Milik, op.cit., p. 30.
115 The regular form should be dadē, but the Aramaic fragments do not always graphically distinguish between waw and yod, cf. M. Sokoloff, "Notes on the Aramaic Fragments of Enoch from Qumran Cave 4", Maarav 1/2, 1978-79, pp. 197-224, p. 200.
116 Cf. note 147, ANET[3], p. 88.
117 Grelot, "La géographie mythique d'Hénoch", p. 56, solves the problem by referring to Heidel's translation of the Old Babylonian version Tabl X, col iv, line 11: "A long journey, (from) the rising of the sun", cf. Heidel, The Epic of Gilgamesh, p. 71. But Speiser translates differently: "A long journey as the sun rises", cf. ANET[3], p. 90.

Two indications point in favour of the direction northwest. One is more general with regard to the geographical area. On his journey Gilgamesh encounters the ale-wife Siduri. This is a Hurrian term for "young woman", used to describe Ḥebat, a name form of Ishtar in Hurrian texts.[118] This would more generally point to the area Lebanon/Syria/Asia Minor, which lies northwest of central Mesopotamia. The second indication is more specific geographically. According to the Epic of Gilgamesh, Tabl XI, line 7, Utnapishtim joined "the assembly of the gods". This may have been meant as a general statement in the sense that Utnapishtim was likened to the gods. The "assembly of the gods" is also in many Mesopotamian texts more generally thought to be in heaven, as for instance in *Enmeduranki and the Diviners*.[119] But the Epic of Gilgamesh is marked by a combination of mythology and vague ideas about geography. The result is a horizontal mythology where areas which in many texts are placed according to a vertical axis in the epic are placed on a horizontal plane. In the Old Babylonian version of the epic the pantheon is located on Mount Hermon, Tabl V, fragment C, reverse, line 13.[120] When Gilgamesh on his second journey travels to seek Utnapishtim who had joined the assembly of the gods, it would not be unlikely that he was thought to go in the same direction.

If this is correct, the Epic of Gilgamesh includes some vague ideas that Gilgamesh crossed the deserted areas northwest of central Mesopotamia, in Mesopotamian texts describes as Sumerian *ḫursag*, Akkadian *ḫuršānu*, "mountain" or "stony desert".[121] In this area he encounters the mountain Mašu, meaning "twins", which may be situated some place among the mountains of Lebanon/Syria. He travels through this mountain, and on the other side he comes to a wonderful garden full of precious stones, Tabl IX, col v, lines 46-51.[122]

A comparison of this geographical sketch with the one found in the Enochic writings yields clear correspondences. In Enoch we

118   Cf. Speiser in ANET[3], note 152, p. 89.
119   Cf. above, p. 187.
120   Cf. ANET[3], p. 504. Cf. Also W.G. Lambert, Babylonian Wisdom Literature, Oxford 1960, pp. 12f.
121   Cf. R.J. Clifford, The Cosmic Mountain in Canaan and the Old Testament, HSM 4, Cambridge, Mass. 1972, pp. 12f.
122   Cf. ANET[3], p. 89.

also have a twin mountain connected to a great desert situated east of the Garden of Eden. In the Noah birth story contained in the Genesis Apocryphon, Paradise is situated in Parwaim, the land from where the gold came (1Q apGen, col ii, line 23).[123] The connection between the Garden of Eden and precious stones and metals is also known in the Old Testament, Ezek 28,13.

But the description of Gilgamesh' journey also contains elements which seem to contradict the location above and which remind us about the epic's complex fusion of myth and geography. To reach Utnapishtim Gilgamesh has to cross the sea, the Waters of Death, Tabl X, col ii, lines 20-27.[124] The use of underworld imagery here depends on the mythic thinking along the horizontal line mentioned earlier. What is more disturbing is the location of Utnapishtim on what seems to be an island. As we have seen previously, this was most likely also thought as the placement of Dilmun, "Paradise", in the Sumerian Flood story. Dilmun is there located in the Persian Gulf.[125] This location of Paradise and the flood hero corresponds at least generally to the situation of Utnapishtim in the Epic of Gilgamesh, Tabl XI, line 196, *ina pī nārāti*, "at the mouth of the rivers", which means the place where the Tigris and Euphrates flow into the Persian Gulf. But this is the opposite direction of the journey which could be traced above. In the light of the whole epic, however, Gilgamesh can hardly have been thought to travel to the Persian Gulf, because then he would have travelled through an inhabited, fertile, flat area.

The most plausible explanation is that we have two traditions that are juxtaposed. One belongs to the Flood story and locates Paradise adjacent to the Persian Gulf. The other belongs to the Epic of Gilgamesh itself and locates Paradise in the Lebanese or Syrian mountains.

This supposed transposition of Paradise has support from other sources. In Ugaritic texts El resides *mbk nhrm*, "at the sources of

---

123   Cf. above, p. 89.
124   Cf. ANET[3], p. 91.
125   Cf. above, pp. 176f.

the rivers".[126] M.H. Pope located this place to the modern Khirbet Afqa in Syria, at the source of the Nahr Ibrāhīm, the ancient river of Adonis.[127] R.J. Clifford argued against this location: "Even though El's abode was localized in Syria by the Ugaritians, it had a mythical, ungeographical character."[128] Clifford believed, I think correctly, that the passage was taken from Mesopotamian poetry: "El lives on the mountain which is described with ancient paradisiacal motifs."[129] We cannot enter into a further discussion about El's abode. Our point is that the paradise motif "at the mouth (or source) of the rivers" in Ugaritic mythology is transposed to concern El's abode somewhere in the mountains of Lebanon or Syria. The Epic of Gilgamesh is accordingly not the only composition which has this transposition. Texts from three different cultural environments seem to locate Paradise in the same area.

En 60,7-8 contains a sequence of strange mythology: "And on that day two monsters will be separated from one other: a female monster whose name (is) Leviathan, to dwell in the depth of the sea above the springs of the waters; and the name of the male (is) Behemot who occupies with his breast an immense desert, named Dendayn, on the east of the garden where the chosen and righteous dwell . . ." The sequence gives the impression of a fusion of different mythological components.

Leviathan and Behemot are mentioned together in Job 40,15-41,26 (TM). Here בהמות, *behemōt* (40,15), means "hippopotamus", and לויתן, *liwyātān* (40,25), means "crocodile", which is apparent from the description of the beasts. *behemōt* is a plural form of *behemā*, "beast", and Job 40,15 is the only place in the Old

---

126   Cf. C.H. Gordon, Ugaritic Textbook, Rome 1965, text No. 129, line 4, p. 196. Translation in ANET[3], Poems about Baal and Anath, b.III AB,C, line 4, p. 129. The same text is also quoted by Clifford, op.cit., p. 48. Clifford also quotes another text, p. 49. For another occurrence, cf. e. II. AB, col iv-v, line 20, ANET[3], p. 133.
127   M.H. Pope, El in the Ugaritic texts, VT.S 2, Leiden 1955, pp. 72-81.
128   Clifford, op.cit., p. 50.
129   Clifford, p. 51. A similar transposition seems to have taken place in Ezek 28,12-19. Here the paradisiacal motif associated with the Garden of Eden, in Gen 2,10-14 located to the sources of the Euphrates and Tigris, is connected to the "holy mountain of God", vv. 14.16. In Ezek 31.3 Assur is described as a cedar on Lebanon, and in the same context compared to the other trees in the garden of God, designated as the trees of Eden, vv. 8-9.

Testament where it is used as a designation of a species.[130]
Leviathan, however, is well known as a mythological sea-monster
in Old Testament texts (cf. Ps 74,12-17; 104,26; Job 3,8). The
passage in Ps 74,12-17 recounts the crushing of Leviathan's heads
when God separated the waters in connection with his act of
creation (cf. Gen 1,6; Ps 104,5-10). The background is clearly to
be found in Ugaritic myths where Anath is said to have crushed
the seven headed serpent, the sea-monster Lotan.[131] The motif
also occurs in an eschatological context in Is 27,1 where it is stated
that on the day of judgment Yahweh shall kill Leviathan, the
serpent in the sea.

This background in Old Testament texts and Ugaritic mythology
sheds light on some of the features of En 60,7-8. The cleaving of
the monster corresponds to Ps 74,12-17 and occurs in the Old
Testament often in the context of creation. This context is maintained in our text both in v. 7 and v. 8. But the text starts with
Ethiopic *bayĕ'tu 'ĕlat*, "on that day", which seems to reflect
Hebrew ביום ההוא, *bayyōm hahū'*, "on that day" in Is 27,1. In Is
27,1 the context is clearly eschatological. Accordingly it seems as if
the composer of En 60,7-8 viewed the primeval cleaving of the
monster and the eschatological cleaving, i.e. annihilation, in one
perspective.

What is also confusing in En 60,7-8 is that one monster is separated into two. I think this motif depends on the composer's
interpretation of the myth. As we have seen, only one of the
monsters, Leviathan, has a mythological background. Within a
mythological framework the fight between gods and monsters has
no fixed time but repeats itself as a part of reality. But when
placed into historical perspective things look entirely different.
God could not have crushed Leviathan in primeval time when Old
Testament texts state that he is still living in the sea. The result is
a compromise. God did not crush the seamonster but separated the
primeval monster in two parts. The one part is Leviathan, living in

---

130 Behemot and Leviathan appear together also in 4 Ezra 6,49-52. This
sequence juxtaposes components from earlier texts: Ps 74,13-14; 50,10 (b^ehemot
is interpreted as a proper name) and our text En 60,7-8. That our sequence
forms a part of the background for the Ezra text is a decisive argument against
Milik's onion that En 60 was composed "in Christian times", Milik, op.cit., p. 30.
131 Poems about Baal and Anath, f. V AB, D, line 39, ANET[3], p. 137; g I[*]
AB, col i, line 38, ANET[3], p. 138.

the sea. From the other part God made the desert Dedayn. This part is given the name Behemot simply because this creature is mentioned together with Leviathan in Job.

We have now located the background for the part of the sequence concerning Leviathan, which is Old Testament and Ugaritic. But the Old Testament never tells that God created anything from the slain monster. In the known Ugaritic texts this motif is also lacking.[132] It is also implausible that the composer knew such a background connected to Leviathan, because then he would hardly have transferred the motif to Behemot. The composer seems to have known a myth in which Leviathan/Lotan was crushed and nothing more. We must accordingly look elsewhere for the second part of En 60,7-8.

If the name Behemot is added to the tradition in 60,8 from the Book of Job, the only fixed point in the passage is the name of the desert. Taking into consideration that the name of the desert is Dedayn, "twin breasts", there must be a pun in the text between the breast of the beast and the name of the desert. This also shows that the tradition must have existed in Aramaic language. The place דדין, dᵉdayīn, "twin breasts", was made of the דד, dad, "breast" of the beast. In the same direction points the other occurrence of the name as דדו אל, dadū'el, "the twin breasts of the god". The twin breasts can originally hardly have been a name of a flat desert, but as the Akkadian Mašu must have been the name of a mountain with two peaks. Moreover, the Ethiopic badw does not necessarily mean "desert", but can also refer to "a desolated place". Accordingly, the deity can hardly have been imagined as male, as the Ethiopic text says, in this stage of the tradition. The breasts as mountain peaks are distinctively female. What we have then is a tradition transmitted in Aramaic in which a mountain was formed out of the breasts of a slain monster/goddess.

This tradition is similar to the creation of the world in the fifth tablet of Enuma Elish. After Marduk has vanquished the sea-monster Tiamat, he created the world out of different parts of her body:

> Putting her head into position
> he formed the[reon the mountai]ns

---

132 Cf. A. Kapelrud, "Creation in the Ras Shamra Texts", StTh 34, 1980, pp. 1-11.

Opening the deep (which) was in flood,
He caused to flow from her eyes
the Euphr[ates (and) T]igris
. . .
He formed at her udder the lofty m[ountain]s,
(Therein) he drilled springs for the wells
to carry of (the water)

(Tabl V, lines 53-55.57-58)[133]

We have accordingly on the Enochic side recorded two traditions which are juxtaposed. One is that Paradise is situated in a garden west of an immense desolated area which is occupied by a mountain called "twin breasts". The other is that the mountain "twin breasts" was created from the breasts of a slain monster. On the Mesopotamian side we have the Epic of Gilgamesh which places a garden and Paradise west of a desolated area occupied by a mountain called "twins"; and Enuma Elish which recounts that from the breasts of the slain monster Tiamat were formed lofty mountains.

It is difficult to know whether these traditions were related on the Mesopotamian side, as well. It is tempting to regard the eyes of Tiamat, which became the sources of the Euphrates and Tigris, as a parallel to "at the mouth (source) of the rivers" in the Epic of Gilgamesh and in Ugaritic texts, and thus find more parallels between the mythic geography in the Epic of Gilgamesh and Tiamat's body. But such speculation in vulnerable.

I think we can conclude, however, that the mythic geography presented in the description of Paradise in Enochic texts has parallels in Mesopotamian ones. I find it also likely to assume that the parallels indicate relationships between the concepts. But I do not believe we should imagine too direct a relationship, for we are dealing with fairly vague ideas of mythology and geography which most likely have been transmitted through several links.

Fortunately, we know that traditions derived from the Epic of Gilgamesh were known i circles producing Enochic literature. In 4Q EnGiants[a], fragment 1, line 2 (Fitzmyer and Harrington, p. 72), the name חובבש, ḥobbābeš occurs as the name of one of the giants, which clearly reflects the monster Humbaba/Huwawa. In the fragments 4Q EnGiants[b.c] Milik claimed to have read the name of the hero himself, written גלגמיס, and גלגמיש "Gilgamīš" (Milik, p. 313).

---

133 Cf. ANET[3], pp. 501ff.

	THE PRIMEVAL HISTORY	
FLOOD STORY	Fragm I	Fragm II
Actors:	giants	giants
Protagonists:	(Belus)	Belus
Cause:		impiety

BABYLON		
Actors/	giants/	Belus/
Protagonists:	survivors	survivor
Activity:	founded	settled in
	Babylon	Babylon
	built the tower	built the tower
		ruled over it
Result:	ruined by god	
	dispersed over	
	the whole earth	

6.   The Background of the Primeval History in Pseudo-Eupolemus

The issue was discussed by B.Z. Wacholder, whose work on
Pseudo-Eupolemus contained an analysis of the Genesis texts, the
parallels in Jewish and Greek literature and the similarities with
Berossos' Babyloniaca.[134] N. Walter subsequently commented on
some of these subjects.[135] I have earlier given a presentation of
Pseudo-Eupolemus and discussed the parallels to Jewish and Greek
sources.[136] My aims is now to uncover how Mesopotamian
traditions may have influenced his account of the Primeval
history. I shall divide the inquiry into three sections corresponding
to the three themes in Pseudo-Eupolemus' primeval account.

134   B.Z. Wacholder, "Pseudo-Eupolemus' Two Greek Fragments on Abraham",
pp. 87-113.
135   N. Walter, "Zu Pseudo-Eupolemus", pp. 284-90.
136   Cf. above, pp. 111-8.

OF PSEUDO-EUPOLEMUS

Genesis	Berossos	Atra-Ḥasis
mankind (giants)	mankind	semi-divine primeval race
Noah	Xisouthros	Ziusudra
impiety		rebellion

mankind (the giant Nimrod) settled down	survivors refounded Babylon	
built the tower		
confusion of tongues dispersed over the whole earth		

6.1   The Story of the Flood and the Tower of Babel

To get a clearer perspective on Pseudo-Eupolemus' account, I present a table to the Primeval history. In this table are included the two fragments attributed to Pseudo-Eupolemus and three accounts of the Primeval history which I think either directly or through written or oral connecting links influenced Pseudo-Eupolemus, namely the Genesis account, Berossos and Atra-Ḥasis.

Commentary: The relationship between Fragment I and II:
There are differences between the fragments.[137] In Fragm I Belus is not directly mentioned in the account of the flood. He is, however, mentioned later in the same fragment: "the Babylonians say that the first (giant) was Belus, who is Chronos, who begat

---

137   Cf. also above, pp. 111f.

Belus and Cham."[138] The first Belus seems to be the same as the one mentioned in Fragm II. He equals the Biblical Noah. Wacholder considered two possibilities concerning the second Belus. He can equal the Biblical Shem or the Biblical Nimrod. Wacholder opted in his main study for the first possibility, since Biblical Noah is the father of Shem and Ham (Gen 5,32).[139] In two later studies, though, he decided for the second possibility, arguing that Belus II must be the Belus of Fragm II who built Babylon.[140] The Genesis account can be interpreted that the giant Nimrod built the tower.[141] But I do not think that there is any possibility of interpreting Fragm II as dealing with two "Beloi", one flood hero and one builder. If Pseudo-Eupolemus originally had a second Belus as the son of Belus/Noah and brother of Cham/Ham, he must be Shem.[142] If this is correct the second Belus does not appear in the accounts of the flood in Fragm I and Fragm II.

The second main difference is that Fragm I recounts that the tower was ruined by an act of God, while nothing explicitly is said about the flood except that the giants escaped it. Fragm II recounts that the dwellings of the giants in Babylonia were destroyed by the gods because of their impiety, while nothing is said explicitly about the tower except that Belus ruled over it. It seems as if we have two variations of the same motif: rebellion - destruction, and that both the flood and the tower story is interpreted according to this pattern.

The difference are not so great as to indicate that the fragments stem from different compositions or different composers. They may very well belong to different sequences of the same work by Pseudo-Eupolemus.

---

138   Translation according to Wacholder, Eupolemus. A Study of Judeo-Greek Literature, p. 314.
139   Wacholder, Pseudo-Eupolemus' Two Greek Fragments", p. 94.
140   Wacholder, "Hellenistic World Chronicles", p. 114; and Eupolemus. A Study, p. 104.
141   Cf. above, p. 113.
142   Wacholder, "Pseudo-Eupolemus' Two Greek Fragments", p. 94, thought that the meaning of the Hebrew term šem, "name", caused the two "Beloi". Pseudo-Eupolemus would then have understood Shem as an indication that the son had the name of his father. This explanation seems a bit artificial. So also Walter, op.cit., pp. 284f.

The relationship of Pseudo-Eupolemus and Genesis:
There are six differences between the two sources: 1) In Pseudo-Eupolemus the flood strikes the giants, in Genesis mankind. 2 The protagonist in Pseudo-Eupolemus is divine or semi-divine Belus, in Genesis the man Noah. 3) In Pseudo-Eupolemus the city of Babylon was founded; in Genesis the people settled down on a plain in the land Shinear. 4) In Pseudo-Eupolemus the tower of Babel is built by the survivors of the flood, the giants/Belus, but in Genesis by people many generations after the flood. 5) In Pseudo-Eupolemus Belus ruled over the tower (Babylon); in Genesis the builders were dispersed before the tower was finished. 6) In Pseudo-Eupolemus the tower was ruined, in Genesis the builders only ceased their building activity.

Some of the differences depend on a combination of motifs extant in the Genesis narratives. In the first case the giants from Gen 6,1-4 are combined with the Flood story.[143] But there remains the question why Pseudo-Eupolemus made this combination. In the fourth case Pseudo-Eupolemus seems to have made the giant Nimrod the builder of the tower (cf. note 143), but this does not explain why he made the survivors from the flood its builders.[144] The fifth case seems to depend on the fourth. According to Gen 10,10 Nimrod was the ruler of Babylon. The sixth case presupposes a transference of the motif "catastrophe" from the Flood story. In both the Flood story (Fragm II) and the tower story (Fragm I) the catastrophe strikes the cities of the Babylonians, Fragm II: "dwellings"; Fragm II: "the city of Babylon". There is no explanation for the second and third cases.

The relationship of Pseudo-Eupolemus and Berossos:
Four main differences to Berossos are apparent:[145] 1) In Pseudo-Eupolemus the flood strikes the giants, in Berossos mankind. 2) In Pseudo-Eupolemus the protagonist is Belus, in Berossos Xisouthros. 3) In Pseudo-Eupolemus the reason for the flood is impiety,

---

143   Cf. above, p. 113.
144   Wacholder, op.cit., p. 90, thought that one of the reasons for the connection Belus - Babylon in Pseudo-Eupolemus could be that he interpreted the name as bā'bel, "Bel came". Walter, op.cit., p. 284, called attention to that Pseudo-Eupolemus used the common hellenistic form "Babylon" as the name of the city, which does not indicate this etymology.
145   For Berossos, cf. above, pp. 176, 232ff.

Berossos gives no reason. 4) Berossos does not recount the building of the tower.

There is, however, one important correspondence on the place where Pseudo-Eupolemus and Genesis differ most: Berossos makes the survivors of the flood the (re)founders of Babylon.

Another subject has to be commented on when comparing the sources: Pseudo-Eupolemus equated Belus with the Greek Chronos and makes him the flood hero and founder of Babylon. Berossos makes Belus the founder of Babylon in his account of creation. Bel is here the same as the Babylonian Marduk in Enuma Elish. Berossos makes Chronos the god who intercedes in the flood story. In this respect Chronos equals Mesopotamian Enki/Ea. The two sources correspond in making Bel the founder of Babylon but differ in the juxtaposition of Belus and Greek gods. The sources also differ in the case of the flood hero. A Babylonian could hardly make Belus, the supreme god of Babylon, the hero of the flood. Pseudo-Eupolemus may have known, however, that the Babylonian flood hero was regarded as divine, which could have facilitated the fusion with Bel.

The relationship Pseudo-Eupolemus and Atra-Ḫasis:
There is one distinguishing point where Pseudo-Eupolemus and Atra-Ḫasis correspond: In both the flood struck semi-divine creatures as a punishment for their crimes. In Atra-Ḫasis the origin of the primeval human race is described in the section before the catastrophes and the flood. Primeval man was made from divine substance and born of a goddess.[146] The same act of creation is reflected i Berossos, but there not so intimately connected with the Flood story.[147] We do not in this context discuss how this divine origin of the primeval human race was understood by the Babylonians themselves. As it seems, they did not distinguish between the primeval race and ordinary human beings. This is explicitly clear in Berossos (cf. note above). But for a recipient belonging to a culture influenced by Old Testament traditions, these creatures made of divine substance and born of a goddess could not be

---

146   Cf. above, pp. 174f.
147   Text: Euseb. (Arm.) Chron. p. 6,8-9,2 and Syncellus p. 49,19. FGH III, C, 1.B, sequences 7-8, pp. 372f. Translation: Burstein, Book I, 2,3a and 3b, p. 15. Cf. also our discussion of the sequence below, p. 292.

regarded as ordinary human beings. They had to be placed into a separate category between gods and men, that of semi-divine giants.

Another indication that Pseudo-Eupolemus utilized Mesopotamian traditions is his statement that the catastrophe struck Babylonian cities. This is implied in Berossos, where the cities are recorded together with kings before the flood. It is a more distinguishing feature in the Sumerian Flood story, however, where only the list of primeval cities precedes the Flood story.

Our analysis shows that all the features that Pseudo-Eupolemus does not share with Genesis correspond to features in Mesopotamian versions of primeval history. The account in Pseudo-Eupolemus must therefore be understood as a combination of Genesis and these traditions. We demonstrate this in the following way:

1. Giants as actors — Atra-Ḥasis: Semi-divine primeval race.
2. Divine or semi-divine Belus as protagonist — Berossos, Atra-Ḥasis: Semi-divine hero.
3. Founding of Babylon — Berossos: Refoundation of Babylon.
4. Babylon/tower built by survivors — Berossos: Survivors built Babylon.
5. Belus ruled the tower (Babylon) — Common Mesopotamian: Belus the founder and supreme god of Babylon.
6. Babylonian cities ruined — Sumerian Flood story: Babylonian cities ruined in the flood.

The list is not, of course, to be understood as indicating that Pseudo-Eupolemus read these Mesopotamian compositions. Its contents are listed only as sources to demonstrate that these features existed in Mesopotamian primeval accounts. What sort of relationship Pseudo-Eupolemus had with the Mesopotamian material will be discussed below.

6.2   Abraham in the Tenth Generation

Freudenthal has pointed out the striking similarity between the description of Abraham in Pseudo-Eupolemus and the notice about the great wise man in Berossos:[148]

---

148   J. Freudenthal, Hellenistische Studien, p. 94.

Pseudo-Eupolemus

δεκάτη δὲ γενεᾷ ... εν
πόλει τῆς Βαβυλονίας ...
γενέσθαι ᾿Αβραάμ ...
εὐγένεια καὶ σοφία
παντας ὑπερβεβηκότα, ὃν
δὴ καὶ τὴν ἀστρολογίαν
καὶ Χαλδαϊκὴν εὑρεῖν

In the tenth generation ... in a
Babylonian city ... Abraham was
born ..., who surpassed everybody in nobility and wisdom, and
who also discovered astrology and
Chaldean (science).149

Berossos

μετὰ τὸν κατακλυσμὸν
δεκάτηι γενεᾶι παρα
Χαλδαίος τις ἦν δίκαιος
ἀνὴρ καὶ μέγας καὶ τὰ
οὐράνια ἔμπειρος
....

....

After the flood in the tenth
generation among the Chaldeans
there was a man who was just
and knowledgeable about heavenly phenomena.150

We have previously discussed the sequence in Berossos in relation
to the Priestly source of Genesis which also counts ten generations
from the flood to Abraham. P could not have known the passage i
Berossos but he seemed to know the underlying Mesopotamian
traditions.151 Pseudo-Eupolemus' account is so close to Berossos'
that it must in one way or another depend on Berossos' work.

6.3   Enoch as Astrologer

I have previously argued that Pseudo-Eupolemus' account of
Enoch as the discoverer of astrology most likely was directly based
on the Astronomical Book, or at least on traditions similar to those
contained in this work.152 In the analysis of the background of
the Enoch portrait in the Astronomical Book we found that Enoch
there was a reflection of the Mesopotamian primeval sage Uanadapa. But Uanadapa was also the background for the angel Uriel
who taught Enoch astronomy.153
Pseudo-Eupolemus equated Enoch with the Greek Atlas. This does
not mean that he claims that Enoch is rooted in Greek mythology,

149   Text: Praep. Ev. 9.17. For text editions, cf. above, note 207, p. 111. The
full text is quoted on p. 113 above.
150   Text: Praep. Ev. 9.16.2 and Josephus, Jewish Antiquities I, 158. For text
edition, cf. above, note 110, p. 193. For an examination of the text, cf. above,
pp. 193ff.
151   Cf. above, pp. 232ff.
152   Cf. above, pp. 115ff.
153   Cf. above, pp. 237ff.

no more than he claims that Belus is rooted in Greek mythology when he equated Belus with Chronos. Like Belus, Enoch is for Pseudo-Eupolemus a Babylonian figure. By making Enoch an equivalent of Atlas, Pseudo-Eupolemus places him into the same semidivine category as Uriel.[154] By comparing the sources to Uanadapa, Uriel and Atlas, I think we can trace the background for this transposition:[155] 1) All three figures are regarded as cosmic guardians. 2) All three are connected to the underworld. 3) All three are teachers of astrology.

The traditions about Uanadapa were in the Astronomical Book split up according to the different emphasis on the mythical and legendary features and assigned to Uriel and Enoch. In Pseudo-Eupolemus the juxtaposition of Enoch and Atlas shows that Enoch here is portrayed in the "mythical role" of Uanadapa. This also indicates that Pseudo-Eupolemus must have had some ideas about the traditions underlying the portrayal of Enoch in the Astronomical Book.

6.4   The Transmission of the Mesopotamian Material

We limit this subject only to concern what can be said on basis of a comparison between Pseudo-Eupolemus and Mesopotamian sources.[156] Schnabel first decided that Pseudo-Eupolemus knew Berossos' Babyloniaca as a written document either directly or through a written connecting link. Later he changed his mind and argued that Pseudo-Eupolemus used oral traditions from Babylonia. He did not say whether these traditions were derived from Berossos' Babyloniaca, or more generally corresponded to the book.[157] Wacholder claimed that Pseudo-Eupolemus undoubtedly used Babyloniaca as a written source.[158] Walter argued the same.[159] I think my analysis has given some indications to determine the relationship.

---

154   Cf. above, p. 116.
155   Cf. also the discussion on pp. 237ff above.
156   The subject is discussed on a broader basis by Schnabel, Berossos und die Babylonisch-Hellenistische Literatur, cf. esp. pp. 108,226,246 where he suggested that Greek authors knew Babylonian material prior to Berossos.
157   Cf. Schnabel, op.cit., pp. 67ff and p. 246.
158   Wacholder, op.cit., pp. 88, 102.
159   Walter, op.cit., p. 289.

There are two features in Pseudo-Eupolemus which definitely point toward a dependence on Berossos. The first is that the survivors of the flood founded Babylon; the second is the description of the great wise man in the tenth generation after the flood. The second case is so close to Berossos that it could indicate a literary dependence.

But these observations have to be balanced by two negative ones. Pseudo-Eupolemus equated Belus with Chronos, while Chronos in Berossos is used about Enki/Ea. Even more in contradiction to Berossos, Pseudo-Eupolemus makes Belus to the hero of the flood. If Pseudo-Eupolemus had read Berossos where Belus naturally equals Marduk as the creator of the world, he could hardly have made this identification.

There is also a third point. Pseudo-Eupolemus seems to have known more Mesopotamian traditions than those recorded in Berossos (as we know him through Polyhistor). He seems to have had some idea about the divine origin of the primeval race which rebelled before the flood, as it is recounted in Atra-Ḥasis. He seems to have known traditions similar to the Sumerian Flood story in which the flood destroyed the Babylonian cities. And he seems to have had some knowledge of a broader mythological tradition about the primary antediluvian sage than what is recorded in Berossos.

If my second observation excludes the possibility that Pseudo-Eupolemus actually read the Babyloniaca, my first observation points in the direction that he used a source which depended on this work. It is difficult to know whether it was written or oral. What we probably can determine is that it was fairly exact in rendering some of the content of the Babyloniaca. My third observation indicates that this connecting source also contained other information derived from Mesopotamian traditions but more vague than those derived from Berossos.

The analysis show that Babylonian traditions must have reached Samaria in the third century B.C. It is possible that the connecting link could be a Greek source, although no allusions to Berossos are known prior to Pseudo-Eupolemus. At any rate the interest in the account is decisively the synchronizing of Babylonian and Biblical primeval traditions presented for readers schooled in hellenistic thought.

Accordingly, Pseudo-Eupolemus' setting differs considerably from that of the Enochic group that to a large extent worked with the same material. He knew one of their works and Mesopotamian traditions underlying this work, but he did not belong to their group and did not adapt the Mesopotamian traditions as a framework for the interpretation of reality as they did.

7. The Mesopotamian Background of the Enochic Traditions in the Book of Jubilees

7.1 The Background of the Enoch Portrait

7.1.1 Enoch as Primeval Sage

According to Jubilees Enoch was the first among men "who learnt writing and knowledge and wisdom and who wrote down the signs of heaven according to the order of their months in a book" (Jub 4,17). Here Enoch is clearly described as the primary primeval sage. I have previously analyzed the passage.[160] The book referred to is the Astronomical Book, and also in other writings and traditions Enoch is associated with "knowledge and wisdom". There are no explicit statements in earlier literature that Enoch was the *first* (although Pseudo-Eupolemus comes close to saying so), and especially that Enoch was the first to learn the art of writing.

I have previously argued that the Mesopotamian primeval sage Uanadapa forms the background of Enoch as composer of an astronomical work containing supreme wisdom.[161] The apkallu's and especially Uanadapa were also regarded as the initiators of culture and civilization, and, consequently, those who brought mankind all kind of wisdom and knowledge.[162] This background also explains the emphasis on *first* in Jubilees. Uanadapa (U-An) appears as the first sage in Bīt Mēseri, Berossos and W 20 030,7.[163] According to Berossos, Oannes (U-An) "gave to men the

---

160 Cf. above, p. 131.
161 Cf. above, pp. 236ff.
162 Cf. above, pp. 200f.
163 Cf. above, p. 193.

knowledge of letters".[164] That this was an established tradition is clear from an inscription by Ashurbanipal who says that he learnt "the art of the wise Adapa, the hidden mystery, the art of writing tablets".[165]

7.1.2   Enoch's Stay with the Angels

The statement that Enoch was with the angels for three hundred years has a complicated background (Jub 4,21). The passage is formed as a commentary on Gen 5,22, where it is said that Enoch walked with the 'älohīm, but the meaning is different.[166] As the passage now reads in P, the meaning is that Enoch had an intimate relationship with God.[167] The author of Jubilees, however, interpreted the passage literally in the sense that Enoch "stayed with the angels". He read the passage in the light of the cosmological sections of the Book of Watchers and the Astronomical Book, in which Enoch travels with the angels and is revealed cosmic geography. The question is why the author of Jubilees made this interpretation. Could it be that the passage "walked with the 'älohīm corresponded to underlying traditions that were open to another interpretation than that of P?

The answer must lie in the cosmological parts of the Enochic writings, since these formed the background for the interpretation in Jubilees. In our concluding remarks on the visionary forms in the Enochic literature we came to the result that the visionary form in the cosmological parts corresponded to two features in the oldest Enochic literature. In the Astronomical Book the traces of a visionary form corresponded to Enoch's communication with a divine figure in the astronomical corpus. In the Book of Watchers the visionary form of Enoch's journeys was an extension of Enoch's throne vision in En 14.[168] Two new elements contributed to this extension; on the formal level a visionary pattern similar to that found in the Book of Zechariah, and on the level of content mythical geography corresponding to other ancient near eastern

---

164   Cf. above, p. 200.
165   Cf. above, p. 189.
166   Cf. above, p. 130.
167   Cf. above, pp. 37f.
168   Cf. above, pp. 150f.

and Greek sources.[169] But the answer to the question why this
kind of literature was attributed to Enoch must lie in the fact that
already in the oldest sources he was introduced as a visionary who
went to heaven (En 14) and a sage who communicated with a
divine being (Astronomical corpus).

Behind these two concepts we find the traditions about Enmeduranki and Uanadapa. I think that the portrait of Enmeduranki
played the dominant role behind the motif "the primeval sage who
travelled with the 'ālohīm. We have previously noted that the text
Enmeduranki and the Diviners contained different elements
corresponding to "walked with the 'ālohīm".[170] One of these
elements was that Enmeduranki was brought by the gods Shamash
and Adad to heaven, where he communicated with the gods.
Afterwards he returned to the earth and taught the divine secrets.
P utilized another feature of this tradition describing Enmeduranki
as the favorite of the gods as the background for "Enoch walked
with God", and used the ascension motif as background for "he
was taken away". There seems to have been a Jewish tradition
which developed the journey motif further adding other mysterious experiences of divine wisdom.

7.1.3   Enoch's Removal to Paradise

The sequence about Enoch's removal to Paradise sheds light on the
Noahitic traditions in which Enoch is located in the same place,
but no removal is recounted. I have previously pointed out three
basic motifs in the account: 1) The flood strikes the Land of Eden
which is to be located east of Palestine in the Mesopotamian area.
2) The hero is removed to the Garden of Eden. 3) The hero
sacrifices on a mountain.[171] All these motifs correspond to the
Mesopotamian versions of the Flood story, which means that
Enoch here is described in the role of Ziusudra.[172]

The wording used about the removal of Utnapishtim in the Epic
of Gilgamesh and about th removal of Enoch is in fact very close.

169   Cf. above, pp. 66f; and my own analysis of a part of the mythic geography, pp. 246-53.
170   Cf. above, p. 230.
171   Cf. above, pp. 134f.
172   Cf. also above, pp. 242f.

Enoch: *watanśĕ'a ĕmā'kala daqiqa 'egᵘāla 'emaḥyāw wawasadnāhu wĕsta ganata 'edom,* "And he was taken from amongst the children of men and we conducted him into the Garden of Eden" (Jub 4,23).[173] Utnapishtim: *ilqûnnima ina rūgi ina pī nārāti uštēši-bŭnni,* "Thus they took me and made me reside far away, at the mouth of the rivers" (Tabl XI, line 196).[174]

7.2   Enochic and Mesopotamian Primeval Writings and Traditions

The author of Jubilees drew a line of tradition from Enoch as primeval sage up to Levi, and thus claimed that the descendants of Levi in his own time were responsible for the Enochic writings and traditions. The line follows a genealogical pattern where father instructs son in the primeval divine secrets. This construction must be regarded as an etiology of the sacred knowledge of the Levitical priesthood. The sacred knowledge is transmitted through both oral instruction and primeval books composed by Enoch and Noah. The content of the tradition is consistent with the content of the primeval books: astronomy, cosmology, predictions, medicine, but also, especially in the oral instruction, cultical and moral teaching. The books were originally composed in the language of creation, Hebrew, but later translated into Aramaic.

The background of this construction in Jewish literature is threefold: 1) Enoch is regarded as a composer of antediluvian books. 2) Enoch visited heaven, read the heavenly tablets, returned to the earth, instructed his son, and demanded that the wisdom should be transmitted to future generations. 3) "Priests" claiming Levitical ancestry traced the origin of their knowledge back to their primeval ancestor Enoch.[175]

The structure of this concept of the origin of wisdom is a fairly exact parallel to the Mesopotamian model, which was based on two traditions. One was associated with the primeval sages, the other

---

173   Cf. also above, pp. 50f.
174   Cf. above, p. 177. Cf. also Grelot, "La légende d'Hénoch", p. 22.
175   Cf. the analysis above, pp. 135-43.

with the seventh antediluvian king Enmeduranki. The sages were primarily associated with primeval books. Enmeduranki was both associated with a written composition, an astrological series, and regarded as the first link in the transmission of oral instruction belonging to the secret knowledge of the Babylonian priesthood. Exactly the same double aspect appears in the description of Enoch. He was regarded as both a composer of primeval books and the first link in the chain of oral instruction. I give below an outline of the similarities between the two concepts:

I   Enoch, Noah and the apkallu's:

1. The revelation of the divine wisdom was dated back in primeval time.[176]
2. The wisdom was revealed through primeval sages.[177]
3. The wisdom was written down in the primeval language.[178]
4. The wisdom was written down in primeval books, i.e. present compositions were dated back pseudepigraphically to primeval authors.[179]
5. The books contained astronomy/astrology, predictions (divination), instruction in medicine and cultic matters (cf. note above).
6. The wisdom was primarily associated with the one primary antediluvian sage who got it from a divine being or divine beings.[180]

II   Enoch and Enmeduranki:

1. The seventh antediluvian figure stayed with divine beings.[181]
2. To him were revealed the divine secrets.
3. Thus he was enabled to predict the future and carry out astrological/-astronomical calculations.
4. He returned to the earth and instructed his son.
5. He started a line of transmission following a genealogical pattern of priestly ancestry up to the time of the present priesthood (at the time of the author).

On the basis of these observations I think there are enough indications to claim that persons regarding themselves as priests and claiming Levitical ancestry, adopted the model of the origin of wisdom which was taught by Babylonian priests and scholars.

176   Cf. above, pp. 201f.
177   Cf. above, pp. 200f.
178   Hebrew and Sumerian respectively, cf. the quotation from Ashurbanipal above, p. 210; and the reference to Hallo, note 165.
179   Cf. above, pp. 209ff.
180   Cf. above, pp. 210ff.
181   For the following, cf. pp. 185-90.

7.3   The Origin of Babylonian Primeval Wisdom

The Book of Jubilees has not only a concept of the origin of
legitimate Enochic/Levitical wisdom, but also one of the origin of
illegitimate Babylonian wisdom.[182] Both had the same origin.
Wisdom was revealed in primeval time when God sent the
watchers to instruct men. The lines were separated when the
watchers transgressed the divine order and perverted their
teaching. True knowledge was preserved by Enoch and his
descendants. perverted knowledge was carved in a rock or stone
slab by the watchers before the flood and rediscovered by the
ancestors of the Babylonians afterwards. Thus it became the
wisdom of the Babylonians.

The elements underlying this concept also seem familiar from
Mesopotamian traditions. The watchers sent to instruct men are
parallel to the apkallu's. Mesopotamian traditions do not recount
the "the fall of the angels", which forms the background of the
perversion of their teaching in Jubilees, but elements in Mesopotamian traditions may correspond to this concept. The difficulty is
that they are allusive, and we do not know exactly to what they
allude.

In Bīt Mēseri the group of four apkallu's is said to have angered
the gods.[183] The reasons that are recounted are obscure. But it
seems clear that they possessed a power that enabled them to
perform provocative acts which caused divine punishment, not
entirely unlike what is said about the human race before the flood
in Atra-Ḥasis.[184] In the Poem of Erra it is recounted that Marduk
dispatched the apkallu's down to Apsu.[185] This action was
connected to the flood and the breakdown of the cosmic order.
The disappearance of the apkallu's seems to have been one of the
reasons for the catastrophe. What is similar in Bīt Mēseri and the
Poem of Erra is that the apkallu's in both cases are associated with
crises sent by gods, but the whole mythical background for the
allusions is not preserved in any text.

---

182   Cf. above, pp. 143ff.
183   Cf. above, pp. 205ff.
184   Cf. above to Pseudo-Eupolemus, pp. 258f.
185   Cf. above, pp. 182f, 200.

Nevertheless, there are elements in these allusions that correspond to the Watcher story in Jubilees. Like the apkallu's the watchers were responsible for the cosmic order, cf. Jub 2,2. The watcher's transgression caused the breakdown of the cosmic law (Jub 5,2-3). Like the apkallu's the watchers also performed a great crime. Finally, like the apkallu's they were dispatched to the nether world. In both the Poem of Erra and in Jubilees this incident is connected to the flood.

The next stage in Jubilees' account has a clear parallel in Berossos. Berossos recounts how the antediluvian writings were buried in Sippar before the flood, dug up again after the flood, and "distributed to mankind".[186] Jubilees does not necessarily depend on Berossos. As we have pointed out previously, all the elements in Berossos' account are known from other sources — the concept of antediluvian writings, Sippar as the seat of antediluvian wisdom not destroyed in the flood, and the rediscovery of monuments of the ancient past (foundation deposits among other things clay tablets and stone slabs). Although we only have the full story recorded by Berossos, he may very well have depended on an established tradition.

I think we can conclude that the author of Jubilees also here had information derived from Mesopotamian traditions.

The elements that the author of Jubilees has parallel to the Mesopotamian traditions are the same kind as those contained in the Enochic writings, which he knew very well. He includes, however, new Mesopotamian elements not contained in these books. I think this is best explained by the assumption that the author also knew oral traditions originating from the same group that was responsible for the Enochic writings and traditions. If I am right in my conclusion that this was a group containing Levites, the author's strong emphasis on the authority of the Levitical priesthood supports this assumption.

---

186   Cf. above, pp. 178ff.

b) The Story of the Primeval Catastrophe and
Its Background

The title may sound a little presumptuous. Few traditions in
Jewish Literature are so obscure in both background and content.
The story also occurs in different variants. Its theme of rebelling
divine figures has obviously served as a magnet attracting a variety
of different motifs in different settings.[187] Having to limit my
exploration, I find it natural to concentrate primarily on En 6-11,
which is the oldest known Jewish text containing the combination
of elements which forms the basic structure of the Watcher story.

1.   The Watcher Story in En 6-11: An Analysis

1.1   The Debate about En 6-11 in Recent Research

In this chapter I shall give a brief survey of some of the debate
about En 6-11. My primary interest is the background of the composition: the question about the combination of different written or
fixed oral sources and more generally the parallels in ancient near
eastern and Greek mythology. I shall concentrate on the discussion
engaged in by P.D. Hanson, G.W.E. Nickelsburg and J. Collins.

P.D. Hanson[188] claimed that En 6-11 contained one basic source, "the Šemiḥazah Narrative", which later was elaborated in two stages. The first elaboration
is to be found in En 10,4-8 where Asael from the list of the angels is identified
as Azazel from Lev 16.[189] The second elaboration of the combined Šemiḥazah/
Azazel narrative added a new theme, the instruction in divine secrets, taken
from a culture hero tradition (En 7,1de; 8,1-2; 8,3; 9,6; 9,8c; 10,7-8).
Hanson defined En 6-11 as an expository narrative of Gen 4-10 which had
received its own structure:

Background note: Sons of Heaven and Daughters of Earth (6,1-2a)
(1) Plot of rebellion by astral deities in heaven and their descent (6,2b-8).
(2) Sexual commingling, birth of giants, devastation caused by the giants,
     earth's plea (7,1; 8,4 minus 7,1de).
(3) Angelic intercession before the Most High, deliverance of Noah, and
     punishment of the rebels and their offspring who are bound and cast to
     earth, ultimately to be punished in the fiery abyss (9,1-10,15 minus 9,6.8c,
     and 10,4-10).
(4) Restoration of the Kingship of the Most High and of Cosmic Order (10,16-
     11,2).[190]

187   For a survey, cf. P. Perkins, "The Rebellion Myth in Gnostic Apocalypses", SBL 1978 Seminar Papers, Vol. I, pp. 15-30.
188   P.D. Hanson, "Rebellion in Heaven, Azazel and Euhemeristic Heroes in
1 Enoch 6-11", JBL 96, 1977, pp. 195-233.
189   Cf. above, p. 100.
190   Hanson, op.cit., p. 197.

The result was "a complete mythic pattern around the theme of rebellion-in-heaven, and consisting of four movements: rebellion, devastation, punishment, restoration".

This mythical pattern of rebellion in heaven Hanson traced to a variety of ancient near eastern myths. Among Hurrian myths (preserved in Hittite) in Kingship in Heaven,[191] the Song of Ullikummis,[192] the Myth of Illuyankas;[193] among Ugaritic myths the Myth of Ashtar the Rebel.[194] Parts of the pattern are also to be found in Babylonian myths, as for instance Atra-Hasis and Enuma Elish. The pattern is also reflected in Old Testament texts: Is 14,5-21; Ezek 28,1-10. 11-19; Ezek 32; Ezek 26,19-21; Is 24,1-3.

Hanson states: "The ubiquitous theme found in many myths throughout the Near East of the second millennium B.C.E. concerning the introduction of cosmic disharmony through rebellion of certain members of the pantheon is revived in the story of Šemiḥazah and his associates."[195] And also: "When this new setting within the Bible and later Judaism is taken into consideration and when the length of time separating the Hurrian, Hittite, Babylonian, and Ugaritic materials from the story about Šemiḥazah is remembered, the consistency with which the four parts of the mythic pattern are applied along this entire millennium-long continuum is quite remarkable."[196] Concerning how this mythic pattern could have entered post-exilic Judaism, Hanson considered it most likely that there was an unbroken line from the ancient near eastern sources through pre-exilic and post-exilic biblical writings all the way down to the Šemiḥazah narrative.[197]

As already noted, Hanson found that this Šemiḥazah narrative was elaborated twice, first by adding the Azazel sequence, then by adding the culture hero tradition. Thus the Šemiḥazah narrative originally had nothing to do with teaching in divine secrets. This was a feature stemming from the latest elaboration of the material. As background for this culture hero tradition Hanson gave a summary of Mesopotamian primeval traditions associated with Ziusudra and the apkallu's, culture heroes in the Phoenician History by Philo of Byblos, leading over to Greek traditions about primeval inventors.

G.W.E. Nickelsburg[198] traced the background of En 6-11 in quite different material. Like Hanson, however, Nickelsburg separated the Šemiḥazah story and the Asael story (the teaching motif) as two different strata. The background of both stories he found in Greek mythology. The battles of the giants suggest the Titanomachia as recorded in Hesiod's Theogony and the Gigantomachia especially as recorded by Apollodorus. The giants' mixed origin suggests Greek stories about the gods' amours with mortal women. With reference to T.F. Glasson, Nickelsburg called attention to the similarity between the mixed marriage in Enoch and Hesiod's Catalogues of Women and Eoiae, II, 5-12.[199] Here the theme of sexual intermingling of demi-gods with the human race is the same as in Enoch.

As background for the Asael story which has the teaching motif as its central scope, Nickelsburg called attention to Gen 4,22-24 where Tubal-Cain is described as a forger of all instruments of bronze and iron. This corresponds to what is said about Asael in En 8,1a. But Genesis does not state that metallurgy was taught by a rebel angel. For a close analogy to this idea and for other parallels to

---

191 Cf. ANET³, pp. 120f.
192 Cf. ANET³, pp. 121-5.
193 Cf. ANET³, pp. 125f.
194 Text and translation i Clifford, The Cosmic Mountain, pp. 163ff.
195 Hanson, op.cit., pp. 202f.
196 Hanson, op.cit., p. 217.
197 Hanson, op.cit., p. 218.
198 G.W.E. Nickelsburg, "Apocalyptic and Myth in Enoch 6-11", JBL 96, 1977, pp. 383-405.
199 Text in H.G. Evelyn-White, Hesiod. The Homeric Hymns and Homerica, pp. 200f.

the Asael material, Nickelsburg referred to the Prometheus myth as described in Hesiod's Theogony and Work and Days. Nickelsburg summarized the description as follows: "Prometheus is wise and clever and uses his wisdom to help mankind. However, in so doing, he rebels against Zeus, and for this rebellion he is punished. Moreover, his benefaction of mankind turns out to be the ultimate source of all evil in this world."[200]

A second important source for Prometheus is Aeschylus' tragedy Prometheus Bound. Here Prometheus is described as the revealer of all cultural benefits: "All arts that men possess are from Prometheus' hand" (line 506).[201] But Prometheus is regarded as a rebel against Zeus. For this rebellion, he is taken out into the wilderness and chained hand and foot to the side of a rock. When he continues his insolence against the high god, Zeus opens up the rock and Prometheus is entombed until a later time when he is subjected to terrible torment (Prometheus Bound, lines 1014-1019).

In Hesiod's version of the Prometheus myth the women Pandora is responsible for all evil and trouble in the world. Nickelsburg regarded this as a clear parallel to En 8,1 in the translation of Gr^{Syn} where Asael teaches the women, who in turn seduce Šemiḥazah and the other angels, thus causing the terrible evils on the earth.

J. Collins[202] discussed various items in his reflection on Hanson's and Nickelsburg's articles. I shall concentrate on those dealing with literary criticism and underlying traditions. Collins agreed with Hanson and Nickelsburg that the cluster of motifs associated with Šemiḥazah is distinct from that associated with Asael and that the two can be ascribed to different traditions. But he doubted that the two traditions could be regarded as distinct sources: "While there may have been earlier versions of the Šemiḥazah story, the only version we have is combined with the Asael material, and I see no compelling evidence that the story isolated by the excision of the Asael material ever circulated in precisely that form. So I would argue that we cannot purposefully discuss the meaning and function of the Šemiḥazah story apart from the Asael material."[203]

Collins did not enter into a detailed discussion of the underlying traditions. Generally he claimed that the existence of Semitic parallels did not preclude the possibility that even better parallels could be found in hellenistic sources: "Since the apocalyptic writers did not follow their sources slavishly we must reckon with the possibility of an eclectic use of traditional material, which may combine motifs from different traditions or may use motifs (or patterns) which could be understood simultaneously against a number of different traditions."[204]

In their responses to Collins, Hanson and Nickelsburg maintained their earlier positions but do not seem to have marshalled decisive new arguments.[205]

When reading the articles of Hanson and Nickelsburg, one gains the impression that on several occasions they have got hold of the opposite ends of the same thread. The extremely difficult question

---

200   Nickelsburg, op.cit., p. 399.
201   Translation in W.D. Anderson, Prometheus Bound. Aeschylus, LLA, Indianapolis/New York 1963, p. 24.
202   J.J. Collins, "Methodological Issues in the Study of 1 Enoch: Reflections on the Articles of P.D. Hanson and G.W. Nickelsburg", SBL 1978 Seminar Papers, Vol. I, pp. 315-22.
203   Collins, p. 316.
204   Collins, p. 320.
205   P.C. Hanson, "A Response to John Collins' 'Methodological Issues in the Study of 1 Enoch'", SBL 1978, pp. 307ff; G.W.E. Nickelsburg, "Reflections upon Reflections: A Response to John Collins' 'Methodological Issues in the Study of 1 Enoch'", SBL 1978, pp. 311-4.

is how to follow this thread through the tangle which lies in between. This question involves the whole problem of the relationships between Mesopotamian, Ugaritic, Hittite and Greek myths. It also involves methodological problems of how to interpret the existence of similar motifs and patterns extant in different myths in entirely different cultures where the known written versions span about a millennium. I have limited my investigation to those case where a text-to-text comparison suggests some sort of direct relationship either by quoting, or through reference to traditions which definitely can be derived from known texts, or where we at least can suppose that texts share the same traditions which easily can be defined and delimited. In all cases the relationship can be defined historically as the transmission of written sources or fixed oral traditions. I have tried to demonstrate how this was possible by indicating the historical and geographical setting for the transmission and the contact between the sources. Comparing mythical patterns as Hanson did is something different and involves a methodology of the generating process of myths, the transmission of myths, and the transposing of mythical components from one myth to another, which is much more complex than what he seems to suggest. If not, the result can easily be that features that look similar in extant text versions were entirely different in the actual setting of the myths.

Accordingly, I shall not deny that En 6-11 shows affinity to ancient near eastern and Greek myths dealing with deposed gods and battles between gods and between giants, but I have not developed a methodology which enables a sound comparison of the vast material involved. Nor do I think that Hanson did. It was his and Nickelsburg's great achievement to call attention to this material, but especially Hanson has left a great task for the subsequent research.

In addition to this general reflection on the issue, more detailed comments are to be made. Concerning Nickelsburg I find both the description of the sexual commingling in Hesiod's Catalogue and the description of Prometheus to be interesting parallels. There are parallels to both features in near eastern mythology. In the first case, however, I think that none of them is so close to Enoch as this one. In the second case the description of Prometheus comes close to the Mesopotamian traditions about the apkallu's. The similarity between Mesopotamian and Greek mythology in this matter was already seen by Pseudo-Eupolemus by making Atlas to the Greek counterpart of Enoch/Uanadapa.[206] More generally, I think that the use of Tartarus as the name of the underworld and prison of the rebelling angels in the Greek translation of En 20,1 demonstrates the affinity between the Enochic theme of imprisonment of the angels and the Greek theme of imprisonment of deposed gods and heroes.[207] It seems as if the literature of third-century Palestine reflects the ongoing amalgamation of near eastern and Greek mythical themes.

I have two basic objections to Hanson's comparison of the rebellion myths and En 6-11. One can be formulated as a question. If En 6-11 contains a pattern of the near eastern rebellion myths which also is reflected in texts from the Book of Isaiah and Ezekiel and transmitted to the Enochic writers through an unbroken current of traditions through pre- and post-exilic Israel, why is En 6-11 based on Gen 6,1-4 and not on the texts which most clearly reflect the rebellion pattern? And why does En 6-11 not even allude to the Biblical texts in Isaiah and Ezekiel which demonstrate the transmission of the rebellion myth in Israel?

The second objection depends on the first. I think Hanson failed to nuance his argument sufficiently when he dealt with the rebellion theme. The word "rebellion" is ambiguous and can cover different motifs. In the Hittite and Ugaritic myths the rebellion is an action to replace the ruling deity. I believe it also occurs in such Biblical texts as Is 14, which may be dependent on the Ugaritic myth about Ashtar the Rebel,[208] and Ezek 28. But this motif is reflected in neither Gen 6,1-4 nor En 6-11. In these two texts the crime is a violation against the divine order, not an attempt to replace the ruling deity. I am aware that the two motifs can be combined. My point is that when the replacement of the ruling deity is the primary concern in the rebellion myths, this should have been reflected in En 6-11 if this text was directly patterned on these myths.

---

206 Cf. above, pp. 206f. For parallels especially between Hesiod's Theogony and Mesopotamian mythology, cf. G. Steiner, "Griechische und orientalische Mythen", AnAb 6, 1957, pp. 171-87; and W.G. Lambert and P. Walcot, "A New Babylonian Theogony and Hesiod", Kadmos 4, 1965, pp. 64-72.
207 Cf. above, p. 66.
208 Cf. Clifford, Cosmic Mountain, pp. 160-6.

These considerations lead to another approach. And I think that the most obvious approach still is the most profitable: Among other aspects En 6-11 is an expository narrative to Gen 4-9. The analysis must start with an examination of the correspondence between these two texts.

1.2   The Relationship of En 6-11 to Gen 4-9

I start the analysis with a table of the allusions in En 6-11 to Gen 4-9[209] (pp. 276-77, pages references to Milik).

Quantitatively about half of the verses in En 6-11 allude to Gen 4-9. I am aware of the limits of such quantification, but it gives an impression of how intimately the two texts are woven together. The next question is what sequences in En 6-11 do not contain allusions to Gen 4-9. I give the following survey:

6,3	the oath of the watchers	A
6,6b	descent on Mount Hermon	E
6,7-8	the list of angelic leaders	E
7,1b	teaching in magic	(A) F
7,3	giants devouring the toil of men	D
7,5ab	sin against animals	A
8,1	teaching in "make up"	A
8,2	fornication	A
8,3	teaching in magic, divination, astrology	(A) F
9,4-5	blessing	B
9,6	revelation of eternal secrets	F
9,7	revelation of magic	(A) F
9,11	transitional notice	C
10,4-6	dispatching of Asael to the nether world and final judgment	(A) E
10,8	the crimes of Asael, his teaching	F
10,9ab	the battle between the giants	D
10,12-14	dispatching of the watchers to the nether world and final judgment	E
10,16-11,2 (-10,17.22)	description of the restored earth	B

209   As previously stated, I do not share Milik's opinion that En 6-11 is composed prior to the latest stage of the Genesis texts, cf. above, pp. 95f. I also think that the table below utterly disproves Milik's assumption. En 6-11 not only corresponds to Gen 6,1-4, but utilizes motifs from all sources to Genesis in ch. 4-9.

Enoch	Sources
6,1	Traces: En^{b}1 ii, 2-3 (p. 165)
6,6a	Traces: En^{a}1 iii, 4 (p. 150)
7,1a	Traces: En^{a}1 iii, 14-15 (p. 150); En^{b}1 ii, 18 (p. 166)
7,2	En^{a}1 iii, 16-17 (p. 150)
7,4	En^{a}1 iii, 19 (p. 150)
7,5c	Gr^{Pan}
7,6	Gr^{Pan}
8,1a	En^{b}1 ii, 26 (p. 167)
8,4	En^{a}1 iv, 5-6 (p. 157) En^{b}1 iii, 5-6 (p. 170)
9,1	En^{a}1 iv, 6-8 (p. 157); En^{b}1 iii, 7-8 (pp. 171-1)
9,2	En^{a}1 iv, 9-10 (pp. 157-8)
9,3	Gr^{Pan}; Gr^{Syn}
9,8	Gr^{Pan}; Gr^{Syn}
9,9	Gr^{Pan}; Gr^{Syn}
9,10	Gr^{Pan}; Gr^{Syn}
10,1-2	Gr^{Pan}; Gr^{Syn}
10,3	Traces: En^{a}1 v, 3-4 (p. 161)
10,7	Gr^{Pan}; Gr^{Syn}
10,9c-10	Traces: En^{b}1 iv, 6-8 (p. 175)
10,11	Traces: En^{b}1 iv, 8-9 (p. 175)
10,15	Gr^{Pan}
10,17	En^{c}1 v, 5-6 (p. 189)
10,22b	Traces: En^{a}1 vi, 5 (p. 162)

Explanations of the groups:
A: sexual commingling and birth of giants
B: date of the incident
C: the crimes of the watchers and giants
D: the complaint from the earth
E: instruction of Noah
F: condemnation of Giants
G: restoration of the earth and the human race

I must first point out the danger of misinterpretation which is
implied in the comparison. The lists cannot be treated in the way
that the occurrence of a passage in the table of allusions excludes
the possibility that this sentence functions within a totally
different system of thoughts in Enoch. It is quite clear that

Genesis	Theme	Group
6,1-2	increase of human race taking wives	A
5,18-19	descent in the days of Jared	B
6,2.4	sexual commingling	A
6,4	birth of giants	A
9,6	murder	C
9,4	drinking blood	C
4,10	complaint from the earth	D
6,11	lawlessness	C
4,22	war equipment of iron and brass	C
4,10	complaint from the earth and from the	
4,10	souls of killed men	D
4,10		
4,10		
6,2-4	sexual commingling	A
6,4	birth of giants	A
4,10	complaint from the souls of killed men	D
6,13-14.18	instruction of Noah	E
6,13-14.18	to escape the flood	
8,21b-22	restoration of the earth	G
6,3	shortening of giants lives	F
6,2.4	sexual commingling	A
6,3	spirits of the giants	F
9,7	fruitfulness of human race	G
9,15b	promise never to destroy the creation	G

although the Enochic text frequently alludes to Genesis, the meaning of En 6-11 could have been determined by other factors. Nevertheless, I find it helpful to have an indication of what kind of material does not correspond to the Genesis text. I place the sequences in the following groups:

A: sequences corresponding to halakcic rules[210]
B: sequences containing conventional language in the Jewish setting
C: transitional notice
D: historical references[211]
E: names and fate of the watchers
F: teaching

Also here it is important to be aware that the occurrence of a sequence in one group does not mean that it cannot relate to another group. For instance sequences corresponding to halakcic rules may contain motifs taken from other traditions than biblical texts. And what is classified as historical references may contain motifs taken from older traditions and applied to the historical circumstances behind the composition. The survey is only intended to give an indication of what material cannot be explained as derived from Genesis, elaborations or halakcic rules, conventional in the Jewish setting, or determined by the actual historical situation. The survey gives this indication. The group of sequences in E and F demonstrates the adaptation of mythical material which cannot be explained in this way. The elements in these groups are: 1) divine beings associated with Mount Hermon; 2) the condemnation of these beings to the nether world; 3) the association of these beings with the teaching of magic, divination and astrology.

The next question is what elements played the dominant role in the formation of the structure of En 6-11. I adopt the four scheme used by Hanson when he defined the structure of the section (cf. above, p. 270): rebellion, devastation, punishment, and restoration. The table below demonstrates that the structure of En 6-11 follows closely the structure of Gen 4-9:

	Genesis	Enoch
rebellion:	6,1-4	6,1-7,2
devastation:	6,5-12	7,3-8,4
punishment:	6,13-8,19	9,1-10,16a
restoration:	8,20-9,17	10,16b-11,2

I do not maintain that this is the structure originally intended by the composers of the Genesis texts, but it appears to be the structure as it was interpreted by the composer of En 6-11. Both

210   Cf. above, pp. 99f.
211   Cf. above, pp. 97f.

the high number of allusions to Gen 4-9 and the similarity of structure suggest that Gen 4-9 must be regarded as the primary source for En 6-11. This does not mean that En 6-11 contains nothing alien to Genesis, nor does it mean that the story in En 6-11 only elaborates the original meaning of Gen 4-9. But it does mean that the key to understanding En 6-11 must lie in how its author interpreted Gen 4-9. When one is aware of the close relationship between the texts, the differences are even more striking.

The first main difference is that the aspects of rebellion and devastation in primeval history are concentrated around the theme from Gen 6,1-4. When the composer deals with the devastating consequences of the watcher incident, he alludes to Gen 4,10.22; 6,11; 9,4.6 (cf. group C and D in our table). This means that the crime of Cain killing Abel, the invention of metallurgy by Tubal-Cain, the lawless conditions before the flood, and the crimes that are prohibited in the Noahitic commandments, are viewed together in one perspective and claimed to have been caused by the watchers and their offspring. This concentration on the theme of Gen 6,1-4 is remarkable when one considers that the composer of En 6-11 clearly used Genesis in its present shape. In Genesis it is not the incident in 6,1-4 which marks the primary crime and changed human conditions, but rather the actions of Adam and Eve in 2-3. There are no allusions to this in En 6-11. The composer of En 6-11 must deliberately have neglected this story and concentrated the introduction of evil into the world around the watcher incident.

The second main difference follows in the same line as the preceding. The composer combined the judgment motif which he perceived in Gen 6,3 with the Flood story (cf. Group E and F on the table). Gen 6,3 is interpreted as the judgment of the giants and combined with the instruction of Noah to escape the flood in Gen 6,13-14.18.

These two main differences from the Genesis primeval history correspond to the inclusion of material alien to Genesis. The composer adds new elements to the crimes of the watchers and giants, such as fornication, violence, and teaching in forbidden knowledge. He also adds a new dimension which forms the greatest difference from Genesis, namely the condemnation of the watchers to the nether world.

But the basis for these differences is an interpretation of primeval history in which the introduction of evil into the world is associated with the rebellion of divine and semi-divine figures who were struck by a primeval catastrophe. Accordingly our next question must be: What caused the composer of En 6-11 to interpret the Genesis narratives in that way?

2.   Gen 6,1-4 and the Primeval Catastrophe

Our analysis of Gen 6,1-4 does not aim to give detailed answers to all the questions associated with the sequence. Rather, it seeks to answer the question already put forward in the preceding chapter and now formulated in a somewhat different way: Are there indications in the text of Gen 6,1-4 which point toward a connection between it and a primeval catastrophe? Since the text is placed just before the Flood story it seems natural to focus its connection to the deluge. But I am not primarily concerned with whether the incident in Gen 6,1-4 can be regarded as one of the reasons for the flood in Genesis. It is likely that the composers thought that way. But this relationship to the Flood story is not in principle different from the other crimes described in the antediluvian period. The stories in Gen 2-3; 4; and 6,1-4 all illustrate transgressions of the divine law and how sin increased in human life and society. But read in this perspective the subject from beginning to end is human life and society, and the flood strikes the human race. The main difference from En 6-11 is that here the catastrophe strikes the watchers and giants. Our question is therefor whether there is anything in Gen 6,1-4 which could have caused this change.

2.1   Literary Sources of Gen 6,1-4

The question has been discussed in detail in commentaries and monographies with differing conclusions.

F. Dexinger regarded 6,2 as belonging to the source L or J, while

vv. 3-4 are ascribed to P.[212] H. Gese regarded vv. 1-4 as a unity
which was added to J.[213] C. Westermann thought that two stories
were woven together i the first source (J). One was an etiology of
the *gibborīm* "giants, mighty heroes", and preserved in 6,1-2.4c.
The other was a story about transgression of limits in human
society. Both stories have vv. 1-2 in common, but the second also
included God's intervention, the report of which was originally
placed where v. 3 now stands. This second story, however, was
later elaborated by the inclusion of mythical material which is
apparent in v. 3 in its present wording and in v. 4a, a passage
telling about the origin of the mythical $n^e f i l \bar{\imath} m$.[214] L. Bartelmus
regarded vv. 1-2.4 as belonging to J. He claimed that v. 3 was not
alluded to in Jewish literature before the Book of Jubilees and
accordingly not known by the composer of En 6-11. The verse was
inserted in Genesis under the influence of this composer's
interpretation of Genesis not long after the composing of En 6-11,
which Bartelmus dated to the second century B.C.[215]

These few examples should be sufficient to illustrate the diver-
gences in the research concerning the issue. I base my own
contribution to the discussion on three observations:

I. As has often been pointed out, the main line of narration which concentrates
on the same theme and contains no syntactical breaks extends from v. 2 to v. 4c:
"And the sons of the gods saw that the daughters of men were beautiful. And
they took for themselves such women as they chose. The sons of the gods went
into the daughters of men and they gave birth by them. These were the <u>gibborīm</u>
from remote times, the men of a (famous) name."

II. Many scholars have also noted that the greatest trouble in the sequence is
caused by v. 3. First, the verse interrupts the line of events described in vv.
2.4bc. Secondly, and this is the basic argument, the verse seems to deal with
something entirely different from vv. 2.4bc. The subject of vv. 2.4bc is the birth
of giants. The principals are the sons of the gods and the daughters of men. The
subject concerned in v. 3 is the life time of man, 'ādām. I think it is artificial to
include automatically either the n^efilīm or the <u>gibborīm</u> here. 'ādām is also in
v. 1 introduced as a group distinct from these groups.[216]

212 F. Dexinger, Sturz der Göttersöhne oder Engel vor der Sintflut?, WBTh 13,
Wien 1966, pp. 54-8.
213 H. Gese, "Der bewachte Lebensbaum und die Heroen: Zwei mythologische
Ergänzungen zur Urgeschichte der Quelle J", now in: Vom Sinai zum Zion,
München 1974, pp. 99-112, p. 108-12.
214 C. Westermann, Genesis, pp. 495, 497, 509, 511f.
215 R. Bartelmus, Heroentum in Israel und seine Umwelt, pp. 25-30, 146, 191-3.
216 Against Gese, op.cit., p. 111, who thought that the n^efilīm were intended.

III. Also v. 4a causes trouble. Syntactically the passage appears to be an addition to v. 4bc. "The n^{e}filīm were on the earth (or in the land) in those days and also afterwards when (the sons of the gods . . .)." At least the sentence must be regarded as a digression, an explanatory note. The closest parallel to this kind of statement may be in Gen 12,6. The sequence starts: "And Abraham passed through the land to the sanctuary at Shechem, to the terebinth-tree of Moreh" and continues: "and the Canaanites at that time were in the land". This statement is historical. The author wished to inform his readers that this happened at the time of the Canaanites. I think Gen 6,4a serves exactly the same purpose. The author wished to inform his readers that this happened at the time of the n^{e}filīm. In Gen 12,6 the aside has nothing to do with the course of events described, but there is no reason to think that it was not made by the original composer of the narrative, cf. the same statement in Gen 13,7. I am inclined to regard 6,4a as an analogous digression made by the original composer. I am also inclined to see a connection between the two. The first incident happened in the primeval time when the n^{e}filīm inhabited the land, while in the story of Abraham we are informed that we have now moved to the period of Canaanite inhabitation.

We are then left with the result that we have two sources, one in vv. 2 and 4, the other in v. 3. The next question is where to place v. 1. There is no direct evidence that the verse could not have belonged to the oldest source and introduced the story about the sons of the gods. If so, it must have been meant as a sort of background notice, because the increase of the human race has thematically nothing to do with the birth of giants. The increase of the human race, however, corresponds thematically to the delimination of the lifespan in v. 3. The evaluation here will depend partly on how one interprets v. 3, which is extremely obscure. But in favour of a connection between v. 1 and v. 3 points the fact that both verses deal with the human race as such, while this is not the subject in vv. 2.4. I am therefore inclined to think that vv. 2 and 4 belonged to the oldest source, while vv. 1 and 3 must be regarded as a later commentary.

I think R. Bartelmus (cf. note 215) has given good reasons for assuming that the oldest version belonged to the Jahwistic source. If one excises Gen 5, Gen 6,2.4 (Bartelmus includes also v. 1) comes directly after the etiological genealogy in Gen 4. The leading question here is the origin of civilization.[217] The origin of the *gibborīm* suits easily into this context. I do not agree, however, with Bartelmus in placing v. 3 in the second century B.C. First, I find it hard to think that such great changes in the *torah* could be

---

217 Cf. above, p. 40 and pp. 218ff.

made and generally accepted at so late a date. Secondly, I find a clear allusion to Gen 6,3 in En 10,9c. The sequence deals with the destruction of the giants. Gr^{Pan} reads: μακρότης γὰρ ἡμερῶν οὐκ ἔστιν αὐτῶν. On the basis of traces to the first word Milik reconstructs: וארכת ימין לא איתי להון,4Q En^b 1iv, line 6 (Milik, p. 175), "and length of days they will not have". En 10,15 deals with the spirits of the giants, which I think allude to the rū^{a}ḥ, "spirit" of Yahweh in 'ādām in Gen 6,3. Like Bartelmus I find it difficult to ascribe v. 3 to the Priestly source. P recounts numbers much higher than 120 for the life time of the postdiluvian patriarchs. The use of "Yahweh" as the divine name before the revelation to Moses (Ex 6,3) does not occur elsewhere in P. But there are also similarities to the Priestly source, such as the interest in numbers, the use of rū^{a}ḥ and bāsār, "flesh" in the context of creation (cf. below). I would not place the composing of v. 3 (and v. 1) too far from P with regard to time and setting. The differences to P especially in the numbers of years seem to indicate that 6,1.3 was written before P.

2.2 The Character of the Oldest Version

R. Bartelmus defines the oldest version as "a mythical etiology". The intention of the narrative was to tell about the origin of the gibbor ī m, the primeval heroes. In a broad presentation of parallels in ancient near eastern and Greek literature, he demonstrated that these kinds of stories served to legitimize the ruling dynasties.[218] Presupposed is that the b^{e}nē hā'^{a}lohī m, "the sons of the gods", are to be understood as divine beings. The use of the phrase in Ugaritic material should give sufficient background for this assumption.

Bartelmus' documentation and analysis are confirmed by two other observations. One, as previously noted,[219] is that the Jahwist uses the designation gibbōr about Nimrod, the first great ruler on earth, Gen 10,8-12. The second is the parallels between the Jahwist and Philo of Byblos. In the Phoenician History the sequence about the giants belongs to the genealogical section telling about the origin of

218 Bartelmus, op.cit., pp. 15-24; pp. 36-78.
219 Cf. above, p. 113.

civilization. I have previously demonstrated the close relationship between this section and the antediluvian section of the Jahwistic source.[220] In the Phoenician History the description of the giants is meant as a report of the achievement of power in human civilization.[221] I think that this is also the case in the Jahwistic source.

In Philo the achievement of power is meant positively. It is a characteristic feature in the Jahwistic source that achievements are regarded in a dialectic perspective. Just as the invention of metallurgy in Gen 4,22 reveals human progress on the one hand, but opens the way for the productions of weapons and precedes Lamech's song of revenge on the other, and the story of the tower of Babel demonstrates human skill on the one hand but is also a manifestation of rebellion, Gen 6,2.4 tells about the achievement of power on the one hand but also alludes to the terrifying danger connected to power on the other. Twice in the Primeval history the Jahwist reports about divine interventions of a negative character, in the Paradise story dealing with knowledge and here dealing with power. It seems as if he intended to emphasize that these two areas of human life and society are the areas where men are most like God and therefore in the most dangerous position.

The *nefilīm* in v. 4a are not explicitly equated with the *gibborīm*. If my earlier suggestion that v. 4a is to be understood as an explanatory historical statement similar to Gen 12,6 is correct, the *nefilīm* seem to be a broader group than the *gibborīm*. If so, the meaning is that in the primeval time of the *nefilīm* some distinguished mighty rulers were born of divine origin.

The designation *nefilīm* occurs once more in the Old Testament, namely in Num 13,33. There the inhabitants of Canaan are described as men of gigantic size, "the *nefilīm*, sons of Enak, from the *nefilīm*". Enak is depicted as a king of Hebron. The wording suggests that the Enakites are described as *nefilīm*, descendants of the *nefilīm*, which seems to mean that people from the primeval race of the *nefilīm* were still living in Canaan at the time of Moses. This corresponds also to the wording in Gen 6,4a: "The *nefilīm* were on the earth (or in the land) in those days *and also*

---

220   Cf. above, pp. 215-22.
221   Cf. J. Ebach, Weltentstehung und Kulturentwicklung bei Philo von Byblos, p. 148.

afterwards." Most likely the Jahwist indicated here that there existed n^{e}fil$\bar{i}$m also at a later date than this primeval period.

The identification of the Enakites as n^{e}fil$\bar{i}$m allows another step in the identification of this group. In Deut 2,10.20f the Enakites are described as r^{e}f$\bar{a}$im, also characterized as ancient gigantic inhabitants of the Canaanite area. There are good reasons for thinking that the n^{e}fil$\bar{i}$m and the r^{e}f$\bar{a}$im were two names for the same thing. Since the discoveries of Ugaritic texts, completely new light has been shed on the problem of the r^{e}f$\bar{a}$im.[222] The meaning of the West-Semitic root RP' is "heal". In Ugaritic texts a distinguished group of rp'um is located in the nether world. They are shades of dead and regarded as divine beings. There are clear indications that this designation was used especially for a special class of spirits, namely those of kings, heroes, warriors and rulers.[223] Among these spirits are also the rp'im qdmyn, "the primeval manes", i.e. the manes of ancient ancestors.[224] The Ugaritic texts also show clearly that the rp'um appear in ancestor worship where they are cared for and invoked for protective reasons and in order to give health and strength.[225]

The n^{e}fil$\bar{i}$m and r^{e}f$\bar{a}$im can accordingly designate primeval ancestors of the Canaanites who were worshipped in hero cult as divine beings. J.C. de Moor suggested that the word n^{e}fil$\bar{i}$m, which looks like an Aramaic passive participle and accordingly would mean "the fallen", originally could have been a designation of those killed in heroic battle.[226] This would correspond very well to the use of the verb n$\bar{a}$fal, "fall" in Ezek 32,20.22.23.24.27, cf. v. 27: "They all fell by the sword and descended to Sheol." "The fallen ones" are often regarded in research as an allusion to Gen 6,4a.[227]

---

222 Cf. the discussion of the material in H. Gese, "Die Religionen Altsyriens", pp. 90ff; and "Der bewachte Lebensbaum und die Heroen", pp. 108-12; N.J. Tromp, Primitive Conceptions of Death and the Nether World in the Old Testament, BibOr 21, Rome 1969, pp. 176-80; M. Astour, "The Nether World and its Denizens at Ugarit", B. Alster (ed.), Death in Mesopotamia, M.CSA 8, Copenhagen 1980, pp. 227-38; J.C. de Moor, "Rapi'uma-Rephaim", ZAW 88, 1976, pp. 323-45.
223 Cf. de Moor, op.cit.,p. 333.
224 Cf. Astour, op.cit., p. 233.
225 Cf. Ebach, op.cit., pp. 257f.
226 Cf. de Moor, op.cit., p. 339.
227 Cf. Westermann, op.cit., p. 511; W. Zimmerli, Ezechiel, p. 789f.

It is difficult to decide to what extent the underworld context is intended by the Jahwist in Gen 6,4a, or whether the notice is meant only as a reference to the primeval inhabitants of the area. Certainly Gese exaggerated when he described the primary issue in Gen 6,1-4 as cult of dead heroes.[228] It is interesting to note that Philo of Byblos also has a reference to worship of antediluvian ancestors: "Now when these men died ... those who were left behind dedicated staffs to them and worshipped the monuments and observed feasts to them yearly."[229] Philo here clearly refers to Semitic customs of ancestor worship[230] within a section closely related to the Jahwistic narrative. This can indicate that the cultic aspect was implied in the memory of the primeval ancestors also in the context of Gen 6,4. What is quite clear is that even if the emphasis is not laid on the cultic underworld aspect in the Jahwistic account, this is certainly an aspect of the $n^e fil\bar{\imath} m$ concept in a broader context.

2.3   The Connection to the Primeval Catastrophe in Gen 6,1.3

The first passage belonging to this source is clear: ויהי כי החל האדם לרב על פני האדמה, "and it happened when mankind began to multiply over the earth". V. 3, however, is extremely obscure. The problem is that two of the words, the verb ידון, $y\bar{a}don$, of the root דון, $d\bar{u}n$, and what seems to be a noun שגם, $\check{s}agam$, are unknown in Hebrew.

Concerning the first, LXX translates καταμείνη, "remain", which presupposes ידור, $y\bar{a}dor$, instead of $y\bar{a}don$. That gives meaning in the context: "my spirit shall not remain in man", but it is clearly a correction of an unintelligible text. Many readings have been proposed.[231] I still think the best solution is to derive the verb from Akkadian $dan\bar{a}nu$ which as a verb means "to be strong" and as a noun has the meaning "strength, might, force, violence".[232]

---

228   Gese, op.cit., p. 110.
229   Cf. above, p. 218.
230   Cf. Astour, op.cit., p. 228.
231   Cf. the discussion in Westermann, op.cit., pp. 506f; Bartelmus, op.cit., pp. 18f.
232   Cf. CAD, sub $dan\bar{a}nu$, pp. 81-6.

There are several verbs in Hebrew and Aramaic which seem to correspond to Akkadian ones in the same way. Akkadian damāmu means "to lament", Hebrew dāmam, has two meanings, "to lament" and "to be silent". The verb dūm, most likely meaning "to be silent", may be a derivation of dāmam. Akkadian ašāšu, "to suffer" appears in Aramaic in two roots with the same meaning, hᵃšaš and hūš. The verb hūš appears in Hebrew with the meaning "to be affected". Akkadian kalālu means in causative (S-stem) "to complete", Hebrew kūl means in causative (hiph'il) "to endure". Akkadian radādu means "to pursue", Hebrew rūd means "to roam". Ethiopic roda has preserved a meaning closer to Akkadian, "to run upon, attack". Akkadian salālu, Hebrew II sālal can both mean "sink". In Hebrew sūlā corresponding to mᵉsōlā means "deep".

The second word is even more problematic. LXX translates the Hebrew phrase בשגם הוא with διὰ τὸ εἶναι αὐτοὺς, "because he is...". To get a similar meaning in Hebrew we have to split up the word into separate particles: ב-ש-גם. Westermann regarded this as the only possibility, although he admits that: 1) This combination of particles does not occur elsewhere; 2) *š* does not occur in the Pentateuch as a relative pronoun; 3) *gam* is difficult in the context (in fact it gives no meaning).[233] We can formulate the three obstacles in the following way: A combination of the three particles ב-ש-גם to בשגם is not known in Hebrew; besides this nothing indicates that this combination should have the meaning "because". Formulated this way the solution must be rejected. There is no linguistic basis for the assumption.

There is, however, one more possibility. The root שגם, ŠGM, *šagam*, has an equivalence in Akkadian. The verb *šagāmu* has the meaning "howl, roar, cry, shout", the nouns *šagīmu* and *šigmu* mean "loud cry, noise".[234] In favour of this derivation is the fact that the stems are identical and that the verb in the same passage also most likely is derived from Akkadian. The translation of the whole sequence belonging to this source may at first glance seem a little strange, but the criteria of content will be given below: "And it happened when mankind began to multiply over the earth... And Yahweh said: 'My spirit shall not be powerful in man for everlasting time because of the noise. He is flesh and his days will be hundred and twenty years'."

233 Westermann, op.cit., p. 507.
234 Cf. AHW, pp. 1125, 1127, 1231. The only place I have found this possibility considered is in J.A. Clines, "The Significance of the 'Sons of God' Episode (Genesis 6:1-4) in the Context of the 'Primeval History' (Genesis 1-11)*, JSOT 13, 1979, pp. 33-46. Clines did, however, reject this possibility: "If this was the case, it is clearly no longer the case, and the sentence, though not crystal-clear, is generally intelligible, p. 40.

I do not think that the text existed independently of Gen 6,2.4. It seems to be an additional commentary to the older version. Nevertheless, a preliminary analysis shows that the sequence by itself makes sense. Yahweh's speech related to the increase of the human race, which is characterized as "noise". The human race has received this ability to increase and "make noise" because it was given the divine powerful spirit. The intention of the speech is clearly to establish a new order diminishing the increase and the noise. The lifespan is delimited to hundred and twenty years.

This commentary on vv. 2 and 4 involves an interpretation of the previous text. The commentator saw a parallel between the divine origin of the *gibborīm* and the divine spirit being powerful in man. This means that he treated the *gibborīm* and *'adām*, the primeval man, as parallels.

It is not difficult to find a parallel to this source. There has been a general agreement among scholars that Gen 6,1 is a parallel to the introductory clause to the section about the crises in Atra-Ḥasis: *mātum irtapis nišu imtīdā*, "when the land extended and the peoples multiplied", Tabl I, v, rev, line 353 and Tabl II, i, line 2 (Lambert, Atra-Ḥasis, pp. 66, 72). I shall argue that also Gen 6,3 corresponds to Atra-Ḥasis. Below I give the translation of the Assyrian Recension according to Lambert (p. 107). The section introduces the crises:

> [Twelve hundred years had not yet passed]
> When the land extended [and the peoples multiplied].
>
> He got disturbed [with] their noise,
> [With] their uproar [sleep] did not overcome him.
>
> Enlil convened his assembly
> And addressed the gods his sons,
>
> 'The noise of mankind has become too intense for me,
>
> I have got disturbed [with] their noise,
> With their uproar sleep does not overcome me.
>
> Command that there be plague,
> Let Namtar diminish their noise.
>
> Let disease, sickness, plague and pestilence
> Blow upon them like a tornado.'

They commanded and there was plague,
Namtar diminished their noise.

Disease, sickness, plague and pestilence
Blew upon them like a tornado.'

The discerning one, the man Atra-ḫasis,
Kept an open ear [to his lord], Ea.

He spoke with his god,
[And] Ea spoke with him.

Atra-ḫasis opened his mouth to speak
[And addressed] Ea his lord,

'Lord, the human race is groaning,
Your [disease] is consuming the land.

Ea, lord, the human race is groaning,
[The disease] from the gods is consuming the land.'
                                    (Rev iv, lines 1-26)

The section in Atra-Ḥasis gives the reason why the gods sent the crises and finally the flood: The people multiplied and disturbed the gods. The Akkadian words used for the disturbance are *rigmu* and *ḫubūru*. This action of mankind caused the reaction of the gods. Enlil convened his assembly and the gods decided to diminish the *rigmu* by sending disease, sickness, plague and pestilence.

Some problems have to be clarified. First, what is the meaning of *rigmu* and *ḫubūru*? Lambert translates them as "noise" and "uproar". *rigmu* means commonly "cry, scream, voice" and is often used metaphorically about Adad's thunder.[235] (In Atra-Ḥasis the verb *šagāmu* is used in the same way, cf. Tabl III, ii, lines 49.53 (Lambert, p. 92)). *ḫubūru* means "noise", but von Soden has argued that the word suggests more than "noise as such" (Lärm als solchen) and rather indicates "noisy activities" (lärmende Aktivitäten).[236] R.A. Oden argued the same.[237] Closest in support of Lambert's translation comes G. Pettinato. According to him the two words mean "Wehgeschrei, Klageschrei, empörtes

235 Cf. R.A. Oden, Jr., "Divine Aspirations in Atrahasis and in Genesis 1-11", ZAW 93, 1981, pp. 197-216, p. 205.
236 W. von Soden, "Der Mensch bescheidet sich nicht. Überlegungen zu Schöpfungserzählungen in Babylonien und Israel", Symbolae Biblicae et Mesopotamicae, Leiden 1973, pp. 349-58, p. 353.
237 Oden, op.cit., p. 205.

Geschrei". He asserts that "der Lärm, der die Götter zornig marcht, ist nicht der Arbeitlärm oder sogar ein freudiger Lärm, sondern ein Lärm der Empörung."[238]

But the interpretation of the "cry" and "noise" as "uproar" or "rebellion" involves another problem. Is not the noise only a consequence of the increase, which is regarded as the real offence against the gods? I agree with Oden's argumentation based on Pettinato and von Soden. When Enlil complains about mankind he refers to their *rigmu* and *huburu,* not to their increase. Besides this, overpopulation is never mentioned in Mesopotamian texts as a phenomenon to be feared.[239] I think the numerical increase is introduced to demonstrate the large extent of human noise, which is to be interpreted as rebellion against the hard conditions that the gods had imposed upon man. "Das bedeutet aber, dass die Menschen damals bereits über ihren ursprünglichen Auftrag, den Götter schwere Arbeit abzunehmen, hinausgingen und selbständig viel mehr unternahmen" (von Soden, p. 353); "die Stelle besagt also, dass die Menschen die Empörung über ihr schweres Schicksal durch Lärm kundgetan haben" (Pettinato, p. 190).

The other occurrences of *rigmu* in Atra-Ḥasis shed light on the content of the word. In Tabl I, line 179 (Lambert, p. 52) the lamentation of the Igigu gods because of the hard conditions is characterized as *rigmu.* In Tabl I, line 77 (Lambert, p. 46) the rebellion of the Igigu gods is characterized by the same word, but here it must mean "war cry". This indicates that the word has two aspects that very well can be united: the cry of despair and the cry of rebellion.

The word is also used in the section dealing with the creation of man. The *rigmu* of the Igigu gods is given to mankind, Tabl I, line 242 (Lambert, p. 60). Explicitly *rigmu* refers here to the cry of despair. But I find it very likely that the composer also intended the other aspect of the word. When the gods solved the problem of suffering in the divine world by imposing "the cry of despair" on the new created human race, they did not consider that out of the cry of despair grows the cry of rebellion, just as happened among the Igigu gods. The composer thus draws a line from the rebellion

238   G. Pettinato, "Die Bestrafung der Menschengeschlechts durch die Sintflut", Orientalia 37 NS, 1968, pp. 165-200, p. 190.
239   Oden, op.cit., pp. 206ff.

of the Igigu gods to the creation of man and, subsequently, to the rebellion of man.

There are in fact other indications that the author drew this line, which becomes clear from the section dealing with the creation of man, Tabl I, lines 189-260. I record lines 223-230 according to Lambert (p. 58):

^{d}we-e-i-la ša i-šu-ú ṭe$_4$-e-ma
i-na pu-úḫ-ri-šu-nu iṭ-ṭa-ab-ḫu
i-na ši-ri-šu ù da-mi-šu
^{d}nin-tu ú-ba-li-il-ṭi-iṭ-ṭa
aḫ-ri-a-t[i-iš u$_4$-mi up-pa-iš-mu]-ú
i-na ši-i-ir i-li e-ṭe-[em-mu ib-ši]
ba- al-ṭa it-ta-šu ú-še-di-š[u-ma]
aš-šu la mu-uš-ši-i e-ṭe-em-mu [ib-ši]

We-ila, who had personality,
They slaughtered in their assembly.
From his flesh and blood
Nintu mixed clay.
For the rest [of the time they heard the drum],
From the flesh of the god [there was] a spirit.
It proclaimed living man as its sign,
And so that this was not forgotten [there was] a spirit.

Man is created from the flesh and blood of the leading rebel god.[240] Atra-Ḥasis follows to some extent the basic pattern in Akkadian myths about the creation of man. Man is created from the blood of a slain god mixed with clay.[241] The divine element in man is accordingly the blood. This is clearly exemplified in Enuma Elish, Tabl VI, lines 27-35:

The Igigi, the great gods, replied to him,
To Lugaldimmerankia, counselor of the gods, their lord:
"It was Kingu who contrived the uprising,
And made Tiamat rebel, and joined the battle."
They bound him, holding him before Ea.
They imposed on him his guilt and severed his blood
   (vessels).
Out of his blood they fashioned mankind.
He imposed the service and let free the gods.[242]

---

240 Cf. W.L. Moran, "The Creation of Man in Atrahasis I 192-248", BASOR 200, 1970, pp. 48-56, pp. 51f.
241 Cf. Lambert, Atra-Ḥasis, pp. 21f; G. Pettinato, Das altorientalische Menschenbild und die sumerischen und akkadischen Schöpfungsmythen, AHA W.PH. Abh.1 Heidelberg 1971, pp. 41-7.
242 Cf. ANET³, p. 68.

Berossos seems to depend on Enuma Elish in his account of creation. The sequence dealing with the creation of man reads as follows (according to version a)[243]:

τοῦτον τὸν θεὸν ἀφελεῖν τὴν ἑαυτοῦ κεφαλήν,

καὶ τὸ ῥυὲν αἷμα τοὺς ἄλλους θεοὺς φυρᾶσαι τῆι γῆι,

καὶ διαπλάσαι τοὺς ανθρώπους

δι᾽ ὃ νοερούς τε εἶναι,

καὶ φρονήσεως θείας μετέχειν.

This god took off his own head
and the other gods (gathered up) the blood which flowed from it
and mixed the blood with earth and formed men.
For this reason men are intelligent
and have a share of divine wisdom.

Berossos, claiming that the divine blood allowed man to share in divine wisdom, hardly depends on Greek philosophy, as Pettinato argues.[244] He has rather underscored a central aspect in the Mesopotamian concept of creation.[245]

In Atra-Hasis man is created both from the flesh and blood of the rebel god. The rebel god is also described as the one who had ṭēmu. The term can have different connotations: "personality, idea, sense, rationality".[246] Von Soden interprets the word here as "die Fähigkeit sachgemäss zu planen".[247] He is followed by Oden (note 35): "the ability to plan, the capacity to scheme."

When man is given "the ability to plan" from the rebel god, this clearly points forward to the rebellion of mankind, as did the rigmu imposed on man.

Man is given not only the ṭēmu of the rebel god, but also his eṭemmu.[248] This is the spirit or ghost of the dead. I think Oden argued correctly about the relationship between ṭēmu and eṭemmu in Atra-Hasis: "... it seems that with the very creation of humans in this Epic comes an indication of the tension within the new

---

243   Text according to Syncellus p. 49,19. FGH III, C, 1.B, sequence 7, p. 372. Translation from Burstein, Book I, 2, 3a, p. 15. Cf. also Burstein, op.cit., note 16.
244   Pettinato, op.cit., p. 44.
245   Cf. the criticism of Pettinato by H.M. Kümmel, "Bemerkungen zu den altorientalischen Berichten von der Menschenschöpfung", WO 7, 1973-74, pp. 25-38, pp. 31f; cf. also A. Heidel, The Babylonian Genesis, 2nd ed., Chicago 1951, pp. 118f.
246   Tabl I, line 223. Cf. Oden, op.cit., p. 202.
247   Von Soden, op.cit., p. 352.
248   Tabl I, lines 228. 236. Von Soden interprets the signs differently and reads edimmu, "wild man, primeval man", op.cit., pp. 350ff. I follow the reading in Lambert, p. 58; Pettinato, p. 45; Moran, p. 50.

class of beings, a tension inevitably to lead to rebellion. Humans are created with the 'spirit' *(eṭemmu)* of the leader god, which spirit is to remind them of the consequences of rebellion. Yet they are created also with the god's 'scheming' *(ṭēmu)*. It is difficult not to see in the play between *eṭemmu* and *ṭēmu* a pun; and it is equally difficult not to see in this pun a presage of the remainder of the Epic," (p. 203).

The *eṭemmu* was taken from the flesh of the god. This is a significantly new feature in Atra-Ḫasis compared to other Akkadian myths. More in correspondence to other myths is the transference of the divine *ṭēmu* to man. I see this as a parallel to Berossos' account, in which the blood gave man share in the divine wisdom.[249]

Atra-Ḫasis accordingly ends up with a tension in man that tends toward dualism. Man possesses the divine *ṭēmu*, which is the spiritual and rational side of man, and he is created with the *eṭemmu*, taken from the flesh of the slain god, which characterizes man as a mortal creature.

I think this outline of Atra-Ḫasis enables us to get a clearer understanding of Gen 6,1 and 3. The Genesis sequences in some cases correspond to Old Testament theology, but those features which seem strange in an Old Testament context have parallels in Atra-Ḫasis.

1. In the Priestly source the increase of the human race is intimately connected to creation, cf. Gen 1,28; 9,7. It is regarded positively as a consequence of God's blessing. In Gen 6, 1 and 3, however, the increase is connected to human activity which causes a negative reaction by god. The wording is close to the sentence which introduces the section of the crises in Atra-Ḫasis. Genesis: "And it happened when mankind began to multiply over the earth". Atra-Ḫasis: "When the land extended and peoples multiplied". The Genesis text implies both aspects of Atra-Ḫasis: the increase of mankind and the extension of the inhabited area.

2. In both Genesis and Atra-Ḫasis this clause introduces a court decision where human action is met with divine reaction.

3. In Genesis the human activity is characterized as šāgam, "cry, noise". There is a parallel to this in Gen 18,20 where the rebellion against the divine order in Sodom and Gomorrah is characterized as zeʿāqā, "outcry". This rebellion caused God to send a catastrophe. The concept is accordingly not unknown in the Old Testament. In Gen 6,3 šāgam can be understood as an Akkadian loanword. In Akkadian the root ŠGM has the same connotations as rigmu, the word that characterizes the human rebellion in Atra-Ḫasis.

249 Cf. Kümmel, op.cit., p. 31.

4. The speech of Yahweh seems to allude to the creation of man. Both rūᵃḥ, "spirit" and bāsār, "flesh", belong to this context. The rūᵃḥ in man corresponds to nišmat hayyīm, "the breath of life", given in the act of creation in J, Gen 2,7. In younger theology, especially from the exilic age and onwards ruᵃḥ is used parallel to and partly replaces nᵉšāmā, "breath", in the context of creation.[250] In the Priestly source all creatures are characterized as "flesh in which there is the spirit of life" (Gen 6,17; 7,15). The rūᵃḥ is the power of life given by creation (Ps 104,29-30; Job 34,14).
    On the other hand, the clause "My spirit shall not be powerful in man for everlasting time in the noise (rebellion)", is strange in an Old Testament context. It is difficult to interpret this in another way that the divine spirit is connected to the rebellion. Man is created with a force that causes the increase and the noise.
    The verb used in the clause seems to be derived from Akkadian danānu, "to be strong, powerful". In Atra-Ḥasis man is created with the ṭēmu of the god. this is the rational side of man, "the ability to scheme", which leads man to rebel. In the Old Testament rūᵃḥ can have similar connotations in an anthropological context. It can designate the rational side of man, his ability to decide and make plans.[251] I regard it as likely that Atra-Ḥasis influenced the strange wording in Gen 6,3 also at this point.

5. In Atra-Ḥasis there is a tendency toward dualism involving ṭēmu, the rational side of man, and eṭemmu, the spirit of death, connected to the flesh of the slain god. A similar kind of dualism we find in Genesis between the divine spirit and the flesh of man. bāsār clearly corresponds to the mortal side of man, which is emphasized in the succeeding clause about the delimitation of man's lifespan.

6. The result of the court decision in Atra-Ḥasis is the diminishing of the human race through crises. The result in Genesis is the delimitation of human lifespan to 120 years. This is not precisely the same, but I find the general idea not entirely different. It is also tempting to regard the 120 years as a reflex from the date 1200 years given in the entry to this section in Atra-Ḥasis (cf. above, p. 288).

7. If we examine the contexts of the sequences in Atra-Ḥasis and Genesis we find that they are the same. In Atra-Ḥasis the sequence about the rebellion of man comes directly before the introduction of Atra-ḥasis, the hero of the flood. In Genesis the sequence comes directly before the introduction of Noah. In Atra-Ḥasis the diminishing of the human race through plagues and illness precedes the flood as the last reaction of the gods. In Genesis the delimitation of the human lifespan also precedes the flood.

I think that on the basis of these observations we have sufficient reason to conclude that Atra-Ḥasis in one form or another forms the background of Gen 6,1 and 3. My next question is why the composer of these verses associated the older Jahwistic version of the birth of the giants with Atra-Ḥasis. I think the reason for this lies in the account of creation of man in Atra-Ḥasis. Man is not

250 Cf. R. Albertz and C. Westermann, "ruᵃḥ Geist", THAT II, cols 726-53, col. 737.
251 Cf. Albertz and Westermann, op.cit., col. 741; H.W. Wolff, Anthropologie des Alten Testaments, 2nd ed., München 1973, p. 67.

only made of divine flesh and blood, he is also born by a goddess.[252] This scheme resembles what is said about the divine origin of the giants in the Jahwistic source.

Our main question for the exploration of Gen 6,1-4 was whether this text could indicate why the author of En 6-11 changed the Genesis Primeval history so that the primeval catastrophe struck the watchers and the giants and not primarily the human race. I think we have found the answer. Gen 6,1 and 3 reveals an exegesis where the incident of the sons of the gods and the birth of giants are interpreted in the light of Atra-Hasis. The rebellion of what must have looked like a race of semi-divine creatures for a Jewish interpreter is equalled to the giants. This opened up for a new understanding of the Primeval history. In Mesopotamian primeval traditions the flood and the crises preceding it were the decisive catastrophe. The theme could be transposed to a new historical setting and expanded, as we have seen previously in the Poem of Erra.[253] This new interpretation of the Primeval history is reflected in the Watcher story in En 6-11. The rebellion of the divine and semi-divine figures have become the point of gravity in the Primeval history. En 6-11 has adopted more material than contained in Atra-Hasis. But the new interpretation of the Primeval history was the decisive point that opened up for other material which could be connected to the theme "rebellion of and condemnation of divine or semi-divine beings in primeval time".

3. The Background of the Watcher Story

The basic feature of the latest stratum of Gen 6,1-4, vv. 1 and 3, is that the primeval catastrophe struck divine or semi-divine beings. This feature depended on an interpretation of Atra-Hasis in which the antediluvian race was understood as divine. The same interpretation of traditions at least similar to Atra-Hasis we have noted in Pseudo-Eupolemus.[254] This interpretation of the

---

252 Tabl I, lines 244-260 and K3399+3934 (S), Obverse iii, lines 1-20, Lambert, op.cit., pp. 60-3; and above, pp. 174f and pp. 258f.
253 Cf. above, pp. 181-4.
254 Cf. above, pp. 258f.

primeval catastrophe is also the key to understanding the Watcher story, as it is first known to us in En 6-11 and reflected in the Noahitic traditions and in the Book of Jubilees. But the Watcher story has attracted material alien to Gen 6,1-4 and Pseudo-Eupolemus. Our aim is now to give an outline of these traditions and to demonstrate how they were related to the point of gravity in En 6-11: the condemnation of divine or semi-divine beings. We shall include the whole Book of Watchers as the broader context.

3.1   The Identification of the Protagonists in En 6-11

Already the opening lines of the Watcher story demonstrate the dependence of En 6-11 on Gen 6,1-4. But in the quotation from Gen 6,1-4 the author of En 6-11 interprets the $b^e n\bar{e}$ $h\bar{a}$'$^a loh\bar{i}m$, "the sons of the gods" or simply "the gods"[255] as, in the Greek translation οἱ ἄγγελοι, "the angels", and υἱοὶ οὐρανοῦ, "sons of heaven" (En 6,2). Later these beings are identified as, Aramaic עירי שמיא, '$\bar{i}r\bar{e}$ $\check{s}^e mayy\bar{a}$, En^c lvi 8 = En 13,10 (Milik, p. 193), "the watchers of heaven". In Gen 6,2 the $b^e n\bar{e}$ $h\bar{a}$'$^a loh\bar{i}m$ appear as an indefinite group with no special characteristics. In En 6-11 this group is identified as a specific group of divine beings with a series of characteristics.

Another group from Gen 6,1-4 which is easy to trace in En 6-11 are the $gibbor\bar{i}m$, "the giants". As in Gen 6,4 these are the offspring of the divine beings and the human women (En 7,2). The line of narration which concentrates on the watchers — the sexual relationship with the women — the giants, is an elaboration of the basic line of narration in Gen 6,1-4. I have previously called this line of narration "the structure of power" because it deals with the origin and character of power in the human world.[256]

But there is a third group in Gen 6,1-4 which seems to have left no traces in En 6-11, namely the Nefilim. In Gen 6,1-4 this designation could not be taken as a second name of either "the sons of the gods" or the giants, but represented a third group. This

---

255   Cf. above, p. 283.
256   Cf. above, pp. 96ff and pp. 283f.

group was closely related to the giants, however, and designated the primeval ancestors in the Canaanite area.[257] As a group similar to the giants it is also interpreted in Jub 7,22.

But this is not the case in En 6-11. Nowhere are the Nefilim mentioned together with the giants, and at first glance they seem not to be mentioned at all. When one examines how closely En 6-11 is related to Gen 6,1-4 this is rather remarkable. One should have expected this group to be represented in En 6-11 as well as the two other groups.

In our analysis of Gen 6,4 we considered the view that the name Nefilim was derived from the root NFL and meant "the fallen ones". In the context of religious history it could be a designation of the primeval ancestors who were killed in heroic battle and had descended to the underworld.[258] Whether or not this is the original meaning of the designation, a derivation from the verb "fall" is certainly the most likely way of interpretation in Hebrew and Aramaic speaking environments.

If we consider once again the differences between Gen 6,1-4 and En 6-11, one of the most striking ones is the fate of the divine beings. Their fate is described in two stages in En 6-11. The stages clearly demonstrate a line from above to below. Firstly the divine beings *came down* from heaven to the top of mount Hermon. Gr[Syn] reads: ἦσαν δὲ οὗτοι διακόσιοι οἱ καταβάντες ἐν ταῖς ἡμέραις ᾽Ιάρεδ, which suggests the following restoration of the partial Aramaic text: והוו כלהן מאתין די נחתו] ביומי ירד, En[a]1iii, lines 3-4 = En 6,6 (Milik, p. 150), "and they were all of these two hundred who came down] in the days of Jared". Secondly the divine beings were thrown down into the prison of the nether world (En 10,4.11-13).

It is rather tempting to see a relationship between "the fallen ones" in Gen 6,4, and those who *came down* and were thrown down into the underworld in En 6-11. On the semantic level this would presuppose that the Aramaic-writing author of En 6-11 saw some sort of correspondence between the verb *nāfal*, "fall", which can be read out of *nᵉfilīm*, and the verb *nᵉḥat*, "come down", which he used about the divine beings.

---

257 Cf. above, p. 282 and pp. 284f.
258 Cf. above, pp. 285f.

In fact, there is such a correspondence in the way that both *nāfal* and *nᵉḥat*, or the Hebrew equivalent *yārad*, which the author certainly knew in the same meaning as *nᵉḥat*, cf. the pun in the line quoted above[259], occur in the context of "falling" or "descending" either from heaven or the earth into the underworld. In Is 14,12 the hubristic rebel king *fell* (Hebrew *nāfal*) from heaven, and was made *to go down* (Hebrew hiph'il of *yārad*) to the nether world. In Ezek 32 the inhabitants of the nether world are those who *fell* by the sword (32,20.22.23.24.27) and *came down* to sheol (32,18.19.21.24.25.29.30). The stereotyped repetition of the two verbs indicates conventional language: The inhabitants of the nether world are the fallen ones and the descended ones.

This indicates the possibility that *nᵉḥat* in En 6,6 could be an interpretation of *nāfal* in Gen 6,4, but it does ot necessarily say that this was the case.

There is clear evidence, however, of a tradition in which the relationship between Gen 6,1-4 and En 6-11 was interpreted in this way. The most clear example is from the targum Pseudo-Jonathan (Ps-J), which in many cases represents the Old Palestinian Targum, current before the Second Jewish War.[260] Besides the example given below, Ps-J's use of En 6-11 in its interpretation of Gen 6,1-4 is clearly demonstrated in the description of the women. Here Ps-J reads: "The daughters of men were beautiful, with eyes painted and hair curled, walking in nakedness of flesh." A similar elaboration of female beauty occurs in En 8,1: "And he showed the women concerning antimony, and concerning eye shadow, and concerning all precious stones, and concerning dye-stuffs."[261]

Our interest is, however, Ps-J's interpretation of Gen 6,4, the passage with the Nefilim. Here Ps-J reads: שמיחזאי ועזאל הינון נפלו מן שמיא והוו בארעא ביומיא האינון, "Shemiḥazai and Azael — they who fell from heaven, were on earth in those days".[262] The text of TM to Gen 6,4 reads: הנפלים היו בארץ

259   Cf. above, pp. 91f, 297.
260   Cf. the discussion in P.S. Alexander, "The Targumim and Early Exegesis of 'Sons of God' in Genesis 6", JJS 23, 1972, pp. 60-71, pp. 70f.
261   Translation according to Milik, based on Aramaic traces (Milik, p. 168).
262   Aramaic text in M. Ginsburger (ed.), Pseudo-Jonathan, Berlin 1903 (repr. Hildesheim/New York 1971), p. 11. Translations: J.W. Etheridge, The Targums of Onkelos and Jonathan ben Uzziel on the Pentateuch, first publ. 1862 (New York 1968), pp. 176f; J. Bowker, The Targums and Rabbinic Literature, Cambridge

בימים ההם, "the Nefilim were on earth in those days". The meaning of the interpretation is clear. Instead of the Nefilim as the subject of the clause Ps-J places the chief angels Shemiḥazai and Azael. The stem NFL, which can be discerned from nefilīm, is used as a verb and transferred to the subordinate clause. Here it is used in the same way as neḥat in En 6,6. According to En 6,6 the angels *came down* from heaven, while according to Ps-J they *fell* from heaven. Ps-J clearly identifies the descending angels in En 6,6 as the Nefilim from Gen 6,4.

The other example is more general, but should be just as conclusive. In a passage dealing with the birth of Noah[263] Genesis Apocryphon reads: הא באדין חשבת בלבי די מן עירין

הריאנתא ומן קדשין ה(י)א ולנפיל(ין)

1Q apGen (proper), col 2, line 1 (Fitz/Harr, p. 104), "So then I thought in my mind that the conception was due to Watchers or it w[a]s due to Holy Ones, or to Nefil[im]". The three names here muse designate the same group of beings and not beings of different kinds. The whole problem in the Noah birth stories is whether he is the offspring of divine beings in the same way as the giants, or the son of Lamech. No other alternatives seem plausible.

We have accordingly the following evidence in our discussion: On the basis of the relationship between En 6-11 and Gen 6,1-4 an interpretation in which the Nefilim are identified as the descended watchers is the most likely one. Placing the two texts into the broader context of the Jewish milieu, we have seen that their relationship was interpreted exactly that way. In a case like this it is difficult to demand more evidence.

We have previously made clear that the Nefilim in the Old Testament also occur under the name Refaim. According to Ugaritic texts they were imagined as divine beings and as the manes of primeval kings and heroes, and located in the underworld.[264] If we turn to En 6-11 and ask where the primeval divinities are located at the time of the author, we get the same answer: They are in the nether world and will stay there until the day of judgment (En 10,12-13).

1969, p. 151; R. le Déaut, Targum du Pentateuque, Tome 1 Genèse, SC, Paris 1978, p. 115.
263 For the Noah birth stories, cf. above, pp. 89f.
264 Cf. above, p. 285.

We have accordingly reached what we can call the second point of gravity in the Watcher story. The first was an interpretation of the primeval catastrophe in which it struck divine or semi-divine beings, based on the latest stratum of Gen 6,1-4, vv. 1 and 3. Here Atra-Ḥasis is interpreted in this way. The second point of gravity is the inclusion of the underworld motif in which the divine beings are identified as a group of beings who came down to the nether world in primeval time. In both cases, however, we are dealing with categories: Primeval catastrophe affecting divine beings; divinities who came down to the nether world in primeval time. These categories are then given their specific form in the Watcher story.

3.2   The Character of the Descended Angels

Our next question is what sort of semi-divine or divine beings the author of En 6-11 had in mind.

The incident told in En 6-11 is located in the mountainous area of Northern Palestine. The watchers descended on Mount Hermon (En 6,6). Asael is thrown down to the underworld in Daduel, which is to be located in the same area.[265] When Enoch wishes to talk to the watchers, he goes to Abel-maīn or "the Waters of Dan" close to Mount Hermon.[266] This indicates that the author may have adopted traditions from the same area.

We have previously noted that Philo of Byblos in his antediluvian section follows closely the Jahwistic account, also reporting about the origin of giants, as in Gen 6,2.4.[267] Philo recounts that the giants gave their names to the mountains they occupied: Cassius (Mount Zaphon), Libanus, Antilibanus and Brathy. J. Ebach has demonstrated that Brathy must be another name of Hermon.[268] In the list of the names of the angels recorded in En 6,7, the eleventh angel has the name Hermani,[269] i.e. the name of Mount Hermon

---

265   Cf. above, pp. 246-50.
266   Cf. above, pp. 103, 142.
267   Cf. above, p. 219.
268   Cf. J. Ebach, Weltentstehung, pp. 134-42.
269   Cf. the list of names based on the Aramaic fragments in Milik, op.cit., p. 152ff and the corrections made by M. Sokoloff, "Notes on the Aramaic Fragments", p. 207.

which is occupied. The eighteenth angel has the more general name Turiel, "Mountain of God", or "God is my Mountain". In Hittite mythology mountain gods are located in the same area and also have the names of the mountains they occupy, such as Hazzi, "Mount Zaphon", and Namnis, probably located in Syria. In Canaanite mythology Baal Zaphon, "the Lord of Zaphon", is the ruler of Mount Zaphon.[270] In the Epic of Gilgamesh the Babylonian pantheon is located on Mount Hermon. The monster Humbaba is located in the same area. In the Enochic Book of Giants Humbaba is recorded as one of the giants.[271]

This should be sufficient to demonstrate that the mountainous area of Northern Palestine occurs in several mythologies as an area occupied by mountain gods and giants.

This local colouring of the Watcher story makes it reasonable to seek the background also of other features in mythology connected to the area, as for instance Hittite mythology. As already demonstrated, two of the names in the list of angels are related to mountains, as was common in Hittite religious thought. What about the other names in En 6,7? Of the 20 names eleven have the names of natural and astronomical phenomena connected to the divine designation 'el: burning heat (No. 3), star (No. 4), thunder (No. 6), lightning-flash (No. 8), lightning (No. 9), rain (No. 12), cloud (No. 13), winter (No. 14), sun (No. 15), moon (No. 16), and day (No. 19).[272] The names reveal a system of deification of the surrounding world, especially concentrating on natural phenomena. Such deification and personification are specific characteristics of Hittite mythology.[273] One example is the treaty of Mūwatalli with Alakšandu in which the leading gods of the Hittite pantheon are invoked. Here occur, among others, the sun god, gods of natural phenomena, and several mountain gods in the same list.[274]

Besides the groups of deified mountains and natural phenomena, there is a group of angels whose names describe functions:

270 Cf. E. von Schuler, "Kleinasien", H.W. Haussig (ed.), Götter und Mythen im Vorderen Orient, WM I, Stuttgart 1965, pp. 143-215, pp. 160f and 171f.
271 Cf. above, p. 253.
272 The numbers as in the list in Milik, cf. note 269.
273 Cf. von Schuler, op.cit., pp. 189f.
274 Cf. H. Otten, "Die Religionen des Alten Kleinasiens", Religionsgeschichte des Alten Orients, Lief. 1, HO 8, Erste Abschnitt, Leiden-Köln 1964, pp. 92-122, p. 105.

Šemiḥazah, "The name saw", (No. 1); Daniel, "God has judged" or
"God is my judge", (No. 7); Asael, "God has made", (No. 10);
Yehaddiel, "God will guide me", (No. 20). The name Daniel could
be the name of the primeval hero and sage referred to in Ezek
14,14; 28,3 and Jub 4,20 and known from the Ugaritic Tale of
Aqhat.[275]
Similar kinds of names occur in an incantation from Bogazköy
which is a part of a magic ritual. At the head of the list there are
recorded Aduntarri, the seer. Then comes Zulki, the interpreter of
dreams, and finally Irpitiqa, the Lord of judgment, Obv. I, lines
49-50.[276] These gods are introduced as *karuilieš DINGIR*[meš],
"the primeval gods", and also as "the Lords of the Earth", i.e.
"the underworld", line 46, cf. lines 56.59. According to Hittite
mythology they were among the gods who ruled the world in
primeval time but were condemned to the nether world by the
Weather god.[277]
The one angel left in the list of angels is Artaqof, "The Earth of
the Mighty one" or "The Earth is mighty", (No. 2). I am inclined
to see the earth here as a reference to the nether world, as is often
the case in the religious environments, cf. for instance the chief
divinity of the underworld in Mesopotamian mythology, Ereškigal,
"Lady of the great earth", i.e. "the underworld", who also was
worshipped by the Hittites.[278]
We turn once more to the group of angels associated with natural
phenomena. A group similar to those mentioned in En 6,7 occurs
in Jub 2 in connection with the creation of the world: "For the
first day he created the heavens which are above and the earth
and the waters and the spirits which serve before him" (Jub 2,2).
These spirits or angels are recorded in two groups. First come the
"angels of the presence and the angels of holiness" (or "of
sanctification"), which in analogy to En 14,12 seem to be the
angels of God's holy council. Then come the angels associated with
natural phenomena — the angels of the spirit of the winds, the
clouds, the darkness, the snow, the hail, the hoar frost, the voices,

275   Cf. ANET³, pp. 149-55.
276   Cf. H. Otten, "Eine Beschwörung der Unterirdischen aus Bogazköy, ZA
NF 20, 1961, pp. 113-57, pp. 121 and 145f.
277   Cf. Otten, op.cit., p. 114; and O.R. Gurney, "Hittite Prayers of Mursili II",
AAA 27, 1940, pp. 4-163, pp. 81f.
278   Cf. von Schuler, op.cit., p. 186.

the thunder, the lightning, the cold, the heat, the winter, the spring, the autumn, and the summer. The list is not only in general of the same kind as that in En 6,7, for several of the natural phenomena are the same: clouds, thunder, lightning, heat, and winter. The difference between the lists is that the one in Jubilees seems to be complete and in this sequence concentrated on only one group of angels, while the list in En 6,7 contains several groups and has only a selection in the group dealing with natural phenomena. The list in Jubilees accordingly helps us to determine the context of the largest group of angels in En 6,7: They were in the act of creation put in charge of the cosmic order, each individual angelic leader over one specific natural phenomenon. The Watcher story thus draws on traditions about a primeval group of divine beings connected to the creation and the cosmic order, and who once in primeval time were dispatched to the nether world.

We have previously called attention to the similarity in names between some of the angels in the list of En 6,7 and the names of some of the primeval gods in Hittite mythology. The primeval gods in Hittite mythology were in primeval time deposed by the younger generation of gods and dispatched to the nether world. It was this primeval group, according to the myth "The Song of Ullikummis", which was responsible for the creation.[279]

The list of angels in En 6,7 seems accordingly to be a rather confusing combination of different sorts of divine beings: divine or semi-divine heroes, divine beings connected to magical practices, and divine beings connected to the creation of the world.

There are, however, two common features for the groups as they can be traced in Enoch's religious environments: 1) They are connected to the primeval time; 2) They are now located in the nether world. It is interesting to notice that Philo of Byblos in his summary of the religion of the ancient Phoenicians and Egyptians mentions the same groups of divinities that occur in Enoch. The ancients "considered as greatest gods those men who had made discoveries valuable for life's necessities or those who had in some way benefited their nations, ... they worshipped them as gods

279 The Song of Ullikummis, (IIIc) KUB XXXIII, 106 iii, last sequence, ANET[3], p. 125; cf. also von Schuler, op.cit., pp. 183 and 205.

even after they had past on. ... Among things of nature they
acknowledged as gods only the sun, the moon, the other planets,
the elements and their combination."[280]

If the theory held by most scholars is correct, that Philo's work to
a large extent reflects the cultural and religious traditions in the
last centuries B.C., [281] this characteristics of the religion of the
ancients should shed some light on the religious environment of
the Watcher story. It should be remembered that Philo of Byblos
had almost the same geographical setting.

The author of the Watcher story has accordingly adapted divine
epithets known from his religious environment and ascribed these
names to the indefinite group "the sons of the gods" from Gen
6,2, interpreted as the same group as the Nefilim in Gen 6,4. The
common denominators of the gods and divine heroes behind the
angelic list and Gen 6,1-4 as interpreted by the author of the
Watcher story, are first, the distinct primeval context, and
secondly, the location of these divine beings in the underworld in
the author's own time.

3.3   The Designation "Watcher"

The Aramaic word for "watcher" is '$\bar{i}r$. The Hebrew/Aramaic verb
עור, '$\bar{u}r$, means basically to "rouse, awake".[282] Often the emphasis can be laid on the aim of the wakening, "rouse to activity",
cf. Judg 5,12; Ps 7,7; 44,24; 59,5. In other cases the verb means
simply "to awake", cf. Zech 4,1; Job 14,12; IQ apGen, col 19, line
17 (Fitz/Harr, p. 110). The Greek translation εγρηγορὸς, corresponding to the verb ἐγείρω, covers the same semantic field. The
Ethiopic translation *tĕguh*, corresponding to the verb *tagha*, covers
partly the same field, but can also have the meaning "to keep
watch", and the noun can have the meaning "watcher". Literally
the Aramaic word '$\bar{i}r$ thus does not mean "watcher" but "he who
rouse" or "awoke", as it is understood also in the Greek translation. There is one occurrence in Aramaic which may indicate a

---

280   Cf. Praep. Ev. 1.9.29, (Attridge and Oden, pp. 32f).
281   Cf. the discussion referred to above, pp. 215f.
282   Cf. Gesenius and Brown (ed.), A Hebrew and English Lexicon of the Old
Testament, sub 'ur, pp. 734f.

meaning closer to what appears to be the function of the "watchers". Among people who had given donations to the Synagogue, the Hammath–Gadara Synagogue Inscription III, line 4 (Fitz/Harr, p. 264), mentions the עיריא, 'īrayyā, which can be a designation of the overseers or guardians of the Synagogue.

Before the publication of the scrolls and fragments from Qumran, the only Aramaic occurrence of 'īr as a designation of an angelic figure, from this period, was Dan 4,10.14.20. The Aramaic material is now much broader:

Dan 4,10.20:   עיר וקדיש מן שמיא נחת
"A watcher and a holy one descended from heaven."

Dan 4,14:   בגזרת עירין פתגמא ומאמר קדישין שאלתא
"The message according to the decision of the watchers, the matter according to the word of the holy ones."

En 10,9 = En^b liv 6 (Milik, p. 175):   בנ(י) עיריא
"the childr]en of the watchers".

En 13,10 = En^c lvi 8 (Milik, p. 193):   לעירי שמ(יא
"to the watchers of hea[ven."

En 22,6 = En^e lxxii 5 (Milik, p. 229):   לרפא(ל לעירא וקדישא
"Raphae]l the watcher and holy one."

En 33,3 = En^e xxvii 19 (Milik, p. 235):   אוריאל חד מן (עירין
"Uriel, one of the] watchers."

En 93,2 = En^g liii 20 (Milik, p. 264):   ומן (ממר עירין וקדישין
"And from] the word of the watchers and holy ones."

4Q Amram^d, frg. 2, line 1 (Fitz/Harr, p. 94)   חזית עירי(ן
"I saw watchers."

4Q Mess ar, col 2, line 16 (Fitz/Harr, p. 101)   כעירין עובדה
"Like watchers his activity."
Line 18:   קדיש ועירי(ן
"A holy one and watchers."

1Q apGen (proper), col 2, line 1 (Fitz/Harr, p. 104):

מן עירין...ומן קדישין

"from the watchers . . . or from the holy ones."
Line 16:   ולא מן כול עירין ולא מן כול בני שמ(ין)
"nor from any of the watchers, nor from any of the sons of hea[ven.".

The occurrences give some hint of the use of the designation "watcher". The designation occurs most frequently in the Watcher story (En 6-11), but is also attested to in the introduction to the later Apocalypse of Weeks (En 93,2). When it occurs in 4Q Mess ar and the Genesis Apocryphon it is in contexts related to the Watcher story. If we include translations, this is also the case in the Book of Jubilees (Jub 4,15). Besides these, the designation occurs in two visions, Dan 4 and the vision of Amram, Levi's grandson. It is interesting that the designation does not occur in the Astronomical Book. Here Uriel, the primeval sage, is called "angel" (En 72,1; 74,2; 75,3). When Uriel and other divine beings are placed in connection to the cosmic order, they are called ראשין, rēʾšîn, "leaders", cf. 4Q Enastrᵇ28 = En 82,11 (Milik, p. 295), and En 72,1; 74,2. The Watcher story and perhaps Dan 4 are the oldest literary compositions in which the designation occurs. It would be too facile to suggest that the other occurrences are literarily dependent on En 6-11, but I think that the evidence points in the direction that the designation was introduced by the group behind the Book of Watchers and used by contemporary and later authors under the influence of this group.

One indication of this becomes apparent when we compare the designations in the Astronomical Book and the Book of Watchers. In the former Uriel is called "angel" and "leader" (cf. references above), while in the latter he is "one of the watchers", and that in a section directly drawing on the Astronomical Book, En 33,3.[283]

En 82,10ff describes how divine beings are placed in charge of the movements of the celestial bodies. The sequence is similar to the names in En 6,7, where the watchers also are called "leaders", especially when it is considered in the context of Jub 2,2.[284] But the divine beings in En 82,9ff are only called reʾšîn, "leaders" (cf. reference above), not "watchers". They are, however, said "to keep watch" over the celestial bodies. The Ethiopic translation here uses the verb

283 Cf. above, p. 68.
284 Cf. above, pp. 302f.

'aqaba, and not the verb corresponding to "watcher" tagha. This should demonstrate that the authors of the Book of Watchers introduced 'ir to designate the
divine beings known from the older Astronomical Book, in which they had a
different name.

The next observation is that 'īr frequently occurs together with
qaddīš, "holy one", used as an angelic designation. This designation in the Book of Watchers clearly corresponds to Old
Testament usage, comp. En 1,9 to Deut 33,2f and Zech 14,5; and
En 14,23 to Ps 89,8. The designation "holy ones" for divine beings
in the Old Testament is often seen in relation to Canaanite religion
where "the holy ones" occur as members of the divine assembly.[285] The use of "holy ones" and "watchers" as parallels in the
Book of Watchers and related scriptures could indicate that the
designation 'īr has a background similar to qaddīš.

So far we have placed the watchers in relation to two groups
which are known from literature older than the Book of Watchers:
1) The divine beings, called rē'šīn, "leaders", whose task is "to
keep watch" over the cosmic order, and especially the celestial
bodies, known from the Astronomical Book; 2) The holy ones, who
are members of the heavenly assembly, known from Old Testament and Canaanite texts. This double relationship is also clearly
reflected in the way the watchers are described in the Book of
Watchers. They are members of God's holy council (En 12;14), and
they are specialists in cosmic geography and astronomy (cf. the
names in En 6,7, and En 17-36).

There is a correspondence between the functions of the watchers
and the designation. Semantically the word "watch" which is used
about the task of the angelic leaders in En 82,10, is not far
removed from "awake", which is the literal meaning of the stem
'WR. In En 14,23 it is said that the holy ones did not leave God
by night or day, which easily also could be related to the meaning
"awake". I think it very likely that the "wakers" in the Book of
Watchers have been understood as "those who keep watch" both in
the heavenly sanctuary (cf. the analogy in the Hammath-Gadara
Synagogue Inscription referred to above, p. 305), and over the
celestial and cosmic order.

---

285   Cf. H.-P. Müller, "qdš, heilig", THAT II, cols 589-609, cols 601f, with
references to Canaanite texts.

But this does not explain the origin of the designation, which is quite a riddle since we have no clear references to the designation "the awake ones" from any text earlier than En 6-11. Moreover, it is not known in any texts outside the Jewish milieu. Since the designation occurs first in En 6-11, it seems plausible that it was introduced in relation to the special event recorded there. We have already noted that one of the points of gravity in the story was the reflection of mythical material in which divine beings in primeval time were dispatched to the nether world. We also noted that the Watcher story here had affinity to Canaanite and Hittite material, not least to Philo of Byblos' Phoenician History, which reflects this kind of material. The phrase "holy ones", frequently used together with '*īrīn*, could point in the same direction.

Philo of Byblos does in fact tell about "watchers". And these figures are really named "watchers" and not "wakers". The relevant passage reads:

Ἦν δέ τινα ζῷα ουκ ἔχοντα αἴσθησιν, ἐξ ὧν ἐγένετο ζῷα νοερά, καὶ εκλήθη Ζοφασημίν, τουτ᾽ ἔστιν οὐρανοῦ κατόπται, (Praep. Ev. 1.10.2)[286] "There were some living creatures which had no perception, from which came intelligent creatures, and they were called 'Zophasemin', that is 'watchers of heaven'." The Zophasemin must here be taken as the name of the intelligent creatures. The word clearly reflects the Aramaic or Hebrew *ṣōfē šamayim*.[287] Philo's translation of *ṣōfē* with κατόπτης is correct. Both words mean "observer" or "watcher". The problem is to what Philo here refers. As usual his account is a mixture of motifs taken from a variegated background. Ebach and others have argued that the passage describes the origin of human beings developed from animals.[288] Although this idea is not alien to the ancients, Ebach's interpretation rides counter to severe obstacles. The most important one is that "the watchers of heaven", according to Philo, came into being before the celestial bodies, whose origin is recorded in the next passage.[289] It is very

286   Text according to Attridge and Oden, p. 37.
287   Cf. Attridge and Oden, p. 77, note 33.
288   J. Ebach, Weltentstehung, pp. 46-53.
289   Cf. for the following the discussion in L.R. Clapham, Sancuniathon: The First Two Cycles, unpubl. diss., Harvard University 1969, pp. 60-75, pp. 61f.

unlikely that Philo thought animals and human beings originated
before the universe was established. Later in his primeval account
(Praep. Ev. 1.10.7) Philo describes Aion and Protogonos as the first
mortal men.[290]

L.R. Clapham has argued convincingly that the watchers of heaven
must be seen in relation to the celestial bodies.[291] The context in
Philo makes this likely, because the origin of "the sun, moon, stars
and great constellations" is recorded in the same sequence. In Philo
the watchers of heaven are also called ζῷα νοερά, "intelligent
living creatures" or "intelligent animals". Exactly the same phrase
is used by Philo of Alexandria about the stars: "Such are the stars:
for they are said to be not only animals but intelligent animals"
(ζῷα νοερά), (de opificio mundi 73).[292] A very similar description is given in a Hermetic cosmogony: "... the father and
demiurge put up for me animal figures sensible and intelligent"
(νοερά).[293] There is accordingly evidence which strongly indicates
that the watchers of heaven either are the celestial bodies themselves, thought to be divine, or divine beings "watching over" the
celestial bodies.

Philo returns to the origin of the "intelligent living creatures" later
in his account, in a passage no less puzzling than the previous one:
"At the crash of the thunder the intelligent creatures previously
mentioned awoke (or "rouse" — ἐγρηγόρησεν). They were
alarmed at the noise, and male and female creatures began to stir
on (or "in") earth and sea". When we compare to the other passage
it seems clear that the creatures without perception changed or
"rouse" into intelligent creatures, that is, something like celestial
gods, as a result of a cosmic thunder storm. At the same time,
however, male and female creatures began to move around on or
in earth and sea. The relationship between the heavenly watchers
and the male and female creatures is not clear. Apparently they
have different locations — the sky versus the earth and sea. If we
accept the explanation that those in heaven are something like
celestial gods, it seems plausible to take the others as chthonic

---

290 Cf. above, pp. 220f.
291 Cf. Clapham, op.cit., pp. 64f.
292 Text in F.H. Colson and G.H. Whitaker, "On the Creation", Philo I, LCL,
London-Cambridge, Mass, 1829 (repr. 1971), p. 58. Cf. also Clapham, p. 65.
293 Text according to Clapham, p. 65.

deities moving around in the earth, i.e. the underworld, and the sea, i.e. the other place where monstrous creatures in animal form were located in ancient mythologies.

There seem to be other allusions to the underworld in Philo's account. In the sequence before his passage about the heavenly watchers Mot is introduced as a muddy and watery mixture (Praep. Ev. 1.10.1). Although the context is confusing, Mot seems clearly to reflect the Canaanite underworld god with the same name, meaning "death", whose abode is in the watery abyss.[294] Philo described Mot as the substance from which the universe was created and placed it in direct relation to the celestial bodies: "Mot shone forth, with sun and moon, stars and great constellations" (Praep. Ev. 1.10.2).

Philo combines different elements in his account, and we must delimit our task to seeking the primary context in ancient near eastern myths. What we seem to have recorded in Philo are the following basic features: Mot signifies both "watery substance" and "the underworld". The combination seems to indicate a confusion of two different conceptions of the threatening powers, the underworld monster and the sea monster. From this monster the universe was created. At the same time the heavenly watchers, the gods of the celestial bodies, originated. They were not created or had their origin from Mot's substance, but existed before as creatures without perception. They are described, however, as part of Mot's domain in their activity. The moment of origin of the watchers is described as a cosmic thunder storm. The celestial gods "awoke". At the same time the chthonic divinities began to move around in the underworld.

Although the picture still is confusing, we begin to see in it the outlines of ancient near eastern creation myths. Clapham called attention to Enuma Elish, and at least I think this myth can serve as an example for a composition containing these outlines.[295] In Enuma Elish the gods were created inside the waters of Tiamat and her male counterpart Apsu (Tabl I, lines 1-28).[296] There came to a cosmic battle, described as a cosmic thunder storm,

---

294   Cf. Clifford, Cosmic Mountain, pp. 79ff.
295   Cf. Clapham, op.cit., pp. 63f. For other traditions similar to Enuma Elish in the same geographical location, cf. above, pp. 252f.
296   ANET[3], p. 61.

between Tiamat and the generation of younger gods (Tabl IV).[297]
Tiamat was defeated, and the universe was created from her body.
In this universe the celestial bodies of the great gods were created,
and they were put in charge of the cosmic order (Tabl V).[298]
Accompanying Tiamat, however, were a series of demon-like
monsters (Tabl I, lines 125-45).[299] They were imprisoned and
their leader sent to the god of death (Tabl IV, lines 117-20).[300]

The structural similarities to Philo's account are as follows: 1) The
cosmos is created out of the substance of a god, symbolizing the
threatening powers and watery substance. 2) The gods existed prior
to the origin of the universe, but they were without any function.
In Philo's words: They were without perception, they had not yet
awoken. 3) There comes a cosmic thunder storm, the gods awake
and get a cosmic function. 4) This cosmic function is connected to
the celestial bodies.

There may also be correspondence between the demonic monsters
in Enuma Elish and the male and female creatures moving in the
earth and sea according to Philo.

When this context of Philo's account is established, we see several
points of contacts between Philo and the Enochic traditions. In
both divine beings are associated with celestial bodies in primeval
time. In Philo the divine beings are called "watchers of heaven",
while in Enoch their task is described as "to keep watch" over the
celestial bodies. The designation ʿīrē šemayyā (cf. En 13,10 = En^c
lvi 8 (Milik, p. 193) literally means "wakers of heaven" but seems
to have been interpreted according to the function of the divine
beings as "watchers of heaven". In both places the existence of a
second group of divinities also is described, closely related to the
heavenly watchers but located to the underworld.

There is one more interesting detail. The origin of the watchers of
heaven is described by Philo as the moment they "awoke" or
"rouse", Greek ἐγρηγόρησεν (Praep Ev. 1.10.4).[301] In Enoch the
divine beings are called "the awake ones" (ἐγρήγοροι). In Philo
this was the moment when the gods became intelligent beings, i.e.

---

297 ANET³, pp. 66f.
298 ANET³, pp. 67f and 501f.
299 ANET³, p. 62.
300 ANET³, p. 67.
301 The correspondence with ʿīr in Enoch was pointed out by Clapham, op.cit.,
      p. 73.

when they were given their task as watchers of the heavenly bodies and consequently the cosmic order. This is also the task of the "awake ones" in Enoch. It seems therefore likely to assume that '*īrīn* in Enoch is a reflection of the same mythical material presented in Philo.

3.4   The Watchers as Teachers

One of the most distinguishing features of the watchers, not alluded to in Gen 6,1-4, was their activity as sages. They revealed "the eternal secrets of heaven", En 9,6. The character of this teaching activity is linked to some of the names of the watchers. In most of the cases there is also a clear correspondence between name and activity.

Watchers and teaching: En 8,1-3 = En^{a}liv, lines 1-5 (Milik, p. 157); En^{b}lii, lines 26-29 (Milik, p. 167).

Asael	"God has made"	taught men to make swords of iron and breastplates of brass, and he showed them metals which are dug out, and how they should work gold to fashion it apt (for uses), and concerning silver, to fashion it for bracelets, and for other adornments of women. And he showed to women concerning antimony, and concerning eye shadow, and concerning all precious stones, and concerning dyestuffs.
Šemiḥazah	"The name has seen"	taught spell-binding and cutting of roots
Hermani	"Of Hermon" also from ḥerām, "ban"	taught the loosing of spells, magic, sorcery, and skill
Baraqel	"Lightning of God" or "Thunder of God"	taught the signs of thunders
Kokabel	"Star of God"	taught the signs of the stars
Zeqiel	"Lightning-flash of God"	taught the signs of lightningflashes
Artaqof	"The earth is mighty"	taught the signs of the earth
Šamšiel	"Sun of God"	taught the signs of the sun
Sahriel	"Moon of God"	taught the signs of the moon

The only cases where there is no clear correspondence between name and activity are in the names of the two chief angels. The name Asael, "God has made", may allude to his activity as smith. The passage is clearly drawn from the statement about Tubal-Cain in Gen 4,22, further elaborated on the background of the sexual motif from Gen 6,2 and 4.[302] The name Šemiḥazah, "The name has seen", indicates some sort of magical practice, but soothsaying would perhaps be closer to the meaning of the name than witchcraft.[303]

The correspondence between names and activities does not point in the direction that the teaching activity is a secondary elaboration not originally connected to the names. There are indications in the material previously discussed that point in the same direction. Philo of Byblos informs us that the primeval divinities whom men worshipped after their death "had made discoveries for life's necessities".[304] The Hittite material demonstrates that the primeval gods who were located in the nether world were invoked in magic rituals connected to mantic wisdom.[305]

The kinds of wisdom described as the teaching of the watchers — spellbinding, healing, different kinds of divination as astrology and taking of omens of weather phenomena — were not a secular enterprise. This wisdom was practiced in a religious context in which the divinities of the nether world played the dominant role. I think this is the background for this feature of the Watcher story. The story records the basic outlines of contemporary religious thought where this kind of wisdom was practiced in relation to primeval divinities once descended to the underworld. But the concept is interpreted in a new critical perspective.

3.5   The Watchers and the Apkallu's

To trace the background of the different elements in the Watcher story is a puzzle, and it is easy to lose the correct perspective of the basic features of the story. None of the parallels traced in

302   Cf. the list above, pp. 275f, and pp. 278ff.
303   Cf. the names of the Hittite underworld gods above, pp. 301f.
304   Cf. above, pp. 303f, 219ff and 286.
305   Cf. above, p. 302.

Phoenician, Canaanite or Hittite mythology can serve as patterns for the Watcher story. The parallels indicate the kind of material which was adapted into the story and the religious context of the story. But the basic structure of the story was not, as far as I can judge, taken from this mythic material.

I have previously defined this structure on the basis of what I have called the two points of gravity in the narrative: 1) that the primeval flood was interpreted as a catastrophe affecting divine or semi-divine beings; 2) that divine or semi-divine beings in primeval time were dispatched to the nether world. The first basic feature could be traced back to a certain interpretation of Atra-Ḥasis. The second basic feature corresponded to Phoenician, Canaanite and Hittite material. But we have not yet encountered mythic material where these two basic features are combined, material which connects the primeval flood to the dispatching of primeval divine figures to the nether world.

The only place where this combination is known to occur is in the mythic material about the apkallu's. I have already given an outline of this material in relation to the origin of the Babylonian primeval wisdom according to the Book of Jubilees,[306] but I find it necessary to repeat the basic features in relation to the Watcher story, as well:

1 The apkallu's are described as the sons of the god Ea.[307]
   The watchers are described as "the sons of heaven".[308]

2 The apkallu's had two primary functions:
   * They were the guardians of the cosmic order.[309]
   * They were the servants in Marduk's temple.[310]

   The function of the watchers is described in the same way:
   * They are put in charge of the cosmic order.
   * They are servants in the heavenly temple.[311]

3 In primeval time both the watchers and the apkallu's visited the earth.[312]

4 Both the watchers and the apkallu's taught men wisdom and skills.[313]

306   Cf. above, pp. 266-70.
307   Cf. above, pp. 198 and 203.
308   Cf. above, p. 296.
309   Cf. above, pp. 199f.
310   Cf. above, pp. 183 and 200.
311   Cf. above, pp. 99 and 307.
312   For the apkallu's, cf. above, pp. 207ff.
313   For the apkallu's, cf. pp. 200f.

5 The watchers mixed sexually with human women. This is not explicitly stated about the apkallu's. The sources seem, however, to presuppose a sexual mingling, since the latest apkallu is a mixture of apkallu and ordinary human being.[314]

6 The watchers rebelled against the divine order. Some of the apkallu's offended the gods.[315]

7 The watchers were condemned to the nether world at the time of the flood. The apkallu's were dispatched to the nether world at the same time.[316]

8 The Watcher story reflects the practice of invoking underworld divinities for magical purposes.[317] The apkallu's were invoked for the same purpose.[318]

The material about the apkallu's recorded above is not taken from one single Mesopotamian composition, but from different ones, some of them of an allusive character. The correspondence between the Watcher story and the apkallu traditions does not point toward a literary dependence. But both the apkallu traditions and the Watchers story combine different elements in a so similar way that a dependence on the level of oral transmission seems likely. There are no other known traditions or compositions than those dealing with the apkallu's which contain these elements in exactly this combination corresponding to the Watcher story.

3.6   How to Read the Watcher Story

We have previously analyzed the underlying patterns and components of the Watcher story. But there remains one problem: How is the whole story to be read?

We have defined the underlying text of the Watcher story, Gen 6,1-4, as a "mythical etiology".[319] Furthermore, we have seen that among other aspects the Watcher Story must be understood as an expository narrative on the Genesis primeval history, above all Gen 6,1-4.[320] In this perspective the Watcher story can be read as

314 Cf. above, pp. 201f.
315 Cf. above, pp. 205f.
316 Cf. above, pp. 182f and 200.
317 Cf. above, p. 313.
318 Cf. above, pp. 191f; note 123, p. 199; and pp. 207ff.
319 Cf. above, p. 283.
320 Cf. above, pp. 275-80.

an etiology as well, one elaborating features of the Genesis texts and incorporating new elements. The intention of the Watcher story would ten be to tell how evil once broke into this world and became a part of it. But it also relates how God intervened and limited the consequences of evil.

There are in fact clear indications that the Watcher story can be read in this way. The story is distinctively linked to antediluvian times: "It happened in the days of Jared", En 6,6. And at that time the rebelling watchers were condemned to the nether world where they should stay for seventy generations until the day of judgement, En 10,12. This is also clearly the perspective behind some of the concluding lines in the part En 12-16: "And now the giants, who are produced from the spirits and flesh, shall be called evil spirits upon the earth, and on the earth shall be their dwelling. Evil spirits have proceeded from their bodies; because they are born from men, and from the holy watchers are their beginning and primal origin; they shall be evil spirits on earth, and evil spirits shall they be called ... And the spirits of the giants afflict, oppress, destroy, attack, do battle, and work destruction on the earth, and cause trouble; and they take no food, but nevertheless hunger and thirst, and cause offenses. And these spirits shall rise up against the children of men and against the women, because they have proceeded from them," En 15,8-9.11-12.[321] In this perspective the giants are an ancient race. What men in the days of the author experience are the consequences of the primeval rebellion — the demons which will trouble men until the day of judgment.

This etiological perspective we also find in the Mesopotamian traditions which are closest to the Watcher story. Atra-Ḥasis explains how the basic conditions of the human race came into being by the creation of man and demonstrates that they could not be broken. It concludes by recounting how the gods created the basic institutions in human society after the flood.[322] The most informative text about the apkallu's the editor classified as an "etiological myth".[323] It explains the origin of the divine beings invoked by the Babylonian mantic priests.

---

321   Translation according to Charles, The Book of Enoch, pp. 36f.
322   Cf. above, pp. 174f, 288-93.
323   Cf. above, p. 191.

The etiological texts draw a line from present phenomena to the time of origin. Consequently it is in the nature of these texts that present and past easily can be woven together. When the etiology deals not only with a phenomenon, but involves human conditions as well, it often takes on a paradigmatic character. The primeval story functions as a didactic poem about human conditions in all times. The technique of narration is: As it happened then, so it is also now. Undoubtedly features of Atra-Ḥasis can be read in this way, as can several of the Genesis stories, such as those relating the Temptation of Eve, Cain and Abel, and the Tower of Babel. Certainly the Watcher story can also be read in this way: Not only in primeval time did the power of evil incorporate itself in false wisdom and ruthless power, but again and again men have to encounter this devastating dimension of reality. But this kind of reading of a primeval story did not influence the character of the composition. The incidents behind Atra-Ḥasis, for instance, are according to the composition itself linked to primeval time, even though the composition reflects the present of the story teller and also is meant partly to have a paradigmatic character. The same is also the case with the Genesis stories. But it is not the case with the Watcher story.

As noted previously, the structure of the Watcher story follows close to the structure of the Genesis narratives.[324] But when the author comes to the renewal of the earth after the flood, he breaks the primeval pattern and incorporates a picture of the future reflecting Old Testament prophecies about the days of salvation.[325] The description of the fruitfulness, righteousness, peace, and universal worship of the Lord in En 10 does not fit into the primeval context; these qualities are distinguishing eschatological characteristics (cf. Is 9,2-7; 11,1-10; 65,17-25; 66,20-23; Am 9, 13-15).

This indicates that the Watcher story was meant to be read also in another perspective besides its etiological and paradigmatic intention. The eschatological era does not belong to primeval time, nor dos it repeat itself as a part of human conditions. It lies distinctively in the future, linked to a radical change in history.

324   Cf. above, pp. 278ff.
325   Cf. also above, pp. 153f.

The author clearly wrote his poem with the expectation that this radical change was soon to come.

That means that the Watcher story was not meant only as an etiology about the origin of evil or a didactic paradigm of the nature of evil, but also as a story about evils in the author's own historical setting. This affected the composition in the way that the figures of the past, the sons of the gods/the watchers and giants, are meant to reflect circumstances of the historical present, such as authorities of false wisdom and devastating power.[326]

The author of the Watcher story accordingly retold the account of the primeval catastrophe in such a way as to reflect current circumstances. The primeval story has two parts, first the catastrophe and then the renewal of the earth. The author sees his own days in the light of the catastrophe, and he longs for the renewal.

This retelling, or transference of the primeval Flood story to a historical situation, we find in another composition, the Poem of Erra. Although the details in the Poem of Erra are different from the Watcher story, the technique of narration is the same. The narration mediates between the primeval catastrophe and the actual historical circumstances in a way that the present is interpreted in the light of the ancient mythical narrative about the primeval catastrophe.[327]

There is one more interesting feature which combines the Watcher story and the Poem of Erra. In En 19,3, which once concluded the Book of Watchers, the material is characterized as "visions", and in En 1,2 the visionary features of the material are emphasized.[328] The Poem of Erra is directly characterized as a vision revealed to the scribe during the night.[329]

The Poem of Erra demonstrates that the transference of the Flood story to a historical setting and the elaboration of this story, adding new elements and broadening the perspective, was not a totally new invention by the author of the Watcher story. This technique of narration was also practiced by Babylonian scribes.[330]

---

326   Cf. above, pp. 96ff.
327   Cf. above, pp. 181-4.
328   Cf. above, pp. 86 and 151.
329   Cf. above, pp. 184 and 211f.
330   Cf. the structure of the Poem of Erra, note 327 above, and also the idioms, which have a close affinity to apocalyptic language.

c) The Origin of the Enochic Traditions and Literature: Synopsis

I. At first glance the Enochic traditions and literature appear as a mixture of motifs occurring in a broad spectrum of other sources of different origins. There are of course Old Testament elements and elements corresponding to post-exilic Jewish writings. But there are also elements corresponding to non-Jewish traditions, such as Mesopotamian, Canaanite, Hittite, Phoenician and Greek. It could be tempting to conclude that the Enochic traditions in their very nature were a collection of highly disparate elements, and that none of these formed the decisive influence. The underlying traditions would thus only be the material used freely by the composers without contributing to the intention or scope of the Enochic traditions and literature. The special character of the Enoch concept would accordingly lie in this concept itself regarded more or less isolated from the underlying traditions.

Our study has demonstrated that this is not the case. In our concluding remarks we shall summarize our previous observations and establish a diachronical model for the growth of the Enochic traditions and literature. It will appear that the influence from non-Jewish cultures on the Enoch concept occurs in different levels. On the one hand we have disparate elements corresponding to Canaanite, Phoenician, Hittite and Greek sources. On the other hand we have fixed traditions which can be traced back to a fairly uniform Mesopotamian concept of primeval time from the period when the Enochic traditions and literature were formed.[331]

---

331 J.C. VanderKam, Enoch and the Growth of an Apocalyptic Tradition (cf. note 44, p. 32) has dealt with many of the same sources and problems as my study. The two studies are written simultaneously and independently. I here give a summary statement about how I see the relation between them.
(1) Both studies are concerned with the origin and growth of the Enochic traditions. Both are based on the latest publications of cuneiform sources from the Mesopotamian area and the Aramaic sources from Qumran. Nevertheless the emphasis of the two studies differs, since VanderKam wrote about the origin and growth of a tradition, while I have written about the Enoch figure. Consequently VanderKam generally devotes more space in analyzing the content of the Enochic books, while I am more concerned about the various roles in which Enoch appears.
In some respects the convergence of the two studies is remarkable. The basic theory is the same, namely that the portraits of Enoch are rooted in Mesopotamian traditions. The accordance is especially close in the analysis of Gen 5,21-24 and the Mesopotamian lists of antediluvian kings, and among them the seventh

II.   The oldest occurrence of Enoch as a primeval ancestor was in
the Jahwistic source, Gen 4,17-18. This source also contained the
oldest version of the story about "the fall of the angels", Gen
6,2.4. Although the composer knew Mesopotamian traditions about

king Enmeduranki as the most outstanding figure. Likewise the two studies often
come to similar results in concrete observations in the Enochic books. Here it
must be of great interest for the research that two scholars independently arrive
at similar conclusions. This surely strengthens the validity of the observations
and conclusions.

(3) Other places the two studies offer different material and observations that
substantiate the same theory, i.e. that the Enoch portraits and traditions grew out
of Mesopotamian wisdom traditions. VanderKam offers here a broad analysis of
Mesopotamian mantic traditions and their sociological setting, and he goes into
detail in tracing the background of the Enochic astronomy in Mesopotamian
sources. Some of this material, especially the Akkadian prophecies, I shall discuss
in detail in my study to the Son of Man. In other places I am hesitant about
seeing too close a connection between Mesopotamian divinatory literature of
various kinds and the concrete content of the Enochic sources. But surely
VanderKam has located the Mesopotamian milieu out of which the Enochic traditions arose. My analysis leads to the result that the fixed point in the Enochic
sources was located in the portrayals of the hero and the roles and functions
attributed to him. Consequently I have devoted more effort to analyzing the
different roles and functions of the Mesopotamian primeval figures. This also
leads me to include analysis of comprehensive models of the primeval history in
Biblical, Mesopotamian, Phoenician, Samaritan and Jewish traditions.

(4) VanderKam's study gives a strong support for the thesis previously advanced
by several scholars that Enoch is basically patterned on Enmeduranki. Several
places we converge in seeing an influence from this figure. But VanderKam
concentrates almost exclusively on the influence of this king. There we disagree.
In his analysis of the Mesopotamian primeval traditions he includes the traditions
about the apkallu's, but there is remarkably little notice of the influence of this
tradition in the analysis of the Enochic sources. VanderKam also notes that
Enoch sometimes is confused with Noah, but he offers no inquiry into the background of the flood hero in the Mesopotamian sources. My conclusions here
point toward a much broader Mesopotamian background for the Enoch portraits
than VanderKam advances.

(5) VanderKam is mostly interested in the portrayal of Enoch as sage, in one
way or another patterned on Enmeduranki. When he inquires into the underlying
material, he consequently concentrates on traditions relating to this function. He
therefore does not substantiate the cluster of motifs associated with the primeval
catastrophe in the Enochic traditions. Since this theme forms an essential part of
the Enochic traditions, VanderKam's exclusion of it has considerable influence
on the final conclusions of his work.

(6) VanderKam arrives at the conclusion that the Mesopotamian impact is
greatest on the oldest Enochic sources, i.e. Gen 5,21-24 and the Astronomical
Book. The later Enochic sources contains an echo of this earlier impact, but are
basically to be regarded as an amalgam of syncretistic Hellenistic and Palestinian
traditions, most notable in the Book of Watchers and Jubilees. I have arrived at
different conclusions, because I have focused more on the primeval catastrophe
theme and the apkallu traditions. This also means that the model of the origin
and growth of the Enochic apocalyptical traditions differs in the two studies.

(7) But these differences between VanderKam's study and mine are nevertheless
differences appearing within the framework of the same basic approach to the
Enochic apocalyptic. Both studies mark a new entry into the problems, which in
many ways distinguish them from earlier attempts to solve the riddle of apocalyptic.

primeval time, as for instance the Flood story, there are no traces of a direct Mesopotamian influence in Gen 4 or 6,2.4. In the first case there is a general correspondence in which great cultural achievements were dated back in antediluvian time, in the second case a correspondence concerning ancestral heroes who in Mesopotamian literature could also be imagined as partly divine. But these features are too general to suppose that the Jahwistic account was patterned on a Mesopotamian model. The structure of the account comes closer to the record about the origin of culture in Philo of Byblos' Phoenician history.[332] And in Gen 6,2.4 the Jahwist seems to have adopted a mythical etiology about the origin of the great heroes among the primeval ancestors of the Canaanites, the *gibbor ī m*. These heroes were imagined as divine beings residing in the nether world.[333]

It is not without significance that the basic features of the later Enochic literature, the origin of culture and the interruption of human history by divine beings, already occurred in the Jahwistic source and there corresponded to Canaanite and Phoenician sources. This gave rise to the adoption of other mythical elements from the same cultural environments when the Enochic traditions and literature developed in post-exilic Judaism.

This is apparent in the Watcher story. Reading Gen 4-9 the composer brought together a wide range of motifs belonging to Palestinian, Syrian and Hittite religion. The protagonists of the story, the sons of the gods, were identified partly as gods and partly as semi-divine heroes once descended to the nether world in primeval time. They were given functions connecting them to the creation and the order of the universe, and they were named after natural phenomena and celestial bodies. They were also associated with cultural achievements, especially the skills of magic and divination. Their location was the mountainous area in Northern Palestine. All of these are features occurring partly in Canaanite and partly in Hittite, Phoenician and Greek sources.[334]

This segment of the Enochic traditions may best be characterized as pieces of Palestinian and Syrian folklore. There are other elements stemming from these popular imaginations as well, such

332   Cf. above, pp. 214ff.
333   Cf. above, pp. 283ff.
334   Cf. above, pp. 270ff, 300ff.

as the mythical geography of the location of Paradise.[335] If we keep in mind that the Palestinian area in the post-exilic period had a mixed population, and had been under both Mesopotamian and Macedonian dominion, it is not surprising to find these syncretistic imaginations, corresponding to Mesopotamian, Hittite, Phoenician, Canaanite and Greek sources.

But these elements have not played the decisive role in the formation of the Enochic traditions and literature. They were a part of the material which was adopted, but did not deliver the model according to which the Enochic traditions were patterned.

III.   We have observed that the Enoch concept developed out of Mesopotamian traditions about primeval time. How these traditions played the formative role towards the Palestinian material can clearly be demonstrated in three places.

1) Enoch occurred for the first time in Gen 4,17-18 within a sequence of the Jahwistic account that corresponded to the model found in Philo's Phoenician history. The second occurrence of Enoch in Genesis was the Priestly source, Gen 5,18-24. By comparing the structure of the two sources we found that the priestly composer had updated the traditions from the Jahwistic source according to a pattern which could be traced in the Mesopotamian sources WB 62, CT 46,5 + 12054, Berossos and W 20 030,7.[336] As demonstrated, it was the Enoch figure of the Priestly source that occurred in the later Jewish and Samaritan literature, not the figure from Gen 4,17-18.[337] Accordingly, although the Jahwistic account formed a part of the background of the Priestly source, the structure of this source was Mesopotamian. And within this structure the Enoch figure corresponded to the Mesopotamian prototypes Uanadapa and Enmeduranki.[338]

2) We have argued that Gen 6,2.4 belonged to the Jahwistic source. The sequence corresponded to Palestinian imaginations about the origin of the mighty heroes in primeval time. To this etiology vv. 1 and 3 were added. These two verses corresponded exactly to sequences in the Mesopotamian Atra-Ḫasis about the

---

335   Cf. above, pp. 246ff.
336   Cf. above, pp. 230ff.
337   Cf. above, pp. 147f.
338   Cf. above, pp. 230ff.

divine origin of the antediluvian human race and its rebellion.[339] This rebellion caused the deluge. Through the additions in vv. 1 and 3 the etiology in vv. 2 and 4 was linked directly to the account of the flood. According to this interpretation the catastrophes caused by the rebellion affected a race of semi-divine beings, and not ordinary humans as in the Jahwistic account. It was this version of the Flood story which formed the basis for the Watcher story.[340]

3) The Watcher story in En 6-11.12-16 was accordingly based on an interpretation of the primeval catastrophe similar to the one that occurred in Gen 6,1.3 added to vv. 2 and 4. We have pointed out that the composer adopted several mythical elements from Palestinian traditions, but these traditions were formed according to a pattern taken from elsewhere. This pattern could be traced in the Mesopotamian traditions about the primeval sages who came from the god Ea, visited the earth, taught men the basic skills, angered the gods, and were dispatched to the abyss at the time of the deluge.[341] The Mesopotamian traditions about the deluge and the sages were originally separate. Each tradition had its own hero, Ziusudra and Uanadapa, corresponding to respectively Noah and Enoch. The contamination of the two traditions by the Jewish transmitters caused a confusion of the two heroes, so that Enoch and Noah could appear in the same roles.

We think that these examples should be sufficient to demonstrate that those places where the Palestinian elements are most notable, these traditions did not deliver the pattern according to which the Enochic traditions were formed. The pattern is clearly to be sought in Mesopotamian traditions about primeval time.

This is also clear where no distinct signs of Palestinian influence occur, as in Pseudo-Eupolemus and the Book of Jubilees. In Pseudo-Eupolemus there are explicit references to Greek mythology, but this was only the framework for his communication. His intended readers were apparently trained in Greek thought.[342] But the basic structure of Pseudo-Eupolemus' primeval account was distinctively not Greek, but Mesopotamian, corresponding

---

339   Cf. above, pp. 286ff.
340   Cf. above, pp. 295ff.
341   Cf. above, pp. 313ff.
342   Cf. above, pp. 260ff.

most directly to Berossos, but also to traditions found in Atra-Ḥasis and the Sumerian Flood story.[343] In Jubilees the Mesopotamian influence is considerable, both in the description of Enoch as a primeval sage, patterned on Uanadapa and Enmeduranki,[344] and as a hero of a deluge, patterned on Ziusudra.[345] The influence did not, however, concern only the Enoch figure, but the whole structure of the primeval history. The account about the divine sages once appearing on earth, performing provocative acts and consequently being dispatched to the abyss is known from the apkallu traditions.[346] The concept of the origin of wisdom centered around the seventh in the antediluvian list who went to heaven and thereafter instructed his son, and started a chain of transmission from father to son up to the priesthood in the composer's own time, is known from the tablet Enmeduranki and the Diviners.[347] Even the rather strange story about the survival of the Babylonian wisdom through the flood has a close parallel in Berossos' account about the books in Sippar, which most likely was based on already existing traditions.[348] The author of Jubilees had certainly read the early Enochic books carefully, but he also had available a broader current of Mesopotamian antediluvian traditions which enabled him to place Enoch in a broader context of the antediluvian period.

These examples should be sufficient to conclude that the Enoch figure from the time of the exile and thereafter was a "Mesopotamian" Enoch patterned on Mesopotamian prototypes and belonging to the Mesopotamian concept of the primeval history.

IV. But the importance of Enoch varies considerably in the sources. In the Priestly source of Genesis the fate of Enoch is only briefly recorded, he did not have any significance for the theology of the document. This was also the case in Hebrew Ben Sira both in the original version and in the version which included Enoch as primeval sage. In both places Enoch was listed together with other

343 Cf. above, pp. 254ff.
344 Cf. above, pp. 263ff.
345 Cf.above, pp. 265f.
346 Cf. above, pp. 268ff.
347 Cf. above, pp. 266ff.
348 Cf. above, p. 178ff, 269.

heroes of the past, but nothing more.[349] Pseudo-Eupolemus' account was in fact dealing with Abraham as the father of civilization. Enoch was incorporated most likely because he had gained such a reputation as a primeval sage that he could not be ignored.[350]

This is significantly different in the Books of Enoch and in Jubilees. Our analysis has clearly demonstrated that Enoch appears for the first time as primary revealer in the Astronomical Book and in the Book of Watchers in the course of the third century. If we are correct in dating the astronomical material of the Astronomical Book to the end of the fourth or the beginning of the third century and in assuming that Uriel and Enoch already were associated with the material at this early stage,[351] there may have existed an Enochic theology already in the Persian age.

There is a possibility that the adaption of the Mesopotamian material into a Jewish Enoch concept took place in Palestine. If so, the Mesopotamian traditions could have been brought to Palestine by Persian or Greek officials, merchants or itinerant wise men. We know that Babylonian traditions reached Palestine in the course of the third century. Pseudo-Eupolemus seems through a connecting link to be dependent on Berossos who wrote his work 281 B.C.[352] But Berossos wrote his work to present Babylonian traditions to the Hellenistic world, and the other Mesopotamian traditions known by Pseudo-Eupolemus may have been of a similar popular character. There are no indications that the Enochic books should be dependent on Berossos. They deal with some of the same topics, but they are not coloured by his attempt to explain the traditions to a Greek audience, as was the case in Pseudo-Eupolemus. Rather, the character of relationship between the Enochic books and the Mesopotamian traditions does point toward a direct contact between Babylonian culture and Jewish thought. Since it is unlikely that the Babylonian traditions first were adopted by Jewish scribes in their Babylonian form and later in Palestine were transformed into a Jewish Enochic concept, we must assume that

349   Cf. above, pp. 119ff.
350   Cf. above, pp. 111ff.
351   Cf. above, pp. 80ff.
352   Cf. above, pp. 261ff.

the contamination of Babylonian and Jewish traditions took place in the Babylonian diaspora.

Two other indications point in the same direction. The first is of a more general character. The Enochic writings show affinity to the visions of Ezekiel and Zechariah, both prophets and priests, the former living in, the latter coming from Babylonia.[353] Although the pre-exilic prophets also could receive their message in visions, none of them used the visionary form so extensively as Ezekiel and Zechariah. The prophets living in the post-exilic period, such as Trito-Isaiah, Joel, Malachi, Deutero-Zechariah and the composer of the so called Isaiah Apocalypse (Is 24-27), did not use the visionary form at all. Ezekiel and Zechariah may reflect a Jewish milieu in Babylonia already in the sixth century that paid special attention to visionary experiences and visionary literature not unlike the milieu behind the Enochic books.

The other indication relates to the Priestly source. In this source which was composed in Babylonia the "Mesopotamian" Enoch appeared for the first time. We have already demonstrated that the composers of the Enochic literature read Gen 5,18-24 in the light of the Mesopotamian traditions which formed the background of the sequence. Accordingly, Gen 5,18-24 was not the only bridge between the Mesopotamian traditions and the Jewish Enoch concept. The question is, however, whether those circles who developed the specific traditions about Enoch as the primary revealer did so because he already was introduced in a Mesopotamian framework in the *Torah*, or whether the priestly author adopted the "Mesopotamian" Enoch traditions because Enoch already at that time had gained authority in Jewish circles.

Why did the priestly author write the Enoch sequence? It could not be because Enoch was already introduced as a distinguished hero in the Jahwistic source, because he was not. Neither could it be that the priestly author himself wanted to develop an Enochic theology, because he did not. It could be that these characteristics belonged to the structure of the antediluvian period in the Mesopotamian sources, but not necessarily. The priestly author followed there traditions similar to WB 62, CT 46,5 + 12054, Berossos and W 20 030,7. None of these sources recount the

---

353   Cf. above, pp. 64, 67, 93, 156f.

removal of the seventh hero to heaven, which is the most distinctive feature of the priestly Enoch sequence.

There are, however, indications pointing toward the second
possibility, that the process of assimilation had already started
when the Priestly source was composed. In the genealogy the
priestly author changed the name Irad to Jared, "descent", and
moved him from the fourth place to the sixth, thus making him
the father of Enoch.[354] There are no explanations for this
rearrangement except the one which occurs in the Book of
Watchers and Jubilees. The name Jared there signified the descent
of the watchers in the generation before Enoch.[355] From Gen
6,1.3 we know that a commentator prior to the Priestly source had
already started to interpret the Jahwistic account in the light of
Atra-Hasis, thus creating the basis for the Watcher story.

We are inclined to think that the priestly author was not the one
who started the process of contamination, he was rather the one
who because of his position in the priestly class and his orthodox
attitude toward the pre-exilic Mosaic traditions, rapidly gained
authority. There must have been others, and among them a group
that paid special attention to the Mesopotamian sages of the
primeval time.

There is one more indication that points in the same direction. In
our analysis of the Enoch traditions in the Astronomical Book we
found that they were not patterned on, but corresponded in several ways indirectly to the priestly Enoch sequence.[356] The great
revealer in the Astronomical Book was, however, not Enoch but
Uriel.[357] The name Uriel for the primeval divine sage, meaning
"light of God", has a fairly direct equivalent in the short name of
the Mesopotamian divine sage par excellence U-An, "light of the
god (heaven)". There were other significant parallels as well: Both
were associated with the lights of heaven, both were in charge of
the cosmic order, both were associated with the underworld or
abyss, both composed an astronomical work.[358] I think that we
here can observe an adoption of the Mesopotamian traditions prior

354   Cf. above, p. 45.
355   Cf. above, pp. 91f.
356   Cf. above, pp. 79f.
357   Cf. above, pp. 62f.
358   Cf. above, pp. 236ff.

to that of the priestly author, an adoption where the name of the primeval sage simply was translated to Aramaic or taken over in its Aramaic form together with the basic characteristics attributed to this sage, without any connection to the Jahwistic account of the primeval history. If so, it may have been the priestly author who chose the "Biblical" name Enoch for the sage, thus influencing the subsequent development of the Enochic traditions.

The parallels to the Palestinian syncretistic traditions indicate that the Enoch literature was written in Palestine. We thus have to reckon with a transference of the Enoch traditions from Babylonia to Palestine. Considering the date of the earliest Enoch literature this transference may have taken place already in the fourth century. It is also more likely to assume a direct contact between Babylonia and Palestine in the fourth century when Palestine was under Persian domain than in the third century when the Ptolemaic kings ruled the area.

One could consider the possibility that the Enochic scribes during a long period had access to Mesopotamian traditions, but it is hard to imagine how these traditions should be available in Palestine. Rather, it seems more likely that the features attributed to Enoch in the course of the third and second centuries, were adopted by Jewish scribes already in Babylonia. We then have to reckon with an oral substratum which was utilized when the Enoch literature was written. The fairly exact correspondences between Enoch reading the tablets of heaven and the composition Enmeduranki and the Diviners demonstrate that the Enochic scribes could utilize "Mesopotamian" Enoch traditions as late as in the second century which were not recorded in written form in the earlier Enoch literature.[359]

When one reads the Enoch literature in the light of the Mesopotamian traditions one easily understands the transition from traditions dealing with Enoch as a hero and a sage to Enochic revelatory literature. The three primary Mesopotamian protagonists of primeval time had all access to the secret knowledge of the gods. The hero of the flood, Ziusudra, had intimate relationship with the god of wisdom Enki, who revealed to him the future

359   Cf. above, pp. 239ff.

plans of the gods.[360] The ancestor of the diviners Enmeduranki travelled with the gods to the heavenly assembly and was revealed the secret knowledge of the gods in divination and astrology.[361] The primary sage Uanadapa was himself divine, coming from the abode of the god of wisdom to teach men the basic cultural benefits.[362] Written compositions were ascribed to both Enmeduranki and Uanadapa. Enmeduranki received a well known astrological work in the divine assembly. Uanadapa wrote several compositions on dictation from a divine being.[363] The same pattern is found in the Enoch literature. The Enochic scribes clearly adopted the Mesopotamian model of pseudepigraphy thus making Enoch the composer of primeval books containing divine revelations as a counterpart to the Mesopotamian sages.

V.   So far we have observed the following levels in the Enochic traditions and literature:

1) A general background for some of the material in Palestinian folkloristic traditions.

2) A formative influence from Mesopotamian primeval traditions.

3) A special current emphasizing the antediluvian heroes and sages as revealers of divine wisdom. In this current we find the special Enochic theology of the Books of Enoch.

The question is what group stood behind this emphasis on Enoch as primary revealer which also implied an emphasis on the primeval history as a period of revelation similar to the Mesopotamian concept.

If we start with the method of elimination, we can exclude the following groups and milieus. It was not the ruling class of Zadokite priests who stood behind the Priestly source of the Pentateuch, nor the milieus represented by Ben Sira and Pseudo-Eupolemus respectively. In both cases the Enoch traditions were included, but they were not the primary subject. Consequently we can exclude the sapiential milieu of Jerusalem and the Samaritan milieu behind Pseudo-Eupolemus. The Essenes of Qumran can be excluded as well, because the Qumran community copied the early Enochic books, they were written considerably earlier. The

---

360   Cf. above, pp. 173ff.
361   Cf. above, pp. 185ff.
362   Cf. above, pp. 200f.
363   Cf. above, pp. 210f.

Egyptian diaspora can also be eliminated, because the "Mesopotamian" Enoch seems unknown in their writings.[364] We do not
know any prophetic movement as late as the third century. In the
earlier post-exilic prophetic writings from the sixth to the fourth
centuries Enoch is not mentioned.

There are not many possibilities left. It could be that the ruling
Zadokite priesthood developed the Enoch traditions and literature
at a later date than the composing of the Priestly source. But no
observations support this theory. The Chronicler who reflects their
positions in the fourth century only mentions Enoch as a name in
his genealogy (1 Chr 1,3), but does not seem to have associated
anything specific with it.

With these negative results in mind, the clear references in Jewish
literature to a connection between Enoch and Levi seem even more
conclusive. The composer of Jubilees drew a line of transmission
from Enoch to Levi.[365] Both the Aramaic and Greek Levi
literature refer to Enoch as a primeval authority supporting the
legitimacy of the Levitical priesthood.[366] In the Aramaic Testament of Qahat (Levi's son) it is confirmed that Levi was the
holder of the primeval books.[367] These direct references to a
connection Enoch — Levi are supported by more general observations. The early Enochic documents demonstrate considerable
cultic interest which would fit well into an origin in circles of
Levitical descent claiming priestly authority.[368] Both the Aramaic
and Greek Levi literature demonstrate a predilection for visions,
visionary journeys and mythical elements similar to the Enochic
literature.[369] We think that these observations taken together
clearly point towards a group claiming Levitical descent which
developed both the Levi and the Enoch traditions. Furthermore,
that members of this group wrote the earliest Enochic books, the
Astronomical Book and the Book of Watchers. They would thus be
the same group Beckwith designated as the "pre-Essenes".[370]

The problem is, as we have pointed out, that the Zadokites in the

364 Cf. above, pp. 125f.
365 Cf. above, pp. 135ff.
366 Cf. above, pp. 137ff.
367 Cf. above, p. 142.
368 Cf. above, pp. 84, 102f.
369 Cf. above, pp. 140ff.
370 Cf. above, pp. 82f.

post-exilic period also traced their ancestry back to Levi.[371] "Levi" may thus have been introduced as the ancestor of the ruling Zadokite priesthood. But as we have already stated, there are no indications that the ruling class of Zadokite priests of Jerusalem composed the Enoch literature. Besides, both the Enoch and the Aramaic and Greek Levi literature reflect a hostility between groups claiming priestly authority, and the group behind the Enoch and Levi traditions seems to be the one in opposition.[372] It is also highly significant that both the Book of Watchers and the Aramaic Testament of Levi locate the primary revelation to Enoch and Levi respectively to the vicinity of Dan, the ancient Levitical sanctuary.[373] There are accordingly good reasons to assume that behind the concept Enoch — Levi stood a group of oppositional priests claiming priestly rights because they were the true descendants of Levi.

If we are correct in the assumption that there existed one main current of Enoch traditions originating in the Babylonian diaspora and later utilized in the Enoch literature in Palestine, we can suppose that this group of Levites was the one who created the Enoch traditions in the diaspora and later brought them to Palestine. As we have seen, such a movement of Levites is recorded in connection with Ezra's coming to Jerusalem in the beginning of the fourth century.[374] Pointing toward a connection Enoch — Ezra is the observation that the earliest part of the Book of Watchers dealing with Enoch, En 12-16, seems to be based on an Ezra — Enoch typology.[375] Whether it was exactly this group that brought the Enoch concept to Palestine is impossible to decide. But the account in Ezra 8,15-20 nevertheless shows that there existed Levitical communities in the Babylonian diaspora, and that Levites moved from Babylonia to Palestine in the fourth century.

In light of these observations it is possible to trace a fairly simple historical process underlying the development of the Enoch traditions and literature. This process can be defined as a process of identification and demarcation. It relates both to the Enoch tra-

---

371 Cf. above, pp. 137f.
372 Cf. above, p. 141.
373 Cf. above, pp. 103f, 142.
374 Cf. above, pp. 157f.
375 Cf. above, p. 101.

ditions and literature and to the two blocks of Mesopotamian traditions utilized by the Enochic scribes, the tradition about the primeval revealers and the tradition about the primeval catastrophe.

Although the pre-exilic claim advanced by the Levites — that
Levi was the ancestor of the priestly class — was commonly
accepted during the exilic period of the sixth century, this did not
lead to a rehabilitation of the Levitical tribe as a priestly tribe. It
led to an alteration of the Zadokite genealogies making Levi an
ancestor of Zadok (cf. 1 Chr 6,1-8). If we are correct in that
members of the Levitical tribe were those who created the concept
of Enoch as a primeval revealer, this incident could have been the
underlying historical factor. The Levites had lost the dispute about
Levi, it would not be unlikely that they sought a new platform for
their identity. This platform existed in the Mesopotamian concept
of the antediluvian history as a period of revelation. We have
observed how the composer of Jubilees, who was familiar with the
early Enoch and Levi traditions, drew a line consisting of physical
descent, transmission of books and oral instruction from Enoch to
Levi corresponding exactly to the one found in the traditions
about Enmeduranki as the ancestor of Babylonian divinatory
priests.[376] This process was surely facilitated by the fact that
other groups within the Jewish community were also impressed by
the Babylonian traditions, as is clearly demonstrated in the Priestly
document. That the Zadokite priests accepted the special character
of the seventh Babylonian sage and king and introduced Enoch,
"the trained one", as a Jewish counterpart did apparently influence the subsequent development. The Levites now had support
for their attempt to seek an ancestor in the primeval time in a
document which rapidly gained authority. If we are correct in that
the oldest adaptation of these Mesopotamian traditions is reflected
through the two parallel figures U-An — Uriel, the Levites now,
under influence of the Priestly source, introduced Enoch as a
parallel figure to Uriel (the Astronomical Book).[377] Later Uriel
was reduced to one among other angels, and Enoch placed as the
primary revealer alone (the Book of Watchers).[378]

The Mesopotamian traditions about the origin of wisdom centered

376   Cf. above, pp. 266f.
377   Cf. above, pp. 238f.
378   Cf. above, p. 66.

around the sage Uanadapa and the king Enmeduranki thus served to give the Levitical group a new platform. They introduced a new concept of history in the Jewish milieu where the basic revelation was dated back in primeval time. This approach was in principle not different from what had taken place at other times in Israel's history. During the settlement in Canaan the Hebrew tribes adopted the Canaanite cultic celebrations, thus broadening their religious perspective to include the fertility of the land. During the early years of the monarchy the priests of the temple in Jerusalem adopted old Jebusite traditions centered around Zion, thus creating a religious basis for the capital of the southern monarchy. What made the approach of the Levitical group different was not this approach itself, but the succeeding historical circumstances. The pre-exilic history of Israel was a period of developing religious traditions. The post-exilic history became a period of collecting and preserving traditions. Of course, this did not happen in one step, neither did it happen in the same way at all levels of post-exilic Jewish society. But the Mosaic and subsequently the prophetic writings gradually became the centre of gravity in the religious life, thus subduing the attempts to add new sacred traditions to the Jewish religion.[379]

The Levitical group developing the Enochic traditions did not give up what they saw as the core of the Jewish faith. This is clearly demonstrated in the process of demarcation which accompanied the process of identification. In the Book of Watchers we have observed that the ancient story about the primeval catastrophe was used polemically in two ways. The fallen watchers seem on one hand to reflect a defiled priesthood, which may have been directed against the Zadokite priests of Jerusalem. On the other hand, the watchers and their offspring represented foreign military power and culture, which accordingly were utterly condemned by the Levitical group.[380] Already the Astronomical Book polemized against "heathen" religious practice by condemning those who worshipped the stars as gods.[381]

But it is highly significant that the concept which primarily was used to make a front against foreign religion and culture, the

---

379   Cf. above, pp. 18ff.
380   Cf. above, pp. 96ff, 99f.
381   Cf. above, p. 76.

Watcher story, was also based on Mesopotamian traditions. Not only was the pattern taken from Mesopotamian traditions, but also the technique of using the story about the primeval catastrophe as a framework for the interpretation of new catastrophes was developed by Babylonian scribes, as clearly demonstrated in the Poem of Erra.[382] This should illustrate how deeply rooted the Enochic scribes were in their Mesopotamian background. The traditions did not only provide them with a new platform for their theology in a positive way, they also constituted the horizon in the polemics against what they understood as demonic power and wisdom.

VI.   It would, however, be an overstatement to regard the early Enochic literature as only a reflection of Mesopotamian traditions. The Enochic scribes transformed these traditions into a new literary Gattung, the Gattung "apocalypse". The Enochic apocalyptical literature accordingly did not develop out of Old Testament prophecy, nor did it develop out of Jewish sapiential traditions.[383] This does not mean that there was no connection with "prophecy" or "wisdom". The Enochic scribes handled topics dealt with both places. Like the Jewish sages they paid attention to cosmology, and like the prophets their message became marked by an eschatological perspective. But the characteristics of the Enochic literature can be explained neither on the background of prophecy nor on the background of sapiential traditions. The characteristics arose out of the transformation of Mesopotamian primeval traditions, partly consisting of mythical material, into a literature marked by a Jewish historical-eschatological perspective of reality. This transformation did not happen in one step, but gradually by emphasizing and selecting elements already extant in the Mesopotamian traditions.

Below we give a survey to demonstrate how the Mesopotamian traditions were transformed according to what became the primary characteristics of the Enochic literature, namely the aspect of revelation.

---

382   Cf. above, pp. 181ff.
383   Cf. above, pp. 36ff, 154ff.

SAGES AND REVELATIONS

Figure	Composition	Theme	Manner of revelation	Corresponding forms
Ziusudra	Atra-Ḥasis	Flood story	Warned through a dream	
Kabti-ilāni-Marduk	Poem of Erra	Primeval catastrophe/ Contemporary catastrophe	Revealed in a night-vision	
Enoch	Book of Watchers	Primeval catastrophe/ Contemporary catastrophe (Watcher story)	Visions of Enoch (Redactional classification, En 1,2; 19,3)	
Enoch	Book of Dreams (En 83-84)	Primeval catastrophe/ Contemporary catastrophe	Revealed in a night-vision	
	Book of Dreams Apocalypse of Animals (En 85-90, 86-88)	Primeval catastrophe (Watcher story)	Revealed in a night-vision	
Enmeduranki	Enmeduranki and the Diviners	Ascension to the heavenly assembly		
Utuaabba/ Adapa	Bit Meseri	Ascension to heaven		
Enoch	Book of Watchers (En 13-14)	Ascension to the heavenly assembly	Night-vision	Corresponding to Ezek 1-2
Enmeduranki	Enmeduranki and the Diviners	Travelled with the gods		
Enoch	Book of Watchers (En 17-36)	Travelled with the angels	Visionary journey	Corresponding to Zech 1-6; Ezek 8-11

Continues

Continued

SAGES AND REVELATIONS

Figure	Composition	Theme	Manner of revelation	Corresponding forms
Enmeduranki	Enmeduranki and the Diviners	Reading the heavenly tablets	Instruction	
Enoch	En 81	Reading the heavenly tablets	Instruction	
Enoch	Epistle of Enoch	Reading the heavenly tablets	Instruction/ vision	
Uanadapa	Catalogue of Texts and Authors	Composer of astronomical work	Dictation/ vision	
Enoch	Astronomical Book	Composer of astronomical work	Instruction/ vision	

1) The first section deals with the primeval catastrophe. In Atra-Ḥasis several crises are recorded leading up to the deluge as the climax. Atra-ḥasis himself is described as a man "giving attention to dreams", i.e. communicating with the gods through the dream as a medium. The fragmentary text introducing the account of the deluge indicates that this was the case when Enki revealed to him the coming catastrophe as well. In Berossos the coming catastrophe is explicitly said to have been revealed through a dream.[384] The composer of the Poem of Erra transfers the primeval catastrophe to his own time to reflect a contemporary catastrophe. The composer Kabti-ilāni-Marduk claims that he got the whole drama revealed in a night-vision.[385]

The Enochic scribe behind the Watcher story, En 6-11.12-16, used the same technique of narration as the composer of the Poem of Erra by transferring the primeval stories about the fall of the

384   Cf. above, pp. 174f, 176.
385   Cf. above, pp. 181ff, 211f.

angels and the deluge to his own time. He did not, however, claim to have seen these incidents in a vision. The composers of the Book of Watchers, however, placed the Watcher story in a visionary framework, at least indirectly, by characterizing the whole book as the visions of Enoch.[386] What was indicated by these composers, was made explicit by the composer of the Book of Dreams. Here Enoch twice sees the primeval catastrophe (in two different versions) in night visions.[387]

The correspondences between the Enochic and Mesopotamian material concern two features that are crucial for the understanding of the Enoch literature. The first one is that it was revealed to the primeval hero, through a dream or vision, that a catastrophe was to come. The other is that this catastrophe could be transferred to a new historical setting through a visionary experience.

The differences lie in the emphasis on vision as a medium of revelation. Even though Enki's communication with Atra-ḥasis through dreams comes close to Enoch's dream-visions, Atra-ḥasis' visionary capacity was not the primary subject in the Mesopotamian traditions. It seems to be a part of a general description of the king as diviner, seer and prophet.[388] There is, however, a growth in the Enochic literature at this point. The Watcher story in En 6-11 originally had nothing to do with visionary experiences. The connection was first indicated by the composers of the Book of Watchers, and made explicit by the composer of the Book of Dreams. This growth also concerns the genre of the composition. Like Atra-Ḥasis and the Poem of Erra the Watcher story is an epical composition and as such has nothing to do with visionary literature. This has changed in the Book of Dreams. Here the story of the catastrophe is structures according to the Gattung "vision".

2) Both the seventh king and the seventh sage of the primeval lists ascended to heaven.[389] The same motif is frequently attributed to Enoch.[390] In the only detailed report about the ascension of Enoch (En 14) the mythical ascension of the primeval heroes is transformed into a visionary ascension. Here the Enochic scribe

---

386 Cf. above, p. 86.
387 Cf. above, pp. 104f, 149f.
388 Cf. the Sumerian flood story above, p. 174.
389 Cf. above, pp. 185ff, 203f.
390 Cf. above, pp. 48ff, 76f, 93f, 109, 119ff.

has introduced the Gattung vision (drawing on Ezekiel) without any preceding visionary elements in the Mesopotamian material.

3) We have previously argued that the journeys of Enoch in En 17-36 within the development of the Enochic literature had to be regarded as an extension of the visionary ascension in En 14.[391] This seems confirmed by the observation that the composition Enmeduranki and the Diviners most likely formed the background both for the ascension and the journey motifs.[392] Accordingly the Enochic scribe has also here transformed the material. Out of a report about a mythical journey he has created a visionary (using a visionary form similar to Proto-Zechariah and Ezekiel).

4) Both in the compositions Enmeduranki and the Diviners and En 81 the reading of the heavenly tablets is accompanied by instruction.[393] The language used to express this situation is parallel to that of vision, cf. the verb "show", even though no visionary experience is intended. This is different in the Epistle of Enoch. Here Enoch's reading of the heavenly tablets is related to his visionary capacity.[394]

5) According to the Catalogue of Texts and Authors Uanadapa surely was believed to have written his works on dictation from a god (most probably Ea). Most likely this concept of inspiration was understood as a visionary revelation in one form or another.[395] We have observed that the language of transmission in the Astronomical Book tended toward the language of vision.[396] The hesitation to classify it as "visionary language" lay in the fact that there were no other marks of vision in the astronomical material. So even though we do not know the exact nature of the described experiences, the intention is clearly in both places to underscore the authority of the astronomical works by tracing them back to a divine being through inspiration.

This analysis should demonstrate that the Enochic scribes gradually reinforced the visionary elements where they were extant in the Mesopotamian material and introduced visionary language where

391   Cf. above, pp. 149ff.
392   Cf. above, pp. 245f, 264f.
393   Cf. above, pp. 240f.
394   Cf. above, pp. 76ff, 151f.
395   Cf. above, pp. 211ff.
396   Cf. above, pp. 63ff.

these elements were lacking. If we bear in mind that the revelatory visionary forms were the primary characteristics of the apocalyptical literature,[397] this process of transformation of the legendary and mythical material concerns the very nature of the Enochic apocalyptic. This process was initiated when circles within Judaism, most likely a group of oppositional Levites, began to see their identity and the framework for their interpretation of reality not in their own native heritage, but in learned Babylonian traditions. Since these circles did not give up their indigenous faith, however, there came a confrontation between the mythical material which was a part of the Babylonian tradition, and the Jewish historical-eschatological perspective of reality. This confrontation was gradually eased by the application of a medium of interpreting reality which was known both by the Babylonians and the Jews, namely that of vision. Through it mythical events became visionary experiences. The mythical universe could be retained but transferred to a visionary universe. The visionary form was applied in different ways. The apocalyptic seer could ascend to heaven and communicate with divine beings just like his Mesopotamian counterparts, but in a visionary experience. He could disclose the far recesses of cosmos, the heavens and the underworld as portrayed in ancient myths, but in a visionary journey. He could disclose the future like the primeval divinators, but through a visionary revelation. Even entire mythical stories, such as that of the primeval catastrophe, could be reproduced, but in the end also this incident was seen in a vision.

The visionary form in the Enochic literature was associated with the eschatological perspective. Like the visionary form the eschatological perspective gradually became a part of the Enochic interpretation of reality.[398] It is clear, however, that the Enochic scribes were not dependent on one fixed pattern of eschatology. The way the eschatological perspective marked the compositions varied considerably.

Enoch's association with eschatology is based on the presupposition that his fate and message were related in different ways to the

---

397   Cf. above, pp. 35ff.
398   Cf. above, pp. 153f.

future. This was the starting point which later was interpreted in an eschatological perspective.[399] Accordingly, the fate and message of Enoch was not used as a framework to "decorate" an already existing eschatological pattern. His fate and message concerned the very nature of the Enochic eschatology.

The Enochic scribes regarded the stories about Enoch and his primeval contemporaries not only as stories about primeval time. In different ways the scribes drew lines from the primeval time up to their own time. We have already observed how this took place in the Watcher story, it was also the case in the other Enochic traditions which more directly concentrated on the figure of Enoch himself. The starting point here is Enoch's ability to foresee the future. This feature occurs in three connections in the Enochic literature:

1) In the Astronomical Book Enoch is enabled to foresee the distant time of the sinners on basis of his training in astronomy, cf. En 80.
2) In En 81 Enoch reads the future of mankind out of the heavenly tablets.
3) In the Book of Dreams Enoch sees the coming catastrophe in night visions.

These three features correspond exactly to the description of the primeval heroes in the Mesopotamian traditions shown on p. 341.

What sharply distinguished the Enochic literature from the Mesopotamian is that Enoch has the ability to foresee not only the immediate future or is associated with techniques to foresee the future in general like his Mesopotamian counterparts, but he is enabled to foresee the distant future and exactly that part of history in which the composers of the books were involved. When the eschatological perspective was adopted into the Enochic literature, Enoch was also enabled to foresee the eschatological drama. This was as already stated a gradual process. The Astronomical Book did not contain eschatology. In the Book of Watchers eschatology is introduced in an ambiguous way, first in relation to

---

399   Cf. above, p. 154.

DIVINATION/PREDICTION			
Figure	Composition	Theme	Prediction
Uanadapa	Catalogue of Texts and Authors	Composer of astronomical work	Astronomy could serve as basis for astrology
Enoch	Astronomical Book	Composer of astronomical work	Astronomy used as basis for prediction (En 80)
Enmeduranki	Enmeduranki and the Diviners	Reading the heavenly tablets	Containing the secrets of divination
Enoch	En 81 and Epistle of Enoch	Reading the heavenly tablets	Containing the secrets of the future
Ziusudra	Atra-Ḥasis	Flood story	The coming catastrophe revealed in a dream
Enoch	Book of Dreams 1. vision (En 83-84)	Primeval catastrophe/ Contemporary catastrophe	The coming catastrophe revealed in a dream

the Watcher story, then in the journeys of Enoch where Enoch travels in space and time to see the eschatological condemnation of the watchers. In the first vision of the Book of Dreams the coming catastrophe seen by Enoch has a double aspect, both as a primordial and eschatological crisis. Eschatology in more conventional form, loosened from the primeval context, occurs for the first time in the Apocalypse of Animals.[400] The transformation of the primeval traditions into eschatological literature was accordingly based on two factors, the first was that the primeval events foreshadowed the eschatological drama, the other was that the hero of primeval time was able to predict this distant future.

400   Cf. above, p. 106.

It seems as if the transformation of the material according to the visionary form and the eschatological perspective is rooted in the same experience of reality. In both cases the reinterpretation related to the same Mesopotamian traditions partly including a mythical perception of reality. This mythical perception is evident in the way that compositions which to some extent deal with humans as protagonists, nevertheless contain a mythical transcendence where humans and gods were mingled, and the borders of the human and the divine reality could easily be crossed. In the Enochic literature this mythical transcendence is transformed on the one hand to a visionary transcendence where the divine and human world only meet in the visionary experience, on the other hand to an eschatological transcendence where patterns, figures and symbols belonging to the mythical transcendence reoccur in the description of the final crisis of history.

Part 2

The Mesopotamian Background
of the Son of Man

ודניאל הבין בכל חזון וחלמות

"And Daniel had insight in
all kinds of visions and dreams"
(Dan 1,17)

I
Introduction

The Unsolved Riddle

One of the most enigmatic figures in Jewish and Christian literature appears for the first time in the vision in Dan 7,1-14. Already
the designation of the figure in v. 13, Aramaic *bar 'ănāš*, which
for convenience sake is commonly translated "son of man", causes
problems concerning the exact meaning of the phrase. The same
figure is the central figure in one of the Enochic books in the
Ethiopic corpus, "the Similitudes of Enoch" (En 37-71). He is also
the central figure in one of the visions in the Apocalypse of Ezra,
4 Ezra 13. In the New Testament the designation "son of man" is
attributed to Jesus mainly in the Gospels and in the Book of
Revelation.

If we exclude the New Testament sources, Dan 7 is the only source
which can be dated with certainty. There is a general agreement in
the research that this chapter got its final form together with the
rest of the Book of Daniel about 167-165 B.C. Since the Similitudes of Enoch did not belong to the Aramaic corpus of Enochic
books found in Qumran, there is great uncertainty about the age
of this source, whether it is understood as a Jewish or Christian
composition.[1] The apocalyptical 4 Ezra is to be dated about 100
A.D. The vision contained in chapter 13 is generally held to be
older, but how old can only be decided by an analysis based on
literary and tradition criticism. The vision in Dan 7 is accordingly
the only source where a pre-Christian date can be taken for
granted. This vision will therefore be the main subject of our
analysis. The vision in 4 Ezra 13 will be consulted as an additional
source to the Son of Man imagery; the Similitudes of Enoch and
the New Testament contain so many problems of their own, that
they require a separate study in their own right and will accordingly not be discussed in this study.

---

1   For the Aramaic corpus of the Books of Enoch, cf. Part I, pp. 31f.

The very title of this part, "The Mesopotamian Background of the Son of Man", indicates a standpoint in the discussion about the phrase "son of man" in Dan 7,13. If the Son of Man has a background, it implies that the phrase is not a mere ad hoc creation by the author of the vision, and also that the figure described is more than a mere symbol, created as contrast to the beasts which precede it in the vision. The more precise determination "Mesopotamian" demonstrates that the background of the figure will be sought in Mesopotamian literature. This does not mean, however, that I intend to revive any of the previous theories about the background of the Son of Man in Mesopotamian traditions. The material presented in this study and the arguments derived from it are entirely new in this context. Formulated briefly, I will argue that the imagery of Dan 7, including the Son of Man, is derived from an Akkadian vision of the nether world and closely related traditions.

I do not start this study with a survey of the research history. There are two reasons for this: Firstly, a research history to the whole Book of Daniel was published in 1980 by K. Koch,[2] and there is not much to add; secondly, since my study starts from an entirely different angle than previous research, such a survey is not needed as an entry into the problems. However, this does not mean that the positions of other scholars will not be discussed, only that the discussion will take place in the course of the concrete work on the text to Dan 7.

Nevertheless, it would be unfair not to warn the reader about the hazardous nature of this attempt to establish a new basis for the understanding of the Son of Man. According to R. Leivestad a distinct apocalyptical figure designated "son of man" existed neither in Jewish literature, nor in the Gospels.[3] So I am doomed to search in vain. The kind of investigation I intend to pursue has received the following verdict by A.A. Di Lella: "Perhaps it may appear harsh, if indeed not unjustified, to describe the quest for an assumed prehistory of this expression as an unusually intricate

---

2 K. Koch, unter Mitarbeit von Till Niewisch und Jürgen Tubach, Das Buch Daniel, EdF, Darmstadt 1980. A discussion of the more recent publications is offered by C. Colpe, "Neue Untersuchungen zum Menschensohn-Problem", ThRv 77, 1981, cols. 353-78.
3 R. Leivestad, "Exit the Apocalyptic Son of Man", NTS 18, 1971-72, pp. 243-67.

and often frustrating enterprise which is nevertheless pursued with vigor by an increasing number of like-minded researchers. But it does seem fair to say that the search is an achingly tedious and not overly productive exercise in literary imagination and scholarly ingenuity".[4]

Di Lella's verdict is understandable. An overview of the vast number of theories relating to the origin of the Son of Man imagery evokes a certain sadness, that so much labour is offered yet so few results achieved. Below I give a list of the solutions that have most often been argued by those scholars who in one way or another have regarded the Son of Man as a reflection of an underlying figure or tradition. The list is not intended to be a complete survey either of theories or scholars, but is offered for the sake of illustration. (For a more complete survey and a discussion I refer to the above-mentioned research history by Koch.)

Traditions about the primeval Man combined with Messianic traditions (Bentzen).[5]

Anthropos, the Cosmic primeval Man (Mowinckel).[6]

Reflection of the Persian Gayomart myth (von Gall).[7]

Persian Anthropos myth, in Babylonia identified with Marduk (Kraeling).[8]

Reflection of a Sungod myth (Gressmann).[9]

Marduk, as he is described in Enuma Elish (Gunkel).[10]

The primeval godman Adapa (Jansen).[11]

---

4   A.A. Di Lella, "The One in Human Likeness and the Holy Ones of the Most High in Dan 7", CBQ 34, 1977, pp. 1-19, pp. 3f.
5   Aa. Bentzen, King and Messiah, London 1955; cf. also; "King Ideology -"Urmensch" -"Troonsbestijgingsfest", StTh 3, 1949, pp. 143-57.
6   S. Mowinckel, He that Cometh, (Nashville-New York 1954, pp. 346-450; cf. also, "Ophavet til den senjødiske forestilling om Menneskesønnen", NTT 14, 1944, pp. 189-343; and, "Urmensch und 'Königsideologie'", StTh 2, 1948-49, pp. 71-89.
7   A. von Gall, Basilieia tou theou, eine religionswissenschaftliche Studie zur vorkirchlichen Eschatologie, Heidelberg 1926, pp. 409-30.
8   C.H. Kraeling, Anthropos and Son of Man, New York 1927, pp. 141-47.
9   H. Gressmann, Der Messias, Göttingen 1929, pp. 343-73.
10   H. Gunkel, Schöpfung und Chaos in Urzeit und Endzeit, Göttingen 1895, pp. 323-35.
11   H.L. Jansen, Die Henochgestalt, Oslo 1939, pp. 86-110.

Baal in Ugaritic myths (Emerton).[12]

The angel Gabriel (Zevit).[13]

Angelic Being as the leader of the holy ones (Coppens).[14]

An angel as celestial patron of the people of Israel (U.B. Müller).[15]

The angel Michael as high priest (Lacocque).[16]

An angel of judgment (K. Müller).[17]

A hypostasis of the glory of God in Ezek 1 (Balz).[18]

A hypostasis of the Divine Wisdom (Muilenburg).[19]

A reflection of Enoch in En 14 (Glasson).[20]

Pseudonym for Daniel (Schmid).[21]

Judas Maccabeus (Sahlin).[22]

I have listed eighteen theories. There are more, at least variants. To start a new inquiry is to be prepared to be listed as number nineteen or more. There must be fairly compelling reasons to run the risk. If the solution was so simple as proposed by Leivestad, Di Lella and many others, that the Son of Man is a symbolic phrase for the holy ones in the interpretation, meaning the pious Israel, and nothing more, I think that the research would have come to a standstill long ago. But neither has this theory gained general

12   J.A. Emerton, "The Origin of the Son of Man Imagery", JThS 9, 1958, pp. 225-42.
13   Z. Zevit, "The Structure and Individual Elements of Daniel 7", ZAW 80, 1968, pp. 385-96.
14   J. Coppens, "Le Fils d'Homme daniélique et les relectures de Dan., VII, 13, dans les apocryphes et les écrits du Nouveau Testament", EThL 37, 1961, pp. 5-51; "Le Fils d'Homme daniélique, vizir céleste?" ALBO 4, Ser. 12, 1964, pp. 72-80; "La vision daniélique du Fils d'Homme", VT 19, 1969, pp. 171-82.
15   U.B. Müller, Messias und Menschensohn in Jüdischen Apokalypsen und in der Offenbarung des Johannes, Gütersloh 1972, pp. 19-60.
16   A. Lacocque, The Book of Daniel, London 1979, pp. 122-34.
17   K. Müller, "Der Menschensohn im Danielzyklus", Jesus und der Menschensohn, für Anton Vögtle, Freiburg 1975, pp. 37-80.
18   H.R. Balz, Methodische Probleme der neutestamentlichen Christologie, WMANT 25, Neukirchen-Vluyn 1967, pp. 79-95.
19   J. Muilenburg, "The Son of Man in Daniel and the Ethiopic Apocalypse of Enoch", JBL 79, 1960, pp. 197-209.
20   T.F. Glasson, "The Son of Man Imagery", NTS 23, 1977, pp. 82-90.
21   H. Schmid, "Daniel, der Menschensohn", Judaica 27, 1971, pp. 192-220.
22   H. Sahlin, "Antiochus Epiphanes und Judas Makkabeus", StTh 23, 1969, pp. 41-68.

acceptance. There is still an awareness among many scholars that the solution is not so simple. Why did the author create the vivid imagery of the vision — imagery which to a large extent is not utilized in the interpretation — if he only wanted to retell the events preceding and succeeding Antiochus IV in symbolical language? And if he wanted to emphasize the visionary imagery as a composition in its own right, which to some degree operates independently of the interpretation, why did he chose an imagery with no resemblances within the Jewish tradition? These are questions which demand an answer, and until this answer is given I am afraid that researchers will continue to run the risk to present solutions that by others will be classified as "achingly tedious exercise in literary imagination".

In my approach to the problem I depart from the main trend among those scholars who assume a background for the Son of Man already from the beginning. This main trend I will define as follows: The imagery and symbolism involved in the vision of Dan 7 are the product of the composer of this text who has collocated either different traditions or different sources extant in nonvisionary form, into a unity. The first step towards a correct analysis of the vision is therefore a diachronic analysis, either of literary-critical or tradition-critical character.

This approach has led some scholars to an elaborate literary criticism, with the result that each scholar is working from his own "private text".[23] Armed with this text it is of course not difficult

---

23 Literary criticism as a means to solve the Son of Man riddle has been particularly favoured in recent German research. P. Weimar, "Daniel 7. Eine Textanalyse", Jesus und der Menschensohn, pp. 11-36, separates two original visions that were combined by a redactor: 1) The Four Beast Vision, vv. 2aBb.3.4abA[*]. 5aAGb.6abA.7aA.bA.11a[*] (only ḥzh hwyt).11b[*]; 2) The Son of Man Hymn, vv. 9.10.13.14aA. The core of the Son of Man Hymn is the commissioning of a heavenly being in the assembly of God by the transmission of rulership. This hymn had originally nothing to do with the succession of kings and empires in the Four Beast Vision.
In the same volume K. Müller (cf. note 17) offers another solution. He separates vv. 9.10.13 as the original Son of Man source. The exclusion of v. 14 from the original text has the consequence that the Son of Man originally had no connection to the transmission of kingship. The only characteristic then left is the court scenery. According to Müller the Son of Man is to be interpreted as an angel of judgement in analogy to Dan 4,10.14.
R. Kearns, Vorfragen der Christologie II, Tübingen 1980, pp. 16f. 83-6. 97-107, comes to nearly the same conclusion as Weimar concerning the Son of Man

to find a new angle to attack the problem. It is more difficult to convince those who either have a different "private text", or think that the text as it stands still is the best one for the analysis of content.

The diachronic analysis of tradition-critical character is often combined with literary criticism, but not necessarily. The approach chosen here is often to separate between the Gattung, structure, symbolism and intention on the one hand, and the underlying mythical imagery on the other.[24] The first level is the creation of

sequence. The main difference is that he includes the two first words in v. 15, "my spirit was troubled", in the original text. This is, however, not without significance. The reaction of the visionary is taken as a part of a Gattung pattern belonging to an alleged original type of Gattung, constitutive for the Son of Man tradition, namely "the Apocalyptical Vision". Kearns finds the same type of Gattung in the alleged oldest stratum of the vision in 4 Ezra 13. Later this type of Gattung in Dan 7 and 4 Ezra 13 was incorporated into other types of Gattungen, "the Symbolic Dream" and "the Apocalypse". The original figure of the Apocalyptical Vision is defined as an apocalyptic "exalted being" (Hoheitswesen) of non-Jewish origin, who later in the framework of the other Gattungen was reinterpreted according to traditions already known in the Jewish milieu.

It is not correct to conclude that because there exist different solutions to a problem all must be wrong. But we cannot overlook the dilemma that as long as the researchers interpret different texts, the possibility of reaching some sort of consensus is minimal. The real problem is the criteria that are used in the literary criticism. These are mostly based on content. There is no parallel text that can shed light on the problem, and there are no syntactical breaks within vv. 1-7 and vv. 9.10.13.14, and between these sections (vv. 8.11.12 will be discussed later) that demand an explanation. There are also no logical "leaps" which are really disturbing. What we have is a text which is extraordinarily rich in associations. This confuses because the associations seem to point in different directions and it is difficult to find the common denominator that combines them into a whole.

This is, however, a characteristic of apocalyptic literature. The enigma of this kind of literature is not solved by distributing the different associations to different independent sources. The associations existed in the mind of the composer and were combined there. We have no criteria to distribute them to different written sources as long as no such sources are found.

24   One of the most favoured theories in recent research is that the imagery of the vision ultimately goes back to the Ugaritic epic cycle about Baal as vanquisher of the Sea-monster Yamm, and subsequently as the receiver of kingship from the highest god El, cf. C. Colpe, "ho hyios tou anthropou", ThWNT 8, Stuttgart 1969, pp. 403-81, pp. 418-22; and, J.J. Collins, The Apocalyptic Vision of the Book of Daniel, Missoula, Montana 1977, pp. 96-106.

I will deal with this material in detail later. here I will only point out the main difficulty in applying this material as the framework for the understanding of the vision. First it must be admitted that there is one correspondence between the Ugaritic myth and the vision. In both cases a god destroys a monster. But as Collins also admits this motif is well attested in Old Testament traditions where Yahweh destroys Rahab or Leviathan in the sea. There is no need to suppose a direct Ugaritic background for this feature.

The sequence which has no parallels in the Old Testament is the one about the man approaching the Ancient of Days to receive kingship. The analogy to the Ugaritic myth demands that the Son of Man is a reflection of Baal, the Ancient

the composer, the second the material he used. Consequently there is a considerable gap between the text as it reads and the assumed underlying material. This gap is given the explanation that the author used the material freely, which of course is a possibility. The disturbing question is that if the underlying material did not share in the Gattung — the visionary form; or the structure-monstrous creatures, throne vision, court-scene, ideal ruler in contrast to rebel prince; or the symbolism — beastmonsters in contrast to "man"; or the intention — to predict the downfall of a hatred king, — why at all did the composer use this material? He must have known that he only obscured what he wanted to reveal. One can of course object that the author wanted to disguise his message in a mysterious language. But still there must be a reason for the adoption of the underlying tradition. At least the author himself must have felt that this tradition offered the framework for a correct interpretation of reality.

This does not mean that I oppose the use of literary and tradition criticism. But when these methods are applied on Dan 7, they must to a large extent be based on internal criteria. The results will therefore have a somewhat hypothetical character. And I find it methodologically unwise to base the rest of the analysis on such observations.

What makes the vision in Dan 7 unique is not each element in isolation, but the combination of the elements. Isolating the elements either as distinct sources or as traditions, makes it possible to find a wide range of more or less close parallels. But that does not mean that these parallels are a part of the background of the vision. The parallels may exist in totally different contexts and within these contexts communicate totally differently from Dan 7.

---

of Days a reflection of El. The question is: If it is correct that the Ugaritic material is to be interpreted in this way, what could it signify for the composer of the vision? According to the analogy Yahweh should confer the supreme cosmic kingship to another god or a divine being, and this act should be the sign for a new era in human history. Has this any connection to the message of the vision as it now reads? On the contrary, the message of the vision is that when the fourth beast challenges the superiority of Yahweh through th proud words, v. 8.11, the succession of terrestrial kings comes to an end. Yahweh then confers not his kingship, which would be an impossible thought for a Jew, but the kingship given to the rulers on earth to the Son of Man. Accordingly the Ugaritic myth would communicate something entirely different from the vision, and the reason why the composer would interpret his reality in the light of this myth is hard to explain.

This may be readily demonstrated: "the sea" occurs in several mythologies with different meanings; "monsters" are frequent in ancient near eastern mythology; descriptions of "the heavenly assembly" are likewise frequent, so are also "court-scenes", "heavenly books" and "divine fire"; "transcendent beings coming with clouds" occurs in several mythologies dealing with nature and vegetation; "visionary figures in human form" are frequent in both Mesopotamian and Jewish visions; "enthronements of rulers" are often described; "rebel kings" are known in the history and literature of both Israel, Egypt and Mesopotamia, — and of course many other countries. What most often has happened in the research is that one of these elements are declared to be *the* underlying source of tradition and used as the key for the interpretation of the whole imagery.

My approach is different. I start with the presupposition that the key to the understanding lies in the way the different elements are combined into a whole.

What characterizes my approach is my claim that the criterion which determines the underlying tradition does not lie in parallels between separate motifs, but in the combination of these. When Dan 7 in the research history is connected to such a wide spectre of mythologies and religious imaginations, it is because this criterion has not been applied.

In concrete terms that means that since Dan 7 is a vision, we are most likely to find the underlying tradition represented in visions. The vision has a clear structure of content: monsters, throne-scene, court-scene, ideal ruler. Where do we find a similar combination of sequences? The basic semantic pattern in the vision is the contrast beast—man. Where do we find a similar semantic pattern? The vision was committed to writing from religio-political motives. Where do we find visions with the same intention?

There must be good reasons to make the attempt to establish one more theory about the background of the Son of Man imagery. The reason I have is the claim to have discovered sources that contain the same combination of elements as occurs in Dan 7. Through the application of these sources I will try to demonstrate both the origin of and the intention behind the imagery of the vision.

The study has three main parts. First an analysis of two Akkadian dream-visions, one of which forms a part of the background of the other. To avoid the temptation to "bend" the material to make it more adaptable for my theory than it is, I first give a historical analysis of the material in its own right. We have to know what was the original meaning of the sources, as far as it can be reconstructed, before we consider how the material was adapted by a later interpreter. The second part consists of a comparison between the Akkadian visions and the vision in Dan 7, also including the vision in 4 Ezra 13. In the third part we consider how the Mesopotamian material was understood by its Jewish adapters, by placing Dan 7 in the context of the Enochic visionary literature from the third century B.C. found in the Book of Watchers.[25]

---

25 Accordingly I do not start with a preliminary analysis of Dan 7. Such an analysis would lead to a series of complicated anticipations of the succeeding material. I have provided an analysis of the main line of the vision, including the main problems, in my article, "Struktur und Geschichte in Dan 7", StTh 32, 1978, pp. 95-117. This article was, however, written before my discovery of the Akkadian visions as the underlying tradition, but formed the basis for my investigation into the Mesopotamian literature in general.
The basic theory about a connection between the Akkadian Vision of the Nether World and Dan 7 was announced briefly in "An Akkadian Vision as Background for Dan 7?", StTh 35, 1981, pp. 85-9.

II
Akkadian Dream Visions

In this part two Akkadian dream visions will be analyzed, the one forming a part of the background of the other. Both visions contain a structure and an imagery which are known from a broad current of tradition dealing with the nether world. This tradition will be referred to insofar as it concerns the visions. The analysis of the background of the visions is important both for the understanding of the visions in general, and for the aim of the whole study: The visions as background for Dan 7. It is important to know as precisely as possible in what way the visions combine motifs known from a broader current of tradition, and where the visions deviate from the conventional structure and imagery occurring in reports about the nether world. This will facilitate the comparison to Dan 7. It is then possible to decide whether the correspondences concern conventional elements, or elements that can only be explained out of the scope of each of the visions.

The philological analyses are not to be regarded as text editions, which would demand another approach to the material. They are rather to be regarded as an up-dating of previous editions. There are several reasons why one could not simply refer to these.

Concerning the first text, the Death-Dream of Enkidu, new tablets have been found which are not considered in the only critical text editions of the Gilgamesh Epic by R.C. Thompson. Many of these tablets are edited one by one, but no critical synopsis is made. Accordingly there is also no translation dealing with all the tablets together.

Concerning the second text, the Vision of the Nether World, the latest edition of the whole text was published by von Soden in 1936. No new tablets have been found, but the knowledge about Akkadian language has increased to such a degree that it is not possible simply to present this edition or later translations based on this edition, without further comments — especially since von Soden himself has suggested new readings in his Akkadisches Handwörterbuch (AHW), as does also the Chicago Assyrian Dictionary (CAD). So even when we are largely dependent upon von Soden's edition, we have also considered later comments.

a) The Death-Dream of Enkidu

1. The Text

1.1 Introduction

1.1.1 Editions

The Death-Dream of Enkidu is a part of the Gilgamesh Epic. In the composition from Nineveh it is written on tablet VII, column iv, lines 11-54. The main edition of the epic is still R.C. Thompson: The Epic of Gilgamish, Oxford 1930. The text is mainly established on the basis of the Neo-Assyrian tablets from Kuyuncik, Nineveh (K. 2589; K. 3389; K. 8590 and 79-7-8,355 concerning our text). Since then there have been discovered more tablets containing our text, but no new edition, which considers all the fragments, has been published. A survey of the situation concerning the whole epic was given by K. Hecker, Untersuchungen zur akkadischen Epik, AOAT, Neukirchen-Vluyn 1974, pp. 26-30. The new tablets containing our text are as follows:

CT 46,24.25: Published by W.G. Lambert in CTBT 46, 1965, plate XXXI.

UET VI 394: Published by C.J. Gadd and S.N. Kramer in UET VI, second part, 1966, plates 278f. The text is transliterated by C.J. Gadd, "Some Contributions to the Gilgamesh Epic", Iraq 28, 1966, pp. 105-121.

Of special importance for our text is the publication of B. Landsberger's notes to the epic "Zur vierten und siebenten Tafel des Gilgames-Epos", RA 62, 1968, pp. 128-135. Here we find a transliteration and a collocation of most of the tablets to our text: The tablets already considered by Thompson in his transliteration; CT 46,24 and UET 394. We also find the transliteration of a fragment published in Thompson's plate 27 of cuneiform texts

79-7-8,320 and now correctly placed; and a new unpublished tablet from
K. 9196 Kuyuncik.

1.1.2 Translations

A survey of the translations is given by K. Hecker, Untersuchungen, p. 26. The problem with these translations is that some of the new discovered fragments were not taken into consideration. That is crucial for our text, because the middle part of the dream is either very badly preserved or not at all preserved in the earlier tablets. Hecker does not mention the translation in the third edition of ANET, 1969, p. 87. This seems to be the most up to date translation of our text. — N.K. Sandars, The Epic of Gilgamesh, PC, London 1972, is to be considered as a retelling rather than a translation. But the tablets 79-7-8,320; CT 46,24.25 and K. 9196 seem not to be considered in this translation. This is crucial for the translation of lines 20-27 in our text.

1.1.3   Working Method

Since there is no edition which contains all the tablets to our text, it is necessary to establish a new text. This concerns lines 11-27 in the Nineveh version where most of the new fragments fit in. From line 31-54 we use the transliteration given by Thompson as our basic text. Lines 28-30 are not preserved in any tablet.
As the basis for our text in lines 11-27 we use the following tablets and transliterations:
K. 2589
K. 3389
K. 8590
79-7-8,355
These tablets are considered by Thompson in his transliteration and by Landsberger in his collocation and transliteration of the tablets.

UET VI 394
This tablet is transliterated by Gadd (Iraq 28, pp. 105ff) and partially by Landsberger.

79-7-8,320
CT 46,24
K. 9196
These tablets are transliterated by Landsberger (CT 46,24 only to line 17 in the Nineveh version).

CT 46,24 (lines 18, 18A, 19)
These lines were transliterated for me personally by Dr. S. Dalley, Oxford University.

As said above, I do not find it necessary to give a new transliteration of lines 31-54. In addition to the tablets already considered by Thompson, there is only one new tablet: CT 46,25. This tablet has few differences compared with Thompson's transliteration: One new reading in line 47 and one in line 46 (the last one is to be considered as a scribal error).
In our rendering of the transliterated text we do not aim to establish a sort of original text. Obviously there have been different text-traditions. In the tablets mentioned above there are slightly differences between the Ur-text (UET 394) and the Nineveh tablets. And if we also consider the Megiddo fragments (transliterated and translated by Landsberger, pp. 131-132), we have yet another text-tradition. Our aim is to try to establish the main Neo-Assyrian text-tradition represented by the tablets found in the late Assyrian library.

1.2   New Text to Lines 11-27

1.2.1   The Transliterated Text

11 [xxx ᵈEn-ki] -dù mar-ṣa-tu ka-ras-su
12 [xxxx-t] i it-ta-lu e-da-nu-uš-šu
13 [i-ta-am-mu] mim-mu-ú kab-ta-ti-šú ana eb-ri-šu

14 [ši-te-me eb-ri] šu-na-ta aṭ-ṭul mu-ši-ti-ya
15 il-su-ú AN-e qaq-qa-ru i-pul
16 ina bi-ri-šu-nu az-za-zi a-na-ku
17 šá 1-en eṭ-lu uk-ku-lu pa-nu-šú
18 a-na ša an-zi-e pa-nu-šu maš-lu
19 rit-ti UR.MAH rit-ta-a-šu ṣu-pur a-ri-e ṣu-pur-a-šu
20 iṣ-bat-ma qim-ma-ti-yá u-dan-ni-na-an-ni ya-a-ši
21 am-ḫas-su-ma kīma kep-pi-e i-šaḫ-ḫi-iṭ
22 im-ḫaṣ-an-ni-ma ki-ma [x(x)] -x-mu uṭ-ṭib-ba-an-ni
23 ki-ma ri-i-mi ú- [kab] -'bi-is' eli-ya
24 ni-tam il-ta-ma-a [ka]l pag-ri-ya
25 šu-zib-an-ni eb-ri [ul tu-še-zi] -ib- [an-ni]
26 tap-laḫ-ma ul [
27 at-ta 'x(y)' [

1.2.2   Text-Critical Notes

11. Text represented by K. 3389.

12. The text is represented by K. 3389. The transliteration is taken from Landsberger. Thompson reads ú at the end of the first uncertain signs, as does von Soden, "Beiträge zum Verständnis des babylonischen Gilgameš-Epos", ZA N.F. 19, p. 228, who with Böhl, Het Gilgamesj Epos, Amsterdam 1958, at the beginning of the line suggests the restoration: [ki-i ina mayyālī-š] ú.
The Ur-version represents another text-tradition, which can not be harmonized with the Nineveh version:
UET 394, line 57: dEn-ki-dù a-šib e-din-[ni]-šu

13. The text is restored on basis of K. 3389 and UET 394. At the beginning of the line the signs are missing in K. 3389. Landsberger thinks he sees i as the first sign. Since the second and the third word in K. 3389 and UET 394 are similar, we find it probable that the first word is similar too. At the beginning of UET 394 Landsberger restores [i-ta-am]-mu. A form of the verb amû (Gt-stem) would suite well in the context, so we have considered this reading as a probability in K. 3389 as well.
After line 13 the Ur-version has a line 13A, which comes instead of the two last words in K. 3389: [i-qa-]ba-aš-šu ana ša-šu.

14. The text is found both in K. 3389, UET 394 and CT 46,24 with slight differences. The signs are missing at the beginning of K. 3389. In both UET 394 and CT 46,24 the line seems to begin with a form of the verb šemû (CT 46,24: "Vage Spuren" — Landsberger), followed by the noun ebri (akk.). We have restored the beginning after Landsberger's suggestion to CT 46,24.

15. The signs are missing at the beginning of K. 3389. But CT 46,24 has clearly il-su-ú and traces of the same verb can be seen in 79-7-8,320 and UET 394.

16. The signs are missing at the beginning of K. 3389. The first clear sign is -nu. Both CT 46,24 and UET 394 have: ina bi-ri-šu-nu, at the beginning of the line, and the beginning of the same phrase can be seen 79-7-8,355.

17. The signs are missing at the beginning of K. 3389. Von Soden suggests the restoration: iš-ten eṭlu (with support from Landsberger). This restoration has support from CT 46,24 and partly from 79-7-8,355. At the beginning of the line 79-7-8,355 has clearly šá (traces also in CT 46,24).

18. The signs are missing at the beginning of K. 3389. (The first clear word is
     panūšu). The line is best preserved in CT 46,24, but traces of it can also be
     read in UET 394, line 63 (Gadd).

19. The signs are missing at the beginning of K. 3389. (The first clear word is
     supur). The line can be restored from the other versions which seems to
     have the same text: CT 46,24, lines 19-20; UET 394, lines 65-66.

20. The signs are missing at the beginning of K. 3389. (The first clear word is
     the verb udanninanni). Traces of the line are represented both in 79-7-
     8,320; CT 46,24; K. 9196; UET 394. As far as one can judge from the traces,
     they seem to have the same text, except that CT 46,24 and UET 394 have
     the suffix for 1. pers. sing. at the end of the noun qimmātū, which is
     omitted in K. 9196; and that K. 9196 also omits enclitic -ma at the end of
     the first verb, which is represented in UET 394 and most probably in 79-7-
     8,320. It seems as if K. 9196 is somewhat special here, giving a slightly
     shorter text.

21. The text is restored from K. 3389; 79-7-8,320; CT 46,24; K. 9196 by
     Landsberger. K. 3389 has only the last part of the word keppi (gen.) and the
     last verb (after Thompson).

22. The text is restored from K. 3389; 79-7-8,320; CT 46,24; K. 9196 by
     Landsberger. The only certain word in K. 3389 is the last verb (after
     Thompson). Landsberger reads the last verb as uttibbanni from ṭâbu. We
     have rendered the transliteration by Thompson: uṭṭibbanni from ṭebû. Cf.
     note 22a to the translation.

23. The text is restored from K. 3389 and K. 9196 by Landsberger. K. 3389 has
     only the last word (after Thompson).

24. The text is restored from K. 3389 and K. 9196 by Landsberger. K. 3381
     contains only the last word (after Thompson).

25. The text is restored from K. 9196 (some traces from K. 3389) by Landsber-
     ger.

26. The text is transliterated from K. 9196 by Landsberger.

27. Text from K. 9196 by Landsberger.

1.3   Translation of the Death-Dream of Enkidu

1.3.1   The Translation

11 [Enki] du, whose mood is bitter,
12 [   ]a lies down all alone.
13 [He tells]a all his troubles to his friend:
14 [Keep listening, friend!]a I saw a dream during my nighttimeb:

15 The heaven howled, the earth echoed.
16 I was standing between them.

17 One Man, whose face was dark,a
18 whose face was similar to that of an Anzu-birda,
19 his hands the paws of a lion, his fingernails the claws of an eagle.

20 He seized my forelock and strove for superiority[a] over me.
21 I hit him and he leaps like a <u>skipping rope</u>[a].
22 He hit me and made me sink[a] like [   ].
23 Like a wild bull he tr[ampl]ed on me.
24 He held round my whole body with a firm grip.

25 "Save me, my friend!" [But you did not save me.][a]
26 You feared and did not [
27 You [
   (line 28-30 is missing on all tablets)
31 [   ][a] he transformed me.
32 [   ] my arms like those of a bird.
33 [   ][a] me, he leads me
   to the house of Darkness, the dwelling-place of Irkalla[b],
34 to the house that they who enter, do not leave,
35 to the road whose way does not return,
36 to the house where the dwellers lack light,
37 where their sustenance (is) dust and their food (is) clay,
38 clothed like birds with wing-feathers for garments.
39 They see no light, dwelling in the darkness.

40 In the ho[use of dust] which I entered,
41 I loo[ked[a]   ][b], crowns were gathered together,
42 [   ][a] those of the crowns who had ruled the country from ancient days.
43 [The substitutes][a] of Anu and Enlil were serving roasted meat.
44 They were serving [   ] and pouring cool water from waterskins.

45 In the house of dust which I entered,
46 resided the first priest and the temple-servant[a],
47 resided the purification priest and the high priest[a],
48 resided the chief priests[a] of the great gods,
49 resided Etana, resided Sumuqan,
50 [resided] the queen of the nether world[a], Ereškigal.
51 [Belet]-Șeri, the scribe of the nether world,
   kneeling before her,
52 [hol]ding [a tablet][a], she reads out before her.
53 [Lifting up][a] her head, she looked at me:
54 [Saying: "Who][a] has brought this one here?"

(The remainder of the tablet in the Assyrian Version is missing.)

1.3.2   Notes to the Translation

12 a.   Von Soden suggests with Böhl the restoration: <u>kî ina mayyālīšu</u> (cf. note
        to line 11). The whole phrase could then be translated: . . . "because he lies
        down on his bed all alone."

13 a.   For the restoration, cf. text-critical note to line 13.

14 a.   The beginning is restored after CT 46,24, cf. text-critical note to line 14.
     b. In the text one should have expected the determinative pronoun <u>ša</u> before
        the genitive <u>mušītīya</u>. This is lacking in K. 3389, but is written in UET
        394.

17 a.   One should have expected the genitive after <u>šá</u>, but Neo-Assyrian tablets
        often do not consider the case-endings. Grammatically <u>šá</u> seems to
        introduce a proleptic genitive. Cf. GAG § 138 1.

18 a.   Cf. below, pp. 374f.

20 a.   The verb is danānu (to become strong). The form must be the preterite of
        the Dt-stem, even though one d is missing at the beginning of the word.
        For the meaning "strive for superiority", cf. CAD sub danānu, p. 86.

21 a.   The Akkadian word is taken by Landsberger as keppû. He translates
        "Springschnur" (skipping rope). Cf. also his article: "Einige unerkannt
        gebliebene oder verkannte Nomina des Akkadischen", WZKM 56, 1960,
        p. 121f. Cf. also sub keppû: CAD pr. 312; AHW, p. 467. S. Dalley gives
        this opinion (with permission): "Landsberger, WZKM 56, p. 121f.,
        supposed that keppû "the toy/game of Ishtar" was a skipping rope. This
        was based on his understanding of a motif that occurs on cylinder seals,
        but that motif is not now considered to show a skipping rope. : it is the
        fringe of a robe. Therefore keppû must be some other game or toy. In
        any event, the translation "skipping rope" made nonsense in the context
        of Gilgamesh Tablet VII col. iv l. 21.

22 a.   The Akkadian form is uttibbanni with or without the emphatic ṭ (ṭ).
        Landsberger derives the verb from ṭâbu, cf. text-critical note to line 22.
        He translates: . . . "heilte er mich". Three derivations seem possible: ṭâbu,
        "do good"; tebû, "stand up"; ṭebû, "sink". To judge from the content
        ṭebû, "sink", is most likely. Several grammatical forms are possible. The
        most likely seems to be the perfect of the D-stem, with the factitive
        meaning "made sink".

22 a.   The restoration is uncertain.

32 a.   The only certain word of the line is the verb uttirranni (D-stem from
        târu, "transform"). Von Soden, "Beiträge", restores: [ana] su!-um[-mi ia-]
        a-ši ut-ter-ra-an-ni. He translates: "in einem Tauberich verwandelte er
        mich".

33 a.   Thompson put a question mark with the first syllable, which makes the
        whole transliteration uncertain. Speiser has obviously another translitera-
        tion. He translates: "Looking at me".
    b. Irkalla is a name for the nether world. It comes from Sumerian eri-gal,
        which means "big city". Cf. W. Röllig, "Irkalla", RLA V, Berlin-New
        York 1977, p. 164; and K. Tallqvist, Sumerisch-akkadische Namen der
        Totenwelt, StOr 5/4, Helsingfors 1934, pp. 34f.

41 a.   Another syntax is possible, taking ana bit epri as complement to appalis.
        naplasu ana can have the meaning "look at", cf. AHW sub palāsu, p. 814.
        The translation would then be: "I looked at the house of dust, which I
        had entered". But our translation is preferable because line 40 seems to
        have the same syntax as line 45.
    b. Speiser restores and translates the line: "I looked at [rulers], their crowns
        put away." The translation "their crowns" would demand the reading
        agūšunu, but the text has clearly agū without the suffix. The second part
        of the line is to be translated: "crowns were gathered together", cf. CAD
        sub kamāsu A, p. 117.

42 a.   Speiser restores: "I saw princes".

43 a.   At the beginning of the line Speiser restores: [di-n]a-an, from dinānu,
        which means "substitute", cf. CAD sub dinānu, p. 148. Unfortunately it
        is not quite clear who is designated in this way. Most likely it is the kings
        who seem to be presupposed in the lines before (so Speiser).

46 a. Ct 46,25 has u̱ lā magāri instead of u̱ lagaru. magāru means "to be disobedient". The form would here be the infinitive. The translation would be: "and not disobedience". The reading does not make sense in the context and is to be considered as a scribal error.

47 a. Thompson transliterates: maḫ-ḫu (ecstatic), accompanied with the determinative for man: lú. CT 46,25 shows that lú here not is to be considered as a determinative, but as the first syllable: lu-maḫ-ḫu, "a priest of high rank".

48 a. The Sumeriogram UH.ME.ZU.ABP[l] rendered by Thompson is to be read gudapšû, cf. von Soden, "Beiträge". The meaning is "chief priest", cf. CAD sub gudapšû, p. 119.

50 a. The akkadian word is erṣetu, which literally means "earth". Often it is used as a designation for "the nether world", cf. note 42a to the translation of the Vision of the Nether World.

52 a. Von Soden restores [ṭup-pa na-] šat, "holding a tablet", at the beginning of the line.

53 a. We restore našât, stative feminine from našû, as also Speiser does.

54 a. Restoration as Speiser.

2. Analysis of Content

2.1 Description of Structure and Content

The text begins with an introduction which gives information about the reception and the telling of the dream: Section A, lines 11-14. This section is formed in the 3rd person. The dream report which follows is formed in the 1st person from line 15 to line 54 where the report breaks off.

The dream report begins with two opening lines which reveal the atmosphere of the vision: Section B, lines 15-16 (formed in the preterite followed by the present tense). Enkidu is placed in the open, in a furious thunder storm.

The next section, C, lines 17-32, begins with introducing the first figure of the vision: "One man", ištēn eṭlu, from the nether world. The first part of this section (lines 17-19) contains the description of this man (formed in stative clauses, lines 17-18 and a nominal clause, line 19). The next part contains the fight between this man and Enkiu (clearly marked by the use of verbal clauses). It describes a course of events. The report about the fight is interrupted by a cry from Enkidu to Gilgamesh for help, followed by a statement that Gilgamesh did not help (lines 25-30?). The outcry seems to presuppose that Gilgamesh was accompanying Enkidu in his dream, although this is not confirmed elsewhere. The description of the fight continues after the interruption, the man is transforming Enkidu into a "bird".

Then follows the description of the descent: Section D, lines 33-39. (The section begins and ends with composed verbal clauses, the part in between has the stative.) This section has a clear poetic structure. The lines 33B-36 all begin with *ana* followed by a noun indicating the end of the journey. The lines 37-39 are formed in *parallelismus membrorum*.

The two following sections are marked with the same opening line, Section E, lines 40-44; Section F, lines 45-54 (?): "In the house of dust which I entered".

The first part of section E seems to describe the fate of the previous kings (lines 41-42). The next part (lines 43-44, formed in verbal clauses) describes a course of events, the royalties are holding a banquet in the nether world.

Section F is also divided in two parts. The first (lines 45-49(50)) has a clear poetic structure. Each line (from line 46) begins with the verb *ašābu* in the stative, followed by *parallelismus membrorum*. The structure of line 50 is uncertain. Since the line contains no verbal elements in the words preserved, it is reasonable to expect a verb at the beginning of the line. The line has then the same structure as the previous lines, only without *parallelismus membrorum*. The description of the dwellers in the nether world then ends with the queen Ereshkigal as the climax. The nest part (lines 51-54(?)) is marked by the introduction of a new figure, Belet-Ṣeri. The part is distinct from the previous one in that it describes a course of events (formed in composed verbal clauses). The content is the judgement in the nether world. The part ends with Ereshkigal becoming aware of the entry of Enkidu. The last question seems to indicate surprise. Does Enkidu arrive too early?

Understood this way, three of the sections seem to have the same structure. They begin with a description formed in stative clauses, followed by a report of a course of events formed in verbal clauses:

Section C
Description: The man
Course of events: The fight

Section E
Description: The kings
Course of events: The banquet

Section F
Description: The priests and Ereshkigal
Course of events: The judgement

The whole text contains the following sections and parts:

A (lines 11-14): Introduction to the vision

B (lines 15-16): Opening of the vision

C (lines 17-32): The man
  1. (lines 17-19): Description of the man
  2. (lines 20-24): The fight
  3. (lines 25-30?): Cry for help
  4. (lines 31-34): Transformation

D (lines 33-39): The descent to the nether world

E (lines 40-44): The kings and the banquet of the nether world
  1. (lines 40-41): Description of the kings
  2. (lines 43-44): The banquet

F (lines 45-54?): The dwellers and the judgement of the nether world
  1. (lines 46-50): Description of the dwellers and the goddess
  2. (lines 51-54?): The judgement

2.2   The Gattung

The text contains a first section which is formed in the 3rd person and the following sections in the 1st person. The first section forms a framework which both incorporates the following sections in the whole epic and introduces them. The text is introduced as a "night-dream": *šunata aṭṭul mušitīya* (I saw a dream during my night-time), line 14.

In his analysis of dreams in the Ancient Near East A.L. Oppenheim[1] describes two main types: The message dream and the symbolic dream. Both types consist of a framework and a dream report as seen in our dream above.[2] Message dreams are defined as follows: They ... "contain without exception a divine message

---

1   A.L. Oppenheim, The Interpretation of Dreams in the Ancient Near East, TAPhS 46/3, 1966.
2   Oppenheim, pp. 186f.

(command or warning) couched in clearly understandable terms which do not necessitate interpretation".[3] The symbolic dreams are different: ... "the 'symbolic' dream of the Ancient Near East is considered a "message" dream with its message not expressed in clear words but transmitted in a specific way by which certain selected elements of the message, such as persons, key-words, actions, etc., are replaced by other elements". The symbolic dream therefore needs interpretation.[4]

The Death-Dream of Enkidu does not fit clearly into any of these two types. Oppenheim writes: ... "neither is it a symbolic dream, nor does it seem to contain a message, but the latter cannot be proved because of the break. Typologically it might best be characterized again as a case of clairvoyance on the level of the dream, a clairvoyance which concerns the future as against the other clairvoyance-dream of Enkidu".[5] The other dream referred to by Oppenheim (in the edition of ANET[3], Tabl. VII, lines 1-15) contains a description of how Enkidu sees and hears the great gods deliberate in their heavenly assembly and decide that he has to die.[6] What links the two dreams together, is that they both contain a vision of another world which reveals the future death of Enkidu, but there are no stylistic similarities.

The dream that comes closest to the Death-Dream of Enkidu is "A Vision of the Nether World" (cf. for text and discussion nest chapter). In both dreams the visionary sees his own future death. One might therefore ask if such dreams could form a separate type of dreams, called "death-dreams".

There are two Sumerian dreams which seem to have a similar theme. The one is "Dumuzi's Dream".[7] In this dream the god Dumuzi gets a premonition of his death. He sees several signs which are interpreted as forewarnings: He is going to be a victim of the demons from the nether world. The dream combines symbolic with non-symbolic elements. Like the two Akkadian

---

3 Oppenheim, p. 191.
4 Oppenheim, p. 206.
5 Oppenheim, pp. 213f.
6 For description, cf. Oppenheim, p. 196. For translation, cf. ANET[3], pp. 85-86.
7 For text, translation and commentary, cf. B. Alster, Dumuzi's Dream. Aspects of Oral Poetry in a Sumerian Myth, Mesopotamia 1, Copenhagen 1972. For description, cf. also Oppenheim, p. 212, and T. Jacobsen, The Treasures of Darkness. A History of Mesopotamian Religion, Yale 1976, pp. 48f.

death-dreams it contains a vision of the visionary's future fate, but
unlike these the figures of the dream are represented by symbols
which need interpretation.

The other dream is called "The Death of Gilgamesh".[8] The
problem is that the text is very badly preserved. As published by
S.N. Kramer it is based on two tablets. The first tablet seems to
have contained a prediction of Gilgamesh's future fate and a
description of his death. The other tablet seems to have dealt with
Gilgamesh in the nether world. On the first tablet it is indicated
two places that a dream is involved. This is in line 34: "— O lord
Gilgamesh, the *meaning* of the dream (is)";[9] and in lines 80-81:
"After its ... had been interpreted ... which he interpreted to
them".[10] Thus a possible interpretation of the whole text is that it
begins with a dream where Gilgamesh sees his future fate which
also includes his death, then comes the interpretation of the dream
by a deity, then the description of the fulfillment of the dream,
first in Gilgamesh's death and then in his descent to the nether
world.

If this interpretation is correct, it seems possible that the whole
text has the same outline as the text to which Dumuzi's Dream
belongs. The last one contains the following basic elements:
Dumuzi has a dream (lines 15-18); he calls for his sister and relates
the dream to her (lines 19-40); she interprets the dream as an
omen foreboding his death (lines 49-69); the dream is fulfilled (the
end: lines 250-261).[11]

We will then have the following common elements in these two
Sumerian dream-stories:

1. Dream report
2. Interpretation
3. Fulfillment

If, however, we compare the two Sumerian dream reports with the
Akkadian death-dreams, there is not enough evidence to suppose

---

8   For text, translation and description, cf. S.N. Kramer, "The Death of Gilgamesh", BASOR 94, 1944, pp. 2-12. For translation and notes, cf. also ANET[3],
pp. 50-3.
9   The translation is taken from Kramer.
10   The translation is taken from Kramer.
11   The analysis is taken from Alster, p. 37.

that these dreams together represent a special Gattung. compared to the Akkadian dreams, Dumuzi's Dream has quite another structure because it is partly a symbolic dream, and in the content the only similarity is that the deputies of the nether world are overwhelming Dumuzi. There is not an actual description of the descent to and the conditions in the nether world.

Concerning the Death of Gilgamesh it is difficult to draw firm conclusions about the actual content. But the dream does not seem to have contained a description of the nether world as the Akkadian dreams. This comes first in the report about the fulfillment of the dream.

But even though these dreams do not have enough features in common to represent a distinct Gattung of their own, they all seem to refer to the same sort of experience and contain the same main motif. The experience is what Oppenheim calls "clairvoyance on the level of the dream",[12] and the motif is the visionary's death. This common theme, the forewarning of the destructive future of the visionary, makes it worth while considering them together.

2.3   The Traditions about the Nether World

Our considerations have led to the conclusion that the structure and basic elements of the Death-Dream of Enkidu are not dependent upon a Gattung-pattern common in other dreams. The background must therefore be sought in other Gattungen. As it will be shown, descriptions of the nether world are represented in several text-types.[13]

I.   A description of a descent to and the conditions in the nether world is given at the end of the Epic of Gilgamesh, Tabl. XII.[14] The text tells about the death of Enkidu and does not fit in the context of the rest of the epic where Enkidu's death occurs under

12   Oppenheim, p. 196.
13   We use the same criteria for classification as S.N. Kramer, "Sumerian Lite-rature. A General Survey", The Bible and the Ancient Near East. Essays in honor of W.G. Albright, New York 1961, pp. 249-66.
14   Cf. ANET[3], p. 97 for introduction to and translation of the Akkadian text. Cf. also the note on p. 507 in ANET[3].

quite different circumstances. It has long been realised that this tablet was taken by the Akkadian author from a Sumerian source. The Sumerian poem was published by S.N. Kramer and given the name "Gilgamesh, Enkidu and the Nether World".[15] The text on Tabl. XII of the Epic of Gilgamesh is taken from the second part of this poem.

The story of the Sumerian poem, briefly sketched, runs as follows: Once upon a time there was a ḫuluppu-tree (a willow?), planted on the banks of Euphrates, it was nurtured by the waters of the river. But it was blown down and flooded. Thereafter the goddess Inanna found it and brought it to Erech, and she planted it in her holy garden. There she tended it most carefully. For when the tree grew big, she planned to make of its wood a chair for herself and a couch. But when the tree had grown big, Inanna found herself unable to cut it down. For at its base the snake had built its nest, in its crown the Anzu-bird had placed its young, in the middle Lilith, the desert demon, had built its house. After the sun-god Utu had refused to help Inanna, Gilgamesh came to her rescue. With a big axe he slew the snake and the Anzu-bird and the demon Lilith flew away. Out of the tree were made two objects called pukkû and mikkû (the meaning is uncertain[16]).
Playing with these tools, Gilgamesh lost them into the nether world through a hole in the ground. Now Enkidu, Gilgamesh's servant, offered him help: He could descend to the nether world and collect the tools. Gilgamesh instructed him about the rules of the nether world, but Enkidu did the reverse of what he had been told. He was then seized by the nether world and unable to reascend. Because of the plea of Gilgamesh, however, the shade of Enkidu was allowed to ascend to the earth. Enkidu then revealed for Gilgamesh the conditions in the nether world.

The exact meaning of the poem is not easy to understand. Like most of the stories in the Gilgamesh-cycle, it seems to have a variegated mythological background. T. Jacobsen traces two lines in the early Gilgamesh-traditions, one where the focus is on Gilgamesh's relation to the nether world, and another where the

---

15 For the text, translation and comments on the first half of the poem, cf. S.N. Kramer, Gilgamesh and the Ḫuluppu-tree, AS 10, Chicago 1938. For description of the whole poem and translation of the second half, cf. S.N. Kramer, Sumerian Mythology, Philadelphia 1944 (paperback ed. 1972), pp. 30-8.
16 T. Jacobsen translates "puck" and "stick" instead of the traditional "drum" and "drumstick". He thinks the objects are tools used in a game which seems to have resembled modern hockey, cf. Treasures, p. 212. An interpretation which goes in quite another direction suggests K. Oberhuber with reference to M. Eliade: The shamans made their drum of wood from the cosmic tree (Weltbaum) ... "Da sein Trommelkasten von dem Holz des Weltbaumes selbst genommen ist, wird der Schamane beim Trommeln auf magische Weise an den Weltbaum versetz ... Es kommt dabei genau so zu Gesängen der Schamanen von ekstatischen Himmelreisen und gefährliche Unterweltsfahrten". Cf. K. Oberhuber, "Gilgamesh", Das Gilgamesh-Epos, WdF 215, Darmstadt 1977, pp. 9-12.

focus is on Gilgamesh's heroic deeds.[17] He ascribes our text to the first line. The background of this tradition he sees in the worshipping of the dead *en* priests in the ancient Sumer. But since the text talks about the death of Enkidu and not of Gilgamesh, the adaptation of the text in the Gilgamesh-traditions seems fairly uncertain.

II.   Among the myths there are three which deals explicitly with the nether world. Two of them are related, that is the Sumerian "Inanna's Descent to the Nether World" and the Semitic "Ishtar's Descent to the Nether World".[18]

The Sumerian myth runs briefly as follows: Inanna, the queen of heaven, desires for an unknown reason to descend to the nether world. For that purpose she dresses in splendid array and puts on all her regalia. Before she leaves she gives her maid Ninshubur instructions about what to do if she does not come back; which gods to appeal to and what she must say to them. On her way through the nether world to the queen Ereshkigal, Inanna has to pass seven gates. At each gate a functionary removes one of Inanna's ornaments or pieces of clothing. Inanna at last arrives before Ereshkigal crouched and stripped bare (just as the ancients were buried). But then she pulls Ereshkigal from her throne and sits on it herself. She has, however, not reckoned with the powerful Anunnaki-gods. They sit in judgement on her and condemn her to death. When she is killed, she turns into a piece of meat hung on a peg in the wall. After being aware that things have gone wrong, Ninshubur, Inanna's maiden, appeals to the gods that they must help Inanna. Enlil and Nanna consider the case as hopeless, but the wise Enki finds a solution. He makes two creatures who, using the rules for hospitality, trick Ereshkigal to bring Inanna back to life.[19] But Inanna is not allowed to ascend from the nether world without offering a substitute. Inanna then ascends together with demons from the nether world and travels around seeking this substitute. At last they find her husband, Dumuzi, who had not been mourning for Inanna's death like the other gods; on the contrary he was enjoying himself thoroughly, sitting in noble raiment on a noble seat. Dumuzi is then handed over to the demons who will carry him to the nether world. (The text of the myth then breaks off.)

Both A. Falkenstein and T. Jacobsen interpret the myth on the background of the Sumerian fertility cult.[20] According to Falkenstein the starting point of the myth is Dumuzi's stay in the

17   Jacobsen, pp. 208-213.
18   For Inanna's Descent, cf. the translation and the notes in ANET[3], pp. 52-7. In an introductory note S.N. Kramer also gives a description of a new tablet which is not considered in the translation. For Ishtar's Descent, cf. the translation in ANET[3], pp. 106-9. Both myths are partly translated and commented on by A. Falkenstein, "Der sumerische und der akkadische Mythos von Inannas Gang zur Unterwelt", Festschrift Werner Caskel, Leiden 1968, pp. 96-110.
19   Cf. A.D. Kilmer, "How was Queen Ereskigal tricked? A New Interpretation of the Descent of Ishtar", UF 3, 1971, pp. 299-309.
20   Cf. A. Falkenstein above, note 18, and Jacobsen, op.cit., pp. 55-63.

nether world. The shepherd Dumuzi is the god of the spring vegetation and in the hot months of the summer he falls into the nether world. First after the rain in the late autumn when the fields again are green, he is revived and again with his herd. The myth offers then an explanation why Dumuzi had to go to the nether world.

The third myth "Nergal and Ereshkigal" is known from two versions, one from Amarna and one from Sultantepe, of which the latter is the larger and the better preserved.[21] It tells, in brief, how Nergal, one of the gods in heaven, became the king of the nether world. The meaning of the myth apart from this theological intention, is difficult to interpret.

III.   The third Gattung where we have descriptions of the nether world, is the lamentations. A special type of lamentation is found on a Sumerian tablet published by S.N. Kramer.[22] On the tablet Kramer found two elegies, inscribed about 1700 B.C., which were the only ones of this kind discovered from Sumer. In the first a son laments his father who possibly has died from wounds received in some kind of struggle. In the second the same man bewails the death of his wife, who seems to have died a natural death. Most of the content is a description of the deathbed and an expression of loss and sorrow among the left-behind. But we also find especially in the first elegy a very interesting description of the nether world (lines 87-98).

Among the other types of lamentation we find descriptions of the nether world especially in those dealing with the death of the god Dumuzi or one of his counterparts.[23] The central theme in these lamentations is the same as in Dumuzi's Dream and the Descent of Inanna: the death of the fertility deity and his descent to, and stay in, the nether world. The setting of these lamentations is quite clear: they belong to the fertility cult.

---

21   Cf. ANET[3], pp. 103-4 and pp. 507-12. For analysis of the content, cf. E. von Weiher, Der babylonische Gott Nergal, AOAT 11, Neukirchen-Vluyn 1971, pp. 48-56.

22   S.N. Kramer, Two Elegies on a Puskin Museum Tablet. A New Sumerian Literary Genre, Moscow 1960. Cf. also his description in "Death and Nether World According to the Sumerian Literary Texts", Iraq 22, 1960, pp. 59-68, esp. pp. 61ff.

23   For translation and interpretation, cf. Jacobsen, op.cit., p. 49-55.

Another Sumerian composition which is very difficult to categorize
is given the name "The Death of Ur-Nammu and his Descent to
the Nether World".[24] The text has much in common with the
elegies and the cultic lamentations: the description of the death,
the loss and sorrow, the descent to and stay in the nether world.
But the style is different. Besides the Death of Gilgamesh (cf.
above), the closest known parallel in style seems to be the
historiographic text known as "The Curse of Agade".[25] This text
also reflects the end of a famous Akkadian king, Naram-Sin. Our
text is written by a poet who is deeply affected by the death of
Ur-Nammu, another of Sumer's great kings.

The poem begins to describe the fear and terror of Sumer and Ur as a consequence of the death of Ur-Nammu who was carried off to the nether world. The
reason for this was that the gods Anu and Enlil had changed their will against
the righteous king. As a result of the great misery is brought upon Sumer. The
poet then turns to the description of the death and burial of the king, followed
by a description of the nether world: First the king holds a banquet for the dead,
then he offers gifts to the leading deities; afterwards the judges of the nether
world determine the fate of Ur-Nammu, among the judges we also find Gilgamesh. But after a while the king begins to bewail his unjust fate. The goddess
Inanna is aware of the injustice, and possibly she blesses the king. (The remainder of the text is fragmentary and its content unintelligible.)

Kramer dates the text not long after the actual death of Ur-
Nammu (about 2000 B.C.). Besides the myth Inanna's Descent to
the Nether World it is the largest and best preserved Sumerian text
about the nether world.

The traditions about the nether world do not belong to any one
particular Gattung, as has been shown. They are used in different
settings and serve different purposes. This is no late development,
since the traditions are widespread already in the Sumerian texts.
It should, however, be possible to consider the different layers in
the history of tradition. If Falkenstein is correct in his understanding of the descent — myths, they offer a sort of theological
interpretation of Dumuzi's stay in the nether world. It is then
obvious that the mythic conception of Dumuzi's stay in the nether
world comes first chronologically. This mythic conception seems to

24   For text, description and notes, cf. S.N. Kramer, "The Death of Ur-Nammu
and his Descent to the Netherworld", JCS 21, 1961, pp. 104-22. For description,
cf. also Kramer, "Death and Nether World", pp. 59-61.
25   Cf. ANET[3], pp. 646-51.

be reflected in the lamentations of Dumuzi's death which had a cultic setting.

The same sort of consideration is also possible concerning Dumuzi's Dream. The course of events narrated there, is also narrated in the cultic lamentations. Also Dumuzi's Dream presupposes the mythic concept of the death of Dumuzi.

If we go on to the elegies, they reflect another setting. They are part of the funeral rites used in the burial of individuals. The same background is reflected in the Death of Gilgamesh and the Descent of Ur-Nammu. In the last text we have not only a reflection of the lamentations connected with the burial, but also a description of the actual burial itself, accompanied by offering to the underworld-deities.

The epic "Gilgamesh, Enkidu and the Nether World" reflects variegated mythological material. The complex character of the epic shows that it has not been a creative source for the under-world traditions. The same can be said about the myth "Nergal and Ereshkigal" of which the main purpose seems to be theological.

In the case of the Death-Dream of Enkidu it is difficult to say anything definite about the age of the text, except that the Ur tablet which seems to have contained the whole text, is dated at about 1100.[26] From the content, however, it is clear that most of the elements of the dream have their parallels in the other underworld-texts. The dream reflects in fact a broad tradition about the nether world, so it seems to be a later composition compared with most of the other texts.

Our considerations have then shown (not surprisingly) that the traditions seem to have had two centres of gravity from the beginning. The one is the lamentations associated with the cult of the dying deity. The other is the funeral rites used for individuals. These two centres of gravity represents man's encounter with death in nature and in human life.

---

26   C.J. Gadd, "Some Contributions to the Gilgamesh Epic", Iraq 28, 1966, p. 107.

2.4   The Basic Elements of the Dream Report

2.4.1   The Opening of the Vision (Sect. B)

The purpose of the opening line is to describe the reaction in nature when "the powers of death" are breaking into this world. This seems clear from the more detailed parallel in the third dream of Gilgamesh which belongs to the same course of events as our dream:

> And the dream that I saw was wholly awesome!
> The heavens thundered, the earth rumbled,
> [Day]light ceased, darkness advanced.
> Lightning flashed, a fire shot up,
> [The clouds] swelled, it rained death![27]

This report has no parallel in the underworld-texts. They contain mostly a report of the descent to the nether world, not a report of the ascent from there.

The report comes closer to the combat motif in some myths, such as Enuma Elish, Tabl. V,[28] and especially the Myth of Anzu:

> When Anzu heard the word of his mouth,
> In the midst of the mountain range
> he let loose a piercing shriek.
> There was darkness, the face of the
> mountain was covered,
> Ninurta the light of the gods, entered the gloom.
> Adad . . . roared, his thunder pursued Anzu.
> In the midst of the conflict, (in the midst of) the war,
> He launched fourteen storm floods,
> Dressed in armour he bathed in blood,
> Clouds of death sent rain,
> the lightening flashes were arrows.[29]

This and similar combat-scenes reflect the ancients' experiences of the natural forces and especially those phenomena in nature which were experienced as dangerous and frightening. The difference between these texts and the texts about the nether world is that the first group represents what we briefly can call the contrast between cosmos and chaos, while the second group represents the contrast between life and death.

---

27   Epic of Gilgamesh, Tabl. V, col. iv, lines 14-18. Translation in ANET[3], p. 83. For our translation, cf. p. 110, note 42.
28   Cf. for translation, ANET[3], pp. 66-7.
29   Myth of Anzu, Tabl. II, lines 48-55. Translation from ANET[3], p. 515.

But the two conceptions were not far removed from each other. This is evident from the Poem of Erra. The following is a report about the conditions that will appear when Marduk leaves his royal seat:

> I shall rise from my seat
> and the government [of heaven and earth] will be dissolved.
> [The waters] will swell and [devasta]te the country.
> The shining [day will turn] into deep darkness.
> [The st]orm will rise and [blot out?]
> the stars in the sk[y].
> The malign [wind] will blow and [obscure?]
> the eyesight of men, the offspring of the living.
> The gallu (-demons) will come up and . . . will grasp . . .
> The bare-loined man who confronts them . . .
> The Anunnaki will come up and strike down
> the offspring of the living.[30]

The first part of the text describes how chaos will take over in nature. The second part describes how the demons and under-world-gods will ascend,[31] so that death will take over in life. Here, accordingly, the two aspects, cosmos/chaos and life/death, are combined.

Among the underworld-gods described in the Poem of Erra are also the Sibitti (the Seven), cf. Tabl. I, line 23-91. These are evil gods who bring disaster and death upon mankind.[32] According to the incantations collected in the "Utukku lemnuti" series, they live in the Apsu and when they rise from the sea, they bring gloom, clouds and windstorms.[33]

The same is the case in the death-dream of Enkidu. Nature reacts violently when the bringer of death ascends.

2.4.2 The Man from the Nether World (Sect. C)

2.4.2.1 The Description

The designation *ištēn eṭlu* which is used about the man has no parallels in other underworld texts, except the Vision of the

---

30 The Poem of Erra, Tabl. I, lines 170-77. Cf. for introduction, translation and notes, L. Cagni, The Poem of Erra, SANE 1/3, Malibu, California 1974, p. 34.
31 The gallu-demons and Anunnaki-gods ascend from the Apsu (the fresh-water under the earth) which is here a designation for the nether world, cf. Cagni, note 55, p. 35.
32 Cf. the description of the gods in Cagni, pp. 18f.
33 Cf. R.C. Thompson, The Devils and Evil Spirits of Babylonia I, London 1903, pp. 42ff.

Nether World. The parallels to this phrase are found in other dreams, which shows that the phrase belongs too the style in certain dream reports (a detailed analysis of the phrase will be given under the discussion of the Vision of the Nether World).

It is possible that the history of the text can give further support for this consideration. In the oldest known version of the text from Ur it is clear, according to J. Gadd, that the phrase *ištēn eṭlu* is lacking. Gadd thinks he sees traces of the word *āribu* which means "crow" or "raven".[34] Instead of the Neo-Assyrian version which reads: "One man, whose face was dark", the Ur version would then read: "One raven, whose face was dark".[35]

The deputy of darkness is compared with an Anzu-bird. The same sentence: "His face was similar to that of an Anzu-bird", is also found in the description of the man in the Vision of the Nether World, line 50. Here also three of the demons are compared with an Anzu-bird: Ḥumuṭ-ṭabal was provided with the head of an Anzu-bird (line 45B); Utukku had hands and feet of an Anzu-bird (line 46B); the last unnamed monster is partly described as having head, hands and feet of an Anzu-bird (line 48B).

Our text and the Vision of the Nether World can give us some idea of how these Anzu-bird-like figures were imagined. In our text the man has the face similar to an Anzu-bird, hands like the paws of a lion and claws of an eagle. In the Vision of the Nether World Utukku has hands and feet of an Anzu-bird and the head of a lion. Obviously we have here a figure composed of features from the lion and the eagle.

The Anzu-bird concept is under discussion both with regard to the correct rendering and pronunciation of the word, the interpretation of the depictions of the figure, and the understanding of the mythological speculations associated with it.

I. The philological problem
In the Sumeriogram AN.IM.DUGUD.MUŠEN the last word is to be understood as a determinative meaning "bird", the second and the third words can be read

---

34 Cf. Gadd, "Some Contributions", transliteration of line 63, p. 113, and note, p. 115.
35 The phrase ukkulu panūšu does not designate a colour. The verb ekēlu means primarily "to be dark" in the sense "to lack light". It can be used about demons because they belong to and bring darkness. In transferred meaning it can also be said about moods, "sombre". In our text the dark face expresses both that the figure belonged to the realm of darkness and that he had evil intentions. Cf. CAD sub ekēlu, p. 64.

as logograms meaning either "fog" or "thundercloud" (cf. below p. III). Previously the first word AN was understood as a determinative for "god". The
Sumeriogram IM.DUGUD could be read syllabic zu-u in Akkadian. In earlier
transliterations the Sumeriogram was then rendered [d]IM.DUGUD (d for "dingir"
= god), and the Akkadian word [d]Zû.
In 1961 B. Landsberger argued that what had previously been read Zû in
Akkadian and IM.DUGUD in Sumerian was to be read Anzû and Anzu(d)
respectively.[36] The reason for this was that on the one hand he gave AN a
phonological value instead of understanding it as a determinative, while on the
other hand he claimed to have found anzu(d) as a gloss to AN.IM.DUGUD.
MUŠEN in a Sumerian list of gods (Landsberger p. 5). The new reading has
gained acceptance[37] although it has also encountered some skepticism.[38]

II. The art-historical problem

From the beginning of the third millennium a beast appears in Mesopotamian
depictions, composed of features from both an eagle and a lion. The beast has
been characterized as the lion-headed eagle. We find this figure depicted in
sculptures in the round, reliefs, paintings and cylinder seals spread all over the
Middle East.[39]
One of the problems concerning the interpretation of the lion-headed eagle is
that although there are many indications that the beast was associated with the
Anzu-bird, we can not always presuppose such an interpretation.[40] And
certainly it would be arbitrary to interpret each representation of the beast in art
against the background of the myths about Anzu. Another problem is that no
example of the lion-headed eagle (with the traditional Sumerian features) is
found in Assyrian art.[41] This is even more confusing since Anzu-birds are
mentioned in several Assyrian texts.
The Neo-Assyrian king Esarhaddon (680-669), for example, wrote that he
restored the temple of Ishtar in Borsippa and decorated it with "lions, Anzu-
birds, 'roaring storms', Laḫmu-monsters and cherubims".[42]
H. Frankfort thinks that the features of the lion-headed eagle, which was often
believed to be a manifestation of a god (cf. below), were transferred to the god

---

36 B. Landsberger, "Einige unerkannt gebliebene oder verkannte Nomina des
Akkadischen", WZKM 57, 1961, pp. 1-21.
37 Support for Landsberger was given by M. Civil, "The Anzu-bird and
Scribal Whimsies", JAOS 92, 1972, p. 271. And C. Wilcke, Das Lugalbandaepos,
Wiesbaden 1969, pp. 61-4.
38 Cf. for example W.G. Lambert, "The Gula Hymn of Bulluṭsa-rabi", Orientalia 36, 1967, pp. 105-32, p. 130.
39 Cf. in general for the depiction of the lion-headed eagle in the art, I. Fuhr-
Jaeppelt, Materialien zur Ikonographie des Löwenadlers Anzu-Imdugud, München 1972. Perhaps the most famous depiction of the lion-headed eagle is represented by a copper relief found in the temple of Ninhursag in Al 'Ubaid (now in
British Museum), cf. S. Lloyd, The Archeology of Mesopotamia, London 1978,
pp. 103-4. For picture and description, cf. also H. Frankfort, The Art and
Architecture of the Ancient Orient, PB, London 1954, pp. 29f and Pl. 27A; cf.
also the depiction on the vase, p. 33 and Pl. 32. For discussion of different
interpretations of the copper-relief and the lion-headed eagle in general, cf.
Fuhr-Jaeppelt, pp. 27-9. The monstrous eagle is also a common motif on cylinder
seals, cf. H. Frankfort, Cylinder Seals, London 1939, Pl. III b, V h, XIV c, XIII
b,g.
40 Cf. Fuhr-Jaeppelt, p. 3f.
41 Cf. Frankfort, Art and Architecture, p. 67.
42 Text in R. Borger, Die Inschriften Asarhaddons, Königs von Assyrien, AfO,
Beih. 9, Graz 1956, p. 33, § 21: Kalach A,10.

Ashur, who can be depicted with wings and feathered body.[43]
But the monsters described by Esarhaddon above belong to another category than
the gods. So since no traditional lion-headed eagle has been found from this
period, the Anzu-birds mentioned in Assyrian texts seem to have been depicted
differently. T.A. Madhloom gives a survey of Neo-Assyrian guardian figures,
which clearly shows how important a role eagle- and lion-features also played in
the new Neo-Assyrian style.[44] So the basic elements were extant also in the
Assyrian art. Frankfort suggests that the figure described in the Death-Dream
could be a griffin.[45] But that is not likely because the griffin has an eagle- and
not a lion-head. The lion-dragon depicted on a relief found in Nimrud, seems to
come closer both to the old Sumerian style and the descriptions in the Death-
Dream and the Vision of the Nether World.[46] The relief shows a monster with
lion-head and lion-paws with claws, wings and feathered body, standing upright
on its hind legs.

III. The mythological problem
The difficulty in interpreting the Anzu-bird is that the figure seems to belong to
different mythological conceptions.[47]
It is clear that the expression IM.DUGUD.MUŠEN and the depiction of the
lion-headed eagle were used as symbols for gods, in the earliest times especially
Ninurta.[48] But there is disagreement about what exactly the Sumeriogram
IM.DUGUD means.[49] The Akkadian equivalent to IM.DUGUD is imbaru. In an
analysis of this word A. Schott[50] claimed that the correct translation was
"fog".[51] A common translation earlier had been "snow-storm". Schott thought
on the background of the new translation that the bird was a mythological
reflection of a tremendous bird of prey.
T. Jacobsen holds another interpretation: "Im-dugud mušen is the thundercloud
personified. The mythopoetic imagination saw it as an enormous vulture floating

---

43 Frankfort, pp. 55f and Pl. 84.
44 T.A. Madhloom, The Chronology of Neo-Assyrian Art, London 1970, pp.
94-116.
45 H. Frankfort, "Notes on the Cretan Griffin", ABSA 37, 1936-37, pp. 106-
22, pp. 121f.
46 Cf. the drawing in Madhloom, Pl. LXIV, 1.B. Landsberger made the same
suggestion, "Einige underkannt oder verkannte Nomina", p. 9; with reference to
E. Unger, "Mischwesen", RLV 8, Berlin 1927, who gives a description of the
figure in § 27, pp. 203f, and a picture, Taf. 61e. A figure with features both
from a lion and a bird of prey, but more human-like, is described by Madhloom, p. 109; drawing, Pl. LXXXi, 2,3.
47 Cf. in general to the Anzu-bird in the myths, T. Fish, "The Zu Bird",
BJRL 31, 1948, pp. 162-71. Although Fish held the traditional view that the Zu-
bird was a god.
48 A good example is the Dream of Gudea, cf. for translation, Oppenheim,
Dreams, pp. 245f; and A. Falkenstein, Sumerische und akkadische Hymnen und
Gebete, Zürich 1953, pp. 141ff. Cf. for description, Oppenheim, Dreams, pp. 189
and 211ff; and Falkenstein, pp. 372ff. In this text Gudea has a dream where he
sees a gigantic human-shaped figure, reaching from the earth to the heaven. The
figure had a headgear like a deity, was winged like the Anzu-bird, and its lower
parts were like the stormflood. The figure is interpreted as Ningursu which is
another name for Ninurta.
49 Cf. R. Borger, Assyrisch-babylonische Zeichenliste, Neukirchen-Vluyn
1978, pp. 161 and 163.
50 A. Schott, "imbaru, Lexicalisches Archiv", ZA 10, 1938, pp. 170-7.
51 This translation has gained wide acceptance, cf. Landsberger, "Einige unerkannt oder verkannte Nomina", p. 1; and sub imbaru in CAD, p. 108; and AHW,
p. 375.

with outstretched wings in the sky. Because its roar, the thunder, is like the roar that issues from the lion's mouth it was imagined with the head of a lion. The name Im-dugud seems to be composed of imi, 'rain', . . . and dugud, 'cloud'".[52]
The connection between Anzu and meteorological phenomena is more recently denied by B. Hruška.[53] Hruška denies both the interpretation of the signs given by Jacobsen above, and that Anzu should incorporate meteorological phenomena. After Hrušška's study a new edition of the first tablet of the Neo-Assyrian version of the Myth of Anzu has been published by W.W. Hallo and W.L. Moran.[54] It appears here that Anzu is accompanied by the four winds and the storm-flood, col. ii, lines 5-11. He is designated as IM erbeti A[nzu] "the fourfold wind A[nzu]", col. ii, line 11. The connection with meteorological phenomena should then be clearly attested.

The difficulty in deciding the correct interpretation is caused by the fact that the imagining of mythological figures changed during the time, and that one figure could have several mythological aspects. For instance, Ninurta, who is connected to Anzu, is both a fertility and a war deity.[55]
But the Anzu in the Myth of Anzu is different from Anzu as a manifestation of a god.[56] In the Myth of Anzu he is called "the evil Anzu" (ANET[3], p. 515, Tabl. II, line 21, and other places). In this myth Anzu is described in the following way: "When Anzu saw him he raged at him, He ground (his teeth) like a demon, his brilliance covered the mountain, He roared like a lion seized with anger".[57] Here the Anzu-bird is described like a demonic monster.

Jacobsen sees a connection between Anzu as a manifestation of the god Ninurta and as an evil monster. The image of the gods in the human mind was changing from the non-human to the human form: "The unworthy non-human form, so difficult to annihilate, became more and more a problem. It was relegated to the status of a mere symbol of the god. Yet still when the god went to war with the army or when oaths were sworn by touching him in law cases, it was the old non-human form, the 'emblem', that was encountered. At last the dislike of the nonhuman form and the difficulty of expunging it made it a foe, a captured enemy. The bird form, Imdugud, became an enemy of the human form, Ningirsu or Ninurta, captured by him in a fight in the mountains . . ."[58]

In both the Death-Dream and the Vision of the Nether World the point of comparison is obviously this terrifying aspect of Anzu. Similar comparisons are found in other texts either in descriptions of fighting soldiers, wild animals or frightening demons.[59] The stress lies on the Anzu-bird as a powerful, wild and frightening creature.

52 T. Jacobsen and S.N. Kramer, "The Myth of Inanna and Bilulu", JNES 12, 1953, pp. 160-88, p. 167, note 27. The same opinion is argued in Jacobsen, Treasures of Darkness, pp. 128f.
53 B. Hruška, Der Mythenadler Anzu in Literatur und Vorstellung des Alten Mesopotamien, Budapest 1975, pp. 35-40.
54 W.W. Hallo and W.L. Moran, "The First Tablet of the SB Recension of the Anzu-Myth", JCS 31, 1979, pp. 65-115; cf. text, p. 81 and commentary, p. 93.
55 Jacobsen, Treasures, pp. 129-34.
56 Cf. for example Das Lugalbandaepos, published by Wilcke, note 37 above; and the Myth of Anzu, translation in ANET[3], pp. 111ff and 514ff.
57 Tabl. II, lines 36-38. Translation from ANET[3], p. 515.
58 Jacobsen, op.cit., pp. 128f.
59 Cf. below, pp. 412ff.

2.4.2.2   The Fight

Man in the Babylonian and Assyrian milieu believed that he was surrounded by supernatural powers. When he was feeling at his best, in full vigour, physically and psychically, he would ascribe this state of body and mind to the presence of good supernatural powers that either filled his body or guarded him. Conversely, when he experienced misfortune and illness, he would believe that he was afflicted by evil powers. The powers, however, were for the Babylonians and for the Assyrians experienced as individuals and given names and functions. So man's ultimate experience, death, was mythologized into an individual creature, and often named Namtar, which is Sumerian and means "fate". So when man encountered death, he encountered Namtar, his fate.[60]

In the Vision of the Nether World Namtar is the first demon described (line 42). He has just fetched a man, holding his hair in one hand and a sword in the other. In the same vision we also meet the boatman of the nether world, Ḥumut-ṭabal, which means "hurry, remove!". So when man experienced death, he was visited from the nether world by demons or ghosts of the dead. When man fought against death, he was fighting deputies from the nether world.

In the texts about the death and the nether world this is especially described in Dumuzi's Dream.[61] Here "the shepherd" Dumuzi sees how his camp will be destroyed. In the interpretation it is said that bandits will attack him, the bandits being demons from the nether world. The struggle is described both in the interpretation (lines 42-65) and in the report about the fulfillment:

> They caught Dumuzi at the house of Old Belili
> The men surrounded him and let the standing waters flow,
> They twist a cord for him, they bind a net for him,
> They weave a ziptum-cord for him,
> They cuts sticks for him.
> The man in front of him throws things against him,
> The man behind him . . .
> His hands are bound in handcuffs,
> His arms are bound in fetters.
>
> > (lines 217-225;
> > cf. also lines 151-164, 180-190)

---

60   Cf. A.L. Oppenheim, Ancient Mesopotamia. Portrait of a Dead Civilization, rev. ed. by E. Reiner, Chicago 1977, pp. 198-206.
61   For Dumuzi's dream, cf. Alster, note 7 above.

2.4.2.3 The Transformation

Enkidu is transformed into a bird-like creature. He is made similar to the dead of the nether world who are "clothed like birds with wing-feathers for garments" (line 38). Oppenheim thought that the transformation also affected the gender of the subject.[62] The reason for this assumption was both textual and archeological. Concerning the archeological evidence he referred to "the numerous small clay-figurines of females with birdshaped heads, shoulders and arms covered with clustered clay-lumps imitating feathers". Unfortunately he made no reference to show what exactly he had in mind. But if he was primarily thinking of the female clay-figurines, which are known from prehistoric times, there seems to be no support in present archeological and art-historical research for the supposition that these figurines should depict the dead or have any connection to death.[63]

On the other side, the textual reasons are present. Oppenheim noticed here that the suffixes in line 37 are female, and he could have added that also the lines 38 and 39 have female forms.[64] But how these forms should be interpreted, whether on philological or mythological grounds, is uncertain. As long as we do not have any other sources which directly give evidence that the dead were imagined as female, it is the best to leave the question open.

Our text is the only one which actually tells about an act of transformation, but the Descent of Ishtar tells also that the dead were clothed like birds (line 10). The explanation for the belief that the dead underwent a transformation seems to lie in the fact that the images of the nether world belonged to two different mythological conceptions. The nether world was the destination of the dead, but it was also the dwelling-place of the demons. The

62 A.L. Oppenheim, "Mesopotamian Mythology", Orientalia 17, 1948, pp. 43-5.
63 Cf. S. Lloyd, The Archeology of Mesopotamia, pp. 47 and 83ff; and A. Moortgat, The Art of Ancient Mesopotamia, London-New York 1969, p. 7. Of greater interest — especially for the description of the winged demons in the Vision of the Nether World are the winged clay-figurines found buried under the floor in the Burnt Palace in Nimrud. Cf. M.E.L. Mallowan, "The Excavations at Nimrud", Iraq 16, 1954, pp. 59-163, pp. 85ff; and Nimrud and its Remains I, London 1966, pp. 226ff. But these Neo-Assyrian figurines seem to have nothing to do with those mentioned above.
64 The female suffixes in line 37 are: bubūssina, "their sustenance"; akalšina, "their food". In line 38 is labšā stative 3. f. pl. of labāšu, "dress". In line 39 is immarā the present 3. f. pl. of amāru, "see".

demons were imagined with wings,[65] and the Babylonians and Assyrians made no sharp distinction between demons and the dead since they both belonged to the nether world. They were afraid of ghosts of the dead just as much as of the demons.[66] Accordingly they imagined the demons and the dead in the same shape.

2.4.3   The Descent to the Nether World (Sect. D)

The poetic section which describes how the man is leading Enkidu to the nether world, has a literal parallel in the Descent of Ishtar: The Death-Dream: lines 33B-39 = The Descent: Obv., lines 4-10.[67] It is interesting to notice that the scribe of Tabl. 79-7-8,335 has seen this identity. The scribe continues to quote line 11 from the Descent of Ishtar after line 39 in the Death-Dream which is the last identical line according to the other tablets.[68] This shows that the scribe has connected the two texts on the literary level.

This does not mean, however, that the Death-Dream must be literally dependent upon the Descent of Ishtar. Traces of the same poetic section can also be seen in the Neo-Assyrian version of Nergal and Ereshkigal found in Sultantepe.[69] There is no reason to assume that the one author quoted from the other. It is more likely that each of the three authors had access to this poetically formed description and used it independently. The section was then a traditional way of describing the descent and it could be used in different connections.[70]

The motif "descent" in the underworld-texts corresponds to the burial customs. Man was buried under the earth, and at least

65   Cf. the terra-cotta relief from Ur of the demon Lilith, a bringer of death, Frankfort, Art and Architecture, p. 56, Pl. 56. The goddess is winged, and the legs, between the knee and talon, are feathered. At her side two owls are depicted, because she reveals herself in the night in the guise of an owl. She is standing on two lions, because her terrifying power is like a lion.

66   Cf. G.R. Castellino, "Prayer Against Appearing Ghosts", Orientalia 24, 1955, pp. 240-74; and R.C. Thompson, The Devils and Evil Spirits of Babylonia, pp. 21-42.

67   A collocation of the different tablets to the Descent of Ishtar and the Death-Dream of Enkidu is given by R. Borger, Babylonisch-Assyrische Lesestücke II, Roma 1963, pp. 86f.

68   Cf. R.C. Thompson, The Epic of Gilgamish, p. 46, note 9.

69   Col. ii, last three lines; col. iii, lines 1-5. For translation, cf. ANET[3], pp. 507ff.

70   Cf. for the same in Sumerian texts, Alster, Dumuzi, pp. 16ff.

important people in chambers.[71] This correspondence is clearly shown in texts about the death of individuals,[72] but also in the myths: The goddess Inanna had to take off all her clothes and regalia and arrived before queen Ereshkigal crouched and naked, just as the ancients were buried.[73] So it is also in our text: The nether world is the house of darkness and dust, where the dwellers had to eat dust and clay.

2.4.4   The Kings and the Banquet of the Nether World (Sect. E)

Both section E and F begin with a description of the dwellers of the nether world. There is also a description of the dwellers and their conditions in the last section of Tabl. XII of the Gilgamesh epic, but of another kind.[74] In our text the intention is to underline that all men of high rank — kings, priests, heroes, — are gathered in the end to this miserable place. This is emphasized even more firmly in section E in the description of the kings: They have lost their crowns and have to act as servants at the tables.

The motif "the banquet of the nether world" corresponds both to the funeral rites and the cult of the dead. The dead were provided with food and drink not only at the time of the entombment but also thereafter.[75] On Tabl. XII of the Gilgamesh epic we read:

> "Him whose spirit has no one to tend (it)
> hast thou seen?"
> "I have seen: Lees of the pot, crumbs of bread
> offals of the street he eats."
>
> (line 154f.)[76]

The connection between offerings to the dead and the banquet in the nether world is clearly shown in the Death of Ur-Nammu:

> Ur-Nammu, (his) coming, they announced to the people,
> a tumult arose in the Netherworld.
> The king slaughters oxen, multiplies sheep.

---

71   Cf. the royal tombs of Ur, S. Lloyd, The Archeology, pp. 153f.
72   Cf. for example the Descent of Ur-Nammu, lines 63-75.
73   Cf. Jacobsen, Treasures, p. 57.
74   Cf. ANET[3], p. 99.
75   Cf. A. Heidel, The Gilgamesh Epic and Old Testament Parallels, 2nd ed., Chicago 1949, pp. 150ff; M. Bayliss, "The Cult of the Dead Kin in Assyria and Babylonia", Iraq 35, 1973, pp. 115-26.
76   Translation from ANET[3], p. 99.

They seated Ur-Nammu at a huge banquet —
Bitter is the food of the Netherworld,
brackish is the water of the Netherworld!
(lines 79-82)[77]

The ordinary food in the nether world was poor, the enjoyable variety came from the offerings. The conception is the same in our text. But there is one striking difference. In the Sumerian text Ur-Nammu was in all ways received as a king, with respect and deference. He was also seated at the table during the banquet. In the Death-Dream of Enkidu the kings had to act as servants. The author of the Death-Dream stresses — in contradiction to the previous tradition — that death makes everybody equal, and therefore that death humiliates the great.

2.4.5   The Judgement of the Nether World (Sect. F)

The description of ruling Ereshkigal sitting on her throne is traditional. We find it in the Sumerian and Akkadian myths about Inanna's or Ishtar's descent to the nether world: Inanna's Descent, line 162 (ANET[3], p. 55); Ishtar's Descent, obv., lines 23,64 (ANET[3], pp. 107f.). We also find it in Nergal and Ereshkigal, col. i, lines 28-29; col. iii, lines 48-50 (ANET[3], pp. 508ff).

In the myths about Inanna and Ishtar, Ereshkigal is seated in judgement: Inanna's Descent, line 162-165; Ishtar's Descent, obv., lines 64-75. Ereshkigal is judge also in the Death of Ur-Nammu, line 137, although in this text Gilgamesh also acts as judge (lines 142-143). In other texts it is the sun-god, Sumerian "Utu", Akkadian "Shamash", who was believed to be the supreme judge of the living and dead.[78]

As she pronounces judgement, Ereshkigal is surrounded by the Anunnaki, the seven judges of the nether world:

---

77 Translation from Kramer, "The Death of Ur-Nammu", p. 118.
78 Cf. Kramer, Two Elegies, lines 88-9, p. 61; cf. also "Death and Nether World", p. 63 and note 10, p. 66. For further examples for the sun-god as judge, cf. G.R. Castellino, "Incantation to Utu", OrAnt 8, 1969, pp. 1-57. For general reference to Utu as judge, cf. lines 7, 21-23, 29, 39, 177. For special reference to Utu as judge of the dead, cf. p. 21 in Castellino. For the connection between the sun-deity, the dead and the nether world in Ugaritic mythology, cf. J.F. Healy, Death, Underworld and Afterlife in the Ugaritic texts. Diss., London 1977, pp. 90-103.

> The pure Ereshkigal seated herself upon the throne,
> The Anunnaki, the seven judges, pronounced
> judgement before her.
>
> > (Desc. of Inanna, lines 162-63;
> > cf. also Desc. of Ishtar, rev., line 31)[79]

The content of the judgement in the myths is of course a little unusual since it concerns a god (cf. Desc. of Ishtar, obv., lines 64-75; Desc. of Inanna, lines 167-68, where Inanna is turned into a corpse that was hung from a stake.)[80] In the texts about the death of individuals there seem to be a common conception of the judgement in the texts with a Sumerian background. In both the Death of Ur-Nammu, lines 133-143; and the first of the elegies, lines 88-103, the judgement concerns the dead man's fate in the nether world and what conditions he will suffer. The last part of Tabl. XII of the Gilgamesh epic gives us some idea about the rules which guided the judges: The conditions in death were thought as a continuation of the conditions in life. A person's status, deeds and way of death determined his position in the nether world.[81]

It is difficult to say anything definite about the nature of judgement in the Death-Dream of Enkidu. The scribe, Belet-Ṣeri, seems to announce the names of the dead when they arrive before Ereshkigal. Whether she also reads out deeds or misdeeds of the dead is uncertain. That would presuppose that Ereshkigal was varying the sentences as in the texts with Sumerian background. The description of the kings as servants above (lines 40-44), can point in another direction: Death itself was the only sentence Ereshkigal imposed on men.

2.5   The Pattern of the Underworld Texts

As pointed out under "description of structure and content" the Death-Dream of Enkidu has a clear structure. The sections C, E and F all feature a description followed by a report of an event. The sections A and B introduce the text, and the highly poetical

---

79   Translation from ANET[3], p. 55.

80   The Jacobsen suggests here the influence from the experience that the thinks has formed parts of the myth. Inanna is "the power of the storehouse" and "her actual death, the final inability of the storehouse to function as food supply, the myth dramatically symbolized by the cut of tainted meat into which she is turned in the netherworld", Treasures, pp. 62f.

81   Cf. A. Heidel, op.cit., pp. 191ff.

section D links section C to the following sections E and F. This structure is peculiar to the Death-Dream and there is no reason to suggest that the author has used some other texts directly as a model.

But just as the dream in most of its details is marked by the traditional image of the nether world, it is also marked by a pattern which is traditional. This pattern relates to the arrangement of the sections:

1. Sect. C: Description of the death
2. Sect. D: Descent
3. Sect. E: Encounter with the dwellers and conditions in the nether world (continues also party in sect. F)
4. Sect. F: The ruling god and the judgement

The same pattern is extant also in the Death of Ur-Nammu where, following the description of the lamentation in Sumer, we have the following sections:

1. Death and burial (lines 17-72)
2. Descent (lines 73-75)
3. The encounter with the dwellers and the conditions in the nether world (lines 76-130: the banquet, gifts for the gods)
4. The ruling gods and the judgement (lines 131-143)

The three last sections are also found in the myths about Inanna's and Ishtar's descent:

* Descent
* Encounter with the dwellers and conditions (the way through the seven gates)
* The ruling god and the judgement

The interrelationship of the sections from the different texts can vary from similar wording to greater or lesser similarity in the content, but the arrangement of the sections points out the cornerstones in the Mesopotamian ideas about death and afterlife: First the death, then the descent; then the encounter first with the dwellers then with the ruler, sitting on the throne, surrounded by attendants, judging the dead.

2.6 The Death-Dream as a Part of the Gilgamesh Epic

The Death-Dream of Enkidu is part of what we can call the "Humbaba story" which covers Tabl. III-VII in the Assyrian version of the whole Gilgamesh epic. In this section dreams play an important role in the forming of the story, in the same way as in the first part of the epic, Tabl. I-II, where the arrival of Enkidu is announced. In the "Humbaba story" we find three dreams of Gilgamesh and three of Enkidu.

A series of three dreams as a part of a narrative is also found in the poem <u>ludlul</u> <u>bēl</u> <u>nemēqi</u>, "I will praise the lord of wisdom".[82] The first two tablets of the poem deal with the narrator's suffering — "Marduk's hand was heavy upon him" (Tabl. III, line 1). The dreams are located on Tabl. III which forms the turning point of the narration (1st dream: lines 8-20; 2nd dream: lines 21-28; 3rd dream: lines 29-44). In these dreams the visionary experiences how Marduk through his messengers announces the end of the sufferings and symbolically frees him. The fulfillment of the dreams is then told in the rest of the poem.
In the Vision of the Nether World there is also in all probability a series of three dreams involved (the first two on the obverse). This would then be a close parallel to the dreams of Enkidu, since both series then end with a descent to the nether world.

The "Humbaba story" to which the Gilgamesh and Enkidu-dreams belong, runs briefly as follows: Gilgamesh and Enkidu make up their minds to go to the Cedar Forest to cut the big cedar trees. The Cedar Forest is the abode of the gods and guarded by the monster Humbaba. With support from the sun-god Utu the two friends make their way over six mountains and come to the seventh where they meet Humbaba, the guard. At encouragement of Enkidu they kill the monster in a fight. The cedar trees were then cut (Tabl. III-V). There follows a new incident where the goddess Ishtar falls in love with Gilgamesh and wants to marry him, but Gilgamesh refuses her offer. Furious because of this Ishtar sends a new monster against Gilgamesh and Enkidu, the Bull of Heaven. But like Humbaba, this monster is also killed by the two heroes (Tabl. VI). Then the gods decide that because of the cutting of the trees and the killing of the monsters, one of the two heroes must die. The choice falls on Enkidu (Tabl. VII).
This is an outline of the story as it is reconstructed in present research.[83] The reconstruction of this section of the epic in particular is difficult because the Assyrian tablets are fragmentary. The reconstruction follows the Assyrian, Old Babylonian and

---

82   The poem is published by W.G. Lambert, Babylonian Wisdom Literature, Oxford 1960, pp. 21-62. Translation also in ANET[3], pp. 596ff.
83   Cf. ANET[3], pp. 78-87.

Hittite tablets. This causes some uncertainty about the arrangement
of the smaller fragments, but the main features of the story seems
to have been as outlined above as early as the Old Babylonian
version.[84]

The Old Babylonian version is again, especially in Tabl. III-V
dependent upon a Sumerian epic tale which is given the name
"Gilgamesh and the Land of Living".[85] The outline of this story
is in fact the same as in the Akkadian and Hittite versions. The
most striking difference is the end of the story, where neither of
the heroes is killed, but both cursed.

All three dreams of Gilgamesh come before the killing of Humbaba and the cutting of the trees. The first dream is only indicated, but not preserved on the Assyrian tablets (Tabl. V, col. i,
lines 6ff). However, the first dream is probably preserved on an
Old Babylonian tablet.[86] In this dream the visionary is fighting
with a wild bull, and suddenly he is rescued by a man. The
interpretation of the dream is that Gilgamesh' father, the divine
hero Lugalbanda (cf. Gilgamesh and the Land of Living, line 90),
will save Gilgamesh from the death.

The second dream is preserved on the Assyrian tablets (Tabl. V,
col. i, line 12ff). The dream tells how a mountain will fall over
Gilgamesh, but suddenly "a man", $i\check{s}t\bar{e}n$ $e\underline{t}lu$, will pull him out
and save his life. Enkidu interprets that they will both seize
Humbaba and kill him (Tabl. V, col. iii, lines 37-43).

The third dream is also preserved on the Assyrian tablets (Tabl. V,
col. iv, lines 13ff). Gilgamesh experiences a thunderstorm. The
thunderstorm represents both the powers of chaos and death.[87]
This time there is no sign of rescue and th immediate reaction of
Gilgamesh is to flee. This dream is also interpreted by Enkidu, but
the interpretation is lost.

---

84 Cf. K. Oberhuber, "Gilgamesch", Das Gilgamesch-Epos, pp. 13ff. For the
development of the text in general, cf. B. Landsberger, "Einleitung in das
Gilgameš-Epos", Das Gilgamesch-Epos, pp. 171-8. For the Hittite version, cf. A.
Kammenhuber, "Die hethitische und hurritische Überlieferung zum 'Gilgameš-
Epos'", MSS 21, 1967, pp. 45-58.
85 Cf. for translation and description, S.N. Kramer, The Sumerians, Chicago
1963, pp. 190-7; and ANET[3], pp. 47-50.
86 W. von Soden, "Beiträge zum Verständnis des babylonischen Gilgameš-
Epos", ZA N.F. 19, 1959, pp. 215-9. Translation also in ANET[3], V, B, 1-9, p.
504.
87 Cf. pp. 372f above.

All three dreams follow the same pattern. They are symbolic warning dreams which predict the future danger of the visionary if he does not change his plans. The first two dreams tell that in the first part of his venture he can expect miraculous divine interference. The third dream shows, however, that at the end he will be left alone without divine support.

Only one of the dreams of Enkidu comes before the killing of Humbaba and the cutting of the trees — Assyrian version Tabl. V, col. iv, lines 1-5. Enkidu experiences a rainstorm. This dream is also a warning like the three dreams of Gilgamesh.

What is supposed to be the second dream of Enkidu is only preserved in a Hittite version. In the present reconstruction of the epic it is placed as the beginning of Tabl. VII, lines 1-15. Both this dream and the Death-Dream, which is the third, come after the Humbaba event. Their pattern is also different from the other dreams. In the second dream Enkidu experiences how the gods in the heavenly council decree his death sentence, in the third he experiences proleptically his actual death.

One of the main difficulties in the interpretation of the Gilgamesh epic is that the texts speak with several voices. The texts all have their own history and each layer in this history has its own voice. The question about the meaning of the whole epic often depends upon which layer in the tradition was allowed to determine the sense.[88]

Nevertheless, although the epic is a composite arrangement of independent traditions, it seems clear that the composition as a whole does have a meaning. The epic has two parts. The first part deals with the heroic deeds of Gilgamesh and Enkidu, the second part with Gilgamesh' search for immortality. The "Humbaba story" and its consequences is the turning-point of the narration.[89] At this point of the story the two friends stood at the pinnacle of power and fame. They had reached the remote and inaccessible cedar forest, they had killed the dreadful monster Humbaba, they

---

88 Cf. for the history of research, K. Oberhuber, "Wege der Gilgamesch-Forschung", Das Gilgamesch-Epos, pp. XIII-XXVI.
89 Cf. for this interpretation, A.L. Oppenheim, Mesopotamia, pp. 255-264; Jacobsen, Treasures, pp. 215-9.

had treated the goddess Ishtar with disdain. There seemed to be
nothing they could not do. But just at this point the disaster breaks
in. Enkidu's death at the height of triumph makes Gilgamesh turn
from his quest for fame to a quest for eternal life.

But he fails here as well. Interpreting the epic in this way, the
first part tells about aspirations to immortality in fame, the second
part about aspirations to immortality in lasting life (Jacobsen). The
intention is thus to underline the limitations of man: the limitation
of man's power over against the power of the gods, the limitation
of man's life over against the power of death.

Thus the "Humbaba story", where the Death-Dream forms the
conclusion, talks about the limitation of man's power. To be sure,
the story contains other motifs too, for example the motif of
"friendship".[90] But the main theme from the Sumerian "Humbaba
story" (Gilgamesh and the Land of Living) is present also in the
Akkadian versions: The heroes go too far in their attempt to reach
immortal fame. They offend the gods.[91] In the Hittite version of
the second dream of Enkidu the heroes' crime is summarized as
follows:

> Anu, Enlil and heavenly Shamash were in council.
> And Anu said to Enlil:
> "Because the Bull of Heaven they have slain,
> and Huwawa they have slain,
> therefore" — said Anu —
> "the one of them who stripped the mountains of cedar
> must die!"[92]

The success leads the heroes to "hubris". They break into the
territory of the gods, kill the divine guard, they treat a goddess
with contempt. The Death-Dream shows the consequences:
Enkidu's "heaven-defying" quest for fame ended in the gloomy
realm of the nether world.

90   Cf. K. Oberhuber, "Gilgamesch", p. 4.
91   Cf. F.M.T. de Liagre Böhl, "Das Problem Ewigen Lebens im Zyklus und
Epos des Gilamesch", Das Gilgamesch-Epos, pp. 237-75, pp. 248ff. Cf. also K.
Oberhuber, "Gilgamesch", pp. 6-8.
92   Translation from ANET[3], p. 85.

b) The Vision of the Nether World

1. The Text

1.1 Introduction

1.1.1 Editions

The text (VAT 10057), which was found in Ashur, was first published by E. Ebeling in Tod und Leben nach den Vorstellungen der Babylonier I, Berlin-Leipzig 1931, pp. 1-19. The edition contained transliteration, translation and notes. Five years after the text was reedited by W. von Soden in ZA N.F. 9 (43), 1936, pp. 1-31, under the title: "Die Unterweltsvision eines assyrischen Kronprinzen". This edition contained a revised transliteration, accompanied by photographs, translation, introduction, and a brief commentary. After that Ebeling published a new transliteration, accompanied by notes: "Kritische Beiträge zu neueren assyrologischen Veröffentlichungen", MAOG 10, 1937, pp. 1-20. This transliteration was again commented on by von Soden in "Altbabylonischen Dialektdichtungen", ZA N.F. 10 (44), 1938, pp. 26-31.
A new transliteration and translation of lines 42-49 in von Soden's edition was given by C. Frank, accompanied by a more detailed commentary: "Lamastu, Pazuzu und andere Dämonen. Ein Beitrag zur babyl.-assyr. Dämonologie", MAOG 14, 1941, pp. 23-41.

1.1.2 Translations

The editions by Ebeling land von Soden contain a translation of the whole tablet, both the obverse and the reverse. The vision is on the reverse. The translation by Frank contains lines 42-49 (the first part of the reverse), as mentioned.
In addition to these editions the reverse of the text is translated by A. Heidel in The Gilgamesh Epic and Old Testament Parallels, pp. 132-6; and by E.A. Speiser in ANET[3], pp. 109f.

1.1.3 Working Method

The basis for this translation is the transliterated text. Problems then arise because the whole text has been edited in two transliterations and a part of it in three. Going through the discussion between Ebeling and von Soden concerning the interpretation of the signs, it seems, however, as if the discussion reached a sort of equilibrium. The new transliteration by Ebeling did not in fact contain many new readings. And in his final comment von Soden accepts some of them. Following this discussion the right working method must be to use von Soden's transliteration as a basic text and adjust it where necessary by readings from the following discussion.
One of the main reasons why von Soden's transliteration differed greatly from the first by Ebeling, was that von Soden used photographs of a newly cleaned tablet. The result is therefore more certain. However, it is a different matter with Frank's transliteration. He used the same photographs as von Soden and accordingly the differences in the interpretation of signs are not so many. Where differing translations between von Soden and Frank depend only on different interpretations of signs, we will therefore be very careful in our conclusions.
However, as far as the translations of Heidel and Speiser are concerned, another working method must be employed. Different translations depend here upon a

different understanding of the transliterated text, since they both have used von Soden as the basic text. In fact it seems as if they did not know Frank's transliteration at all (understandable for Heidel — 1946).

Even though the discussion of the signs has been hard, it seems right to say that the difficulty in understanding the reverse of the text does not primarily arise from differing interpretation of signs. The difficulties arise firstly because of the lacunas, secondly because of dialectical peculiarities in the language and thirdly because of the strange content.

1.2   Translation of the Vision of the Nether World

1.2.1   The Translation

41 [Kum]māya[a] lay down and he saw a night-vision[b]. In his dream [   ][c]. I saw its terror. [   ].[d]

42 Namtar,   the vizier of the nether world[a], the <u>creator</u>[b] of the decrees, I saw. And a man[c] was standing before him. He[d] was holding the hair of his head in his left hand, in his right hand [he was holding] a sword.

43 [Na]mtartu[a],   the concubine, was provided with the head of a Kuribu, the hands (and) feet (were) those of a man.
Mūtu[b]   was provided with the head of a serpent-dragon[c], the hands[d] (were) those of men[e], the feet [   ][f].

44 [Šēdu][a],   an evil one, the head (and) hands (were) those of men. He was wearing a crown. The feet (were) those of an eagle[b]. With his left foot he was treading on a <u>sea-monster</u>[c].
Alluḫappu[d]   was provided withe the head of a lion, the hands (and) feet (were) those of men.

45 Saghulḫaza[a]   (had) the head of a bird, with wings outspread, he was flying to and fro[b]. The hands (and) feet (were) those of men.
Ḫumuṭ-ṭabal[c],   the boatsman of the nether world, was provided with[d] the head of an Anzu-bird[e]. The hands (and) feet [   ][f].

46 E[ṭem]mu[a]   was provided[b] with the head of an ox. The hands (and) feet (were) those of men.
Utukku,   an evil one, the head (was) that of a lion. The hands (and) feet (were) those of an Anzu-bird.
Šulak   (was) an ordinary lion, standing on his hind legs.

47 [Mā]mītu[a]   (had) the head of a goat. The hands (and) feet (were) those of men.
Nedu,   the doorkeeper of the nether world, (had) the head of a lion, the hands of men, the feet of a bird.
Mimma lemnu[b],   his two heads, the first head (was) that of a lion, the second head [   ].

48 [Muḫ]rā[a]   (had) three feet. The two forefeet (were) those of a bird, the hindfoot (was) that of an ox. He was possessing terror and dreadful splendor.
Two gods[b],   their name I do not know. The first (had) the head, hands (and) feet of an Anzu-bird. In his left hand [   ].

49   The second was provided with the head of a man. He was wearing a crown. In his right hand he was carrying a mace. In his left hand [   ]a.

[In] all fifteen gods were standing (there). I saw them and I called out to them.

50 One mana,   his body was black like pitch. His face was similar to that of an Anzu-bird. He was wearing a red robe. In his left hand he was holding up a bow. In his right hand he was hol[ding] a sword. [With his left foot he was treading on   ]b.

51 When I raised my [ey]es, the warrior Nergal was seated on a royal thronea. He was wearing a royal crown. In both his hands he was holding two furious maces. Each two heads [   ], each two headsb [   ].

52 [   ]a they were cast down. [From ... of] his [a]rms lightning was flashing. The Anunnaki, the great gods, were knee[ling] at his right and his left side [   ].

53 The underworld was filled with fear and it lay prostrate before the son of princesa.

The mighty [   ]b seized me by my forelocks and drew me into his presence.

54 I saw him and my legs began trembling. The fearsome sheen of his terror overwhelmed me. I kissed the feet of his [gre]at divinity and prostrated. I stood upa. He was looking at me and shaking his

55 [he]ad at me. Then he raised his [c]ry, like a fu[ri]ous storm

56 he shrieked terribly against me. He drewa [towa]rds me the sceptre which befits his majesty, that which is full of terror, like the horned serpent, in order to kill [me]. Išum, his counselor, he who upholds paternity, who saves life, who loves truth, so be it!b, he saidc: "Put not the man do death, you po[wer]ful king

57 of the nether world! Let the inhabitants all over the land hear [the word]a of your [gl]ory!" He soothed like the clear water of a well the heart of the all-powerful, the almighty, who captures the wicked.

58 Nergal [deliv]ered this his statement: "Why have you dishonoured her, my honorable, beloved wife, the queen of the nether world

59 [   ]? [A]t her exalted command, which does not alter, let Biblu, the executioner of the nether world, entrust you to Lugalsula, the gatekeeper, and then he will lead you out through the Ištar

60 -Aya-gate. [For]get and forsake me not! Then I will not decree the death sentence. At the command of Šamaš, let disturbance

61 dishonesty and rebellion [   ] together blow over youa! May sleep not be poured out over you because of their terrible noise.

62 This [spirit]a which you saw in the nether world, is that of the exalted shepherd:
to whom my father [   ], the king of the gods, givesb full responsibility;

63 [w]hom from sunrise to sunset he allows to look over the lands in their totalitya [   ], and he r[ul]esb over everything;

64 to [w]hom, in view of his priesthood, Aššur [decr]eesa the celebration of the holy New-Years festivalb in the open country, in the garden of fertility, an image of Lebanon. [   ] in all eternity.

65 And Yabru, Humban, Naprušu, guarding his body, preservea his seed and saveb his army and camp, so that in the battle a charioteer does notc come near him.

66 [   ]^a your begetter^b, <u>the t[al]l one</u>^{c}, wise in speech, broad in understanding, with a well-informed mind, examining the
67 drawings of the formation of the earth^d, [   ] when he closed his ear for his sp[ee]ch^a, he ate the taboo (and) stamped on the abomination^b.

Suddenly the fearsome sheen of his^c terrible kingship shall throw^d you^e down to the win[ds]^f.

68 Let this speech lay to your hearts as a thorn! Go away to the upper (world) until I shall remember you!" he said [   ]^a.

69 I awoke . . .,
like a man^a who sheds blood^b, who roams alone in the marshes, a henchman seizes him and his heart pounds, or
70 like a young offspring of a pig, which is mounting its female, it insides constantly blows up and it ejects "clay" from its mouth and from its behind the whole time . . .

71 He uttered a lamentation, saying: "Woe, my heart!" And he darted out into the street like an arrow and gathered the dust of the road and square into his mouth, the whole time giving
72 forth a frightful cry: "Woe! Alas!" Calling: "Why did you decree this for me!", he praised bitterly before the population of Aššur the heroic deeds of Nergal and Ereškigal, who had helped^a this very prince.

73 And that scribe, who earlier had accepted a bribe when he stood^a in the office of his father with the wisdom and insight which
74 Ea gave to him, he laid to his heart [the words]^a of praise and spoke in his heart as follows: "So that the oath shall
75 not come close to me and not strike me for evil, I will always do^a the deeds [which Nergal] demanded." And he went to the royal palace and repeated: "Let this be an occasion for averting the evil^b."

1.2.2   Notes to the Translation

41 a. The name of the visionary is given clearly on the obverse, line 27. It is pronounced in different ways. I use the pronunciation <u>Kummāya</u>.

   b. Von Soden and Speiser let the sentence end with <u>ina</u> <u>šuttišu</u>, "in his dream". I follow Ebeling and Heidel who let the sentence end with the verb, which is the natural word-order in Akkadian.

   c. In the photograph published by von Soden all the signs between <u>ana</u>, "to", and <u>rašubbatsu</u>, "his/its terror", are uncertain. Ebeling claims that when he read the tablet before it was cleaned, he could clearly see more signs. In his first edition he translates: "In seinem Traume stieg er in die Erde hinab . . .". Heidel suggests the same.

   d. After the sentence which ends with <u>appalis</u>, "see", about fifteen signs are missing. Accordingly it is difficult to know what the first section of the vision is dealing with. It does not seem to be a description of an underworld-god: In line 49 it is said that the vision so far contains fifteen gods. The description of the gods has then to begin with Namtar in line 42. Therefore it is most likely that line 41 contains the descending and description of the nether world.

42 a.   ersetu, "earth", is a common name for "the nether world". Cf. K. Tallquist: Sumerisch-akkadische Namen der Totenwelt, pp. 8-11.

    b.   The verb banû, "create", is uncertain. Frank reads tamû, "speak". He also translates sukallu with "messenger" and not with "vizier". Accordingly he translates: "Namtar, den Boten der Unterwelt, den Verkünder(?) der Gebote, sah ich". Cf. on sukallu, "messenger" or "vizier", AHW, p. 1263.

    c.   The ordinary word for "human being", amēlu, is used. So also in the comparisons below.

    d.   The subject must be Namtar.

43 a.   Von Soden will not now read namtartu here, cf. AHW, sub namtaru, p. 729.

    b.   Mūtu means "death".

    c.   The Akkadian word is mušḫuššu.

    d.   Both Ebeling, von Soden and Frank read qātā-šu amēle (plural) — "his hands like those of men", without comments. qātā is in the construct state to the following genitive amēle. The suffix -šu accompanying a status constructus is irregular grammar.
The other combinations of qātā/šepā, "feet", and amēle are either as direct status constructus: qātā šepā amēle (lines 44, 45, 46, 47), or with the pronoun ša: qātā ša amēle (lines 44, cf. 43). Perhaps therefore the text should emended to read qātā-šu <ša> amēle.

    e.   Frank transliterates all the logograms for "man/human being" with plural determination in the abstract feminine form amēlūti (gen.). The concrete masculine amēle (gen.) seems to be preferable because a phonetic complement is absent.

    f.   At the end of the line Frank thinks he sees the logogram for "lion".

44 a.   Von Soden thinks with some uncertainty to see "Šedu". Ebeling and Frank leave it open.

    b.   All translators refrain from translating this word. The signs are A.ŠI. MUŠEN. The last sign is the determinative for "bird". The sign complex A.ŠI can be read ÉR, which may be a scholarly way of writing erû = eagle. Cf. S. Dalley, "Two Points in the Text of 'A Crown Prince's Vision of the Nether World'", RA 74, 1980, p. 190.

    c.   The Akkadian word is kušû. Both Ebeling and von Soden have this transliteration. The translation differs: Ebeling: "serpent", von Soden: "crocodile" (so also Heidel and Speiser). It is difficult to identify the animal. The word seems to be the same as the Sumerian KUŠU, which can mean an aquatic animal (cf. CAD, sub kušû, p. 602). We have chosen a general translation: "sea-monster". Frank transliterates duššu (in plural), which he thinks designates some species of antelope.

    d.   alluḫappu means "net". It is the demon who captures man in the net of death.

e. Ebeling and von Soden transliterate the sign as the number "four". They
    translate: "four hands" (so also Heidel and Speiser). The same sign do also
    occur in line 45 and 46. It seems better, however, to follow Frank who
    reads the sign as the logogram GAR for šakānu, "provide", in the stative
    3 p. sing. šakin. The same verb occurs in syllabic writing in line 43.

45 a. Saghulḫaza is the Sumerian name. Read in Akkadian it would be mukīl-
       reš-lemutti. It has the meaning: "he who promotes evil".

   b. The verb is naprašum, "fly". The Ntn stem has iterative meaning: "Going
       on flying / fly to and fro".

   c. The name is composed of imperative forms of the verbs ḫamātu, "hurry"
       and tabālu, "remove": "Hurry! Remove!" It is the name of the god who
       is (too) quick to remove man to the nether world.

   d. Cf. 44 e.

   e. We follow the transliteration argued by Landsberger, "Einige unerkannt
       gebliebene oder verkannte Nomina des Akkadischen," WZKM 57, 1961,
       pp. 1-21. Cf. above, pp. 374f.

   f. Frank reads here amēlūti, "human being". A sign for "man/human" at
       the end of the line is most likely.

46 a. The reading is uncertain. Von Soden believes he can identify a part of the
       sign. Frank left it open, but considers the possibility of reading eṭemmu.
       This demon occurs often together with utukku, and is often described as
       alpu, "bull". The meaning is "ghost / spirit of a dead man".

   b. Cf. 44 e.

47 a. Frank is not certain about the reading here, which is suggested by both
       Ebeling and von Soden.
       Māmītu means "oath", the god mentioned here is accordingly the "oath-
       demon". Cf. E. Reiner, Šurpu. A Collection of Sumerian and Akkadian
       Incantations. Graz 1958, p. 55.

   b. Mimma lemnu means "something that is evil".

48 a. The signs are partly damaged. There seems to be a common agreement
       about the syllable -ra at the end, accompanied by the sign for plural. The
       suffix šu on šēpā shows that it is a singular demon. We have then one
       god with a plural name. This may be the demon Muḫrā. The name is
       derived from the plural imperative of the verb maḫāru, "face, approach".
       The plural sign and the plural imperative could indicate that Muḫrā is a
       demon with two faces. In the Poem of Erra Muḫrā is described as an
       underworld guard. L. Cagni: The Poem of Erra, p. 49. Cf. S. Dalley,
       "Two Points", p. 190.

   b. The text means one god with two bodies, a "siamese god".

49 a. Frank transliterates namṣari šutallup and gives the translation: ". . . had
       drawn a sword", at the end of the line. Unfortunately he does not explain
       the form šutallup which does not seem to exist. Von Soden transliterates
       ina maḫrišu "in front of him", but is uncertain about the signs here.

50 a. The Akkadian word is here eṭlu and not amēlu which is used in the
      description of the demons above, cf. 42 c. eṭlu means literally "man /
      young man", and is often used in the meaning "hero". Cf. the analysis
      under content, below, pp. 414f.

   b. The interpretation of the signs in the last sentence is uncertain. Frank and
      von Soden have a partly different transliteration and translation of the
      sentence. What is common in the transliteration, is the suggestion of
      reading the words šumēli (gen), "left (foot)" and kabis (stative), "trea-
      ding".

51 a. In his first transliteration von Soden renders šarrūti-šu, "of his royalty".
      Later he agrees with Ebeling only to read šarrūti without the suffix.

   b. In his first transliteration von Soden does not render the last qaqqadu,
      "head". Later he agrees with Ebeling in the possibility of reading the
      logogram SAG.DU (= qaqqadu) here. Frank thinks that Nergal here is
      carrying two maces, and upon each mace there are two knobs depicting
      animal-heads.

52 a. About 21 signs are missing.

53 a. Von Soden has the sentence begin with arallu, "nether world" and end
      with siššu, which he translates with "Entsetzen": "Die Unterwelt war voll
      der Furchtbarkeit; vor dem Fürstensohn lag gewaltiges Entsetzen". Heidel
      and Speiser have also the same syntax, but they translate "silence" or
      "stillness" instead of "Entsetzen". This syntax does not seem preferable.
      It is more likely to have the sentence end with nadi (stative), "prostra-
      ted", since the statives generally end a clause in our text. arallu is then
      subject to both mali (stative), "filled", and nadi. A new sentence begins
      with the words transliterated by von Soden as siššu dannu (. . . "the
      mighty").

   b. The signs are not clear. Von Soden transliterates siššu, but this word
      gives no meaning in the context.

54 a. Von Soden suggests aziz and translates: "stand ich auf". To judge from
      the context it is unlikely that Kummāya here is allowed to stand up. That
      would be a sign of grace in clear contrast to the rest of the sentence. The
      form aziz, if it is to be read here, must be the preterite of uzuzzum.
      Preterite with only one z occurs two other times in our text: line 72 and
      73. Cf. 72 a. and 73 a.

56 a. The verb "drew" does not fit quite well in the context. But there seems
      to be no doubt about the reading išāta (pret. vent.) of the verb šātum,
      "draw".

   b. Von Soden reads u kīam, but suggests the rendering šī lū kīam, which is
      to be translated: "So be it!". Cf. GAG § 124 c.

   c. The text renders: Išum . . . iqtabi eṭlu lā tušmâta. Ebeling takes eṭlu,
      "man", as subject to iqtabi (perf. of qabûm = to say). The direct speech
      begins then with lā tušmâta (Šin-stem, pres. of mâtu = die): "Don't kill!"
      The noun eṭlu is then a designation for Išum. This syntax depends partly
      upon another transliteration of parts of the text by Ebeling. As the text is
      transliterated by von Soden this syntax is not possible. If eṭlu is subject
      for iqtabi, it must be an apposition to Išum, but as an apposition it should
      be placed before the verb, together with the other appositions. The only

possible rendering is to take etlu as a part of the direct speech as object
to lā tušmâta. The noun etlu is then a designation for Kummāya.

57 a.   Before tašrīhīka, "your glory", one can expect something like amātum,
"word".

61 a.   The verb is liddibani. The form is precative. Von Soden derives it from
edēpu, "blow", and sees it as a compound of the G and D stem: The
prefix li from G, the double dd from D (AHW sub edēpu, p. 186).
Another derivation is possible, from dabābu, "conspire". The form would
then be liddib (G stem, precative) + ani (ventive). CAD sub dabābu, p.
11). In both cases the form is irregular.

62 a.   The following sentence requires a word like etemmu, "spirit of the
dead", here.

   b.   The grammatical forms of the verbs in line 63B-67 are difficult to
determine. Von Soden translates line 62B-67A in the past tense and line
67B in the future. Heidel and Speiser have the same translation. This
translation is problematic. A classification of the verbs will be as follows:

1) Verbs where signs are damaged and the forms impossible to decide:
i-b [e(?)]-lu, "rule?"; [i(?)-ši(?)]-mu or [i(?)-ša(?)]-mu, "decree?"

2) Verbs that can be both the present and the preterite:
ušamsū, "give responsibility" — from masû, Sin-stem, pret./pres. subj.
uštabrū, "let look" — from barû, St-stem, pret./pres. subj.

3) Verbs where the forms are certain:
Present:
ušallamū, "preserve" — from šalāmu, pres. pl.
ušezzabū, "save" — from šuzubu, pres. pl.
esahhap, "throw down" — from sahāpu, pres. sing.
Preterite:
iqruba, "come near" — from qerēbu, pret. vent.
iphû, "close" — from pehû, pret. subj.
īkula, "eat" — from akālu, pret. vent.
ukabbisa, "stamp" — from kabāsu, D-stem, pret. vent.

This classification shows:
I. Verbs that can be classified with certainty as the present, govern lines
65A (from Yabru) and 67B.

II. Verbs that can be classified with certainty as the preterite, govern
lines 66 and 67A. Concerning line 65B cf. p. IV.

III. The verbs in present tense in line 65A (from Yabru) are linked to the
damaged verb at the beginning of line 65A (from Yabru) through the
enclitic particle -ma at the end of this verb. This makes it likely that we
should take this verb as the present too, restoring [i-ša]-mu instead of
von Soden's [i-ši]-mu. This verb governs line 64 (cf. 63 a). Line 64 seems
to have the same syntactical structure as line 62B and 63: Introduced by
ša with following subjunctive. As shown above the verbs in 62B-63 can
be either the present or the preterite. The close connection to line 64-65
seems to make it most likely to classify the verbs as the present.

IV. So far it seems as if we have the present in line 62B-65, the preterite
in line 66-67A and the present in 67B. The only problem is the preterite

iqrub in line 65B. The line seems to be subordinate to 65A (so von Soden, Heidel, Speiser). The use of tenses in subordinate clauses in the Neo-Assyrian period is often confusing, but this does not overshadow the fact that we should have expected the present iqarrab. A strange preterite where we should have expected the present, is also to be found in line 75A (cf. note 75 a).

Von Soden explains the two present forms in 65A (from Yabru) as the present without indication of time (Durativ in der Vergangenheit, cf. GAG § 78 e). In fact he has the preterite in the subordinate clause 65B govern the whole part 62B-65: He interprets the present as past, restores the damaged verbs as preterite forms and interprets the uncertain forms as the preterite. There are two difficulties connected with this:

1) If the other verbs are kept in the preterite, the section 62B-65 seems to be a sort of historical report. It is no indications in the text itself why the author then should change from the preterit to the durative.

2) There is no doubt that the present in 67B indicates time and that the time there is the present-future, as usual with the present. We should expect the author to have used the tenses in the same way within the same section, when there are no indications of the converse.

To put it briefly: According to the text as we have it, we are left with the dilemma that we must either let the present verbs in 65A govern line 62B-65, which gives a strange use of the preterite in the subordinate clause 65B, or to let the preterite in 65B govern the part 62B-65, which gives a strange use of the present in 65A. We feel that the arguments are strongest for the first solution.

In our translation we have chosen a pragmatic approach and translated lines 62B-65 in the present, which allows both a past and a future interpretation. The section 66-67A is without doubt held in the preterite.

63 a. The translation here is difficult both because of unclear signs and complicated syntax. Von Soden transliterates: kīma bilti uštabrū, and translates: "(die Länder) wie eine Traglast ausgehalten hat". In the transliteration he puts a questionmark with bilti, ("Traglast") "load", and in the notes he admits that the translation is uncertain. Heidel follows von Soden: ". . . carried like a load". Speiser underlines the uncertainty with bilti with an open space in the translation. The verb uštabrū he does not translate with "carry" as von Soden and Heidel, but with "fatten": "who all the lands . . . fattened like [   ]." All three take the shepherd from line 62A as the subject. To this we make the following comments:

1) The word biltu is uncertain in this connection and can not govern the understanding of the whole clause.

2) The verb uštabrū is clear. It means neither "carry" nor "fatten", but is the St-stem of barû, "see", in the pres. or pret. subj. The meaning is causative: "to let see".

3) It is likely that the gods are subject here as in line 62B and lines 64-65A. In line 63B the "shepherd" must, however, be subject.

63 b. Cf. 62 b.

64 a. Cf. 62 b.

b. The phrase epēš akīt . . . can be understood in two ways. It can mean "to celebrate the akitu — festival", or "to build the akitu — temple". The final judgement about which is to be preferred, must depend upon a stylistic and historical analysis.

65 a. Cf. 62 b.

b. Cf. 62 b.

c. Cf. 62 b.

66 a. The beginning of the clause is damaged. Von Soden restores [u(?) šu]-u and has the phrase introduce a new person as in line 73: "Aber [e]r, dein Erzeuger . . .".

b. The word zarû can also mean "ancestor", cf. CAD sub zarû, p. 72.

c. The translation does not fit well in the context. The signs are not clear. The suggested transliteration by von Soden is sīhu, "tall". J. Bottero, "Antiquité Assyro-Babyloniennes", École Pratique des Hautes Études IVe Section Sciences Historiques et Philologiques, Annuaire 1972-73, p. 98, translates, "avancé en âge".

d. We have chosen a "narrow" translation of the noun usurtu. The corresponding verb is esēru, "draw". The noun can also have a broader meaning: "sign", "plan", cf. CAD sub esēru, p. 347. Together with the phrase markas qaqqari, (markasu, "link, centre"; qaqqaru, "earth") the clause can refer to knowledge about written documents containing the divine plans for the earth. Cf. Oppenheim, Ancient Mesopotamia, p. 204.

67 a. Cf. note 67 c.

b. We have chosen a "narrow" translation. The first phrase reads asakku īkula, (asakku, "taboo"; akālu, "eat"). This phrase can be used in a broader sense: "to infringe a taboo". The next phrase reads anzilla ukabbisa, (anzillu, "abomination"; kabāsu, "tread", here D-stem, "stamp"). This phrase can also be understood in a broader sense: "to commit an abomination". Exactly what sort of acts are described in this way, can not be determined on basis of the wording. It is, however, clear that the text tells about a severe rebellion against the gods with cultic implications. Cf. CAD sub asakku, p. 327; sub anzillu, p. 153; sub akālu, p. 255.

c. The text has melammē šarrūtisu. melammū is the supernatural awe-inspiring sheen inherent in things divine and royal. Connected to šarrūtu, "kingship", it can describe the dignity of both gods and human kings. As in line 65 melammū used together with the verb šahāpu, "throw down, overwhelm", can describe the immediate impact of a god on man. The combination melammē šarrūti or melammē belūti, "lordship", can also describe the terror of an earthly king, coming over his enemies, cf. CAD sub melammū, p. 11.

The problem is to decide what the suffix here and in qabīšu, "his speech", in line 67A refers to. Line 54 tells about the "fearsome sheen" of Nergal. In the lines 60-61 there is a prediction about the misfortune similar to the one in 67B. There the threat comes from Nergal. But Nergal can not be the one referred to in line 67B, because he is the one speaking. We are then left with two possibilities: The suffix can refer to Assur, the king of the gods in the lines 62 and 64. If this is the case, the rebel king can expect the god's punishment in the future. The problem is, however,

that Assur is not focussed upon in the preceding lines 62-65. The figure
dealt with is the ideal king. If he is meant, the prediction in line 67B
foretells a future visitation of the terror of the ideal king. Although the
text is open to both interpretations, the last one seems preferable when we
take the context into consideration. In any case, the act of the rebel king
is regarded as a crime against the divine will. And the punishment is a
reaction to this crime.

d. Cf. 62 b.

e. "you" is here plural.

f. The text is transliterated adi šārī, literally "to the winds". The translation
"everywhere" is suggested by Ebeling and followed by Speiser. Von
Soden translates "ganz und gar", Heidel "altogether". The meaning seems,
however, to be "to nothingness". The meaning of the whole phrase is
accordingly: "annihilate completely". Cf. AHW sub šāru, pp. 1192f; and
Oppenheim, The Interpretation of Dreams, p. 234.

68 a. Von Soden's transliteration reads: iq-ba-[am(?)-ma(?)]. The ending of the
verb qabûm, "say", is accordingly uncertain. The suggested last enclitic
particle -ma is the reason why von Soden, Heidel and Speiser link this
verb to the succeeding sentence: "He spoke to me and then I woke".
Bearing in mind that where von Soden suggests -ma, the text has a
lacuna, we must assess the reference of iqba ... on the basis of syntax
and content. It seems then more likely that the verbs should be taken as
the end of the direct speech of Nergal, than as the beginning of Kummāya's autobiographical report.

69 a. The Akkadian word is eṭlu.

b. The text has tāpik damē, "shed blood". The same simile is used in Sargon
II's report about this eighth campaign; transliteration: F. Thureau-Dangin,
Une relation de la huitième campagne de Sargon, Paris 1912, p. 26;
English translation: D.D. Luckenbill, Ancient Records of Assyria and
Babylonia II, Chicago 1927, p. 83. The simile reads in context: "Like a
man who shed blood, he left Turushpâ, his royal city; like (an animal)
fleeing from the hunter, he hid in the recesses of this mountain".

72 a. The text has ana resuti ... izizu, "stood to assistance". The preterite izuzu
with only one z is not registered by von Soden in his grammar (GAG,
Varbalpar. 35), but is registered in AHW as a rare form.

73 a. The text has ezizu, the preterite form, cf. note 72 a.

74 a. Von Soden restores eg[err]ê. egerrû is an accidental omen, cf. sub egerrû
in CAD, p. 44. This restoration does not make sense in the context. The
text demands something like amatū, "words".

75 a. The text has eteppuš from epēšu, "do". The form is pret., Gtn-stem. The
translation should then be in the past tense, but this seems very strange in
the context. Von Soden, Heidel, Speiser, all translate the future, cf. the
use of pret. in the line 65B, note 62 b.

b. The text reads literally: "Let this be for my namburbi". Namburbi was
the ritual which was used to avert an evil that was predicted. Cf. R.I.
Caplice, The Akkadian Namburbi Texts: An Introduction, SANE 1/1,
Malibu, California 1974.

2.   Analysis of Content

2.1   Description of Structure and Content

The text begins with an introductory line which reveals the nature
of the following report (section A): It is a report about a night-
vision, Akk: *tabrīt mūši*. The text also gives the name of the
person who experienced the vision: Kummāya, although this is a
"cover-name" with unknown meaning.
The introduction is kept in the 3rd person while the following
report from line 41B is autobiographical. This autobiographical
style lasts until line 70. The end of the text, dealing with the
reaction of the visionary, is again kept in the 3rd person. The
author of the tablet gives the impression that he has both heard
the dream as recounted by the visionary, and has been witness to
the enormous effect the vision had on the visionary (cf. line 74).

The opening of the vision (section B) is damaged. the only words
left contain a reference to the terror, Akk: *rašubbatsu*. The suffix
-*šu* at the end can both mean "his" or "its". Accordingly the
reference can be either to a figure or to the underworld more
generally. Since the list of underworld-gods first begins in line 42,
the last solution is more likely (cf. grammatical note 41 d.).

The list of underworld-gods (section C) lasts from line 42 to line
49. It has clearly the style of enumeration. Syntactical the sentences are kept either as nominal or as stative clauses. No course of
events is reported. The enumeration contains fifteen gods (cf. line
49B). Each one begins with mentioning the name of the god and
then describes how he is composed. There are some exceptions
from this pattern. The last god is given no name (line 49A).
Namtar is acting as executioner (described in stative clauses, line
42). Šedu is treading on a seamonster (described in a stative clause,
line 44). Saghulhaza is flying (described in the present-iterative,
line 45). But this does not effect the style of enumeration. The
first scene of the vision is accordingly static like a motionless picture. When the enumeration is ended the sum "fifteen" is given.
There follows then a short reference to the reaction of the visionary: He calls out to the underworld-gods, in despair and adoration.

The vision continues with the picture of one man (section D). The number "one" seems here to have a special semantic function in comparison to the gods: There are fifteen *ilū* and one *eṭlu*. The description of the man is kept in the same style as that of the underworld-gods (in stative clauses). But there are differences. When the gods are described, it is expressed in genitive relations. They have the heads, hands and feet *of* a man or a beast. The author gives information about how they are "built". This is not the case concerning the man. He has not the face *of* an Anzû-bird as the gods have their limbs of Anzû-birds, "his face was similar to that of an Anzu-bird" — *mašālu*, "be similar" (line 50). The description of the man has its own style which makes it an independent section of the vision.

A new section is clearly marked in line 51 with the reference to the visionary: He raised his eyes and saw a new picture: The underworld-king Nergal on his throne (section E). This section also contains a description kept in stative clauses, but the pattern from the description of the underworld-gods lacks. We get no information about how Nergal is composed or what he exactly looks like, only about his frightening appearance.

In the section (F, from line 53B(?)) the style is changed. The picture is not static, the figures move and talk. The visionary himself is no longer a mere spectator to the drama, he is an actor. The content of the scene is the judgement of the visionary and the intercession of Išum, Nergal's counsellor.

The following section (from line 58) is a long speech of Nergal (section G). The section falls into two parts, according to the two references which are given.
The first part (lines 58-61) has a direct reference to the visionary, Kummāya (line 58). He has dishonoured Ereshkigal, Nergal's wife. Therefore he is threatened with a death-sentence, which because of the intercession of Išum is altered. The future will bring him rebellion instead of immediate death.
The second part (lines 62-68) begins with a description of a king seen in the vision. In form it is a sort of interpretation. He is

described as the ideal king who is given kingship and priesthood from the gods and is under divine protection (lines 62-65). What is confusing in this section is that the verbs seems to indicate the future although they refer to a dead person (cf. grammatical note 62 b.).

In line 66 a new person seems to be introduced. Unfortunately the beginning of the clause is damaged, but the reasons to assume a new person are as follows: The ideal king from line 62ff is already introduced, so it does not seem necessary to introduce him one more time. The lines 67B and 68A contain a prediction and an admonition. The address is not singular but plural (cf. grammatical note 67 e.). Obviously the one person must be Kummāya (cf. line 68B). The other person can not be the ideal king, because he is dead. Then there must be another person involved in the speech and the only possibility for this is in the lines 66-67.

The whole second part of Nergal's speech has then the following content: It starts with the description of the ideal king (lines 62-65). He is then contrasted with the rebel king (lines 66-67). The rebel king is the father of the visionary. They are going to suffer together because of the crime (67B-68A).

The section G ends with a command that Kummāya shall leave the nether world. In due time Nergal will again remember him.

The next section (H) describes the reaction of the visionary, clearly marked with a reference to the visionary: I awoke ... (for the beginning of this section, cf. grammatical note 68 a.). The first part of this section is a simile (lines 69-70). The visionary feels like a murderer who is taken after a long flight, or like a pig who fails in the sexual act after a long try.

In the next part (lines 71-72) the style is changed from autobiographical to description in 3rd person. Here too the content is the reaction of the visionary.

The last section (I) of the vision contains the epilogue of the scribe (lines 73-75). The scribe reports how the message of the prince (line 72) changed his attitude.

The whole text contains the following sections and parts:

A. Introduction (Biographical report): line 41A

B. Opening of the vision (autobiographical report in the following): line 41B

C. The fifteen underworld-gods: lines 42-49

D. The one man: line 50

E. Nergal on the throne: lines 51-53A

F. The judgement: lines 53B-57

G. The speech of Nergal:
   Part 1:   Accusation: Crime against Ereshkigal: line 58
             Punishment: Future rebellion in the reign of the ruler: lines 59-61
   Part 2:   Accusation: Crime against the will of the ideal king and the gods:
                            lines 62-67A
             Punishment: Future annihilation of two rebellious rulers: lines
                            67B-68

H. The reaction of the visionary:
   Part 1:   Autobiographical report: lines 69-70
   Part 2:   Biographical report: lines 71-72

I. The epilogue of the scribe: lines 73-75

When we compare the pattern in this vision with the pattern in the
other Akkadian underworld-vision, the Death-Dream of Enkidu,
we find similarities in the arrangements of the sections. Also the
Vision of the Nether World follows the pattern which the Death-
Dream of Enkidu shared with the other underworld texts, (cf. pp.
383ff).

1. The descent to the nether world
2. The encounter with the dwellers and the conditions in the nether world
3. The encounter with the ruling god and the judgement.

Using this pattern as a model for our text, we see clearly what
makes our text so complex. It is above all the second part of
section G. If we omit this part, we get a fairly simple structure:
The descent, the encounter with the underworld-gods, the
encounter with the ruling god, the judgement with the intercession, the speech of the underworld-judge with the determination
of the visionary's future fate, the reaction of the visionary. It is
the break with this common pattern which above all is marked in
section G, which makes the interpretation of our text so complicated.

2.2   The Gattung

In the analysis of the Gattung of the Death-Dream of Enkidu we came to the conclusion that the dream was neither clearly a symbolic dream nor a message dream, but a sort of clairvoyance on the level of the dram where the visionary saw his own future death (cf. above, pp. 363ff).

Our vision shares the same pattern as the Death-Dream to a certain extent, but the events at the end of the vision give an altered perspective. By the intercession of Išum the sentence of Nergal is altered. He does not decree the death-sentence as we can suppose Ereshkigal did for Enkidu. Instead Nergal warns and admonishes the visionary and predicts a future filled with misfortune until he in due time will collect the visionary again (lines 60-61, 68).

The vision has then the same structure as the dreams Oppenheim characterizes as "message-dreams". These dreams contain a vision of the deity and an audition of his message in the form of warnings, admonitions and predictions just as in our text.[93]

But section G, part 2, in our text differs from this structure. The message which normally belongs to the "message-dreams" concerns the visionary and has him and his situation in focus. It is also clear and distinct. The last part of Nergal's speech concerns the visionary only indirectly. The immediate reference is to two other rulers who are contrasted. The description of these rulers is vague and does not clearly reveal their identity. In this section the dream functions as a medium for the revelation not only concerning the visionary himself, but concerning a part of the history in which he is involved.

There are no direct parallels to this in other dreams. But some of the elements have similarities with other texts, although they are not so close.

An example where the Gattung "dream" is used as a frame for a text with historical relevance, is found in the Poem of Erra. The poem is in itself a "mythological" text which tells how the god of scorched earth Erra took over the government of the world from

---

93 Cf. A.L. Oppenheim, The Interpretation of Dreams in the Ancient Near East, pp. 197ff; and the translation of the dreams number 8-12, pp. 249f.

Marduk. But the text has also historical relevance. It interprets a part of the history as a reflection of the divine drama in heaven.[94] At the very end of the poem the scribe reveals the nature of the text:

> Kabti-ilani-Marduk the son of Dabibi
> (was) the composer of this tablet:
> (The deity) revealed it to him during the night,
> and in the morning, when he recited (it),
> he did not skip a single (line).
> Nor a single line (of his own) did he add to it.
>   (Tabl. V, lines 42-44)[95]

Here the Gattung "night-vision"[96] is used as a medium for the gods to reveal the meaning of the history in which the visionary was involved. And it is used to underline the authority of the revelation.

Another example which is worth considering actually includes some of the content of our dream. In our vision one of the figures is clearly identified as a dead king. We have at least one other Mesopotamian dream with the same content. The dream was inscribed on a stela erected by the Neo-Babylonian king Nabonidus. The whole text tells about Nabonidus' rise to power. The section of the dream report which concerns the dead king runs as follows:

> In the same dream, when my royal predecessor
> Nebuchadnezzar and one attendant (appeared to me)
> standing in a chariot,
> the attendant said to Nebuchadnezzar:
> "Do speak to Nabonidus, that he should
> report to you the dream he has seen!"
> And I answered him, saying:
> "In my dream I beheld with joy
> the Great Star, the moon and Marduk
> high up on the sky and it (the Great Star)
> called me by my name.[97]

---

94 Cf. L. Cagni, The Poem of Erra, pp. 13f; and my discussion of the Poem of Erra in Part I, pp. 181ff.
95 Translation from Cagni, p. 60.
96 The transliteration of the second sentence in our quotation is in šāt mūši ušabrīšūma, "revealed to him during the night". Transliteration from L. Cagni, L'epopea di Erra, SS 34, Roma 1969, p. 126. The verb ušabri is the Š-stem of barû, "look at", which in connection with mūšu, "night", or similar words is a technical term for "reveal in a dream" or "vision", cf. CAD, sub barû, A. 5.b, p. 118.
97 Cf. col. vi. For translation, cf. ANET[3], pp. 309f. For description, cf. Oppenheim, Dreams, pp. 203-5.

The content of the dream seems to be that Nabonidus had had a dream vision where he experienced a miraculous astrological event. In the same dream his predecessor Nebukadnezzar arrives and interprets the dream for him.

Compared to our vision there are no direct similarities in style or description, apart from that a king appears in both dreams. What the dreams have in common is a religious presupposition and a political intention.

The presupposition lies in the religious reverence of dead kings in the Neo-Assyrian and Neo-Babylonian period.[98] This reverence is reflected in the royal funeral cult in which certain kings had a special interest. Ashurbanipal writes:

> "I made arrangements for the funeral offerings
> and libations for the ghosts of my royal predecessors,
> which had fallen into abeyance;
> I did good to god and man,
> to dead and living.
> Why are sickness, sorrow, loss and expense
> always connected with me?"[99]

On the stela erected by Nabonidus in Harran it is written:

> "Afterwards they died (the Assyrian kings);
> none of their children, none of their families
> and of their officials to whom —
> when they had been put into office —
> they had given rich gifts,
> performed actually as much
> as a fumigation-offering,
> whereas I brought monthly,
> without interruption — in my best garments
> — offerings to their souls,
> fat lambs, bread, fine bear, wine, oil,
> honey and all kind of garden fruits,
> and established as perpetual offerings
> abundant fumigations (yielding) sweet smells for them
> and placed . . . before them."[100]

---

98   Cf. M. Bayliss, "The Cult of the Dead Kin in Assyria and Babylonia", pp. 122ff.

99   For transliteration and translation, cf. M. Streck, Assurbanipal II, VAB, Leipzig 1916, pp. 251f (reverse line 1-5). English translation from Bayliss, op.cit., p. 123.

100   Cf. col. iii, lines 7-19. For transliteration, translation and commentary, cf. B. Landsberger, Die Basalstele Nabonids von Eski-Harran, Memoriam Halil Edhem, Vol. 1, Ankara 1947, pp. 115-51. The English translation is taken from ANET[3], p. 312.

The similarity between the dreams in political intention does not mean that the dreams show similar political point of views. It lies in the attitude to the royal predecessor. In both cases he was the ideal king from whom the living king needed appreciation.

The analysis of the Gattung has then given the same result as the description of the structure and content: If we exclude section G, part 2, the dream has a simple structure. Concerning the Gattung, it follows the pattern from the message-dreams; concerning the traditions, it follows the pattern from the underworld texts. What makes the text special is that this pattern "underworld dream" is used as a frame for a political message with a broader historical reference. The elements isolated are not without parallels, but the composition is highly original.

2.3   The Basic Elements of the Dream Report

2.3.1   The Underworld Gods (Sect. C)

Fifteen underworld-gods are counted.[101] The enumeration follows a stereotyped structure. The description is mostly kept in stative clauses, the comparison in genitive relations. The pattern used in the description of the figures is as follows:

name

head of	lion (4x), man (2x), Anzu-bird (2x), Kuribu, serpent-dragon, bird, ox, goat
hands of	man (8x), Anzu-bird (2x)
feet of	man (5x), Anzu-bird (2x), eagle, bird, ox
attitude	holding a mace, a sword, left foot on a seamonster, flying
(headdress	wearing a crown (2x))

The order "name, head, hands, feet" is found in the description of all monsters (except Namtar at the beginning). The attitude of four of the monsters is mentioned. The headdress of two monsters is mentioned in connection with the description of the head.

101   For discussion of each of the gods, cf. C. Frank, "Lamastu, Pazuzu und andere Dämonen", pp. 23-41.

In the description of the heads the author shows great variation: Eight different features are mentioned, although features from lion and bird dominate. In the description of the hands and feet there is, however, monotony: most of the monsters have features from human beings, although features from birds are also represented. If we consider all limbs together, features from men, birds (eagles — Anzu-birds have eagle-features) and lions predominate.

This way of describing gods has a close parallel in a List of Gods (Göttertypentext) excavated in Ashur as our tablet was, but is also represented on tablets found elsewhere.[102] Also this text contains enumeration of gods with description in the stative and comparison in genitive relations. The pattern used in the description of the gods is as follows:

```
*head and headdress
 face
 hair and decoration of face
*hands
 body
 garment
*feet
*attitude
*name
```

We have marked the points which are represented also in our text. The order is the same, except for the placing of the name which comes first in our text. The difference is that the List of Gods is much more detailed in its description.

Unfortunately we do not know the purpose of the List of Gods. The style has similarities with descriptions of how to make images of gods for prophylactic purposes as a part of an incantation ritual.[103] But there are given no references to such a purpose in the List of Gods. The connection is difficult to decide.

The connection between the List of Gods and our text is also difficult to decide. But since the similarities concern both syntax, order and phrases it seems clear that the texts share the same

102 Cf. F. Köcher, "Der babylonische Göttertypentext", MIOF 1, 1953, pp. 57-103.
103 Cf. O.R. Gurney, "Babylonian Prophylactic Figures and their Rituals", AAA 12, 1935, pp. 31-96. Such figures were found during the excavations at Nimrud, cf. M.E.L. Mallowan, "The excavations at Nimrud", pp. 85ff; and Nimrud and its Remain I, London 1966, pp. 266ff.

linguistic conventions. A direct influence from the older List of Gods upon the vision is possible, but difficult to prove.

The difficulty in deciding the nature of the connection between these texts rests upon that they share the same attitude towards the divine. The gods and semi-gods were not experienced in abstract terms, but represented concretely through statues, paintings and reliefs. Obviously behind such conventions lay the depiction of the divine creatures for cultic purposes, and these conventions are also reflected in the human mind, and in the linguistic style. Therefore the transmission of conventions need not be textual, but cultural.

2.3.2   The Unique Man (Sect. D)

2.3.2.1   Previous Identifications

As far as we know, there is no previous thorough discussion of this figure of the dream. But short remarks have been made in the general notes to the text.

E. Ebeling[104] thought that the man was identical with Išum, Nergal's counsellor in lines 56B-57. The reason for this opinion was that he connected the name Išum, derived from $i\check{s}\bar{a}tu$, "fire", with the red robe the man was wearing. The man was "der Feuerrote". Another reason why Ebeling chose this solution could be that he had $etlum$ as the term for $I\check{s}um$ in line 56B. This translation is, however, impossible on the basis of the new transliteration of the text by von Soden (cf. grammatical note 56 c.). We are far from convinced that the text gives any grounds to suppose that the author should have made the following associations: Išum — fire — red — red robe — the man. The evidence of the text goes in another direction. When Išum is mentioned in line 56B, there are no references to an earlier occurrence, but he is thoroughly introduced in the same way as the other main figures of the text when they are described for the first time (cf. lines 50, 51, 66, 73).

B. Landsberger identified the man as Nergal's executioner (Scharfrichter Nergals) who was a negro (the black colour).[105]

---

104   E. Ebeling, Tod und Leben nach den Vorstellungen der Babylonier I, p. 6, note q.

105   B. Landsberger, "Einige unerkannt gebliebene oder verkannte Nomina des Akkadischen", pp. 8f.

There is nothing explicit in the description of the man to support
this interpretation. There are indications which oppose it. Firstly,
the equipment of the man (sword and bow) points to a warrior
rather than to an executioner, as does the attitude (treading on the
victim). Secondly, Biblu is explicitly mentioned in the text as the
executioner (line 59). He has the sign for "god", DINGIR, linked
to his name. So has also Namtar who acts as an executioner in the
beginning of the vision (line 42), and Išum when he is mentioned
in line 56B. "The man" does not have this sign. We think therefore
we can conclude that Landsberger's interpretation lacks positive
support in the text and that there are indications against it.

K. Frank suggested that "the man" might be identical with the
figure at the beginning of the Death-Dream of Enkidu.[106] This
suggestion has been confirmed by the publication of the new
tablets to the dream (cf. our transliterated text to the Death-
Dream).

The following sentence occurs in both texts: *ištēn eṭlu ... ana ša
anzî panūšu mašlū*, "One man ..., whose face was similar to that
of an Anzu-bird". The identical wording means that the texts are
related in one way or another, but it does not mean that the figure
described in this way is necessarily the same in both texts.

A. Heidel suggested that the man might be identical with the ruler
described in the lines 62ff. More recently J. Bottero has argued for
the same view.[107] I think this is the solution which has the best
textual support.

2.3.2.2 Textual Evidences

In the speech of Nergal, lines 62ff, it is explicitly said that the
ruler there described is seen in the vision. This part of the speech
is formed as an interpretation to a sequence in the vision: "this ...
which you saw in the nether world". In the vision all figures
before line 62, except "the man", have the determinative for
"god". So among the figures mentioned, "the man" is the only one
who could be identified as a human king.

There are two lacunas in the text: About 15 signs are missing at
the end of line 41. But fifteen signs are not sufficient to introduce

---

106   Frank, Lamaštu, Pazuzu und andere Dämonen", p. 40.
107   Heidel, The Gilgamesh Epic, p. 134, note 109; J. Bottero, "Antiquité
Assyro-Babyloniennes", p. 96.

and describe such an important figure of the vision. Apart from that it is most likely that we have here an opening description of the nether world. The other lacuna is larger. About 21 signs are missing in line 52. But this section contains the description of Nergal. We can therefore conclude that there is nothing which indicates that the description of the king, presupposed from line 62, should have been in the lacunas. Accordingly there is no other figure in the vision that "the man" that can be identified as the king in line 62ff.

"The man" is introduced as "one man" (ištēn eṭlu) in contrast to the fifteen gods (ilū). The contrast *ilu* — *eṭlu* seems to have been formed deliberately (cf. below). That means, however, that *eṭlu* has to be understood as another kind of figure than *ilu*, *eṭlu* can not designate a "god".

The noun *eṭlu* occurs two other times in the vision. First as a designation for Kummāya in line 56B (cf. grammatical note 56 c.), then in the simile in the line 69. Both times *eṭlu* designates "a man" as a human being.

We think that after this analysis we can consider it certain that "the man" in line 50 is identical with the king described in lines 62ff.

2.3.2.3   The Description of The Man

The man's body is described as "black like pitch". Landsberger thinks therefore that the man was a negro (Landsberger, our note 105). There are no indications in the text to support this interpretation. In the text the black body is mentioned together with the "face similar to that of an Anzu-bird". The Anzu-bird was depicted by the Sumerians as an eagle with lion-head, and the features of the eagle and the lion seem to be extant also in the Assyrian image of the monster (cf. above, pp. 375f). Therefore it seems reasonable to assume that the man shares the black colour of the eagle. The description of the man in the Death-Dream of Enkidu, line 17: "One man, whose face was dark", seems to have inspired our author, considering that the next line has identical wording in the two visions. The dark face in the Death-Dream symbolized ill fortune, as does also the black colour generally in

Akkadian texts.[108] The first part of the description of the man, which concerns his body, seems then to be formed on the basis of the Anzu-bird symbolism and the intention to present the man as "a bringer of misfortune". In the context this means that the vision of the man is an unfavourable sign for the visionary.

The use of the Anzu-bird symbolism will in general underline that the man is frightening and powerful (cf. above, p. 377). This symbolism is not necessarily dependent upon the underworld framework which gives the context here. In several reports from Assyrian kings we find Anzu-bird comparisons when they describe battles.

In an inscription of Ashurnaṣirpal it is written: "My warriors flew against them like the Anzu-bird".[109] And in the "Tukulti-Ninurta Epic", col. ii, line 37, the fighting soldiers are described as follows: "They are raging, fierce, strange in shape like the Anzu-bird".[110]

An interesting report about the battle at Ishḫupri is found in the inscriptions of Esarhaddon. This report is again strongly dependent upon a report of Sennacherib describing the battle at Ḥalule.[111] The report of Esarhaddon reads (German translation from Borger):

Ich wurde wütend wie ein Löwe,
zog den Panzer an, setze den Helm,
eine notwendige Kampfausrüstung, auf mein Haupt,
und fasste mit meiner Hand den mächtigen Bogen
und den starken Pfeil, die Assur, der König der Götter,
mir verliehen hatte.
Wie ein wütender Adler, ging ich sintflutgleich
im Spitze meines Heeres.
. . . Unter ihrem starken Beistande
sturmte ich wie ein grimmig sich erhebender Sturm
in ihre Mitte.

(lines 6B-10, 17B)[112]

---

108   Cf. E. Unger, "Farben", RLA III, Berlin-New York 1957-71, pp. 24ff.
109   Cf. E.A.W. Budge and L.W. King, The Annals of the Kings of Assyria, London 1902, p. 223, rev. line 25.
110   Cf. E. Ebeling, "Bruchstücke eines Politischen Propagandagedichtes aus einer Assyrischen Kanzlei", MAOG 12, 1938, pp. 1-41. More examples of comparisons between fighting soldiers and Anzu are given by Hruška, Der Mythenadler Anzu, pp. 46f.
111   Cf. D.D. Luckenbill, The Annals of Senacherib, Chicago 1924, pp. 44f; The Oriental Institute Prism Inscription, col. v, lines 67-69.
112   Translation from R. Borger, Die Inschriften Asarhaddons, p. 65; Anhang: Nin. E, Kol. ii.

Here we have the basic elements which occur in the description of the Anzu-bird: The roaring lion, the fierce eagle and the storm which is accompanying the beast (for the last cf. also the report of Sennacherib).

The man was wearing a red robe. A red garment was also worn by the incantation-priest for protection against the evil demons.[113] Generally the red was regarded as a colour with favourable effect.[114] In our context it can symbolize protection against the underworld-gods, but more likely it is thought as a "warrior-garment" for protection against the enemies.

The armour of the man is the armour of a soldier. A description which comes close to our text may be found in a dream report from a priest to Ashurbanipal:

> The goddess Ishtar who dwells in Arbela entered the room,
> quivers hanging at her right and left,
> holding the bow in her (one) hand,
> The sharp sword drawn (ready) for battle.[115]

The attitude of the man is the attitude of a victor. In the List of Gods (cf. pp. 407f) it is said about the god Ninurta who in the Myth of Anzu conquered the Anzu-bird (cf. p. 372): "With his foot he is treading on the Anzu-bird".[116] A depiction which may reflect the same myth is found on several cylinder seals. The motif is a god, equipped as a warrior, treading with one foot on a monster.[117] The victory-stela of Naram-Sin which was erected in Sippar to celebrate the victory over the mountain people Lullubi shows the same attitude. The same motif is later carved upon a wall of a rock at the gateway to Asia.[118] The stela shows Naram-Sin placed on a mountain. The king is depicted as a divine hero, with horned helmet. He is armed with a bow, axe and arrows. With his left foot he is treading on the dead bodies of his defeated enemy.

---

113 Cf. L. Waterman, Royal Correspondence of the Assyrian Empire I, Michigan 1930, p. 21; letter 24, line 15.
114 Cf. Unger, "Farben", p. 25.
115 The translation is taken from Oppenheim, Dreams, p. 249; for description, cf. pp. 200f.
116 Cf. Köcher, "Göttertypentext", rev., col. ii, line 9, p. 67.
117 Cf. Ilse Fuhr-Jaeppelt, Materialien zur Ikonographie des Löwenadlers Anzu-Imdugur, pictures 214-19, pp. 208-19.
118 Cf. A. Mortgat, The Art of Ancient Mesopotamia, plates 155-7, pp. 51ff.

Taking the different features in the description of the man together, we get the following picture: He has the frightening features of the Anzu-bird, he wears a protective red robe against his enemies, he is equipped as a warrior, his attitude is that of a glorious victor. The man is certainly depicted as a frightening, powerful and victorious hero.

2.3.2.4   The Phrase *ištēn eṭlu*

A. *ištēn*

Grammatically *ištēn* is to be classified as the cardinal number "one" in status absolutus masculinum.[119] It can also be used as an indefinite article "a". In some connections it is used as a sort of emphasizing article with the meaning "unique, outstanding", etc.[120] This is especially the case of the status rectus form *ištānu*.[121]

B. *eṭlu*

eṭlu means literally "young man" or just "man". Used about an ordinary human being it refers to the grown up man. The word can also be used about kings and gods. They are then qualified as full grown males at the peak of their physical powers. Often the word is used as a honorific designation with the connotation "hero".[122] With this connotation the word is a frequent designation for the Assyrian kings.[123] *eṭlu* shares part of the semantic field of *amēlu*, the ordinary Akkadian word for "man / human being": Both words can refer to the grown up man; both words can designate men in leading positions, but amēlu is not common as a designation for a king, it is then an administrative title, meaning "governor".[124] Thus *eṭlu*, as a royal title, corresponds to the designation of the figure in the interpretation as "the exalted shepherd" (line 62), which is a common title for the king as well.

---

119   W. von Soden, GAG § 69, p. 91.
120   Cf. CAD, sub ištēn, p. 275ff.
121   Cf. von Soden, op.cit.
122   Cf. CAD, sub eṭlu, p. 407ff.
123   Cf. M.-J. Seux, Épithètes Royales. Akkadiennes et Sumériennes, Paris 1967, pp. 91-3.
124   Cf. for amēlu, T. Jacobsen, "Inuma Ilu awīlum", Ancient Near Eastern Studies in Memory of J.J. Finkelstein, Connecticut 1977, pp. 113-7, p. 115, note 16.

C. ištēn eṭlu

The phrase *ištēn eṭlu* is a fixed term in several Akkadian dream reports. A survey of the occurrence of the phrase is given below.

A. Old Babylonian dream report (most likely the first dream of Gilgamesh, indicated in the Neo-Assyrian tablets, Tabl. V, col. i, line 6ff). Our translation is from ANET[3], p. 504. Cf. for transliteration, translation and notes, W. von Soden, "Beiträge zum Verständnis des babylonischen Gilgamesh-Epos", ZA 53, 1959, pp. 215-9. (Cf. our short description, p. 386.)

B. Gilgamesh' second dream. Gilgamesh epic, Tabl. V, col. i, lines 12ff; Interpretation: Tabl. V, col. iii, lines 37-43. Our translation is from ANET[3], pp. 82-3. Cf. for translation and description, A.L. Oppenheim, Dreams, pp. 247f and 215ff.

C. D. The dreams of a righteous sufferer. Ludlul bēl nēmeqi, Tabl. III, lines 8-44. Our translation is from W.G. Lambert, Babylonian Wisdom Literature, Oxford 1960, pp. 21-62. Translation also in ANET[3], pp. 596ff.

E. A dream of Nabonidus. (On the basalt stela in Istanbul, col. vi in ANET[3].) Our translation is from ANET[3], pp. 309f. Cf. for translation and description also Oppenheim, Dreams, pp. 250 and 203f.

F. The Death-Dream of Enkidu. Cf. our own translation and discussion.

G. The Vision of the Nether World. Cf. our own translation and discussion.

The figure: In the dreams E, F, G below the figure is rendered partly syllabically as *1-en eṭ-lu*. The form of the first word is status absolutus. In the dream B both words are written as logograms *1-en* LU.GURUŠ. In the dreams C and D the first word has the form of status rectus.

In status rectus *ištānu* functions like an "emphasizing article" with the meaning "a unique" (cf. above). This seems also to be the case in the other dreams (for the moment we exclude dream G). There are no other figures or any other circumstances involved that should demand the stress on "one". But it is quite clear the intention of the dreams to emphasize the figure itself. The translation "a unique man" will therefore be in accordance with the semantic value of the phrase in these dreams.

Since dream G has the same phrase with partly the same structural function within the dream, it seems also here correct to consider *ištēn* as an "emphasizing article". But unlike the other dreams the man is here contrasted to the fifteen underworld-gods. In this dream the word *ištēn* seems to have a double function: In the first place to emphasize the figure, dependent upon the style of the Gattung; in the second place to contrast the man against the underworld-gods. The semantic value seems therefore to be "one unique man".

Pattern	A 1st Dream of Gilgamesh	B 2nd Dream of Gilgamesh	C The Righteous Sufferer 1st Dream	D 2nd Dream
Introduction	My friend, I saw a dream	A second dream I saw		A second time [I saw a dream]
Figure		ištēn eṭlu	ištānu eṭlu	ištānu eṭlu
Description		The fairest in the land was he; his grace [. . .]	. . . of out- standing physique. Massive in his body, clothed in new gar- ments	Holding in his hand a tama- risk rod of purification
Activity	(He was seiz- ing [. . .] strength, my flank). He tore out the [. . .] He provided food . . . [he] drank, [he] gave me [to dr]ink from his waterskin	From under the mountain he pulled me out, gave me water to drink; my heart qui[eted]. On the ground he set my feet	(Section damaged)	The water he was carrying he threw over me, pronoun- ced the life- giving incan- tation and rubbed [my body]
Interpretation	The one who gave you to drink from his waterskin, he is your god who brings honour. We should join (with him) Lugalbanda	(General: The dream is favour- able)		

E	F	G
Dream of Nabonidus	Death-Dream of Enkidu	Vision of the Nether World
	I saw a dream during my nighttime	he saw a night-vision
ištēn eṭlu	ištēn eṭlu	ištēn eṭlu
	. . . whose face was similar to that of an Anzu-bird, his hands (were) the paws of a lion, his fingernails were) of an eagle	. . . his body was black like pitch. His face was similar to that of an Anzu-bird. He was wearing a red robe. In his left hand he was holding up a bow. In his right hand he was holding a sword
(he) came to my assistance, saying to me: "There are no evil portents in the impending constellation".	He seized my forelock and strove for superiority over me . . . (cf. lines 20-33 in our translation)	(Described as a king, lines 62-65)
		This [spirit] which you saw in the nether world, is that of the exalted shepherd . . .

In dream A no figure is mentioned in the preserved text. Several signs are missing where this could have been done. There is no evidence to suggest the reading *ištēn eṭlu* from the text itself. But the dream is most likely the first of Gilgamesh' dreams, since it has exactly the same structure and partly the same content as the second dream. So the figure described in the dream can very well be parallel to *ištēn eṭlu* in the second dream.

The description: The description may concern the body (dreams B, C, F, G), the garment (dreams C, G) and the equipment (dreams D, G) of the man. The description of the body and garment tells whether the vision of the man is favourable or not: the beauty (dream B, C) versus the frightening (dreams F, G). The equipment tells about the identity of the figure (dreams D, G).

The activity: In four of the dreams the man is active (A, B, D, F), in one he is announcing a message (E). In three of the dreams the man acts as a "saviour" (A, B, D). In two of these dreams the activity is the same: The man cares for the visionary and gives him water (A, B). (The man here used about the main figure of the vision since we include dream A). In the "message-dream" the man is also a bringer of fortune (E). One of the dreams here forms a contrast: Here the man acts as an enemy (F).
In dream G no activity is reported here. The description of the man, including some of the features from dream F, depicts him as an unfavourable sign for the visionary. The description of the man in the interpretation, however, shows the opposite: In view of the composer of the tablet he is the ideal king, a "saviour".

The interpretation: Three of the dreams are interpreted (A, B, G). In two it is explicitly said whom the main figure of the vision is (A, G). A third dream gets a favourable interpretation, which more generally shows that the man is a bringer of fortune (B).

Identification: Since two of the dreams are explicitly interpreted, the identification of two of the dream figures seems clear. In dream A it is Lugalbanda, Gilgamesh' dead father, who was believed to be his tutelar god. In dream G it is a dead king in the nether world. In the other dreams it is only possible to get a more general impression. In dream D the man is clearly described as a purification-priest. In dream F he is clearly described as a deputy from the nether world. In dream E the man appears in the same dream as the dead king Nebuchadnezzar. Later in the dream one of the king's attendants are introduced as a mediator between the visionary and Nebuchadnezzar. Although it is not explicitly said in the dream, there are reasons to suppose that it is the attendant who is designated as *ištēn eṭlu* earlier in the dream.

Variations: This scheme shows "the standard pattern" for the use of *ištēn eṭlu* in the dreams. There are some variations. In a dream reported by Ashurbanipal the visionary is called *ištēn eṭlu*.[125] This corresponds to a certain extent with our vision where Kummāya also is called *eṭlu* (line 56B).

In the third dream of the righteous sufferer the dream figure is described in this way:

```
iš-te-e[t] batūltu ba-nu-ù zi[mu-šá]
ni-ši-iš [    ] i-liš ma[š-lat]
šar-rat niši-m [eš           ]
```
                              Tabl. III, lines 30a-32[126]

A unique young girl, [her] counten[ance] was beautiful,
like a human being [   ] similar to a god
a queen of the peoples.

The text continues:

33. She entered and [sat down] . . .
34. She spoke my deliverance [. . .]
35. "Fear not", she said, I [will . . .]
36. (   )
37. She said, "Be delivered from your very wretched state,
38. Whoever has seen a vision in the night time."[127]

---

125   Cf. Oppenheim, Dreams, p. 249f and 201f.
126   The text is from the more recently identified tablet BM 54821. This tablet is considered by Lambert in his addenda to Babylonian Wisdom Literature, p. 345. In the transliteration we have only rendered the signs which belong to words which with certainty can be identified.
127   The translation is from Lambert, op.cit., p. 51. In line 34 we read the preterite which is confirmed by BM 54821, cf. Lambert, addenda, p. 345. In line 36 we refrain from a translation since the preserved text gives no meaning, cf. Lambert, addenda.

The pattern of this text is exactly the same as in the other dreams. It comes closest to the dream E, since this also is a "message-dream". The only difference is that the dream figure is classified as *ištet batūltu*, "a unique young girl", instead of *ištānu eṭlu*, "a unique young man". The description of the girl is interesting. She is both like a human being and like a god in her beauty. Obviously there is no difficulty in combining the two aspects: The outstanding beauty of a human body was a reflection of the outstanding beauty of the gods.

In the same third dream another dream figure is introduced. He is named and accordingly familiar to the contemporaries of the author (unfortunately not for us): Urnindinlugga, the Babylonian (?). He is an incantation-priest of profession. In the dream he announces the deliverance of the visionary, like the young girl. This person is also called *eṭlu* (line 40).

Conclusions:

1)   There is no need to doubt that the description of the dream figures generally has its background in real dream experiences, either as dream visions of figures of outstanding beauty or, by contrast, with frightening features.

2)   On the literary level the language of the dream experiences has undergone a standardization. The main figure of the vision is emphasized as "unique" *(ištēn)* and most commonly designated as "a young man" *(eṭlu)*. Since the favourable dreams are in clear majority, it seems most likely that this standardization has developed within this type of dreams. The textual indications from the Death-Dream of Enkidu give support for this assumption (cf. above, p. 374). The designation *eṭlu* is then also transferred to unfavourable dreams as an extension of the Gattung-pattern. If this observation is correct, the designation *eṭlu* originally corresponded to the beauty of the dream figure: It was a young man at the peak of his physical development. Support for this opinion is given in the third dream of the righteous sufferer where the dream figure is described as *batūltu*, "a young girl". The young girl in this dream both resembles a human being and a god. She represents in other words the ideal beauty. The same is the case of *eṭlu:* The young man of the dreams represents the ideal of beauty and strength for both human and gods.

3) The man is a mediator between the gods and the visionary. He is their representative. His task can be carried out either through an act or a message, and it can be either favourable or unfavourable. Dream G has a combination of both aspects: The man is favourable in view of the composer, but unfavourable for the visionary.

4) There is no clear evidence that the designation *ištēn eṭlu* should represent an already fixed conception which can be isolated from the dreams. In that case we should have expected some sort of identity between the figures that are designated in this way.

But there are some indications that may support a connection between *eṭlu* in the dreams and the dead. This is certainly the case in the Death-Dream and in the Vision of the Nether World. But such an interpretation is also possible in two other dreams.

If we are correct in that the Old Babylonian dream (A) is the first dream of Gilgamesh and renders the same pattern as the second, there are reasons to assume that the saviours of the two dreams are meant to be the same person. The *ištēn eṭlu* of the second dream would then be Lugalbanda, Gilgamesh' dead father.

The *ištēn eṭlu* of the dream of Nabonidus (E) appears in the same dream as the dead king Nebuchadnezzar, possibly as his attendant. He could therefore also belong to the nether world.

The only dreams left where there are no indications of a connection to the dead, are the dreams of the righteous sufferer. Here it is difficult to decide whether the dream figures are living or dead persons.[128]

The indications mentioned are not to be regarded as conclusive evidence. But if *ištēn eṭlu* was a designation for dead people appearing in dreams, it would have explained the transference of

---

[128] Lambert denies the latter: "We know nothing that lends support to the idea that these were dead worthies who in their disembodied state cared for this unfortunate man. The shades of the Babylonians troubled the living if not provided with burial and offerings, but never helped them"; Babylonian Wisdom Literature, p. 23. This statement does not seem quite in accordance with the following rendering in a letter: [The crown prince] explained [it as follows]: "The gods Aššur (and) Šamaš ordained me to be the crown prince of Assyria because of her (= the dead queen's) truthfulness." (And) her ghost blesses him in the same degree as he revered the ghost: "May his descendants rule over Assyria!" (As it is said), fear of the gods creates kindness, fear of the Anunnaki-gods returns life." Cf. for transliteration and translation, S. Parpola, Letters From Assyrian Scholars to the Kings Esarhaddon and Ashurbanipal, Part I: Texts, AOAT 5/1, Neukirchen-Vluyn 1970, Nr. 132, p. 106.

the designation from the favourable dreams to the dreams of the nether world.

5) Within the dreams the use of *ištēn eṭlu* in the Vision of the Nether World is special in three ways. In the first place it is emphasized through the contrast *ilu — eṭlu* that the man, although he belongs to the realm of the gods, is a human being. In the second place the designation is in correspondence with the Gattung-style in the other dreams and must be read in this context. In the third place the *eṭlu* is identified as a king. And the Assyrian kings very often used *eṭlu* as a designation for themselves.

The semantic value of *ištēn eṭlu* in the Vision of the Nether World can therefore be summarized as follows:

1. *ištēn eṭlu* =   one man / human being in contrast to the underworld-god, the monsters (*ištēn* = "one"; *eṭlu* = "man / human being").

2. *ištēn eṭlu* =   the unique man in a dream experience as mediator between the gods and men (*ištēn* = "unique"; *eṭlu* = "ideal man").

3. *ištēn eṭlu* =   the ideal king, designated "the exalted shepherd" in the interpretation of the dream (*eṭlu* = "hero").

2.3.3   Nergal on the Throne (Sect. E)

The vision of Nergal contains the traditional elements of the description of the ruling god of the underworld: The god is sitting on a royal throne, wearing the royal insignia; he is surrounded by the Anunnaki-gods and provokes adoration and fear among the dwellers of the nether world, (cf. above, pp. 382f).

Nergal is holding two maces in his hands. The most likely interpretation of the text is that each mace had two animal-heads (cf. grammatical note 51 b.). The common symbol for Nergal is a staff with lion-head. There are examples of depictions of a mace with two lion-heads, either worn by a god or as a symbol for a god. Whether Nergal is the god represented in these depictions is under discussion.[129] Our text might be a support for this assumption.

---

129   Cf. E. von Weiher, Der babylonische Gott Nergal, pp. 45ff.

In our text it is Nergal and not as is usually the case Ereshkigal who is the head of the underworld-pantheon. The belief in Nergal as an underworld-god is well attested as early as the Old Babylonian period, and is reflected in the myth Nergal and Ereshkigal (cf. above, p. 369). In the Sumerian "Death of Ur-Nammu" (cf. above, p. 370) Nergal is described as the first of the underworldgods. He has the title: "Nergal, Enlil of the nether world" (line 89). This means that Nergal is the lord of the nether world, just as Enlil is the lord of the earth. In Old Babylonian texts he is also described as judge and the god who determines the fate of men.[130]

In later texts Nergal is also described as the god of light and fire.[131] He surrounds himself with a terrifying sheen. This was especially combined with the image of Nergal as a star deity, identified with the planet Mars. So just as to the human eye the fire-light of the planet seemed to flash the god himself was flashing. As it is said in a prayer to Nergal:

ki-ma birqi it-ta-nab-riq lētā-šu

"His cheeks are always flashing as lightning."[132]

Which comes very close to our text:

i(?)-di-š birqu i-bar-ri-iq

"(from?) his sides lightning was flashing." (line 52)

The combination $birqu — barāqu$ (lightning — flash) is often used in describing the gods which were connected with the natural forces, especially the god Adad.[133] But this seems not to be the case in our text, since Nergal not was believed to be a "weathergod", but a god of light and fire.

But the two aspects of reality of the ancients, the divine manifestation through frightening natural forces (theophany), and through the powers of death, can be combined (as we have shown in the

---

130 Weiher, op.cit., pp. 14f.; 20f.
131 Weiher, op.cit., pp. 73-6. In this respect Nergal could also be identified with Gibil, the god of fire. Cf. Weiher, p. 75. On the god Gibil, cf. K.L. Tallqvist, Die Assyrische Beschwörungsserie Maqlû, ASSF XX, No. 6, 1894, pp. 23-30.
132 Cf. Weiher, op.cit., p. 77.
133 For examples, cf. CAD, sub birqu, 1b, p. 259.

Death-Dream, cf. above, pp. 372f). This seems to be the case in the second dream of Gilgamesh, where the lightning is both connected with the thunderstorm and the breaking through of the powers of death:

> The heavens thundered, the earth rumbled,
> daylight ceased, darkness advanced,
> lightning flashed, fire shot up,
> it rained death.
>
> (Tabl. V, col. iv, lines 15-18)[134]

2.3.4 The Judgement (Sect. F)

The scene of judgement begins as expected according to the pattern of the text: The visionary is taken before the throne of Nergal to receive his death-sentence. But in the moment the visionary is going to be killed, the course of events is interrupted by Ishum.

The god Ishum is described as Nergal's counsellor (line 56B). In the Poem of Erra he is regarded as Erra's counsellor, but in this poem Nergal and Erra are to a certain extent regarded as the same god.[135]

The role of Ishum in our text is so closely related to the role of Ishum in the Poem of Erra that our text seems to be dependent upon this poem: compare our lines 56B-57 with the Poem of Erra, Tabl. I, lines 100-103; Tabl. III, fragment C, lines 34-37; Tabl. IV, lines 128-129.

The reason for this introduction of Ishum as a moderator of the fury of Nergal and the following alteration of the death-sentence, is to be sought in the setting of the story. The other underworld-texts were either fictions (myths, legendary epics) or they dealt with already dead persons. Then the descent-experience could either be the description of the death itself, or a premonition of the death as the immediate consequence. This is different in our text, because it also deals with history. The narrator had to adjust the story to what really happened. This can be an indication for the dating of the composition. Since the visionary is not going to

---

134   For the Akkadian text, cf. CAD, sub barāqu, 1,1', p. 104; and sub mūtu, d, p. 318.
135   Cf. L. Cagni, The Poem of Erra, pp. 14-8.

suffer death as an immediate consequence, or a later death is not reported, he was most likely alive when the text was written. Otherwise the scribe would scarcely have failed to report his death.

2.3.5 The Speech of Nergal (Sect. G)

2.3.5.1 The Crime against Ereshkigal

The first part of the speech is a continuation of the scene of judgement in the previous sequence. Nergal acts as judge. Influenced by Ishum he releases Kummaya from the nether world (cf. also line 68B). But he predicts an unfavourable future for the visionary as punishment for his crime (lines 60-61). He will experience disturbance, dishonesty and rebellion in his reign.

The crime mentioned is that the visionary has dishonoured Ereshkigal, the queen of the nether world (line 58). This refers to Kummaya's desire to descend to the nether world in a vision, which is reported on the obverse of the tablet, lines 27ff.[136] From the description there it is clear that this provoked the anger of the gods (line 29). The reason why Kummaya had this desire is difficult to read out of the badly preserved text, but it seems as if he wanted approval from the nether world for some task he was going to carry out. The actual descent shows that he got the opposite.

2.3.5.2 The Ideal King and the Rebel King

A. The traditional elements:
The description of the ideal king (lines 62-65) reproduces the basic elements in the Assyrian king ideology:

The king is given kingship from the highest god (line 62B).
The kingship includes rulership over all countries (line 63).
The kingship includes priesthood for the gods (line 64).
The kingship includes divine protection (line 65).

The same ideology is clearly demonstrated in the Assyrian coronation ritual. While crowning the king the priest says:

---

136 Cf. von Soden, "Die Unterweltsvision", transliteration, p. 15 and translation, p. 21.

(kingship from the gods:)
"The diadem of thy head — may Assur
and Ninlil, the lords of thy diadem,
put it upon thee for hundred years.
Thy foot in Ekur (the Assur temple)
and thy hand stretched towards Assur,
thy god — may they be favoured."

(priesthood:)
"Before Assur, thy god, may thy priesthood
and the priesthood of thy sons find favour."

(rulership:)
"With thy straight sceptre make thy land wide."

(protection:)
"May Assur grant thee quick satisfaction, justice and peace."[137]

The description of the next king (lines 66-67), who forms the antithesis to the first, also contains traditional elements, although of another kind. The wisdom of the king has a nearly verbatim parallel in a bilingual text (Sumerian/Akkadian) which is published under the name The Etiological Myth of the "Seven Sages".[138] The text describes the activity of the seven semidivine apkallu's (sages) who lived in Sumer in primeval time. Unfortunately the tablet was very damaged. We use the restoration of the text according to E. Reiner (cf. note 138):

```
 1- 2  [     ], the purification priest of Eridu
 3- 4  [. . .] who ascended to heaven
 5- 6  They are the seven brilliant apkallu's,
        purādu-fish of the sea,
 7- 9  [sev]en apkallu's "grown" in the river,
        who insure the correct functioning of
        the plans of heaven and earth.
10-13  Nunpirggalnungal, the apkallu from Enmerkar,
        who brought down Ištar from heaven into Eanna;
14-17  Piriggalnungal, stemming from Kiš,
        who angered Adad in the heaven so that he let
        no rain and (hence) no vegetation be in the
        country for three years;
18-23  Piriggalabzu, stemming from [Eridu] who . . .
        and thus angered Ea in the Apsu so that he . . .
```

137   The text was published by K.F. Müller, Das Assyrische Ritual I. Texte zum Assyrischen Königsritual, MVÄG 41/3, Leipzig 1937. Text 1: Königsritual aus der Zeit der Nachfolger des Tukilti-Ninurta 1: col. ii, lines 30-36, p. 13. The English translation is taken from H. Frankfort, Kingship and the Gods, Chicago 1948, new ed. 1978, p. 247; cf. in general to the ideology of kingship, pp. 243-8, 265-74, 313-33.
138   E. Reiner, "The Etiological Myth of the 'Seven Sages'", Orientalia 30, 1961, pp. 1-11. Cf. also Part I, pp. 191ff.

24-27 The fourth (is) Lu-Nanna, (only) two-thirds
apkallu, who drove the ušumgallu-dragon from
Eninkarnunna, the temple of Ištar of Šulgi.
28-31 [. . .] of human descend, whom (pl.) the lord Ea
endowed with a broad understanding.

A comparison between our text and this text shows the following
similarities:

Vision, line 66:

mu-de-e a-ma-ti ra-pa-áš uz-ni pal-ku-u ka-ra-áš
ta-šim-tì ša ^{iṣ}uṣurāti^{meš} šá mar-kas qaq-qa-ri ḫi-i-ṭu

"wise in speech, broad in understanding, with a well-informed mind,
examining the drawings (plans) of the formation of the earth." (Cf. grammatical note 66 d.)

The seven sages:

9 muš-te-ši-ru uṣurat AN-e ù KI-tìm
"who insure the correct functioning of the plans of heaven and earth."

31 ^{d}É-a be-lum uz-na ra-pa-áš-tu ú-šak-li-lu-šu-nu-ti
"the lord Ea had endowed with a broad understanding."

Similar wordings:

rapaš uzni "broad in understanding"	uzna rapašta "broad understanding"
uṣurāti ša markas qaqqari "the plans of the formation of the earth"	uṣurat šamê u erṣeti "the plans of heaven and earth"

We do not claim that the scribe of our text has quoted from this
actual tablet, but the similarities should show that the king in our
text is "modelled" after the tradition about the sages.

This is even more convincing since at least certain Assyrian kings
were described as sages. In a letter to Ashurbanipal his grandfather, Sennacherib, is described in this way:

Assur in a dream, called the grandfather
of the king, my lord; a sage; the king, the lord
of the kings, is an offspring of a sage and Adapa:
you have surpassed the wisdom of the . . .
and the whole scholarship.[139]

139 For the text, cf. S. Parpola, Letters from Assyrian Scholars, letter 117, p.
83. For translation, cf. also ANET^3, pp. 450 and 606.

In an oracle to Esarhaddon he is also compared with a sage,[140] and the same is written in an anonymous letter to a Neo-Assyrian king.[141] In the same way Ashurbanipal boasted of knowing the mystery of the apkallu's, the art of writing tablets.[142]

Thus it seems clear that the king in our text is said to possess the divine wisdom like the wisdom of the sages of the ancient times.

The mythical conception of the seven sages which the text quoted above partly reproduces and partly alludes to, is variegated, and is not to be brought into a single formula. But on the background of the text quoted it is possible to reconstruct some of the basic elements which are also represented in other texts where the sages are dealt with.

1. In the lines 5-6 it is said that the apkallu's lived in Apsu (the fresh water). This is attested both in an incantation ritual and in Berossos' myth about Oannes which reflects the Mesopotamian myths about the apkallu's.[143]

2. The first apkallu's were of divine origin. Apsu was the dwelling place of the god of wisdom, Ea. They were created by Ea in the sea and bestowed with divine wisdom. This is attested in the Poem of Erra, Tabl. I, line 162; and the Myth of Adapa, Tabl. A, lines 1-9.[144] Cf. also line 31 on our tablet quoted above.

3. The apkallu's ascended from the sea. This is attested by Berossos. It is presupposed in our text where the apkallu's are associated with ancient Sumerian temple-cities and kings. Our text describes also a development in the "history of the apkallu's", from divine to human, cf. lines 24-27, 28-31.

4. At least one of the apkallu's ascended to heaven, cf. 1-2; 3-4. This is the main motif in the Myth of Adapa where Adapa ascends to heaven to reach immortal life. He failed and is presumably sent back to Eridu or to Apsu. (The end of the myth is not preserved.)

5. The apkallu's offended the gods. This is the most surprising "news" that comes from our text. It is stated explicitly in lines 14-17, 18-23. But it seems also to be the meaning of the report of the acts of the other sages.[145]

6. The sages were dispatched back to Apsu.[146] This is referred to in the Poem

---

140   Cf. ANET[3], p. 450, "Oracles concerning Esarhaddon", col. iv, line 20.
141   Parpola, op.cit., letter 321, p. 277.
142   Cf. M. Streck, Assurbanipal II, pp. 362f, col. i, and p. 254, 13.
143   Cf. Gurney, above, note 103. On Berossos, cf. S.M. Burstein, The Babylo-niaca of Berossos, SANE 1/5, Malibu, California 1978, pp. 13-14.
144   Cf. my discussion in Part I, pp. 197ff.
145   The Poem of Erra, Cagni, p. 34; the Myth of Adapa, ANET[3], p. 101.
146   The conception of the Apsu seems to have undergone a transformation from the Old Babylonian to the Neo-Assyrian time. In the Old Babylonian texts the Apsu is the dwelling-place of Ea as the god of wisdom. There seems to be no connection between the Apsu and the nether world. Accordingly "water" is not mentioned in the old underworld-texts. In the Neo-Assyrian time there seems to

of Erra in a speech of Marduk: "I dispatched those (renown) ummânū (-sages) down into the Apsu: I did not ordain them up again" (Tabl. I, line 147).[147]

Accordingly there was a tradition about the apkallu's where they were described both as possessors of divine wisdom and offenders of the gods. It seems then very likely that the description of the second king in the vision is "modelled" after the sages not only concerning the king's wisdom, but also concerning his rebellion.

In fact, there is another text, which contains the same pattern. That is the so called "Verse Account of Nabonidus".[148] Here the last Neo-Babylonian king Nabonidus is portrayed as a rebel king. "He did against the will of the gods and he performed an unholy action" (col. i). Instituting a new cult with a new image of a god "he built an abomination, a work for unholiness" (col. ii). In the further report about his acts it is written:

> (It was) he (who) stood up in the assembly to praise hi[mself]
> (Saying): "I am wise, I know, I have seen (what is) hi[dden]
> (Even) if I do not know how to write (with the stylus),
> yet I have seen se[cret things].
> The god Ilte'ri has made me see a vision,
> he ha[s shown to me] everything.
> [I am] aw[are] of a wisdom which greatly surpasses
> (even that of the series) U_4 sar. ^{d}A.num. ^{d}En.líl. lá
> which Adapa has composed.
>
> (col. v)[149]

There can be no doubt that the text means that Nabonidus claimed to be bestowed with a wisdom like that of the apkallu's. In fact, more than that: It is said that Nabonidus claimed himself to be wiser than the apkallu's (cf. the last line). This seems also to have

be a confusion of the two conceptions. In the Poem of Erra the Apsu is the dwelling-place of Ea, but also the nether world (cf. the Death-Dream, note 31, p. 373). In the List of Gods from Ashur (cf. above, pp. 407f) it is said about two of the monsters: "They are the two laḫmu (-monsters) of heaven and earth (erṣetu, "nether world"), of the apsû, belonging to Ea". Cf. also CAD, sub apsû, p. 195. The myth of Adapa, Tabl. A, line 9, can also be interpreted in this way, since Adapa is mentioned together with the underworld-judges, Anunnaki.

147   Cf. Cagni, op.cit., p. 32.
148   The text was published by S. Smith, Babylonian Historical Texts, London 1924, pp. 24-97. The latest translation is in ANET[3], pp. 312-15.
149   The translation is taken from ANET[3], p. 314. The series referred to is an unknown astrological series; cf. W.W. Hallo, "On the Antiquity of Sumerian Literature", JAOS 83, 1967, pp. 167-76, p. 176. Cf. the discussion of the sequence in Part I, pp. 212f.

been said about Sennacherib (cf. the letter to Ashurbanipal), but
there is one important difference: The boasting of the supreme
wisdom of the Neo-Assyrian kings was regarded as an legitimate
part of the king ideology. This is even so in our vision where the
wisdom of the rebel king is not doubted. In the "Verse Account of
Nabonidus" on the other hand his claim to possess divine wisdom
is clearly regarded as hubris.

The two "rebel kings", the second king in our vision, and
Nabonidus, seem therefore to have been portrayed with two basic
features: The supreme wisdom and the rebellion against the gods.
In the description of the supreme wisdom there are direct references to the myths about the apkallu's. Most likely the motif of the
rebellion has also been influenced by the same myths (which of
course does not exclude some sort of historical background for the
reports).

B. The historical setting:
Although the text is structured according to a traditional kingship
ideology and mythological conceptions, it contains historical
allusions. The allusions can be enumerated as follows:

1. The god Ashur is one of the chief gods, line 64.

2. The king built an akitu temple / celebrated the akitu festival (cf. gramma-
    tical note 64 b.), line 64.

3. The king was protected by the gods Yabru, Humban, Naprušu in a battle,
    line 65.

4. The second king mentioned is the father of the visionary, line 66.

5. The visionary shared the responsibility for the reign with his father, lines
    67B-68A.

The allusions are in fact vague, but considered together it seems
possible to locate the historical background.

1)   When the god Ashur is one of the chief gods, the tablet must
be Assyrian and deal with Assyrian kings. In line 11 on the
obverse it is said that Nineveh was the capital. Nineveh was
chosen capital under Sennacherib and destroyed during the fall of
the Assyrian empire. Thus the tablet is Neo-Assyrian, the kings

Neo-Assyrian, the historical limitations 704 (beginning of Sennacherib's reign) — 612 (fall of Nineveh).

2) Within these years there is one occasion in relation to the akitu
festival (New-years festival) in Assyria which has special significance. That is the building of the bīt akītu (akitu temple) in the
city Ashur by Sennacherib. This has both textual and archeological
attestation. On the foundation stone of the temple there was found
an inscription of Sennacherib, where a section reads:

> I constructed entirely of mountain limestone,
> and I raised it up mountain-high.
> Two irrigation ditches I dug around its sides,
> and encircled it with a garden of abundance
> and orchard(s) of . . ., with luxurious
> plantations I surrounded its sides.[150]

The temple was excavated during the excavations in Ashur by
Walther Andrae (1903-1914). Andrae gives a thorough description
of the temple and its artificial garden.[151] Concerning the temple
one of the striking features is the imitation of the central motifs of
the Babylonian cult, transformed from the god Marduk to the god
Ashur.

3) The three gods mentioned as the protectors of the king are
Elamite gods.[152] Humban is in fact the head of the Elamite
pantheon. The reference to the Elamite gods includes the Elamites
as a political factor as well, in one way or another. This would
scarcely have happened after the completely looting of the Elamite
area and Susa, the capital, by Ashurbanipal in 642-639.
The protection of the Elamite deities could of course be an
allusion to a coalition between the Assyrians and the Elamites. But
no such coalition is known. On the contrary, during this whole
period the Elamites supported the Chaldean and Babylonian forces
and fought against the Assyrians.

---

150   Cf. D.D. Luckenbill, The Annals of Senacherib. "The Temple of the New
Year's Feast"; pp. 135-43. Our quoting: Text a, line 33-35, p. 137.
151   W. Andrae, Das wiedererstandene Assur, Leipzig 1938, repr. München
1977, pp. 219-24.
152   Cf. von Soden, "Die Unterweltsvision", p. 30, note to line 65. For Yabru
(Jabnu), cf. W.G. Lambert, "Jabnu", RLA V, Berlin-New York 1977, p. 229.
For Humba(n), cf. W. Hinz, "Humban", RLA IV, 1972-75, pp. 491f.

It may, however, also mean that the Neo-Assyrian scribe of our tablet claimed that a favourable outcome of a battle with the Elamites meant that the Elamite gods supported the Assyrians.

The reading of our text is somewhat strange here because it does not boast of a complete victory of the Assyrian king, which would suit the rest of the style in this section. It rather seems as if the king and his army were very close to a defeat, but were at last rescued.

There was a battle between the Assyrians and the Elamites in this period which is well attested in the sources. That was the battle at Ḫalule (692). In his annals Sennacherib boasts of a complete victory over the Elamites.[153] The scribe of the Babylonian Chronicle, however, held another opinion, writing: "In an unknown year Humban-nimena mustered the troops of Elam (and) Akkad and did battle against Assyria in Ḫalule. He effected an Assyrian retreat".[154] The historians seem to give the Babylonian scribe more credence than the Assyrian scribe of the annals of Sennacherib.[155]

The cautious style of our text about the rescue of the king could suit very well with the actual events in the battle at Ḫalule.

4)   If the first king is Sennacherib, the second king must be his descendant, Esarhaddon. He was made crown prince in charge of Babylon in 689, and king after Sennacherib was murdered in 681. The description about the rebellion is a common description about a crime against the gods and it does not give any exact historical information.

5)   The visionary, Kummāya, is then the son of Esarhaddon. Two of Esarhaddon's sons had political influence and both were made crown princes in 672: Ashurbanipal should have responsibility for Assyria, Shamash-kum-ukin for Babylonia. Since the scribe locates the events behind the dream report to Assyria (cf. line 72), it is most likely that the visionary is Ashurbanipal.

---

153 Cf. Luckenbill, the Annals of Senacherib, pp. 44-7, col. v,58-vi,35. It was in the report about this battle Sennacherib described himself with the features of an Anzu-bird, cf. above, pp. 412f and note 111.
154 A.K. Grayson, Assyrian and Babylonian Chronicles, TCS 5, New York 1975. Chronicle 1, col. iii, lines 16-18, p. 80.
155 Cf. A.T. Olmstead, History of Assyria, Chicago 1923, repr. 1975, pp. 290-295. H.W.F. Saggs, The Greatness that was Babylon, London 1962, pp. 120-21.

If our considerations so far are correct, the three persons involved in this section are:

Sennacherib, 704-681: The ideal king
Esarhaddon, 680-669: The rebel king
Ashurbanipal, crown prince 672; king 668-627: The visionary

The scribe draws the picture of the dead Senacherib as the ideal king over against Esarhaddon and Ashurbanipal. The date which is presupposed in the dream report must then be the years 672-669 when Esarhaddon and Ashurbanipal ruled together.

There was one overwhelming political problem during this period where Sennacherib's politics differed from that of Esarhaddon and Ashurbanipal, and where opinions were divided among the influential Assyrians: that was the relation to Babylonia.
The Babylonians revolted against Sennacherib in 703 and onwards. This led finally to the sacking of Babylon in 689. The city was destroyed and the statues of the gods moved to Ashur (above all the statue of Marduk). This caused that the main Babylonian cultic celebration, the akitu festival, was interrupted for twenty years.[156] Esarhaddon was put in charge of Babylonia from 689. In 681 Sennacherib was murdered. The Babylonian Chronicle states that he was murdered by one of this sons.[157] The annals of Ashurbanipal seem to indicate that this was done in Babylon.[158]

After becoming king Esarhaddon changed the religious politics of his father and began to rebuild Babylon again (how seriously he took this task is under discussion).[159] When Ashurbanipal followed his father as king in 669, one of the first tasks he carried

---

156 Cf. the reports in the Babylonian Chronicles, Grayson, op.cit., Chr. I, col. iii, line 22, p. 80; Chr. 14, lines 31-33, p. 127; and the same repeated in Chr. 16, lines 1-8, p. 131. For Sennacherib's religious politics, cf. J.A. Brinkmann, "Senacherib's Babylonian Problem: An Interpretation", JCS 25, 1973, pp. 89-95; and J. Oates, Babylon, London 1979, pp. 119ff.
157 Cf. Grayson, op.cit., Chr. 1, col. iii, lines 34-37, p. 81. The murderer was most likely Sennacherib's son Arad-Ninlil, cf. S. Parpola, "The Murderer of Senacherib", Death In Mesopotamia, ed. B. Alster, M. CSA 8, Copenhagen 1980, pp. 171-81.
158 Cf. the report about Sennacherib's death, ANET[3], p. 288.
159 The religious politics of Esarhaddon is discussed in B. Landsberger, Brief des Bischofs von Esagila an König Asarhaddon, MNAW.L 28, No. 6, Amsterdam 1965; cf. also Oates, Babylon, pp. 120f.

out, was to remove the statues of the gods back to Babylon.[160]
Later Ashurbanipal's relation to Babylon partly changed under the
revolt of his brother Shamash-kum-ukin and the seizure of
Babylon in 648.[161]

If these are the historical events underlying our text, the dream-
report has the following historical setting:

Sennacherib	was the ideal king who was appointed by the gods to rule both Assyria and Babylonia. He was the king who destroyed the rebellious Babylon. He removed the statues of the Babylonian gods to Ashur and in this way demonstrated the supremacy of the Assyrian gods.
Esarhaddon	was the rebel king who changed his father's religious politics. He did treachery against Assyria and the Assyrian gods.
Ashurbanipal	followed in his father's footsteps in the new politics towards Babylonia and accordingly in the rebellion against the will of the Assyrian gods.

The scribe of the tablet does nothing to hide his sympathy. But his
epilogue at the end of the tablet seems to indicate a change in his
attitude (lines 73-75). The report about Nergal's speech caused him
to support the old religious politics of Sennacherib.[162] The tablet
has accordingly a political intention on showing that the gods
warned against the religious politics of Esarhaddon which Ashurbanipal seemed to intend to continue.

It is not possible to decide whether the scribe built upon a report
about a real vision of Ashurbanipal or whether the whole tablet is
fiction. In support of the first assumption it could be mentioned
that the two basic elements in the text are attested in the sources
about Ashurbanipal: The belief in visions as a medium for divine
revelation, and the reverence of the dead kins (Ashurbanipal
seems to emphasize this more than the other Neo-Assyrian kings).
We also know that when Ashurbanipal seized Babylon during the
revolt of his brother Shamash-kum-ukin, he referred to a dream
which he interpreted as a divine revelation.[163]

---

160   Cf. Grayson, Babylonian Chronicles, Chr. 14, lines 31-33, p. 127; Chr. 16,
lines 1-8, p. 131. For Ashurbanipal's religious politics, cf. Oates, op.cit., pp.
121ff.

161   Cf. the text referred to in our note 158.

162   For von Soden's attempt to identify the scribe, cf. "Unterweltsvision", pp.
9ff.

163   Cf. the report from Ashurbanipal's fifth Campaign, col. iii, lines 27-127,
No. 790; D.D. Luckenbill, Ancient Records of Assyria and Babylonia II, p. 302.

C. The style of the section:

In our grammatical analysis of this section we came to the conclusion that the verbs of lines 62-65 should most likely be classified as the present tense (with one exception in the subordinate clause 65B, cf. grammatical note 62 b.). If the verbs are kept in the present this raises a tension between the style of the section and what we can most probably interpret as its historical setting. The Akkadian present is used equivalent to English future, but that the section should be kept in the future, does not seem to suit well with the fact that it seems to deal with past events.

As an explanation of this problem, we can consider the following solutions:

1) The section is to be interpreted as the future in sense. The section is then a prediction about an ideal king to come. This raises two problems:

*Historically the section does not seem to describe the future, but past events.

*The context of the section shows that the king is dead.

The first problem can, however, be solved. Predictions of past events, vaticinia ex eventu, are well attested in Akkadian prophecy.[164] Grayson describes the style as follows: "The author, in other words, uses vaticinia ex eventu to establish his credibility and then proceeds to his real purpose, which might be to justify a current idea or institution, or as it appears in the Dynastic Prophecy, to forecast future doom for a hated enemy" (p. 6). There is as far as we can see nothing that contradicts the suggestion that our section in isolation could be a prophecy (if we exclude the introductory words). The elaborate style with the vague historical references could rather support it.

The problem is, however, the context. The Akkadian prophecy is a device whose purpose was to give credibility to the author of the historical report and authority to certain historical features. But in our text the device is divulged because the king is dead and then has to be a past person.

Theoretically it would of course be possible to consider that even though the king is depicted in a vision of the nether world, the

---

164   Cf. A.K. Grayson, Babylonian Historical Literary Texts, TSTS 3, Toronto 1975, pp. 3-37; and A.K. Grayson and W.G. Lambert, "Akkadian Prophecies", JCS 18, 1964, pp. 7-30. Cf. also our discussion on pp. 472ff and 488ff.

king could ascend from there to get "power and glory". But ascension or resurrection is not attested in this way in Mesopotamian literature. At least within the limits of the genuine Mesopotamian mythology this seems an impossible interpretation.

2) Another solution is to regard the section as taken from elsewhere. The author has ten "borrowed" a prophecy about Sennacherib and adjusted it to an original vision, also including lines 66-68A and the sequence about "the man" in the vision. There is textual support for an assumption like this. It would have explained the origin of the complex structure of the dream report and the abrupt change from autobiographical to biographical report between lines 70 and 71. There could then have existed an original dream report which the author of the tablet used for his purposes.

3) The third solution is that the author has used the style from the prophecies to underline the "message" of the vision. This combination of the style of the prophecies and of historical report could be the reason for the break in tenses which is certain at least i line 65B where grammatically we have the preterite.

A parallel to this as a semantic feature seems to be a text published under the title "Nebuchadnezzar King of Justice".[165] The first intelligible part of this epic text, col. ii, lines 1-21, is kept in the present. The style also resembles that of the prophecies. In isolation it would be natural to read it as a prophecy. Together with the rest of the text this is however impossible: "Thus the presents in ii, 1-21 are not future in sense, as one could naturally take them at the first reading, but describe the bad old days against which the model king is to be judged so much the better" (Lambert, our note 165, p. 2).

But there are differences. Although the text above shows that the style of prophecy can be used as a "historical report", this is not done in contradiction to the known grammatical rules. The events which the text describes are of such a character that it would not be unnatural to describe them as what Lambert calls "habitual present" (which seems to be the same as von Soden's "Durativ in der Vergangenheit"). In our text, however, the intention is not to describe "what usually happened", but quite the opposite, as it

165   W.G. Lambert, "Nebuchadnezzar King of Justice", Iraq 27, 1965, pp. 1-11.

seems: to describe the outstanding events connected with the ideal king.

The author of our text could therefore have chosen the style of prophecy not out of linguistic conventions, but to underline a feature in the vision. (This could also be the purpose with regard to solution 2.) If our previous considerations about the historical background of the text are correct, the intention must have been to describe Sennacherib as the king who acted in accordance with the divine plans. That would in fact be very necessary as a defence for a king whom many Assyrians and Babylonians (following the sacking of Babylon) regarded as a rebel against the gods.

2.4 The Message of the Vision

We have previously seen that the vision follows the basic pattern of underworld reports known from myths and lamentations, and above all from the Death-Dream of Enkidu. That concern the descent to the nether world, the description of inhabitants, and of the ruler of the underworld sitting on his throne in judgement. The break with this pattern is primarily connected to the introduction of the unique man in line 50, and the identification of him as the ideal king in lines 62-65, in contrast to the rebel king in lines 66-67A.

The explicit message of the dream is revealed in the speech of Nergal. It consists of two sequences, each having the structure: Accusation — predicted punishment (cf. above, p. 403). The first sequence is centered around the god Nergal himself. He acts as judge on behalf of his wife. The visionary has offended the goddess and is therefore to suffer disturbance, dishonesty and rebellion in his future reign. The other sequence is centered around the unique man / ideal king. The visionary and his father have been disobedient and offended the gods. Therefore "the fearsome sheen" shall annihilate the two rulers.

The first prediction, that the visionary, because of his crime against the underworld gods, will be visited by their evil powers in his future life, should be clear. The second prediction is, however, more obscure. According to the structure the ideal king and the rebel king are here contrasted. It seems therefore most probably to take the disobedience (line 67A) as directed against the ideal king. If so, "the fearsome sheen" that will come over the two kings must be related to the same figure (cf. grammatical note 67 c.). The passage then predicts a visitation of the ideal king upon the two rebels.

This interpretation is not an impossible assumption. What the visionary sees in the nether world is the *eṭemmu*, "spirit", of the dead king (cf. grammatical note 62 a.). The prediction then refers to this spirit. That the fate of a successor is dependent upon the benevolence of the spirit of his predecessor is a well established fact in Mesopotamian view of life.[166] The spirit of the ancestor would visit the living for good or to evil. The political implication of this belief was that the successor in rulership needed the appreciation of the dead predecessor to succeed.[167]

As we have noticed, the *ištēn eṭlu* in our vision is partly patterned on the same figure in the Death-Dream of Enkidu (cf. above, pp. 411f). There "the unique man" was a deputy from the nether world who had ascended to collect Enkidu (cf. above, pp. 373f). The vision of the frightening unique man and the prediction connected to it seems to have a similar implication in the Vision of the Nether World. Thus the Vision predicts a visitation of the ideal king through his spirit on the rebel rulers.

2.5   The Vision as a Part of the Whole Tablet

The difficulty in interpreting at least some of the sections in our vision is caused by the very badly preserved text on the obverse of the tablet. The text is so fragmentary that it is not possible to draw conclusive evidence from it.

What is clear is that we have a narration about the events that led to the vision reported on the reverse. The first five lines of the narration are unintelligible. Lines 6-12 deal with the acts of what

---

166   Cf. Aa. Skaist, "The Ancestor Cult and Succession in Mesopotamia", Death in Mesopotamia, pp. 123-38.
167   Cf. above, pp. 405ff; cf. also note 128, p. 421. A somewhat different translation of the sequence quoted is given in CAD, sub eṭemmu, p. 397. But this does not concern our point.

is most likely one of the persons mentioned in line 62-67. It tells that he collected treasures against the will of the gods. Whether the person is the visionary (Ashurbanipal) or his father (Esarhaddon) is not easy to decide. Von Soden thinks that the visionary is most likely the person involved because he is given responsibility from someone else (line 6), and he acts *like* a king (line 8), a description which would suit better for a crown prince than for a king.[168] But it could seem as if the visionary (Kummaya) is introduced first in line 27, cf. the introduction: "Kummaya, son of ...". Another possibility would then be that the lines describe the years of Esarhaddon as crown prince (689-681), but this would mean that the obverse of the tablet dealt with a rather long period of time, which is not confirmed by the rest of the fragmentary text. What can be said fairly certainly about this section is that it describes a crime most likely of the visionary or his father. The text is not intelligible again before line 27 where Kummaya is mentioned. The text tells, though very fragmentarily, how Kummaya prepared a vision of the nether world, an act that both in intention and performance dishonoured the gods (lines 27-34). There follows a report about two dream experiences (1. dream: lines 35-37; 2. dream: lines 38-40). The vision of the nether world on the reverse is then the third dream experience.

Examples of narrations where dreams play an important role are given in the analysis of the Death-Dream of Enkidu (cf. above, pp. 364f and 384ff). The closest parallel is the Death-Dream itself. Here too a descent-dream comes as the conclusive dream after two previous dream-experiences. And here too the descent is regarded as a punishment for the crime of the visionary. But the story about Enkidu is fiction with no relation to historical circumstances. So even though the vision is dependent upon the Death-Dream, the motifs are transferred to another setting and used with another intention. The theme of our text has also a parallel in the Death of Ur-Nammu and His Descent to the Nether World (cf. above, p. 370) where a descent of a ruler is also reported, but there seem to be no direct relations between the texts.

The vision itself has the Gattung-features of a dream. But the dream forms a part of a narration. The narration itself shows

---

168   Von Soden, "Unterweltsvision", p. 5.

clearly epic features.[169] A.K. Grayson, starting with a wide
definition of an epic as "a lengthy poetic narrative", talks about
three groups of epics: 1) Those which are purely mythological in
character (usually classified as myths). 2) Those which have a
historical or legendary quality about them while also containing
mythological material (as for example the Epic of Gilgamesh).
3) Those which are concerned with historical heroes, and mythological themes are absent.[170]

The Babylonian historical epics which form the pattern for
Grayson's definition of a historical epic, were the product of the
learned scribal activity in Babylonia. They have their own style
which is not represented in our text. But there are several texts
which are related to the historical epics.[171] One of the most
interesting of these concerning our text is the Verse Account of
Nabonidus (cf. above, pp. 429f).

Our text has an epic style, but does not clearly belong to any of
the groups mentioned by Grayson. If we should try to place it in
the "scheme" it has elements from both group two and three: The
text has a clear historical context as group three, but contains
mythological elements as group two.

The similarities between the Verse Account of Nabonidus and our
text could show that the texts are related in one way or another, at
least that they are influenced by the same traditions. They have
the same epic style; they have the supremacy of the national god
and his cult as the central theme (this they have in common with
the historical epics;[172] they both contain the motif of the supreme
wise rebel king; they both deal with the last king of an empire
(Assyria continued to exist after Ashurbanipal, as is well known,
but the decline came in the second half of his reign); they are
both written in support of a particular religious politics.

Although the text seems to presuppose the years when Ashurbanipal was crown prince under Esarhaddon, this does not mean that
the text as a whole was written at that time. In fact there are

---

169   Von Soden, op.cit., pp. 2f.
170   Cf. A.K. Grayson, Babylonian Historical Literary Texts, pp. 41ff.
171   Cf. Grayson, op.cit., pp. 6f; cf. also the texts mentioned in connection with
the prophecies in Grayson and Lambert, "Akkadian Prophecies", pp. 8f.
172   Cf. Grayson, Babylonian Historical Literary Texts, p. 43.

indications that point toward a later date. The description of Esarhaddon as a rebel king by an Assyrian scribe on a tablet that was kept in Ashur, is not likely as long as Esarhaddon was still king. The predictions about rebellion and disturbance (lines 60-61) and the completely annihilation of the dynasty of Esarhaddon and Ashurbanipal (line 67B) also suit better if they took shape in a later time. As is commonly known Ashurbanipal did experience radical change in the Assyrian empire, from the greatest extension in power to the decline through inner weakness and outer pressure. The text could then offer an explanation for this unexpected change.

But even though the text was written before Ashurbanipal's death and certainly before the "fall" of the Assyrian empire in 612, the threatening predictions of the text could for later readers be understood as predictions about the "fall" not only of a king but of the empire itself. The tablet was found in Ashur, but that does not mean that copies of it could not have survived and been read later in the Neo-Babylonian time. For later readers who were not informed about the actual historical background of the text, it gives a strange testimony about the last Assyrian kings.

The text describes the descent to the nether world of a king who offended the gods. It tells about the rebel king who even though he possessed the supreme wisdom, revolted against the gods. And it tells about the (prophesied) ideal king, called "the unique man", who was determined to rule a worldwide kingdom.

III
The Akkadian Dream-Visions
and the Aramaic Dream-Vision in Dan 7

a) Dan 7 in Relation to the Underworld Visions

1. Direct Comparison of the Texts

1.1 Introduction

We have in the previous chapters described the two Akkadian dream-visions in their own environment without any reference to what influence they may have had outside the Mesopotamian region. We will claim that this is a correct methodical approach. Often in the research of comparative religion questions about parallels and relations between texts belonging to different socio-religious environments are mixed up with the analysis of the texts themselves.

Our aim in the analysis of the Mesopotamian material has not been to establish a sort of Babylonian-Assyrian concept of the nether world. The dangers connected with such an approach are obvious. First the scholar establishes a sort of religious concept, then he claims that this concept was known in the described society, then he claims that people belonging to a different society have known this concept in one form or another, and on this basis he draws the parallels.

We have tried to work out the historical meaning of two concrete texts which in the Mesopotamian milieu were related. Our main issue in this chapter will be to see if and in what way there may be similarities between these two Akkadian dream-visions and the night-vision in Dan 7.

To work with similarities between concrete texts has a great advantage compared to working out similarities between religious concepts or ideas. The comparison can be much more detailed and take into consideration questions about text-types, semantic patterns, stylistic features and concrete correspondences between words and phrases.

It is however important to be aware that relations between texts can be established in different ways, and further, that the influence of one text upon another implies a particular inter-pretation of the first text.

In our comparison between the Akkadian texts and Dan 7 we do not start with a theory about what sort of relation there may be between the texts. The possibilities are many: They can represent the same Gattung and accordingly show similar Gattung-features; they can have adopted similar sorts of traditions and show similarities in semantic patterns; there can be an indirect text to text relation with written or oral sources in between; or the author of the one text can have read the other. The decision here must come after the linguistic and historical analysis.

Our concrete approach on the linguistic level will first be to analyze the similarity in Gattung, then in pattern and stylistic features, and then the similarities in words and phrases.

Since we are comparing two texts with Dan 7, we must remain open to the possibility that their relation to Dan 7 may be different in kind. We must also consider the possibility that the author of Dan 7 can have associated material related to the two Akkadian visions.

In the following comparison we designate the three visions according to the visionaries:

E — The Death-Dream of Enkidu
K — The Vision of the Nether World (after Kummāya)
D — Dan 7

1.2   The Gattung

A. Basic classification:

Introduction: Introducing the visionary and the circumstances. Biographical.

D: "Daniel saw a dream and visions of his head on his bed," v. 1
K: "Kummāya lay down and saw a night-vision," line 41.
E: ". . . Enkidu, whose mood is bitter, . . . lies down all alone," lines 11-12.

Opening: Reception of the vision. Autobiographical.

D: "I was seeing in my visions during the night," v. 2.
K: "I saw," line 42.
E: "I saw a dream during my night-time," line 14.

Division of scenes:

D: "I was seeing," (connected with other words signifying division of scenes and sequences within the scenes), vv. 4, 6, 7, 9, 11, 13.
K: "I raised my eyes," line 51.
E: ――――

Reaction: After the vision-picture:

D: "My spirit was troubled within me, I Daniel, and the visions of my head dismayed me," v. 15.
K: "I saw him and my legs began trembling," line 54.
E: ――――

Reaction: After the whole vision-experience:

D: "I Daniel, my thoughts dismayed me greatly and I turned pale," v. 28.
K: "He uttered a lamentation, saying: "Woe, my heart." (Biographical) line 71.
E: ――――

Above we have listed phrases and sentences that most often accompany the Gattung "vision". To the basic pattern of this Gattung belong the introduction of the visionary, an opening about the reception of the vision and an ending that tells about the reaction of the visionary. All three visions share the first two elements, D and K the third, but probably it was also the end of E (the tablet is broken). In the introduction and opening D and K are classified as "night-visions". They report also a reaction of the visionary within the vision-experience.

D has a clear structure dividing the whole vision into scenes and dividing the first and fourth scenes into sequences. Each scene and sequence is introduced by a formula beginning with "I saw". This artificial structure is not found in E or K. But K has a formula similar to D introducing a section (line 51, sect. E). This formula occurs before the vision of the throne where also D has a formula.

The three texts share a basic pattern for visions. They are all night-visions. But besides this they show individual variations. D and K have more in common than D and E.

B. Further classification:

D is as a whole to be classified as a symbolic vision in the sense that the imagery is given an interpretation. But not all of the features of the text need interpretation and the interest in understanding the features of the text varies greatly. The first scenes of the vision are only given a general interpretation (v. 17). The vision of the throne is of such a character that no interpretation is necessary (v. 9-10). The real interest of the interpreter lies in interpreting the last beast/horn/king in the vision in contrast to the holy ones, which in the interpretation substitute "the man" seen in the last scene.

The classification of the two Akkadian dream-visions in this respect is difficult. In our analysis we have stated that they are neither clearly symbolic dreams, nor clear message dreams. E is here difficult to classify because the tablet is broken. K shows similarities with the message-dream, the main content of which is the revelation of a divine message in unsymbolic speach, but there are also differences. This concerns especially section D and G2 (cf. above, p. 403). Here we have a feature in the vision, the man, which is later interpreted as the ideal king. The difference between D and K is accordingly that D is a symbolic dream with non-symbolic features, while K has similarities with the message-dream, but also contains symbolic features. The similarity is found in the features emphasized in the interpretation; K: The man as the ideal king in contrast to the rebel king (K, line 62-67); D: The holy ones as a substitute for the man in contrast to the rebel king.

The basic content of K is a vision of the divine assembly. Such visions of the supreme god, sitting on his throne, surrounded by attendants are well attested in Old Testament and Jewish texts, as well as in Mesopotamian.

In our description of the Mesopotamian underworld-traditions we saw that this motif was the climax of the description of the underworld (cf. above, pp. 383f). E has here the pattern from the underworld-traditions, making the vision of the god on the throne a part of the climax.

Also in K the direct vision of the god on the throne comes at the end, but we get the impression that the visionary stays in the courtroom the whole time, first seeing the beast-demons standing down in the hall, then the man higher up towards the throne, and then at the end the supreme god on his throne surrounded by attendants.

D also contains a vision of the divine assembly. Like K and E the vision of the god on the throne makes a climax of the vision (although in K and D it can scarcely be characterized as *the* climax). But unlike K the monsters are not a part of the divine assembly in D.

We conclude: D differs in further classification of Gattung from K and E in that sense that D as a whole is primarily a symbolic vision, K and E are not. However, D contains one non-symbolic scene which is similar to the dominating non-symbolic scene in K: the divine assembly. K contains one symbolic feature, which is similar to the most emphasized feature in D: The contrast between the ideal king and the rebel king. E on the other hand contains only the element of the throne vision.

C. The dream-experience:

In all three texts the dream is experienced as a vision and an audition. In the audition the visionary is directly addressed. More remarkably, in all three visions the visionary himself acts within the framework of the vision: he moves into the picture he sees. In E this feature is dominating: The whole first part describes the fight of the visionary and his transformation. In K the same motif of fight occurs after the throne vision: The visionary is forced in front of the throne. In D this feature is more restrained: Daniel moves in front of the throne to ask for the interpretation of the vision, v. 16. The similarity between the three visions is that in all three the visionary ends up in front of the throne.

D. The intention:

The basic difference between E and K on the one hand and D on the other is that E and K concern the visionary's future (although K is here of a mixed character), while the visionary in D sees someone else's future.

In the analysis of the Gattung of E and K (cf. pp. 363ff) we found that there was not evidence to classify the dreams as a special Gattung "death-dreams". But together with other Mesopotamian dreams they can on the basis of their content be called "dreams of destruction".

In this respect the two Akkadian dreams are closer to Dan 4 than Dan 7. The basic pattern of the dream-story in Dan 4 is also represented in ancient Sumerian dream-stories which also have a premonition of the destructive future of the visionary as the central theme.

A closer examination shows, however, that it is E and D that are most opposed to each other in this respect and that K has a position in between. As shown in the analysis of structure and Gattung (cf. above, pp. 400-7) K follows the basic pattern of E to some extent: The visionary is taken to the nether world in front of the throne of the supreme god to receive his judgement. But this pattern, which in many respects resembles the pattern in other underworld-texts, is used as the starting point for a highly original composition in K. The dream-report is taken into a larger epic story written by a scribe who wants to interpret events in his contemporary political history by means of the divine message in the vision (cf. above, pp. 438ff). The vision in K does not end up by predicting the immediate death of the visionary, as is the meaning in E. In K the death-sentence is postponed and related to historical circumstances around three rulers in which the visionary was involved as one of them. At the end the vision predicts not only the destruction of the visionary, but also of another person, the rebel king. This use of the Gattung "vision" to interpret a period of history out of religious-political interests is the same in K and D. The prediction of destruction over the rebel king is a similar case.

By way of conclusion we set up a table to show the correspondence of the Gattung-features. The table must of course be read in light of the previous description.

	Comparison of Gattung Features		
	E	K	D
Basic classification	Night-vision	Night-vision	Night-vision
	Introduction	Introduction	Introduction
	Opening	Opening	Opening
		Scenes (2)	Scenes (5)
	?	Reaction (x2)	Reaction (x2)
Further classification	?	Partly symbolic	Symbolic
	Throne-scene	Throne-vision	Throne-scene
Experience:	Vision + audition	Vision + audition	Vision + audition
	Action by the visionary (dominating)	Action by the visionary	Action by the visionary (restrained)
Intention:	Destruction of visionary	Destruction of visionary	
		Destruction of another person	Destruction of another person
		Religious-political intention	Religious-political intention

1.3   Structure of Content

A. The action of natural forces

D begins by reporting how the four winds of heaven are stirring up the sea. The symbolism of four occurs here for the first time and continues through the description: four winds, four beasts, four wings and four heads of the third beast. There is no symbolism of four either in E or K.

The image of this opening section is of a heavy storm. K contains no motif like this. Most probably it has a short description of the terror of the nether world here. E, however, has a somewhat similar image: "The heaven howled, the earth echoed", line 15. On the background of the more detailed report in the opening of Gilgamesh' third dream which contains the same line, it seems clear that E reports about a heavy thunder-storm (cf. above, pp. 372f). In both E and D the meaning is to report the action of natural forces which leads into the following vision.

B. The monsters

D continues to report about monsters. Both K and E have a report about monsters at this place.

In D the monsters are coming up out of the sea. In E it is not explicitly said that the beast-man is coming up from the nether world, but the context points clearly in that direction (cf. above, pp. 373f). In K the monsters are not coming up from the nether world, but the visionary is descending to the nether world, a motif which occurs later in E.

In all three texts the monsters are described in detail. In all three texts they have both animal and human features. D and K come closest since several monsters are counted, listed one after the other.

In D one of the monsters in transformed from beast to man-like. E also reports about transformation. During the fight with the beast-man the visionary is transformed from man to beast. K contains no report about transformation.

After the section about the beast-man, E continues to report about the descent to the nether world and the conditions in the nether world. This has no parallel in D.

After the list of monsters K reports about "one man" described as a victorious warrior. At this place there is no similar report in D.

C. The god on the throne

All three texts report about the supreme god on the throne. In E it is only mentioned without further description. In D and K the god is described, and the surroundings: fire, attendants. In D the report contains movement, the thrones were set in place and the god took his seat. In both E and K the god is sitting on the throne.

D. The judgement

All three texts tell about judgement immediately after the throne vision. In both D and E the sentence is read out of a protocol.

In E we get no further information about the judgement except that it concerns the visionary (the tablet is then broken). Also in K the judgement concerns the visionary in the first instance. This is different in D where the judgement comes over the last beast symbolizing a king. In the report about the circumstances surrounding the judgement there are no similarities between D and K.

In all three visions the reason for the judgement is rebellion against the god(s). In D the one really accused is a king in rebellion against the god. The judgement implies the destruction of his power and person (burning in fire, v. 11). K is complicated at this place. On the one hand it announces the judgement over the visionary, following the pattern from E. On the other hand K implies historical and political circumstances: The visionary is temporarily freed, but a political life in misfortune is predicted for him (lines 60-61). This theme is taken up again at the end of the vision. The visionary shares political responsibility with his father who is described as a ruler in rebellion against the gods (cf. line 66-67; and above, pp. 430ff). The following future is predicted for the two rulers: "Suddenly the fearsome sheen of his terrible kingship shall annihilate you completely (line 67B; cf. grammatical note 67 f.).

Since the circumstances around the judgement are confusing we repeat the main features:

Differences:
— The description of the judgement is different in style and details in K and D (E is here broken).
— The visionary is involved in the judgement in E and K, while the judgement falls on one of the monsters in D.

Similarities:
— The judgement is read from a protocol in E and D.
— The rebellion motif is implied in the accusation in E, K, D.
— The judgement means the annihilation of a rebel king in K and D.

E. The ideal ruler

In both K and D the report about the ideal ruler comes after the scene of judgement.

The difference is that in D this is a part of the vision, while K has it as a part of the speech of the god who interprets a feature in the vision. The difference in style is that D reports about movement: The ruler is coming to the throne of the god. In K the ruler is standing by the throne.

The similarities are that in both texts the ruler is designated with a word for "man" (in K presupposed from line 50). In style both texts seem to reflect the enthronement of a king where the king is given universal and lasting kingship (cf. above, pp. 425f). In style D is a prediction. This seems also to be the case concerning the style in K (cf. grammatical note 62 b., and above, pp. 435ff).

In the analysis above we have listed both similarities and differences. To make a decision about a possible relation easier, we offer below a comparative table of the similarities in pattern. As with the previous table this must also be read in relation to the description above. In the table we use parentheses to indicate features that have to be read out of context or do not occur at the same place as the corresponding feature in D.

1.4 Words and Phrases

D. v. 2: "The four winds of heaven were stirring the great sea."
K: ———
E: "The heaven howled, the earth echoed," line 15.

D. v. 4: The first beast:
Comparison with K:
Basic features:
As already noticed the greatest difference in style between D and K is that K gives a static description, while D contains both static descriptions and reports of events. But the movements reported in D are described within the framework of the symbolism used in K.
The beast in D is described as a lion with eagle wings. Lion and eagle features are the basic features used in the description of the Anzu-bird (cf. above, pp. 375f). In K features from the Anzu-bird occur 3x, eagle 1x, bird 3x, lion 4x.
The beast is raised from the ground and placed on its hind legs like a man. Features of man/human are represented by nine of the fifteen monsters in K. Most frequently they are combined with hands and feet.
The whole description in D contains features from lion, eagle and man. These are also the features mot frequently mentioned in K.

COMPARISON OF PATTERN OF CONTENT

Sequences	Features		
	D	K	E
1. Action of nature	Winds		Thunder-storm
2. Monsters	Descrp. of monsters	Descrp. of monsters	Descrp. of monster
	Listing of monsters	Listing of monsters	
	Transformation	Transformation	
		Descrp. of the man	Descrp. of the nether world
3. God on the throne	God on the throne	God on the throne	God on the throne
	Descrp. of the god	Descrp. of the god	
	Surroundings: Fire, attendants	Surroundings: Fire, attendants	
4. Judgement	The supreme god as judge	The supreme god as judge	The supreme god as judge
	Read from a protocol		Read from a protocol
	Accusation: Rebellion	Accusation: Rebellion	Accusation: Rebellion
	Accused: rebel king	(Accused: rebel king)	
	Judgement: Annihilation in fire	(Judgement: Annihilation)	
5. The ideal ruler	Designation: Man	(Designation: Man)	
	Style reflects enthronement	Style reflects enthronement	
	Universal and everlasting kingdom	Universal and everlasting kingdom	
	Style indicating future	Style indicating future	

Individual features:
D: The wings:
K: "Sagulḫazza . . . with wings outspread he was flying . . .," line 45.

D: Lion-eagle:
K: "Utukku . . . the head was that of a lion. The hands and feet were those of an Anzu-bird," line 46B.
"Nedu . . . the head of a lion, the hands of a man, the feet of a bird," line 47B.
(Two gods): "The first had the head, hands and feet of an Anzu-bird" (lion-headed eagle), line 48B.

D: ". . . a lion . . . was raised upon two feet . . ."
K: "Šulak was an ordinary lion, standing on his hind legs," line 46C.

Comparison with E:
Description:
The beast-man in E is composed of the basic features of the Anzu-bird: ". . . whose face was similar to an Anzu-bird, his hands were the paws of a lion, his fingernails were the claws of an eagle," lines 18-19. In our analysis of Anzu-birdlike creatures represented in Neo-Assyrian art, we found that the relief from Nimrud came closest to the description in E (cf. above, p. 376). The relief shows a monster with lion-head and lion-paws with claws, wings and feathered body, standing upright on its hind legs. The resemblance between the beast-man in E and the first monster in D is accordingly close:
Both have a lion body.
Both have wings.
Both are standing upright on the hind legs.
In E the monster is called "a man", eṭlu, in D the beast ends up like "a man", 'ǟ nāš.

Transformation:
The report of the transformation in D is closely related to the description of Nebuchadnezzar's transformation in Dan 4:
Dan 7,4: ". . . a lion and wings of an eagle on it."
Dan 4,30b:
    "Until his hear was long as eagle(-feathers),
    and his nails long as birds(-claws)."
Dan 7,4: "A human heart was given to it."
Dan 4,13: "A beast's heart shall be given to him."

Also E tells about transformation, but it is only described with reference to the outer appearance. The direction is the same as in Dan 4: from man to beast. The text in E is partly damaged, but the following words are clear: ". . . he transformed me . . . my arms like those of a bird," lines 31-32. Enkidu is apparently changed into the same shape as the other dwellers of the nether world. They are "clothed like birds with wing-feathers for garments," line 38.

If we consider the texts involved here together, we have the following features represented:
Dan 7,4: Lion with eagle wings.
Dan 4,30b: Hair as eagle feathers, nails as bird-claws.
E: The man:
    Face of an Anzu-bird (lion),
    paws of a lion,
    nails like the claws of an eagle.
The dwellers:
    Clothed like birds with wing-feathers for garment.

We notice that all the beast-features mentioned in Dan 7,4 and Dan 4,30b are represented in E: The lion-body, the eagle-wings, the feathers, the bird-claws.

D. v. 5: "Raised on one side . . ."
This image is curious. The beast is not raised on the hind legs as the first beast, which has some kind of meaning on two levels: within the beast imagery it suggests readiness to fight; within the vision symbolism it suggests the attitude of a human being. The second beast is raised on either its left or right side, leaning over to the other, which gives it a strange limping attitude. K has no wording like D, but it reports a monster which standing upright would have the same limping attitude. The monster Muḫrā has only three feet, the one hind foot is missing (line 48A).

D. v. 5: "Three ribs in his mouth between his teeth."
There is no identical wording in K, but th first monster has also grasped a victim: "He was holding the hair of his head in his left hand," line 42B.

D. v. 5: "And it was said to it: "Stand up, devour much flesh!"
There is no identical wording, but the name of one of the monsters, Ḫumut Tabal, contains a similar imperative expression: hurry, remove! line 45.

D. v. 6: "Four bird wings on its back."
K/E: Cf. the first beast.

D. v. 6: "Four heads on the beast."
K: "Mimma lemnu, his two heads, the first was that of a lion, the second head . . .", line 47C.

D. vv. 7-8:   The last beast
Comparison with K:
General description:
The fourth and last beast in D is given no name, while the three others are named "lion, bear, panther". It seems as if the terrifying and bizarre features of the fourth beast makes it impossible to characterize with a name. In K all the monsters are given names, except the completely abnormal last monster. The description of this monster begins: "The two gods, their name I do not know," line 48B.
The description of the last monster in D differs from the previous. The last monster is of a more complex character. It is not one creature only that is described, but two creatures, the second linked to the first.
The last monster in K is different from the previous ones. It is not only composed of features from beast and man as the others, it is also composed of two bodies like a siamese twin.

Individual features:
D: "Terrible and dreadful and exceedingly strong."
K: (Muḫrā) "He was possessing terror and dreadful splendour." line 45A.
D: "And the rest it stamped with its feet."
K: (Šedu) "With his left foot he was treading . . .", line 44A.
D: "Ten horns on it."
None of the monsters described in K are explicitly said to have horns. But two of the monsters, among them the last monster, are provided with a crown. The demons were in Mesopotamia imagined as divine and therefore often described and depicted with the special divine crown as headdress. This is generally the case in the List of Gods from Ashur (cf. above, pp. 407f). This crown was a horned crown.
If the author of d has imagined the horns as a part of a horned crown, this would correspond more general to the character of the last complex monster. Clearly this monster is described as hubristic. The horned crown, only to be worn of gods and deified kings, could underline this hubristic character of the last beast/king.

COMPARISON OF MONSTER-FEATURES

	D	K	E
1st monster	lion with eagle-wings	lion-eagle	lion-eagle
	lion raised upon two feet	lion standing on hind legs	lion-eagle standing upright
	upon two feet like a man	feet like a man	one man
2nd monster	raised on one side	monster missing hind leg	
	ribs in his mouth	grasping the hair of a victim	
	stand up, devour!	name of monster: hurry, remove!	
3rd monster	four bird-wings	monster with wings	
	four heads	monster with two heads	
4th monster	no name of last monster	no name of last monster	
	two creatures described	last monster composed of two bodies	
	terrible and dreadful	possessing terror and dreadful splendour	
	stamped with its feet	with its left foot it was treading	
	ten horns	(horned) crown of last monster	
	human eyes and a mouth that spoke	second part of last monster: head of a man	

D: The eleventh horn, which is the second part described of the last monster, seems to be imagined with a human head:
   "Eyes like human eyes on the horn and a mouth that spoke great (words)."
K: About the second part of the last monster in K it is written:
   "The second was provided with the head of a man," line 49A.

D.v.9.:   "Thrones were set in place."
There are, as far as we can see, no parallels in underworld texts to the setting in
place of thrones. But the plural <u>thrones</u> in D has parallels. The Descent of Ishtar
reads: "Ereshkigal opened her mouth to speak, saying these words to Namtar, her
vizier: "Up Namtar, knock at Esagina (Palace of Justice). Adorn the thresholds
with coral stone. Bring forth the Anunnaki and seat them on thrones of god!"
rev., lines 29-34. A collegium of judges is also described in the court scene in
the Descent of Ur-Nammu (cf. above, pp. 382f).

D. v. 9:   "An Ancient of Days took his seat."
K: "The warrior Nergal was seated on a royal throne," line 51.
E: "(resided) the queen of the nether world, Ereshkigal," line 50.

A description of movement as in D, "took his seat", occurs in the court scene in
the Descent of Inanna: "The pure Ereshkigal seated herself upon the throne,"
line 162 (cf. above, p. 383).

D. v. 9:   "His throne flames of fire and its wheels burning fire; a river of fire
streamed out and went out from before him."
K: "(From) his arms lightning was flashing," line 52.

In several Akkadian texts Nergal is imagined as a god of light and fire (cf.
above, p. 423).

D. v. 10:   "Thousands upon thousands served him and myriads upon myriads
were standing before him."
K: "The Anunnaki, the great gods, were kneeling at his right and at his left side
   . . .   The underworld was filled with fear and it lay prostrate before the son
   of princes," lines 52B-53A.

D. v. 10:   "The court sat."
K/E: in both visions the report of the god on the throne introduces a scene of
judgement. The seating of the court is reported in the Descent of Ishtar (lines
29-34, cf. above to v. 9).

D. v. 10:   ". . . books were opened"
E: "Belet-Ṣeri, the scribe of the nether world, kneeling before her (Ereshkigal),
   holding a tablet, she reads out before her," lines 51-52.

D. v. 11b: "The beast was killed and its body destroyed, it was given to the
burning fire."
K: "Suddenly the fearsome sheen of his terrible kingship shall annihilate you
   completely," line 67B (cf. grammatical note 67 f.).

D. v. 13:   ". . . one like man"
K: "One man," line 50.

D. v. 14:   "Dominion and glory and kingdom were given to him."
K: ". . . the exalted shepherd: whom my father . . ., the king of the gods gives
   full responsibility," line 62.

D. v. 14:   ". . . all peoples, nations and tongues shall serve him."
K: ". . . whom (the king) from east to west he (the god) allows to look over the
   lands in their totality . . ., and he (the king) rules over everything," line 63.

D. v. 14:   "His dominion is an everlasting dominion which shall not pass away,
his kingdom such as shall never be impaired."
K: ". . . in all eternity", line 64.

2.   A Preliminary Discussion of the Relationship

The correspondences between Dan 7 and the Vision of the Nether World occur within four sections of the texts: the monsters, the god on the throne, the judgement, the ideal ruler.

In the description of the monsters there are so many similarities that we think we can conclude that the texts share the same basic imagery. This, however, does not automatically mean that the texts are related in one way or another. Some of the basic features mentioned are fairly common in descriptions of monsters in the Ancient Near East. That concerns especially the lion-eagle imagery. There are, however, details given in the texts that taken together could point toward a relationship, even though some of them also are represented in other texts: the lion standing on hind legs, the combination feet and man, a limping monster — three legs, monsters with several heads, the description of monsters as terrible and dreadful and stamping with their feet, monsters grasping a victim. The parallels between the last-described monster in the two texts are also outstanding: Both are distinguished from the others by their bizarre appearance, both lack names, both embody two creatures, both have horns (the horned crown), the second part of this monster is described in both texts with human features concerning the head. In our opinion these parallels are so significant that they may indicate a dependence — especially when we take into consideration that they occur in two night-visions with the same sequence of basic content.

In the description of the god on the throne there are also correspondences in the basic imagery: The supreme god on the throne, surrounded by attendants, the fire, the adoration. But the correspondences in phraseology are not so close as in the previous section. Visions of the divine assembly are also represented elsewhere in Jewish literature. If we argue for a relationship between the Vision of the Nether World and Dan 7 as a whole, it seems clear that other sources can have influence Dan 7 in this sequence just as much or even more than the Akkadian vision.

In the description of the judgement there seem to be do direct correspondences in phraseology. There is also a difference since one of the monsters is killed in Dan 7, which is not recounted in the Vision of the Nether World. The unique man has, however, defeated a creature which most likely is a monster (cf. line 50).

Nevertheless, if we argue for a relationship between the texts, the author of Dan 7 must have interpreted the Akkadian vision according to a new setting and added new material.

There are, however, also striking similarities in motifs. In both texts the judgement comes over the supremely wise rebel king. The occurrence of this motif in a vision following the vision of the ruling god on the throne is so distinctive that it can indicate a relationship.

In the description of the ideal ruler the correspondences are in style rather than direct phraseology. Both texts describe how the supreme god transfers universal kingship to a ruler. In both texts the ruler is called "a man". The phraseology used in both texts is traditional in relation to the milieu of the texts. But the appearance of an ideal ruler in a vision, described in contrast to a rebel king, is more distinctive. The crucial issue here, however, is how we understand the designation "man". If it could be made clear that the Akkadian *ištēn eṭlu* which is used about the king within the Akkadian vision corresponds to Aramaic *bar 'ănāš* which is used about the ruler in Dan 7 within the vision, this would be a fairly decisive argument for a relationship between the texts. The Vision of the Nether World would then be the only occurrence outside the Jewish-Christian milieu.

When we compare the Death-Dream of Enkidu to Dan 7, the first thing to consider is the difference between the Death-Dream and the Vision of the Nether World. Even though there are found no parallels to the Death-Dream as a whole outside the Gilgamesh cycle, the text adheres closely to the traditions of the nether world in Mesopotamia, a part of it even reciting a traditional poem (cf. above, p. 380). The Vision of the Nether World is, however, a singular text, linked to a specific historical situation. Accordingly there is a higher degree of possibility that the parallels between the Death-Dream and Dan 7 may depend on the adaptation of similar traditions without any form of direct relationship between the texts.

The parallels between these two texts are not nearly as many as between the Akkadian vision and Dan 7. The first similarity in the opening, the action of natural forces, can be explained as a motif introducing a special type of dreams and does not demonstrate any relationship.

The next similarity concerning the first beast in Dan 7 and the beast-man in the Death-Dream is more remarkable. Here the features are so close that it is difficult to conclude other than that the author of Dan 7 must have written under the influence of a similar sort of imagination as the author of the Death Dream. If we include Dan 4, there are similarities even down to such specific features as the nails/claws. That is even more conclusive since both texts contain the motif of transformation. On the other hand the Anzu-bird symbolism represented in the Death-Dream occurs in many texts. And even though the Death-Dream is the only text known to us which explicitly describes a transformation within this imagery, a similar transformation is implied in the underworld traditions where the dwellers are described with bird-like features. The next distinctive parallel occurs in the scene of judgement where something is read from a court protocol. This motif is also only explicitly reported in the Death-Dream, but it is not so remarkable that it could not have occurred in a broader tradition about the judgement of the dead.

Concerning the Gattung- and pattern-similarities, these do not depart from the similarities between the Vision of the Nether World and Dan 7 (except the opening). We must therefore conclude that although there are significant similarities also between the Death-Dream and Dan 7, these do not demonstrate a likely dependence.

b) Dan 7 in a Mesopotamian Context

1. Introduction

The analysis so far indicates some sort of relationship between the Vision of the Nether World and Dan 7. The analysis needs, however, to be supplemented by a broader investigation of the context of the Daniel vision. If a theory of dependence is correct, we should expect that the various elements of content i Dan 7 functioned within a framework similar to the Vision of the Nether World. This means that there is not only an "outward" correspondence in Gattung, structure and phrases, but also an "internal" correspondence in "message". Of course a complete identity in message cannot be expected, because of the different historical and cultural setting of the visions, but a dependence of Dan 7 on the Akkadian vision must have influenced the content of the former.

What we need therefore, is an investigation of the various elements of content in Dan 7 compared to the Vision of the Nether World. But since we still not have given an independent analysis of Dan 7 such a direct comparison would run the danger of circular arguments. We therefore need to establish a broader context of Dan 7 than the Akkadian vision, based on an analysis of the elements of content in Dan 7 themselves. The aim is not to investigate how this vision communicated in its Jewish setting, but to shed more light on the background of the vision, this time with Dan 7 itself as the starting point. This will enable us to test whether Dan 7 communicates within a framework corresponding to the Akkadian vision, and if this is the case, to establish a new basis for the understanding of the vision.

The special character of Dan 7 is that a mythical pattern is applied to historical circumstances. But as it will appear it is not possible to separate a purely mythical stratum from a purely historical. The interrelationship between "myth" and "history" is more complex. The historical references make use of historiographical patterns which contain mythical allusions. Nevertheless, it seems profitable to start the analysis with those elements of content in which the historical features are most dominant such as the description of the rebel king, the four kingdoms and the ideal king, and then proceed to the elements in which the mythical features dominate, such as the sea, the monsters, the four winds of heaven and the clouds accompanying the Son of Man.

2. The Rebel King

The succession of beasts in the vision of Dan 7 has its climax in the fourth beast and the eleventh horn growing out of the head of this beast. The beast surpasses the others in cruelty (v. 7) and the eleventh horn speaks words of rebellion (v. 8.11). The interpretator of the vision from v. 19 concentrates on this beast and the horn.

There is a general agreement in research that this beast signifies Antiochus Epiphanes. But there has also been an awareness among some scholars that the description of Antiochus Epiphanes is not to be taken exclusively as a historical report. When Antiochus in the Book of Daniel is portrayed as a rebel king, he is described according to a role or pattern developed prior to the actual events leading up to the Maccabean revolt.

The pattern of the "rebel king" in the Book of Daniel has been analyzed by J.C.H. Lebram.[1] He found that in a general way the pattern reflected the fate of the ungodly in sapiential literature. More directly he traced the background of the pattern as it was applied to Antiochus back to Egyptian sources. According to Lebram the pattern was first developed around the Persian king Cambyses because of his cruel acts against the Egyptians, and later in Egypt transferred to Antiochus. The pattern was then adopted by the composers of the Book of Daniel in their description of Antiochus.

In his article Lebram concentrated mainly on the question: why did pious Jews so soon portray Antiochus with the typical characteristics of a rebel prince? In this perspective it seems likely that the description of Antiochus in Egyptian and Greek sources as cruel, an enemy of the gods and oppressor of the people has influenced the composers of the Book of Daniel. Lebram did, however, not discuss in detail the question of the original source of the pattern of the "rebel prince" as it unfolds in the Book of Daniel. At the end of the article he referred to H. Lewy who claimed that the traditions centered around the last Babylonian king Nabonidus constituted the origin of the pattern.[2] The question then arises whether Nabonidus formed only the origin of the traditions as they were developed in Egypt, or whether there could be a more direct current of tradition from the Mesopotamian provenance to the Book of Daniel.

H. Lewy's article is primarily an investigation of the background of the Persian legends about the king Kay Kaus, recorded by the historiographer Firdausi in the tenth century A.D.[3] In the story about this king she found the following characteristics (in selection):[4]

---

1 J.C.H. Lebram, "König Antiochus im Buch Daniel", VT 25, 1975, pp. 737-72.
2 Lebram, op.cit., p. 769.
3 H. Lewy, "The Babylonian Background of the Kay Kâûs Legend", ArOr 17, 1949, pp. 28-109.
4 Lewy, op.cit., pp. 31f.

* Kay Kaus was passionately interested in observations of the moon, the sun and the stars. The interest became so intense that he undertook a flight to heaven in order to see the moon and the sun and to count the stars one by one.
* Kay Kaus rebelled against the religion in al-'Irâq.
* He undertook a military expedition against Arabia.
* Seated on a golden throne he attempted to ascend to heaven.
* He constructed a lofty tower which is located by some of the sources in the vicinity of the city of Babylon.
* He was stricken by a temporary but complete dementia.

Knowing the Babylonian and early Persian sources dealing with Nabonidus, one can hardly deny the similarities between the descriptions of Nabonidus in these sources and the Kay Kaus legends. But the reflection of Nabonidus in Kay Kaus has also adopted elements from a broader current of tradition in the long history of transmission, as Aa. Bentzen made clear.[5]

Lewy did not only trace one current of tradition from Nabonidus into late Persian legends, she also traced another which led to the tale about the insanity of Nebuchadnezzar i Dan 4. That Nabonidus and not Nebuchadnezzar was the actual historical king behind the tale in Dan 4 had already gained some acceptance in research in the first half of our century, while still being under discussion.[6] After the publication of the fragment 4QOrNab, the Prayer of Nabonidus, from Qumran by J.T. Milik in 1956 there can be no doubt that traditions about Nabonidus form at least a part of the background of Dan 4.[7] The best preserved part of the text reads:

> The words of the p[ra]yer said by Nabonidus,
> the king of A[ssyria and Baby]lon, the [great] king,
> [when he was smitten] with malignant boils
> by the ordinance of G[od Most Hi]h in [the city] of Teima.
> [With malignant boils] I was smitten for seven years,
> and unlike [man] I was made;

---

5 Cf. Aa. Bentzen, "Der böse Fürst", StTh 4, 1950, pp. 109-19, who especially drew attention to the wide spread motif of the divine throne of the king and the ascension of a king to heaven in the Middle Ages.
6 Cf. W. Baumgartner, "Ein Vierteljahrhundert Danielforschung", ThRv 11, 1939, pp. 59-83, 125-44, 201-28, pp. 128ff.
7 For text editions, cf. J.T. Milik, "'Prière de Nabonide' et autres écrits d'un cycle de Daniel", RB 63, 1956, pp. 407-15; B. Jongeling, C.J. Labuschange and A.S. van der Woude, Aramaic Texts from Qumran I, SSS, Leiden 1976, pp. 121-31; J.A. Fitzmyer and D.J. Harrington, A Manual of Palestinian Aramaic Texts, BibOr 34, Rome 1978, p. 2. A discussion of the relationship between Nabonidus, the Prayer of Nabonidus and Dan 4 is found in R. Meyer, Das Gebet des Nabonid, SSAW.PH 107/3, Berlin 1962; W. Dommerhausen, Nabonid im Buch Daniel, Mainz 1964; A. Mertens, Das Buch Daniel im Lichte der Texte vom Toten Meer, SBM 12, Stuttgart 1971, pp. 34-42. A more complete bibliography to the extensive literature to the subject is found in Fitzmyer and Harrington, op.cit., pp. 191ff.

[but I prayed to God Most High],
and he pardoned my sins.
He had a diviner, who was a Jewish [man]
fr[om the exiles, and who said to me]:
Make a written proclamation that honour,
gr[eatness and glory] be given to the name
of G[od Most High].[8]

We have accordingly on the one hand late Persian traditions about a rebel king going back to Nabonidus, and on the other, evidence that Nabonidus was at least partly used as the historical model behind the presumptuous king in Dan 4. Our next question concerns the relation between the king described in Dan 4 and the rebel king described in Dan 7. This question is, however, best answered by placing the two texts in a broader context. Dan 4 shares a pattern describing rebel kings with other Old Testament texts. Dan 7 concerns, at least in the final redaction of the vision, Antiochus Epiphanes, who is described several places in the Hebrew part of the book. We shall first concentrate on Dan 4, comparing this text with Is 14, Ezek 28 and 31 (pp. 464-467).

The comparison demonstrates that Dan 4 relates to an already existing pattern of rebel kings. This pattern cannot have hade Nabonidus or the break-down of the Babylonian empire as its background because the texts in Ezekiel are to be dated earlier.[9] But the reason why this pattern was used in Dan 4 must lie in the traditions about Nabonidus. According to the Prayer of Nabonidus, quoted above, Nabonidus suffered from a severe illness as punishment for his sins, and only when he confessed his sins was he released.

Comparing the pattern of rebel kings used in Dan 4 to the statements about Antiochus Epiphanes, we can see that the description of Antiochus follows exactly the same pattern (p. 468).

8   I have used the English translation of Jongeling et al. in Aramaic Texts from Qumran with two exceptions. In line 2 in my text I read with Milik, "Prière de Nabonide"; "the king of Assyria and Babylon", instead of "the king of the land Babylon". In my line 6 I read with Fitzmyer and Harrington, A Manual: "and unlike man I was made", instead of "I came to be like the animals", Milik's reading: "far from man I was placed", should also be considered.
9   Cf. W. Zimmerli, Ezechiel, BK XIII/2, Neukirchen-Vluyn 1969, pp. 680 and 755.

THE REBEL KING IN THE

Characteristics	Is 14 (the king)		Ezek 28 (the king)	
	13-14a:		**14b:**	
Ascent or	ואתה אמרת	And you said	בהר קדש	You were on
placement	בלבבך	in your heart:	אלהים היית	the holy
in high	השמים אעלה	"I will ascend		mountain of
position	ממעל	to the heaven,		the gods.
	לכוכבי אל	high above the		
	ארים כסאי	stars of God I		
	ואשב בהר	will set my		
	מועד	throne. I will		
	בירכתי	sit on the		
	צפון אעלה	mountain of		
	על במתי	the assembly,		
	עב	in the far		
		recess of the		
		north. I will		
		ascend high		
		above the		
		cloud-banks.		

OLD TESTAMENT

Ezek 31 (the tree)	Dan 4 (5) (the tree)
3:	8:
וגבה קומה towering high and	ורומה ימטא And its top reached
ובין עבתים between the clouds	לשמיא the heaven.
היתה צמרתו was its crown.	

Continued Characteristics	Is 14 (the king)		Ezek 28 (the king)	
	16b:		4:	
Supreme wisdom/ power	הזה האיש מרגיז הארץ מרעיש ממלכות	Is this the man who shook the earth, who made king- doms quake.	בחכמתך ובתבונתך עשית לך חיל	With your wisdom and skill you have created power for yourself.
	14b:		2:	
Like God	אדמה לעליון	I will make myself like the Most High.	ותאמר אל אני	And you say: "I am a god."
	11:		2:	
Hubris	גאונך	Your high- ness	גבה לבך	Your heart is high
	12:		16:	
Fall	איך נפלת משמים	How you have fallen from heaven ...	ואחללך מהר אלהים	I brought you down in dis- grace from the mountain of the gods.
	11:			
	הורד שאול גאונך	Your highness has been brought down to sheol		
			8:	
			לשחת יורדוך	They will bring you down to the grave.

Ezek 31 (the tree)		Dan 4 (5) (the tree)	
6:		**19:**	
ובצלו ישבו	And in its shadows	ורבותך רבת	Your greatness has
כל גוים	all great nations	ומטת לשמיא	grown and reached
רבים	dwelled.	ושלטנך לסוף	the heaven, and
		ארעא	your power to the
			end of the earth.
10:		**5, 20:**	
רם לבבו	His heart is high in	רם לבבה	His heart was high
בגבהו	his highness		
12:		**11:**	
ויכרתהו	Strangers from	גדו אילנא	Hew down the tree,
זרים עריצי	ruthless nations	וקצצו ענפוהי	cut off its branches!
גוים	hewed it down.		
15:			
ביום רדתו	On the day he		
שאולה	descended to sheol		
. . .			

THE REBEL KING IN THE BOOK OF DANIEL

Ascent or placement in a high position (8, 10)	ותגדל עד צבא השמים	And it grew great up to the host of heaven.
Supreme wisdom/ power (8, 23b, 25a)	מבין חידות	One who understands mysteries.
	ועל שכלו והצליח מרמה בידו	Because he is wise, treachery shall succeed by his hand.
Like God (11, 36)	ויתרומם ויתגדל כל אל	He shall exalt and magnify himself above every god and against the God of gods he will talk blasphemies.
	ועל אל אלים ידבר נפלאות	
Hubris (8, 25)	ובלבבו יגדיל	He shall be great in his heart.
Fall (11, 45b)	ובא עד קצו ואין עוזר לו	And he will meet his end with nobody to help him.

So far we have demonstrated the following: 1) Both the description of the king in Dan 4 and of Antiochus in Dan 8-11 follow an Old Testament pattern of descriptions of rebel kings which was developed prior to the fall of the Babylonian empire; 2) This pattern was adopted into Dan 4 because it had affinity to the traditions about Nabonidus underlying the story told there. The next question to be put is whether there are parallels between the description of Nabonidus in Mesopotamian sources and the description of Antiochus in the Book of Daniel.

In the comparison below we use the two cuneiform texts which reflect the position of the Marduk priesthood in Babylon and the Persians as primary sources, the Verse Account of Nabonidus[10] and the Cyrus Cylinder.[11] In one case we also include a statement from the Harran Stela.[12] Our aim is not to analyze the historical background of Nabonidus, nor of Antiochus. The statements of the texts may sometimes have close contact with historical reality, sometimes looser contact and sometimes none at all. Our only interest is in the pattern according to which the two kings, who in some circles were highly unpopular, were described.

The descriptions of the two kings are not without contact with historical reality. But nobody can fail to see that the descriptions are not objective reports of historical events. They are strongly coloured by the positions of the opponents of the kings. The acts of the kings are interpreted on the basis of a distinct political and religious standpoint. However, in that case it is highly remarkable that the acts are interpreted in exactly the same way by two entirely different groups, belonging to two different cultures: Babylonian priests and officials loyal toward the new Persian regime, and pious persecuted Jews. Both kings entered kingship without legal rights, both became oppressors of their country, both showed negligence to the former gods, both uttered blasphemies against the highest god, both altered the established religious practice, both worshipped an unknown god, both placed an abominable statue of a god in the temple, both interrupted the regular offerings, both claimed wisdom and insight in mysteries superior to ordinary man, and even regarded themselves as superior to divine beings.

10 Cf. ANET[3], pp. 312-15.
11 Cf. ANET[3], p. 315.
12 Cf. ANET[3], p. 562.

NABONIDUS AND THE REBEL KING IN THE BOOK OF DANIEL

Characteristics	Rebel king in Daniel	Nabonidus
Descent	11, 21: In his place there will arise a contemptable figure. He is not given the dignity of kingship, but in a time of peace he secures his kingship by a stratagem.	Cyr cyl: A weakling has been installed as the <u>enu</u> of his country. Har st. (i): For me, Nabonidus, the lonely one who has nobody, in whose heart was no thought of kingship, the gods and goddesses prayed (to Sin) and Sin called me to kingship.
Oppressor	8, 24: And his power shall wax mighty; and he shall destroy terribly, and in all he does he shall succeed; and he shall destroy mighty ones and the people of the holy ones.	Vers Acc (i): [. . . law (and)] order are not promulgated by him. [. . . <u>he made perish the common people</u> through w]ant, the nobles he killed in war. Cyr cyl: . . . daily he used to do evil against his (Marduk's) city . . . He [tormented] its [inhabitant]s with a yoke without relief, he ruined them all.
Negligence of the former gods	11, 37: He ignores the gods of his fathers.	Vers Acc (i): [. . . against the will of the g]ods he performed an unholy action. Vers Acc (v): (Yet) he (continues to) mix up the rites, he confuses the (hepatoscopic) oracles [. . .]. The most important ritual observances he orders to an end . . . Cyr cyl: [the correct images of the gods he removed from their thrones, imi]tations he ordered to place upon them.

Continued

Characteristics	Rebel king in Daniel	Nabonidus
Blasphemies	11, 36: And against the God of gods he utters blasphemies.	Vers Acc (v): As to the (sacred) representations in Esagila — representations which Ea-Mummu (himself) had fashioned — He looks at the representations and utters blasphemies. Cyr cyl: . . . for Ur and the other sacred cities inappropriate rituals . . . daily he did blabber [incorrect prayers].
New religious practice	7, 25: He plans to alter the times and law	Vers Acc (ii): "I shall omit (all) festivals, I shall order (even) the New Year's Festival to cease!"
Worship of an unknown god	11, 38: . . . but the god of fortresses he honors in place thereof, a god whom his fathers did not know, he honors.	Vers Acc (i): [He made the image of a deity] which nobody had (ever) seen in this country. Vers Acc (ii): Not (even) the learned Adapa knows his name.
The abominable statue and cult	11, 31: Armies from him arise and profane the sanctuary, the fortress, and do away with the regular offering and set up an abomination that causes desolation.	Vers Acc (ii): He built this abomination, a work of unholiness . . . Vers Acc (i): [He introduced it (the image) into the temple] he placed (it) upon a pedestal. Cyr cyl: He interrupted in a fiendish way the regular offerings. The worship of Marduk he [chang]ed into abomination.
Supreme wise	8, 23b: . . . one who understands mysteries . . . 8, 25a: Because he is wise, treachery shall succeed by his hand.	Vers Acc (v): (Saying): "I am wise, I know, I have seen (what is) hi[dden]. . . . I have seen secret things.
Superior to gods	11, 36: He shall exalt and magnify himself above every god.	Verse Acc (v): [I am] aw[are] of a wisdom which greatly surpasses (even that of) (the series) . . ., which Adapa has composed.

The most likely explanation of these similarities is that we have two kings who in some respects acted similarly and, therefore, were ascribed the same role by their opponents, the role of the rebel king. We have already noticed that Antiochus Epiphanes was described in a role similar to rebel kings known from earlier Old Testament texts. Now we can see that other aspects of his reign are described in the same way as Nabonidus was portrayed in sources from the early Persian period. In Dan 4 we have noticed that the features from the rebel king pattern were used because they had affinity to the Nabonidus traditions. There seems to be a similar sort of collocation of the Old Testament pattern and Nabonidus traditions in the description of Antiochus.

There are still more observations to support this theory. In recording history the Babylonian scribes sometimes used a special style. The history was recorded in the style of predictions. Since we know that the compositions were written after the events and not before, they contain accordingly the technique of *vaticinia ex eventu*, predictions after the event. The predictions were divided according to reigns, and a new period often begins with "a prince will arise". The description of reigns follows a pattern according to which they are described in conventional language as "good" and "bad". As a consequence of the style of prediction the rulers involved are never named and the historical references rather vague. Nevertheless, the compositions refer to real historical circumstances.[13] In their new edition of some of these prophecies Grayson and Lambert called attention to the similarity especially to Dan 8,23-5 and 11,3-45. In order to illustrate the similarity in style we quote one extract from Text A in the edition by Grayson and Lambert[14] and one extract from the Book of Daniel:[15]

> A prince will arise and will exercise kingship for 13 years.
> There will be an attack of Elam on Babylonia
> and the booty of Babylonia will be carried off.

---

13   Cf. A.K. Grayson and W.G. Lambert, "Akkadian Prophecies", JCS 18, 1964, pp. 7-30; and R.D. Biggs, "More Babylonian 'Prophecies'", Iraq 29, 1967, pp. 117-32.
14   Cf. Grayson and Lambert, op.cit., p. 10; cf. also W.W. Hallo, "Akkadian Apocalypses", IEJ 16, 1966, pp. 231-42. For a more detailed comparison with Daniel; Cf: W.G. Lambert, The Background of Jewish Apocalyptic, London 1978, pp. 9-17.
15   Grayson and Lambert, op.cit., p. 14.

The shrines of the great gods will be ruined
and Babylonia will be defeated.
There will be chaos, upset and trouble in the land,
and the upper classes will loose power.
Some other unknown person will arise,
will seize power as if a king,
and will kill of the nobility.

(Col. ii, lines 9-15)

A mighty king will arise,
and he will rule a great empire and do as he pleases.
When he has arisen, his kingdom shall be scattered,
and divided in four according to the four quarters of heaven.
It will not pass to his descendants,
nor be as mighty as when he ruled himself.
For the kingdom will break down
and pass on to others.

(Dan 11,3-4)

The assumption that the style of prophecy in Dan 8 and 11, written in the technique of *vaticinia ex eventu*, was influenced by the style of Babylonian written prophecies — it is to be remembered that this style is unknown in earlier Old Testament texts, has been utterly confirmed by one of the latest publications of a Babylonian prophecy, the so called Dynastic Prophecy, by Grayson in 1975.[16] This prophecy was composed in the Hellenistic age, the exact date is difficult to decide because the end is broken. What makes this prophecy especially interesting is that it deals with the rise and fall of partly the same empires as in the Book of Daniel: Assyria, Babylonia, Persia, Macedonia. In this succession of empires two periods are singled out as particularly bad, that is the reign of the last empire, the Macedonian, cf. col. iii, lines 9-22; and the reign of Nabonidus. We quote the sequence dealing with Nabonidus and a sequence dealing with the rebel king in the Book of Daniel in order to demonstrate the similarity in style.

A re[bel] prince will arise ([. . .]).
The dynasty of Harran [he will establish].
For seventeen years [he will exercise sovereignty].
He will oppress the land
and the festival of Esa[gil he will cancel].
A fortress in Babylon [he will build].
He will plot evil against Akkad.

(Col. ii, lines 11-16)

16 The text is published in A.K. Grayson, Babylonian Historical-Literary Texts, TSTS 3, Toronto 1975, pp. 24-37; cf. also the introduction, pp. 13-23.

A king will arise who is bold faced
and who understands mysteries.
His power will wax mighty,
and he will destroy terribly;
in all he does he will succeed.
He will destroy mighty ones
and the people of the holy ones.
Because he is wise, treachery
will succeed by his hand.

(Dan 8,23b-25a)

There is accordingly a general correspondence between the "predictions" in Dan 8 and 11 and the Babylonian "predictions". Both can be classified as "written prophecy", composed with the same stylistic features in the same technique of *vaticinia ex eventu*. At the latest stage of the history of this Gattung in Babylonia it was applied to the rise and fall of the great empires, beginning with Assyria and ending with Macedonia. Within this "prophecy" Nabonidus is singled out as particularly bad and designated as "a rebel prince". In the Book of Daniel the same Gattung is applied to approximately the same period of history, and generally following the rise and fall of the same empires. Here as well a ruler is singled out as a rebel king. We think there are indications that not only the Gattung of Babylonian written prophecy has influenced the Book of Daniel in general, but also more specially the description of Antiochus Epiphanes. If this is the case, we may also have the answer to how the Nabonidus traditions could have influenced this stage of the Book of Daniel: they could have been adopted into the book as a part of the pattern used in the written prophecies.

Let us now recall our observations:

1. A pattern of description of rebel kings known from earlier Old Testament texts is used both in Dan 4 and in 7-11. In Dan 4 this pattern is applied to Nebuchadnezzar, in Dan 7-11 it is applied to Antiochus Epiphanes.
2. From the Qumran fragment "the Prayer of Nabonidus" it is evident that the Old Testament pattern "rebel king" was adapted into Dan 4 because it had affinity to the Nabonidus traditions underlying this story.
3. In nine different cases the description of Antiochus as rebel king adheres closely to the description of Nabonidus as rebel king in cuneiform sources from the early Persian period.
4. The description of Antiochus as a rebel king occurs within the Gattung written prophecy dealing with the rise and fall of the great empires leading finally to the Macedonian.
   Nabonidus is described within a Babylonian written prophecy dealing with approximately the same period of history. In this prophecy Nabonidus is designated "rebel prince".

These observations should be sufficient to assume that what is evident in Dan 4 is also the case in Dan 7-11, namely that features derived from the traditions about Nabonidus were utilized in the description of Antiochus Epiphanes.

This does not mean, however, that the traditions were adopted into the Book of Daniel at one fixed point, i.e. that it was the same composer who utilized features from the Nabonidus traditions both in Dan 4 and in Dan 7-11. Our observations only demonstrate that these traditions were known to the composers of the Book of Daniel, they could have been known in the milieu behind the Daniel traditions over a long period of time. An analogy is the Mesopotamian traditions about the primeval wise kings and sages that were utilized in the portrayal of Enoch in the Enoch traditions over a long period.[17] Since the Nabonidus traditions were applied to Nebuchadnezzar in Dan 4 and to Antiochus Epiphanes in Dan 7-11, it is not unlikely to assume that they were used by different composers to different times. The portrayals of the two kings are also different, because Nebuchadnezzar is described with more sympathy.

Concerning our subject, it is quite clear that in the interpretation of the vision, in Dan 7,21.24-25, the rebel king is meant to be Antiochus Epiphanes; furthermore that the description is formed under the influence of historical experiences connected to this king. This is also the case with regard to the historical information given within the vision in v. 8. There is general agreement in the research that this sequence describes Antiochus' rise to poser.[18] But with regard to the actual crime mentioned in the sequence we have to judge more carefully. The speaking of great or proud words in vv. 8b and 11a was surely meant to refer to Antiochus by the composers of Dan 7 in its final shape. But the motif is so general that it was not necessarily caused by any particular act of Antiochus, even though it was applied to him.

---

17 Cf. Part I, pp. 324ff.
18 This is generally accepted in research, cf. the following commentaries: Aa. Bentzen, Daniel, HAT 19, Tübingen 1952, pp. 65ff; N.W. Porteous, Das Buch Daniel, ATD 23, 2nd ed., Göttingen 1968, pp. 92ff; O. Plöger, Das Buch Daniel, KAT 18, Gütersloh 1965, pp. 116ff; J.A. Montgomery, A Critical and Exegetical Commentary on the Book of Daniel, ICC, Edinburgh 1927, pp. 311-15; L. Hartman and A.A. Di Lella, The Book of Daniel, AncB 23, New York 1978, pp. 213-17; A. Lacocque, The Book of Daniel, London 1979, pp. 153f.

In v. 8 the passage read: ופם ממלל רברבן, "and a mouth that was speaking great (things)". In v. 11a the passage reads: מן קל מליא רברבתא די קרנא ממללה, "because of the utterance of great words that the horn was speaking". In Ps 12,4 a similar phrase is used as a general characteristic of the ungodly: לשון מדברת גדלות, "a tongue speaking great (things)". The phraseology also occurs twice in the Enochic Book of Watchers: (ועל כול מלין רברבן וקשין (די מללו עלוהי, "Because of all] great and hard [words they spoke against him", En 1,9 = 4Q En°1i, line 17 (Milik, p. 184), restored on the basis of Gr^Pan. And: ותע)ברון עלוהי רברבן וקשין <בפום> טמתכן,[19] "but] you [tr]ansgress against Him with great and hard (words) with your unclean <mouth>, En 5,4 = 4Q En^ali, line 13 (Milik, p. 146). Boasting as an act of arrogance and rebellion against the gods was, as we have seen, also a part of the Nabonidus' portrait in the Verse Account. Such a boasting is also ascribed to Nebuchadnezzar in Dan 4,26.

Accordingly, the great words ascribed to the horn in Dan 7,8.11 were not necessarily caused by any particular act of Antiochus Epiphanes. The phraseology is conventional and describes a ruler who is arrogant and rebellious in his power. We can therefore conclude that although the phraseology in Dan 7,8.11, as it reads now, was meant by the final redactors as a description of Antiochus, the actual crime mentioned is so general that it could suit any rebellious king. We can therefore not exclude the possibility that the motif "rebel king" reflected in the "great words" could have belonged to a stage of the vision in Dan 7 prior to the identification with Antiochus Epiphanes, if Dan 7 had such a pre-history.

So far we have observed and argued on the basis of these observations that Nabonidus actually was portrayed as a rebel king in cuneiform sources from the Persian and Hellenistic period, and that traditions from these sources seem to have influenced the late Persian legends about Kay Kaus and the concept of the rebel king in the Book of Daniel. The next question is whether this pattern or at least traces of it existed prior to Nabonidus and the fall of the Babylonian empire.

---

19 I emend with Milik, The Books of Enoch, p. 146, and Knibb, The Ethiopic Book of Enoch II, Oxford 1978, p. 65, bjwm to bpwm.

THE TREE IN EZEK 31 AND DAN 4

Ezek 31	Dan 4

3a:
Behold, Assur, a cedar on Lebanon,

7a:
Behold, a tree in the midst of the
earth, <u>and its height was great</u>.[2]

3b-4a, 5a:
<u>with fair branches</u>,[1]
a shading forest,
<u>its top reached among the clouds</u>.[2]
The water nourished it,
<u>the deep made it grow tall</u>[3] . . .
<u>So it towered high above all
the trees in the forest</u>.[2]

8-9a:
<u>The tree grew and waxed strong</u>,[3]
<u>and its height reached unto heaven,
and the view of it to the whole earth's
end;</u>[2]
<u>the leafage of it fair</u>,[1]
and its fruit much,
and food in it for all.

6:
<u>In its branches all the birds
of the sky made their nests</u>,[4]
<u>and under its leafage all the beasts of
the field gave birth to their young,
and in its shadow dwelt all great
nations</u>.[5]

9b:
<u>And under it the beasts of the field
were taking shade</u>,[5]
<u>and in its branches the birds of the sky
were dwelling</u>,[4]
and from it all flesh obtained food.

10-13:
Therefore, thus says Yahweh, the Lord:
<u>"Because it towered high, and set its
top among the clouds, and its heart was
high because of its height</u>,[6]
I gave it in the hand of a mighty one
among the nations, so that he could
deal with it according to its wickedness
and drive it away.

19:
It is you O king,
<u>who has been so great and strong,
whose greatness has grown and reached
the heaven</u>,[6]
<u>and whose power has reached the end
of the earth</u>.[5]

And foreigners, the most terrible
among the nations, <u>cut it down, and
cast it on the mountains, and its
branches fell down in all the valleys,
and its leafage was torn apart in all the
watercourses of the land</u>,[7]
<u>and all the peoples of the earth
descended from its shadow and rejected
it</u>.[8]
<u>Upon its fallen trunk all the birds of
the sky made their dwelling, and to its
leafage came all the beasts of the
field</u>.[9]

11-12:
And thus he said:
<u>"Hew down the tree, cut off its
branches, strip off its leafage and
scatter its fruit!"</u>[7]
<u>The beasts shall depart from beneath it,
and the birds from its branches</u>.[8]
But let a stump with its roots be left in
the earth in a bond of iron and brass,
in the grass of the field. Let him be
wet with the dew of the sky,
<u>and with the beasts shall be his lot, in
the grass of the earth</u>.[9]

(The numbers signify corresponding passages.)

On the Jewish side we have already noticed that the pattern occurs in a description of the fall of the Assyrian empire, written in the exile in Babylonia, Ezek 31.[20] This description of Assur as a tree, which in the present context occurs within an oracle against Pharaon, has a word-to-word correspondence to the description of the tree symbolizing Nebuchadnezzar in Dan 4 (cf. comparision above). The texts are so close that there must be a relationship, but not necessarily so that the composer of Dan 4 quoted the present text of Ezekiel. The poem about the fall of Assyria in Ezek is adopted into an oracle against Pharaon as an example of the fate of a hubristic nation. The poem may very well have existed independently and circulated among the Jews in Babylonia, and in this form have been the source behind Dan 4. In any case, the poem demonstrates that the pattern rebel king or rebel nation, which once was used in the description of the fall of Assyria, by the composer of Dan 4 was connected to the Nabonidus traditions in the writing down of the story there.

Let us examine more closely the imagery of the vision in Dan 4. In the vision the king is symbolized as a huge tree. Beneath it the beasts of the field are taking shade, in its branches the birds of the sky have their dwelling, and from it all flesh obtain food (vv. 8-9). This imagery is well known from Mesopotamian texts and representations. As the shepherd of the nation the king is described and depicted as a tree protecting and caring for his people. The representations, especially on cylinder seals, demonstrate clearly that the king was imagined as the tree of life.[21] How this feature is emphasized in Dan 4 is apparent in the comparison with Ezek 31 above. In Dan 4 the king as a tree is feeding the beasts (nations), a

---

20   TM and all other text witnesses read 'aššūr in 31,3. W. Eichrodt, Ezekiel. A Commentary, OTL, London 1970, pp. 422f; and W. Zimmerli, Ezechiel, pp. 747f, nevertheless emend the text to te'aššūr, a kind of tree also mentioned in Ezek 27,6. Zimmerli assumed that the reason for the false text could be haplography. The taw at the beginning of 'aššūr fell out because of the he at the end of the preceding word hinneh. I doubt whether it is correct to use haplography as criterion for textual emendation when the text is smooth and gives full meaning, and when all other text witnesses conform the reading of TM. Nothing in the content contradicts that Assur here is referred to as an example of the fate of the hubristic nation. In Ezek 32,22 Assur is mentioned as the first great empire which fell and descended to the nether world. In Ezek 30,24-26 the Pharaon of Egypt is threatened by the power of the Babylonians. Accordingly it is natural to continue to remind of the fate of the Assyrians who fell by the power of the Babylonians in Ezek 31.

21   Cf. I. Seibert, Hirt-Herde-König, DAWB.SSA 53, Berlin 1969, pp. 17-53.

motif lacking in Ezek 31.

The conception of the tree in Dan 4 as primarily a tree of life sheds light upon another aspect of the imagery lacking in Ezek 31, and whose content has been difficult to decide. In Dan 4,12 it is said that the stump of the tree should be left in a bond of iron and brass. There have been many interpretations of this strange feature. It has been suggested that Nebuchadnezzar had to be kept in chains as a madman, or that it was customary in ancient arboriculture to bind a stump with a chain to keep it from splitting.[22] The last proposal runs counter to the fact that this practice can not be attested in any sources. The first interpretation runs counter to the interpretation of Dan 4,12 in v. 23 where the stump is interpreted as a positive sign. In more recent research one has, therefore, made v. 23 determine the interpretation of v. 12, and claimed that the stump is a sign that Nebuchadnezzar will get back his kingship.[23] But that does not explain the metal band.

Let us once more consider the imagery. The tree is hewn down, leaving a stump behind; the branches are cut off, and the stump of the tree, left as a naked trunk, is surrounded by a metal band. This was what the Assyrian sacred trees must have looked like, whose remains were excavated in the residence city of Sargon, Dur Sharrukin, or modern Khorsabad. Such trees were found at the entrances to the temples of Sin and Shamash. In the excavation report by G. Loud the tree is described as a naked trunk of a cedar tree encapsulated in a bronze band or in bronze rings.[24] This sacred tree played an important role in the ritual of the New Years Festival. The tree was a symbol of fertility, and the decoration of the tree with the bronze band — in Khorsabad having the pattern of bark — and leafage — in Khorsabad gold leaves were found near by — should secure and promote the revival of nature in the year to come.[25]

---

22 For references to earlier research, cf. Montgomery, op.cit., p. 233. The first opinion is argued in more recent research by Hartman and Di Lella, op.cit., p. 176.
23 So Montgomery, op.cit., p. 233; Bentzen, op.cit., p. 43; Porteous, op.cit., p. 54; Plöger, op.cit., p. 75; Lacocque, op.cit., p. 78.
24 G. Loud, Khorsabad I. Excavations in the Palace and at the City Gate, Chicago 1936, pp. 94, 104.
25 Cf. S. Smith, Early History of Assyria, London 1928, pp. 123f; H. Frankfort, Cylinder Seals, London 1939, pp. 204ff; E.O. James, The Tree of Life, Leiden 1966, p. 42.

This sheds new light on the imagery of the naked trunk or stump encapsulated in a metal band in Dan 4. The tree is hewn down and the branches cut off, but a stump is left as was the case with the Assyrian sacred tree. This imagery was a hopeful sign because the sacred tree was a tree of life. Consequently the composer of the story in Dan 4 can let the stump in the metal band signify a future restitution of Nebuchadnezzar, cf. v. 23.

The rite of the encapsulated trunk was Assyrian. It is not attested among the Babylonians. Together with the observation already made, that the imagery of the king as the tree of life in Dan 4 was dependent on the poem about Assyria in Ezek 31, this points in the direction that the composer of Dan 4 combined traditions relating to the fall of Assyria with traditions about Nabonidus.

That exilic Jews portrayed Assyria as a hubristic nation that received its just fate, as Ezek 31 shows, is not remarkable. The Judean prophet Isaiah had already portrayed Assyria as a rebellious nation, cf. Is 10,5-15. This attitude also had support from the Babylonians. After many years under Assyrian supremacy hatred against the Assyrians had grown strong. A literary reflection of this anti-Assyrian attitude is found in a Babylonian prophecy, called the Uruk prophecy, in which the "bad" kings are the Neo-Assyrian ones. These are contrasted with the "good" kings of the Neo-Babylonian empire.[26]

---

26   The prophecy is from Uruk and dates from the Neo-Babylonian period. A succession of "bad" kings are described, preceding two "good" ones. H. Hunger and S.A. Kaufman identified the first bad king as Erību-Marduk, king of Babylon in the middle of the eighth century. The succeeding bad kings were assumed to be Babylonian as well, with exception of the last one, whom they suggested could be Tiglath-Pilesar III. The two good kings were identified as Nebuchadnezzar II and Amel-Marduk. Cf. the text edition by H. Hunger and S. Kaufman, "A New Akkadian Prophecy Text", JAOS 95, 1975, pp. 371-5. The test was also published by Hunger in Spätbabylonische Texte aus Uruk I. Ausgrabungen der Deutschen Forschungsgemeinschaft in Uruk-Warka 9, Berlin 1976, No. 3, pp. 21ff. The interpretation advanced by Hunger and Kaufmann is not without problems, as they themselves admitted. If the interpretation is correct, there would be a gap in the text between the reigns of Tiglat-Pilesar and Nebuchadnezzar which is hard to explain. Furthermore, the last king is strongly idealized, which accords badly with Amel-Marduk, who was rather unimportant and ruled two years only. W.G. Lambert has suggested another interpretation, which seems more likely, cf. Lambert, The Background of Apocalyptic, pp. 10ff. The first king is identified as the Babylonian Merodach-baladan II. Then follows a succession of four bad kings who are the last kings of the Assyrian empire: Sargon II, Sennacherib, Esarhaddon and Ashurbanipal. The first good king is the Babylonian Nabopolassar, and the strongly idealized king at the end is Nebuchadnezzar II. According to this interpretation the pattern "bad kings / good

We have observed how the author of Dan 4 combined traditions about Assyria with traditions about Nabonidus. There are at least indications that a similar sort of combination occurred among the Babylonians as well. We have previously called attention to the similarities between the Vision of the Nether World and the Verse Account of Nabonidus. Both compositions are written in the same epical style, they have the supremacy of the national god and his cult as the central theme, they both contain the motif of the supreme wise rebel king, they both deal with the last king or kings of an empire, and they are both written in order to make clear that the break-down of the empire is caused by the crimes of these kings.[27]

A transference of propaganda against Assyrian kings to propaganda against Nabonidus is also possible on historical grounds. The last Assyrian stronghold was Harran. This was also the city which Nabonidus was most closely attached to. Most probably he was connected to Harran by descent through his mother. Nabonidus' reverence of Sin as the supreme god also fits this pattern. Sin was worshipped as one of the most important gods by the last Assyrian kings.[28] From the Dynastic Prophecy we know that Nabonidus among later Babylonians was not regarded as a Babylonian king at all. In this Prophecy Nabonidus is described as the founder of the dynasty of Harran, who will plot evil against Akkad (Babylonia).[29] This connection between Nabonidus and Harran, the last Assyrian stronghold, makes the assumption even more plausible, that traditions once centered around Assyrian kings were transferred to Nabonidus.

There is one indication that the Assyrians did not only initiate the concept "rebel king" in the Jewish milieu, but also contributed one distinct motif belonging to that concept. We have previously noticed that Antiochus Epiphanes was described as "wise" and as the one who "understands mysteries" in Dan 8, 23b. 25a. This

kings" is applied to the change from the Assyrian to the Babylonian empire. The Neo-Babylonian kings, and especially Nebuchadnezzar, are contrasted to the bad Assyrian rulers.

27 Cf. above, pp. 429f and 440.

28 For Nabonidus' connection to Harran and the Assyrian dynasty, cf. K. Galling, "Politische Wandlungen in der Zeit zwischen Nabonid und Darius", Studien zur Geschichte Israels im persischen Zeitalter, Tübingen 1964, pp. 1-60, pp. 1-8.

29 Cf. above, p. 473.

corresponded to what was said about Nabonidus' boasting in the Verse Account.[30] The motif occurs, however, earlier than Nabonidus in the description of the king of Tyre as a rebel king in Ezek 28,3. The passage reads: "Behold, you are wiser than Daniel, and nothing is a secret to you."[31] The "Daniel" referred to here must be the primeval hero also mentioned in Ezek 14,14, and known from the Ugaritic Tale of Aqhat.[32] Also Jub 4,20 mentiones a primeval figure with the same name. As Zimmerli has suggested[33] it seems likely that Daniel is chosen as the primeval hero here because of his connection with the cities at the Syrian coast where the ancient Ugaritic traditions were located. The problem is, however, that no Ugaritic or Phoenician traditions are known in which a king compares himself in wisdom with a primeval sage.

Ezek 28 was, however, not composed in Palestine, but in Babylonia which makes a Mesopotamian provenance for this motif possible. The comparison in terms of wisdom with ancient sages was a characteristic of the late Assyrian kings. They boasted of a wisdom like or superior to the semi-divine primeval sages and especially the primeval sage *par excellence* Adapa.[34] We have previously noticed that this was also the context of Nabonidus' boasting of superior wisdom and insight in hidden things.[35] In the texts dealing with the last Assyrian kings this boasting was regarded as legitimate. In the Verse Account of Nabonidus it is regarded as hubristic, and recounted together with the other crimes of Nabonidus.

The same motif, the rebel king bestowed with the wisdom of the primeval sages, occurs in the Vision of the Nether World, lines 66-67.[36] Ezek 28,3 is closer to the pattern in this text than to the Verse Account. Both in the Vision of the Nether World and in Ezek 28,3 the wisdom like or superior to the primeval sage(s) is mentioned together with rebellion, but not explicitly regarded as hubristic as in the Verse Account.

---

30   Cf. above, p. 471.
31   The meaning of the last verb ʿmm is unclear. The translation is the same as in Eichrodt, op.cit., p. 388, and is based on criteria of content. For a discussion of the verb, cf. Zimmerli, op.cit., p. 663.
32   Cf. ANET³, pp. 149-55.
33   Cf. note 31 above.
34   Cf. above, pp. 427ff.
35   Cf. above, pp. 429f.
36   Cf. above, p. 427.

This may be another indication that the strands that were later woven together into the pattern "rebel king" had their origin in traditions connected to the last Assyrian kings.

Both on the Jewish and the Mesopotamian side the origin of the pattern "rebel king" seems to relate to the same historical circumstances. The central figure behind these traditions was the last Babylonian king Nabonidus. His strange politics and religious attitude, together with the fact that he was at least partly responsible for the break-down of the Babylonian empire, gave rise to traditions in which he was portrayed as a rebel against the gods and the one who received the just punishment. But Nabonidus was not the only source for this pattern. He rather served as a magnet attracting motifs associated with the pattern. At least some of these motifs seem to relate to the Assyrian kings. We thus have to reckon with several stages in the formation of the rebel king pattern: The first stage relating to the last Assyrian kings and the break-down of the Assyrian empire, the next and most formative stage to Nabonidus and the break-down of the Babylonian empire. Through these events and the traditions arising out of them the type "rebel king" was created, which could subsequently be applied to other rulers, legendary or historical.

The Vision of the Nether World and Dan 7 both relate to the traditions about the rebel king, but the texts are to be placed at two different stages in the development of the pattern. The Vision of the Nether World attests that the motif "the supreme wise rebel king" already existed at the end of the Neo-Assyrian period. Dan 7 shares in the pattern "rebel king" as it was applied to Antiochus Epiphanes. Thus the analysis of the pattern in a broader context has demonstrated that the texts relate to the same history of tradition. But the analysis has also shown that the Jews who appropriated the Vision of the Nether World into the Daniel traditions as a text, or more likely as a tradition, can hardly have known its Assyrian setting. Nabonidus was the historical model behind the pattern "rebel king" as it was applied to Nebuchadnezzar and Antiochus Epiphanes in the Book of Daniel. It therefore seems likely that Nabonidus and the break-down of the Babylonian empire was the context of the Jewish adoption of the Vision of the Nether World or traditions derived from it. If this was the case, the Vision of the Nether World must have been understood as a story about the last Babylonian kings corresponding to Dan 2 and 4-5 by the Jews who first transformed Mesopotamian traditions into Daniel traditions.

3. The Four Empires and the Ideal King

In the interpretation of the vision the four beasts are explained as four kings (v. 17). A similar division of history occurs in Dan 2 where the four metals are explained as four empires, Aram $malk\bar{u}$ (vv. 39-40). In Dan 2 the first empire is represented by Nebuchadnezzar (v. 38). The same king must be intended as the first in Dan 7, since the transformation of the first beast in v. 4 clearly reflects the fate of Nebuchadnezzar in Dan 4, except that there the transformation goes in the opposite direction.[37] According to Dan 5,26-27 the empire was taken from Belshazzar, understood as the last Babylonian king, and given to the Medes and the Persians. According to Dan 6,1 the Medes were the first to take the kingdom after the Babylonians.

In the Hebrew part of the book the same kingdoms are referred to. In Dan 8,20 Media and Persia are again listed, succeeded by Macedonia, v. 21. The succession Persia—Macedonia is also intended in Dan 11,2-3.

The same pattern is also reflected in the dating of the stories, dreams and visions: Babylonia: Nabuchadnezzar (ch. 1, 2, 3, 4); Belshazzar (ch. 5, 7, 8) Media: Darius (ch. 6, 9); Persia: Cyrus (ch. 10-12). It is thus evident that the Book of Daniel as a whole presupposes a fixed pattern of successive empires in the order: Babylonia - Media - Persia - Macedonia.

J. Swain was the first to demonstrate that a similar pattern is presupposed by Greek and Latin historiographers. His study has

---

37 For the four empires in the Book of Daniel, cf. K. Koch, "Spätisraelitisches Geschichtsdenken am Beispiel des Buches Daniel", HZ 193, 1961, pp. 1-32, pp. 7-20; H.S. Kvanvig, Struktur und Geschichte in Dan 7", pp. 99f. A four scheme is also applied to the same period of history in the Apocalypse of Animals, En 89,59-90,19, cf. Part I, pp. 108f.

later gained general acceptance.[38] The pattern is reflected as early as about 180 B.C. in a fragment stemming from the Roman historiographer Aemelius Sura. The difference to the list in the Book of Daniel is that the Greek and Roman historiographers have Assyria and not Babylonia as the first kingdom, reading: Assyria - Media - Persia - Macedonia.

The position of Babylonia as the first empire in the Book of Daniel seems to depend upon the important role of this empire in this book, a feature to which we shall return later. The inclusion of the Medes both in the Book of Daniel and in the Greek and Latin sources seems to reflect a Persian point of view since this people was closely attached to the Persians.[39]

D. Flusser has argued that Or Sib IV,49-89, which recounts the succession of the empires Assyria - Media - Persia - Macedonia, is derived from a Persian source. The sequence contains the same combination of a scheme of four and a scheme of ten as later Persian sources.[40] The scheme of ten is also attested to in another Sibyl, written down by a certain Servius about 400 A.D., but there combined with the scheme of metal ages, which also occurs in Persian sources. Earlier than Flusser S.K. Eddy had argued for a setting of the underlying Persian source of the scheme of four empires in the Persian resistance against the Macedonian empire at the end of the third century B.C. Eddy also argued for the same setting of other texts reflecting Persian resistance, such as Or Sib III,388-400, and the Oracle of Hystaspes.[41]

---

38 J.W. Swain, "The Theory of the Four Monarchies. Opposition History under the Roman Empire", CP 35, 1940, pp. 1-21; cf. also W. Baumgartner, "Zu den vier Reichen von Dan 2", ThZ 1, 1945, pp. 17-22; M. Noth, "Das Geschichtsverständnis der alttestamentlichen Apokalyptik", 1954, = Gesammelte Studien zum AT, 2nd ed. 1960, pp. 248-73; K. Koch, op.cit.
39 Cf. M. Noth, op.cit., pp. 251-59.
40 D. Flusser, "The Four Empires in the Fourth Sibyl and in the Book of Daniel", IOS 2, 1972, pp. 148-75. The combination "four" and "ten" also occurs in Dan 7, cf. vv. 7-8.
41 S.K. Eddy, The King is Dead, Lincoln 1961, pp. 3-36. The Oracle of Hystaspes is referred to by several of the early Christian apologists, among them Lactantius (240 to c. 320 A.D.). Together with other sources of apocalyptic character the Oracle was used in his Divinae Institutionis VII, 15-21. It was quoted as an oracle against the Roman empire. In the research the name Hystaspes is generally seen as a transformation of the Persian Vistāšpa, the king who supported Zoroaster. The Oracle is commonly held to be of Persian origin, although it also has attracted motifs of Hellenistic origin. Cf. for text, J. Bidez and F. Cumont, Les mages hellénisés II, Paris 1938, pp. 359-76; for discussion and analysis, H. Windisch, Die Orakel des Hystaspes, VNAW.L 28, No. 3, 1929;

An attestation of the scheme of four in a genuine Persian source is found in a Pahlavi work (about 9th century A.D.), called Zand-ī Vohūman Yašn. The text is accordingly a *zand*, "interpretation", of a lost book of the Avesta, the Vohūman Yašt. The Pahlavi text is in its present shape composed during the Sassanide period, but the original version is considerably older.[42] The text is presented as a vision seen by Zoroaster. It contains the scheme of the four metals, which is attested to already in Hesiod's Work and Days (about 700 B.C.),[43] and there applied to the four metal ages.[44] In the Vohūman Yašt this scheme is applied to successive kings. The vision of Zoroaster reads:

> Aūhrmazd showed the wisdom
> of all-knowledge until Zaratūhst.
> Through it, he saw the trunk of a tree
> on which there were four branches:
> One of gold, one of silver,
> one of steel and one of iron mixed.
> Thereof he considered that he saw this in a dream.[45]

The resemblance with the dreams in Dan 2 and 4 is clear: The four metals signifying four periods as in Dan 2; the tree as in Dan 4. But it is clear that Zoroaster's dream is not connected to the scheme of four empires, only to successive kings within the

G. Widengren, Die Religionen Irans, RM 14, Stuttgart 1965, pp. 199-207; J.R. Hinnels, "The Zoroastrian Doctrine of Salvation in the Roman World", Man and his Salvation, Studies in Memory of S.G.F. Brandon, Manchester 1973, pp. 125-48, (with English translation); K. Müller, "Die Ansätze der Apokalyptik", Literatur und Religion des Frühjudentums, J. Maier and J. Schreiner (eds.), Würzburg 1973, pp. 31-42, pp. 33-6.

S.K. Eddy dates the Oracle in its original Persian form to the end of the third or the beginning of the second century B.C., op.cit., pp. 32ff. The Oracle was then directed against Macedonia as the hostile empire and not against Rome. This date — approximately the same time as the appearance of the Jewish historically centered apocalyptic — makes the Oracle an interesting parallel to Jewish apocalyptical texts, cf. G. Widengren, "Iran and Israel in Parthian Times with Special Regard to the Ethiopic Book of Enoch", Religious Syncretism in Antiquity, B.A. Pearson (ed.), Missoula, Montana 1975, pp. 85-129.

42   The text is translated into German by G. Widengren, Iranische Geistwelt, GML, Baden-Baden 1961, pp. 181-84. For a survey of Persian "apocalyptic" literature, cf. J.J. Collins, "Persian Apocalypses", Semeia 14, 1979, pp. 207-17.

43   Work and Days, 106-201. For text, cf. H.G. Evelyn-White, Hesiod. The Homeric Hymns and Homerica, LCL, London-Cambridge (Mass.), 1914 (1977), pp. 10-17.

44   For the four ages, cf. B. Gatz, Weltalter, goldene Zeit und sinnverwandte Vorstellungen, Spudasmata 16, Hildesheim 1967, pp. 1-86.

45   The English translation is taken from Flusser, "The Four Empires", p. 166.

Persian empire.[46]

In Dan 2,31-45 the scheme of four metal ages is combined with the scheme of four empires. This combination does not occur in Dan 7. In both Dan 2 and Dan 7 the scheme of four empires, however, is combined with the idea of kings representing world empires. This combination does not occur in either the Roman, Greek or Persian sources. This idea is again in the Aramaic part of the Book of Daniel associated with the prominent position given to the Babylonian king Nebuchadnezzar.

In Dan 2,37 the golden head of the statue seen in the dream is interpreted as Nebuchadnezzar who is given *malkūtā ḥisnā wetāqpā wīqārā,* "the kingdom, power, strength and honour". A similar wording occurs in Dan 5,18. Nebuchadnezzar was given *malkūtā ūrebūtā wīqārā wehadrā,* "the kingdom, greatness, honour and glory". In Dan 7,4 Nebuchadnezzar, represented as a beast, is transformed into a human shape and given a human heart. Since the semantic pattern of the vision is based on the pattern man - beast, Nebuchadnezzar's transformance can hardly be accidental. The figure transformed to a human being in the beginning of the vision corresponds to the distinguished man at the end of the vision.[47]

The connection between the Son of Man and Nebuchadnezzar is fully confirmed by the wording used about the Son of Man. He is given *šāltān wīqar ūmalkū,* "rulership, honour and kingdom", v. 14, designations clearly resembling those used about Nebuchadnez-zar's kingdom. This does of course not mean that the Son of Man is thought only as a "shadow" or reflection of Nebuchadnezzar. There are distinct differences between the two figures because the Son of Man is both a transcendent and an eschatological figure. But the Son of Man is not without analogies in the human world. The composer has deliberately drawn a line from the kingship of Nebuchadnezzar to the kingship of the Son of Man.

So far we can conclude: Dan 7 contains a scheme of four applied to four empires. A similar scheme is found in Greek and Roman sources, and in Or Sib IV, which seems to have adopted a Persian

---

46 The last period is interpreted as the period of evil spirits, Eddy, op.cit., p. 19, takes this as a reference to the Macedonian empire. The three first kings are, however, Persian.
47 Cf. Kvanvig, "Struktur und Geschichte", p. 114.

source. The application of the scheme of four to a period of the contemporary history and subsequently to the four world empires seems to have Persian provenance. Dan 7 does,however, combine this scheme with new elements: The world empires are represented by kings, Nebuchadnezzar is regarded as the world emperor *par excellence*, the four world empires and their kings are followed by a fifth ruler and empire, greatly surpassing the others, but nevertheless comparable with the glory of Nebuchadnezzar and the Babylonian empire.

This eschatological outlook, in which the fifth empire and the Son of Man appears, is unique to the Book of Daniel, and must be explained on the background of Old Testament prophetic eschatology.[48] But some of the other elements mentioned above seem to correspond to Babylonian sources.

This has a bearing on the prominent place of Babylonia in the Book of Daniel. We have earlier discussed the relationship between the "predictions" in the Book of Daniel and the Babylonian prophecies.[49] The correspondences between the Dynastic Prophecy and the Book of Daniel seem especially close. Both compositions recount the rise and fall of the great empires. Both compositions cast Babylonia in the leading role. Both compositions reflect hostility against the Macedonian empire, recorded as the last of the series in both texts (cf. Dynastic Prophecy, col. iii, lines 9-23 and col. iv).

We have also noticed that the empires in the Book of Daniel are represented by kings. The Babylonian prophecies recount the rule

---

48   The portrayal of the Son of Man in v. 14 as an eschatological king of salvation is often in the research connected with the "Messianic Prophecies" in the Old Testament, cf. for instance Is 9,2-7; 11,1-9; Jer 23,5-6; Ezek 37,24-25; Mich 5,1; in Jewish literature especially Ps Sal 17; cf. Aa. Bentzen, King and Messiah, pp. 73-80; and H.R. Balz, Methodische Probleme der neutestamentlichen Christologie, p. 71. There is a correspondence between these messianic prophecies and Dan 7,14 in the topic "eschatological king of salvation". But the Son of Man lacks the basic characteristics of the royal salvation figure in these prophecies, namely the Davidic descent. The correspondence therefore points rather towards a general influence from the prophetic heritage, especially in the historical-eschatological perspective of Dan 7, than towards a direct influence from the Messianic Prophecies and the traditions centered around the Judean Davidic kingship.

49   Cf. above, pp. 472ff; cf. also the discussion of the relationship between the Dynastic Prophecy and the scheme of the four world empires in G.F. Hasel, "The Four World Empires of Daniel 2 against its Near Eastern Environments", JSOT 12, 1979, pp. 17-30.

of kings. When this Gattung was applied to the period of the great empires, as in the Dynastic Prophecy, a combination king—empire was created similar to the Book of Daniel.

Also the prominent place of Nebuchadnezzar in the Book of Daniel corresponds to the Babylonian point of view. A strong idealization of Nebuchadnezzar and his reign occurs in a Babylonian composition given the name "Nebuchadnezzar, the king of justice".[50] Even more interesting for our subject is that such an idealization occurs in the Uruk Prophecy as well. The prophecy starts by "predicting" a favourable Babylonian reign, succeeded by four "bad" Assyrian kings. Then follows the Neo-Babylonian reign which is described as "good".[51] The prophecy ends by "predicting" the following reign clearly reflecting the kingship of Nebuchadnezzar:

> After him his son will arise as king in Uruk
> and he will become master of the world.
> He will exercise rule and kingship in Uruk
> and his dynasty will be established for ever.
> The kings of Uruk will exercise rulership like the gods.
> (Reverse, lines 16-19)[52]

The prophecy is especially interesting considering the relationship between Nabuchadnezzar and the future ruler, the Son of Man, in the Book of Daniel. There are of course differences between the description of the reign of Nebuchadnezzar and that of the Son of Man in Dan 7,13-14 both in wording and in structure of thought. Dan 7,13-14 describes real future, while the Uruk prophecy is written according to the style of *vaticinia ex eventu*. The Daniel sequence contains an eschatological outlook which implies a radical "break" in history before the reign of the Son of Man. This is not the case in the Uruk prophecy. The Son of Man is also a transcendent figure coming with the clouds of heaven and entering before God. But these differences are not of the kind that they rule out the possibility that the description of the Son of Man as the last king ruling a universal and everlasting kingdom may have been influenced by the style of the Babylonian prophecies, as well as other features in the Book of Daniel.

The Uruk prophecy is written in the style of *vaticinia ex eventu*,

---

50 Cf. above, p. 436.
51 Cf. above, note 26, p. 480.
52 The translation is taken from H. Hunger and S.A. Kaufman, "A New Akkadian Prophecy Text", pp. 372f.

but it is intended to be read as a real prophecy like Dan 7,13-14. The Uruk prophecy is not eschatological, but its strongly idealized description of the last reign comes close to the style of Jewish eschatological prophecies. The king in the Uruk prophecy is not a transcendent figure, but the kings of Uruk will nevertheless "exercise rulership like the gods", which seems not far removed from the idea behind Dan 7,13-14. And it is not to be overlooked that this is said about Nebuchadnezzar in the Uruk prophecy, who in the Book of Daniel functions as a signal within history of the eschatological kingdom of the Son of Man.

In our analysis of the Vision of the Nether World we argued that the composer had "borrowed" the style of the Babylonian prophecies in the description of the ideal king seen in the vision.[53] The sequence about the ideal king and his universal and everlasting kingdom granted by the gods could accordingly be read as a description of a future king, although historically it described the reign of Sennacherib. We will later discuss in detail how the Vision of the Nether World or traditions derived from it could have been interpreted by later readers who did not know the historical circumstances to which it alluded. Here we shall only call attention to one possibility. For a later recipient of the Vision the predicted rebellion in the reign of the visionary and the predicted annihilation of the visionary and his father could easily have been interpreted as a prediction about the fall of the Assyrian empire.[54] If so, the ideal king would be a king belonging to the next empire, the Babylonian. This would correspond to the interpretation of history in the Uruk prophecy in which the bad Assyrian kings were followed by the good kings of the Babylonians, and in which Nebuchadnezzar is described in the same idealized manner as the ideal king in the Vision of the Nether World.

Our investigation of the four empires and the ideal king thus leads to the same conclusion as the analysis of the rebel king pattern. The material in the Book of Daniel, such as the scheme of four empires, the connection between king and empire, the emphasis on the Babylonian empire and the idealization of Nebuchadnezzar, points toward a Mesopotamian provenance of the traditions. The

53 Cf. above, pp. 435ff.
54 Cf. above, pp. 440f.

traditions reflect partly a Persian (the scheme of four) and partly a Babylonian point of view. That Persian and Babylonian priests and officials could join in a common political and religious attitude we have observed earlier in the Verse Account of Nabonidus and the Cyrus Cylinder.[55] In these compositions the contrast is not between the Neo-Babylonian and the Persian reign, but between Nabonidus, portrayed as a rebel king, and Cyrus described in a strongly idealized manner as the liberator of the Babylonians (especially in the Cyrus Cylinder).

There seems accordingly to be a tendency to contrast rebel kings and ideal kings: The rebel kings of Assyria against the ideal king of Babylonia; Nabonidus, the rebel king, against Cyrus, the ideal king of Persia. Both the Vision of the Nether World in its contrast between the last rebellious Assyrian kings and the ideal king, and Dan 7 in its contrast between Antiochus Epiphanes and the Son of Man share in this pattern. But also here, as was the case with the rebel king pattern, there seems to be a stage in between, a stage which reflects the traditions of the Babylonian and early Persian empire.

4. The Son of Man

The phrase "son of man" in Dan 7,13 is a literal translation of two nouns connected by a genitive, Aramaic *bar 'ǎnāš*.

The genitive in the connection, *'ǎnāš*, is the ordinary Aramaic word for "man, human being". The word can also be used with a collective meaning "someone, mankind, people".[56] A good indication of its semantic value can be obtained by comparing Hebrew TM Job with the Aramaic Targum of Job:[57]

	TM Job		11Qtg Job
19,19:	כל מתי סודי	col. 2,8:	כל אנש
32,13:	לא איש	col. 21,5:	לא (א) נש
34,11:	אדם	col. 24,5:	אנש
35,8:	לא איש/לא אדם	col. 31,4:	לא אנש

---

55   Cf. above, pp. 469ff.

56   Cf. C. Colpe, "ho hyios to anthropou", ThWNT VIII, Stuttgart 1969, pp. 403-81, pp. 404f; and: "Der Begriff 'Menschensohn' und die Methode der Erforschung Messianischer Prototypen", Kairos 11, 1969, pp. 241-68, pp. 245f; K. Koch, Das Buch Daniel, p. 225.

57   I use the edition by Fitzmyer and Harrington, pp. 10-46.

Aramaic '*ănāš* is here used equivalent to both hebrew '*ādām*, "human being", and to '*īš*/*m*e*tīm* (pl.), "man/men".

The noun *bar* means literally "son", but placed in a genitive connection to a collective noun it functions so as to single out one part of the collective body.[58] The genitive connection *bar* '*ănāš* thus means "one member of mankind". The problem is whether this phrase or the later spelling of the phrase in Palestinian Aramaic *bar naš*[59] has another meaning than the simple noun '*ănāš* used in the singular meaning "human being, man" or undetermined "someone". Scholars disagree at this point, some claiming that the two phrases are identical in meaning,[60] others that the genitive connection emphasizes the singular aspect more

---

58   Cf. S. Segert, Altaramäische Grammatik, Leipzig 1975, 6.3.5.1.2, pp. 338f.

59   Kearns, Vorfragen I, has advanced a quite different theory. The nouns bar '*ănāš* and bar naš have usually been regarded as two different spellings of the same phrase. Kearns argues that the noun barnaš reflects a word with a meaning and etymology different from that commonly attributed to bar '*ănāš*, "man, human being". The origin of the word is found in the Ugaritic word bnš, "royal vassal, royal tenant", which developed into Aramaic brnš with the meaning "vassal king" in the eight century B.C. in Syria. The word is however not attested in this form. The only attestation is on the Sefire Stela from the middle of the eighth century in the form bar '*ănāš*. The meaning of this phrase, which was adopted into the Official Aramaic of Palestine, was the same as brnš. The word had nothing to do with the identical written phrase bar '*ănāš*, "son of man", which was formed under the influence of Hebrew ben '*ādām*. With reference to Dan 7,13 this means that bar '*ănāš* there is to be read in the light of brnš, "royal vassal", and not in the light of the Hebrew construction "son of man".

Kearns himself has called attention to the hypothetical character of the theory. In a foot-note at the very beginning of his analysis he remarks that the theory remains a hypothesis (note 1, p. 9). This is indeed so.

Since the form bar '*ănāš* is composed out ot two nouns, the one well attested in the meaning "son" and the other well attested in the meaning "man", and since bar '*ănāš* in Aramaic texts is used as a translation of Hebrew ben '*ādām*, "son of man", this word can not serve as a basis for a totally different understanding. The burden of proof must lie with the different form brnš. This word is not, however, attested in Old or Official Aramaic. What Kearns does is to presuppose a non attested brnš as attested and to use this word as the key to understand the attested bar '*ănāš*, which is identical in form to the phrase meaning "son of man", but has nothing to do with this phrase, since it is derived from the (not attested) brnš. That is indeed hypothetical. For a more detailed discussion cf. C. Colpe, "Neue Untersuchungen zum Menschensohn-Problem", cols. 373-78.

60   Cf. for instance C. Colpe, "ho hyios tou anthropou", p. 406; A.A. Di Lella, "The One in Human Likeness and the Holy Ones of the Most High in Dan 7, pp. 1ff; G. Vermez, "The Use of br nš / br nš' in Jewish Aramaic", Appendix E, in M. Black, An Aramaic Approach to the Gospels and Acts, 3rd ed., Oxford 1967, pp. 310-28. Vermez demonstrates that in several places the phrase is used as a circumlocution for "I", which has significance for the use of the phrase in the New Testament as a self-designation for Jesus, cf. also G. Vermes, Jesus the Jew, Fortress Press ed., Philadelphia 1981 (first publ. 1973), pp. 160-91; cf. also the discussion of the issue by J. Bowker, "The Son of Man", JThS 28, 1977, pp. 19-48, pp. 28-35.

than the simple noun.[61] Concerning Dan 7,13 the question is whether the author had any particular reason to use the genitive connection or whether he could just as well have used the simple 'ănā̄š.

One reason why the question is difficult to decide is that the relevant material is scanty. The occurrences of the genitive connection are fairly frequent in post-Christian Jewish sources, but rare in earlier sources. Only one occurrence is known ante-dating the Book of Daniel, the Sefire Stele III from the mid-eighth century B.C.[62] Here it is not possible to decide whether the phrase *bar 'ănā̄š* means simply "someone" or emphasized the singular aspect "one single man". In the massive bulk of literature from the Qumran library the phrase occurs only three times, once in the Genesis Apochryphon, spelled *bar 'ănōš*, col. 21, line 13 (Fitzmyer/Harrington, p. 118); and twice in the Targum of Job, col. 9, line 9 and col. 26, line 3 (Fitzmyer/Harrington, pp. 18,22). Here also the exact value of the phrase is difficult to decide.

Therefore, these few occurrences allow no conclusions, except the one that the rare use of the phrase in itself seems to indicate that it cannot have belonged to the every-day language in Aramaic. "Man, human being, someone" was commonly expressed through simple 'ănā̄š and not through the genitive connection *bar 'ănā̄š*.

The material does allow us, however, to go one step further. In the two occurrences in the Targum of Job the Aramaic phrase is used as a translation of Hebrew *ben 'ādām*. This indicates that the translator regarded the phrases as equivalent. So far as the Hebrew phrase is concerned we are better off because the phrase is used over hundred times in the Old Testament.

The lexigraphical statistics concerning *ben 'ādām* are interesting and demonstrate that the phrase "son of man" did not belong to the every-day language in Old Testament Hebrew either. It occurs in two distinct contexts: 1) In poetic passages, 14 times; 2) In addresses to the prophet Ezekiel, 93 times.[63] In its poetic usage the phrase always occurs in the second half of

---

61 Cf. Koch, op.cit., pp. 224-7.
62 Cf. H.D. Donner and W.R. Rölling, Kanaanäische und Aramäische Inschriften I, 2nd ed., Wiesbaden 1966, Nr. 224, line 16, p. 45.
63 The phrase also occurs once or twice in the Book of Daniel: In Dan 10,16 if we emend bᵉnē 'ādām to ben 'ādām, cf. note 69; and in Dan 8,17, cf. below.

a synonym parallelism, in which simple designations for "man, human being", such as *'īs, 'ᵃnōš, gābār*, occur in the first half.[64] This usage is interpreted variously. A.A. Di Lella understood the phrase "as a lofty designation for man in poetic and solemn contexts".[65] This is hardly precise enough considering the distinct usage of the phrase. J. Kühlwein thought that the phrase was used to designate man as an individual.[66] This is correct as far as the relationship between *ben* and *'ādām* is concerned: *ben* is one individual member of the collective *'ādām*, "mankind". But it is far from certain that *ben 'ādām* emphasizes this individual aspect more than the simple words for "man, human being" in the first half of the parallelism.

What is striking in this usage is that the genitive connection always occurs in the second half of the parallelism. This leads to the conclusion that the usage must be related to the poetical style of the passages. The characteristics os this style is that the second half of the verse functions as an underscoring of the first half. This means that *ben 'ādām* functions to underscore the meaning implied in the simple word for "man" used in the first half of the verse. It is a heavier phrase which stresses the connotations connected with the simple phrase. What this heavier phrase emphasized, must be decided by the context. It can be the powerful man, the weak man, the happy man, man in relation to God, the one man in relation to the many etc.

The second context is that of the addresses to the prophet Ezekiel. He is constantly addressed as "you, son of man". It is possible to regard the phrase here as an underscoring of the contrast between man and God.[67] The phrase would then have been used to stress the unique situation that a terrestrial man is confronted by God. But this aspect does not seem to be underscored in the acts of

---

64   Cf. Num 23,19; Is 51,12; 56,12; Jer 49,18.33; 50,40; 51,43; Ps 8,5; 80,18; 146,3; Job 16,21; 25,6; 35,8.

65   Di Lella, op.cit., p. 2; cf. also Colpe, op.cit., p. 404.

66   J. Kühlwein, "ben, 'Sohn'" THAT I, cols. 316-33, cols. 320 and 323.

67   Thus W. Eichrodt, Ezekiel, p. 61: "Now that title already expresses, in the same words and manner as Ps 8,5, the weakness of the creature to whom the mighty Lord shows such condescension"; and W. Zimmerli, Ezechiel, p. 70: "Der Akzent liegt aber nicht auf dem Merkmal des einzelnen, sondern auf dem '*ādām*, zu dem unausgesprochenen das Gegenwort '*el* (Jes 31,3; Ez 28,2) mitgehört werden muss". We find it doubtful, however, that one should presuppose such a contrast in texts, in which one element of the contrast (in this case '*el*, "God"), is not articulated.

revelation. Certainly, Ezekiel reacts as a human being when he is confronted by the glory of God (Ezek 1,26). But this reaction, which serves to emphasize the human nature of the recipient of revelation, is more prominent in the descriptions of Isaiah and Jeremiah (cf. Is 6,5; Jer 1,6) than here. There is, however, another aspect that is emphasized more often in the revelatory speeches in the Book of Ezekiel, namely the contrast between Ezekiel and the rest of the people (cf. for instance 2,3-8; 3,4-10). Ezekiel is *the* man singled out from the rest of the people as a messenger from God. This understanding is supported by the reflection of the commissioning of Ezekiel in the commissioning of Enoch (En 15,1). Here Enoch is designated as "man of truth", and portrayed as the one chosen by God to reveal his will.[68]

The phrase is also used once about Daniel, Dan 8,17. Here the context may indicate that it is the contrast between the terrestrial man and the divine being that is emphasized.[69]

We now return to the question why *bar* '$^{\text{ă}}na\check{s}$ is used in Dan 7,13. This question must be distinguished from the question why a phrase for "man" occurs there at all, although the two questions are not totally unrelated. Why did the author use *bar* '$^{\text{ă}}na\check{s}$ and not simply '$^{\text{ă}}na\check{s}$? If we use Hebrew as analogy, *bar* '$^{\text{ă}}na\check{s}$ must be regarded as a heavier phrase than simple '$^{\text{ă}}na\check{s}$, used to reinforce an aspect of this or equivalent words. What it was that was emphasized had to be decided on the basis of the context. Now, the semantic pattern "man—beast" is clearly emphasized in the vision. But this did not necessarily demand the heavier phrase as v. 4 demonstrates, where simple '$^{\text{ă}}na\check{s}$ is used as a part of the pattern. The reason for the heavier phrase must rather be sought in the relation between simple '$^{\text{ă}}na\check{s}$ and *bar* '$^{\text{ă}}na\check{s}$ in the vision.

The first beast is raised to its feet *k'*$^{\text{ă}}na\check{s}$, "like a man", and given *l*^{e}*bab* '$^{\text{ă}}na\check{s}$, "the heart of a man", v. 4. The eleventh horn had

---

68 Cf. H.S. Kvanvig, "Henoch und der Menschensohn", StTh, 38, 1984, pp. 101-31, pp. 105f.

69 There may be one more occurrence of <u>ben</u> '$\underline{\text{ā}}$dām, in Dan 10,16. TM reads plural b^{e}<u>ne</u> '$\underline{\text{ā}}$dām, "sons of man", which seems strange in the context. LXX has a different reading <u>keiros anthropou</u>, which presupposes yad '$\underline{\text{ā}}$dām, "hand of a man". Theodotion, Vulgata and Aquila read singular "son of man", while the Peshitta (the Syriac translation) only reads "man". If singular <u>ben</u> '$\underline{\text{ā}}$dām is original, it must be understood in analogy to '$\underline{\text{i}}\check{s}$ '$\underline{\text{ā}}$$\underline{\text{h}}$ād, "one man" or "a particular man" in Dan 10,5. Like '$\underline{\text{ā}}\underline{\text{h}}$ād, <u>ben</u> would serve to emphasize the general '$\underline{\text{ā}}$dām. But the original reading can not be reconstructed with certainty.

eyes, $k^e{}^{\prime}ayn\bar{e}$ '$\check{a}n\bar{a}\check{s}a$, "like the eyes of man", v. 8. In these cases, where '$\check{a}n\bar{a}\check{s}$ is used generally, it is "any man". When the author used another wording in v. 13 it must be because "man" there was not intended as "any man". It is hard to avoid the impression that the author must have had "one particular man" in mind, who distinguished himself from ordinary man, and therefore used the heavier phrase.

The next question to decide is why at all a phrase for "man" was used as a designation in v. 13. We here see that the phrase functions within three semantic patterns.

1) The semantic pattern belonging to the Gattung "vision"
bar '$\check{a}n\bar{a}\check{s}$ corresponds to a stylistic feature extant in several of the visions in the Book of Daniel, in which the dominant figure described is perceived in the image of a "man". The same feature also occurs in the visions of Ezekiel.[70]
The survey below should demonstrate clearly that the phrase "son of man" in Dan 7,13 is a part of a well attested stylistic feature of these visions. In the reports about the visionary experiences the dominant figures are said to have appeared for the visionary in the likeness of a man. The phrases used for "man" are not intended to reveal the identity of the figure, only his appearance. They can accordingly be used of different figures appearing in visions but all belonging to the transcendent realm.
There is, however, one basic difference between Dan 7,13 and the other occurrences. In the other cases the visionary figures confront the visionary. They are heavenly messengers in the visionary experience. In the Book of Daniel their appearance and acting are described in the following way:

8,15-16:   And behold! Standing in front of me someone who looked like a man. And I heard the voice of a man over Ulai that cried out: "Gabriel, explain the vision for the man!" Then he came to the place where I stood, and when he came, I was afraid, and I prostrated myself. But he said to me: "Pay attention, son of man . . ."

70   This is also the case in the Enochic Apocalypse of Animals. The seven arch-angels are described as "white men", cf. En 87,2; 90,21. Within the visionary imagery Moses is changed from a sheep to a man, the image of the divine beings, 4Q En ^{C} 4, line 10 (Milik, p. 205) = En 89,36a. Cf. Part I, pp. 106f.

EZEKIEL

1,4:	The four living ones	דמות אדם	"in the resemblance of a man"
1,8:	The four living ones	ידו אדם	"hand of a man"
1,26:	God	דמות כמראה אדם	"in the resemblance of what looked like a man"
8,2:	Heavenly being	דמות כמראה איש	"in the resemblance of what looked like a man"
9,2:	Heavenly being	איש אחד...לבש בדים	one man clothed in linen", cf. 9,3; 10,2.6.7
10,8:	Cherub	תבנית יד אדם:	the resemblance of the hand of a man," cf. 8,21

DANIEL

5,5:	Heavenly being	אצבען די יד אנש	"fingers of the hand of a man"
7,13:		כבר אנש	"like a son of man"
8,15:	Heavenly being	כמראה גבר	"what looked like a man"
8,16:	Heavenly being	קול אדם	"the voice of a man"
10,5:	Heavenly being	איש אחד לבוש בדים	"one man clothed in linen", cf. 12,6.7
10,16:	Heavenly being	כדמות בני אדם	"in the resemblance of the son(s) of man"
10,18:	Heavenly being	כמראה אדם	"what looked like a man"

10,5-6:   And I raised my eyes and saw, and behold! One man, clothed in linen with a belt of Ophir gold round his waist. His body gleamed like topaz, his face shone like lightning, his eyes flamed like fire, his arms and legs sparkled like bronze, and when he talked the sound of his words was like the sound of a crowd.

10,16:   And behold! Someone in the resemblance of the son(s) of man touched my lips . . .

10,18:   And he who looked like a man touched me one more time and gave me strength. He said: "Do not be afraid, man beloved, peace be with you, be strong, be strong!"

The basic difference from Dan 7,13 is that the man seen there does not perform an act directed toward the visionary. The visionary is only a witness to the scene seen in the vision.

2) The semantic pattern belonging to the structure of content

The most apparent reason to call the figure in Dan 7,13 a "man" is that he forms a contrast to the preceding figures, which are designated ḥewan, "beasts". This contrast also appears in v. 4 where the first beast in transformed to a man and given a human heart.

3) The semantic pattern implied in the scene itself

The first four visionary figures are explicitly interpreted as kings, v. 17. This is not directly said about the Son of Man, but he appears to have the same role. In v. 14 he is given šålṭan, "dominion", yeqar, "honour", and malku, "kingdom". In v. 6 the third beast/king is given šålṭan, and in v. 12 the šålṭan of the beasts/kings are taken away from them just before the appearance of the Son of Man.

The wording has several parallels in the Aramaic part of the Book of Daniel. King Nebuchadnezzar is especially singled out as the one who received "power and glory" (Dan 2,37; 5,18). The meaning of the wording is demonstrated in Dan 4,33. The "power and glory" were given to Nebuchadnezzar at the time when he was reinstated as king. This is in fact one of the leading themes in the Aramaic part of the Book of Daniel. The act of God in history is to establish kings in their kingdoms, or to take away their dominion (Dan 2,21; 4,14.22; 6,1; 7,6.12).[71]

---

71   Cf. Kvanvig, "Struktur und Geschichte in Daniel 7", pp. 110-15.

Whatever the Son of Man is taken to signify in the real world outside the imagery of the vision, within the vision he stands in analogy to the four preceding figures, portrayed as a king receiving kingship from the Ancient of Days.

The correspondence between Nebuchadnezzar and the Son of Man[72] also seems to contribute to the "man-imagery" in the vision of Dan 7. As noted Nebuchadnezzar is transformed from beast to man in Dan 7,4. This transformation corresponds to Dan 4,30. Both in Dan 4 and Dan 7 the "man-imagery" is closely connected to the ideology of kingship.[73] In Dan 4 the king looses his royal status together with his human status, and after having confessed his sins he received both (cf. v. 33). In Dan 7,4 the passage "and the heart of a man was given to it" occurs at the same place and with the same syntax as the passage about the royal power given to the third beast.[74]

In a recent study of Dan 7 P.A. Porter has convincingly demonstrated that the "man-imagery" in Dan 4 belongs together with the dominant image of the vision, the tree of life.[75] Both the "man-imagery" and the tree of life were used in Mesopotamian texts and representations to describe the king in the role of the shepherd of the people. As shepherd the king was "man" presiding over men

---

72 Cf. above, p. 487.
73 Cf. Kvanvig, op.cit., p. 115.
74 For the structure, cf. Kvanvig, op.cit., pp. 102f.
75 Cf. P.A. Potter, Metaphors and Monsters. A Literary-Critical Study of Daniel 7 and 8, CB.OT 20, Lund 1983, pp. 109-14. For the "tree of life" in Dan 4, cf. above. pp. 477ff. Potter claims that the animal metaphors of Dan 7 and 8 also find their origin in the "root metaphor of the shepherd". The parallels between Dan 7 and 8 and the Apocalypse of Animals (En 85-90) are crucial for this argument, op.cit., pp. 48-60. Potter is certainly correct in seeing a close relationship between the texts, cf. also Part I, p. 109. But I am not convinced that this implies the parallels in the shepherd imagery advanced by Potter. There are several obstacles:
* In the Apocalypse of Animals the shepherds are not described as beasts.
* The beasts signifying foreign power in the Apocalypse of Animals are not described as monstrous. They are basically normal beasts.
* In Dan 4 the shepherd is described as "man", his subjects are described as beasts. When the "man—shepherd" metaphor is repeated in Dan 7 as Potter correctly claims, it is highly unlikely that the beasts there signify shepherds as well as the man.
* The widespread occurrence of animal imagery in the description of kings in the Ancient Near East is not limited to the "shepherd metaphor". In the identification of beast with king the author of Dan 7 could have applied the animal imagery without any implication of "the metaphor of the shepherd".

and animals.[76] This interpretation of the imagery also corresponds very well to the meaning of the texts most closely related to Dan 4: Dan 2,37-38 where Nebuchadnezzar is described as the golden head of the statue; and the glorifications of Nebuchadnezzar in Jer 27,5-7; 28,14. In these sequences Nebuchadnezzar does not only rule over nations as world emperor, he even has the power over the beasts of the field.

When Nebuchadnezzar's status as "man" in Dan 4 and 7,4 clearly describes his royal role as shepherd, this must also concern the "second man" seen in the vision, "the one particular man", in v. 13. Accordingly the designation "man" given to the universal ruler in Dan 7,13-14 shares in a semantic pattern where "man" is used as a royal designation for the shepherd of the nations.

In our direct comparison between the Vision of the Nether World and Dan 7 we listed the Akkadian phrase *ištēn eṭlu* used about the ideal king there as a parallel to *bar'ănāš* in Dan 7,13.[77] Generally there is a correspondence between *eṭlu* in Akkadian and *'ănāš* in Aramaic because both words can mean "man". The two other words in isolation have nothing in common. In Dan 10,5 we have a direct equivalent to the whole Akkadian phrase in Hebrew, where the angel appearing in the vision is called *'īš 'āḥād*, "one man". Our analysis of the value of the phrase *bar 'ănāš* in Dan 7 has however indicated that the function of *bar* in relation to *'ănāš* does not differ much from the function of *ištēn* in relation to *eṭlu*. *ištēn* means "one", but can also function as "an emphasizing article" with the meaning "outstanding, unique",[78] thus it emphasized that one particular man is meant. In isolation *bar* has a totally different meaning, but added to *'ănāš* it changes the general meaning "man" to "one particular man".

The term "man" functioned both in the Vision of the Nether World and in Dan 7 within several semantic patterns. It now remains to compare these.

76 Cf. I. Seibert, Hirt-Herde-König, pp. 7-15, 23-35.
77 Cf. above, p. 451.
78 Cf. above, pp. 414f.

In our analysis of the phrase *ištēn eṭlu* we found that the phrase occurred in several Akkadian dream-reports.[79] In the reported visions the phrase pointed back to dream-experiences of figures appearing in human form. On the literary level this experience was expressed according to a convention where the figure was given prominence through the use of *ištēn* and described as *eṭlu*, a man at the peak of his physical power. The figure described as *eṭlu* acted or brought a message on behalf of the god.

There are thus close similarities between the figures seen in the Akkadian visions and those seen in the Hebrew visions of the Book of Daniel:

* They are designated as men / human beings according to their appearance.
* Their impressive appearance is reinforced by the description of their bodies and garments (cf. esp. Dan 10,5; 12,6-7 — Akkadian dreams B, C, F, G).
* They are the protagonists of the visions, carrying out a task on behalf of a god, either as an act or through a message to the visionary.
* Their actions could include consolation of the visionary (cf. esp. Dan 10,5 — Akkadian dreams A, B, C, D).

We do not claim that there is any sort of relationship between the Akkadian dreams and the Hebrew visions. Our aim is to show that they have developed a similar Gattung-style in the description of visionary figures. That means that the words for "man/human" are used in the same way within the same Gattung pointing toward the same basic experience. The only difference is that within the Akkadian visions the language has undergone a complete standardization in the use of only one phrase *ištēn eṭlu*, whereas in the Aramaic and Hebrew visions we find different parallel designations: *'ᵉnāš, bar 'ᵉnās, 'īš 'āḥad, 'īš, gäbär, ben 'ādām, 'ādām*. The conclusion must be that *ištēn eṭlu* used in Akkadian visions has the same connotations as the Aramaic and Hebrew words for "man/human", and that the phrases in this usage must be regarded as functionally equivalent.

In our analysis of *ištēn eṭlu* in the Akkadian visions we saw that although the Vision of the Nether World shared the same Gattung pattern as the other dreams, the phrase *ištēn eṭlu* also functioned within other semantic patterns. This is already signalled by the role of *ištēn eṭlu*. In the other visions the man was carrying out a task

---

79 Cf. above. pp. 415ff.

directed toward the visionary, in the Vision of the Nether world
the man's "task" is directed toward other people.

In our conclusions about the use of *ištēn eṭlu* in the Vision of the
Nether World we summarized as follows:[80]

1. According to the Gattung:
    ištēn eṭlu = "the unique man" in a dream experience described as a messenger
    from god to man.
2. According to the structure of content:
    ištēn eṭlu = the one man / human being described in contrast to the demons,
    the monsters.
3. According to the direct description:
    ištēn eṭlu = the ideal king designated as "the exalted shepherd".

In the Aramaic and Hebrew visions we find that although Dan 7
shares the same Gattung pattern as the other dreams and visions,
the phrase *bar 'ᵉnāš* also functions within other semantic patterns.
This is already signalled by the role of *bar 'ᵉnāš*. In the other
visions the man-like figures are carrying out a task in direct
relation to the visionary, in Dan 7 the man's "task" is directed
toward other people. In our analysis of *bar 'ᵉnāš* in Dan 7 we have
reached the following conclusions:

1. According to the Gattung:
    bar 'ᵉnāš corresponds to transcendent figures, appearing in visions as manlike,
    acting as a messenger from God to man.
2. According to the structure of content:
    bar 'ᵉnāš forms a contrast to the beast-monsters.
3. According to the direct description:
    bar 'ᵉnāš designates an ideal king described as the shepherd of the nations.

There can be no other conclusions than that the phrases *bar 'ᵉnāš*
and *ištēn eṭlu* do not only carry the same meaning generally, but
that within Dan 7 and the Vision of the Nether World they
function according to exactly the same semantic patterns. No other
texts are known where this specific combinations of semantic
patterns occurs.

---

80   Cf. above, p. 422.

5. The Sea and the Monsters

In Dan 7,3 the four monsters are coming up out of the sea, *min yammā*. In Hebrew and Aramaic the noun *yam* usually carries a plain geographical meaning, "ocean", or "lake", Hebrew: Ps 104,25; Job 14,11; Aramaic: 1QapGen (proper) col. 21, line 1 (Fitzmyer/Harrington, p. 120). In Dan 7,2 the sea is called *yammā rabbā*, "the great sea". This phrase is often used as the name for the Mediterranean Sea, cf. Num 34,6; 1QapGen (proper), col. 16, line 12 (Fitzmyer/Harrington, p. 108); col. 21, lines 11.16 (Fitzmyer/Harrington, p. 118). *yam* can also designate the subterranean water, Ps 24,2. Used in this way the word is parallel to *tᵉhōm rabbā*, "the great abyss", cf. Am 7,4; Is 51,10.

In near eastern imagination the sea was, however, not only a neutral area. It was involved in a series of mythological concepts. In TM Job 38,8, and the corresponding Targum of Job, col. 30, line 6 (Fitzmyer/Harrington, p. 36), *yam* is conceived as the power of chaos. In TM Job 26,12, and corresponding Targum of Job, col. 10, line 3 (Fitzmyer/Harrington, p. 18), *yam* is described as the abode of the sea monster Rahab. That *yam* also in Dan 7 has mythological connotations is quite clear because of the connection with the monsters. The difficulty is to decide the nature of the mythical concept implied.

As early as 1895 H. Gunkel argued that the background of this imagery was to be sought in the myth about the sea monster Tiamat in Enuma Elish.[81] Gunkel based his argumentation firstly on the link between Dan 7 and texts about sea monsters in the Old Testament, cf. Is 51,9-10; Ps 89,9-12; Job 9,13-14; 26,12-13; Is 27,1; Ps 74,12-17, and the wind connected to the primeval abyss, *tᵉhōm*, in Gen 1,2. Secondly he claimed that this concept of the sea either as the abode of sea monsters, or as a chaotic power itself, reflected the Tiamat myth.

In later research a direct influence from this myth is rightly questioned. The fight against the sea monster in the Old Testament does not seem to reflect the fight against Tiamat, but has much closer parallels in Ugaritic myths about the slaying of the dragon

---

81 H. Gunkel, Schöpfung und Chaos in Urzeit und Endzeit, Göttingen 1895, pp. 323-33.

Lotan and Baal's victory over his rival Yamm.[82] It is also rightly questioned whether the water-deep, $t^eh\bar{o}m$, in Gen 1,2 had anything to do with the sea monster Tiamat.[83]

On the basis of the relationship between the sea and the monsters in Dan 7 and sea monsters in the Old Testament, and the background of this material in Ugaritic myths, J.A. Emerton argued that Dan 7 as a whole reflected Ugaritic myths about Baal as the vanquisher of the sea dragon and Yamm.[84] We shall return to Emerton's article later in dealing with the Son of Man imagery. With regard to the sea and the monsters in Dan 7, we cannot see any particular reason to connect this material directly to Ugaritic myths. The correspondences to the myth about the slaying of the sea monster are of such a kind that the spread of this myth in Israelite milieu — as attested in the Old Testament — should be sufficient as background. There are three correspondences, which are all fairly general: 1) The sea is the abode of sea monsters; 2) The monsters are killed, cf. Dan 7,11b; 3) Sea monsters could be used as symbols for foreign rulers, cf. Is 30,7; Ezek 29,3; 32,2; and probably Is 27,1.

The central motif in Dan 7 is lacking, however, in the myths about the slaying of the sea monster, namely that the monsters are coming up out of the sea to spread disaster on earth. The sea monsters in the Old Testament, Ugaritic and Mesopotamian myths always belong to the sea because they are regarded as personifications of the sea. The dominant motif in Dan 7, the ascending monsters, derives from a different mythological gird. We have referred to this mythological gird several times earlier. In Mesopotamian mythology Apsu, the subterranean water-deep, was regarded as the abode of strange composite creatures of different kinds. These could be of benevolent or malevolent character. The frightening aspect of Apsu and the monsters belonging to it appears in those contexts where Apsu is either equated with the nether world or is regarded as a transitional area for monsters

---

82   Cf. O. Kaiser, Die mythische Bedeutung des Meeres in Ägypten, Ugarit und Israel, BZAW 78, Berlin 1959, pp. 140-52; cf. also Part I, pp. 250ff.

83   Cf. A. Heidel, The Babylonian Genesis, 2nd ed., Chicago 1951 (Phoenix ed. 1963), pp. 102-14; C. Westermann, Genesis, BK I, Neukirchen-Vluyn 1967, pp. 145f.

84   J.A. Emerton, "The Origin of the Son of Man Imagery", JThS, 9, Oxford 1958, pp. 225-42, pp. 228f.

ascending from the nether world. We have already noticed the connections between Apsu, the nether world and monsters with regard to the Sibitti in the series Utukku lemnuti, and various kinds of demonic beings in the Poem of Erra.[85] In the Poem of Erra the Sibitti are instructed as follows:

> They stood before him and he fixed their destinies.
> He summoned the first one and he gave (him) instructions:
> "wherever you may go and spread terror, have no equal!"
> To the second he said: "Burn like fire, blaze like a flame!"
> With the third he spo[ke]: "Take a lionlike aspect, and may
>   he be annihilated who looks at you!".
> To the fourth he said: "At the wielding of your fierce weapons,
>   may the mountain be razed to the ground!"
> To the fifth he said: "Blow like the wind, check the (entire)
>   orbit (or the world)!"
> To the sixth he ordered: "Strike upwards and downwards: spare nobody!"
> He charged the seventh with a viper venom (saying):
>   Kill (all) that lives!"
>
> (Tabl. I, lines 30-38)[86]

A similar demonic attack is described in the Shurpu incantations:

> Dimetu has come out of the apsû
> Mimetu is on his way down from heaven.
> Aḫḫazu is breaking through the earth.
>
> (Tabl. VII, lines 1-6)[87]

Aramaic *yam* in Dan 7 is therefore to be regarded as functionally equivalent to Apsu in several Mesopotamian texts. The "sea" in these cases is the abyss, the abode of monstrous creatures. The choice of *yam* corresponding to Apsu here as a designation for the abyss instead of *'ar'ā*, "the earth, underworld", corresponding to Akkadian *erṣetu*, is determined by the fact that in Israel the sea and not the underground was imagined as the abode of monstrous creatures. However, it should be noticed that the kings in the interpretative clause to Dan 7,3 in v. 17 are said to arise *min 'ar'ā*, which can be read as "out of the earth", i.e. "the underworld". We think that this basic imagery of the sea in Dan 7 as the abyss and dwelling place of monstrous demonic creatures has subsequently given rise to other allusions to monsters in the sea, for instance to the myth about the slaying of the sea monster.

---

85 Cf. above, p. 373.
86 Translation according to Cagni, The Poem of Erra, pp. 26ff.
87 Text according to E. Reiner, Šurpu. A Collection of Sumerian and Akkadian Incantations, Graz 1958, p. 55.

Thus Dan 7,3-8 describes is a demonic attack on the earth from the world below. We have previously noticed that the monsters are described with features closely resembling those of the monsters in the Vision of the Nether World.[88] But in Dan 7 the monsters do not remain in the nether world, but emerge from below to bring disaster on earth. This way of interpreting disastrous political events was not unusual in Mesopotamian milieu, as is demonstrated in the Poem of Erra.[89] In fact such a visitation from the nether world was also predicted by Nergal in the Vision of the Nether World: "At the command of Šamaš, let disturbance, dishonesty and rebellion [   ] together blow over you! (line 61) . . . "Go away to the upper (world) until I shall remember you!" (line 68).[90]

6.   The Four Winds and the Clouds of Heaven

In his influential article of 1958 J.A. Emerton argued that the whole imagery of the vision in Dan 7 was dependent on the Ugaritic material from Ras Shamra.[91] The vision reflected the enthronement of Baal after his victory over the sea-monster Yamm and the prince of death Mot. In the scene of enthronement Baal took the place of El as the supreme god. The setting of the tradition was the New Year's Festival, on which the kingship of Baal and Yahweh was celebrated in Canaanite and Israelite religion respectively. According to this interpretation of the referential background of Dan 7 "he who comes with the clouds" in Dan 7,13 is to be regarded as a reflection of Baal.

More recently A.J. Ferch has examined this theory anew.[92] Ferch calls attention to the complexity of the Ugaritic material and the difficulties associated with its interpretation. He refutes all the distinct parallels previously suggested between Dan 7 and the

---

88   Cf. above, pp. 451ff.
89   For the Poem of Erra, cf. above, pp. 404f; and Part I, pp. 181ff.
90   Cf. above, pp. 437f.
91   J.A. Emerton, "The Origin of the Son of Man Imagery". The same theory is later argued by several influential scholars, cf. for instance C. Colpe, "ho hyios tou anthropou", pp. 418-22; and J.J. Collins, The Apocalyptic Vision of the Book of Daniel, pp. 96-106. Cf. also our preliminary discussion above, note 24, pp. 350f.
92   A.J. Ferch, "Daniel 7 and Ugarit: A Reconsideration", JBL 99, 1980, pp. 75-86.

Ugaritic myths: The description of the sea and the monsters and the judgement of the fourth monster have no direct parallels in the Baal cycles; there is no record in Ugaritic myths of an enthronement of Baal, which would correspond to the Son of Man receiving kingship; the Canaanite texts do not substantiate the claim that El abdicates his throne or transfers his kingship to Baal.

Ferch's article is later discussed by J.J. Collins.[93] Collins admits that there is no reproduction of the Ugaritic myths in Dan 7, but that has not been the point in the comparison: "... no scholar has ever denied that there is 'discontinuity' between Dan 7 and Ugarit, or indeed that the discontinuity is more significant than the continuity in determining the present meaning of the text. All that is claimed is that the imagery of Daniel has traditional associations and that these associations are one significant factor in the communicative power of the text"[94] ... "Even Ferch admits resemblance between the 'one like a son of man' and 'Ancient of Days' on the one hand and Baal and El on the other. Further, it is indisputable that the sea (yamma‘) of the vision is cognate to the name of Baal's adversary Yamm. I do not believe that these are the only similarities, but even this constellation requires explanation".[95]

Generally we agree with Collins that Dan 7 contains mythological allusions with communicative power. But there remains a problem: How vague must the parallels be before a specific mythological concept cannot be meaningfully used as a referential background? Let us examine Collins' example above.

The resemblance between the Son of Man and Baal lies in that both are connected with clouds. There are at least two different concepts where a figure comes with the clouds. The more common one is in mythologies dealing with vegetation, in which the god of rain and thunder is manifested in clouds. The other is that Enoch in En 14 is accompanied by winds and clouds when he is taken away to the heavenly assembly.[96] If we assume that Dan 7,13 alludes to the first concept (which does not necessarily exclude the

---

93   J.J. Collins, "Apocalyptic Genre and Mythic Allusions in Daniel", JSOT 21, 1981, pp. 83-100, pp. 89-94.
94   Collins, op.cit., p. 91.
95   Collins, op.cit., p. 93.
96   Cf. below, pp. 560f.

second), there is no specific allusion to Baal, only a general allusion to a divine being coming with clouds.

The resemblance between the Ancient of Days and El lies in that El sometimes has the epithet "father of years" and is sometimes portrayed as old. That a supreme god of a pantheon is portrayed as old in relation to the younger generation of gods is again a wide spread phenomenon. It is for instance a distinct characteristic of Marduk in the Poem of Erra.[97] The epithet "father of years" resembles "Ancient of Days", but is not identical. We will later demonstrate that there existed Aramaic designations of Yahweh from approximately the same period as Dan 7 that are just as close as the Ugaritic epithet.[98]

If we assume that Baal really received kingship after El in the Ugaritic myths, neither is this a specific Canaanite phenomenon. In Enuma Elish Marduk, equipped with the armour of the natural forces, received kingship after the victory over Tiamat.[99] It is, however, highly unlikely that the scene of enthronement in Dan 7,13-14 had anything to do with these myths. The scene in Dan resembles that of an enthronement of an terrestrial king because the Son of Man takes over kingship after four previous terrestrial kings (v. 17), and because the kingship is political rather than cosmical (v. 14). If there is any relationship here, the motif must have been so strongly transformed that the background is scarcely recognizable.

The last case mentioned by Collins is that the sea, *yammā*, in Dan 7 is a cognate to the name of Baal's adversary Yamm. This is certainly correct, but we would phrase it differently: Both words correspond to the common word for "sea". The link needs not be closer than that — especially when the sea is personified in Ugaritic myths but not in Dan 7; and when there are no correspondences between the imagery of the beasts in Dan 7 and that of Yamm in the Ugaritic myths; and when Baal, who should be the parallel figure to the Son of Man, vanquished Yamm, while nothing like this is said about the Son of Man in Dan 7.

When we consider these correlations to mythical motifs of various kinds, we do not see that "this constellation requires explanation",

---

97 Cf. L. Cagni, The Poem of Erra, p. 19.
98 Cf. below, pp. 562f.
99 Enuma Elish, Tabl. IV and V. ANET[3], pp. 66f and p. 502.

to use Collins words. None of the correspondences are specific enough to give a decisive hint about the kind of material which lies behind Dan 7. Nor can we see that the way the motifs occur in Dan 7 gives any link to specifically Ugaritic myths. We agree with Collins that Dan 7 alludes to a mythic concept which is a part of the communicative power of the text, but we will seek the underlying tradition elsewhere.

Let us once more consider the imagery of the vision in Dan 7. First *'arba' rūḥē šemayyā*, "the four winds of heaven", appear (v. 2). These are followed by *'arba' hēwān ... min yammā*, "four beasts ... from the sea" (v. 3). The number four is repeated in the description of the third beast. It has four wings and four heads (v. 6). The sequence of the beasts is followed by the appearance of the Ancient of Days in his chariot (vv. 9-10). At the end of the vision *'im 'anānē šemayyā kebar 'ānāš ātē*, "with the clouds of heaven one like a son of man came" (v. 13).

This imagery has a close parallel in the first vision of Ezekiel, Ezek 1. The vision starts with a description of a theophany, in which Yahweh comes in his divine chariot. First a *rūaḥ se'ārā*, "storm-wind", appears, accompanied by *'anān gādōl*, "a great cloud" (v. 4). In the storm *'arba' ḥayyōt*, "four living ones", are visible. The number four is repeated in the description of the living ones. They have four wings and four faces (v. 6). The living ones make the divine chariot roll (vv. 15-21), and support the fundament on which Yahweh is seated in this throne chair (vv. 22-28).

Now it is clear that elements of different origins are combined in the vision of Ezekiel. O. Keel has thoroughly examined the background of the imagery and come to the conclusion that the basic imagery can be described as "living creatures supporting a fundament on which a divine throne is placed".[100] This motif occurs in the art of Anatolia, northern Syria and Mesopotamia.[101] According to Keel a later commentator of the vision added the wheels to the chair thus creating the impression of a chariot rather than a chair.

---

100 O. Keel, Jahve-Visionen und Siegelkunst. Eine neue Deutung der Majestätsschilderungen in Jes 6, Ez 1 und 10 und Sach 4, SBS 84/85, Stuttgart 1977, pp. 191f, 271ff.
101 Keel, op.cit., pp. 168-77.

We are not convinced that the image of the divine chariot is a later addition. The divine chariot or chariots occur in Old Testament descriptions of theophanies (Ps 68,18; Hab 3,8; Is 66,15). In Zech 6,1ff the four winds are described as four chariots. Keel has obviously found it difficult to unite the static picture of a fundament supported by composite figures and the dynamic picture of a chariot rolling on wheels. There is in fact one representation from Mesopotamia which combines these two features. A relief from Khorsabad depicts the royal procession of Sargon. Here the throne chair is depicted as a chariot. The seat of the chair is supported by an animal figure with straight legs (Ezek 1,7). The arm-rests of the chair are supported by figures in human form. Since the chariot is depicted one-dimensionally from the side, only one wheel is visible (Ezek 1,15). And strange enough, the chariot does not roll, but is carried by attendants.[102]

We are therefore inclined to see two basic images combined in Ezek 1. The one is as Keel claims, the divine throne supported by composite beings. The other is God seated in his chariot appearing in a storm. The two images could be united because the throne could also have the shape of a chariot and be carried in a procession by attendants (cf. Ezek 1,9.19-21).

This double background of the visionary imagery is also reflected in the description of the four living ones. A part of their function is to support the fundament of the throne (vv. 22-23.26), but they are also closely connected to the theophany. This becomes clear when one examines the connection between the $ḥayyōt$, "living ones", and the $rū^aḥ$, "wind" or "spirit" in the vision.

The first image of the vision is that of a $rū^aḥ$ $s^e'arā$, "storm-wind" (v. 4). Inside this storm-wind appear the four living ones as attendants of the chariot. In vv. 12 and 20 it is said that the $ḥayyōt$ went in whatever direction the $rū^aḥ$ would go. In vv. 20f it is described how the wheels moved in exactly the same way as the $ḥayyōt$ because the $rū^aḥ$ of the $ḥayyōt$ was in the wheels. In Ezek 3,12.14 the $rū^aḥ$ came to Ezekiel, lifted him up and carried him away. We do not think it is possible to give $rū^aḥ$ in these contexts differing interpretations by understanding it in some instances as

---

102 Cf. G. Perrot and C. Chipez, Histoire de l'art dans l'antiquité II: Chaldée et Assyrie, Paris 1884, p. 100. I am grateful to Prof. M. Greenberg at the Hebrew University of Jerusalem, who called my attention to this representation.

only a natural phenomenon and in others as a spirit. The $r\bar{u}^a h$ acts both as a wind and as a personified spirit. Accordingly, the $r\bar{u}^a h$ hahayyā, "the wind-spirit of the living one", in Ezek 1,20 must be understood as an aspect of the living one. The four living ones act as wind-spirits.

Two other occurrences support this interpretation. In Ezek 8,2 Ezekiel beholds a man, who is described in the same way as God in Ezek 1. But here God himself is scarcely meant. In 8,3 the man is connected to the $r\bar{u}^a h$. The man stretched out his hand and seized Ezekiel by his forelock. The next line reads: "A $r\bar{u}^a h$ lifted me up . . .".

The other occurrence is from the Book of Zechariah. In the vision in Zech 6,1-8 Zechariah beholds four chariots, v. 1. In the interpretation of the vision these four chariots are explained as the four $r\bar{u}\dot{h}\bar{o}t$ $ha\check{s}\check{s}amayyim$, "the four 'wind-spirits' of heaven", who act as the servants of Yahweh, v. 5. As in Ezek we have here also the connection between servant of Yahweh, chariot, and $r\bar{u}^a h$.

The four winds accompanying a divine figure are well known from Mesopotamian texts. They belong to the concept of the coming of the weather-god. In Enuma Elish Marduk is accompanied by the four winds when he comes in his divine chariot, Tabl. II, lines 105ff, and Tabl. IV, lines 113ff.[103] In the Old Babylonian Susa Version of the Myth of Anzu the four winds are the companions of Ninurta, Tabl. III.[104]

The four living ones in Ezek are thus described according to two models. They are attendants supporting the divine chair, which could be a part of a chariot, and they incorporate the four winds of heaven accompanying God coming in his divine chariot. It is accordingly easy to understand how the two concepts could be merged.

As already noticed these figures accompanying God are called $\dot{h}ayy\bar{o}t$. The plural is commonly translated "living creatures",[105] because the feminine adjective $\dot{h}ayy\bar{a}$ is a derivation from $\dot{h}ayy$, "life". But the plural is most often used with the meaning

---

103   ANET³, pp. 62, 66.
104   ANET³, p. 517; cf. also Hruška, Der Mythenadler Anzu, pp. 173f.
105   Cf. for instance Zimmerli, Ezechiel I, pp. 1ff: "Lebewesen"; Eichrodt, Ezekiel, pp. 49ff: "living creatures".

"beasts".[106] The word can therefore be understood in the same way as *hewā* in Dan 7, which is derived from the same root and also has the meaning "beast".[107] This can hardly support a theory of literary dependence between the texts, but rather points in the direction that the composite beings in both texts were understood as "animal-like".

We have accordingly the following basic imagery in Ezek:

storm-wind
great cloud
the four winds
the four "animal beings" — four wings, four faces
God in his divine chariot

In Dan we have the following basic imagery:

the four winds of heaven
the four "animal beings" from the sea — four wings, four heads
God in his divine chariot
the clouds of heaven
the Son of Man

We do not claim that Dan 7 is dependent on Ezek 1.[108] The correspondence is in the basic imagery, which is used differently in the two texts. This becomes clear when we notice that the features in Ezek are united into one coherent picture of God coming in his chariot, accompanied by his attendants. In Dan 7, however, the features are collected into two groups forming a contrast to each other:

the *four* winds of *heaven*   the *four* beasts from the *sea*
the clouds of *heaven*

the Son of *Man*   the *beasts*

---

106   Cf. G. Gerleman, "ḥjh, leben", THAT I, cols. 549-57, col. 553.
107   Cf. E. Vogt, Lexicon Linguae Aramaicae Veteris Testamenti, Rome 1971, sub ḥayy, p. 63, and sub hewā, p. 64.
108   Cf. the discussion about the relationship between Dan 7 and Ezek 1 in Kvanvig, "Henoch und der Menschensohn", pp. 114-19.

So far the analysis should have demonstrated the following:

1. The correspondence to Ezekiel should have demonstrated that the basic imagery of Dan 7 has its origin in the imaginary world centred around the supreme god surrounded by his attendants, and the coming of a divine figure in a theophany.
2. The symbolism of four belongs to this imaginary world. This means that although this symbolism corresponds to the scheme of the four empires,[109] it is not necessarily derived from this scheme. The parallels in Ezek point rather in another direction. The symbolism of four was adopted into the vision in Ezekiel in connection with the four winds. We are inclined to draw the same conclusion in Dan 7. There are four beasts corresponding to the four winds of heaven.
3. The four winds of heaven and the clouds of heaven belong together and accompany the Son of Man in what resembles a theophany. This means that the Son of Man is contrasted to the beasts in two ways, both in the contrast man—beast, and in the contrast four winds of heaven — four beasts from the sea. It also means that the four winds of heaven and the clouds of heaven are crucial for the understanding of the identity of the Son of Man.

In isolation the imagery of the four winds and the clouds could signify the appearance of Yahweh as in Ezek 1, or of some other god which manifests weather phenomena. Yahweh must, however, be excluded if we take the text of Dan 7 seriously. Here God is distinctively separated from the figure coming with the clouds. In Mesopotamian milieu gods like Marduk and Ninurta are parallels, because they are accompanied by the four winds. Of greater interest, however, is Ninurta's counterpart in Mesopotamian mythology, the Anzu-bird.

According to T. Jacobsen the Anzu-bird personified the thunder-cloud. In the Neo-Assyrian Version of the Anzu-myth he also embodied the four winds.[110] Moreover, in the Vision of the Nether World the unique man is likened to the Anzu-bird, line 50. The comparison corresponded on the one hand to other Neo-Assyrian descriptions of warriors resembling the Anzu-bird in their storm-like attacks;[111] on the other hand to the description of the man in the Death Dream of Enkidu, who confronted Enkidu in the thunder-storm.[112] We have therefore the following features in the Assyrian vision compared to Dan 7: *Vision of the Nether World:* Within a vision dealing with composite beings of malevolent character a universal

---

109 Cf. above, pp. 484ff.
110 Cf. above, pp. 376f.
111 Cf. above, pp. 411ff.
112 Cf. above, pp. 373f.

ruler is described and designated "the unique man". He is likened
to the Anzu-bird, corresponding to warriors in their stormlike
attacks and to the man confronting Enkidu in the thunder-storm.
In Mesopotamian mythology the Anzu-bird personifies the
thunder-cloud and embodies the four winds. *Dan 7:* Within a
vision dealing with composite beings of malevolent character a
universal ruler is described and designated as "one like a man".
His entrance is heralded by the four winds of heaven and he
comes with the clouds of heaven.

7. The Flying Man from the Sea in 4 Ezra 13

The resemblances between the description of the Son of Man in
Dan 7 and the man rising from the sea in 4 Ezra 13 have generally
been recognized in the research. But the problems surrounding this
strange text in the Apocalypse of Ezra seem even greater than
those in Dan 7. That concerns both the date, transmission and
content of the vision.

7.1   The Versions and the Date and Setting of the Vision

The text is extant in a series of translations of which the Latin,
Syriac and Ethiopic are the most important.[113] Among these the
Latin text is generally regarded as the most valuable, followed by
the Syriac.[114] Most scholars think that the extant translations go
back to lost Greek versions.[115] It is further generally accepted

---

113   For the Latin text we use: Vulgata II, 1931-74; for the Syriac: A.M. Ceri-
ani, Monumenta sacra et profana, Vol. V, Fasc. I, Milano 1868; Ethiopic: A.
Dillmann, Veteris Testamenti Aethiopici. Libri Apocryphi, tomus V, Berlin 1894.
Translations of the Syriac, Ethiopic, Arabic and Armenian versions are available
in B. Violet; Die Esra-Apokalypse. Erster Teil. Die Überlieferung, Leiden 1910.
114   Cf. in general for the versions, G.H. Box, The Ezra-Apocalypse, London
1912, pp. iv-xi; B. Violet, Die Esra-Apokalypse, pp. xv-xlvi; and, Die Apokalypsen des Esra und des Baruch in deutscher Gestalt, GCS, Leipzig 1924, pp.
xiii-xxviii.
115   Cf. Box, op.cit., pp. xi-xiii; Violet, Die Esra-Apokalypse, pp. xiii-xv; and,
Die Apokalypsen des Esra und Baruch, pp. xxix-xxxi. This was strongly denied
by J. Bloch who argued that the Latin version was a direct translation of an
Aramaic original, cf. J. Bloch, "Was there a Greek Version of the Apocalypse of

that the apocalypse was composed in a Semitic language. There is, however, disagreement whether this language was Hebrew or Aramaic. Most scholars seem to argue for Hebrew,[116] but it cannot be denied that several creatures are better explained by supposing an Aramaic background.[117] In one way or another there must have been Aramaic influence on the Semitic version preceding the Greek translation, even when the Semitic version most likely existed in Hebrew.[118]

The whole Apocalypse of Ezra[119] is commonly dated either to the end of the first century AD, or to the beginning of the second. There has, however, been considerable disagreement as to how the composition should be defined. One current in the research has regarded it as a collocation of several distinct written sources.[120] Another current has emphasized its unity, composed by one hand, without denying preceding traditions.[121]

Ezra?", JQR 46, 1956, pp. 309-20; and, "The Ezra-Apocalypse, was it written in Hebrew, Greek or Aramaic?", JQR 48, 1957/57, pp. 279-84. This opinion runs counter to the fact that 4 Ezra is quoted in Greek by the Church fathers, cf. F. Zimmermann, "Underlying Documents of Ezra", JQR 51, 1960/61, pp. 107-34, pp. 107f. 4 Ezra is retranslated into Greek by A. Hilgenfeld, Messias Judaeorum, Leipzig 1869.

116 Arguing for a Hebrew original were: Box, op.cit. pp. xiii-xx; Violet, Die Apokalypsen des Esra und des Baruch, pp. xxxi-xxxxix; A. Kaminka, "Beiträge zur Erklärung der Esra-Apokalypse und zur Rekonstruktion ihres hebräisches Urtextes", MGWJ 76/77, 1932/33, Vol. 76: pp. 121-38, 206-12, 494-511, 604-7; Vol. 77: pp. 339-55.

117 Arguing for an Aramaic original was: L. Gry, Les dires prophétique d'Esdras I-II, Paris 1938.

118 A compromise has been argued by F. Zimmermann, "Underlying Documents of IV Ezra". Zimmermann argued for a Hebrew original subsequently translated into Aramaic, then to Greek and Latin. To decide whether the original composition was in Hebrew or Aramaic on basis of a translation is extremely difficult. As a parallel we can refer to 1 Enoch. A scholar as distinguished as R.H. Charles argued that several sections of this book were originally written in Hebrew, cf. R.H. Charles, The Book of Enoch, Oxford 1912, pp. ivii-lxx. The finds of the Aramaic fragments of Enoch have demonstrated that the Enoch corpus as a whole was originally written in Aramaic.

119 I.e. 4 Ezra 3-14. The chapters 1-2 and 15-16 are Christian additions.

120 This trend has been strongly influenced by the analysis of R. Kabisch, Das vierte Buch Esra auf seine Quellen untersucht, Göttingen 1889. Kabisch distinguished five different sources, the longest one called the Salathiel-Apocalypse that contained most of the material in ch. 3,1-10,24. Following Kabisch was Box, The Ezra Apocalypse, pp. xxi-xxviii.

121 So H. Gunkel, "Das vierte Buch Esra", E. Kautzsch (ed.), Die Apokryphen und Pseudepigraphen des Alten Testaments II, Leiden 1900, pp. 335-52. Following Gunkel was Violet, Die Apokalypsen des Esra und des Baruch, pp. xlii-l; land more recently, E. Brandenburger, Die Verborgenheit Gottes im Weltgeschehen, Zürich 1981, pp. 23-37.

There is a general agreement among scholars that the material in 4 Ezra 13 antedates the final writing down of the whole Apocalypse of Ezra. Most scholars maintain that at least parts of 4 Ezra 13 have existed either as a fixed oral tradition or as a written source.

On the basis of literary criticism C.H. Box separated three levels in the text: 1) The vision; 2) The interpretation; 3) Further comments to the interpretation by the redactor of the Ezra Apocalypse (vv. 13b-24.26b.29-32.36.48).[122] The distinction between the vision as the oldest stratum of the text and the interpretation as a later addition is also argued more recently by M. Stone, U.B. Müller and R. Kearns.[123]

If the interpretation of the vision is not original we cannot use it as a key to understand the features of the vision, nor can the date and origin of the vision be decided through an analysis of the date and setting of the Ezra Apocalypse as a whole or 4 Ezra 13 as a whole. There are no internal criteria in the vision of 4 Ezra 13 that can indicate date and setting. The only criterion we have, therefore, is the relationship to Dan 7. If the vision in 4 Ezra 13,1-13a has to be defined as a later elaboration of the text of Dan 7, nothing definite can be said about the age of this elaboration. If, however, the Ezra vision not is an elaboration of the Daniel text, the vision has to be defined as an independent source for the Son of Man imagery. It is then a possibility that the vision could have a date and origin not too far removed from the original setting of the Daniel traditions.

7.2   The Relationship Between Dan 7 and 4 Ezra 13

Dan 7 shows a distinctive resemblance to 4 Ezra 13 especially in vv. 1b-3a of the Ezra vision. I give below a critical evaluation of the text witnesses.

---

122   Cf. Box, op.cit., pp. 280-6.
123   Cf. M. Stone, "The Concept of Messiah in IV Ezra", J. Neusner (ed.), Religions in Antiquity, Leiden 1968, pp. 295-312, pp. 303ff; U.B. Müller, Messias und Menschensohn in jüdischen Apokalypsen und in der Offenbarung des Johannes, Gütersloh 1972, p. 108; R. Kearns, Vorfragen zur Christologie II, Tübingen 1980, p. 54.

Latin:
   et somniavi somnium nocte.
   Et ecce de mari ventus exsurgebat,
   ut conturbaret omnes fluctus eius.
   Et vidi, et ecce
   convolabat ipse homo cum nubibus caeli.

Translation:
   And I dreamed a dream by night,
   and behold, from the sea a wind rose,
   so that it stirred all its waves.
   And I saw, and behold,
   this man flew with the clouds of heaven.

Syriac:
   I saw a vision by night,
   and behold, a great wind rose in the sea,
   so that it stirred all its waves.
   And I saw, and behold,
   the wind let ascend from the heart of the sea
   someone in the resemblance of a man
   And I saw, and behold,
   this man flew with the clouds of heaven.

Ethiopic:
   I dreamed a dream by night,
   and behold, a great wind came out of the sea,
   and all its waves were stirred.
   And I saw,
   this wind came out of the sea
   in the resemblance of a man
   And thereafter,
   this man flew with the clouds of heaven.

The notable difference between the versions lies in the second passage in Syr and Eth, which is not recorded in Lat. Two questions arise: 1) Was this passage originally part of the vision?; 2) If so, what was the original wording of the passage?

I.   There are three reasons why the second clause must have been part of the original vision: 1) All the text witnesses, Syr, Eth, Arab[1], Arab[2], Armen, except the Latin record the passage; 2) In the Latin version the introduction of the man presupposes that he is known, cf. *ipse homo,* "this man"; 3) The Latin version states later in the text that the man came from the sea, v. 5.

II.   It is more difficult to decide what was the original wording. Syr reads here: *hy rwḥ' 'sqt mn lbh dym' 'yk dmwt' dbrnš',* "this wind let ascend from the heart of the sea someone in the resemblance of a man".

Eth reads: *yĕwaḍḍĕ' wĕ' ĕtu nafās 'ĕmbāḥr kama 'amsāla bĕ'ĕsi,* "this wind came out of the sea in the resemblance of a man". The greatest difference between the readings lies in the verbal forms: In Syr the wind "let someone ascend", in Eth the wind "came". In Greek this would presuppose different verbs. A Greek retranslation of the Syriac version could be: οὗτος ἄνεμος ἀνήγειρεν ἐκ καρδίας θαλάσσης ὡς ὁμοίωμα ἀνθρώπου, while a retranslation of the Ethiopic version could be: οὗτος ἄνεμος ἀνέβαινεν ἐκ τῆς θαλάσσης ὡς ὁμοίωμα ἀνθρώπου. In Hebrew or Aramaic, however, the same verb would have been used, only in two different forms: In Hebrew עלה, 'alā, "ascend", either in hiphil which would correspond to the causative form in Syriac, or in qal which would correspond to the form in Ethiopic; in Aramaic the same two forms of the verb סלק, s⁵laq, "ascend", the same verb which is used in Syriac.[124] It is therefore reasonable to assume that the different versions go back to different Greek texts which have interpreted the same Semitic verb differently, either as normal active or as causative. This assumption is supported by the fact that both Arab[1] and Armen presuppose a Greek text similar to the Ethiopic version and not to the Syriac.

But what was the original Semitic form of the verb? The only criterion we have to answer the question is to decide what is the *lectio difficilior*, i.e. to decide what would be the most likely alteration carried out by a translator belonging to a Jewish-Christian milieu. What was most likely, to alter "the wind making someone like a man to ascend" into "the wind ascending like someone like a man", or the other way round? We have at least several cases in the Jewish tradition that correspond to the first idea.

In 2 Kings 2 the prophet Elijah ascends to heaven in a storm, s⁵ʿārā, vv. 1.11. After his disappearance his disciples suggest that the *rūᵃh*, "the wind-spirit" of Yahweh had carried him away, v. 16.

In Ezek 3,14 the prophet Ezekiel is removed to the exiled in Tel Aviv in Babylonia. The Hebrew text reads: ורוח נשאתני ותקחני ואלך, "the wind-spirit lifted me up and carried me away, and I went ...". Later Ezekiel is removed to Jerusalem also by the *rūᵃh*, Ezek 8,3.

In En 14 Enoch is taken to heaven. The removal is described in

---

124   For the assimilation of l in Syriac slq*, cf. C. Brockelmann, Syrische Grammatik, Leipzig 1960, § 25, pp. 17f.

the following way in Gr^{Pan}: ἄνεμοι ἐν τῇ ὁράσει μου ἐξεπέτασάν με καὶ ἐπῆραν με ἄνω καὶ εἰσήνεγκάν με εἰς τὸν οὐρανόν, v. 8.[125] Traces of the passage are visible in the Aramaic fragment 4Q En^c 1vi,21,[126] so that the text can be restored in the following way in Aramaic:

(ורוחיא בחזיתי אפרחוני ונטלוני) לעלה

ואובלוני ואע(לו)ני ב(שמיא

"And wind spirits in my vision let me fly, and lifted me] up, and carried me away, and made me en[ter] into [heaven".

Since these instances are the most detailed descriptions we have in the Jewish tradition about supernatural removal of a terrestrial hero, I think we can conclude that the idea that the wind carried somebody away or made somebody ascend was the traditional one. Accordingly a Greek text reading ἄνεμος ἀνήγειρεν ... ὡς ὁμοίωμα ἀνθρώπου, "the wind lifted ... someone like a man up", would correspond to a traditional pattern. The Messiah, as the figure is interpreted, cf. vv. 32.37.52, is coming, carried by a wind, like other heroes in the Jewish tradition.

Is it a likely assumption that this reading, if it was the original one in the Semitic version, was altered to "the wind came out of the sea in the resemblance of a man"? In the first case the wind is the instrument that brings "the man", in the second case the wind itself has the image of a man. There are no analogies to the second reading in the Jewish or Christian tradition. And it must have been extremely hard to swallow, because here the Messiah, as the figure is interpreted in 4 Ezra, is said to be a "wind".[127] I think the only explanation for the existence of this reading after the figure had been identified as the Messiah must be that it was the original one. If that was the case, the original Semitic version had the qal form of the verb, and this was read as a causative form by one of the Greek translators, thus altering the offensive original into a more traditional pattern.

---

125   Greek text according to M. Black, Apocalypsis Henochi Graece, Leiden 1970.
126   Aramaic text according to J.T. Milik, The Books of Enoch, Oxford 1976, p. 194.
127   I think this must be the reason why the Latin version omits the clause. It can not be that the man came from the sea, because this is recorded in the Latin version v. 5. The Greek text known by the Latin translator must have had another offensive reading.

On the basis of this analysis we can give a critical translation of
4 Ezra 13,1b-3a. The translation is mostly based on the Syriac
version since, as we have seen, the Latin version is here less
reliable. But in the central passage about the coming of the man
we use the form of the verb from the Ethiopic version.

> I saw a vision by night,
> and behold, a great wind rose in the sea,
> so that it stirred all its waves.
> And I saw, and behold,
> this wind came up out of the heart of the sea
> in the resemblance of a man.
> And I saw, and behold,
> this man flew with the clouds of heaven.

On basis of this translation we can suggest the following underlying Greek text:[128]

Ἐθεώρουν ὅρασιν τῆς νυκτὸς
καὶ ἰδοὺ ἐν τῇ θαλάσσῃ μέγας ἄνεμος ἐξηγείρετο,
ὥστε συνταράσσειν πάντα τὰ κύματα αὐτῆς.
Ἐθεώρουν καὶ ἰδοὺ
ὁ ἄνεμος ἀνέβαινεν ἐκ καρδίας θαλάσσης
ὡς ὁμοίωμα ανθρώπου.
Ἐθεώρουν καὶ ἰδοὺ
συνέπτη ἐκεῖνος ὁ ανθρώπος σὺν ταῖς νεφέλαις
τοῦ οὐρανοῦ.

Our aim in this chapter is to compare the text of 4 Ezra 13 to
Dan 7. To carry out this comparison we need to establish a Semitic
version of the Ezra sequence. If 4 Ezra 13 is a later commentary
on the text of Dan 7, this commentary could have been written in
Hebrew. If, however, the vision of 4 Ezra 13 was an independent
entity, a parallel vision to Dan 7, this vision may very well like
Dan 7 have existed in Aramaic. Since it is the last assumption we
are going to test, we retranslate the Greek version into Aramaic.
there should be no need to underline the provisional nature of this
enterprise.[129]

---

128   Our translation differs partly from the one given by Hilgenfeld, Messias
Judaeorum, p. 97, because our text critical analysis has led to another critical
text.
129   The verbs qwm and slq are those used in the Syriac version.

חזה הוית חזו עם ליליא וארו
רוח רבה קימה בימא
ומגיחה לכול גללוהי
חזה הוית וארו
רוחא דא סלקה מן לבב ימא
דמא אנש
חזה הוית וארו
עם ענני שמיא אנשא דנה פרח הוה

A comparison with the parallel passage in Dan 7 will therefore be as follows:

Aramaic text

Dan 7,2-4.13	4 Ezra 13,1b-3a
חזה הוית בחזוי עם ליליא וארו	חזה הוית חזו עם ליליא וארו
ארבע רוחי שמיא	רוח רבה קימה בימא
מגיחן לימא רבא	ומגיחה לכול גללוהי
	חזה הוית וארו
וארבע חיון רברבן	רוחא דא
סלקן מן ימא	סלקה מן לבב ימא
שנין דא מן דא	דמה אנש
קדמיתא כאריה	
חזה הוית בחזוי ליליא וארו	חזה הוית . וארו
עם ענני שמיא כבר אנש	עם ענני שמיא אנשא דנה
אתה הוה	פרח הוה

Translation

Dan 7	4 Ezra 13
I saw in my vision by night, and behold:	I saw a vision by night, and behold:
The four winds of heaven stirred the great sea.	A great wind rose in the sea and stirred all its waves.

	I saw, and behold:
And four great animal beings came up out of the sea the one different from the other.	This wind came up out of the heart of the sea
The first one was like a lion ...	in the resemblance of a man.
I saw in the visions of the night, and behold:	I saw, and behold:
With the clouds of heaven someone like a Son of Man was coming.	With the clouds of heaven this man was flying.

First of all it is quite clear that the visions describe the same figure, designated k^ebar '$\check{a}n\bar{a}\check{s}$, "someone like a son of man", and $d\bar{a}m\bar{a}$ '$\check{a}n\bar{a}\check{s}$, "someone resembling a man". The question is how the visions are related. Is the vision in 4 Ezra 13 a later commentary on Dan 7?

1) In Dan 7 the hostile forces come from the sea, the man comes with the clouds of heaven. In 4 Ezra 13 the picture is reversed. Here the man comes from the sea, while the hostile forces come from the four quarters of heaven, v. 5.[130] It is hard to see why a later commentator should have made this alteration.

2) In Dan 7,18 the man is placed in direct connection to the holy ones. For a later commentator who did not know the background of the vision, the connection must have been understood as very intimate. But how could this commentator place the man in the sea? This is certainly not the place for the holy ones, whether they are interpreted as "angels" of "people".

3) The climax in Dan 7 is the entrance of the man before the throne of God, v. 14. This is not mentioned at all in the Ezra vision. It is hard to believe that a commentator who concentrated so much on the nature of the man, would have missed this point.

---

130 The Latin version reads "from the four winds of heaven". But Latin ventus clearly presupposes Hebrew or Aramaic $r\bar{u}^a\d{h}$, which means both "wind" and "quarter", cf. Part I, note 65, p. 62.

4) In Dan 7,13 the man comes with the clouds of heaven. There are good reasons to assume that he was also associated with the winds of heaven in v. 2. But we find it very unlikely that a Jewish commentator who saw in this figure the exalted saviour of the people of God, should on the basis of this imagery come to the conclusion that the man actually *was* a wind.

5) The verb used in 7,13 "come" is a general description. The verb in 4 Ezra "fly" seems to presuppose a more mythologically coloured imagery, which is better explained as a stage prior to Dan 7, than as a later commentary.

6) The Ezra vision does not correspond to any known text in the Jewish or Christian tradition, while the imagery in Dan 7 is utilized in both the New Testament and the Similitudes of Enoch. If the author of the Ezra vision altered the text from Dan 7, we should have expected that his alterations corresponded in one way or another to a broader tradition. This is not the case. Precisely in those respects in which the Ezra vision differs from Dan 7, the Ezra vision is unique.[131]

The analysis points in only one direction: The author of the Ezra vision has not utilized Dan 7 in its present shape.

Could the influence have worked in the opposite direction, from the Ezra vision to Dan 7? This seems unlikely as far as the whole vision vv. 1-13a is concerned. If Dan 7 was patterned on this vision, we should have expected parallels to other parts of the Ezra vision and not only to vv. 1b-3a. As far as we can see, there are no direct parallels outside this sequence.

Could Dan 7 be dependent upon only vv. 1b-13 in the Ezra vision? This presupposes that this sequence once existed in isolation either as a written source or as a fixed oral tradition. There are, however, no indications that this has been the case. We have then only one possibility left: The vision of Dan 7 and the vision of 4 Ezra 13 are two independent visions dealing with the same protagonist, the man. The relationship between them can be defined as follows:

---

131 There seems to be no influence the one way or the other between the vision in 4 Ezra 13 and the Similitudes, cf. J. Theisohn, Der auserwählte Richter, Göttingen 1975, pp. 144-8. On the relation between Dan 7 and the Similitudes, cf. Theisohn, pp. 31-48; on the Son of Man in the Gospels, cf. pp. 152-60.

1. Since the essential point, the coming of the one like a man, and the imagery connected to this man, is the same in both visions, they must derive these features from a common source.

2. Since the wording is so close, the visions must have their origin in the same milieu.

3. Since the correspondences are limited to specific passages within the visions, the composers must have emphasized different features from the preceding source and combined it with different kinds of new material.

These conclusions have the following significance for the understanding of the vision in Dan 7:

1. Since the man in the Ezra vision appears without any connection to the beasts and the holy ones, the theory that the man is a mere symbol for the holy ones as opposed to the beasts can be excluded.[132] The man is conceived as an individual, the designation is not only a symbolic phrase.

2. Since the parallels between the Ezra vision and Dan 7 do not concern the entrance of the man before the Ancient of Days, but the coming of the man and his relationship to the sea, the wind(s) and the clouds, the theory that the oldest source to the Son of Man is to be found in Dan 7,9-10.13-14 (v. 14 is sometimes excluded) must be rejected.[133] The throne scene and the entrance scene may very well reflect the preceding source, but so do also other features of the Daniel vision, namely the sea and the wind(s).

3. The origin of the man is not recorded in Dan 7. Indirectly he is associated with the sea through the winds, presupposing that the winds in v. 2 and the clouds in v. 13 belong together. The Ezra vision is decisive on this point: the man comes from the sea, the same realm as the beasts in Dan 7.

7.3   The Identification of "The Man" in Earlier Research

We do not intend to summarize the whole research history relating to the origin of the imagery in 4 Ezra 13. The man in the Ezra vision is most often seen in relation to the Son of Man in Dan 7, and the problems connected to the two figures are discussed together. A more complete list of theories concerning the identity of the figure may be found in the introductory chapter.[134] This does not, however, mean that the special character of the Ezra vision has not been recognized. This concerns primarily the obscure sequence dealt with in the preceding chapter. The enigmatic character of this sequence has given rise to a series of proposals concerning the identification of the figure.

132   For this theory, cf. above, pp. 384f.
133   For this theory, cf. above, note 23, pp. 349f.
134   Cf. above, pp. 347f.

I. As in Dan 7 the theory that the ultimate source behind the Man imagery was the concept of the Primordial Man, has had many supporters, especially in the earlier research.[135] There have clearly been problems, however, in connecting this hypothetical mythic concept to the coming of the man from the sea. S. Mowinckel suggested two parallels: One from a Mandean source where Mana, a supposed variant of the Primordial Man, is said to dwell in the sea; another from Persian sources, where the "saviour" Saoshyant, a figure which supposedly also had features from the Primordial Man, was born from the waters of a lake.[136] We must admit that we have difficulties in seeing the connection between the two sources; and even more so in seeing the resemblance to 4 Ezra 13.

The whole concept of the Primordial Man has been carefully examined by C. Colpe. His conclusion is clear: There existed no concept of a Primordial Man in Oriental, Jewish or Hellenistic sources which could have formed the background of an apocalyptic Son of Man.[137]

A variant of this theory was advanced by H.L. Jansen. He argued that the background of the Son of Man imagery was to be sought in Babylonian texts about the "god-man" Ea-Oannes who in primeval time ascended from the sea.[138] In Part I we have examined the sources dealing with the primeval sage Uanadapa (Oannes).[139] Our study clearly demonstrated: 1) The concept of Ea-Oannes as described by Jansen did not exist; 2) Uanadapa was a sage whose characteristics differed considerably from those connected with the man in the Ezra vision.

II. Another theory was argued by H. Gressmann, adapted to the theory discussed above.[140] According to him the man in 4 Ezra 13 is described as a god, more precisely as a sun god. He ascends from the sea, flies with the clouds of heaven, fights against a great

---

135 Cf. for instance Box, op.cit., pp. 282ff; P. Volz, Die Eschatologie der jüdischen Gemeinde, Tübingen 1934 (repr. Hildesheim 1966), pp. 186-90; S. Mowinckel, He that cometh, Nashville - New York 1954, pp. 420-37.

136 Cf. Mowinckel, op.cit., pp. 391f.

137 C. Colpe, "Der Begriff 'Menschensohn' und die Methode der Erforschung Messianischer Prototypen".

138 H.L. Jansen, Die Henochgestalt, Oslo 1939, pp. 105-9.

139 Part I, pp. 28ff, 191ff.

140 H. Gressmann, Der Messias, Göttingen 1929, p. 372.

army, and, so it seems, descends to the sea or nether world again. There he gathers the dead in order to deliver them. Then he ascends to the sky. According to Gressmann this course is clearly the orbit of the sun. The battle is that of the sun defeating the demons in order to redeem the souls of men. Also the connection between the man and the fire, cf. vv. 9-10, supports a connection to the sun.

There are several difficulties in this theory. Gressmann had to presuppose several elements not recorded in the Ezra vision to get the orbit of the sun. It is not said in the vision that the man descends to the sea and then again ascends to the sky. Consequently no orbit is described at all. Besides this the imagery of "winds, clouds, fire" rather points toward the manifestation of a weather god than of a sun god.[141]

III. J.A. Emerton also applied his theory about a Ugaritic background of the Son of Man imagery to the Ezra vision.[142] According to him the imagery is best explained as a rain-cloud theophany. Such theophanies were associated with Yahweh in the Old Testament and with Baal in Canaanite mythology. The storm clouds are blown over Palestine from the west (Luk 12,54), and appear to the onlooker to arise from the sea, cf. 1 Kings 18,44(!). We think that Emerton as in Dan 7, is basically right here in connecting some of the imagery to a divine being manifesting meteorological phenomena. The reference to 1 Kings 18,44 where a cloud is 'olā miyyam, "ascending from the sea", is also an interesting parallel to the scenery of the vision. But we cannot see any specific reason to connect this imagery with Baal. If anything, the Ezra vision makes this connection more tenuous than Dan 7. In the Ugaritic myths the sea is a monster defeated by Baal. In the Ezra vision the sea is not defeated. The man comes from the sea and he defeats a great multitude coming from the four quarters of heaven. Besides this, the Ezra vision does not record a cloud raising from the sea as does 1 Kings 18,44, but a "wind" coming up out of the heart of the sea. This feature can hardly be explained in terms of the imagery of meterological phenomena.

---

141 Cf. the rejection of the theory by Müller, Messias und Menschensohn, pp. 111ff.
142 Cf. Emerton, "The Origin of the Son of Man Imagery", pp. 236ff; cf. also above, pp. 503f, 506f.

IV. None of the solutions recorded above have gained broad approval. This dilemma has long been felt by several scholars and given rise to approaches of another kind.

J. Keulers regarded the Ezra vision generally as a compilation of different motifs taken from earlier eschatological and apocalyptical texts, above all from Dan 7. The motif "sea" was taken over from Dan 7,3. It had lost its original meaning as the abode of the sea-monsters and other evil forces.[143] U.B. Müller came to the same conclusion: "Der Apokalyptiker hat ein Visionsbild konstruiert, wobei er die einzelne Züge des Bildes den verschiedensten, ursprünglich nicht zusammen-gehörenden Schrifttexten des AT entnommen hat".[144]

We have previously argued that the Ezra vision is not composed on the basis of Dan 7. But apart from this, — can we suppose that the author worked so mechanically that he only collected different motifs from different texts without any specific idea about the meaning of the new text he was creating? This could have been so if he had composed a traditional text, made up of conventional phrases placed together in conventional order. But this is not the case. If Müller is correct, the composer created a *novum* within Jewish literature without any idea about what it really meant. The composer had the man ascend from the sea for purely "formal reasons", because the context (Dan 7,2), spoke about the sea.[145] We find it more plausible to assume that the text had a meaning, but as yet undiscovered.

R. Kearns has suggested a more complex solution to the problem.[146] According to him the Ezra vision combines different Gattungen. Kearns designates the original vision which existed in oral form, as "apocalyptical vision" (Apokalyptisches Gesicht). This vision recounted the coming of the man, the gathering of the great multitude and the battle. Kearns does not identify the man precisely, but designates him as "the apocalyptical supreme being" (das apokalyptische Hoheitswesen). While still an oral tradition the original vision was changed into another Gattung, which Kearns

---

143 J. Keulers, Die Eschatologische Lehre des Vierten Esrabuches, Inaugural Dissertation, Freiburg im Breisgau 1922, pp. 124, 129f.
144 Müller, op.cit., p. 113.
145 Müller, op.cit., p. 120.
146 Kearns, Vorfragen II, pp. 52-62, 138-50.

calls "the symbolic dream-theophany" (Gleichnistraum-Theophenie). As the name indicates this new Gattung has attracted different elements, some from the Gattung "symbolic dream" and some from the Gattung "theophany". At this level the man was identified as Yahweh.

According to Kearns the elements from the Gattung "theophany" are fundamental for the understanding of the vision at this level: Yahweh is carried by winds from his abode, and flies with the clouds of heaven. His countenance causes trembling, his voice brings destruction by fire. A hostile multitude gathers to do battle with him, but he creates a big mountain (identified by Kearns as Sinai), flies up unto this mountain, and destroys the enemies.

There is one element in particular which according to Kearns contradicts the pattern of theophany, and that is the coming of the man *from the sea*. The sea is never recorded as the abode of Yahweh. Kearns explains this feature on the basis of the combination of the two Gattungen "symbolic dream" and "theophany". The motif "a wind coming from the sea" belongs to the Gattung "symbolic dream". Kearns defines this feature as "fixed" (erstarrt), it belongs to the formal characteristics of the Gattung. By the juxtaposition of features from the two Gattungen the wind from the sea was equated with the wind that carried Yahweh (the man). As a result of this confusion the image of the man ascending from the sea was formed.[147]

We have severe doubts about Kearns' analysis of the history of tradition underlying the visions of Dan 7 and 4 Ezra 13,[148] but for the moment we will concentrate on his arguments concerning the man coming from the sea. Kearns explains its origin in two stages: Firstly the author adopted the motif "a wind coming from the sea". This motif had, however, no inherent meaning. It is a cliché belonging to the stylistic features of the Gattung "dream-vision". Secondly be means of this cliché the author changed the traditional pattern of theophany into a unique statement that Yahweh came from the heart of the sea. The author did so unconciously, because neither the first cliché, nor the new unique statement had any specific meaning in the vision.

---

147   Kearns, op.cit., p. 143, note 196.
148   Cf. above, note 23, pp. 349f.

The first problem to be faced in Kearns' analysis is the treatment of visionary features as "fixed" (erstarrte) features of content. We would generally be very cautious using such a category in exegesis, because it can be used to explain away troublesome elements of a text. We will not deny that Gattungen contain not only formal characteristics such as specific grammatical forms, a specific syntax, specific formulas; but also features of content where the same motif occurs within several texts belonging to the same Gattung. Within a Gattung such a motif may be conventional and in the analysis it must be treated as belonging to the style of the Gattung. But this does not automatically mean that the motif has lost its meaning. It means that the Gattung structure constitutes the framework of the meaning.

That is a more general consideration. There are, however, more specific problems in Kearns' analysis. What criteria does Kearns have to define the motif "wind coming form the sea" as "fixed"? If this motif was part of the stylistic level of the text, it must be frequent in texts belonging to the same Gattung. Where does this phrase occur elsewhere? The answer is simple: Nowhere. Certainly, Dan 7,2 tells of winds stirring the sea, but not explicitly winds coming up out of the sea. How can a motif which only occurs in one single text be "fixed"?

Then to the second stage in Kearns' argumentation. By means of a cliché the composer has changed the location of Yahweh from heaven or Sinai into the sea. He has thus broken the traditional pattern of theophany and created a unique statement, which had, however, no specific meaning in the text. He has only created a new cliché.[149] My question is simple: What secret knowledge about the thoughts of the composer does Kearns have, since he is able to decide which words carry a meaning and which do not?

The attempts to explain the opening passage of the Ezra vision as merely "formal" without any specific meaning can hardly be evaluated in isolation from the rest of the research. Until now scholars have failed to find a convincing background to the passage. As a result another approach emerged which sought to play down its significance.

---

149 According to Kearns, p. 59, note 193, the origin of the man from the sea is also found among the "fixed elements" (erstarrte Innhalte) of the vision.

7.4   The Provenance of the Man from the Sea

We are primarily asking about the background of the imagery of the man, not about the meaning of the whole vision of vv. 1-13a. As previously noticed, the first sequence of the vision, vv. 1b-3a, runs parallel to Dan 7. In the following sequences the man is clearly placed in a framework different from Dan 7. There is, however, a continuity in the description of the man between the first sequence and the following ones. The coming of the man in vv. 3b-4 causes trembling and fire. The same imagery is taken up again in vv. 9-10 in connection with the assault of the hostile multitude. The sequences run as follows:[150]

The Origin, vv. 1b-2:
  I saw a vision by night,
  and behold, a great wind rose in the sea,
  so that it stirred all its waves.
  And I saw, and behold,
  this wind came up out of the heart of the sea
  in the resemblance of a man.

The Appearance, vv. 3-4:
  And I saw, and behold,
  this man flew with the clouds of heaven.
  And wherever he turned his countenance to look
  everything seen by him trembled.
  And wherever his voice went out from his mouth,
  all that heard his voice melted away,
  as the wax melts when it feels the fire.

The Appearance, vv. 9-10:
  . . . And lo! when he saw the assault
  of the multitude as they came,
  he neither lifted his hand,
  nor held any spear nor any warlike weapon;
  but I saw how he sent out of his mouth
  as it were a fiery stream,
  and out of his lips a flaming breath,
  and of his tongue he shot forth a form of sparks.

The imagery connected with the appearance of the man seems more familiar than the one connected to the origin. The clouds, voice (thunder), fire, storm, belong to the imagery of theophany, as Emerton and Kearns clearly demonstrated (cf. for instance Ps

---

150   In the translation of vv. 4.9.10 we follow G.H. Box, "IV Ezra", R.H. Charles (ed.), The Apocrypha and Pseudepigrapha of the Old Testament II, Oxford 1913, pp. 616f.

18,11-16; 68,34; Deut 33,26; Is 19,1).[151] More precisely the imagery is that of a divine warrior appearing in a theophany. But the identity of the figure is not revealed. That the figure is described in a way similar to Yahweh (Kearns) or to Baal (Emerton) does not mean that he actually is thought to be Yahweh or Baal. The imagery is conventional and say no more than that the figure appears in the role of a divine warrior.

For more specific information about the nature of the figure we have to turn to the sequence dealing with the origin.

The figure comes from the sea, Aramaic *yammā*. The sea must have the same meaning here as in Dan 7. There we argued that the sea was functionally equivalent to Akkadian Apsu, the subterranean water. In Mesopotamian mythology Apsu was the abode of different kinds of creatures. The god of wisdom Ea and the seven sages lived in the Apsu,[152] as did various kinds of demons.[153] Originally Apsu was thought to lie above the underworld, but the two kinds of subterranean abodes could be confused so that Apsu and designations for the nether world could be used as synonyms.[154]

In Old Testament texts the sea, as a mythological dwelling, is primarily the abode of monsters.[155] But like Mesopotamian mythology the subterranean waters were thought to lie above the nether world (cf. Job 38,16-17), and could be used as a parallel or synonym to death and nether world (cf. Job 26,5-6; Ps 18,5-6; 69,3.16; 88,7-8).[156] In 4 Ezra 13,3a the wind comes from "the heart of the

---

151 Emerton, op.cit., pp. 236f; Kearns, op.cit., p. 143, note 143.
152 Cf. Part I, pp. 197f.
153 Cf. above, p. 373; cf. also CAD, sub apsû, p. 195, a.5'. To the discussion of "the sea" in Dan 7, cf. above, pp. 503ff.
154 Cf. above, note 146, pp. 428f; an CAD, sub. apsû, p. 196, b.2'.
155 Cf. above, pp. 503f.
156 On the connection "sea, water" and "nether world", cf. S. Mowinckel, Psalmenstudien I-II, Kristiania 1921 (repr. Amsterdam 1961), p. 262; J. Kroll, Gott und Hölle, Leipzig-Berlin 1932 (repr. Darmstadt 1963), p. 325, note 2. N.J. Tromp, Primitive Conceptions of the Nether World in the Old Testament, Rome 1969, pp. 63f, — maintains that the strict nether world connotations are extremely weak with yam. It may be correct that the nether world connotations are stronger with other words for "water", but that does not mean that they are lacking with yam, cf. for instance the text quoted by Tromp, Jon 2,4, where he does not notice that the expression 1ᵉbab yamîm, "in the heart of the seas", is parallel to the nether world. Generally we do not think it correct to distinguish so sharp between the different words for "water" as Tromp does. The basic idea is the subterranean waters lying above the nether world, which caused the confusion of the two concepts.

sea". In both Jon 2,3-4 and Ezek 28,8 *leb yammīm*, "heart of the
seas" corresponds to other expressions for the nether world.[157]

In Mesopotamian imagination the nether wold was the abode both
of demons in monstrous shape and of the dead. The first feature
has its parallel in the monsters in Dan 7. In the Ezra vision the
man can not be understood as a demonic creature, but coming
from the same realm as the monsters he may very well be a dead
man ascending from the nether world.

In the Latin version both the man, v. 5, and the wind, v. 2, come
from the sea. In all the other versions the coming of the wind and
the man is brought together in one clause. We have previously
argued that the original combination of the wind and the man read
"the wind came up out of the heart of the sea in the resemblance
of a man".[158] The Latin version reads *ventus* for "wind". The
underlying Greek text must have had ἄνεμος. The Aramaic (or
Hebrew) original word must, however, have been *rūaḥ* (like the
Syriac version). We have previously proposed the following
Aramaic original text: רוחא דא סלקה מן ימא דמה אנש

As commonly known *rūaḥ* in Hebrew and Aramaic does not only
mean "wind", but also "spirit". A wind coming up out of the
heart of the sea gives no sense. A spirit coming up out of the sea,
as a designation for the nether world, gives, however, good sense.
In 4Q En^e 1xxii, lines 3-4 (Milik, p. 229) = En 22,5 Enoch sees
רוח אנש מת, "a spirit of a dead man" (Abel) in the nether world.
According to GrPan (the Aramaic text is lacking) the nether world
in this text is the abode of τα πνεύματα τῶν ψυχῶν τῶν νεκρῶν,

---

157 In Jon 2,3-4 the phrase is used together with other expressions for "water"
as a parallel to bäṭän šeʾōl, "womb of the nether world"; in Ezek 28,8 the phrase
is used parallel to šaḥat, "grave, nether world". One can argue that the imagery
of "water" and "sea" is natural in view of the context in both places, and that
yam therefore only refers to a natural phenomenon with no allusion to the nether
world. A closer examination of the clauses, however, yields another result. Jon
2,3-4 as a whole describes a descent to the nether world, cf. bäṭän šeʾōl in v. 3
and šaḥat in v. 7. Within this section the "water symbolism" and "death symbolism" are clearly juxtaposed: "You did cast me into the deep, meṣūlā, into the
heart of the seas, leḇab yammim, the stream, nahar, was around me, all your
breakers, mišbārīm, and waves, gallīm, passed over me . . ., the waters, mayim,
surrounded me up to my neck, the deep, tehōm, was round about me".
Ezek 28,8 has a parallel in Ezek 26,19-20. There the descent of the king of Tyre
into the underworld is juxtaposed to drowning in the deep, tehōm. In both Jonah
and Ezekiel the natural motif "drowning" has attracted associations to nether
world and death symbolism connected to "water".
158 Cf. above, pp. 517ff.

"the spirits of the souls of the dead", En 22,3. In En 15,9 evil spirits, πνεύματα πονηρά, will proceed from the bodies of the giants and dwell on the earth. In both cases the spirits, Aramaic rūḥīn, are spirits of the dead — in the first case of a righteous person, in the second case of the destructive giants.

Reports about the rising of spirits or ghosts are rare in Old Testament and Jewish literature. There is one well known example, however, the raising of the spirit of Samuel on the request of Saul. The short dialogue between the necromancer and Saul runs as follows:

אלהים ראיתי עלים מן הארץ
ויאמר לה מה תארו
ותאמר איש זקן עלה

I see a divine being ascending from the underworld."
And he said to her: "What is his appearance?"
And she answered: "An old man is ascending."
(1 Sam 28, 13b-14a)

The structure of the vision resembles the structure of the sequence in the Ezra vision. First the ascension of the spirit or ghost, then the description of his appearance, in both cases as "a man".

References to ghosts from the nether world are frequent in Mesopotamian literature.[159] A direct report about an ascending ghost is for instance found in the Epic of Gilgamesh, Tabl. XII:[160] *utukku ša Enkidu kī zaqīqi ultu erṣetim itteṣa.*[161] "When the spirit of Enkidu, like a wind, issued forth from the nether world ..." (line 84).

We have accordingly two concepts which are united in the Ezra vision. The first sequence tells about the rising of a *rūaḥ*, "spirit", from the nether world in the resemblance of a man. In the succeeding sequences this man is described in the conventional imagery for divine beings which manifest meteorological phenomena. The combination of these two concepts is not traditional, and as far as we know, the only text which united elements from these two concepts is the Vision of the Nether World. The correspondences are as follows:

---

159 Cf. A. Heidel, The Gilgamesh Epic, pp. 150-57; cf. also above, pp. 378ff.
160 On this tablet, cf. above, pp. 366ff.
161 Text from R.C. Thompson, The Epic of Gilgamish, p. 69.

1. The scenery of the Vision of the Nether World is the underworld, situated below the water, cf. Ḫumut-Tabal, the boatsman in line 45B. The place of origin in the Ezra vision is the sea, signifying the nether world.
2. In the Vision of the Nether World the visionary sees the etemmu, "the spirit", of the ideal king, cf. line 62. In the Ezra vision the visionary sees a rūᵃḫ, "a spirit".
3. In the Vision of the Nether World the spirit has the shape of ištēn etlu, "a unique man", line 50. In the Ezra vision the rūᵃḫ has the shape of an ᵃnāš, "a man".
4. In the Vision of the Nether World "the unique man" has features from the Anzu-bird, the storm bird which signifies the storm clouds, line 50. In the Ezra vision the man flies with the clouds and manifests storm and lightnings.
5. In the Vision of the Nether World the imagery of the Anzu-bird corresponds to the description of the unique man as a victorious warrior, line 50. In the Ezra vision the man acts as a victorious warrior.
6. In the Vision of the Nether World it is predicted that the etemmu of the man will visit the earth again, causing the destruction of his enemies, cf. line 67B.[162] A parallel to this is the ištēn etlu in the Death-Dream of Enkidu who comes in a thunder storm to collect Enkidu to the nether world.[163] In the Ezra vision the rūᵃḫ, appearing as a man, ascends to defeat his enemies.

The correspondences are so close that they indicate a relationship between the texts — especially when we take into account the fact that the Vision of the Nether World seems to be the only text known form the Mesopotamian side that combines these features and the Ezra vision is the only text known from the Jewish side.

Consequently the Ezra vision sheds light on Dan 7. One of the great riddles in this vision is the place of origin of the Son of Man. The animal beings come from the sea (v. 3), but the son of Man comes *with* the clouds of heaven (v. 13). Our analysis of the imagery of the man in a previous chapter indicated that he was connected both to the clouds of heaven and to the four winds of heaven. Dan 7,2 reads:

ארבע רוחי שמיא מגיחן לימא רבא, "the four winds of heaven stirred the great sea". This is commonly interpreted as if the four winds blew upon the sea.[164] But this interpretation is not inevitable. The movement can go in the opposite direction as in Job 38,8 (TM): ויסך בדלתים ים בגיחו מרחם יצא, "who shut in the sea with doors, when it *came gushing* from the womb". In the Targum of Job (11 QtgJob, col. 30, line 6, Fitzmyer/Harrington, p.

162 This seems to be the most plausible interpretation of the passage, cf. above, pp. 398f, note 67c and pp. 437f.
163 Cf. above, pp. 373f.
164 So already in the ancient translations, LXX: enepeson, "fell upon, blew upon"; Theodot: proseballon, "strike against"; Vulgata: pugnabant, "fought with".

36) the phrase בגיחו יצא is substituted by what must be taken as a haf'el form of the verb גיח, the same form as in Daniel. The text reads:

התסוג בדשין ימא ב(ה)גחותה מן רחם תהומא

"Is it you who shut in the sea with doors, when it *came gushing* from the womb of the deep". The four winds in Dan 7, a characteristic of the Anzu-bird connected to the Son of man,[165] could just as well have been thought to stir the sea when they broke the surface of the sea from below, instead of stirring it when they blew upon it from above. This possibility is confirmed when we read Dan 7 in the light of 4 Ezra 13. Here the man is actually said to stir the sea when he comes from below.

The Ezra vision also helps to resolve another problem in Dan 7, the question of the significance of the comparative particle k^e, "like", in k^ebar '$^a\bar{n}\bar{a}\check{s}$. In Dan 7 the particle is connected to several of the visionary figures: $k'ary\bar{e}$, "like a lion", v. 4; $k^{e'\bar{a}}\bar{n}\bar{a}\check{s}$, "like a man", v. 4; kin^emar, "like a panther", v. 6. In v. 5 the particle is replaced by the functionally equivalent דמיה (feminine participle), $d\bar{a}my\bar{a}$, "resembling". In 4 Ezra 13,2 we have proposed an original Aramaic form of the verb דמה. The same root occurs in the Syriac version. This would accordingly be identical to Dan 7,5 and functionally equivalent to k^e used elsewhere in Dan 7.

What we have described in both the Ezra vision and Dan 7 are transcendent figures ascending from the nether world. In the Ezra vision the nature of the figure is defined. He is a $r\bar{u}^ah$, "a spirit". But when the spirit appears to human eyes he makes himself manifest in a shape resembling something in the natural world: He has the likeness of a human being. The verb $d^em\bar{a}$ and the particle k^e thus serve to describe the nature of the appearance of the transcendent beings: They are not simply animals (lion, bear, panther) or human beings, because they are transcendent beings. But they appear "like" or "in the resemblance of" animals and human beings. The manner of appearance — either as dangerous monstrous animals or as a man — reveals the nature of the transcendent figure: either as a malevolent demonic creature, as is the case with the animal beings, or as, at least for the visionary, a benevolent saviour figure, as is the case with the man.

---

165 Cf. above, pp. 513f.

c) The Background of Dan 7 in the Vision of the Nether World

1. Summary of Corresponding Features

In the two preceding sections we have presented the observations that point in favour of a dependence of Dan 7 on the Vision of the Nether World. The two visions demonstrate close correspondence not only in Gattung, structure of content and imagery, but also in the basic elements of content. Many of the features of Dan 7 that previously have been obscure have their meaning uncovered in the light of the Akkadian vision and corresponding traditions. To help the reader's own evaluation I repeat below the basic findings:

	Dan 7	Vision of the Nether World
Gattung	Night-vision	Night-vision
	Symbolic	Partly symbolic
	Throne-scene	Throne-vision
	Vision/audition	Vision/audition
	Religious-political intention: Fall of an empire	Religious-political intention: Decline of an empire

Common to both visions

| Structure of content | Listing and description of monsters
God on the throne, surrounded by fire
Attendants offering adoration
Judgement
Accused and annihilated: Rebel king
Ideal king designated "man"
Given universal and everlasting kingdom
(In the Vision of the Nether world the description of the ideal king comes before the judgement of the rebel king.) |

Special features
Monsters:

	Dan 7	Vision of the Nether World
1st Monster:	lion with eagle-wings	lion-eagle
	lion raised upon two feet	lion standing on hind legs
	upon two feet like a man	feet like a man
2nd Monster:	raised on one side	monster standing without hind leg
	stand up, devour!	name of monster: hurry, remove!

3rd Monster:	four bird-wings	monster with wings
	four heads	monster with two heads
4th Monster:	no name of last monster	no name of last monster
	two creatures described	last monster comprising two bodies
	terrible and dreadful	possessing terror and dreadful splendour
	stamped with its feet	with its left foot it was treading
	ten horns	(horned) crown of last monster
	human eyes and a mouth that spoke	second part of last monster: head of a man
Throne-scene:	an Ancient of Days took his seat	the warrior Nergal was seated on a royal throne
	his throne flames of fire and its wheels burning fire; a river of fire streamed out and went out from before him	from his arms lightning was flashing
	thousands upon thousands served him and myriads upon myriads were standing before him	the Anunakki, the great gods, were kneeling at his right and at his left side . . . The underworld was filled with fear and prostrated before the son of princes
Judgement:	the beast was killed and its body destroyed, it was given to the burning fire	suddenly the fearsome sheen of his terrible kingship shall annihilate you completely
Ideal king:	one like a man	one man
	dominion and glory and kingdom were given to him	the exalted shepherd: whom my father . . ., the king of the gods gives full responsibility
	all peoples, nations and tongues shall serve him	. . . whom (the king) from east to west he (the god) allows to look over the lands in their totality . . ., and he (the king) rules over everything
	his dominion is an everlasting dominion which shall not pass away, his kingdom such as shall never be impaired	in all eternity

Themes:

The rebel king is portrayed according to a pattern known both from biblical and ancient near eastern texts. He is supremely wise, oppressor of the people and commits an abomination against the god. The style of the description os that of prophecy, based on the technique of vaticinia ex eventu, corresponding to Babylonian written prophecies.

The pattern "rebel king" goes back to Nabonidus, especially as he is portrayed in the Verse Account of Nabonidus and the Dynastic Prophecy, and further to the latest Neo-Assyrian kings.

The rebel king is portrayed in a way that corresponds to later descriptions of rebel kings in Babylonian, Persian and Jewish traditions. He is supremely wise, but commits an abomination against the god.

The description of the king has its closest parallel in the description of Nabonidus in the Verse Account of Nabonidus.

The description of the ideal king is added to the scheme of four kings or empires known from Greek and Persian sources. The same scheme is also found in the Dynastic Prophecy which records the rise and fall of the great empires up to the Macedonian. The ideal king is contrasted to the rebel king, which corresponds to a general tendency in the Babylonian prophecies of contrasting good and bad kings. The reign of the ideal king has a historical parallel in the reign of Nebuchadnezzar, who is described as the world emperor par excellence in the Book of Daniel. A similar idealized description of Nebuchadnezzar is found in Babylonian sources, especially in the Uruk prophecy.

The description of the ideal king occurs within a sequence which resembles the Babylonian written prophecies. Although the historical identification of the king demonstrates that he was a figure of the past (Senacherib), the description is nevertheless given the present-future tense. Read in this way the ideal king is contrasted to rebellious Neo-Assyrian kings. This pattern is also found in the Uruk prophecy where Nebuchadnezzar is contrasted to the bad kings of the Neo-Assyrian empire.

The ideal king is designated bar ʾănāš, literally to be translated "son of man". The word bar does, however, not mean "son" in this connection, but emphasizes the unique character of the figure ʾănāš.

The ideal king is designated ištēn etlu, literally to be translated "one man". The world ištēn can, however, also be used in a non-numerical sense in the meaning "unique, outstanding".

The phrase "man" for the ideal king functions within three semantic patterns:

The phrase "man" for the ideal king functions within three semantic patterns:

According to the Gattung bar ʾănāš corresponds to transcendent figures, appearing in visions in human form, acting as messengers from God to man.

According to the Gattung ištēn etlu is "the unique man" in dream-experiences, described as a messenger from god to man.

Within the structure of content bar ʾănāš represents a contrast to the demonic monsters.

Within the structure of content ištēn etlu is "the one man" described in contrast to the demonic monsters.

As a direct description bar ʾănāš designates an ideal king described as the shepherd of the nations.

As a direct description ištēn etlu is the ideal king, called "the exalted shepherd".

The monsters have their origin from the sea, which is generally held to be the abode of monstrous creatures in the Old Testament and in Jewish tradition. In this context Aramaic yamm corresponds to Akkadian Apsu, the subterranean water-deep. In Mesopotamian mythology Apsu both signifies the abode of composite beings, and is used as a parallel phrase to "underworld". This second aspect can also be implied in "the sea" in the Old Testament and in Jewish tradition.

The monsters have their abode in the underworld. The vision predicts a visitation from the underworld on the two rebellious kings.

The one like a man, the ideal king, comes with the clouds of heaven, accompanied by the four winds of heaven. The imagery resembles a theophany where a divine warrior manifests meteorological phenomena.	The one man, the ideal king, is described with the features of the Anzu-bird. This imagery is often used in the description of frightening and victorious warriors. The Anzu-bird is a personification of the thunderclouds and embodies the four winds.

4 Ezra 13	Vision of the Nether World
The man has his origin in the sea, which signifies the underworld.	The man appears in the underworld.
The death-spirit of the man ascends from the underworld in order to destroy the enemy.	The spirit of the dead king shall visit upon the earth in order to destroy the king's enemies.
The spirit appears in the form of a man.	The spirit has the form of a man.
The man comes with clouds and manifests storms and lightning.	The man is described with the features of the Anzu-bird, which in Mesopotamian mythology signifies the thundercloud and manifests storms and lightning.
The man acts as a victorious warrior.	The man is described as a victorious warrior.

2.   The Transition of the Vision from a Mesopotamian to a Jewish Setting

The parallels between the visions do not indicate a literary dependence. They are, however, so outstanding that they indicate a dependence in one way or another. No other alternatives seem possible, since it is the Vision of the Nether World as a composition that corresponds most directly to Dan 7, and not the underlying patterns and traditions. The Vision of the Nether World is a unique composition arising out of the application of visionary forms and mythical patterns upon a fixed situation in history. Accordingly there must have been some transference of traditions derived from this vision in its Akkadian form, or in an Aramaic translation or summary, to the composer of Dan 7.

The problem is that no such traditions are known. We do not possess any Mesopotamian sources reflecting later elaborations of the Vision of the Nether World, nor any Jewish "Vorlage" to Dan 7. 4 Ezra 13 reflects some of the motifs from the Vision of the Nether World closer to this vision than Dan 7, but 4 Ezra 13 was not used as a source by the composer of Dan 7.

The problem must, however, not be exaggerated. If the Vision of the Nether World gave rise to later traditions, it is not unlikely to assume that they were preserved in the Aramaic language, which was the spoken language at that time. If the traditions were written down in Aramaic, it is not surprising that they have not survived, because of the material used. Nevertheless, the lack of sources constituting a link between the Vision of the Nether World and Dan 7 has methodological consequences. The burden of proof for a dependence lies in the comparison of the two visions, and not in considerations about how the transmission took place. What can be maintained in general terms is that a transmission was possible, since the Book of Daniel has at several points adopted Mesopotamian traditions resembling themes dealt with in the Vision of the Nether World.

The lack of text-external evidence demands cautious conclusions. We shall begin our approach with two basic observations derived from our previous analysis:

1. Dan 7,2-14 reflects the Vision of the Nether World as a whole. All basic elements of content are adopted, mostly in the same order. A reinterpretation of the elements has taken place in Dan 7, but no entirely new elements were added. This means that the listing and description of monsters, the throne-scene, the ideal king, the rebel king and the judgement belonged to the unity that was transformed into Dan 7 in its whole history of transmission.
2. In the Book of Daniel there is a close relationship between Dan 7 and the dream-stories in ch. 2 and 4-5. These stories and the traditions adopted into them deal with the fall of the Babylonian empire. This may indicate that Dan 7 at one stage in its pre-history dealt with the same topic.

These two observations indicate that the historiographical pattern from the Vision of the Nether World was loosened from its original historical setting and applied to a new one before it got its final form in Dan 7. This is not without parallels. The huge tree in Ezek 31 did originally symbolize the Assyrian empire, but was in Dan 4 applied to the Babylonian king Nebuchadnezzar. The two dream-visions in Dan 2 and 4 reflect in one way or another Zoroaster's vision in the Persian tradition, but were also applied to

Nebuchadnezzar. In Dan 2 this pattern was extended by the scheme of four empires embracing a larger period of history. The pattern of the "rebel king" could be applied to various kings throughout history. The Babylonian prophecies contained a pattern which could be applied to different historical periods both in their Babylonian setting and in the adoption of this Gattung in the Book of Daniel. This demonstrates a basic fact: The Book of Daniel contains historiographical patterns which could be applied to different historical situations. That this also was the case with the pattern contained in the Vision of the Nether World is accordingly not an unlikely assumption.

It should be remembered that the actual historical setting is not disclosed in the vision. Moreover, the vision certainly contained predictions about the future fall of the rebel rulers (cf. lines 67B-68). It is also possible to read the sequence about the ideal king (lines 62-65) as a prophecy about a king to come. Consequently the vision contains features that easily could have inspired later readers to new interpretations.

The vision was first applied — as can be traced in the original composition of the vision itself — as a prediction of the decline of the Assyrian empire.[166] The vision dealt with events about 670 B.C. when Ashurbanipal was the crown prince. It was most likely written down at the end of Ashurbanipal's reign in order to interpret the last troublesome years of his reign as a fulfillment of the vision.

If we assume that traditions from the vision survived the fall of the Assyrian empire and were transmitted to the Babylonians, the pattern could easily have been interpreted differently. The vision dealt with rebellious Assyrian kings contrasted with an ideal king. The sequence about the ideal king could be read as a prophecy about a king to come. A similar pattern is known from the Babylonian Uruk prophecy, where Nebuchadnezzar is described as the ideal king in contrast to the rebellious Assyrian rulers.[167]

This could have been the setting of the traditions when they became known to the Jewish recipients, but it is tempting to include one more stage in the transmission of the material.

166 Cf. above, pp. 440f.
167 Cf. above, pp. 489ff.

The vision deals with three rulers. One is the visionary. He is the crown prince, but apparently in charge of government in his area. The other is the actual rebel, who is the father of the crown prince and accordingly the king. He is portrayed as a man bestowed with divine wisdom, but nevertheless as a rebel against the gods. The third protagonist is the ideal king, who is described as a universal ruler, victorious in battle, and strange to say under the protection of the leading gods of the Elamite (Persian!) area.[168]

This pattern, which originally reflected the circumstances in Assyria in the first part of the seventh century, also fits another historical situation exactly. By the fall of the Babylonian empire three rulers were involved. The one was the crown prince Belshazzar, who during a long period had ruled Babylonia from Babylon. The other was his father Nabonidus, who was the king, but during a long period of his reign had stayed in Teima in the Arabian desert. As already observed, Nabonidus was portrayed by the Marduk priesthood as a rebel king, boasting of divine wisdom.[169] The third was Cyrus, the Persian(!) king, who on the Cyrus Cylinder is portrayed as the ideal king in contrast to the rebellious Nabonidus.

If traditions derived from the Vision of the Nether World were applied to this situation, this must have taken place in the Persian period; therefore our next question is whether there existed Persian notions which could have contributed to this reinterpretation of the vision.

Of special interest are representations associated with the early persian kings Cyrus and Darius; concerning Cyrus, the gatehouse "genius" of Palace R at Pasargadae; concerning Darius, representations of a royal hero fighting monsters at Persepolis.

The relief at Pasargadae shows a bear-footed winged figure wearing a robe and a crown. The wings are carved in the same manner as the Assyrian genius wings, the robe is meant to recall the garb of the Elamite kings, the crown reproduces the Egyptian *hekhemet*-crown, a symbol of the war-cry. The figure was surmounted by the inscription: "I Cyrus, the king, an Achaemenian".

---

168   Cf. above, pp. 430ff.
169   Cf. above, pp. 469ff.

There is no consensus among scholars about what exactly the figure signifies and how the figure and the inscription are to be related. It is agreed that the dominant features of the figure resemble the Assyrian winged genii, benevolent creatures guarding the doorways of the Assyrian palaces, but then the opinions differ. D. Stronach regards the figure basically as a genius: "... the winged figure was a genius: an apotropaic, protective spirit ultimately based on the magical guardians of Assyria".[170] At the same time the most important contemporary message of the winged figure was almost certainly political. The Egyptian crown in particular signified the suddenly extended horizons of the Achaemenid dynasty. Concerning the relation between the figure and the inscription Stronach denies that the inscription identified the figure as Cyrus. The inscription was not a unique label associated with this doorway or relief alone, but a common inscription that is known from other gates and palaces at Pasargadae.[171]

Stronach is cautious in stressing the political significance of the figure and its association with the ideology of kingship. Other scholars have maintained a more direct connection between the figure and the concept of kingship in the early Persian period. Among them M. Mallowan regarded the figure as a phantom of Cyrus, a guardian angel of the king, signifying his kingship.[172] He implied the possibility that this ideology of kingship was reflected in Herodotus' story about Cyrus' prophetic dream, predicting the empire of Darius as well: "... he saw the eldest of the sons of Hystaspes wearing wings on his shoulders, the one wing overshadowing Asia and the other Europe" (Herodotus I, 209).[173]

M.C. Root's examination of the figure tends towards the same conclusions.[174] She calls attention to the fact that the figure has features of different origins and is not only a copy of the Assyrian guardian genius. Moreover, the figure is facing into the building, while the Assyrian genii always confront the visitors, due to their

---

170   Dr. Stronach, Pasargadae, Oxford 1978, pp. 44-55, p. 54.
171   Stronach, op.cit., p. 53.
172   M.E.L. Mallowan, "Cyrus the Great", Iran 10, 1972, pp. 1-18, pp. 1-6.
173   Text in A.D. Godley, Herodotus I, LCL, London-Cambridge, Mass., 1914 (1977), pp. 262f.
174   M.C. Root, The King and Kingship in Achaemenid Art, AcIr 19, Leiden 1972, pp. 303ff.

protective function. Root concludes: "The figure remains enigmatic. But — whether it represents a syncretic deity, some
metaphorical vision of an abstract idea of imperial domain, or a
vision of Cyrus himself in a mythical aspect of ideal kingship —
the Pasargadae "Genius" is an Achaemenid creation emerging from
and responding to the demands of empire as Cyrus saw them".[175]
Root also includes other representations in her discussion of
"mythical visions of kingship and power" in Persian art.[176] At
Persepolis representations of the well known motif "hero fighting
monster" were found. The same motif of a figure stabbing or
overcoming a beast in a mythical-heroic manner is found on
several seal types inscribed with the name of an Achaemenid king.
The heroic struggle represented on the Persepolis reliefs have
immediate antecedents in Neo-Assyrian art. Here the king is often
depicted in ritual combat. But the beasts defeated by the king are
not portrayed as monstrous creatures, they are real beings. Only
gods, genii and mythical heroes fight monsters.
Here the Persian representation differ. On several of the seals the
hero is wearing a royal crown, clearly signifying his royal status.
The hero portrayed on the Persepolis reliefs lacks the royal crown,
instead he wears a low band similar to that worn by the palace
attendants of the reliefs. The hero also wears strapped shoes
common to all other figures in Persian dress in Achaemenid
sculpture, instead of the royal strapless shoes. Root regards these
features as deliberately reflecting a certain concept of Darius'
kingship. In the tomb inscription of Darius he is given the
designation "a Persian man". Root sees a connection between this
inscription and the reliefs: "the literary metaphor and the sculp-
tural vision of the archetypal hero of 'a Persian man' may
conceivably reflect an Indo-Iranian concept of kingship the
prestige of whose memory Darius (followed by his successors)
consciously wished to evoke".[177] The king is the heroic archetype
of the Persian man. The motif of the king portrayed as this man
and fighting monsters on the doorjambs signified for the intruder
the king's power to protect his domain from creatures who
symbolized any and all hostile forces. "We see here in a sense an

175   Root, op.cit., p. 303.
176   Root, op.cit., pp. 303-8.
177   Root, op.cit., p. 305.

image of the king-as-victor transposed to a cosmic plane . . .".[178]
The Persian representations demonstrate a concept where mythical symbols of divine power are connected with the power of kingship. On the relief at Pasargadae the power of Cyrus' kingship was symbolized by a winged figure, resembling Cyrus' prophetic dream of Darius wearing wings overshadowing his world-wide kingdom. On the reliefs at Persepolis the power of Darius' kingship was symbolized by the mythical motif of "hero fighting monsters". In both cases the representations reflected Neo-Assyrian art, but nevertheless with different presuppositions. In Neo-Assyrian art winged figures and heroes fighting monsters signified divine power, which was distinguished from the power of the king. In the Persian representations the connection between the two aspects was closer, even though the reliefs do not present the king as divine. On the Persian reliefs the symbolism is balanced by the depiction of the king as "a Persian man", which demonstrates the human character of the figure.

What make these representations interesting with regard to the Vision of the Nether World is that the mythical concept of power and the power of kingship in this vision is combined in the same way as in the Persian representations. The ideal king of the vision is a human being, designated "man", but he is nevertheless connected to a mythical imagery of power. He is likened to the mythical Anzu-bird and is portrayed as a victor over a monster, in an attitude resembling the god Ninurta defeating a monstrous creature.[179] If the Pasargadae relief really depicted the protective spirit of Cyrus, as Mallowan suggested, the resemblance to the Vision of the Nether World is even closer, because the vision deals with the spirit of the dead king.

Assuming that traditions derived from the Vision of the Nether World were once interpreted in the light of the fall of the Babylonian empire, this early Persian concept of kingship could have constituted the framework for the understanding of the ideal king of the vision. Whether he was associated with a historical king, for instance Cyrus, is impossible to decide with certainty. If the vision in this context was transposed to a Jewish setting, the

---

178   Root, op.cit., pp. 307.f
179   Cf. above, pp. 413f.

possibility can not be excluded. From the prophecies of Deutero-Isaiah we know that Cyrus was highly praised in circles among the exiled Jews, cf. Is 41,1-5; 44,28-45,7. He was even described as the anointed of Yahweh (Is 45,1), an appellation commonly reserved for the native kings of the Davidic line in earlier Jewish tradition. But it is also possible that the theological reflection of history that led Deutero-Isaiah to praise Cyrus as the agent of Yahweh, was given an eschatological interpretation. In this case the ideal king of the vision would be understood as a future king, even though the imaginary features were based on a historical model. On the Persian side we know from the Oracle of Hystaspes that there arose eschatologically-coloured expectations about the Great King to come.[180] The Oracle in its original form can hardly be dated earlier than the end of the third or the beginning of the second century B.C. But it nevertheless demonstrates that the Persians also developed an eschatological concept in which a saviour king played the dominant role.[181]

That the fall of the Babylonian empire was the historical focus reflected in the earliest Danielic traditions does not give a decisive answer to the question about the date of origin of these traditions. They can have emerged at a later time. The Aramaic part of the Book of Daniel seems clearly to reflect Persian and Babylonian traditions from a later period. The dream-visions in Dan 2 and 4 resemble Zoroaster's dream-vision.[182] The scheme of four empires adopted into Dan 2 and 7 has most probably a Persian provenance.[183] The Babylonian Dynastic Prophecy recounting the rise and fall of the great empires was composed as late as the beginning of the Macedonian period.[184]

A Persian influence from this period may also have taken place in 4 Ezra 13. M. Philonenko has called attention to the resemblance between this vision and the Oracle of Hystaspes.[185] There are no parallels in the Oracle to the opening of the vision in 4 Ezra 13, the ascension of the man from the sea, but there are similarities to

---

180   Cf. above, note 41, pp. 485f.
181   Cf. S.K. Eddy, The King is Dead, pp. 58-61.
182   Cf. above, p. 486.
183   Cf. above, p. 485.
184   Cf. above, p. 473.
185   M. Philonenko, "L'apocalyptique", Études d'Histoire des Religions de l'Université des Sciences Humaines de Strasbourg, 1977, pp. 129-35.

the rest of the visionary imagery. In the vision Ezra sees an immense multitude attacking the man (v. 5). He flies up on a mountain from which he destroys the multitude by fire (vv. 6-11). Thereafter he calls to him a peaceful multitude (vv. 12-13). The Oracle prophecies a Great King descending from heaven accompanied by fire and angels. The king descends on a mountain in the midst of the earth, to which the righteous have fled. The great hordes of an evil king surround the mountain. The Great King destroys the multitude by fire and sword (Div. inst. VII, 17.19).

Philonenko dates the Oracle to the first century B.C., and assumes that the author of 4 Ezra 13 may have known it in a Greek or Aramaic version. But as Eddy has argued, it is possible to date the original Persian oracle much earlier, seeing in it a reaction against Macedonia that was later transformed to a reaction against Rome.[186] We will also date the vision of 4 Ezra 13 much earlier than assumed by Philonenko.[187]

The resemblance between the vision of the flying man and the Oracle is not so close as to suppose a dependence. But the corresponding features may indicate an adoption of similar motifs. As we have seen, the two basic motifs in 4 Ezra 13 and the Oracle were extant in early Persian ideology of kingship: the connection between the power of kingship and the divine power, symbolized through the winged figure, and the portrayal of the king in the mythical role of a hero fighting a monster, that signified his power to destroy any enemy. If this is the case, the vision of 4 Ezra 13 has developed along similar lines as Dan 7. The vision is based on traditions derived from the Vision of the Nether World, but influenced by Persian traditions.

Since both the scheme of four empires, the extension of the Babylon Gattung "written prophecy" to deal with the rise and fall of the great empires, and the Oracle of Hystaspes, presuppose the Macedonian empire, the visions in Dan 7 and 4 Ezra 13 can not have been written earlier than the Macedonian period. But this dating seems to contradict our previous observations. The most likely historical situation underlying the transition of the Vision to a Jewish setting, was the change between the Babylonian and Persian empire. This change took place i the sixth century B.C., and even though the Jewish traditions reflecting this change could have been formed at a some later time, it seems quite unlikely that they should be dated as late as in the third century after the Macedonians had gained control over the Orient. The Jewish traditions must have been formed at an earlier date when the change between Babylonia and Persia was still the most impressive historical event. This indicates that the Jewish traditions resulting in Dan 7 must have been formed in two stages, the first stage in the Persian period, reflecting the change between Babylonia and Persia, the second stage in the Macedonian period, where the historiographical pattern was extended to include the Macedonian empire.

Accordingly, the Jewish vision underlying Dan 7 must have existed without the scheme of four empires and kings being implied. Consequently, we have to concentrate on the visionary imagery alone, excluding v. 17 where the beasts are interpreted as kings. Previously we have demonstrated that the four beasts in Dan 7 could very well have been formed independently of the scheme of four empires, and could have been interpreted according to this scheme only later.[188]

This leads us once more to consider the visionary imagery in Dan 7, compared to visions with a similar imagery. The following visions shall be included:

* The Vision of the Nether World, which forms the main source for Dan 7.
* The vision in Ezek 1, which has adopted a mythical imagery resembling the imagery in Dan 7, but without any connection to the Vision of the Nether World.[189]
* The vision in Zech 6,1-8, which relates to Dan 7 in the same manner as Ezek 1.
* The vision in 4 Ezra 13, which is dependent on the Vision of the Nether World in its basic imagery, and reflects some of the features in a more original way than Dan 7.[190]

The first part of the Vision of the Nether World starts with a section where fifteen monsters composed of animal and human features are listed. These monsters are demons and act as servants

188 Cf. above, pp. 509ff.
189 Cf. note 188.
190 Cf. note 187.

Vision of the Nether World	Ezek 1	Zech 6
		Four winds of heaven
15 monsters in the underworld. Last monster composed of two bodies	4 "animal beings": composite creatures embodying the four winds	
One man likened to the Anzu-bird (embodying clouds and the four winds) in the underworld	Attendants of Yahweh	Agents of Yahweh
Throne-scene: the ruling god	Throne-scene: the ruling god	
Judgement: visionary		
Ideal king: universal and everlasting kingdom		
Judgement: visionary and rebel king	Judgement: Israel (ch. 2-3)	

of the ruling god of the underworld, Nergal. This section is followed by a new one in which one man is described with the features of an Anzu-bird. In Mesopotamian mythology this bird signified the thundercloud and embodies the four winds.

Ezek 1 recounts the coming of God in his throne chariot. He is accompanied by four attendants, beings composed of animal and human features. These "animal beings" (ḥayyōt) embody the four winds. We can here observe a general correspondence to the imagery in the Vision of the Nether World. They both relate to the same kind of mythical imaginations: in both instances the ruling

Reconstruction	4 Ezra 13	Dan 7
The coming of the flying man from the underworld, embodying the four winds, accompanied by the four animal beings	A flying man coming like a wind from the sea Hostile multitude from the four quarters of the earth	Four winds of heaven 4 "animal beings" coming from the sea. Last monster embodies two individuals
Throne-scene: the ruling god		Throne-scene: the ruling god
Judgement: visionary and rebel king	Destruction of the hostile multitude	Judgement: rebel king
Era of salvation: the enthronement of the man, his universal and everlasting kingdom	Era of salvation: vindication of the victims	Era of salvation: the coming of the man with clouds, enthronement, universal and everlasting kingdom

god is surrounded by composite beings; in both instances there is a connection to the four wind, in Ezek directly through the four animal beings, in the Akkadian vision indirectly through the Anzu-bird symbolism, which is connected to several of the monsters as well as the man.

Zech 6 demonstrates that the four winds of heaven are connected to Yahweh as his agents in the Jewish tradition. Ezek 1 is therefore not unique at this point.

4 Ezra 13 recounts the coming of the flying man from the sea. He comes like a wind-spirit. The imagery relates to the man seen in

the Vision of the Nether world.[191] The man, likened to the Anzu-bird, standing in the nether world, has become the flying man from the sea. The vision continues to recount the appearance of an immense hostile multitude from the four quarters of the earth. The imagery is not totally unrelated to the other visions. The four quarters are called *'arba' rūḥīn*, in Aramaic, cf. Enastr[b] 23, lines 2 and 4,[192] a phrase that also means "the four winds", cf. Dan 7,2. The four winds are also connected to the four quarters of the earth, cf. En 18,2-3. But the use of the imagery in 4 Ezra 13 differs from the other visions. The vision introduces a sharp contrast between the man on the one side and the multitude from the four quarters on the other.

Dan 7 contains the same basic imagery as the Vision of the Nether World and Ezek 1: The four winds of heaven and the animal beings. The four winds must be read in the light of the Anzu-bird imagery attached to the man in the Akkadian vision and the flying man in 4 Ezra 13. This means that the four winds belong together with the clouds and the coming of the man at the end of the vision in Dan 7. Thus the coming of the man is signalled even in the opening of the vision. The four animal beings correspond externally in two directions. They correspond on the one hand to the four animal beings in Ezek 1, which are benevolent beings; they correspond on the other hand to the hostile multitude in 4 Ezra 13. The vision of the Nether World is ambiguous at this point. The monsters are on the one hand the servants of the ruling god, on the other, dangerous malevolent beings contrasted to the man. Within this vision both aspects could be united because the monsters, the ruling god and the man were all a threatening omen for the visionary, since he was involved in the judgement. 4 Ezra 13 and Dan 7 differ in this respect. Here the visionaries are not involved in the course of events, and the judgement and the destruction strike other figures of the visionary imagery.

This seems to be the crucial point in the transition of the traditions from the Akkadian vision to Dan 7. At one point in the history of tradition the vision changed character from a vision which also foretold the visionary's own future, to a vision only foretelling

---

191   Cf. above, pp. 530ff.
192   Cf. Milik, The Books of Enoch, p. 289.

someone else's future. This change led to an emphasis on the contrast already contained in the Akkadian vision, the contrast between the man and the monsters. The monsters became the "enemy" of the man. It also implied the creation of a new internal correspondence within the visionary imagery. The Akkadian vision contained an internal correspondence between the mythical described man in the vision and the ideal king in the interpretation given by Nergal. The change of the vision implied one more step: The rulers in the judgement scene were brought in relation to the monsters seen previously in the vision. The Akkadian vision itself may give a hint about how this could have happened. The first part of the scenario ends up by recounting a monster composed of two bodies and thereafter the man. Nergal's speech starts with the ideal king, who was the man, and proceeds with two closely related rulers. The next step implied that the two rulers were identified as the siamese monster, which is in fact the model we find in Dan 7,7-8.11, if we exclude the historical references. The question in then whether this change took place at the moment of transition from a "Mesopotamian" to a Jewish setting, or whether it happened at a later date in the Jewish transmission.

The question is not difficult to answer. The link between the monsters and rulers is signalled in Dan 7 through v. 17 in the interpretation, which belonged to the Macedonian stage of the vision. Moreover, if we are right that the vision in its point of transition reflected the same historical situation as Dan 2 and 4-5, it would be reasonable to assume the same basic structure. In Dan 4 and 5 the structure is simplest. In Dan 4 Nebuchadnezzar's vision of the cutting down of the tree signified that he would lose his kingdom. In Dan 5 Belshazzar's vision of the inscription on the wall signified the fall of the Babylonian empire. In Dan 2 we are inclined to see a similar simple structure in the original vision. The crushing of the statue signified the loss of empire. This simple structure was then extended by the scheme of four in the same manner as Dan 7. In Dan 2; 4 and 5 the ruler sees his own future as in the Vision of the Nether World. We assume that the Jewish vision underlying Dan 7 once had a similar structure.

We have previously argued that the Akkadian vision could well be read in the light of the change between the Babylonian and Persian empire, substituting Belshazzar, Nabonidus and Cyrus for the three protagonists in the Assyrian setting, Ashurbanipal, Esarhaddon and Sennacherib. If so, Belshazzar must be regarded as the visionary in this setting. It is to be noted that Dan 7,1 dates the vision of the reign of Belshazzar, and so presupposes the same historical situation behind both Dan 7 and 5.

These considerations lead to the tentative conclusion that the visions that once formed the background of the Aramaic part of the Book of Daniel are to be regarded as "dreams of destruction".[193] The ruler was forewarned through these dreams that the end of his kingship was at hand, either as a warning, or as an irrevocable decision made by the highest God.

With regard to the original shape of Dan 7 this would demand the structure assumed under the heading "reconstruction" in the scheme above. In the first section of the vision we have assumed that the coming of the man was more clearly articulated than in Dan 7 in analogy to 4 Ezra 13. Belshazzar thus sees the coming of the man from the underworld, embodying the force of the four winds and accompanied by the demons of the underworld. This vision is a signal about the final fate of his and his father, Nabonidus', kingdom. In the court scene the ruling god decides their destruction, which then follows. Thereafter the man is given everlasting and universal kingship.

We have argued that the man at this stage of the vision could have been identified as Cyrus, or at least been inspired by his rise to power. The statement in the Akkadian vision that the ideal king was under the protection of the Elamite gods makes this interpretation possible. But there are features in the vision that oppose an identification with a historical king. The reason is that 4 Ezra 13, Dan 7, and most probably the original Jewish vision underlying these, combine two elements of the Akkadian vision in a special way. The first element is that the vision could be interpreted in such a way that the death-spirit of the ideal king should take revenge on the rebel rulers.[194] The other is that the description of the kingship of the ideal king could be interpreted as a prophecy about a kingship to come.[195] These two elements are reflected in the first and final sequences of the Jewish visions.

193 Cf. above, pp. 363ff, 446f.
194 Cf. above, pp. 437f.
195 Cf. above, pp. 435ff.

The final sequence, the kingdom of the ideal king, could easily be applied to or inspired by a historical ruler, for instance Cyrus. But the connection between this sequence and the first creates difficulties, because this connection implies some sort of ascension of the future king from the underworld. It is difficult to figure out how this feature was interpreted when these two elements were combined. We have to remember that the vision was not created on the basis of Cyrus rise to power, but applied to or inspired by this situation. A direct correspondence between the visionary imagery and the historical situation is therefore not to be expected, but there must have existed some ideas about a general correspondence between the imagery and the historical events.

We have previously called attention to the fact that Cyrus was regarded by the Marduk priesthood as a legitimate Babylonian king over against the rebellious Nabonidus.[196] The spirit ascending from the nether world and manifesting itself in the new kingdom, could have signified this connection between Cyrus and the earlier Babylonian kings.[197] If so, the vision would express the belief that Cyrus ruled through the appreciation and under the protection of the death-spirit of the earlier Babylonian kings.

We have tried to establish a diachronical model of how the Vision of the Nether World developed into Dan 7. Needless to say, the model is hypothetical. But nevertheless, it is based on the criteria we have at our disposal, concerning both the historiographical patterns and the visionary imageries. We do not think that the original Jewish vision existed in written form. The vision in Dan 7 is in its structure a uniform composition, which does not indicate that it is a secondary elaboration of an earlier written source. More probably the original Jewish vision was transmitted orally in Jewish circles that had close contacts with the Mesopotamian milieu from which the vision first was adopted. The transformation of the vision into Dan 7 indicates a change of setting. The vision was loosened from its Mesopotamian context and given a new meaning in relation to the Jewish faith in the Macedonian period.

---

196   Cf. above, pp. 469ff, 490f.
197   For the importance of the appreciation of the royal predecessors, cf. above, pp. 406f.

IV
The Vision in its Jewish Setting

a) The Problem

The traditions derived from the Vision of the Nether World introduced a strange and enigmatic image into Jewish theology. How was this image understood when it was detached from its Mesopotamian environment and transposed to a more genuine Jewish experience of life and history?

We have already touched the problem at various points. The traditions from the Akkadian vision were interpreted according to the same scheme of history as Dan 2: Four kingdoms, the last one divided, followed by an era of salvation.[1] The concept of an ideal king, ruling in this era of salvation, was also well known by the Jews through the Messianic prophecies.[2] We have also observed that both in the oracles of Jeremiah and of Deutero-Isaiah gentile rulers, respectively Nebuchadnezzar and Cyrus, could be described in idealized terms as the agents of Yahweh. Cyrus was even described as the anointed of Yahweh, an appellation commonly reserved for the Davidic kings.[3] So there existed a framework that corresponded to some features of the new image.

But not all features of the new image fit this framework. It is even correct to state that the most distinctive characteristics of the man seen in the vision did not fit the framework. The man is manifestly a transcendent figure, he is associated with death and underworld, he stands by the throne of God. The vision of his appearance is a sign of liberation for the oppressed people, because the oppressor will be destroyed.

1 Cf. above, pp. 484ff.
2 Cf. above, note 48, p. 488.
3 Cf. above, pp. 499f, 546f.

This vision of the transcendent man by the throne of God was a new image in Jewish religious thought. It did not emerge from a reinterpretation of older Jewish traditions, but was adopted from a foreign culture. The people who adopted the image and brought it in direct relation to their experiences in the Macedonian period must, however, have had religious categories that in one way or another corresponded to this new image. A new image must have some relation to older images in order to be reproduced. This leads to the question about the religious milieu in which Dan 7 was composed.

We shall, however, not start this discussion with a final answer about when the vision in Dan 7 was composed, — whether it happened during the reign of Antiochus IV, or whether those passages that clearly refer to this king, vv. 7-8. 11a, were added later, — an observation which would allow a dating earlier in the Macedonian period. We shall rather ask about the context of Dan 7 in contemporary religious thought, which is not to be regarded as a mere reflection of the contemporary historical events, but is rooted in earlier traditions, an observation whose validity should have been sufficiently demonstrated in the previous chapters.

The discovery and publication of the Aramaic fragments from Qumran to the Books of Enoch have created a new opportunity to analyze the evolution of the Jewish apocalyptic literature, a genre to which the Book of Daniel belongs. Previously the Book of Daniel was often held to be the earliest apocalyptic work. The Aramaic Enoch fragments demonstrate that at least two Enochic books were composed before the final redaction of the Book of Daniel, namely the Astronomical Book and the Book of Watchers both to be dated in the third century B.C., and that one book was composed about the same time as Daniel in its final form, the Book of Dreams.[4] This sheds new light on the origin of apocalyptic in general and the composing of the Book of Daniel in particular. The apocalyptic way of interpreting reality was not a result of one decisive historical experience, for instance the persecutions under Antiochus IV, but was developed during a long period. The Book of Daniel is not to be regarded as the composition which gave rise to apocalyptic literature, but emerged in a

4 Cf. Part I, pp. 31f, 110f.

religious context where apocalyptic traditions were transmitted and apocalyptic literature written quite apart from the Danielic traditions.

The central figure in these early apocalyptic traditions and compositions was Enoch. The image of Enoch as the primary revealer of the divine secrets was also a new image in Jewish religion, and like the image of the transcendent man this image was also adopted from Mesopotamian traditions.[5] This leads us to our next question: Can the Enochic traditions shed light on the religious context of Dan 7 and the understanding of the image of the transcendent man?

b) Dan 7 and the Book of Watchers

1.   Protagonists and Scenario

1.1   Enoch and the Son of Man

As previously stated, two Enochic books were written in the third century B.C., the Astronomical Book and the Book of Watchers. The former contains mostly astronomical calculations with no resemblances to Dan 7, the latter tells the story about the watchers who in primeval time descended on earth to bring the human race the divine secrets. It is this story which is of special interest in regard to Dan 7.

The protagonist of the story, as it is unfolded in the whole book, is Enoch, who is well known from a broad current of Jewish traditions as the primary revealer of the wisdom of God. This Enoch figure was introduced in Judaism in the fourth century B.C., and his background is Mesopotamian.[6]

Ultimately the Jewish image of Enoch was based on two Mesopotamian prototypes: The seventh primeval king, Enmeduranki, and the first or seventh (the order differs) primeval sage, Uanadapa. Both figures are connected to the origin of wisdom in the human world.

---

5   This should be amply demonstrated in Part I. I refer to the concluding chapter, pp. 319ff.
6   For the following brief outline of the background of the Enoch figure I refer to the analysis in Part I.

Even though the Danielic and the Enochic traditions have the same geographical provenance, they relate to different Mesopotamian traditions. There is no common source for the Son of Man and Enoch. The question is, however, whether the images connected to the two separate figures through the history of transmission could have been interrelated.

There are some features belonging to the background of the Enoch figure that have affinity to the Vision of the Nether World and Dan 7. The first of the Mesopotamian prototypes, Enmeduranki, was a king who, like the Son of Man, was brought into the divine assembly in heaven.[7] The other prototype, Uanadapa, became a symbol of divine wisdom, which formed the basis for the boastful claim of divine insight by the Assyrian kings.[8] Their comparison with the wisdom of Uanadapa lies implicit in the description of the rebel king in the Vision of the Nether World,[9] and is made explicit in the description of Nabonidus in the Verse Account.[10] It was also the ultimate source for the hubris of the rebel king in the Book of Daniel.[11] In the Mesopotamian mythical tradition Uanadapa and the other primeval sages were located in Apsu, the subterranean water deep.[12] According to Berossos Uanadapa (Greek: "Oannes") ascended from the sea to teach men the benefits of culture.[13] In the Vision of the Nether World the man and the monsters were located in the underworld, in Dan 7 the monsters ascend from the sea, and in 4 Ezra 13 the man comes from the sea.[14]

These similarities do not demonstrate a dependence of Dan 7 on Mesopotamian primeval traditions, nor do they indicate that the composer of Dan 7 was directly inspired by these traditions. But they could have facilitated a fusion of Danielic and Enochic traditions, given that the Danielic transmitters had any knowledge

---

7   Cf. Part I, pp. 185ff.
8   Cf. above, pp. 427f, and Part I, p. 189.
9   Cf. above, pp. 426ff.
10   Cf. above, pp. 429f, and Part I, pp. 212f.
11   Cf. above, pp. 460ff, and below, p. 582.
12   Cf. above, pp. 428f, and Part I, pp. 197ff.
13   Cf. Part I, pp. 200f.
14   This feature was by H.L. Jansen, Die Henochgestalt, Oslo 1939, pp. 105ff, taken as an indication that the Son of Man was patterned on the god-man Ea-Oannes (Adapa). According to the present knowledge of the sources this theory can no longer be maintained, cf. Part I, pp. 28ff.

about this Mesopotamian material. This can not be proved, but not excluded either, since, as we have seen, the Danielic transmitters were well acquainted with Mesopotamian traditions. The final answer about a fusion of Danielic and Enochic traditions must, however, be based on a direct comparison of Dan 7 and Enochic texts.

The Son of Man and Enoch have one distinct characteristic in common: They were both brought into the assembly of God. In my article "Henoch under Menschensohn" I have analyzed the relationship between En 14, where Enoch is brought to heaven in a vision, and Dan 7. In the analysis I also included Ezek 1, because of the resemblance both to Dan 7 and En 14.[15] The analysis gave the following results:

The visionary imagery of En 14 was directly based on Ezekiel's vision in Ezek 1.[16] Between Dan 7 and Ezek 1 there were corresponding features in the visionary imagery, but not of the kind that suggested a direct dependence of Dan 7 on the text of Ezek 1.[17] The correspondences between Dan 7 and En 14 were so close that they indicated a literary dependence.[18] The analysis thus demonstrated a diachronic model where En 14 depended on Ezek 1 and Dan 7 on En 14.[19] The resemblances between Dan 7 and Ezek 1 are best explained on the one hand as effected through En 14 as a connecting link, on the other hand as the adoption of similar motifs from the same religious environment.[20]

The closest parallels between Dan 7 and En 14 are in the throne-scenes, Dan 7,9-10.13-14 and En 14,18-25. A comparison between these two sequences demonstrates not only the same imagery, but also the use of the same words and phrases.[21]

---

15   H.S. Kvanvig, "Henoch under der Menschensohn".
16   Kvanvig, op.cit., pp. 4-15.
17   Kvanvig, op.cit., pp. 15-20.
18   Kvanvig, op.cit., pp. 21-33. This opinion has also been advanced by T.F. Glasson, The Second Advent: The Origin of the NT Doctrine, London 1945, 3rd ed. 1963, and in "The Son of Man Imagery": Enoch xiv and Dan vii", NTS 23, 1977, pp. 82-90.
19   Kvanvig, op.cit., pp. 34f.
20   Cf. above, pp. 509ff, and pp. 549ff.
21   The Aramaic text to En 14 is mostly a retranslation of the Greek text evaluated in the light of the Aramaic fragments to the Books of Enoch and in the light of the Ethiopic translation. The Greek text is edited by M. Black, Apocalypsis Henochi Graece, Leiden 1970. The Ethiopic text is edited by R.C. Charles, The Ethiopic Version of the Book of Enoch ... together with the fragmentary Greek and Latin Versions, Oxford 1906; and by M. A. Knibb, The Ethiopic Book of Enoch. A New Edition in the Light of the Aramaic Dead Sea Frag-

Dan	Hen
חזה הוית עד די כרסון רמיו	חזית ואדיקת כרסא רם
ועתיק יומין יתב	ורבותא רבתא יתבת
לבושה כתלג חור	לבושה... חור מן תלגא רבא
כרסיה שביבין די נור נהר די נור...נפק	ומן תחות כרסא נפקין שבלין די נור דלק
גלגלוהי נור דלק	גלגל כשמשא מנירא
נהר די נור...מן קדמוהי	נור רב קדמוהי יקומון
ורבו רבון קדמוהי יקומון	ורבו רבון קדמוהי יקומון
וקדמוהי הקרבוהי	חד קדישין הקרבני

I looked until thrones were set in place	I looked and I saw a high throne
An Ancient of Days took his seat	The Great (old) Majesty took his seat
His raiment was like the white snow	His raiment . . . was whiter than any snow
His throne flames of fire, a river of fire . . . went out	From underneath the throne streams of burning fire went out
Its wheels burning fires	A wheel like the shining sun
A river of fire . . . from before him	A great fire stood before him

ments, Vol I: Text and Apparatus, Vol II: Introduction, Translation and Commentary, Oxford 1978. Traces of the vision in Aramaic are found on the fragment 4Q En^c1vi, Milik, The Books of Enoch, pp. 192-99. A synopsis comparing the Aramaic and Greek texts to Dan 7 and En 14 is given in Kvanvig, "Henoch und der Menschensohn", pp. 24-7.

Ten thousand times ten thousand stood   Ten thousand times ten thousand stood
before him   before him

They brought him near to him   One of the holy ones brought me near

The similarities between the passages are so close as to consider a
direct quoting:

Line 1:   Visionary formula + identical noun.
"   2:   Appellation of God + identical verb.
"   3:   Identical description of God + comparison with identical adjective and
          noun.
"   4:   Similar subject + identical verb.
"   5:   Identical subject + comparison with similar content.
"   6:   Similar subject + identical attribute.
"   7:   Identical wording
"   8:   Subject of similar content + identical verb.

There are reasons to think that the appellations of God in the
second line are closer than it seems. In Dan 7,9 the appellation
עתיק יומין, 'attīq yōmīn, "ancient of days", has caused great
uncertainty among researchers, since it is unique to this text. In En
14,20 the appellation is translated to Greek ἡ δόξα ἡ μεγάλη and
to Ethiopic 'ābiya sĕbḥat, both meaning "Great Glory" or
"Majesty". The adjective must certainly be retranslated רב, rab,
"great" in Aramaic. On the basis of En 22,14, where also the
Aramaic text is extant, 4Q En^d1xi, line 2 (Milik, p. 218), the noun
must be retranslated רבותא, rebūtā, "greatness". The Aramaic
appellation in En 14,20 is accordingly רבותא רבתא, rebūtā
rabbetā.
There are two significant observations to be made concerning this
appellation. Firstly, the use of this adjective and noun in appellations of God are frequent in Jewish texts. They are mostly used in
contexts where God is praised as the Lord of time and history. His
greatness lies in his capability to see the whole of history, from the
distant past to the present and future.[22] Secondly, the adjective
rab occurs in several Aramaic languages as well as in Palestinian
Aramaic in the meaning "old".[23] In these cases the adjective

22   Cf. the references in Kvanvig, op.cit., p. 28.
23   Cf. the references in J.T. Milik, Recherches d'Épigraphie Proche-Orientale
I, Paris 1972, pp. 28, 98f; and H. Ingholt, "Some Sculptures from the Tomb of
Malkû at Palmyra", Mélanges offerts à Kazimierz Michalowski, Warszaw 1966,
pp. 457-76, pp. 470-6. For references from Palestinian Aramaic, cf. Kvanvig,
op.cit., p. 29.

refers to old people, i.e. *rab* functions semantically like German "gross" in "Grossvater" and English "grand" in "grandfather". A Hebrew expression comes close to this usage; in Job 15,10 old people are called *kabbīr yāmīm*, "great on days", i.e. "ancient of days".

These two aspects are united in the description of God in the Targum of Job, 11QtgJob, col. 28, lines 3-4 (Fitzmyer/Harrington, p. 34):

הא אלהא רב הוא יומוהי סגיא(יא לא נו)דע
ומנין שנוהי די לא סוף

"Look, God is great, and his many days [we do not kn]ow, and the number of his years (is) endless". Here the greatness of God is connected to his "many days" and his "number of years", i.e. the greatness of God lies in his unlimited age. And because of this unlimited age he is able to overlook the whole history.

This explains how *rebūtā rabbetā* in En 14,20 could have been transformed to *'attīq yōmīn* in Dan 7,9. The "Great Majesty" could be read as the "Old Majesty", in the meaning "the Majesty of distant times". Especially because the composer of Dan 7 was dealing with the secrets of history and wished to underscore that the Ancient of Days was the Lord of the whole history.

Dan 7,9-10.13-14 combine two motifs from En 14: The vision of God in his throne chamber, and the arrival of the man, in Dan 7 *bar 'ănāš*, in En 15,1 "man of righteousness", *'ănāš quštā*, to this throne-chamber. This combination is only known from these two texts. The other throne-visions known from the Old Testament and from the Jewish tradition, such as 1 Kings 22,19-22; Is 6; Ezek 1; En 60,1-4, do not contain the motif of arrival to the throne-chamber. The Levi traditions, relating the ascension of Levi to heaven, cf. the Greek Testament of Levi, 2-5, and the fragmentary Aramaic Testament, 4Q TLevi ar[a], col. ii (Fitzmyer/Harrington, p. 90), do not contain a throne-vision. Accordingly there is no evidence to claim that En 14 and Dan 7 both relate to an underlying pattern, because such a pattern can not be proved to have existed.

This observation is confirmed through the analysis of the background of En 14. Although this text has adopted the general characteristics of the Gattung "throne-vision", the text is not merely a compilation of these general characteristics. En 14 was written under the direct influence of Ezek 1. The special features of En 14 are brought about by the fusion of features taken from Ezek 1 with the core of the Enochic traditions, namely the ascension of the seventh patriarch to heaven, already mentioned in Gen 5,24. We must therefore conclude that both direct comparison between En 14 and Dan 7, as well as comparison with other texts, demonstrate that Dan 7 is dependent on En 14.

This dependence is crucial for our understanding of how the vision underlying Dan 7 was interpreted when Dan 7 was composed. The composer had received a vision of a transcendent man by the throne of God, to which there were no parallels in the main current of Jewish traditions derived from the Old Testament period. The only analogy was the Enoch figure, also recently adopted into the Jewish traditions by the Jews in the Mesopotamian diaspora. The composer of Dan 7 interpreted the vision of the transcendent man in the light of the visionary imagery of the transcendent Enoch.

The comparison does not allow the conclusion that the composer of Dan 7 regarded the Son of Man and Enoch identical. The Son of Man has retained his royal characteristics from the Vision of the Nether World. He is not portrayed as a sage, as is Enoch. The transference of the Enochic imagery to the Son of Man demonstrates first of all that the Danielic composer needed the Enochic category of "one particular man staying with God in heaven" to express his own vision in a genuinely Jewish context. But the transference of this Enochic concept to the Son of Man leads to the next question, whether there are further contacts between the phraseology and structure of thought in Dan 7 and the Enochic traditions.

1.2   The Holy Ones

The phrase "holy ones", which plays an important role in the interpretation of the vision in Dan 7, cf. vv. 18.21.22.25.27, occurs many times in the Book of Watchers. We list the occurrences below.

En 1,2 = 4Q En^a1i, line 2 (Milik, p. 142):

ומן מלי (עירין) וקדישין

"and from the words of [the watchers] and holy ones"

En 1,9 = 4Q En^c1i, line 15 (Milik, p. 184):

עם רבו)את קדישו(הי

"with thousa]nds of [His] holy ones"

En 9,3 = 4Q En^a1iv, line 10 (Milik, p. 158):

ואמרו לקדי)שי ש(מיה

"and they said to the hol]y ones of h[eaven"[24]

En 12,2: Gr^{Pan} reads: μετὰ τῶν ἀγίων, "with the holy ones"

En 14,23: Gr^{Pan} reads: οἱ . ἅγιοι τῶν ἀγγέλων, "the holy ones of the angels"

En 14,25: Gr^{Pan} reads: εἷς τῶν ἀγίων, "one of the holy ones"

En 22,6 = 4Q En^e1xxii, line 5 (Milik, p. 229):

לרפא)ל לעירא וקדישא

"to Raphae]l, the watcher and holy one"

In all cases the holy ones are heavenly beings. They have the following functions:
* They are members of the heavenly assembly, En 12,2; 14,23.25.
* They are mediators between god and man, En 1,2; 9,3; 14,25; 22,6.
* They are active in the judgement, En 1,9; 9,3.

If for the present we exclude Dan 7, the designation "holy one" is attested in two contexts in the Book of Daniel. In Dan 4,10.20 the angelic being announcing judgement over Nebuchadnezzar is called עיר וקדיש, "a watcher and a holy one". In 4,14 it is stated that this announcement is according to the decision of the קדישין, "the holy ones". In Dan 8,13 the angelic beings, who act as interpreters of the vision, are designated with קדוש, "holy one".

---

24 The Aramaic traces seem to indicate the longer text, which is preserved in Ethiopic, but not in Greek.

The first attestation equals the third function in the Book of
Watchers, the second equals the second function.

We shall later return to the question of the meaning of the
designation in Dan 7. But so far both the occurrence of the
designation in the two related vision, En 14 and Dan 7, and the
other correspondences between the Book of Daniel and the Book
of Watchers, indicate some sort of connection between the groups
designated in this way in both texts.

1.3   The Sinners and the Giants

The Book of Watchers draws a contrast between the holy ones on
the one hand, and the watchers, their offspring the giants and an
unidentified group of "sinners" on the other. Here also there are
correspondences to Dan 7.

In the scene of judgement in En 1,9 the sinners are accused
because of:

כול מלין) רברבן וקשין (די מללו כלוהי

"[all] the great and hard [words that they spoke against him",[25]
4Q En^{c}1i, line 17 (Milik, p. 184). The same theme is taken up
again in Enoch's speech of judgement in En 5,4:

ותע)ברון עלוהי רברבן וקשין<בפום> טמתכן

"[but] you [tr]ansgress against Him with great and hard (words)
with your unclean <mouth>",[26] 4Q En^{a}1ii, line 13 (Milik, p. 146).

Dan 7 has a similar wording in the description of the rebellion of
the eleventh horn: ופם ממלל רברבן, "and a mouth that spoke
great (words)", v. 8; מן קל מליא רברבתא די קרנא ממללה,
"because of the sound of the great (words) that the horn spoke",
v. 11.

The devastating acts of the giants are according to Gr^{Pan} described in the following way:

οἱ γίγαντες ἐτόλμησαν επ᾿αὐτούς, καὶ κατησθίοσαν
τοὺς ανθρώπους,

---

25   Cf. Gr^{Pan}: "and the hard words which they have spoken". The verse is also
quoted in the New Testament, Jude 15: "and concerning all the hard things
which the impious sinners have spoken against him". The Ethiopic translation
differs both from the Aramaic original and from the two Greek translations.

26   We emend bjwm to bpwm with Milik, The Books of Enoch, p. 146, and
Knibb, The Ethiopic Book of Enoch II, p. 65.

"the giants turned against them and devoured mankind", En 7,4.
And subsequently: καὶ ἀλλήλων τὰς σάρκας κατεσθίειν,
"and to devour one another's flesh", En 7,5. Only traces remain of
the Aramaic original, but it seems clearly to have contained the
same text:

והוו גבריא) קשרין לקטלה לאנשא ו(למכל אכון,

"But the giants conspired to slay men and to devour them", 4Q
Enᵃ1 iii, lines 18-19 (Milik, p. 150);   ולמכל בשר(הן אלין לאלין,
"and to devour the flesh [of one another", line 21.

This description of the huge devastating monsters in the Book of
Watchers is not far removed from the description of the monsters
in Dan 7. The third monster is commanded: קומי אכלי בשר שגיא,
"rise up, devour much flesh!", v. 5. About the last monster it is
said אכלה, "it devoured", v. 7.

1.4   The Punishment

The watchers are cast down into the nether world. There they will
stay until the day of judgement. The punishment is described as
burning in fire, Grᴾᵃⁿ to En 10,13:

τότε ἀπαχθήσονται εἰς τὸ χάος τοῦ πυρὸς, "then they shall
be led off to the abyss of fire"; and to En 10,6:

καὶ ἐν τῇ ἡμέρᾳ τῆς μεγάλης τῆς κρίσεως ἀπαχθήσεται
εἰς τὸν ἐνπυρισμόν, "and on the great day of judgement he
shall be led off to the fire".

This comes close to the way the punishment is described in Dan 7:

קטילת חיוא וחובד גשמה והיבת ליקדת אשא,

"the beast was killed and its body destroyed and given to the
burning fire", v. 11b.

In En 18,8-16 the fire is connected both to the throne of God and
to the punishment of the watchers: "But the middle one reached to
heaven like the throne of God, like alabaster, and the summit of
the throne was of sapphire. And I saw a flaming fire" (according
to Grᴾᵃⁿ), En 18,8-9a; "I saw there seven stars like great burning
mountains ... The angel said: 'This place is the end of heaven and
earth: this has become a prison for the stars and the host of
heaven" (according to Grᴾᵃⁿ), 18,13-14. The same connection
between the throne of God and the fire of punishment occurs in
Dan 7,10-11.

1.5   The Salvation

The era of salvation comes both in En 10,17-11,2 and En 25,3-4 immediately after the final judgement. This is also the case in Dan 7,14. In this era of salvation all nations shall worship the Lord: "And all children of men shall become righteous, and all nations shall offer adoration and shall praise me, and all shall worship me", En 10,21.[27] This corresponds to what is said about the dominion of the Son of Man: "all peoples and all nations and tongues shall worship him", Dan 7,14.

These similarities to various themes in the Book of Watchers indicate a correspondence not only between Dan 7 and En 14, but also in a broader scale between Dan 7 and the Book of Watchers as a whole. We are inclined to think that the composer of Dan 7 was both acquainted with parts at least of the Book of Watchers in written form, and that he belonged to a milieu not far removed from the group behind this book.

2.   The Structure of Thought in Dan 7 and the Book of Watchers

The similarities in words and phrases between the two compositions do not indicate simply that Dan 7 contains parallels on the surface of the text. On the contrary, the two compositions seem to deal with the same problems of reality, and to work along the same lines in their interpretations of reality.

The Watcher story (En 6-11) which constitutes the basic composition of the book, on which the later parts are dependent,[28] was most probably written during the Diadochan wars at the end of the fourth century.[29] The composer interpreted the suffering during these wars by using the story about the primeval catastrophe as a mirror. The retelling of the ancient story also implied a reinterpretation. The story about the sons of the gods in Gen

---

27   Milik claims to see the traces of "shall become righteous", in 4Q En^{a}1vi, line 4 (Milik, p. 162). This agrees with the Ethiopic translation. Gr^{P}an reads <u>latreuontes</u>, "serve".

28   Cf. Part I, pp. 85f.

29   Part I, pp. 95ff.

6,1-4 and the Flood story were combined in a way that presupposed the Mesopotamian Atra-Ḥasis.[30] The result was that the catastrophe struck divine beings and not ordinary humans. The human beings were given the role of those who suffered under the crimes of the devastating divine forces. This new structure of the primeval catastrophe resembled other mythical stories about divine and semi-divine beings dispatched to the nether world in primeval time, known from Canaanite, Hittite and Greek religion.[31] The closest parallel is, however, the Mesopotamian traditions about the apkallu's, the divine sages, who lived on earth in primeval time, but were dispatched to the abyss in connection with the flood, and since then stayed in the abyss.[32] The technique of narration behind the Watcher story, using a story about the primeval catastrophe as a mirror to interpret present reality, has a parallel in the Mesopotamian Poem of Erra.[33]

The composer of the Watcher story and the later composers of the whole Book of Watchers accordingly utilized underlying traditions dealing with underworld-creatures and monstrous giants to interpret the historical circumstances in their own time. The devastating military, political and cultural impact of the new Hellenistic rulers, fighting for supremacy over Palestine, was regarded as an embodiment of underworld forces.

When we read the Book of Watchers in this perspective, we see that the difference to Dan 7 lies not in the actual message of the composition, but in the material used. The composers of the Book of Watchers combined the ancient story about the primeval catastrophe with imaginations about the underworld and applied this material to their own time. The composer of Dan 7 used a vision of the nether world as the underlying source. Both composers did, however, portray the new Hellenistic rulers in the imagery of monsters and underworld forces. In both compositions the heathen military, political and cultural might is said to embody demonic power.

As a contrast to these demonic forces both Dan 7 and the Book of Watchers introduce the holy ones. Their roles are not described in

30   Cf. for the following, Part I, pp. 286ff.
31   Part I, pp. 296ff.
32   Part I, pp. 300ff.
33   Part I, pp. 315ff.

exactly the same way, but in both texts they are involved in the process of bringing forth the era of salvation. The two protagonists of the compositions act on their side: Enoch, staying in heaven with the holy ones (En 12,1-2), and later ascending to the divine assembly in a vision (En 14), acts as God's agent in pronouncing judgement over the watchers and giants (En 15-16); the Son of Man enters the divine assembly and receives the everlasting kingdom together with the holy ones after the final judgement.

The eschatological drama has two phases: First the destruction and punishment of the evil forces governing present reality (En 10,1-16a; Dan 7,11), then the outbreak of the era of salvation for all nations (En 10,16b-11,2; Dan 7,14.18).

The resemblance in wording and structure of thought does not however, mean that there are no differences between the two compositions. Besides the fact that the compositions recount two different stories, at least three significant differences can be noted:

1. The scenery of the throne-visions: En 14,18-25 describe the divine assembly in the heavenly temple, while Dan 7,9-10 describe the final judgement, taking place in a court-room.
2. The protagonists: Enoch is comissioned as a messenger of judgement, En 15,1-2, while the Son of Man is a king, who received a kingdom, 7,14.
3. The holy ones: In En 14,23 these are serving God in the heavenly temple, while in Dan 7,18 they receive the kingdom.

In the two first cases we see clearly that although the composer of Dan 7 has "borrowed" the language from En 14, the original meaning from the Vision of the Nether World is retained: The scene of the ruling god is still a court scene, the unique man i still a king. This departure from the Book of Watchers even in the sequences where a dependence can be demonstrated, cautions against using the Book of Watchers wholly to determine the content of Dan 7. This is also true of the third point, the holy ones. Even though the same term is used in both texts, their function is described differently. And just as the man entering before the throne of God in Dan 7 is not Enoch, but the ideal king, so the holy ones, occurring within the same scenario, are not necessarily angels as in En 14, but can be another or a broader group of beings. The very differences from En 14 within sequences dependent on this text, may demonstrate the scope of Dan 7. This scope seems intimately connected to the identity of the holy ones.

What we can conclude so far, is that the Book of Watchers reflect a milieu, whose religion and political attitudes coincide with Dan 7. This confirms our previous attempt to establish a diachronic model of the growth of Dan 7. In this model we assumed that the contrast between the man and the monsters was emphasized by the composer of Dan 7 over against the previous vision by the identification of monsters and kings.[34] In our analysis of the relationship to the Book of Watchers we have noticed that this contrast-motif, where political power is clothed in demonic imagery, is one of the basic characteristics uniting the two compositions.

c) The Son of Man and the Holy Ones

1. The Grammatical Problem

Unfortunately the identity of the group called the "holy ones" is just as obscure as the identity of the Son of Man. A series of problems are involved. They begin with the grammatical meaning of the phrases where the word "holy" occur.

Simple קדישין, qaddīšīn, is used in Dan 7,21a and 22c. The construct state קדישי עליונין, qaddīšē 'älyōnīn, occurs in 7,18a.22b.25b, and the double construct עם קדישי עליונין, 'am qaddīšē 'älyōnīn, in 7,27a. In the Hebrew part of the book the construct עם קדישים, 'am qᵉdošīm, occurs in 8,24 and עם קדש, 'am qodäš, in 12,7. Individual figures are described as Aramaic קדיש/קדישין, qaddīš/qaddīšīn, in 4,10.14.20, and as Hebrew קדוש, qādōš, in 8,13. Gods are described as qaddīšīn in 4,5.6.15; 5,11.

The simple noun qaddīšīn (pl) means "holy ones". The construct qaddīšē 'älyōnīn is more obscure. The construct is usually translated as genitivus possessivus in accordance with LXX ἅγιοι ὑπίστου, "the holy ones of the Most High". But this is not strictly the literal meaning. 'älyōnīn is plural, in isolation it means "the highest ones". By those who translate singular "Most High" the plural grammatical form is either explained as an attraction (from the plural qaddīšē), or taken as a pluralis majestatis

---

34 Cf. above, pp. 549ff.

influenced through Hebrew grammar.[35] But these explanations are
not quite convincing.

With a singular meaning *'älyonīn* would be equivalent to singular
עליא, *'illāyā*, "the Most High", which occurs several times in the
Book of Daniel, 4,14.21.22.24.31; 7,25.; and also in other Jewish
writings, 4Q Amram[b], frg. 2, line 6 (Fitzmyer/Harrington, p. 94);
1Q ApGen, col. 2, line 4 (Fitzmyer/Harrington, p. 104). If the
plural *'älyonīn* had the same meaning as the singular form as an
appellation of God, the author changed an established divine
epithet from singular to plural simply through attraction. Moreover, the singular form is also known from a construct relation, cf.
the Damascus Document, XX, line 8, reading קדושי עליון,
qᵉdōšē 'älyōn.[36] Here the meaning is "the holy ones of the Most
High". The singular *'älyōn* is used frequently as a divine epithet in
Aramaic.[37] Accordingly the linguistic proofs do not indicate that
the plural and the singular forms should have the same meaning.
When the Jewish writers had "god" in mind, they wrote a singular.
It is unlikely that this established practice should have been
changed simply through attraction.

The assumption that *'älyonīn* should be *pluralis majestatis* also has
a weak basis. *Pluralis majestatis* is unknown in Biblical Aramaic,
where the plural אלהין, *'ᵃlāhīn*, means "gods", and not "God" as
most often with the equivalent word in Biblical Hebrew.[38]
Moreover, there does not exist a *pluralis majestatis* *'älyonīm* in
Hebrew, that could have influenced the Aramaic phrase.

If *qaddīšē 'älyonīn* is not to be read as a *genitivus possessivus* with
the *nomen rectum* in singular meaning, it can still be read as
possessivus with the noun in plural meaning, i.e. "the holy ones
belonging to the high ones". But here are also other alternatives:
Reading *genitivus partitivus* would mean "the holy ones among the
high ones"; reading *genitivus epexegeticus* would mean "the holy

---

35 Cf. Bauer-Leander, Grammatik des Biblisch-Aramäischen, § 305g; F. Rosenthal, A Grammar of Biblical Aramaic, § 22, p. 17 and § 187, p. 57; S. Segert, Alt-
Aramäische Grammatik, § 6.3.2.3.4, p. 334.
36 For the text, cf. E. Lohse, Die Texte aus Qumran, p. 104.
37 Cf. to 'el 'älyōn, 1QapGen, col. 12, line 17 (Fitzmyer/Harrington, p. 108); col.
20, lines 12.16, (p. 114); col. 21, line 2, (p. 116), line 20, (p. 120); col. 22, line 15,
(p. 124).
38 Cf. Segert, note 1 above.

high ones".[39]

The reading as *genitivus partitivus* may have support from En 14. There the composer seems to distinguish between ordinary angels, ἄγγελοι, who had no access to the throne chamber (v. 21), and οἱ ἅγιοι τῶν ἀγγέλων, who did not leave God by night or day (v. 23). οἱ ἅγιοι τῶν ἀγγέλων or in Aramaic *qaddîšê mal' akîn* can be read as *genitivus partitivus* in the light of the simple ἄγγελοι, i.e. "the holy ones among the angels".

A strict analogy to this is, however, not to be found in Dan 7. In the Aramaic phrase *qaddîšê mal' akîn* it is the *nomen rectum* that also designates a group of its own, "the angels". In Dan 7 it is the *nomen regens*, "the holy ones", that is used in isolation. A group called simply *'älyônîn*, "the high ones", is not mentioned.

If two groups should be involved in Dan 7, the only way to distinguish them is in the two different designations, simple *qaddîšîn* and the construct *qaddîšê 'älyônîn*. If so, the use of *qaddîšîn* in both cases would spell out the relationship between the groups, while the *nomen rectum* in the construct would separate them. But it is still not clear what kind of genitive is used in the designation of the second group.

This problem is closely related to the identity of the group designated in 7,27a as *'am qaddîšê 'älyônîn*. The most frequent meaning of *'am* is "people". M. Noth did, however, advance the translation "host", and understood the word as a designation for angels.[40] The references in Jewish literature given by Noth as support for this theory were later examined by C.H.W. Brekelmans, who came to the conclusion that עם in these cases was to be read as *'im*, "with", and not *'am*.[41] Accordingly there should be no reason to deviate from the common translation "people", understood as a group of human beings.

Therefore the accurate interpretation of these genitives has a major bearing on the identity of the holy ones. We have the following alternatives for the double construct *'am qaddîšê 'älyônîn:*

39 These possibilities were already advanced by O. Procksch, "Der Menschensohn als Gottessohn", CuW 3, 1927, pp. 425-81, p. 429. The same possibilities are also considered by K. Koch, Das Buch Daniel, pp. 238f.
40 M. Noth, "Die Heiligen des Höchsten", GesSt, TB 6, München 1960, pp. 274-90, pp. 284f.
41 C.H.W. Brekelmans, "The Saints of the Most High", OTS 14, 1965, pp. 305-29, pp. 319-22.

1. Both constructs are to be read as <u>genitivus</u> <u>epexegeticus</u>. This would require the paraphrases "the people consisting of the holy high ones", which would mean that all phrases relate to "men".
2. The first construct is to be read as <u>genitivus</u> <u>epexegeticus</u>, the second as <u>genitivus</u> <u>partitivus</u> or <u>possessivus</u>. This would require the paraphrases "the people consisting of the holy ones among the high ones", or "consisting of the holy ones belonging to the high ones". Here two groups would be involved. "the holy ones" are identified as "people", which forms one group over against "the high ones" as the second.
3. Both constructs could be read as <u>genitivus</u> <u>possessivus</u> or <u>partitivus</u>. This would require the paraphrases "the people belonging to (or 'among') the holy ones, belonging to (or 'among') the high ones". In this case we are dealing with three groups: the people, the holy ones and the high ones.

There are two occurrences in the Hebrew part of the book that point in favour of reading the first construct as *genitivus epexegeticus* (options 1 and 2 above). In 8,24 Antiochus destroys "mighty ones" and *'am qᵉdošīm*, "the people of the holy ones". This phrase seems to have the same meaning as *'am qodäš*, "the holy people", in 12,7. This at least gives support from the Book of Daniel itself for the reading "the people consisting of the holy ones" at this place relate to human beings.

If the first construct here is *genitivus epexegeticus*, some alternatives may be excluded concerning the second genitive. It does not seem likely to designate a group of human beings as "the high ones" (option 1). The second genitive must accordingly be read as a *genitivus partitivus* or *possessivus*. "The people of the holy ones", i.e. "the holy people" is among or belonging to "the high ones".

The problem is then whether this analysis can be transferred to the other occurrences in Dan 7. There are several questions involved:

1. Has the addition of the noun <u>'am</u> before the construct qaddīšē 'älyōnīn changed the character of this construct, i.e. could the construct have been meant differently in the other instances it is used?
2. Does <u>'am</u> qaddīšīn designate the same group as simple qaddīšīn?

1) It seems unlikely that the construct qaddīšē 'älyōnīn has changed character through the doubling of the construct by adding <u>'am</u>. Therefore this construct must be read as "the holy ones among (or 'belonging to') the high ones". There are two groups involved.
2) It is not obvious that <u>'am</u> qaddīšīn and qaddīšīn should automatically be identical. Rather it can be argued that <u>'am</u> is added in order to spell out one dimension of qaddīšīn. The noun could thus have an explanatory function, stating that in this case we are dealing with "the holy people". Could the composer have felt this explanation necessary because the phrase qaddīšīn was ambiguous in the preceding text?

These considerations allow us to advance our theory, which will be substantiated in the next chapter. The holy ones are divided into two groups, whose fate runs parallel with the events recorded in the text. On the one hand there are "the holy ones among the high ones" in 7,18.22b.25. These holy ones are residing in heaven. On the other hand there are "the holy ones" in 7,21.22c. These are residing on earth. At the end of the text the composer unites the two groups by adding *'am* to the phrase *qaddîšê 'älyônîn*. The eschatological kingdom is given to the holy people among the high ones consisting of both the heavenly and the terrestrial groups.

2. The Identity of the Holy Ones

The question of the identity of "the holy ones" can not be settled before examining the meaning of the phrase in other Jewish writings. But unfortunately, neither does the usage of the phrase outside Dan 7 give decisive criteria to determine its meaning. The phrase can be used about three kinds of groups:

1. Angels. This is certainly the case in Dan 4,10.14.20; 8,13 and in all the occurrences listed previously from the Book of Watchers.
2. Pious men and priests. It is used of pious men in the Epistle of Enoch, En 93,6; 99,16; 100,5; and in the Qumran War Scroll, 1QM X,10, and of priests in 1QM IX, 7-8.[42]
3. Men residing with the angels or in Paradise. Men dwelling with the angels are recorded in the Similitudes of Enoch, En 39,4-5; and in Paradise in the Testament of Levi 18,11-18; and in the Testament of Dan 5,11-12.

These three possibilities are not of equal value with regard to the Book of Daniel. Statistically the designation "holy" for angels clearly outnumbers those cases it refers to men. The third use is only attested in the Similitudes and the Testaments, writings whose origin and date are obscure. This usage may therefore be interpreted as a late development, taking place either within Jewish or Christian circles, if not at least the idea can be demonstrated in earlier writings.

The three interpretations applied to Dan 7 all have their advocates among recent scholars. We present below outlines of the arguments advanced by C.H.W. Brekelmans, L. Dequeker and J.J. Collins.

---

42 Text in Lohse, op.cit., pp. 201f. The designation "holy" occurs frequently in the Qumran writings. Mostly it designates angels. In some instances it is possible that men are intended, cf. the discussion in Brekelmans, note 41 above, and Dequeker, note 44 below.

I.   The crucial argument advanced by Brekelmans[43] for the interpretation that "the holy ones" equals "pious Israel" is that the eschatological dominion of Israel or the elect of God is a fixed theme in Jewish writings: Wisd Sol 3,8; 5,6; 6,20-21; En 38,5; 48,9; 91,12; 92,4; 95,7; 108,12; 1QM I,5; XII,14-16; IXX,7-8; Dam Doc XX,33-34; 1Q 28b V,21. The idea of the dominion of the angels in the eschatological era is, however, practically unknown in this period.

Moreover, Dan 7,27 certainly implies the *people*, and the verb בלא in 7,25 must in view of the Akkadian equivalent *balû* or *belû* be translated "wear out" or "destroy", which does not indicate angels as the object.

II.   L. Dequeker[44] concentrates his analysis on the argument most often advanced against the angelic interpretation of "the holy ones". In 7,21 it is said that the horn (Antiochus IV) made war against the holy ones and prevailed over them. In 7,25 it is said that the horn wore out "the holy ones of the Most High" (Dequeker's interpretation of the phrase). This, it has been argued, clearly indicates that the holy ones are pious Jews persecuted by Antiochus IV.

Dequeker's objection is that 7,21.25 do not refer to Antiochus' acts against the Jews, but to his attack on the angelic host described in 8,9-12. The visionary scene in 8,9-12 is interpreted in 8,23b-25. According to TM Antiochus' acts are here directed against *'am qᵉdošîm*, "he shall destroy mighty ones and the people of the holy ones", v. 24c. Dequeker suggests, however, an emendation of the text. LXX reads "the people of the holy ones" in 24c, but has a succeeding line reading:

καὶ ἐπὶ τοὺς ἁγίους τὸ διανόημα αὐτοῦ, "and his thoughts against the holy ones". Dequeker regards the first *'am qᵉdošîm* as an addition both in TM and LXX, and introduces the simple *qᵉdošîm* from LXX as a part of the original text. Thus in the original text Antiochus launched an attack against "the holy ones", which are to be understood as the same group as the angelic host in 8,10. Accordingly 8,9-12.23b-25 describes an attack on the holy ones understood as angels. The same attack is described in 7,21.25.

43   Brekelmans, op.cit., pp. 326-9.
44   L. Dequeker, "'The Saints of the Most High' in Qumran and Daniel", OTS 18, 1973, pp. 108-87, pp. 173-87.

There remains the problem of how to interpret 'am qaddīšē
'ālyōnīn in 7,27. Dequeker regards this verse as an addition
belonging to what he calls the Maccabean level. The later commentator wanted to explain that the coming and the enthronement
of the Son of Man de facto meant that the Jewish people would be
freed and be given the kingdom.

According to Brekelmans the weakest point in the angelic interpretation was that the "dominion given to the angels" theme was
unknown in Jewish literature. Dequeker replies that Dan 7 is not
about the dominion of the angels at all. The theme is the dominion
of God over all nations. The kingdoms of this world are governed
by evil forces. They are embodied in the four heathen kings and
represented through the beasts. The kingdom of god is represented
by the Son of Man, and "governed" by the angels, the good
forces, who are the tutelary spirits of the sacred people. This is the
most typical aspects of Jewish angeiology in the late biblical
period: the doctrine about the guardian angels of the nations. In
the Book of Daniel this doctrine is attested in Dan 10,13.20.21;
11,1. The mission of the holy ones of the Most High is thus to be
minsters of the divine kingdom; they are to be governors of the
people of God after the heathen rulers have been destroyed.

III.   J.J. Collins follows to a large extent the same line of
interpretation as Dequeker, with regard to the attack on the holy
ones in Dan 7 and 8.[45] This is primarily meant as an attack on the
angels. The idea corresponds to Judg 5,19-20 and to the Qumran
War Scroll where the heavenly host is fighting against the enemies
of Israel together with the chosen people. In Dan 8,10 the idea is
turned the other way round: The enemy of Israel is attacking the
heavenly host. Collins finds the same idea in 11,36, interpreting 'el
and 'elīm as angels.

But Collins devotes more attention to the two last problems
discussed by Dequeker: Israels' role represented by 'am in 7,27 and
the dominion of the holy ones. The drama described in the Book
of Daniel takes place on two levels: in heaven where the patron
angels are bringing forth the final victory, cf. 12,1, and on earth
where the pious Jews are fighting for survival. But these two

---

45   J.J. Collins, "The Son of Man and the Saints of the Most High in the Book
of Daniel", JBL 93, 1974, pp. 50-66.

levels are seen in a single perspective. Ultimately the heavenly battle and the terrestrial battle are one. The two perspectives are also united in 7,27. The people share in the kingdom of the angels, and thus the interpretation in 7,27 serves merely to spell out the human dimension of the more complete reality mentioned in the vision v. 22 and in the interpretation in v. 18. Collins considers the same double aspect to be present in 8,24, if 'am q^{e}došīm is to be read there.

The primary reason why the two levels were united lies according to Collins in the eschatology of the Book of Daniel. According to 12,3 "the wise will shine like the splendor of the firmament and those who lead the many to justice will be like the stars forever". This verse must be read in the light of 8,10 where the angels are equated with the stars. Similar promises are given elsewhere, for instance in the Epistle of Enoch, En 104,2, where the righteous are promised that they "will shine as the stars of heaven", and in v. 6 that they "will become companions to the host of heaven".[46] In the Similitudes of Enoch the dwelling places of the righteous are with the holy angels, En 39,5; and in the Assumption of Moses Israel is elevated to the stars, 10,9. Accordingly, when the eschatological kingdom is given to the holy ones, both the angels and the just are included.

However, this double perspective seems also to be present in the events preceding the great eschatological change. Collins refers here to Qumran writings where the heavenly host mingles with the elect both in the final battle and in cultic celebrations.[47]

The discussion so far enables us to draw some preliminary conclusions:

* Since "the holy ones" are angels in the Book of Watchers, which is the Jewish composition most closely related to Dan 7, and since they are angels in the Book of Daniel itself (4,10.14.20; 8,13) and most frequently in Jewish literature from this period, the designation is likely to include angels in Dan 7 as well.
* In Dan 7,27 "the people of the holy ones" must include the righteous Israelites.

---

46 The last reference is only extant in the Ethiopic translation, and not in the Greek.
47 Cf. the War Scroll, 1QM II, 4-7 (Lohse, pp. 206ff), XV, 14-15 (Lohse, p. 216); The Rule of the Community, 1QS, XI, 7-8 (Lohse, p. 40); the Hymns, 1QH, III, 21-22 (Lohse, p. 122).

* Whatever group the phrase strictly designates, it seems to be related to both
angels and men. An interpretation where the designation actually includes a
composite group of angels and men, as Collins argues, is therefore not
unlikely, since the just are included in the heavenly community of angels both
in Dan 12,3 and in other Jewish writings.

As seen above, a crucial question in the discussion is how to
interpret the war-motif. Is Antiochus' attack directed against the
holy people on earth (Brekelmans), against the angels (Dequeker),
or against both groups (Collins)? To answer this question we need
to examine afresh the sequences related to the war-motif, i.e. Dan
7,8e.11a; 7,20; 7,21-22; 7,25; 8,10-12; 8,24-25; 11,31; 11,32-35;
11,36b-37. We consentrate on the three basic elements of these
sequences: reshaping religious service, making war, speaking proud
words.

Reshaping religious service:

Dan 7,25c: ויסבר להשניה זמנין ודת
   "and he shall intend to alter times and law."

Dan 8,11b: וממנו הרים התמיד וחשלך מכון מקדשו
   "and he took away from Him the regular offering,
   and the place of the sanctuary was profaned."

Dan 11,31:   וזרעים ממנו יעמדו וחללו המקדש
                                      המעוז והסירו התמיד ונתנו השקוץ משמם
   "armies from him will arise, and profane the sanctuary,
   the castle, and remove the regular offering, and erect
   the abomination of desolation."

Dan 11,37:   ועל אלהי אבתיו לא יבין
   "he does not observe the gods of his fathers"

Making war:

Dan 7,21:   וקרנא דכן עבדם קרב עם קדישין ויכלה להן
   "this horn was making war with the holy ones and prevailed
   over them."

Dan 7,25b: ולקדישי עליונין יבלא...ויתיהבון ביד
   "and the holy ones of the high ones he shall wear out ... and
   they shall be given into his power ..."

Dan 8,10:   ותגדל עד השמים ותפל מן הצבה
                                       ומן הכוכבים ותרמסם

"and it waxed mighty up to the host of heaven and it threw some from the host down on the earth, and of the stars, and he stamped on them."

Dan 8,24c: והשחית עצומים ועם קדשים

"and he shall destroy mighty ones and the people of the holy ones."

Cf. Dan 11,32–35: Persecution of the "wise ones".

Speaking proud words (presumptuous attitude):

Dan 7,8e: ופם ממלל רברבן

"and a mouth speaking great (words)."

Dan 7,11a: מן קל מליא רברבתא די קרנא ממללה

"because of the sound of the great words that the horn spoke."

Dan 7,20:   ופם ממלל רברבן

"and a mouth speaking great (words)."

Dan 7,25:   ומלין לצר עליא ימלל

"and he shall speak words against the Highest One."

Dan 8,11:   ועד שר הצבא הגדיל

"and he shall grew mighty against the chief of the host."

Dan 8,25c: ועל שר שרים יעמד

"and he shall stand up against the chief of chiefs."

Dan 11,36b: ויתרומם ויתגדל על כל אל
                                       ועל אל אלים ידבר נפלאות

"and he is haughty and magnify himself against every god, and speaks blasphemies against the God of gods."

As previously demonstrated, the "rebel king" pattern underlies the description of Antiochus IV in the Book of Daniel.[48] Therefore the correct interpretation of these passages hangs on the question of how this "rebel king" pattern relates to the actual historical experiences of the Jews living during the reign of this king and composing the book. The historiographical pattern coincides with historical experience at two points.

The first is the historical fact described in 11,31 that Antiochus IV let his soldiers attack the temple and change the religious service of the temple. This coincides with the motif of "the king as a rebel against the gods" in the rebel king pattern. The second is the historical fact described in 11,32-35 that Antiochus IV persecuted the pious Jews loyal towards the temple and its services. This coincides with the motif of "the king as oppressor of his own people" in the pattern. The two aspects describe an attack of the rebel king in two directions: An attack on the divine order and an attack on his own people. These are the two basic components underlying the passages cited from the Book of Daniel, and our task is to determine what component underlies which sequence.

* We start with the sequence in 8,24. Since the passage in 8,24c is fully consistent in TM, we see no reason to emend the text. If so, the text deals with ʿam qᵉdošīm, which is to be understood as "the holy people". The sequence thus deals with the persecution of the pious Jews.

* The visionary imagery in 8,10-12 is more obscure. The sequence combines the motifs of "making war" in 8,10, of "presumptuous attitude" in 8,11a, and of "reshaping religious service" in 8,11b.
The second motif, "the presumptuous attitude", must be regarded as an explication of the "speaking of proud words" motif. This is the only one associated with the king in the vision of Dan 7, cf. vv. 8e.11a. As in 8,11 this motif is closely connected to that of "reshaping religious service" in 7,25 and 11,36-37. In 7,20 and 8,25c the presumptuous attitude stands more in isolation within the context. The combination of the two other motifs, the war-motif and the religious-service-motif in 8,10-11, has two roots.
The first is the theology adhering to the temple. The temple is the point of intersection between heaven and earth. The temple as a whole, including its sacred objects and rites, shares in the celestial and cosmic order.[49] By profaning the temple and altering its service, the celestial and cosmic order was attacked. The guardians of this order were the angels.[50] Therefore the attack on the temple was also an attack on the angelic host.

48 For the rebel king, cf. above, pp. 460ff.
49 Cf. J. Maier, "Tempel und Tempelkult", Literatur und Religion des Früh-Judentums, J. Maier und J. Schreiner (eds.), Würzburg 1973, pp. 371-90, pp. 383-7.
50 Cf. especially the Enochic Astronomical Book, En 82,9ff, and the discussion in Part I, pp. 72ff, 304ff.

The second is the "rebel king" pattern according to which Antiochus is
described. According to this pattern the rebel king ascends to heaven and
through this hubristic act he provokes the ruling god.[51] The pattern combines
several elements, both historical and mythological. On the mythological side
the traditions about the primeval sages, the apkallu's, were influential.[52] One
of the incidents related of the apkallu's was that one of them ascended to
heaven.[53] Another was that several apkallu's in their superhuman power
provoked the gods. These provocative acts were focused especially on the cult,
a feature which seems to have influenced both the description of the rebel
king in the Vision of the Nether World and of Nabonidus in the Verse
Account.[54] In the description of the four apkallu's, irregular treatment of
cultic objects is explicitly mentioned. It is also recorded about one of the
apkallu's that he brought down Ishtar from heaven.[55]

If we thus read 8,10-12 as a combination of historiographical and mythical
elements on the one hand and historical experiences on the other, we see how
the two aspects run parallel. Historically Antiochus attacked the temple and
altered the services. In the light of the religious, mythical and traditional
notions he thus acted as a rebel king, breaking into the divine realm and
attacking the angelic host guarding the temple and its service.

It is significant that 8,10-12 forms the visionary imagery which is interpreted
in 8,24-25. In this interpretation only a reminiscence of the attack on the
divine order remains in the words "and he shall rise up against the chief of
chiefs" in 8,25c. Beyond that the interpretation deals with the king's attacks on
people, and in this context his attack on the holy people in 8,24c. The
composer has clearly seen a correspondence between the two aspects. The
visionary imagery records his attack on the host of heaven, the interpretation
his attack on the holy people on earth.

Dan 7,21-22 and 7,25 also form a vision (cf. the introduction to v. 21) and an interpretation.

* We begin with the interpretation in 7,25. Here the same three motifs are
  combined as in 8,10-12: "speaking proud words", "making war" and "reshaping religious service". This leads to the conclusion that the sequence in 7,25
  deals with the same topic as 8,10-12, i.e. the attack on the divine order. If so,
  "the holy ones among the high ones" must be a group in heaven similar to the
  angelic host in 8,10-11.

* In the vision in 7,21 only one of the motifs is extant, namely the war against
  the holy ones. This differs from 8,10-12 and 7,25, but corresponds to 8,24.
  Consequently the passage refers to Antiochus IV's persecution of the pious
  Jews.
  Thus the correspondence between visionary imagery and interpretation is the
  same in 7,21; 7,25 as in 8,10-11; 8,24, only in the opposite order. In Dan 8 the
  visionary imagery recorded the attack on the divine order, while the interpretation concentrated on the attack on the pious Jews. In Dan 7 the order is
  converse, but the same correspondence obtains between the two aspects.

---

51   Cf. above, pp. 463ff.
52   Cf. above, pp. 426ff, 482f.
53   Cf. Part I, pp. 203f.
54   Cf. Part I, p. 205, and above, line 67, p. 392 and note 67b, p. 398; and pp.
433f, 470ff.
55   Cf. Part I, p. 205.

This analysis gives us a clearer perspective on what is going on in Dan 7. The first sequence of the interpretation, vv. 17-18, summarizes the vision by stating that the Son of Man's rise to power will lead to the transfer of the kingdom from the terrestrial kings to the heavenly group "the holy ones among the high ones". The vision in 7,21-22 and the interpretation in 7,25-27 deepen this theme.

In 7,21 it becomes clear that the "holy ones among the high ones" have a counterpart on earth, simply called "the holy ones". These are persecuted by the rebel king. But at the end justice will be given to the holy ones in heaven and the kingdom to the holy ones on earth (v. 22).

In 7,25 it becomes clear that the rebel king also attacks the heavenly group of holy ones, through his attack on the temple. But at the end the kingdom will be given to the people of the holy ones among the high ones (v. 27), which means that the kingdom will be given to the united group of holy ones, both the terrestrial and the celestial.

It thus becomes clear that the composer of vv. 19-27 has deliberately portrayed the fate of the terrestrial and the celestial groups in parallel to each other. Both groups suffer under the attack of the demonic king (vv. 21.25), and both receive justice and the kingdom at the end (vv. 22.27).

3.   The Son of Man and the Vindication of the Holy Ones

There remains the question of the relationship between the Son of Man and the holy ones. This question is crucial because the term "the holy ones" was used by the composer to designate the group to which he himself belonged. Analyzing the relationship thus enables us to determine how the Son of Man was understood by the composer or composers of Dan 7 in its final shape. And it enables us to give an overall interpretation of Dan 7 as a unit.

The basis for the analysis must be the relation between vv. 9-10.13-14 in the vision and v. 18 in the interpretation, because v. 18 is the first place where "the holy ones" are used as an exchange for the Son of Man.

The first thing to notice is the difference in style between v. 18

and the preceding v. 17 in the opening of the interpretation. V. 17 has the common form of a *pesher*, a commentary: "These great beasts, that are four: Four kings will rise from the earth". V. 18 does not continue in the same style, but retells the basic content of v. 14 with the holy ones in the same position as the Son of Man. This demonstrates that the Son of Man was not understood as a visionary manifestation of the holy ones. The composer breaks the style of the preceding passage, because the relationship between the visionary image and the interpretation was to be understood differently. The composer no longer interprets the vision such that the visionary manifestation is explained through another word, but in such a way that the interpretation reveals the significance of the visionary manifestation. The transference of kingship to the Son of Man signified that the time had come for the transference of kingship to the holy ones. The Son of Man is thus not a symbol for the holy ones, but his appearance is a signal for the holy ones.

This means that although vv. 9-14.18 belong to different scenes and sequences of the composition, the verses nevertheless constitute a thematic unit: God arrives (vv. 9-10), the last beast is destroyed (v. 11), the dominion is taken from the other beasts (v. 12), the kingdom is given to the Son of Man (vv. 13-14), and subsequently to the holy ones (v. 18).

The character of this unit is explicitly marked at three points: "Chairs are set in place" in the opening of the sequence (v. 9). This in order to prepare the court-room for the "tribunal who is seated" (v. 10). The court starts by "opening the books" (v. 10). The unit is accordingly a description of the final judgement.

As noted previously, the court scene corresponds to the underlying traditions of the Mesopotamian underworld. In the Descent of Ishtar the underworld judges come and are seated, like God and the tribunal in Dan 7,9.[56] In the Vision of the Nether World the ruling god of the underworld is seated in judgement, from him issues fire, and in front of him the underworld is prostrated in adoration.[57] In the Death Dream of Enkidu Ereshkigal is seated in judgement, and the sentences read from a protocol.[58]

We have previously noticed that the description of God on the

---

56   Cf. above, pp. 382f.
57   Cf. above, pp. 422ff.
58   Cf. lines 50-52, p. 359.

throne in Dan 7,9-10 was closely related to the description of God in En 14,18-25.[59] The difference between the texts is that the location is changed. En 14 describes God in the heavenly temple, while Dan 7,9-10 describes God coming in judgement.

This means that the composer of Dan 7 has applied the description of God in En 14 to another setting. This new setting, the final judgement, is, however, described elsewhere in the Book of Watchers.

In En 1,3b-9 the judgement is described in two sequences, both following the same pattern: 1) The coming of God (vv. 3b-4a), in a theophany (vv. 4b-7b), judgement of all men (v. 7c), salvation of the righteous (v. 8), 2) The coming of God with thousands of his holy ones (v. 9), judgement of all men (v. 9bA), condemnation of the sinners (v. 9bB-d).

In En 25,3-4 the two aspects, the salvation of the righteous and the condemnation are taken together in the same sequence: The coming of God (v. 3), the great judgement (v. 4a), the condemnation (v. 4b), the tree of life given to the righteous and humble (v. 4c).

When we apply the same pattern to Dan 7,9-14.18 we get the following result: The coming of God (v. 9ab), surrounded by fire (vv. 9c-10a), the judgement (v. 10bc), condemnation of the wicked (vv. 11-12), "salvation" given to the Son of Man (vv. 13-14), "salvation" given to the holy ones (v. 18).

This new setting of the description of God, which we find in Dan 7 as compared with En 14,18-25, implies a change of function of the figures involved. In En 14,23 the holy ones of the angels are described as those who have access to the throne of God. No such group is described in connection with the throne in Dan 7,9-10. The group of holy ones occurs in 7,18 outside the throne scene. If we assume that En 14,18-25 forms a part of the background of Dan 7, the composer must have changed the location of the holy ones deliberately. He must have also changed their function, since in v. 18 they are given the kingdom.

En 14,22 tells about myriads upon myriads standing before the throne of God. These are not explicitly identified in the throne scene in En 14. Two explanations are possible. The myriads could be the angels who did not have access to the immediate presence

59   Cf. above, pp. 560ff.

of God in v. 21a, or they could be "the flesh", i.e. human beings, also without access, mentioned in v. 22b. In En 1,9 God comes with myriads of his holy ones to execute judgement, but it is difficult to use this verse as a key to the more subtle divisions of heavenly beings in En 14.

The reference to "the flesh" in v. 21b is obscure. The whole verse could have been meant rhetorically: Neither the angels in heaven, nor the men on earth could see God. But v. 21a seems to refer to something specific: in contrast to the holy ones among the angels (v. 23) the ordinary angels had no access to the throne chamber. The division into three categories (holy ones among the angels, ordinary angels, the flesh, i.e. ordinary men) is probably an analogy with the terrestrial temple: only a special group of the priests had access to the most holy part of the temple, whereas the other priests and the ordinary man had no access. When applied to the heavenly temple, this could mean that not only the first two groups, the two kinds of angels, but also the third group, ordinary man, were present in heaven. If so, "flesh" in this context must stand for the dead, residing with the angels. The material does not lead to any certain conclusions, but there is a possibility that the myriads standing before the throne of God could be dead men. At least the text is open to this interpretation.

In Dan 7,10 "a thousand thousands worship him (God), and myriads upon myriads stand before him". In En 1,9 "myriads of holy ones" are coming with God to execute judgement. In Dan 7,10 God seems to come alone, or together with a tribunal of judges. The myriads do not come with God, however; they are standing before him as in En 14,22. In Dan 7,10 the thousands and myriads could be angels. The following passages, however, tend to point in another direction. The thousands and myriads are standing before God, then the tribunal is seated and the court protocols opened. If the myriads are not merely a kind of heavenly back-drop, but have a real function within the sequence, they mst be the group whom the judgement concerns, i.e. they must be those awaiting the final judgement.

This interpretation would give the unit vv. 9-14.18 an inner logic: God arrives in the final judgement, myriads of men are waiting before his throne; the judgement takes place, the beasts which have killed and destroyed on earth are condemned, the everlasting

kingdom is given to the Son of Man, and to the holy ones among
the high ones, who are those given justice (cf. v. 22!) in the final
judgement. The question is whether this interpretation can be
substantiated.

In the light of the Mesopotamian underworld traditions an
interpretation where the multitude who are standing before the
throne of God represents the dead waiting for judgement, would
be likely. In the Vision of the Nether World the underworld —
which also includes the dead — is prostrated before the underworld judge.[60] In the Death Dream of Enkidu the court protocol
relates to the judgement of the dead who appear before the judge
Ereshkigal.[61]

The vision in 4 Ezra 13 is obscure at this point. After the man has
destroyed the hostile multitude he calls to himself "another
multitude which was peaceable. Then the faces of many men drew
nigh to him, some of whom were glad, some sorrowful, some were
in bonds, while some brought others who were to be offered" (vv.
12-13). The sequence is reminiscent of Is 66,18-23 (cf. esp. v. 20)
where all peoples come to Jerusalem to worship the Lord in the
eschatological era. The same theme also occurs in Is 25,6-8. Here
all peoples are invited to the eschatological celebration on Zion
after Yahweh has destroyed death for ever. Read in this light the
peaceful multitude in 4 Ezra 13,12-13 could also include the dead,
rising up to take part in the eschatological celebration. If we bear
in mind that the man himself ascends from the nether world,[62]
this is not an impossible interpretation.

We have previously seen that the structure of Dan 7 follows closely
the structure of the Watcher story and the Book of Watchers. In the
Watcher story the eschatological drama, i.e. the destruction of the
giants, the imprisonment of the watchers, the final judgement and
the outbreak of the era of salvation, is put into effect because of
the lamentation of the victims of the watchers and giants (En 9,3).
These victims are the dead souls (En 9,10). They are pleading their
cause to the holy ones. In En 9,3 traces are preserved in Aramaic:

ואמרין לקד)שי ש(מיא)...די קבלן (נפשו בני אנשא)
וא(מרן

---

60 Cf. lines 52-53, p. 391.
61 Cf. lines 50-52, p. 359.
62 Cf. above, pp. 530ff.

4Q En^a liv, lines 10-11 (Milik, p. 158):[63] "And they said to the ho]ly ones of he[aven...: 'The souls of the sons of men] are complaining and sa[ying]". The holy ones then bring the case of the souls of the dead before God, and the eschatological drama starts. In En 12,1-4 Enoch is introduced, who dwells with the angels in heaven (v. 3). In the section En 12-16 he is the one who acts as the agent of God, bringing the message of the judgement to the watchers and giants.

There is therefore a connection between the holy angels and Enoch on the one hand, and the souls of the victims on the other. The holy ones and Enoch act on behalf of the dead victims to establish justice over against the evil forces on earth.

A similar concept is found in the description of the underworld in En 22. In the underworld Enoch sees the souls of the dead. The vision is explained as follows by the angel Raphael:

והא אלן אנון פחתיא לבית עגנון לכדן עב(י)דן עד
יום די יתדינן ועד זמן יום קצא ד(י) דינא רבא
מנהון יתעבד

4Q En^e lxxii, lines 1-3 = En 22,4 (Milik, p. 229): "And behold, these are the pits of their incarceration; they have been fashioned in this manner until the day they will be judged, and until the time of the day of the end of the great judgement, which will be exacted of them". Among the spirits of the dead Enoch sees one particular spirit (lines 4-5 = En 22,5):

תמן חזית רוח אנש מת קבלה (ו)אנינה ע(ד) שמיא
סלך ומזעק וקב(ל)

"There I saw the spirit of a dead man making accusation, and his lamentation ascending up to heaven, and crying out unceasingly and making accusation". The spirit is identified by Raphael as the spirit of Abel, who was killed by his brother Cain (En 22,7).

In En 9,3.10 the motif of the dead victims pleading their cause to God is also taken from the Genesis narrative about Cain and Abel where Abel's "blood" is crying to Yahweh

קול דמי אחיך צעקים אלי מן הארץ

"the voice of the blood of your brother is crying to me from the earth", Gen 4,10.[64] In the Watcher story and the Book of

---

63   For this restoration, cf. also the traces in 4Q En^b liii, lines 10-11 (Milik, p. 171).
64   For the relationship between En 6-11 and Gen 4-9, cf. Part I, pp. 275ff.

Watchers this motif functions in two ways, neither of which excludes the other. On the one hand the Watcher story is to be read as an etiological narrative which tells of the origin of evil and consequently sheds light upon the evil of every age. In this perspective Abel is the symbol for all those who have suffered death unjustly by violence. On the other hand the Watcher story is a retelling of the ancient narrative of the primeval catastrophe relating to one particular historical situation, namely the Diadochan wars. In this perspective Abel stands especially for the innocent victims of these wars.[65]

The Book of Watchers does not contain a clear promise about a restitution of the souls of the righteous. But it seems presupposed when it is stated that the souls will remain in the underworld until the day of judgement. A restitution is also implied in En 22,13 where it is stated that one group of the sinners will not be raised from the underworld. The righteous dead may be included among the righteous and humble who are give the fruits of the tree of life in En 25,4-5.

The Book of Watchers does apparently reflect the earliest stage of development of a notion about the fate of the righteous, dead and alive, on the day of judgement and thereafter. A later stage in this development is reflected in the Epistle of Enoch, where the souls of the righteous are promised restitution directly, together with the righteous still living (cf. En 103-104), and where in the era of salvation the righteous will be like the angels (cf. En 104,1-6). The explicit use of the designation "holy" for the heavenly and eschatological community in the Similitudes and the Testaments corresponds to this development (cf. En 38,4-5; 39,4; 41,2; 45,1; 48,1.4.7.9; 50,1; 51,2; 58,3.5; 62,8; Test Lev 18,11-14; Test Dan 5,11-12). The righteous dwell in a transcendent realm either with the angels or in Paradise, and they are designated "holy" in the same way as the angels.

Thus far we may conclude as follows: The Mesopotamian traditions underlying Dan 7 point in the direction that the great multitude standing before the throne in 7,10 are men waiting for the judgement. In the Mesopotamian traditions these men are dead. The vision in 4 Ezra 13 tells of a gathering of a great multitude for

---

65   For this interpretation of the Watcher story, cf. Part I, pp. 96ff, 315ff.

the era of salvation. The multitude may in this context include the pious dead. In the Book of Watchers, which is the Jewish composition closest to Dan 7, the souls of the dead victims play an important role in the eschatological drama. Their cause together with the cause of the righteous still living on earth will be vindicated on the day of the great judgement when the evil forces and the oppressors are condemned. In the Epistle of Enoch this theme is even clearer. Here it is also stated that in the era of salvation the righteous will be like the angels. If we take these indications together, they suggest that the great multitude in 7,10 are men, presumably both living and dead, waiting for vindication over against the destructive beasts, and that the holy ones among the high ones in 7,18 may at least include men residing among the angels and vindicated on the day of judgement.

There is one more text which clearly supports this interpretation. The promise of the kingdom and justice to be given to the holy ones ends the Aramaic part of the Book of Daniel. The Hebrew part ends with a similar promise, 12,1b-3. The sequence begins with a general statement about the holy people to which Daniel belongs: "At that time your people will be saved, all those found written in the book" (v. 1b). The "book" can hardly be anything other than the court-protocol referred to in Dan 7,10. There the text read "books", which may allude to both a "book of death" and a "book of life". The sequence proceeds by recounting the fate of the dead: "And many of those who sleep in the ground of dust shall awake, some to everlasting life, and some to reproach, to everlasting abhorrence" (v. 2). The idea seems to be the same as in En 22 which is written earlier than Dan 12. There are three main groups: 1) The righteous, who will be vindicated in the final judgement (En 22,5-7.9b.12); 2) The sinners, who have escaped punishment in their lives and will be condemned in the final judgement (vv. 10-11); 3) The sinners, who have suffered in their lives. These will not be raised up for the great judgement (vv. 12-13). In Dan 12,2 one group is raised to salvation, another to condemnation, and the rest seem to remain in the dust.

In the next passage the fates of the "wise ones" and "those who have made the many righteous" are described: "And the wise will shine like the splendour of the firmament, and those who have made the many righteous like the stars forever" (v. 3). The "wise ones", *maškilīm,* are clearly a self-designation of the group to which the visionary belongs, cf. 11,33.35; 12,10. This group will, through heavy persecutions, cf. 11,35, endure to the end, cf. 12,10. The second designation, "those who have made the many righteous", *maṣdīqē hārabbīm,* can mean something like "those who have instructed many in righteousness", cf. 11,33. We have, however, the same wording in Is 53,11 in connection with the martyrdom of the Servant of Yahweh, who through his death "made the many righteous". The phrase may therefore refer explicitly to the effect of the martyrdom of "the wise ones". In any case, the verse as a whole does refer to the fate of both the dead raised from the dust and the living who endure until the end. They will both "shine like the splendour of the firmament", and "like the stars". Through En 104,1-6 and Dan 8,10 we know that these phrases simply mean "be like the angels".

Therefore it seems clear that Dan 12,1b-3 describes the same event as the court-scene in Dan 7,9-14.18: in the final judgement the victims of the oppressors, both the living and the dead, will receive their vindication over against the oppressors. They will live in the era of salvation together with the angels.[66]

This use of the designation "holy", as a designation of the community of saints and angels, also explains why it was attached to the pious Jews before the judgement. In 7,18 this designation included the vindicated victims after the judgement. The designation could be transferred with no great difference to the victims just before or after their martyrdom. What unites both uses and also makes Dan 7 a thematic unity, is the theme of vindication for those who lived in loyalty to God and who suffered and died unjustly.[67]

---

66 M. Black, "The Throne-Theophany Prophetic Commission and the Son of Man", Jews, Greeks and Christians, Essays in honor of W.D. Davies, Leiden 1976, pp. 57-99, makes similar observations from different premises. His conclusions are, however, misleading: ". . . what Daniel was contemplating was nothing less than the apotheosis of Israel in the end time, a 'deification', as it were, of 'the Saints of the Most High'", p. 62. We do not think that the designation "holy", which could also be used about pious men living on earth, or the inclusion of men in the community of angels, meant that the eschatological community of men was "deified". The closest parallel here is Enoch, who dwelt with the angels in heaven, En 12,1-3, but still a human being, cf. En 15,1-2.

67 This thematic unity is correctly perceived by C.F.D. Moule, "Neglected Features in the Problem of the 'Son of Man'", Neues Testament und Kirche, Festschrf. f. R. Schnackenburg, Freiburg 1974, pp. 413-28, pp. 418f.

There is also a thematic unity between this reading of Dan 7 and the Son of Man concept. This is true of the relationship both with the unique man in the Vision of the Nether World and with Enoch in the Book of Watchers. In the Vision of the Nether World "the man" is a murdered king who is contrasted with the destructive demon monsters. He is even portrayed as a victor over a monstrous creature.[68] His spirit will also punish the rebel rulers for their crimes. In the current of tradition this man has been interpreted as the one who will defeat the forces of death and evil.[69] His ascension from the nether world is taken as a sign of vindication for the victims, who already have died because of, or are suffering under, the powers of death and violence in this world. In this role the unique man resembles Enoch, not only because of his transcendent setting by the throne of God, but also in function: Both figures were taken to the throne of God and given the mission to vindicate the victims. The difference is that the Son of Man is a king taking over kingship from the beasts which preceded him, while Enoch acts as a prophet and sage.

We have not let considerations of literary criticism determine our interpretation of Dan 7. We are still inclined to regard vv. 7bB–8.11a as an addition, or more correctly as an outworking of material already extant in the underlying vision, because of the syntactical break in v. 11 and the stylistic peculiarities in vv. 7bB–8.[70] If so, the vision has as a written document been updated to include the period under Antiochus IV, having dealt in its original written form with the Greek empire under the impact from Alexander the Great, who is the fourth beast. But this question is not crucial for the interpretation of the vision. What is crucial is, firstly, that all the basic elements of the vision have survived in the course of transmission from its Mesopotamian to its Jewish setting; secondly, that the vision, when it was written down, was given its final structure in a milieu closely related to the group behind the Book of Watchers, dealing with the ultimate questions of reality in the same way.

---

68   Cf. line 50, p. 391, and p. 413.
69   Cf. above, pp. 549ff.
70   Cf. H.S. Kvanvig, "Struktur und Geschichte in Dan 7", pp. 106–110.

This concerns the demonisation of heathen power, and consequently the transcendentalization of the conflict in reality. The conflict in history is no longer as generally in the earlier Old Testament tradition a conflict between human interests, but a reflection of a transcendent conflict between demonic forces and the holy ones. As a result of this conflict there are victims among men on earth. In the Book of Watchers these victims are innocent men in general, suffering unjustly under the demonic forces embodied in the terrestrial rulers, in Dan 7 in its final form these victims are the pious Jews, the martyrs who gave their lives in loyalty to God.

This is the setting of the Son of Man. His ascension from the realm of death to the throne of God is a sign for the martyrs and those struggling in the situation of martyrdom. His ascension signifies the ultimate victory over the forces of death and evil, and consequently the vindication of the martyrs. Their fate will be the same as the fate of the Son of Man, they will share in his kingdom.

d) The Origin of the Son of Man Vision: Synopsis

I.   The Danielic apocalyptic represented in Dan 7 contains an imagery based on traditions reaching far back into Mesopotamian mythology. A diachronic survey of the emergence of these traditions indicates distinct levels in the formation of the material. The oldest level in which the underworld imagery appears can be designated as the mythical level, because the imagery is formed through myths of the underworld. The next level can be designated "the dream-level" — represented in our particular current of tradition by the Death-Dream of Enkidu — because the mythical imagery here occurs in a dream story. The third level can be classified "the visionary level", because the dream language is now taken up into a literary unit classified as "vision", with a special religio-political intention. However, this level has to be divided into two stages, the one Mesopotamian, represented by the Vision of the Nether World, and the other Jewish, represented by Dan 7, with the original vision behind 4 Ezra 13 at an intermediate stage.

This division into separate levels does not, however, imply that the development is not a continuum. It only emphasized those links in the current of tradition where the imagery has undergone the greatest changes. These links have affected the formal characteristics of the material, the scenery and the special image of the unique man.

II. The texts belonging to the mythical level demonstrate a variety of forms. There are short poems such as Gilgamesh, Enkidu and the Nether World, myths such as Inanna's or Ishtar's Descent to the Nether World, and Nergal and Ereshkigal, lamentations such as the Sumerian elegies published by Kramer, lamentations of Dumuzi's death, and the Death of Ur-Nammu.[71] The variety of forms shows the spread of the underworld imaginations already taking place in the literary production of Sumeria and early Babylon. It will not be our concern here to analyze the correspondence between the form and the content. We shall confine ourself to some basic observations.

In compositions which contain an actual description of the underworld, some elements of content occur consistently regardless of the genre: the encounter with death itself either through a deputy of the nether world or through a descent to the nether world, or both; the encounter with the dwellers and conditions of the nether world; and at the end, the confrontation with the ruling god of the underworld and his judgement.[72]

The underworld texts concern both gods and humans. In the first case we are dealing with pure myths. These poems reflect in different ways the same basic pattern of the dying and rising fertility deity. The myths serve as a transcendental framework for the change of seasons.

In the second case the compositions still reflect a mythical perception of reality, even though men and not gods are protagonists. The compositions convey a transcendental framework for the experience of death in human life. The underworld and its inhabitants are not only understood as the final destiny of man, but also as a power in life, through the visitation of underworld gods, demons and the spirits of the dead.[73]

From the earliest stage the mythical figures of the underworld

71   Cf. above, pp. 366ff.
72   Cf. above, pp. 383f.
73   Cf. above, pp. 378ff.

occur in dreams. In both the Sumerian dreams preserved — Dumuzi's Dream and the Death of Gilgamesh — the dream functions as a forewarning about the dreamer's actual death.[74] The existence of dream stories already at this stage demonstrates the close relationship between mythical perception and expression of reality, and dream experiences.

This should warn against making too sharp a distinction between the Death-Dream of Enkidu and the mythical compositions. If the myth and dream language are interrelated, the mythicists could have borrowed images and themes from dream experiences, just as well as the composers of dream stories could have borrowed from myths. Nor can we exclude the possibility that dreams such as the Death-Dream of Enkidu could have actually been dreamt, in which case the unconscious was expressing itself in threatening images of death and nether world.

But we have no access to the original dream experiences, only to the literary units, and in this case a literary unit set in the framework of the Gilgamesh legends. In this literary unit we observe how sequences, phrases and themes conform with the earlier traditions about the nether world. Whatever kind of experiences may have lain behind, the composer of the Death-Dream of Enkidu formed this literary composition under the influence of a traditional pattern extant in legends and myths. He thus structured the dream experience in accordance with this existing tradition.

Even though the language of dreams and myths is interrelated, there is a difference in the perception of the transcendental images. In myths the interplay between transcendental and terrestrial figures is "natural", because reality is ultimately formed by transcendental forces. In dreams the crossing of the frontier to the other world is marked by a special experience distinguishing itself from every-day life.

On the stylistic level the adaptation of the underworld images into a dream-story is most notable in the autobiographical style. The whole scenery is perceived through an "I", which gives the composition intensity. This emphasis on the dreamer himself as the focal centre of the events seems to be typical for at least many dream stories. This is also the case in symbolic dreams where the

74 Cf. above, pp. 364ff.

dreamer can be represented through one of the symbols of the scenery.

The Vision of the Nether World is classified as a "vision", which seems to single out the experience it describes as special compared with ordinary dreams. There is, however, close resemblance between this Vision and the Death-Dream of Enkidu both in structure and imagery.[75]

The greatest change, compared with the pattern occurring in myths, lamentations and dreams, lies in the inclusion of "the unique man" in the vision and the interpretation of this man as an ideal king in contrast to the rebel rulers in the speech of Nergal. Through this inclusion the vision changes function from a vision which merely foretells the visionary's own death to a vision with a broader religious and political message.

If the vision-story should be based on a real dream experience, it is probable that the composer used one of the visionary images, that of the *ištēn eṭlu*, as the basis for his own political message which is unfolded in the interpretation.

The result of this change from the ordinary pattern was that the actual experience and fate of the visionary was no longer the only concern of the story. Just as important, or even more important, was the religious and political message of the vision and its fulfillment later in history.

The vision in Dan 7 goes one step further in this process. The actual experience of the visionary is of minor importance, the emphasis lies distinctly on the visionary imagery itself and its meaning for the history in which the visionary is involved. In Dan 7 not only a part of the imagery is relevant for future history — as in the Vision of the Nether World — but the whole imagery has historical and eschatological significance.

This survey of formal and stylistic characteristics demonstrates in fact a fairly simple pattern:

* The poems and lamentations share in a mythical perception of reality and demonstrate how man's natural environments and his own fate were formed through the actions of underworld forces.

* The dream stories demonstrate that through a dream experience, man could receive a revelation of how his own confrontation with the underworld forces would take place.

75   Cf. above, pp. 400ff.

* The Vision of the Nether World extends parts of the visionary underworld imagery to apply to a concrete period of history. The vision thus describes how this period is dependent on the acts of the underworld gods.

* The vision in Dan 7 utilizes the underworld imagery as a whole, as a key to interpret history.

III. The basic pattern of the myths is also discernible in the dream stories and visions: description of underworld beings, description of the ruling god, the judgement. There is also a stable tradition concerning the concrete imagery: the underworld beings are composed of animal and human features, often resembling some kind of winged creatures; the ruling god is sitting on a throne, surrounded by attendants. But even though the images are stable, they represent different kinds of reality.

In the poems and lamentations we can distinguish between two kinds of reality. In the myths about the dying deity the underworld scenery represents the death of vegetation that occurs every year. In these widespread myths the reality is based upon the fate of the deity and the actions of the underworld gods. Reality experienced through ordinary perception and reality experienced through mythical imagination were not separated into two distinct levels, but were two aspects of the same reality participating in each other. In a sense the mythical side was more real, because reality was formed through transcendental activity.

In the stories where an individual man is confronted by demons of the underworld, the underworld imagery does not constitute a part of ordinary reality, but reveals the threatening forces that break into one's individual life to destroy it. But also in these stories reality is perceived in a mythical perspective, because sickness, accidents and death are forced upon men from the world below.

In the dreams the dreamer is given immediate access to this mythical reality. Initially one might not see any tension between myths and dreams. But the dream implies a distinction between ordinary experience and extraordinary dream experience that could lead to a clearer distinction between immanent and transcendental reality as well. In any case, in the dream the underworld forces are not represented by objects or events belonging to everyday life, but communicate directly to the dreamer. The dream is thus the direct bridge to the underworld.

The Vision of the Nether World certainly shares the basic perception of reality represented in the dreams. Nevertheless there are
some interesting differences in the way the imagery is used. The
vision contains a confrontation between political history and transcendental reality. Through the vision the forces ultimately governing political history are revealed to the visionary. Reality is two
dimensional: on the one hand the earthly rulers acting according to
their political decisions, on the other hand the underworld forces
breaking into terrestrial reality, molding political history.

The use of the imagery in Dan 7 is ambiguous. On the one hand
the interpretation of the vision gives the impression that the vision
itself is purely symbolical. This would mean a break in relation to
the Mesopotamian traditions. The images in the vision would thus
not have any life of their own, they would only be a picture
serving to interpret reality. But this conclusion is too simple. Our
analysis of the visionary imagery has demonstrated that it was not
constructed on the basis of historical experience, but existed prior
to the historical events that it interpreted.[76] Read in the light of
the Mesopotamian traditions one gets the impression that the vision
of Dan 7 in itself communicates a message. It reveals to the
visionary an attack on the earth from the underworld.[77] Subsequently this attack was interpreted as the rise of four kings
governing four empires. The transcendental figures manifested
themselves in terrestrial counterparts.

Unlike the Vision of the Nether World Dan 7 does not represent
two separate dimensions, one transcendental and one immanent,
but these two dimensions are combined into one image: the
demonic kings. One might be tempted to classify Dan 7 as a
historical myth but this would veil the special character of the
composition. Dan 7 demonstrates a conscious interpretation of a
mythical dream imagery in order to interpret history. The scenery
is indeed still mythical, but the composition in which it occurs is
visionary. The other-worldly character of the rulers was not
something given out of a general experience and interpretation of
reality, but had to be revealed to the visionary as a hidden secret
from the highest god.

76   Cf. above, pp. 540ff.
77   Cf. above, pp. 554f.

IV. We are in the fortunate position to be able to give a fairly precise description of how the image of the unique man was created. The occurrence of this image in the Vision of the Nether World and in Dan 7 is based on both mythical, dream visionary and historical elements.

It was a common belief in Sumerio-Babylonian religion that death was imposed on man through deputies from the nether world. In the moment of death these deputies confronted man and brought him to the world below.[78]

In the Death-Dream of Enkidu the *ištēn eṭlu*, "the unique man", is clearly conceived as such a deputy. In the concrete description of the man the composer adds new mythological elements. The man appears in a thunderstorm in the resemblance of the Anzu-bird, which in Mesopotamian mythology represents a personification of the thunderstorm.[79] The designation *ištēn eṭlu* was not, however, taken from this mythological background. It is an appellation belonging to the Gattung dream story. In numerous Akkadian dream stories the leading figure of the dream, the messenger from the gods, was called *ištēn eṭlu*.[80] When the underworld traditions were fashioned as a dream story in the Death-Dream of Enkidu, the Anzu-like deputy from the nether world was given the appellation of the dominant figure of dreams, the *ištēn eṭlu*.

This collocation of underworld traditions and dream language formed the background of the Vision of the Nether World. But the Vision adds yet another element. The *ištēn eṭlu* was identified as an ideal king. This identification was possible on the linguistic level, because on the one hand *eṭlu* was frequently used to designate kings, and on the other hand, because the kings often were likened to the Anzu-bird in their frightening power.

Through this identification the dream imagery was imbued with new meaning. The *ištēn eṭlu* was no longer only a mere deputy from the gods, but the spirit of the dead king. As such *ištēn eṭlu* had to be contrasted to the other figures seen in the vision. There were fifteen *ilū*, but only one *eṭlu*. The visitation from the nether world upon the visionary and his father, which was predicted in

78 Cf. above, p. 378.
79 Cf. above, pp. 374ff.
80 Cf. above, pp. 415ff.

the vision was to be carried out by the *ištēn eṭlu* understood not
as a divine deputy, but as the death spirit of the king.[81]

This relevance of the vision for the future was rather complex
since the description of the ideal king in the speech of Nergal was
formed in a language resembling the Akkadian prophecies.[82] The
intention behind the use of this style seems to have been the wish
to elevate the dead Sennacherib as a king whose reign was
according to the will of the gods. The result was in fact that the
vision, read out of context, predicted not only the visitation of the
death spirit of the king, but also the rise of the king to rule a
glorious new kingdom. Such a non-contextual interpretation was
facilitated by the fact that none of the figures of the vision were
identified. The vision was an enigma.

V.   One way to interpret this enigma within the framework of
Mesopotamian religion could be to see a connection between the
death spirit of the king and the rise of a new historical king. The
spirit of the dead king would thus have manifested itself in the
rise of a new kingdom. Such version of the vision is not preserved,
but it would have been a possible link between the vision in its
original context and the traditions that were adopted into 4 Ezra 13
and Dan 7.[83]

These two Jewish visions utilized somewhat different features of
the Vision. The original vision in 4 Ezra 13 seems in some respect
to be closer to the preceding Mesopotamian vision than Dan 7.
Here the basic image of the death spirit, appearing in the shape of
a thunderbird, ascending from the underworld, is preserved.[84]
Dan 7 contains in this respect a more non-mythological imagery.
The man is still associated with the Anzu-bird imagery through
the four wind-spirits and the clouds, but he is no longer characterized as a spirit himself.[85]

But as a whole the vision in Dan 7 reflects more of the Mesopotamian background than 4 Ezra 13. The semantic pattern according
to which the man is described in the Vision of the Nether World is

81   Cf. above, pp. 437f.
82   Cf. above, pp. 435ff, 472ff, 488ff.
83   Cf. above, pp. 554ff.
84   Cf. above, pp. 530ff.
85   Cf. above, pp. 513f.

taken over in Dan 7. The man is a visionary figure, he stands in contrast to the monsters and he is an ideal king.[86]

Turning now to the message, there are some basic features that demonstrate continuity between the Akkadian and Jewish visions. In all three visions the appearance of the man signifies the destruction of his enemies. In all three cases the man comes from the nether world to carry out his mission.[87] In the Akkadian vision and Dan 7 the enemy is defined as a rebel king.[88] In these two visions the appearance of the man is also accompanied by a description of his glorious reign.

But this does not belie the fact that the image of the man is given a new setting in the Jewish context. In Dan 7 this is apparent through the application of the Enochic traditions to Mesopotamian imagery. Thus "the man" appears as a parallel figure to Enoch, who was taken up to heaven to reside among the holy ones, and given the task to pronounce judgement over the demonic monsters on earth on behalf of suffering men. In this context the man became a sign, not only of destruction of the rebel king, but also a sign of liberation of the oppressed people.

But the composer of Dan 7 seems to go still further. He combined the two basic images from the Mesopotamian vision — namely "the man" ascending from the underworld and "the man" as a king in a glorious kingdom — with the basic theme from the Book of Watchers, namely the vindication of those who had suffered and died innocently. Thus he created a new image in Jewish eschatology: The ascension of "the man" as a sign of vindication of the martyrs.

Needless to say, this image became an enigma in Jewish theology. The background of the image can be traced in detail, but that does not mean that the figure itself is identified. In Jewish eschatology this is not without analogy. Even though the mission of the Servant of the Lord in Is 53 most probably is to be explained in terms of Old Testament prophetic traditions, the figure itself is not identified. In neither cases is the figure simply conceived as a reoccurrence of a past figure or an eschatological reflection of a contemporary figure. In both cases the identity of the figures is a

---

86 Cf. above, pp. 495ff.
87 For Dan 7, cf. above, pp. 534f.
88 Cf. above, pp. 483f.

secret. The images were signs crying out to be identified — a task left for subsequent interpreters, as may clearly be seen in the many attempts to interpret Is 53 and Dan 7 in Jewish and Christian theology.

Roots of Apocalyptic

Our examination of the roots of apocalyptic has been based on two currents of tradition, the traditions centered around the Enoch figure and those centered around the Son of Man in Dan 7. The limitation of the Jewish sources investigated demands cautious conclusions with respect to the general value of the results for apocalyptic literature as a whole. So far as the Enochic traditions are concerned we have examined only the earliest literary sources. So far as the Danielic traditions are concerned we have concentrated mostly on one text, Dan 7. Since we are dealing with the "roots", we have not examined the development of Jewish eschatology in exilic and post-exilic time, nor concentrated on the growth of prophetic visionary literature. In non-Jewish cultures we have commented on Persian revelatory literature, but not made this a subject in its own right. Egyptian sources have not been analyzed at all.

Still, the limitation of our inquiry has not been accidental. It has been determined by two factors: 1) The Enochic literature is the oldest apocalyptic literature in Judaism, and it is therefore inevitable that we should start the inquiry here; likewise as Dan 7 is the first fully developed apocalyptical text within the Danielic traditions, an inquiry into the roots of the Danielic apocalyptic has to include Dan 7 as the main source. 2) In the analysis of both currents of tradition we have concentrated on fixed underlying sources, which form the main background. We have not extended the investigation to include all factors that may have influence the emergence of apocalyptic.

Thus we claim that the limitation of scope strengthens the validity of the results. This limitation has made it possible to work out the background in detail, carefully analyzing each step in the growth of the traditions.

We have analyzed each of the two blocks of tradition in isolation. The only exception is the third section of Part II where the Enochic traditions had to be included, because of their influence on Dan 7. The analysis of each block has clearly demonstrated that the Danielic and Enochic apocalyptic developed out of different kinds of Mesopotamian traditions. There is no common source for Jewish apocalyptic, neither in any particular myth, nor in any particular religious concept or tradition. The Enochic traditions are rooted in Mesopotamian traditions about primeval time, the Danielic traditions of Dan 7 in Mesopotamian underworld traditions and visionary literature.

Yet this is not the only conclusion of our investigation. Although the roots are to be found in different traditions, they are found in both cases in texts and depictions belonging to the Sumerian-Babylonian-Assyrian continuum of tradition. The roots are distinctly older than often presumed, and were adopted into Judaism at an earlier stage than often presumed. Thus we may surely conclude that the roots of the Enochic and Danielic apocalyptic lie in the Mesopotamian area, and that the special character of apocalyptic is caused by the inclusion of traditions stemming from this area.

But our analysis enables us to go further still in our conclusions. When the roots are to be found in two distinct blocks, it is even more interesting to ask about the common denominators of both blocks. Somewhere such denominators must have existed, because even though the Enochic and Danielic apocalyptic show distinct characteristics, they both represent the same kind of Jewish revelatory literature. Eventually the two lines even intersect each other in the latest stratum of Dan 7. These denominators cannot relate primarily to the content of the sources used by the Jewish apocalyptical scribes, because the content differs. They must lie in the kind of material used and in the way this material is interpreted in the course of tradition. Accordingly we must compare the characteristics of the two blocks of material, and then try to trace common pattern.

With reference to the formal characteristics, it is not difficult to see the difference between the Danielic and Enochic literature. The Book of Daniel contains legends, dream stories and visions, forming three separate Gattungen, although the dreams and visions share the same basic pattern. These dreams and visions are structured according to a visionary pattern throughout, which means that it is not possible to separate a non-visionary stratum in the texts without destroying their whole structure.

This is significantly different in the Enochic material. In the earliest sources dealing with Enoch, Gen 4,17; 5,21-24; Pseudo-Eupolemus and Ben-Sira, Enoch is not described as a visionary, nor is he involved in a visionary drama. The first Enochic book, the Astronomical Book, has only vague traces of a visionary pattern. The Book of Watchers, written shortly afterwards, contains a variety of forms. The first book consisting of visions is the Book of Dreams, written about hundred years later than the first Enochic literature. When one applies a diachronic model to the material, it is not difficult to see how the visionary forms have expanded in the growth of the traditions and literature, transforming mythical and legendary literature into visionary literature.

These different characteristics of the Danielic and Enochic literature are easy to explain considering the different background of the two blocks. We have demonstrated that the Mesopotamian source utilized in Dan 7 already existed as a visionary unit when it was adopted into Judaism. The unit, going back to the Vision of the Nether World, existed from the beginning as a vision. We have assumed that this was also the case with Dan 2 and 4 considering their parallels with Zoroaster's vision. They were both produced under the influence of visionary traditions.

This was not the case with the background of the Enoch literature. With regard to form, the background demonstrates the same variety as the Enoch literature itself. This is caused by the fact that the fixed points in the background material were primarily connected with primordial figures that could be adapted to different kinds of material.

Focussing upon this difference makes it easier to determine exactly what is common in the two currents. This can be shown in a table that gives a brief outline of the Danielic traditions of Dan 7 and of the Enochic traditions. The basis for the outline is to be found in the concluding chapters to Enoch and the Son of Man.

	DANIEL	
	General	The unique man
Mesopotamian Level		
Mythical or legendary narrative	Gods or humans descending to the nether world	Deputies from the nether world
Dream or visionary implications	Death dreams foretelling the death of the dreamer (The Death-Dream of Enkidu)	"Unique men" appearing in dreams The "unique man" as deputy from the nether world
Vision	The Vision of the Nether World used to interpret history	The "unique man" as visionary figure and as ideal king
Jewish Level		
Mythical or legendary narrative		
Dream or visionary implications		
Vision	Dan 7: Vision used as a key to interpret history	The Son of Man as visionary figure and ideal king

ENOCH

Heroes				Catastrophe-theme
Enmeduranki and Uanadapa ascending to the heavenly assembly (Enm. and the Div.; Bīt Mēseri)	Enmeduranki reads the heavenly tablets (Enm. and the Div.)	Uanadapa reveals the divine secrets (Berossos)	Ziusudra, hero of the flood (general)	Primeval flood catastrophe (general)
		Uanadapa as composer of an astronomical work through revelation (Catal. of Texts and Auth.)	Ziusudra warned through a dream (Atra-Ḫasis; Berossos)	Primeval catastrophe revealed in a visionary framework (Poem of Erra)
Enoch is taken to God (Gen 5,21ff)	Enoch reads the heavenly tablets (En 81)	Enoch reveals the divine secrets (Ben Sira; Pseudo-Eup.; Jub)	Enoch, hero of the primeval catastrophe (En 12-16; Jub)	Primeval catastrophe (En 6-11)
	Enoch reads the heavenly tablets in a vision (Epistle of Enoch)	Enoch is shown an astronomical work (Astronomical Book)		Primeval catastrophe in visionary framework (En 6-11 + 1-5; 12-19)
Enoch's visionary ascension to the heavenly assembly (En 14)			Enoch sees the primeval catastrophe in visions (Book of Dreams)	Primeval catastrophe as a visionary theme (Book of Dreams)

The influence of the Mesopotamian traditions bears upon the core of both the Enochic and Danielic literature, namely the basic themes and structure of content. For the sake of illustration one could compare the Old Testament prophetic traditions, which gave rise to the historical-eschatological perspective of reality that also became a part of apocalyptic. The prophets could use images from non-Yahwistic religions, but their message was not based on fixed patterns that existed independently of the historical situation they addressed. Their preaching, although having traditional features in form and content, nevertheless grew out of concrete historical experience. The Danielic and Enochic traditions developed differently. Here the more genuine Israelite features were fused with already established patterns and served to transform them in accordance with the Jewish faith.

To examine the roots of apocalyptic is thus to examine the history of this process, and how it affected form, imagery and the concept of reality.

1. With regard to form the scheme above demonstrates how legendary and mythical traditions were transformed in both cases to visions. We can observe in detail the different stages of this gradual process. In both cases the mythical and legendary material had dream of visionary implications from the very earliest stage. The difference is that the basic structure of Dan 7 already existed in visionary form in the Mesopotamian environment, while the "Enochic" traditions first found their decisive visionary form after they were adopted into Judaism.

2. The change of forms also meant a transformation of imagery. Initially the traditions functioned within a mythical universe. As a part of this universe they served to preserve, legitimize and explain basic features of reality. Reality was brought about by the acts of the gods or semi-divine beings in a transcendental realm or in mythical, primeval time. In the course of tradition these transcendental images were applied to history, and in the Jewish setting also to the eschatological time.

These features occur in different manner in the sources, but the main lines can be traced in both blocks of tradition. A more concrete impression can be gained from a comparison between the underworld theme in the Danielic traditions and the catastrophe theme in the Enochic traditions.

Underworld theme	Catastrophe theme
Myths telling of the death of gods as the basic reason for change of seasons and death in nature (Vegetation myths)	Primeval flood-story telling of the primeval catastrophe causing the fundamental features of present reality (Atra-Ḥasis)
Visionary transference of the underworld images to interpret a certain period of history (Vision of the Nether World)	Transference of the flood theme to interpret a certain period of history. The catastrophe implying a demonic attack on the earth. Placed in a visionary framework (Poem of Erra)
Visionary transference of the underworld images directly applied to history, where the images were represented through terrestrial figures facing the eschatological drama (Dan 7)	Application of the catastrophe theme, implying a demonic imagery, to history, where the demonic images were reflected in the acts of terrestrial figures facing the eschatological drama. Placed in a visionary framework (Book of Watchers)

The same three stage pattern can be traced in both cases. It gives a significant illustration of how different themes could function in a similar way. It also demonstrates how the application of mythical imagery to historical change started in the Mesopotamian milieu, and was reinforced by the Jewish scribes.

3.   Myths imply a dual perception of reality. The two sides of reality, the transcendental and the immanent, overlap. The terrestrial reality directly represents the transcendental reality, and is directly shaped by the acts of transcendental beings. Of course humans can play a role in the mythical story, as for instance in Atra-Ḥasis, but the gods always have the last word. This means that the basic crises in reality not are solved in this world, but in the transcendental realm.

Although we run the risk of oversimplifying the material, we believe that the Old Testament traditions in this sense are non-mythological. Surely the Israelites saw whole reality governed by supernatural forces, above all Yahweh. But the fundamental crises in reality are nevertheless understood as belonging to this world, and they had to be solved in this world. For instance, the Israelites did not as far as we know create a myth about a struggle between Baal and Yahweh, which would have been possible bearing in mind the mythological climate, and tempting bearing in mind the rivalry between the two gods. The conflict was understood as a conflict between the worshippers of the two gods.

What separates the apocalyptical literature from the earlier Old Testament traditions is the adoption of the dual perception of reality found in the myths. Besides the extensive use of the visionary form and mythical images, this dual perception of reality is the most distinctive feature of apocalyptical literature. The crisis in reality is no longer seen as a crisis begun and ended in this world, but ultimately brought about through the intervention of divine beings, and solved through the destruction of these beings. This is exemplified by the demonic kings and kingdoms in the Book of Daniel fighting against the holy ones, and the fallen angels and their monstrous offspring in the Book of Watchers, also opposing a group of holy ones.

But because of the monotheistic structure of Jewish religion the dual image of reality acquired a specific character. In the Mesopotamian myths a crisis in reality could be traced back to gods opposing each other: Ereshkigal opposing Inanna in the Descent of Inanna; Ea opposing Enlil in Atra-Hasis; Marduk opposing Tiamat in Enuma Elish; Erra opposing Marduk in the Poem of Erra. The gods were to be feared, not to be worshipped for their moral standards.

This perception of reality was excluded for the apocalyptic scribes if they wanted to hold fast to the core of their Jewish faith. They could not explain the transcendental crisis underlying reality as a conflict between gods acting according to their own non-human logic, but had to take the supremacy of Yahweh and his just world-rule for granted. Accordingly, starting with one positive pole in reality, the transcendental crisis had to be explained in terms of a negative one. The dual perception was changed towards a dualistic one. We state "towards", because the monotheistic conviction that Yahweh was the only god of the created world made it impossible to include a negative pole of equal strength and force as Yahweh.

This shift from a dual perception of reality to a modified dualism forms the greatest break between the Mesopotamian and Jewish form of the traditions. It can be observed in the Book of Watchers in the reinterpretation of the primeval catastrophe and apkallu traditions, where the ambiguous figures of the antediluvian period were distinctly formed as one "demonic" group opposing the one God and his holy ones; and in Dan 7, where the frightening, but nevertheless revered underworld gods of the Vision of the Nether World, appeared as demonic rulers, here also opposing the one God and his holy ones.

These three characteristics, the visionary form, the mythical imagery and a modified dualistic perception of reality correspond closely to each other. The transcendental forces shaping reality could only be perceived through a visionary experience and only described in mythical images.

The emergence of the apocalyptical traditions and literature presupposes both a direct contact with Mesopotamian culture in the Babylonian diaspora, and the syncretistic tendencies in Palestine in the post-exilic centuries. But these more general conditions are not sufficient to explain why this kind of literature was created. Although we have not focused upon the sociological factors underlying the emergence of apocalyptic, we believe our analysis can shed some light on this question.

If we accept the three characteristics noted above, that apocalyptic is characterized by the visionary form, the mythical imagery, and a modified dualistic perception of reality, we observe that both the Enochic and Danielic traditions became apocalyptic in their growth in the Jewish milieu. The apocalyptic characteristics were not created altogether at the very moment the traditions were taken over from the Babylonian setting. This means that we are not necessarily dealing with one simple basic historical factor that caused both the adoption of the Mesopotamian traditions and the gradual shaping of these traditions into apocalyptic. There must have been several factors involved.

Why did Jewish circles adopt these Mesopotamian traditions? In our study on Enoch we found that Jews claiming Levitical ancestry adopted the traditions in order to gain a new religious platform over against the Zadokite priests. There are no traces of a similar pattern in the Book of Daniel. Although we must be cautious at this point, because only parts of the book have been fully examined, the Book of Daniel seems to have adopted the Mesopotamian material for different reasons. If we are correct that Dan 2; 4-5 and 7 once formed a cycle of "visions of destruction", the concern of the Danielic scribes was from the very beginning the acts of God in pagan history. They took over pagan prophetic and visionary traditions revealing the divine plans of history and shaped them according to their own faith.

Thus the factors underlying the initial shaping of the Enochic and Danielic traditions seem to differ. But there are nevertheless two similarities. In both cases the traditions were shaped by a minority group over against a dominant majority, and in both cases new questions arising out of radical new experiences demanded answers that could not be given by reproducing the old Israelite traditions. In short, we have minority groups creating a new theology trying to establish new religious platforms. It seems as if already here we have the germ of later apocalyptic.

Thus at the point of transition from a Babylonian to a Jewish setting the elements which were later to develop into apocalyptic were already at hand: the mythical-visionary traditions based on a dual perception of reality, taken over from the Mesopotamian environment; the necessity to transform these traditions in accordance with a Jewish historical perspective of reality; the "dualistic experience" of a minority group facing conflict with a majority.

But the emergence of apocalyptic in the fully developed form which we find in Dan 7 and the Book of Watchers cannot be explained simply as an internal traditional development of these already existent tendencies. New decisive experiences had to be added. On the historical level these experiences came under the dominion of the Macedonian rulers, first during the Diadochan wars, then during the persecutions under Antiochus Epiphanes.

Here the Jews faced a heathen empire occupying Palestine with formidable religious, cultural and political strength. This challenge caused new disruptions in the Jewish society with differing attitudes toward the new emperors. For the scribes of the Danielic and Enochic traditions this frightening experience gave the decisive impetus towards developing a system which on the one hand took the overwhelming impact of the heathen power seriously, on the other hand not giving up their faith in the God of Israel as the Lord of history. The modified dualistic system was created by which the heathen impact represented demonic power subduing just men who stood under the rulership of God and the holy ones of heaven.

Thus the apocalyptical universe emerged in a moment when evil was experienced as a power transgressing human limits. It was the experience of non-human evil. The mythical and visionary traditions taken over from the Babylonian diaspora gave the apocalyptical scribes the opportunity to create a religious universe where these frightening non-human experiences could be included. As a result a new kind of hope rose in Jewish society, by which the transcendental impact of evil was confronted with a transcendental power of justice. In the Enochic traditions this hope was represented by the sage Enoch, living in the transcendental realm of God, and pronouncing judgement over the demonic forces. In the Danielic traditions this hope attached to the Son of Man, the transcendental ideal king, who through his ascension from the realm of death would be a sign of liberation for the faithful struggling in the throes of martyrdom.

Abbreviations

AAA	Annals of Archeology and Anthropology, University of Liverpool
AAH	Acta antiqua academiae scientarum Hungaricae
ABSA	Annal of the British School at Athens
AcIr	Acta Iranica
AcOr	Acta orientalia
AfO	Archiv für Orientforschung
AHAW.PH	Abhandlungen der Heidelberger Akademie der Wissenschaften. Philosophisch-historische Klasse
AHW	W. von Soden. Akkadisches Handwörterbuch
ALBO	Analecta Lovaniensia biblica et orientalia
AnAb	Antike und Abendland
AnBib	Analecta biblica
AncB	Anchor Bible
ANET	Ancient Near Eastern Texts Relating to the Old Testament
AnOr	Analecta orientalia
AOAT	Alter Orient und Altes Testament
ArOr	Archiv orientální
AS	Assyriological Studies
ASSF	Acta societatis scientarum Fennicae
ATD	Das Alte Testament Deutsch
AThANT	Abhandlungen zur Theologie des Alten und Neuen Testaments
Attridge/Oden	Philo of Byblos. The Phoenician History
BaghM	Baghdader Mitteilungen
BASOR	Bulletin of the American Schools of Oriental Research
BHTh	Beiträge zur historischen Theologie
BibOr	Biblica et orientalia
BJRL	Bulletin of the John Rylands Library
BK	Biblischer Kommentar
BSt	Biblische Studien, Neukirchen
Burstein	The Babyloniaca of Berossos
BWANT	Beiträge zur Wissenschaft vom Alten und Neuen Testament
BZ	Biblische Zeitschrift
BZAW	Beihefte zur Zeitschrift für die alttestamentliche Wissenschaft
CAD	Assyrian Dictionary of the Oriental Institute of the University of Chicago
CB.NT	Coniectanea Biblica. New Testament Series
CB.OT	Coniectanea Biblica. Old Testament Series
CBQ	Catholic Biblical Quarterly
CBQ.MS	Catholic Biblical Quarterly. Monograph Series
CeB	Century Bible
CP	Classical Philology
CTBT	Cuneiform Texts from Babylonian Tablets in the British Museum

CuW	Christentum und Wissenschaft
DAWB.SSA	Deutsche Akademie der Wissenschaften zu Berlin. Schriften der Sektion für Altertumswissenschaft
DJD	Discoveries in the Judean Desert
EdF	Erträge der Forschung
EnAnC	Entretiens sur l'Antiquité classique
EThL	Ephemerides theologicae Lovanienses
Euseb.(Arm.)Chron	Eusebius' Chronica According to the Armenian Translation
FGH	Fragmente der griechischen Historiker
Fitzmeyer and Harrington	A Manual of Palestinian Aramaic Texts
FoBib	Forschung zur Bibel
FRLANT	Forschungen zur Religion und Literatur des Alten und Neuen Testaments
GAG	W. von Soden. Grundriss der akkadischen Grammatik
GCS	Griechische christliche Schriftsteller der ersten drei Jahrhunderte
GML	Geist des Morgenlandes
Gr^{Pan}	Greek Text to 1 Enoch According to Codex Panopolitanus
Gr^{Syn}	Greek Text to 1 Enoch According to Syncellus
HAT	Handbuch zum Alten Testament
HK	Göttinger Handkommentar zum Alten Testament
HNT	Handbuch zum Neuen Testament
HO	Handbuch der Orientalistik
HSAT	Die Heilige Schrift des Alten Testaments
HSM	Harvard Semitic Monographs
HThR	Harvard Theological Review
HThS	Harvard Theological Studies
HUCA	Hebrew Union College Annual
HZ	Historische Zeitschrift
ICC	International Critical Commentary
IEJ	Israel Exploration Journal
IOS	Israel Oriental Studies
JAOS	Journal of the American Oriental Society
JBL	Journal of Biblical Literature
JCS	Journal of Cuneiform Studies
JJS	Journal of Jewish Studies
JNES	Journal of Near Eastern Studies
JQR	Jewish Quarterly Review
JRAS	Journal of the Royal Asiatic Socity
JSHRZ	Jüdische Schriften aus hellenistisch-römischer Zeit
JSJ	Journal for the Study of Judaism
JSOT	Journal for the Study of the Old Testament
JThS	Journal of Theological Studies
KAT	Kommentar zum Alten Testament
KDVSMfM	Det Kongelige Danske Videnskabers Selskab Matematisk-fysiske Meddelelser
LCL	Loeb Classical Library
LLA	Library of Liberal Arts
LXX	Septuaginta
MAOG	Mitteilungen der altorientalischen Gesellschaft
M.CSA	Mesopotamia. Copenhagen Studies in Assyriology
MGWJ	Monatsschrift für Geschichte und Wissenschaft des Judentums
Milik	The Books of Enoch
MIOF	Mitteilungen des Instituts für Orientforschung
MNAW.L	Mededelingen der k. nederlandse Akademie van Wettenschappen. Afdeling Letterkunde

MSS	Münchener Studien zur Sprachwissenschaft
MU	Münchener Universitätsschriften
MVÄG	Mitteilungen der vorderasiatisch-ägyptischen Gesellschaft
NTS	New Testament Studies
NTT	Norsk teologisk tidsskrift
OrAnt	Oriens antiquus
OrBOr	Orbis biblicus et orientalis
OTL	Old Testament Library
OTS	Oudtestamentische Studien
PB	Penguin Books
PC	Penguin Classics
PLO	Porta linguarum orientalum
Praep Ev	Eusebius. Praeperatio Evangelica
PsVTGr	Pseudepigrapha Veteris Testamenti Graece
RA	Revue d'assyriologie et d'archéologie orientale
RB	Revue biblique
RevQ	Revue de Qumran
RGG	Religion in Geschichte und Gegenwart
RLA	Reallexikon der der Asyriologie
RLV	Reallexikon der Vorgeschichte
RM	Religionen der Menschheit
RSR	Recherches de science religieuse
SANE	Sources and Monographs on the Ancient Near East
SBAr	Studies in Biblical Archaeology
SBL	Society of Biblical Literature
SBM	Stuttgarter biblische Monographien
SBS	Stuttgarter Bibelstudien
SBT	Studies in Biblical Theology
SC	Sources chrétiennes
SeptVTG	Septuaginta Vetus Testamentum Graecum
SS	Studi semitici
SSAW.PH	Sitzungsberichte der sächsischen Akademie der Wissenschaften zu Leipzig. Philosophische-historische Klasse
SSS	Semitic Studies Series
StOr	Studia orientalia. Helsingfors
StP	Studia Pöhl
StTh	Studia theologica
Syncellus	Eusebius' Chronica According to Syncellus' Chronicle
TAPhS	Transactions of the American Philosophical Society
TB	Theologische Bücherei
THAT	Theologisches Handwörteruch zum Alten Testament
ThR	Theologische Rundschau
ThRv	Theologische Revue
ThStKr	Theologische Studien und Kritiken
ThWAT	Theologisches Wörterbuch zum Alten Testament
ThWNT	Theologisches Wörterbuch zum Neuen Testament
ThZ	Theologische Zeitschrift. Basel
TM	Textus Masoreticus
TPAPA	Transactions and Proceedings of the American Philological Association
TS	Theological Studies
TSTS	Toronto Semitic Texts and Studies
UET	Ur Excavations. Texts
UF	Ugarit Forschungen
UTB	Uni-Taschenbücher
VAB	Vorderasiatische Bibliothek
VNAW.L	Verhandelingen der k. nederlanse Akademie van Wettenschappen. Afdeling Letterkunde

VT	Vetus Testamentum
VT.S	Vetus Testamentum Supplementum
WBTh	Wiener Beiträge zur Theologie
WdF	Wege der Forschung
WM	Wörterbuch der Mythologie
WMANT	Wissenschaftliche Monographien zum Alten und Neuen Testament
WO	Welt des Orients
WUNT	Wissenschaftliche Untersuchungen zum Neuen Testament
WZKM	Wiener Zeitschrift für die Kunde des Morgenlandes
ZA	Zeitschrift der Assyriologie
ZAW	Zeitschrift für die alttestamentliche Wissenschaft
ZDMG	Zeitschrift der deutschen morgenländischen Gesellschaft
ZNW	Zeitschrift für die neutestamentliche Wissenschaft
ZThK	Zeitschrift für Theologie und Kirche

Bibliography

a) Texts, Translations and Anthologies

Bible and Judaism

Allegro, J.M.   Discoveries in the Judean Desert of Jordan V. Qumran Cave 4, Oxford 1968.

Barthélmy, D. and J.T. Milik   Discoveries in the Judean Desert I. Qumran Cave 1, Oxford 1956.

Berger, K.   Das Buch der Jubiläen, JSHRZ II/3, Gütersloh 1981.

Beyer, K.   Die aramäischen Texte vom Toten Meer. Göttingen 1984.

Black, M. (ed.)   Apocalypsis Henochi Graece. Fragmenta Pseudepigraphorum quae supersunt Greaeca. Una cum historicum et auctorum judaeorum hellenistarum fragmentis collegit et ordinavit A.-M. Denis, Leiden 1970.

Bowker, J.   The Targums and Rabbinic Literature, Cambridge 1969.

Box, G.H.   The Ezra-Apocalypse, London 1912.

Cerani, A.M.   Monumenta sacra et profana, Volume V, Fasc. I, Milano 1868.

Charles, R.H. (ed.)   The Apocrypha and Pseudepigrapha of the Old Testament I-II, Oxford 1913 (1964).

— The Book of Enoch, Oxford 1912.

— The Book of Jubilees, London 1902.

— The Ethiopic Version of the Book of Enoch . . . together with the Fragmentary Greek and Latin Versions, Oxford 1906.

— The Ethiopic Versions of the Hebrew Book of Jubilees, Oxford 1895.

— The Greek Versions of the Testament of the Twelve Patriarchs, Oxford 1908 (repr. Darmstadt 1960).

Colson, F.H. et al.   Philo I-X, with an English Translation, with two supplementary volumes transl. by R. Marcus, LCL, London-Cambridge (Mass.) 1929 (repr. 1961-71).

Déaut, R. le   Targum du Pentateuque, Tome 1 Genèse, SC, Paris 1978.

Dillman, A.   Veteris Testamenti Aethiopici. Libri Apocryphi, tomus V, Berlin 1894.

Ellinger, K. and W. Rudolph (eds.)   Biblia Hebraica Stuttgartensia. Textum Masoreticum cur H. Rüger. Masorum elabor. G.E. Weil, Stuttgart 1977.

Etheridge, J.W.   The Targums of Onkelos and Jonathan ben Uzziel on the Pentateuch (first publ. 1862), New York 1968.

Fitzmyer, J.A.   The Genesis Apocryphon of Qumran Cave 1, BibOr 18A, 2nd rev.ed., Rome 1971.

Fitzmyer, J.A. and D.J. Harrington   A Manual of Palestinian Aramaic Texts, BibOr 34, Rome 1978.

Ginsburger, M. (ed.)   Pseudo-Jonathan, Berlin 1903 (repr. Hildesheim New York 1971).

Hammershaimb, E. et al.   De gammeltestamentlige Pseudepigrafer i oversættelse med innledning og noter, København 1953ff.

Herford, R.T.   Pirke Aboth. The Ethics of the Talmud: Sayings of the Fathers, New York 1945 (1962).

Hilgenfeld, A.   Messias Judaeorum, Leipzig 1869.

Jonge, M. de   Testamenta XII Patriarcharum, PsVTGr 1, Leiden 1964.

Jongeling, B. et al.   Aramaic Texts from Qumran I, SSS, Leiden 1976.

Kautzsch, E. (ed.) Die Apokryphen und Pseudepigraphen des Alten Testaments I-II, Tübingen 1900 (repr. Darmstadt 1962).

Kittel, R. (ed.) Biblia Hebraica. Textum Masoretium cur. P. Kahle, Stuttgart 1937 (1966).

Knibb, M.A. The Ethiopic Book of Enoch. A New Edition in the Light of the Aramaic Dead Sea Fragments, Vol. I: Text and Apparatus, Vol. II: Introduction, Translation and Commentary, Oxford 1978.

Lohse, E. Die Texte aus Qumran, Darmstadt 1971.

Milik, J.T. The Books of Enoch. Aramaic Fragments of Qumran Cave 4, Oxford 1976.

— "'Prière de Nabonide' et autres écrits d'un cycle de Daniel", RB 63, 1956, pp. 407-15.

— "Le Testament de Lévi en araméen: Fragment de la grotte 4 de Qumrân", RB 62, 1955, pp. 398-406.

— "4Q Visions d'Amram et une citation d'Origine", RB 79, 1972, pp. 77-97.

Nestle, E. Novum Testamentum Graece, 25th ed., Stuttgart 1966.

Rahlfs, A. Septuaginta, 9th ed., Stuttgart 1935.

Segal, M.S. Säfär ben Sira haššalem, Jerusalem 1959.

Smend, R. (ed.) Die Weisheit des Jesus Sirach. Hebräisch und Deutsch, Berlin 1906.

Swete, H.B. (ed.) The Old Testament in Greek According to the Septuagint, 3rd ed., Cambridge 1905.

Thackeray, H.St.J. Josephus I. Against Apion, with an English Translation, LCL, London-Cambrige (Mass.), 1927-28 (1976).

— Josephus IV. Jewish Antiquities, with an English Translation, LCL, London Cambridge (Mass.), 1930 (1967).

Violet, B. Die Apokalypsen des Esra und des Baruch in deutscher Gestalt, GCS, Leipzig 1924.

— Die Esra-Apokalypse. Erster Teil. Die Überlieferung, Leiden 1910.

Vulgata I-II, 1931-74.

Walter, N. Fragmente jüdisch-hellenistischer Historiker, JSHRZ I, Gütersloh 1976.

Wevers, J.W. (ed.) Genesis, SeptVTG I, Göttingen 1974.

Yadin, Y. The Ben Sira Scroll from Masada, Jerusalem 1965.

Ziegler, J. (ed.) Sapientia Jesu Filii Sirach, SeptVTG XII/2, Göttingen 1965.

Mesopotamian Provenance

Alster, B. Dumuzi's Dream. Aspects of Oral Poetry in a Sumerian Myth, Mesopotamia I, Copenhagen 1972.

Biggs, R.D. "More Babylonian Prophecies", Iraq 29, 1967, pp. 117-32.

Borger, R. Babylonisch-assyrische Lesestücke II, Roma 1963.

— "Die Beschwörungsserie Bīt Mēseri und die Himmelfahrt Henochs", JNES 33, 1974, pp. 183-96.

— Die Inschriften Asarhaddons, Königs von Assyrien, AfO, Beiheft 9, Graz 1956.

Budge, E.A.W and L.W. King The Annals of the Kings of Assyria, London 1902.

Böhl, F.M.T. de Liagre Het Gilgamesj Epos, Amsterdam 1958.

Burstein, S.M. The Babyloniaca of Berossos, SANE 1/5, Malibu, California 1978.

Cagni, L. L'epopea di Erra, SS 34, Roma 1969.

— The Poem of Erra, SANE 1/3, Malibu, California 1974.

Castellino, G.R. "Incantation to Utu", OrAnt 8, 1969, pp. 1-57.

Civil, M. "The Sumerian Flood-Story", in W.G. Lambert and A.R. Millard, Atra-Ḥasis. The Babylonian Story of the Flood, Oxford 1969, pp. 138-45.

Dijk, J. van Sumerische Götterlieder, AHAW.PH, Abh. 1, Heidelberg 1960.

Ebeling, E. "Bruchstücke eines politischen Propagandagedichtes aus einer assyrischen Kanzlei", MAOG 12, 1938, pp. 1-41.
— "Kritische Beiträge zu neueren assyriologischen Veröffentlichungen", MAOG 10, 1937, pp. 1-20.
— Tod und Leben nach den Vorstellungen der Babylonier I, Berlin-Leipzig 1931.
Falkenstein, A. Sumerische und akkadische Hymnen und Gebete, Zürich 1953.
Finkelstein, J.J. "The Antediluvian Kings: A University of California Tablet", JCS 17, 1963, pp. 39-51.
Frank, C. "Lamastu, Pazuzu und andere Dämonen. Ein Beitrag zur babyl.-assyr. Dämonologie", MAOG 14, 1941, pp. 23-41.
Gadd, C.J. "Some Contributions to the Gilgamesh Epic", Iraq 28, 1966, pp. 105-21.
Gadd, C.J. and S.N. Kramer Ur Excavations. Texts VI, London 1966.
Grayson, A.K. Assyrian and Babylonian Chronicles, TCS 5, New York 1975.
— Babylonian Historical Literary Texts, TSTS 3, Toronto 1975.
Grayson, A.K. and W.G. Lambert "Akkadian Prophecies", JCS 18, 1964, pp. 7-30.
Gurney, O.R. "Babylonian Prophylactic Figures and their Rituals", AAA 12, 1935, pp. 31-96.
Hallo, W.W. and W.L. Moran "The First Tablet of the SB Recension of the Anzu Myth", JCS 31, 1979, pp. 65-115.
Hunger, H. Spätbabylonische Texte aus Uruk I. Ausgrabungen der deutschen Forschungsgemeinschaft in Uruk-Warka 9, Berlin 1976.
Hunger, H. and S. Kaufmann "A New Akkadian Prophecy Text", JAOS 95, 1975, pp. 371-5.
Jacobsen, T. The Sumerian King List, AS 11, Chicago 1939.
Jacobsen, T. and S.N. Kramer "The Myth of Inanna and Bilulu", JNES 12, 1953, pp. 160-88.
Köcher, F. "Der babylonische Göttertypentext", MIOF I, 1959, pp. 57-103.
Kramer, S.N. "The 'Babel of Tongues': A Sumerian Version", JAOS 88, 1968, pp. 108-11.
— "The Death of Gilgamesh", BASOR 94, 1944, pp. 2-12.
— "The Death of Ur-Nummu and his Descent to the Netherworld", JCS 21, 1967 pp. 104-22.
— Gilgamesh and the Huluppu-Tree, AS 10, Chicago 1938.
— Two Elegies on a Puskin Museum Tablet. A New Sumerian Literary Genre, Moscow 1960.
Kraus, F.R. "Zur Liste der älteren Könige von Babylonien", ZA, NF 16 (50), 1952, pp. 29-60.
Lambert, W.G. Babylonian Wisdom Literature, Oxford 1960.
— "A Catalogue of Texts and Authors", JCS 16, 1962, pp. 59-77.
— "Enmeduranki and Related Matters", JCS 21, 1967, pp. 126-38.
— "The Gula Hymn of Bullutsa-rabi", Orientalia 36, 1967, pp. 105-32.
— "Literary Style in the First Millenium Mesopotamia", JAOS 88, 1968, pp. 123-32.
— "Nebuchadnezzar King of Justice", Iraq 37, 1965, pp. 1-11.
— "A New Fragment from a List of Antediluvian Kings and Marduk's Chariot", Symbolae Biblicae et Mesopotamicae, Francisco Mario Theodoro de Liagre Böhl dedicatae, Leiden 1973, pp. 271-5.
— "A New Source for the Reign of Nabonidus", AfO 22, 1968-69, pp. 1-8.
Lambert, W.G. and A.R. Millard Atra-Hasis. The Babylonian Story of the Flood, Oxford 1969.
Lambert, W.G. and P. Walcot "A New Babylonian Theogony and Hesiod", Kadmos 4, 1965, pp. 64-72.
Landsberger, B. Die Basaltstele Nabonids von Eski-Harran, Memoriam Halil Edhem, Vol. I, Ankara 1947.
— "Zur vierter und siebenten Tafel des Gilgamesch-Epos", RA 62, 1968, pp. 128-35.

Landsberger, B. and Th. Bauer "Zu neuveröffentlichten Geschichtsquellen der Zeit von Asarhaddon bis Nabonid", ZA, NF3 (37), 1927, pp. 61-98.

Langdon, S. "The Chaldean Kings before the Flood", JRAS 42, 1923.

— Oxford Edition of Cuneiform Texts II, Oxford 1923.

Lenzen, H.J. XVIII. vorläufiger Bericht über die von dem Deutschen Archeologischen Institut und der Deutschen Orient-Gesellschaft aus Mitteln der Deutschen Forschungsgemeinschaft unternommenen Ausgrabungen in Uruk-Warka, Berlin 1962.

Luckenbill, D.D. Ancient Records of Assyria and Babylonia II, Chicago 1927.

— The Annals of Senacherib, Chicago 1924.

Müller, K.F. Das assyrische Ritual I. Texte zum assyrischen Königsritual, MVÄG 41/3, Leipzig 1937.

Neugebauer, O. Astronomical Cuneiform Texts I, London 1955.

Parpola, S. Letters From Assyrian Scholars to the Kings Esarhaddon and Ashurbanipal, Part I: Texts, AOAT 5/1, Neukirchen-Vluyn 1970.

Reiner, E. "The Etiological Myth of the 'Seven Sages'", Orientalia, NS 30, 1961, pp. 1-11.

— Šurpu. A Collection of the Sumerian and Akkadian Incantations, Graz 1958.

Sandars, N.K. The Epic of Gilgamesh, PC, London 1972.

Sjöberg, A. and E. Bergmann The Collection of the Sumerian Temple Hymns, New York 1969.

Smith, S. Babylonian Historical Texts, London 1924.

Soden, W. von "Altbabylonische Dialektdichtungen", ZA, NF 10 (44), 1938, pp. 26-31.

— "Beiträge zum Verständnis des babylonischen Gilgameš-Epos", ZA, NF 19, 1959, pp. 209-35.

— "Die Unterweltsvision eines assyrischen Kronprinzen", ZA, NF 9 (43), 1936, pp. 1-31.

Streck, M. Assurbanipal II, Leipzig 1916.

Thompson, R.C. The Devils and Evil Spirits of Babylonia I, London 1903.

— The Epic of Gilgamish, Oxford 1930.

Thureau-Dangin, F. Une relation de la huitième campagne de Sargon, Paris 1912.

Waterman, L. Royal Correspondence of the Assyrian Empire I, Michigan 1930.

Wilcke, C. Das Lugalbandaepos, Wiesbaden 1969.

Other Sources Relating to the Ancient Near East

Attridge, H.W. and R.A. Oden Jr. Philo of Byblos. The Phoenician History, CBQ.MS 9, Washington DC, 1981.

Bidez, J. and F. Cumont Les mages hellénisés II, Paris 1938.

Cowley, A. Aramaic Papyri of the Fifth Century B.C., Oxford 1923.

Donner, H.D. and U.R. Rölling Kanaanäische und aramäische Inschriften I, 2nd ed., Wiesbaden 1966.

Gordon, C.H. Ugaritic Textbook, Rome 1965.

Jacoby, F. Die Fragmente der griechischen Historiker III, C, Band I-II, Leiden 1958.

Mras, K. Eusebius Werke. Achter Band. Die Praeperatio Evangelica. Erster Teil, GCS, Berlin 1954.

Otten, H. "Eine Beschwörung der unterirdischen aus Bogaszköy", ZA, NF 20, 1961, pp. 113-57.

Pritchard, J.B. (ed.) Ancient Near Eastern Texts Relating to the Old Testament, 3rd ed., Princeton 1969.

Rosenthal, F. An Aramaic Handbook I/1, PLO, Wiesbaden 1967.

Widengren, G. Iranische Geistwelt, GML, Baden-Baden 1961.

Greek Provenance

Anderson, W.D.   Prometheus Bound. Aeschylus, LLA, Indianapolis, New York 1963.
Evelyn-White, H.G.   Hesiod. The Homeric Hymns and Homerica, with an English Translatiton, LCL, London-Cambridge (Mass.) 1914 (1977).
Godley, A.D.   Herodotus I, with an English Translation, LCL, London-Cambridge (Mass.) 1926 (1975).
West, J.W.   Hesiod. Theogony. Edited with Prolegomena and Commentary, Oxford 1966.

b) Works of Reference

Bauer, H. and P. Leander   Grammatik des Biblisch-Aramäischen, Halle 1927 (repr. 1962).
Borger, R.   Assyrisch-babylonische Zeichenliste, Neukirchen-Vluyn 1978.
Brockelmann, C   Syrische Grammatik, Leipzig 1960.
Civil, M. et al.   Assyrian Dictionary of the Oriental Institute of the University of Chicago, Chicago 1956ff.
Dillmann, A.   Chrestomatia Aethiopica. Edita et glossario explanata, Leipzig 1866 (repr. Darmstadt 1974).
–   Grammatik der äthiopischen Sprache, Leipzig 1899 (repr. Graz 1959).
–   Lexikon linguae Aethiopicae cum indice Latino, Leipzig 1865.
Edzard, D.O. and G. Farber   Repertoire géographique des textes cunéiformes 2. Die Orts- und Gewässernamen der 3. Dynastie von Ur: TAVO (Tübinger Atlas zum Vorderen Orient), Beih. B 7/2, Wiesbaden 1974.
Edzard, D.O. et al.   Repertoire géographique des textes cunéiformes I. Die Orts- und Gewässernamen der präsargonischen und sargonischen Zeit: TAVO, Beih. 7/1, Wiesbaden 1977.
Gesenius, W. and F. Brown (eds.)   A Hebrew and English Lexikon of the Old Testament, Oxford 1907 (1966).
Hammond, N.G.L. and H.H. Scullard (eds.)   The Oxford Classical Dictionary, 2nd ed., Oxford 1970.
Jastrow, M.   Dictionary of Talmud Babli, Yerushalami, Midrashic Literature and Targumim, New York 1950.
Koeler, L. and W. Baumgartner (eds.)   Lexicon in Veteris Testamenti Libros, Leiden 1953.
Liddell, H.G. and R. Scott   A Greek-English Lexicon, new rev. ed. by H.S. Jones, Oxford 1940.
Limet, H.   L'Anthroponymie sumérienne dans les documents de la 3ᶜ dynastie d'Ur, Paris 1968.
Rosenthal, F.   A Grammar of Biblical Aramaic, PLO 5, Wiesbaden 1961 (1974).
Segert, S.   Altaramäische Grammatik, Leipzig 1975.
Seux, M.-J.   Epithètes Royal. Akkadiénne et Sumèriénnes, Paris 1967.
Soden, W. von   Akkadisches Handwörterbuch, Wiesbaden 1965ff.
–   Grundriss der Akkadischen Grammatik, AnOr 33/47, Roma 1969.
Vogt, E.   Lexicon linguae Aramaicae Veteris Testamenti, Roma 1971.

c) Books and Articles

Ackroyd, P.A.   Israel under Babylon and Persia, Oxford 1970.
Adler, W.   "Enoch in Early Christian Literature", P.J. Achtemeier (ed.), SBL 1978. Seminar Papers Vol. I, Missoula (Mont.), 1978, pp. 271-5.

Albertz, R. and C. Westermann "rūaḥ, Geist", THAT II, München 1976, cols. 726-53.
Alexander, P.S. "The Targumim and Early Exegesis of 'Sons of God' in Gen 6", JJS 23, 1972, pp. 60-71.
Andreae, W. Das wiedererstandene Assur, Leipzig 1938 (repr. München 1977).
Astour, M. "The Nether World and its Deniziens at Ugarit", B. Altster (ed.), Death in Mesopotamia, M.CSA 8, Copenhagen 1980, pp. 227-38.
Balz, H.R. Methodische Probleme der neutestamentlichen Christologie, WMANT 25, Neukirchen-Vluyn 1967.
Barr, J. Biblical Words for Time, SBT, First Series 33, 2nd rev. ed., Edinburgh 1969.
— "Jewish Apocalyptic in Recent Scholarly Study", BJRL 58, 1975.
— Philo of Byblos and his 'Phoenician History', repr. from BJRL 57, No. 1, Manchester 1974.
Bartelmus, R. Heroentum in Israel und seiner Umwelt, AthANT 65, Zürich 1979.
Bauer, G.L. Hebräische Mythologie des alten und neuen Testaments, Leipzig 1802.
Baumgartner, W. "Ein Vierteljahrhundert Danielforschung", ThRv 11, 1939, pp. 59-83, 125-44, 201-28.
— "Zu den vier Reichen von Dan 2", ThZ 1, 1945, pp. 17-22.
Bayliss, M. "The Cult of the Dead Kin in Assyria and Babylonia", Iraq 35, 1973, pp. 115-26.
Beckwith, R.T. "The Earliest Enoch Literature and its Calendar", RevQ 10, 1981, pp. 365-403.
— "The Significance of the Calendar for Interpreting Essene Chronology and Eschatology. RevQ 10, 1980, pp. 167-202.
Bentzen, Aa. "Der böse Fürst", StTh 4, 1950, pp. 109-19.
— Daniel, HAT 19, Tübingen 1952.
— King and Messiah, London 1955.
— "King-Ideology — 'Urmensch' — 'Troonsbestijgingsfest'", StTh 3, 1949, pp. 143-57.
Betz, O. Offenbarung und Schriftforschung in der Qumransekte, WUNT 2, Tübingen 1960.
Black, M. "The Throne-Theophany Prophetic Commission and the Son of Man", Jews, Greeks and Christians, Essays in honor of W.D. Davies, London 1976, pp. 57-99.
Block, J. "The Ezra-Apocalypse, was it written in Hebrew, Greek or Aramaic?", JQR 48, 1957/58, pp. 279-84.
— "Was there a Greek Version of the Apocalypse of Ezra?" JQR 46, 1956, pp. 309-20.
Böhl, F.M.T. de Liagre "Das Problem Ewigen Lebens im Zyklus und Epos des Gilgamesch", Das Gilgamesch-Epos ed. K. Oberhuber, WdF 215, Darmstadt 1977, pp. 237-75.
Borger, R. "Geheimwissen", E. Weidner and W. von Soden (eds.), RLA III, Berlin 1964, pp. 188-91.
Bottero, J. "Antiquité Assyro-Babyloniènnes", École pratique des hautes Études IVᵉ Sciences Historique et Philologique, Annuaire 1972-73, pp. 93-131.
Bousset, W. and H. Gressmann Die Religion des Judentums im späthellenistischen Zeitalter, HNT 21, Tübingen 1926.
Bowker, J. "The Son of the Man", JThS 28, 1977, pp. 19-48.
Brandenburger, E. Die Verborgenheit Gottes im Weltgeschehen, Zürich 1981.
Brekelmann, C.H.W. "The Saints of the Most High", OTS 14, 1965, pp. 305-29.
Brinkmann, J.A. "Senacheribs Babylonian Problem: An Interpretation, JCS 25, 1973, pp. 87-95.
Brockington, L.H. Ezra, Nehemiah and Esther, CeB, London 1969.
Campenhausen, H. Freiherr von Die Entstehung der christlichen Bibel, BHTh 39, Tübingen 1968.

Caplice, R.I.   The Akkadian Namburbi Texts: An Introduction, SANE 1/1, Malibu, California 1974.

Castellino, G.   "Prayer Against Appearing Ghosts", Orientalia 24, 1955, pp. 240-74.

Charles, R.H.   Religious Development between the Old and New Testament, London 1914.

Childs, B.S.   Introduction to the Old Testament as Scripture, Philadelphia 1979.

Civil, M.   "The Anzu-bird and Scribal Whimsies", JAOS 92, 1972, p. 271.

Clapham, L.R.   Sanchuniathon: The First Two Cycles, unpubl. diss., Harvard University 1969.

Clark, W.M.   "The Flood and the Structure of the Pre-patriarchal History", ZAW 83, 1971, pp. 184-211.

Clines, J.A.   "The Significance of the 'Sons of God' Episode, Genesis 6:1-4, in the Context of the 'Primeval History' (Genesis 1-11)", JSOT 13, 1979, pp. 33-46.

Clifford, R.J.   The Cosmic Mountain in Canaan and the Old Testament, HSM 4, Cambridge (Mass.) 1972.

Cody, A.   The History of the Old Testament Priesthood, AnBib 35, Rome 1969.

Collins, J.J.   "Apocalyptic Genre and Mythic Allusions in Daniel", JSOT 21, 1981, pp. 83-100.

—   The Apocalyptic Vision of the Book of Daniel, Missoula (Mont.) 1977.

—   "Introduction: Towards the Morphology of a Genre", Semeia 14, 1979, pp. 1-20.

—   "The Jewish Apocalypses", Semeia 14, 1979, pp. 21-59.

—   "Metholodological Issues in the Study of Enoch: Reflections on the Articles of P.D. Hanson and G.W. Nickelsburg", P.J. Achtemeier (ed.), SBL 1978 Seminar Papers Vol. I, Missoula (Mont.) 1978, pp. 315-22.

—   "Persian Apocalypses", Semeia 14, 1979, pp. 207-17.

—   "The Son of Man and the Saints of the Most High in the Book of Daniel", JBL 93, 1974, pp. 50-66.

Cölln, D.G.C.   Biblische Theologie, D. Schulz (ed.), Leipzig 1836.

Colpe, C.   "Der Begriff 'Menschensohn' und die Methode der Erforschung messianischer Prototypen", Kairos 11, 1969, pp. 241-68.

—   "ho hyios to anthropou", ThWNT 8, Stuttgart 1969, pp. 403-81.

—   "Neuere Untersuchungen zum Menschensohn-Problem", ThRv 77, 1981, cols. 353-78.

Coppens, J.   "Le Fils d'Homme daniélique et les relectures de Dan., VII, 13, dans les apokryphes et les écrits du Nouveau Testament", EThL 37, 1961, pp. 5-51.

—   "Le Fils d'Homme daniélique, vizir céleste?", ALBO 4, Ser. 12, 1964, pp. 72-80.

—   "La vision daniélique du Fils d'Homme", VT 19, 1969, pp. 171-82.

Corrodi, H.   Kritische Geschichte des Chiliasmus I, Frankfurt-Leipzig 1781.

—   Versuch einer Beleuchtung der Geschichte des Jüdischen und Christlichen Bibelkanons I, Halle 1792.

Cullmann, O.   Christ and Time, 3rd rev. ed., London 1967.

Daley, S.   "Two Points in the Text of 'A Crown Prince's Vision of the Nether World'", RA 74, 1980, p. 190.

Deimel, A.   "Die babylonische und biblische Überlieferung bezüglich der vorsintflutlichen Urväter", Orientalia 17, 1925, pp. 33-47.

Delling, G.   Zeit und Endzeit, BSt 58, Neukirchen-Vluyn 1970.

Dequeker, L.   "'The Saints of the Most High' in Qumran and Daniel", OTS 18, 1973, pp. 108-87.

Dexinger, F.   Sturz der Göttersöhne oder Engel vor der Sintflut? WBTh 13, Wien 1966.

Dijk, J. van   "Le motif cosmique dans la pensée Sumerienne", AcOr 28, 1964, pp. 39-44.

Dimant, D.   "1 Enoch 6-11: A Methodological perspective", P.J. Achtemeier (ed.), SBL 1978 Seminar Papers Vol. I, Missoula (Mont.) 1978, pp. 232-39.

Dommerhausen, W.   Nabonid im Buch Daniel, Mainz 1964.

Ebach, J.   Weltentstehung und Kulturentwicklung bei Philo von Byblos, BWANT 6, Stuttgart 1979.

Ebeling, E.   "Ebabbara", E. Ebeling and B. Meissner (eds.), RLA II, Berlin-Leipzig 1938, p. 263.

Eddy, S.K.   The King is Dead, Lincoln 1961.

Edzard, D.O.   "Enmebaragesi von Kiš", ZA, NF 19, 1959, pp. 9-26.

Eichhorn, J.G.   Einleitung im Alten Testament III, Leipzig 1787.

Eichrodt, W.   Ezekiel, A Commentary, OTL, London 1970.

Eissfeldt, O.   Baal Zaphon, Zeus Kasios und der Durchzug der Israeliten durchs Meer, Halle 1932.

—   Einleitung in das Alte Testament, 3rd rev. ed., Tübingen 1964.

Ellis, R.S.   Foundation Deposits in Ancient Mesopotamia, New Haven-London 1968.

Emerton, J.A.   "The Origin of the Son of Man Imagery", JThS 9, 1958, pp. 225-42.

Falkenstein, A.   "Der sumerische und der akkadische Mythos von Inannas Gang zur Unterwelt", Festschr. W. Caskel, Leiden 1968, pp. 96-110.

Farber-Flügge, G.   Der Mythos 'Inanna und Enki' unter besonderer Berücksichtigung der Liste der me, StP 10, Rome 1973.

Feldmann, L.H.   "Abraham the Greek Philosopher in Josephus", TPAPA 99, 1968, pp. 143-56.

Ferch, A.J.   "Daniel 7 and Ugarit: A Reconsideration", JBL 99, 1980, pp. 75-86.

Fisch, T.   "The Zu Bird", BJRL 31, 1948, pp. 162-71.

Fitzmyer, J.A.   "Implications of the New Enoch Literature from Qumran", TS 38, 1977, pp. 332-45.

Flusser, D.   "The Four Empires in the Fourth Sibyl and in the Book of Daniel", IOS 2, 1972, pp. 148-75.

Frankfort, H.   The Art and Architecture of the Ancient Orient, PB, London 1954.

—   Cylinder Seals, London 1939.

—   Kingship and the Gods, Chicago 1948.

—   "Note on the Cretan Griffin", ABSA 37, 1936-37, pp. 106-22.

Freudenthal, J.   Hellenistische Studien, Heft 1, Jahresbericht des jüdisch theologischen Seminars, Breslau 1874.

Fuhr-Jaeppelt, I.   Materialien zur Ikonographie des Löwenadlers Anzu-Imdugud, München 1972.

Gall, A. von   Basileia tou theou, eine religionsgeschichtliche Studie zur vorkirchlichen Eschatologie, Heidelberg 1926.

Galling, K.   "Bagoas und Ezra", Studien zur Geschichte Israels im persischen Zeitalter, Tübingen 1964, pp. 149-84.

—   "Politische Wandlungen in der Zeit zwischen Nabonid und Darius", Studien zur Geschichte Israels im persischen Zeitalter, Tübingen 1964, pp. 1-60.

Gatz, B.   Weltalter, goldene Zeit und sinnverwandte Vorstellungen, Spudasmata 16, Hildesheim 1967.

Gerleman, G.   "ḥjh, leben", THAT I, München 1971, cols. 549-57.

—   "šeʾōl, Totenreich", THAT II, München 1976, cols. 837-41.

Gese, H.   "Anfang und Ende der Apokalyptik, dargestellt am Sacharjabuch", ZThK 70, 1973, pp. 20-49.

—   "Der bewachte Lebensraum und die Heroen: Zwei mythologische Ergänzungen zur Urgeschichte der Quelle J", Wort und Geschichte, Festschr. K. Ellinger, Neukirchen-Vluyn 1973, also in: Vom Sinai zum Sion, München 1974, pp. 99-112.

—   "Natus ex virgine", Probleme biblischer Theologie, Festschr. G. von Rad, München 1971, pp. 73-89.

—   "Die Religionen Altsyriens", Die Religionen Altsyriens, Altarabiens und der Mandäer, RM 10, 2, Stuttgart 1970.

Glasson, T.F. The Second Advent: The Origin of the NT Doctrine, London 1945, 3rd ed. 1963.
— "The Son of Man Imagery", NTS 23, 1977, pp. 82-90.
Gossens, G. "Les recherches historiques à l'époque neo-babyloniènne", RA 42, 1948, pp. 149-59.
Goudoever, J. van Biblical Calendars, 2nd rev. ed., Leiden 1961.
Greenfield, J.C. "Aḥiqar in the Book of Tobit", De la Torah au Messie, Mélanges Henri Cazelles, Paris 1981, 329-36.
Greenfield, J.C. and M.E. Stone "The Books of Enoch and the Traditions of Enoch", Numen 26, 1979, pp. 89-103.
— "The Enochic Pentateuch and the Date of the Similitudes", HThR 70, 1977, pp. 51-65.
— "Remarks on the Aramaic Testament of Levi from Geniza", RB 86, 1979, pp. 214-30.
Grelot, P. "La géographie mytic d'Hénoch et ses sources orientales", RB 65, 1958, pp. 33-69.
— "Hénoch et ses écritures", RB 82, 1975, pp. 481-500.
— "La légende d'Hénoch dans les apokryphes et dans la Bible: Origine et signification", RSR 46, 1958, pp. 5-26, 181-210.
— "Parwaim des Chroniques à l'Apocryphe de la Genèse", VT 11, 1961, pp. 30-8.
Gressmann, H. Der Messias, Göttingen 1929.
Gry, L. Les dires prophétiques d'Esdras I-II, Paris 1938.
Gunkel, H. Genesis, HK 1/1, 3rd ed., Göttingen 1910.
— Schöpfung und Chaos in Urzeit und Endzeit, Göttingen 1885.
Gunneweg, A.H.J. Leviten und Priester, FRLANT 89, Göttingen 1965.
Gurney, O.R. "Hittite Prayers of Mursili II", AAA 27, 1940, pp. 4-163.
Hallo, W.W. "Akkadian Apocalypses", IEJ 16, 1966, pp. 231-42.
— "Antediluvian Cities", JCS 23, 1970-71, pp. 57-67.
— "Beginning and End of the Sumerian King List in the Nippur Recension", JCS 17, 1963, pp. 52-7.
— "On the Antiquity of Sumerican Literature", JAOS 83, 1963, pp. 167-76.
Hanson, P.D. The Dawn of Apocalyptic, rev. ed., Philadelphia 1979.
— "Introduction", Visionaries and their Apocalypses, Philadelphia-London 1983, pp. 4-15.
— "Jewish Apocalyptic Against its Near Eastern Environment", RB 78, 1971, pp. 31-58.
— "Old Testament Apocalyptic Reexamined", Interpretation 25, 1971, pp. 454-79,.
— "Rebellion in Heaven, Azazel, and Euhemeristic Heroes in 1 Enoch 6-11", JBL 96, 1977, pp. 195-233.
— "A Response to John Collins' 'Methodological Issues in the Study of Enoch'", SBL, 1978. Seminar Papers Vol. I, Missoula (Mont.) 1978, pp. 307-14.
Haran, M. "Behind the Scenes of History: Determining the Date of the Priestly Source", JBL 100, 1981, pp. 321-33.
Harnisch, W. Verhängnis und Verheissung der Geschichte, FRLANT 97, Göttingen 1969.
Harrington, D.J. "The Wisdom of the Scribe according to Ben Sira", J.J. Collins and G.W.E. Nickelsburg (eds.), Ideal Figures in Ancient Judaism, Chico 1980, pp. 181-8.
Hartman, L. Asking for a Meaning. A Study of Enoch 1-5, CB.NT 12, Uppsala 1979.
Hartman, L. and A.A. Di Lella The Book of Daniel, AncB 23, New York 1978.
Hasel, G.F. "The Four World Empires of Daniel 2 Against its Near Eastern Environments", JSOT 12, 1979, pp. 17-30.
Healy, J.F. Death, Underworld and Afterlife in Ugaritic Texts, Diss. London 1977.

Hecker, K. Untersuchungen zur akkadischen Epik, AOAT, Neukirchen-Vluyn 1979.

Heidel, A. The Babylonian Genesis, 2nd ed., Chicago 1951.

– The Gilgamesh Epic and Old Testament Parallels, 2nd ed., Chicago 1949.

Hengel, M. Judentum und Hellenismus, WUNT 10, 2nd rev. ed., Tübingen 1973.

Hilgenfeld, A. Die jüdische Apokalyptik in ihrer geschichtlichen Entwicklung, Jena 1857.

Himmelfarb, M. "A Report on Enoch in Rabbinic Literature", P.J. Achtemeier (ed.), SBL 1978. Seminar Papers Vol. I, Missoula (Mont.) 1978, pp. 259-69.

Hinnels, J.R. "The Zoroastrian Doctrine of Salvation in the Roman World", Man and his Salvation, Studies in Memory of S.G.F. Brandon, Manchester 1973, pp. 125-48.

Hinz, W. "Humban", RLA IV, Berlin-New York 1972-75, pp. 491f.

Hölscher, G. "Die Entstehung des Buches Daniel", ThStKr 92, 1919, pp. 113-38.

– Geschichte der israelitischen und jüdischen Religion, Giessen 1922.

Hruška, B. Der Mythenadler Anzu in Literatur und Vorstellung des Alten Mesopotamien, Budapest 1975.

Hultgård, A. "Forms and Origins of Iranian Apocalypticism", D. Hellholm (ed.), Apocalypticism in the Mediterranean World and the Near East, Tübingen 1983, pp. 387–412.

– "The Ideal 'Levite', The Davidic Messiah and the Savior Priest in the Testament of the Twelve Patriarchs", J.J. Collins and J.W.E. Nickelsburg (eds.), Ideal Figures In Ancient Judaism, Chico 1980, pp. 93-110.

Hurvitz, A. "The Evidence of Language in Dating the Priestly Code", RB 81, 1974, pp. 24-56.

Ingholt, H. "Some Sculptures from the Tomb of Malkû at Palmyra", Mélanges offerts à Kasimièrz Michalowski, Warsaw 1966, pp. 457-76.

Jacobsen, T. "The Eridu Genesis", JBL 100, 1981, pp. 513-29.

– "Inuma Ilu awilum", Ancient Near Eastern Studies in Memory of J.J. Finkelstein, Connecticut 1977, pp. 113-17.

– The Treasures of Darkness. A History of Mesopotamian Religion, New Haven-London 1976.

James, E.O. The Tree of Life, Leiden 1966.

Jansen, H.L. Die Henochgestalt. Eine vergleichende religionsgeschichtliche Untersuchung, Oslo 1939.

Janssen, E. Das Gottesvolk und seine Geschichte, Neukirchen-Vluyn 1971.

Jaubert, A. "Le Calandrier des Jubilés et de la secte de Qumrân. Ses origines biblique", VT 3, 1953, pp. 250-64.

Jenni, E. "'āb, Vater", THAT I, München 1971, cols. 1-17.

– "'ōlām, Ewigkeit", THAT II, München 1976, cols. 228-43.

Kabisch, R. Das vierte Buch Esra auf seine Quellen untersucht, Göttingen 1889.

Kaiser, O. Die mythische Bedeutung des Meeres in Ägypten, Ugarit und Israel, BZAW 78, Berlin 1959.

Kaminka, A. "Beiträge ur Erklärung der Esra-Apokalypse und zur Rekonstruktion ihres hebräischen Urtextes, MGWJ 76, 1932, pp. 121-38, 206-12, 494-511, 604-7; 77, 1933, pp. 339-55.

Kammenhuber, A. "Die hethitische und hurritsche Überlieferung zum 'Gilgames-Epos'", MSS 21, 1967, pp. 45-58.

Kapelrud, A. "Creation in the Ras Shamra Texts", StTh 34, 1980, pp. 1-11.

– "hāwwah", ThWAT II, Stuttgart 1977, cols. 794-8.

Kearns, R. Vorfragen der Christologie I-II, Tübingen 1978/80.

Keel, O. Jahve-Visionen und Siegelkunst. Eine neue Deutung der Majestätsschilderungen in Jes 6, Ez 1 und 10 und Sach 4, SBS 84/85, Stuttgart 1977.

Keulers, J. Die eschatologische Lehre des Vierten Esrabuches, Inagural Diss., Freiburg im Breisgau 1922.

Kienast, B. "Überlegungen zum 'Fluch des Adapa'", Festschrift Labor Matouš, Budapest 1978, pp. 181-200.
— "Die Weisheit des Adapa von Eridu", Symbolae Biblicae et Mesopotamicae, Francisco Mario Theodoro de Liagre Böhl dedicatae, Leiden 1973, pp. 234-9.
Kilian, R. "Die Priesterschrift. Hoffnung auf Heimkehr", J. Schreiner (ed.), Wort und Botschaft des Alten Testaments, Wartburg 1967, pp. 226-43.
Kilmer, A.D. "How was Queen Ereskigal tricked? A New Interpretation of the Descent of Ishtar", UF 3, 1971, pp. 299-301.
Kinet, D. Ugarit — Geschichte und Kultur einer Stadt in der Umwelt des Alten Testaments, SBS 104, Stuttgart 1981.
Kirk, G.S. Myth. Its Meaning and Functions in Ancient and other Cultures, Cambridge 1970 (paperback ed. 1973).
Klein, R.W. "Ezra and Nehemia in Recent Studies", Magnalia Dei. The Mighty Acts of God, in memory of G.E. Wright, New York 1976, pp. 361-76.
Koch, K. "Einleitung", K. Koch and J.M. Schmidt (eds.), Apokalyptik, WdF, Darmstadt 1982, pp. 1-29.
— "Die Hebräer vom Auszug aus Ägypten bis zum Grossreich Davids", VT 19, 1969, pp. 37-81.
— "Die mysteriösen Zahlen der judäischen Könige und die apokalyptischen Jahreswochen", VT 28, pp. 433-41.
— "Priestertum II. In Israel", RGG³, Tübingen 1956-62, col. 577.
— "Ratlos vor der Apokalyptik", Gütersloh 1970.
— "Sabbatsstruktur der Geschichte", ZAW 95, 1983, pp. 403-30.
— "Spätisraelitisches Geschichtsdenken am Beispiel des Buches Daniel", HZ 193, 1961, pp. 1-32.
Koch, K. et al. Das Buch Daniel, EdF, Darmstadt 1980.
Komoróczy, K. "Berosos and the Mesopotamian Literature", AAH 21, 1973, pp. 125-52.
Kraft, R.A. "Philo (Josephus, Sirach, and Wisdom of Salomon) on Enoch", P.J. Achtemeier (ed.), SBL 1978. Seminar Papers Vol. I, Missoula (Mont.), 1978, pp. 253-7.
Kraeling, C.H. Anthropos and Son of Man, New York 1927.
Kramer, S.N. "Death and Nether World According to Sumerian Literary Texts", Iraq 22, 1960, pp. 59-68.
— The Sumerians, Chicago 1963.
— "Sumerian Literature. A General Survey", The Bible and the Ancient Near East, Essays in honor of W.G. Albright, New York 1961, pp. 249-66.
— Sumerian Mythology, rev. ed., Philadelphia 1969 (paperback ed. 1972).
Kraus, H.-J. Geschichte der historisch-kritischen Erforschung des Alten Testaments, 2nd ed., Neukirchen-Vluyn 1969.
— Gottesdienst in Israel. Grundriss einer alttestamentlichen Kultgeschichte", 2nd rev. ed., München 1962.
Kroll, J. Gott und Hölle, Leipzig-Berlin 1932 (repr. Darmstadt 1963).
Küchler, M. Frühjüdische Weisheitstraditionen, OrbBOr 26, Göttingen 1979.
Kühlwein, J. "ben, Sohn", THAT I, München 1971, cols. 316-33.
Kümmel, H.M. "Bemerkungen zu den altorientalischen Berichten von der Menschenschöpfung", WO 7, 1973-74, pp. 25-38.
Kutsch, E. "Der Kalender des Jubiläenbuches und das Alte und Neue Testament", VT 11, 1961, pp. 39-47.
Kvanvig, H.S. "An Akkadian Vision as Background for Dan 7?", StTh 35, 1981, pp. 85-9.
— "Henoch under der Menschensohn", StTh 38, 1984, pp. 101-31.
— "Struktur und Geschichte in Dan 7", StTh 32, 1978, pp. 95-117.
Lacocque, A. The Book of Daniel, London 1979.
Lambert, W.G. "Ancestors, Authors and Canonicity", JCS 11, 1957, pp. 1-14.
— The Background of Jewish Apocalyptic, London 1978.
— "A New Look at the Babylonian Background of 'Genesis'", JThS 16, 1965, pp. 287-300.

— "Jabnu", RLA V, Berlin-New York 1977, p. 229.
— "The Seed of Kingship", XIXe Rencontre Assyriologique Internationale, Paris 1974, pp. 427-40.
— "Three Literary Prayers of the Babylonians", AfO 19, 1959-60, pp. 47-66.
Landsberger, B. Brief des Bischofs von Esagila an König Asarhaddon, MNAW.L 28, No 6, Amsterdam 1965.
— "Einige unerkannt gebliebene oder verkannte Nomina des Akkadischen", WZKM 56, 1960, pp. 109-29, and WZKM 57, 1961, pp. 1-21.
— "Einleitung in das Gilgamesch-Epos", Das Gilgamesch-Epos, ed. K. Oberhuber, WdF 215, Darmstadt 1977, pp. 171-8.
Lebram, J.C.H. "Aspekte der alttestamentlichen Kanonbildung", VT 18, 1968, pp. 173-89.
— "König Antiochus im Buch Daniel", VT 25, 1975, pp. 737-72.
Lehmann-Haupt, C.F. "Berossos", E. Ebeling and B. Meissner (eds.), RLA II, Berlin-Leipzig 1938, pp. 1-17.
Leivestad, R. "Exit the Apocalyptic Son of Man", NTS 18, 1971-72, pp. 243-67.
— "Das Dogma von der prophetenlosen Zeit", NTS 19, 1973, pp. 288-99.
Lella, A.A. Di "The One in Human Likeness and the Holy Ones of the Most High in Dan 7", CBQ 34, 1977, pp. 1-19.
Lenormant, F. Die Magie und Wahrsagekunst der Chaldäer, Jena 1878.
Lewis, J.P. A Study of the Interpretation of Noah and the Flood in Jewish and Christian Literature, Leiden 1968.
Lewy, H. "The Babylonian Background of the Kay Kâûs Legend", ArOr 17, 1949, pp. 28-109.
Lloyd, S. The Archeology of Mesopotamia, London 1978.
Liedke, G. "ḥqq, einritzen, festsetzen", THAT I, München 1971, cols. 626-33.
Loewenstam, S.E. "Philo of Byblos", Comparative Studies in Biblical and Ancient Oriental Literatures, Neukirchen-Vluyn 1980, pp. 390-404.
Loud, G. Khorsabad I. Excavations in the Palace and at the City Gate, Chicago 1936.
Lücke, F. Versuch einer vollständigen Einleitung in die Offenbarung des Johannes, 2nd ed., Bonn 1852 (1932).
Lührmann, D. "Henoch und die Metanoia", ZNW 66, 1975, pp. 103-16.
Madloom, T.A. The Chronology of Neo-Assyrian Art, London 1970.
Maier, G. "Die zweite Tafel der Serie bīt mēseri", AfO 13, 1939-41, pp. 139-52.
Maier, J. "Tempel und Tempelkult", J. Maier and J. Schreiner (eds.), Literatur und Religion der Frühjudentums, Würzburg 1973, pp. 371-90.
Maier, J. and K. Schubert Die Qumran-Essener, UTB 224, München 1982.
Mallowan, M.E.L. "Cyrus the Great", Iraq 10, 1972, pp. 1-18.
— "The Excavations at Nimrud", Iraq 16, 1954, pp. 85-92.
— "Nimrud and Its Remains I", London 1966.
— "Noah's Flood Rediscovered", Iraq 26, 1964, pp. 62-82.
Marböck, J. "'Henoch — Adam — der Thronwagen'. Zu frühjüdischen pseudepigraphischen Traditionen bei ben Sira", BZ 25, 1981, pp. 103-11.
Mayer, W.R. Texte aus dem Reš-Heiligtum in Uruk-Warka; BaghM, Beiheft 2, Berlin 1980.
McCullough, W.S. The History and Literature of the Palestinian Jews from Cyrus to Herod, Toronto 1975.
Mertens, A. Das Buch Daniel in Lichte der Texte vom Toten Meer, SBM 12, Stuttgart 1971.
Meyer, R. Das Gebet des Nabonid, SSAW.PH 107/3, Berlin 1962.
Milik, J.T. Recherches d'épigraphie Proche Orientale I, Paris 1972.
— Ten Years of Discovery in the Wilderness of Judea, SBT 26, London 1959.
Montgomery, J.A. A Critical and Exegetical Commentary on the Book of Daniel, ICC, Edinburgh 1927.
de Moor, J.C. "Rapi'uma — Rephaim", ZAW 88, 1976, pp. 323-45.

Moore, J.F.   Judaism I, Cambridge 1927 (1962).

Moortgat, A.   The Art of Ancient Mesopotamia, London-New York 1969.

Moran, W.L.   "The Creation of Man in Athrahasis I 192-248", BASOR 200, 1970, pp. 48-56.

Moule, C.F.D.   "Neglected Features in the Problem of the 'Son of Man'", Neues Testament und Kirche, Festschrift für R. Schnackenburg, Freiburg 1974, pp. 413-28.

Mowinckel, S.   Han som kommer, København 1951.

— He that Cometh, Nashville-New York 1954.

— "Ophavet til den senjødiske forestilling om Menneskesønnen", NTT 14, 1944, pp. 184-243.

— Psalmenstudien I-II, Kristiania 1921 (repr. Amsterdam 1961).

— "Urmensch und 'Königsideologie'", StTh 2, 1948-49, pp. 71-81.

Muilenburg, J.   "The Son of Man in Daniel and in the Ethiopic Apocalypse of Enoch, JBL 79, 1960, pp. 197-209.

Müller, H.-P.   "Magisch-mantische Weisheit und die Gestalt Daniels", UF 1, 1969, pp. 79-94.

— "Mantische Weisheit und Apokalyptik", VT.S 22, 1972, pp. 268-93.

— "Märchen, Legende und Enderwartung", VT 26, 1976, pp. 338-50.

— "qdš, heilig", THAT II, München 1976, cols. 589-609.

Müller, K.   "Die Ansätze der Apokalyptik", Literatur und Religion des Frühjudentums, J. Maier and J. Schreiner (eds.), Würzburg 1973, pp. 31-42.

— "Geschichte, Heilsgeschichte und Gesetz", J. Maier and J. Schreiner (eds.), Literatur und Religion des Frühjudentums, Würzburg 1973, pp. 73-105.

— "Der Menschensohn im Danielszyklus", Jesus der Menschensohn, f. A. Vögtle, Freiburg 1975, pp. 37-80.

Müller, W.B.   Messias und Menschensohn in jüdischen Apokalypsen und in der Offenbarung des Johannes, Gütersloh 1972.

Neugebauer, O.   The 'Astronomical' Chapters of the Ethiopic Book of Enoch (72-82), KDVSMfM 40:10, København 1981.

— The Exact Sciences in Antiquity, Copenhagen-Princeton-London 1951.

— "The History of Ancient Astronomy: Problems and Methods", JNES 4, 1945, pp. 2-38.

— "Notes on Ethiopic Astronomy", Orientalia, NS 33, 1964, pp. 49-71.

Newsom, C.A.   "The Development of 1 Enoch 6-19: Cosmology and Judgment", CBQ 42, 1980, pp. 310-29.

Nickelsburg, G.W.E.   "Apokalyptic and Myth in 1 Enoch 6-11", JBL 96, 1977, pp. 383-405.

— "Enoch, Levi, and Peter: Recipients of Revelation in Upper Galilee", JBL 100, 1981, pp. 575-600.

— Jewish Literature between the Bible and the Mishnah, Philadelphia 1981.

— "Reflections upon Reflections: A Response to John Collins' 'Methodological Issues in the Study of 1 Enoch'", SBL 1978. Seminar Papers, Vol. I, Missoula (Mont.) 1978, pp. 311-14.

North, R.   "Prophecy to Apocalyptic via Zechariah", VT.S 22, 1972, pp. 47-71.

Noth, M.   "Das Geschichtsverständnis der alttestamentlichen Apokalyptik", 1954: Gesammelte Studien zum AT, 2nd ed., TB 6, München 1960, pp. 248-73.

— "Die Heiligen des Höchsten", 1955: Gesammelte Studien zum AT, 2nd ed., TB 6, München 1960, pp. 274-90.

— "Zur Komposition des Buches Daniel", ThStKr 98/99, 1926, pp. 143-63.

Oates, J.   Babylon, London 1979.

Oberhuber, K.   "Gilgamesch", Das Gilgamesch-Epos, ed. idem, WdF 215, Darmstadt 1977, pp. 9-12.

— "Wege der Gilgamesch-Forschung", Das Gilgamesch-Epos, ed. idem, WdF 215, Darmstadt 1977, pp. xiii-xxvi.

Oden, R.A. Jr.   "Divine Aspirations in Atrahasis and in Genesis 1-11", ZAW 93, 1981, pp. 197-216.

Olmstead, A.T.   History of Assyria, Chicago 1923 (repr. 1975).

Oppenheim, A.L.   Ancient Mesopotamia. Portrait of a Dead Civilization, rev. ed., Chicago 1977.

— The Interpretation of Dreams in the Ancient Near East, TAPhS 46/3, 1966.

Otten, H.   "Die Religionen des Alten Kleinasiens", Religionsgeschichte des Alten Orient, Lief. 1, HO 8, Erster Abschnitt, Leiden-Köln 1964, pp. 92-122.

Otto, R.   Reich Gottes und Menschensohn, München 1933.

Parpola, S.   "The Murderer of Senacherib", Death in Mesopotamia, ed. B. Alster, M.CSA 8, Copenhagen 1980, pp. 171-81.

Parrot, A.   The Flood and Noah's Ark, SBAr 1, London 1955.

Perkins, P.   "The Rebellion Myth in Gnostic Apocalypses", SBL 1978. Seminar Papers Vol. I, Missoula (Mont.) 1978, pp. 15-30.

Perlitt, L.   "Sinai und Horeb", Beiträge zur alttestamentlichen Theologie, Festschrift W. Zimmerli, Göttingen 1977, pp. 302-22.

Perrot, G. and C. Chipez   Histoire de l'art dans l'antiquité II: Chaldée et Assyrie, Paris 1884.

Pettinato, G.   Das altorientalische Menschenbild und die sumerischen und akkadischen Schöpfungsmythen, AHAW.PH.Abh. 1, Heidelberg 1971.

— "Die Bestrafung des Menschengeschlechts durch die Sintflut", Orientalia, NS 37, 1968, pp. 165-200.

Philonenko, M.   "L'apocalyptique", Études d'Histoire des Religions de l'Université de Science Humains de Strassbourg, 1977, pp. 129-35.

Plöger, O.   Das Buch Daniel, KAT 18, Gütersloh 1965.

— "Priester und Prophet", Aus der Spätzeit des Alten Testaments, Göttingen 1971, pp. 8-42.

— "Siebzig Jahre", Aus der Spätzeit des Alten Testaments, Göttingen 1971, pp. 63-73.

— Theokratie und Eschatologie, WMANT 2, Neukirchen-Vluyn 1968.

Pope, M.H.   El in the Ugaritic Texts, VT.S 2, Leiden 1955.

Porteous, N.W.   Das Buch Daniel, ATD 23, 2nd ed., Göttingen 1968.

Potter, P.A.   Metaphors and Monsters. A Literary-Critical Study of Daniel 7 and 8, CB.OT 20, Lund 1983.

Procksch, O.   "Der Menschensohn als Gottessohn", CuW 3, 1927, pp. 425-81.

Rad, G. von   Das erste Buch Mose. Genesis, ATD 2/4, Göttingen 1949.

— Genesis. A Commentary, OTL, 2nd rev. ed., London 1963.

— Theologie des Alten Testaments II, 5th ed., München 1968.

— Weisheit in Israel, Neukirchen-Vluyn 1970.

Rau, E.   Kosmologie, Eschatologie und die Lehrautorität Henochs. Traditions- und formgeschichtliche Untersuchungen zum äth. Henochbuch und zu verwandten Schriften, unpubl. diss. Hamburg 1974.

Reimers, S.   Formgeschichte der prophetischen Visionsberichte, unpubl. diss. Hamburg 1976.

Reiterer, F.V.   'Urtext' und Übersetzungen. Sprachstudie über Sir 44, 16-45, 26 als Beitrag zur Siraforschung, MU, München 1980.

Rendtorff, R.   Das überlieferungsgeschichtliche Problem des Pentateuch, BZAW 147, Berlin-New York 1977.

Ringren, H.   "Akkadian Apocalypses", D. Hellholm (ed.), Apocalypticism in the Mediterranean World and the Near East, Tübingen 1983, pp. 387-412.

Robinson, G.   The Origin and Development of the Old Testament Sabbath, unpubl. diss. Hamburg 1975.

Roland, W.P.   A Commentary to Philo Byblius' 'Phoenician History', unpubl. diss. University of Southern California 1968.

Röllig, W.   "Irkalla", RLA V, Berlin-New York 1977, p. 164.

Root, M.C.   The King and Kingship in Achaemenid Art, AcIr 19, Leiden 1972.

Rost, L.   Einleitung in die alttestamgntlichen Apokryphen und Pseudepigraphen, Heidelberg 1971.

Rowland, C.   The Open Heaven, London 1982.

— "The Visions of God in Apokalyptic Literature", JSJ 10, 1979, pp. 137-54.

Rowley, H.H.   "The Chronological Order of Ezra and Nehemiah", The Servant
    of the Lord and other Essays on the Old Testament, 2nd rev. ed., Oxford
    1965, pp. 137-68.
— The Relevance of Apocalypic, 3rd rev. ed., London 1964.
Rudolph, K.   "Apokalyptik in der Diskussion", D. Hellholm (ed.), Apocalypiti-
    cism in the Mediterranean World and in the Near East, Tübingen 1983, pp.
    771-89.
Rüger, H.P.   Text und Textform in hebräischen Sirach, BZAW 112, Tübingen
    1970.
Russel, D.S.   The Method and Message of Jewish Apocalyptic, London 1964.
Sachs, A.   "Babylonian Horoscopes", JCS 6, 1952, pp. 49-75.
Sahlin, H.   "Antiochus Epiphanes und Judas Makkebeus, StTh 23, 1969, pp. 41-
    68.
Schmid, H.   "Daniel der Menschensohn", Judaica 27, 1971, pp. 192-220.
Schott, A.   "imbaru, Lexikalisches Archiv", ZA 10, 1938, pp. 170-77.
Seibert, I.   Hirt — Herde — König, DAWB.SSA 53, Berlin 1969.
Semler, J.S. (ed.)   Versuch einer biblischen Dämonologie. Mit einer Vorrede und
    einem Anhang von D.J.S. Semler, Halle 1776.
Skaist, Aa.   "The Ancestor Cult and Succession in Mesopotamia", Death in
    Mesopotamia, ed. B. Alster, M.CSA 8, Copenhagen 1980, pp. 123-38.
Smith, S.   Early History of Assyria, London 1928.
Soden, W. von   "Der Mensch bescheidet sich nicht. Überlegungen zu Schöp-
    fungserzählungen in Babylonien und Israel", Symbolae Biblicae et Mesopota-
    micae, Francisco Mario Theodoro de Liagre Böhl dedicatae, Leiden 1973, pp.
    249-58.
Sokoloff, M.   "Notes on the Aramaic Fragments of Enoch from Qumran
    Cave 4", Maarav 1/2, 1978-79, pp. 197-224.
Steck, O.H.   Der Schöpfungsbericht der Priesterschrift, FRLANT 115, Göttingen
    1975.
— "Weltgeschehen und Gottesvolk im Buch Daniel", Kirche, Festchr. G.
    Bornkamm, Tübingen 1980, pp. 53-78: Wahrnehmungen Gottes im Alten
    Testament, TB 70, München 1982, 262-90.
Stegemann, H.   "Die Bedeutung der Qumranfunde für die Erforschung der
    Apokalyptik", D. Hellholm (ed.), Apocalypticism in the Mediterranean World
    and in the Near East. Tübingen 1983, pp. 495-530.
Steiner, G.   "Griechische und orientalische Mythen", AnAb 6, 1957, pp. 171-
    87.
Stone, M.E.   "The Concept of Messiah in IV Ezra", Religions in Antiquity, ed.
    J. Heusner, Leiden 1968, pp. 295-312.
— Scriptures, Sects and Visions. A Profile of Judaism from Ezra to the Jewish
    Revolts, Philadelphia 1980.
Stronach, D.   Parargadae, Oxford 1978.
Sundberg, A.C.   "The Bible Canon and the Christian Doctrine of Inspiration",
    Interpretation 29, 1975, pp. 352-71.
— "The Old Testament of the Early Church, HThS 20, Cambridge 1964.
Suter, D.   "Fallen Angel, Fallen Priest: The Problem of Family Purity in 1
    Enoch 6-16", HUCA 50, 1979, pp. 115-35.
Swain, J.W.   "The Theory of the Four Monarchies. Opposition History under the
    Roman Empire", CP 35, 1940, pp. 1-21.
Tallquist, K.   Die assyrische Beschwörungsserie Maqlû, ASSF 10, No. 6, 1894.
— Sumerisch-akkadische Namen der Totenwelt, StOr 5/4, Helsingfors 1934.
Theison, J.   Der auserwählte Richter, Göttingen 1975.
Thoma, C.   "Der Phariseismus", J. Maier and J. Schreiner (eds.), Literatur und
    Religion des Früjudentums, Würzburg 1973, pp. 254-72.
Tromp, N.J.   Primitive Conceptions of Death and the Nether World in the Old
    Testament, BibOr 21, Rome 1969.
Unger, E.   "Farben", RLA III, Berlin-New York 1957-71, pp. 24-6.
— "Mischwesen", RLV VIII, Berlin 1927, pp. 203f.

VanderKam; J.C. Enoch and the Growth of an Apocalyptic Tradition, CBQ.MS 16, Washington DC 1984.
— "Enoch Traditions in Jubilees and other Second Century Sources", P.J. Achtemeier (ed.), SBL 1978. Seminar Papers Vol. I, Missoula (Mont.) 1978, pp. 229-51.
— "The Righteousness of Noah", J.C. Collins and G.W.E. Nickelsburg (eds.), Ideal Figures in Ancient Judaism, Chico 1980, pp. 13-32.
Vatke, V. Die Religion des Alten Testaments, Berlin 1835.
de Vaux, R. Ancient Israel. Its Life and Institutions, London 1961 (paperback ed. 1973).
Vermez, G. Jesus the Jew, Fortred Press ed., Philadelphia 1981 (first publ. 1973).
— "The Use of bar nāš / bar nāšā in Jewish Aramaic", in M. Black: An Aramaic Approach to the Gospels and Acts, Oxford 1967, pp. 310-28.
Volz, P. Die Eschatologie der jüdischen Gemeinde, Tübingen 1934 (repr. Hildesheim 1966).
Wacholder, B.Z. "Biblical Chronology in the Hellenistic World Chronicles", Essays on Jewish Chronology and Chronography, New York 1976, pp. 106-36.
— Eupolemus. A Study of Judaeo-Greek Literature, New York-Jerusalem 1974.
— "Pseudo-Eupolemus' Two Greek Fragments on the Life of Abraham", HUCA 34, 1963, pp. 83-113.
Walter, N. "Zu Pseudo-Eupolemus", Klio 43-45, 1965, pp. 282-90.
Weiher, E. von Der babylonische Gott Nergal, AOAT 11, Neukirchen-Vluyn 1971.
Weimar, P. "Daniel 7. Eine Textanalyse", Jesus und der Menschensohn, f. A. Vögtle, Freiburg 1975, pp. 11-36.
Wendland, P. Die hellenistisch-römische Kultur in ihren Beziehungen zum Judentum und Christentum, HNT 2, Tübingen 1912 (4th ed. 1972).
Westermann, C. "'ādām, Mensch", THAT I, München 1971, cols. 42-57.
— Genesis, BK I, Neukirchen-Vluyn 1971.
Wette, W.M.L. de Biblische Dogmatik Alten und Neuen Testaments, Berlin 1818.
Widengren, G. "Iran and Israel in Parthian Times with Special Regard to the Ethiopic Book of Enoch", Religious Synchretism in Antiquity, ed. B.A. Pearson, Missoula (Mont.) 1975, pp. 85-129.
— "Leitende Ideen und Quellen der iranischen Apokalyptik", D. Hellholm (ed.), Apocalypticism in the Mediterranean World and the Near East, Tübingen 1983, pp. 77-162.
— Die Religionen Irans, RM 14, Stuttgart 1965.
Windisch, H. Die Orakel des Hystaspes, VNAW.L 28, No 3, 1929.
Wolff, H.W. Anthrologie des Alten Testaments, 2nd ed., München 1973.
Würtwein, E. Der Text des Alten Testaments, 3rd rev. ed., Stuttgart 1966.
Yadin, Y. Masada. Herod's Fortress and the Zealots last Stand, London 1966 (Abacus ed. 1978).
Zenger, E. "Die späte Weisheit und das Gesetz", J. Maier and J. Schreiner (eds.), Literatur und Religion des Früjudentums, Würzburg 1973, pp. 43-56.
Zevit, Z. "The Structure and Individual Elements of Dan 7", ZAW 80, 1968, pp. 385-96.
Zimmerli, W. Ezechiel, BK XIII, Neukirchen-Vluyn 1969.
Zimmermann, F. "Underlying Documents of IV Ezra", JQR 51, 1960/61, pp. 107-34.
Zimmern, H. "Die altbabylonischen vor- (und nach-)sintflutlichen Könige nach neuen Quellen", ZDMG, NF 3 (78), 1924, pp. 19-35.
— "Urkönige und Uroffenbarung", E. Schrader (ed), Die Keilschriften und das Alte Testament III, Giessen 1902, pp. 530-43.

Source Index

Contents

Myths and Epics